IN HARMONY

An Integrated Approach to Reading and Writing

THIRD EDITION

KATHLEEN T. McWHORTER

Niagara County Community College

330 Hudson Street, NY NY 10013

VP & Portfolio Manager: Chris Hoag
Development Editor: Janice Wiggins
Marketing Manager: Fiona Murray
Program Manager: Erin Bosco
Project Coordination, Text Design, and Electronic Page Makeup: Integra-Chicago

Cover Designer: Pentagram
Cover Illustration: Christopher DeLorenzo
Manufacturing Buyer: Roy L. Pickering, Jr.
Printer/Binder: LSC Communications, Inc.
Cover Printer: Phoenix Color/Hagerstown

Acknowledgments of third-party content appear on pages 589–590, which constitute an extension of this copyright page.

Library of Congress Cataloging-in-Publication Data
Names: McWhorter, Kathleen T., author.
Title: In harmony: an integrated approach to reading and writing/by Kathleen T. McWhorter.
Description: Third edition. | Upper Saddle River, New Jersey: Pearson,
    [2019] | Previous edition: 2015.
Identifiers: LCCN 2017023422 | ISBN 9780134679204 (Soft Cover)
Subjects: LCSH: Reading (Higher education) | English
    language—Rhetoric—Study and teaching (Higher)
Classification: LCC LB2395.3 .M393 2019 | DDC 418/.40711–dc23
LC record available at https://lccn.loc.gov/2017023422

5 2020

Rental Edition
ISBN 10: 0-13-467920-2
ISBN 13: 978-0-13-467920-4

Access Card
ISBN 10: 0-13-498440-4
ISBN 13: 978-0-13-498440-7

A la Carte
ISBN 10: 0-13-474667-8
ISBN 13: 978-0-13-474667-8

Annotated Instructor's Edition
ISBN 10: 0-13-474673-2
ISBN 13: 978-0-13-474673-9

Brief Contents

Detailed Contents

PART FOUR   SENTENCE BASICS AND GRAMMAR ESSENTIALS   364

Preface

Purpose

In Harmony is the first text in a two-part series that features a comprehensive, integrated approach to reading and writing that is developed through structured, sequential instruction and guided practice. *In Harmony* focuses on sentence- and paragraph-level reading and writing skills, while the second text, *In Concert,* focuses on paragraph- and essay-writing skills.

Re-visioning *In Harmony* for the Third Edition

The first edition of *In Harmony* was a unique and successful response to the need for a textbook that combined college reading and writing skills. While the book was well received by many instructors, the market continued to evolve since its publication. The second edition moved significantly closer toward integration of skills through a change in pedagogy with each chapter teaching reading and writing through the medium of student and professional readings. The third edition furthers the integration by strengthening the thematic approach initiated in the second edition and adding new features designed to meet the changing needs of our target audience.

The thematic approach sharpens the focus of the instructional material, producing a book that more effectively addresses the needs of the evolving integrated reading/English curriculum. I am pleased to have created a book that integrates these skills—a book that demonstrates that reading and writing do work together—in harmony.

New to the Third Edition

Each of the following changes and new features moves the third edition of *In Harmony* further toward integrated thematic instruction.

- **Updated Thematically Related Readings.** The student and professional essays in all chapters now focus on a single theme, providing instructors with material that can be used for discussion, as well as teaching comparison and contrast, synthesis, and an analysis of ideas and sources.

    The themes are

    - interpersonal relationships
    - living between two worlds
    - digital communication
    - food waste

- life on the grid
- toward a healthier lifestyle
- benefits of creative expression
- the world of dating
- paying it forward
- decline of personal privacy

The thematic organization of each chapter now includes the following new or revised features:

- **Thematic Introduction.** Each chapter theme is briefly introduced before the first reading providing context and background information for the theme. This introduction engages students and focuses their attention on the theme.

- **Look It Up! Feature.** For each theme, students are given a topic related to the chapter theme to explore on their smartphones (or using that of a classmate for those who do not have smartphone access) and asked to formulate a written response. This activity gives academic relevance and validity to smartphones as a research tool and as an aid to reading, research, and writing.

- **Making Connections Between the Readings.** Following the second thematic reading in each chapter is a set of paragraph- and essay-writing activities. These activities enable students to compare and contrast the readings, analyze the writing features of the readings, and synthesize ideas.

- **Revised Thematic Reader.** A new theme has been added to Part Six, Thematic Reader. The new theme of poverty in America provides readings on three related topics: childhood poverty, event poverty, and food poverty in college.

- **NEW! Ten Professional Readings.** In general, the professional essays new to this edition are more challenging and more representative of readings that might be assigned in academic courses. New essay topics include emoji as a language, freegans, effects of Google, paying it forward, childhood poverty, event poverty, food poverty among college students, love across cultures, human-dog relationships, and physician dishonesty.

Features

The third edition of *In Harmony* presents deep integration of reading and writing skills designed to meet the needs of developing readers and writers and includes the following features.

- **Integrated Reading and Writing Process Instruction. Part One** provides an introduction to both reading and writing skills and offers important vocabulary instruction and practice for readers and writers. **Part Two** guides students in reading, writing, organizing, and revising paragraphs. **Part Three** addresses reading, thinking, and writing about essays. **Part Four** combines sentence and grammar coverage in the context of reading and writing sentences. **Part Five** offers a handbook on grammar basics.

- **Deep Integration of Reading and Writing in Chapters 1 and 2. Chapter 1, "An Overview of the Reading Process (with Writing),"** presents the steps in the reading process (pre-, during, and after) and shows students how to write while reading to identify (highlight, annotate) and organize (map, outline) key information. It also shows students how to write to condense, summarize, and recall information after reading (paraphrase, summarize, review, and reflect). The professional essay, "Liking and Loving: Interpersonal Attraction," provides practice in applying reading and writing skills. **Chapter 2, "An Overview of the Writing Process (with Reading),"** begins by connecting the writing process to the reading process, showing the similarities in the stages of the two processes and in the terminology used in both. The chapter integrates reading and writing using the professional essay "Afghanistan: Where Women Have No Choice" as an annotated model of good writing and by following a student writer from prewriting through revision.

- **Use of Student and Professional Essays to Teach Chapter Skills. Chapters 1–10** effectively integrate reading and writing. The professional reading and/or the student essay appears in the front of the chapter to become the focus of instruction. Students can study the professional reading as an effective writing model, and instructors can use it for instruction in and practice with the reading strategies taught in the chapter. Students can study the student essay as an achievable model for their own writing, and the writing instruction in the chapter draws on this essay for examples and practice exercises as students create their own paragraphs or essay.

- **Thematic Reader.** Because an increasing number of instructors prefer to teach writing in the context of reading and responding to professional articles and textbook selections, this edition includes a revised **Part Six**, titled **"Thematic Reader: Writing in Response to Reading."** The two other themes in the reader are on expected and unexpected relationships and medical ethics. The reader starts out with a new theme on poverty in America and provides readings on three related topics: childhood poverty, event poverty, and food poverty among college students. The two other themes in the reader are on expected and unexpected relationships and medical ethics. This rich offering of professional articles and textbook excerpts provides instructors an opportunity to choose the readings best suited to their students' needs and skill levels. Each theme is followed by exercises and activities in a similar format to those accompanying the professional readings within the chapters. Synthesis activities and essay writing assignments follow each theme.

- **Coverage of Critical Thinking.** To handle college-level work and to be well prepared for freshman composition classes, students need to be able to think critically about what they read as well as respond in writing to what they have read. Critical-thinking skills are introduced in **Chapter 1. Chapter 9** addresses specific critical-thinking skills for both reading and writing. Questions that encourage students to think and write critically are included in the "Thinking Critically: An Integrated Perspective" section that follows each professional reading.

- **Visual Literacy.** Reading and interpreting visuals are introduced in **Chapter 1**, where students learn to read and interpret a variety of visuals and to think critically about them. Each chapter opens with a visual that demonstrates the purpose of the chapter; within chapters, the marginal icon "Visualize It!" identifies useful maps and diagrams; and the apparatus of each professional reading contains a question about interpreting visuals.

- **Vocabulary Coverage.** Because a strong vocabulary is important to both readers and writers, vocabulary-building skills are emphasized throughout the book. **Chapter 3** presents an introduction to vocabulary and provides strategies for decoding the meaning of unfamiliar words, including using context clues, word parts, and dictionaries and thesauruses. It also discusses denotative and connotative meanings and the use of creative language. A Strengthening Your Vocabulary section follows each professional reading.

■ **Sentence and Grammar Coverage.** Part Four focuses on sentence-level reading and writing skills. **Chapters 11–15** provide thorough coverage of essential sentence skills and major sentence error identification and correction topics, while more specific aspects of correctness and clarity are treated in **Part Five: A Brief Grammar Handbook.**

■ **Coverage of Writer's Techniques.** The exercises and activities following the professional readings include the section, "Thinking Critically: An Integrated Perspective." Questions in this section guide students in analyzing the strategies and techniques the writer used in the essay, encourage students to think and write critically, provide an opportunity for journal writing and discussion, and include questions about visuals that accompany the reading.

■ **Introductory Material on Reading and Writing Using Sources.** As preparation for college courses that require the use of sources in writing academic papers, **Chapter 10** offers a brief overview of identifying appropriate sources, taking notes, using quotations, and avoiding plagiarism.

Chapter Features

Every chapter includes the following features in addition to those related to the thematic structure of the book:

■ **Visual and Engaging Chapter Openers.** Each chapter opens with a photograph or other image that emphasizes the thematic topic, generates interest, and connects the topic of the chapter to their experience. This feature gets students writing immediately about chapter-related content.

■ **Learning Objectives Tied to Interactive Summaries.** Learning objectives at the beginning of each chapter (and repeated next to relevant section heads) identify what students can expect to learn and correspond directly to the end-of-chapter interactive summaries that students can use to check their recall of chapter content.

■ **Visualize It!** Many chapters contain idea maps that show how paragraphs and essays are organized from both a reading and a writing perspective. The professional readings also contain partially completed maps for students to finish.

■ **"Need to Know" Boxes.** These boxes summarize key concepts and strategies in an easy reference format.

■ **Linked Writing Exercises.** Writing in Progress exercises guide students step by step through the writing process.

■ **Collaborative Activities.** Many chapters contain collaborative activities designed to help students apply skills and learn from their peers.

■ **Read and Revise.** Chapters 4–15 each contain a Read and Revise activity in which students are asked to read, analyze, and revise sample student writing that contains errors that pertain to the topics taught in the chapter.

- **Writing About the Reading at MyLab Reading & Writing Skills.** All of the exercises (except for Examining the Reading Using an Idea Map) that follow each of the professional readings can now be completed online in MyLab Reading & Writing Skills.

- **MyLab Reading & Writing Skills.** MyLab Reading & Writing Skills is an online homework, tutorial, and assessment program designed to engage students and improve results. Within its structured environment, students practice what they learn, test their understanding, and pursue a personalized study plan that helps them better absorb course material and understand difficult concepts.

- **A Personalized Learning Experience.** MyLab Reading & Writing Skills can improve students' reading and writing by offering personalized and adaptive instruction, with integrated learning aids that foster student understanding of skills and ideas.

- **Self-Study or Instructor-Driven Learning.** MyLab Reading & Writing Skills can be set up to fit your specific class needs, whether you seek reading and writing support to complement what you teach in class, a way to easily administer many sections, or a self-paced environment for independent study.

- **Integrated Reading and Writing Content.** MyLab Reading & Writing Skills delivers content that reflects the way in which an integrated reading/writing curriculum is delivered. Assignments in the MyLab enable students to practice their reading skills and write in response to that reading—thus offering real integration that better promotes transference of those skills to college level work.

- **Reading Levels in Annotated Instructor's Edition.** A Lexile® measure—the most widely used reading metric in U.S. schools—provides valuable information about a student's reading ability and the complexity of text. It helps match students with reading resources and activities that are targeted to their ability level. Lexile measures indicate the reading levels of content in MyLab Reading & Writing Skills and the longer selections in the Annotated Instructor's Editions of all Pearson's reading books. See the Annotated Instructor's Edition of *In Concert* and the *Instructor's Manual* for more details.

Instructor Support and Professional Development

Pearson is pleased to offer a variety of support materials to help make teaching reading and writing easier for instructors and to help students excel in their coursework.

Annotated Instructor's Edition (ISBN 0133955990/9780133955996). The AIE offers in-text answers to all exercises, practice sets, and reading/writing assignments. It also indicates which activities are offered simultaneously in MyLab Reading & Writing Skills. It is a valuable resource for experienced and first-time instructors alike.

Online Instructor's Manual (ISBN 0133944972/9780133944976). The material in the IRM is designed to save instructors time and provide them with effective options for teaching the integrated reading/writing course. It offers suggestions for setting up their course, provides sample syllabus models, provides lots of extra practice for students who need it, and is an invaluable resource for adjuncts.

Test Bank (ISBN 0133944999/9780133944990). An abundance of extra practice exercises are included in the Test Bank for *In Harmony*. The Test Bank can also be used to create tests in Pearson's MyTest (9780133945003/0133945006) test creation tool.

PowerPoint Presentation (ISBN 0133944980/9780133944983). PowerPoint presentations have been created to accompany each chapter of *In Harmony* and consists of classroom ready lecture outline slides, lecture tips, classroom activities, and review questions.

Answer Key (0133944964/9780133944969). The Answer Key contains the solutions to the exercises in the student edition of the text. Available for download from the Instructor Resource Center.

Professional Development

Pearson offers a variety of professional development programs and resources to support full- and part-time instructors. These include Pedagogy & Practice, an open-access digital resource gallery [http://pedagogyandpractice.pearson highered.com/], and our Speaking About English online conference series, featuring scholar/educators addressing pedagogical topics via web-based presentations. These conferences are held twice a year and are free to attend. Information about future conferences, as well as archives of past sessions, can be found on the conference website [http://www.pearsonhighered.com/speakingabout/english/]. Updated information about any and all of these Partnership Programs can always be found on our catalog page [http://www.pearsonhighered.com/english/].

MyLab Reading & Writing Skills
https://www.pearsonmylabandmastering.com/northamerica/myskillslab/
Reach every student by pairing this text with MyLab Reading & Writing Skills

MyLab™ is the teaching and learning platform that empowers you to reach *every* student. By combining trusted content with digital tools and a flexible platform, MyLab personalizes the learning experience and improves results for each student. When students enter your course with varying skill levels, MyLab can help you identify which students need extra support and provide them targeted practice and instruction outside of class. Learn more at www.pearson.com/mylab/reading-and-writing-skills.

- **Empower each learner:** Each student learns at a different pace. Personalized learning pinpoints the precise areas where each student needs practice, giving all students the support they need—when and where they need it—to be successful.

- MyLab diagnoses students' strengths and weaknesses through a pre-assessment known as the **Path Builder**, and offers up a personalized Learning Path.Students then receive targeted practice and multimodal activities to help them improve over time.

- MyLab Reading & Writing Skills uses **The Lexile® Framework** for Reading to diagnose a student's reading ability. After an initial Locator Test, students receive readings and practice at their estimated reading level. Throughout the course, periodic diagnostic tests incrementally adjust their level with increasing precision.

- **NEW!** Available for select MyLab courses, **Skill Builder** offers adaptive practice that is designed to increase students' ability to complete their assignments. By monitoring student performance on homework, Skill Builder adapts to each student's needs and provides just-in-time, in-assignment practice to help build confidence.

- **Teach your course your way:** Your course is unique. So whether you'd like to build your own assignments, teach multiple sections, or set prerequisites, MyLab gives you the flexibility to easily create *your* course to fit *your* needs.

- **Improve student results:** When you teach with MyLab, student performance improves. That's why instructors have chosen MyLab for over 15 years, touching the lives of over 50 million students.

Acknowledgments

I would like to express my gratitude to my reviewers for their excellent ideas, suggestions, and advice on the preparation of this text and earlier editions:

Lisa Barnes, Delaware County Community College; Michalle Barnett, Gulf Coast State College; Craig Barto, Charleston Southern University; Cindy Beck, Pulaski Technical College; Gail Bradstreet, Cincinnati State Technical and Community College; Jill Buchert, Wor-Wic Community College; Shiela Bunker, State Fair Community College; Michelle Cantu-Wilson, San Jacinto College; Teresa Carrillo, Joliet Junior College; Sharon M. Cellemme, South Piedmont Community College; Dorothy Chase, College of Southern Nevada; Marlys Cordoba, College of the Siskiyous; Leslie Daughtry-Brian, Lone Star College Kingwood; Barbara, Doyle Arkansas State University; Andrea Dunford, John Tyler Community College; Margot A. Edlin, Queensborough Community College–CUNY; Kim Edwards, Tidewater Community College; Adam Floridia, Middlesex Community College; Marianne Friedell, College of the Mainland; Teresa Fugate, Lindsey Wilson College; Laura Girtman, Tallahassee Community College; M. Elizabeth Grooms, Cameron University; Barbara Hampton, Rend Lake College; Jessie M. Harding, LCNE Southington, CT; Curtis Harrell, NorthWest Arkansas Community College; Annaliese Hausler-Akpovi, Modesto Junior College; Beverly J. Heam, University of Tennessee at Martin; Eric Hibbison, J. Sargeant Reynolds Community College; Carlotta W. Hill, Oklahoma City Community College; Elizabeth Huergo, Montgomery College; Pamela Hunt, Paris Junior College; Julie Jackson-Coe, Genesee Community College; Magdalena Jacobo, San Bernardino Valley College; Kim Jameson, Oklahoma City Community College; Courtney R. Johnson, Montgomery College; Janice Johnson, Missouri State University; Stanley Johnson, Southside Virginia Community College; Suzanne Jones, Collin College; Sally Kloepfer, Tiffin University; Teresa Kozek, Housatonic Community College; Vicky M. Krug, Westmoreland County Community College; Debbie Lamb, Ousey Penn State Brandywine; Frank Lammer, Northeast Iowa Community College; Terri LaRocco, University of Findlay; Debra F. Lee, Nash Community College; Glenda Lowery, Rappahannock Community College; Agnes Malicka, Northern Virginia Community College; Patricia A. Malinowski, Finger Lakes Community College; Barbara Marshall, Rockingham Community College; Dominique Marshall, Lenoir Community College; Jennifer McCann, Bay de Noc Community College; Nancy McKenzie, Tarrant County College South Campus; Laura Meyers, Hawkeye Community College; Linda Miniger, Harrisburg Area Community College; Carol Miyake, Laramie County Community College; Julie Monroe, Madison Area Technical College; Sharon Moran, Hayes Community College of Baltimore County; Debbie Naquin, North Virginia Community College; Gayle Norman, South Arkansas Community College; Carl Olds, University of Central Arkansas; Catherine G. Parra, Northern Virginia Community College; Lisa Parra, Johnson County Community College; Herman Pena, UT Brownsville and Texas Southmost College; Elizabeth Price, Ranger College; Sonya Prince, San Jacinto College; Sue Rauch, Germanna Community College; Regia J. Ray, Dalton State College; Joan Reeves, Northeast Alabama Community College; Adalia Reyna, South Texas College; Vanessa Ruccolo, Virginia Tech; Rebecca Samberg, Housatonic Community College; Anna Schmidt, Lone Star College–CyFair; Cheryle Snead-Greene, Prairie View A&M University; Penny Speidel, John Tyler Community College; Emmie D. Stokes, Augusta Technical College; Dr. Catherine Swift, University of Central

Arkansas; Alexandr Tolj, John Tyler Community College; Dayle K. Turner, Leeward Community College; Usha Wadhwani, New Jersey City University; Jeanine Williams, The Community College Baltimore County; Lisa Williams, Kirkwood Community College; Lucretia Williams, College of the Abermarle; Michelle Zollars, Patrick Henry Community College; Lark Zunich, Long Beach City College.

I would also like to thank the students who wrote and revised the essays included in this book: Kate Atkinson, Alex Boyd, Sarah Frey, Santiago Quintana Garcia, Amanda Keithley, Alaina Mayer, Juliette Simmons, and Claire Stroup. I also wish to thank the unique and talented team that helped me revise the book. Thank you to Jeanne Jones for her assistance in drafting and preparing the manuscript; her attention to detail is remarkable, and she has suggested many needed improvements. Kathy Tyndall, retired department chairperson of the Pre-Curriculum Department of Wake Technical Community College, who has years of teaching experience and a keen understanding of the integration of reading and writing, served as a consultant and offered valuable advice and guidance throughout the revision. She shared her approach to integrating reading and writing and helped me develop a revised chapter structure.

I also wish to thank Jeanne Jones for her valuable assistance in drafting, revising, and preparing the manuscript. I also value the professional and creative efforts of Ohlinger Publishing. In particular I thank Carolyn Merrill, Editor-in-Chief; Marita Sermolins Bley, Managing Editor; and Erin Bosco, Program Manager, all highly skilled, knowledgeable specialists, for their support and careful guidance of this book through the development and production process. I value the contributions of Janice Wiggins, development editor; through daily collaboration and brainstorming, she helped me develop and execute a revision plan to achieve a strong integration of reading and writing skills. I also offer thanks to Angel Chavez and her team at Integra for their highly professional and creative efforts in guiding the book through the production process.

Kathleen T. McWhorter

An Overview of the Reading Process (with Writing)

1

Lisa Payne Photography/Pearson Education

LEARNING
GOALS

Learn how to ...

■ **GOAL 1**
Use the reading process and read actively

■ **GOAL 2**
Use pre-reading strategies

■ **GOAL 3**
Use interactive strategies during reading

■ **GOAL 4**
Use post-reading strategies

■ **GOAL 5**
Think critically

THINK About It!

Study the photo above showing a mother with her son. Write a few sentences commenting on the relationship of the mother and son. Did you observe that the mother seems to have a loving relationship with her son and that she is involved in his life? The mother is actively engaging with her son.

In a similar way, active readers get actively involved with the material they are reading. They interact with the author's ideas. They think, question, challenge, criticize, and take specific steps to understand, remember, and evaluate what they read. This chapter will give you some tips on how to become an active reader. The skills you will learn will also help you to write in response to what you read.

The theme of this chapter is interpersonal relationships. The photograph above shows one type of interpersonal relationship—between parent and child. In this chapter, the professional reading will explore a different aspect of interpersonal relationships—the dynamics of liking and attraction.

What Are the Reading Process and Active Reading?

Reading is more than turning to an assigned textbook chapter or opening a Web page, reading it, and then closing it.

The Reading Process

Reading is a multi-step process that involves activities before you begin to read, while you are reading, and after you finish reading, as detailed in The Reading Process figure. Throughout the reading process, *understanding* the author's ideas is only part of the process. Once you grasp the author's message, you are ready to think critically by interpreting, analyzing, and evaluating that message. (Chapter 9 is devoted to sharpening your critical thinking skills.)

The Reading Process

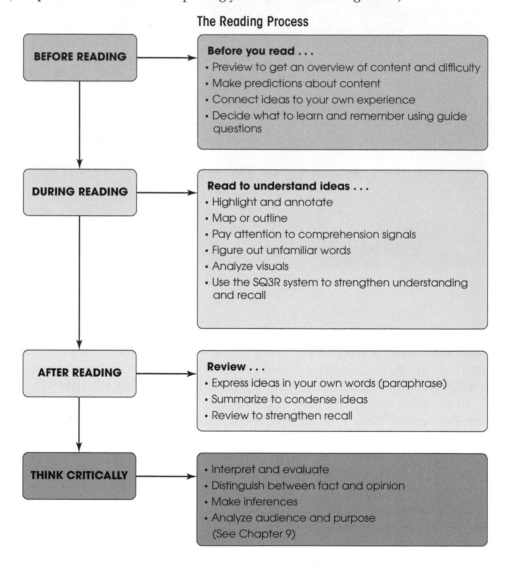

BEFORE READING

Before you read . . .
- Preview to get an overview of content and difficulty
- Make predictions about content
- Connect ideas to your own experience
- Decide what to learn and remember using guide questions

DURING READING

Read to understand ideas . . .
- Highlight and annotate
- Map or outline
- Pay attention to comprehension signals
- Figure out unfamiliar words
- Analyze visuals
- Use the SQ3R system to strengthen understanding and recall

AFTER READING

Review . . .
- Express ideas in your own words (paraphrase)
- Summarize to condense ideas
- Review to strengthen recall

THINK CRITICALLY
- Interpret and evaluate
- Distinguish between fact and opinion
- Make inferences
- Analyze audience and purpose
  (See Chapter 9)

Active Reading: How to Get Started

Active reading requires thinking; it is an active process of identifying important ideas written by others and interpreting, comparing, and evaluating them. Before you read, it is helpful to get an overview of the content and difficulty of the material, make predictions, determine what you need to learn and remember, and connect the content to your own experience. While reading, be sure to highlight and annotate, outline or map, analyze visuals, and use a reading study system (SQ3R) to strengthen your comprehension and recall. When you finish reading, it is helpful to express ideas in your own words, summarize, and review, all of which help you to think critically about what you have read.

EXERCISE 1-1	Analyzing How You Read

Directions: Using the "Need to Know" box, analyze how you read and place a check mark beside items that you already do. Place an asterisk (*) next to items you'd like to learn to do.

! NEED TO KNOW

Active Reading: An Overview

ACTIVE READING INVOLVES ...	CHECK
1. Reading each assignment differently. For each assignment, determine the following:	
■ Why it was assigned	
■ What you need and want to learn	
■ What you need to do with the information (pass a test, write an essay, apply the information)	
■ How the material is organized	
■ How difficult the material is	
■ What you already know	
2. Thinking and asking questions as you read. Do this by doing the following:	
■ Identifying what is important	
■ Recognizing when something is confusing or not understandable	
■ Determining how the key ideas are organized	
■ Drawing connections between ideas	
■ Anticipating what is to come next	
■ Relating ideas to what you already know	
3. Sorting the information as you read. Identify what you need to learn and remember by using these techniques:	
■ Highlighting	
■ Outlining	
■ Mapping (drawing diagrams that show how ideas are organized)	
■ Summarizing	
4. Reviewing after reading. To build retention and recall, use these strategies:	
■ Do a quick one- to three-minute review immediately after reading	
■ Review your highlighting, outlining, notes, and maps periodically to keep information fresh in your mind	
■ Test yourself. Find out what you know and don't know before attending class or taking an exam	

Throughout the chapters in this text, you will learn many strategies to help you use the suggestions on the previous page.

EXERCISE 1-2   Analyzing Assignments

WORKING TOGETHER

Directions: Working in small groups, consider each of the following reading assignments. Discuss ways to get actively involved in each assignment.

1. Reading two poems by Maya Angelou for an American literature class

   _____

   _____

2. Reading the procedures for your next biology lab

   _____

3. Reading an article in *Time* magazine assigned by your political science instructor in preparation for a class discussion

   _____

   _____

4. Reading an online article about leadership styles as part of your research for a management paper

   _____

   _____

Pre-Reading Strategies

■ GOAL 2
Use pre-reading
strategies

Just as you probably would not buy a car without checking its mileage, mechanical condition, and warranty, you should not begin reading without knowing what the material is about and how the author organized it. This section will show you how to preview, make predictions, ask questions, and discover what you already know about what you will read.

Preview Before Reading

Previewing is a way of quickly familiarizing yourself with the organization and content of written material *before* beginning to read it. It is an easy method to use and will make a dramatic difference in how effectively you read.

How to Preview

When you preview, try to

   ■ find only the most important ideas in the material.
   ■ note how the text is organized.

To do this, look only at the parts that state these important ideas and skip the rest. Previewing is a fairly rapid technique; it should take only a minute or two to preview any reading selection in this text. In fact, previewing is so fast that you should *not* take time to highlight or make notes. To preview an article or textbook chapter, follow the steps in the following "Need to Know" box.

! NEED TO KNOW

How to Preview

1. **Read the title and subtitle.** The title explains what a chapter or article is about. The subtitle, if there is one, suggests additional perspectives on the subject. For example, an article titled "Brazil" might be subtitled "The World's Next Superpower." In this instance, the subtitle tells which aspects of Brazil the article discusses.

2. **Read the first paragraph.** The first paragraph or introduction of a reading may provide an overview and offer clues about how a chapter or article is organized. If it is lengthy, read just the first few sentences.

3. **Read section headings.** Section headings, like titles, identify and separate important topics and ideas.

4. **Read the first sentence under each heading**. The first sentence following a heading often further explains the heading. It may also state the central thought of the section it introduces.

5. **If the reading lacks headings, read the first sentence of each of a few paragraphs on each page.** You will discover many of the main ideas of the reading.

6. **Notice typographical aids.** Typographical and visual aids are those features of a page that help to high-light and organize information. Typographical aids include *italics*, **boldfaced type,** marginal notes, colored ink, underlining, and numbering. Visual aids include maps, photographs, diagrams, and charts.

7. **Read the final paragraph or summary.** The final paragraph may review the main points of the reading or bring it to a close.

Chapter Theme: Interpersonal Relationships

In this chapter, you will read a professional essay on the topic of interpersonal relationships. Throughout your life, you will develop relationships on many different levels and be attracted to people for many different reasons. These relationships may include family members, friends, work colleagues, team members, classmates, and those with whom you have a romantic attraction. Some of these relationships will last a lifetime, and other, more casual relationships may fade over time. As you read the essay in this chapter, consider the reasons that people are attracted to one another and the scientific research that the authors use to explain "liking and loving." Also, annotate the reading, recording your thoughts on the topic, to be prepared to write about it or a related topic.

Look it up!

Use the search engine on your smartphone (or work with a classmate who has a smartphone) and look up "How have relationships changed over the past 50 years?" Read two or three entries. Based on what you read, how have interpersonal relationships changed over the years? What factors contributed to these changes? Write a few lines about the interpersonal relationships in your life.

EXAMINING PROFESSIONAL WRITING

The following selection, taken from a psychology textbook, explores the factors surrounding attraction and love. It is a good example of the type of writing you will be asked to read in this text, and it will be used throughout this chapter to demonstrate techniques and to give you practice in reading and learning from college textbooks.

Thinking Before Reading

Study the highlighted parts of the essay and, using the "Need to Know" box above, see if you can explain why each of the sections and sentences is highlighted. After you have previewed the essay, connect it to your own experience by answering the following questions:

a. What factors influence your choices in the people you want to know better?

b. How would you define *love*?

Liking and Loving: Interpersonal Attraction

Saundra K. Ciccarelli and J. Noland White

1   Prejudice pretty much explains why people don't like each other. What does psychology say about why people like someone else? There are some "rules" for those whom people like and find attractive. Liking or having the desire for a relationship with someone else is called interpersonal attraction, and there's a great deal of research on the subject. (Who wouldn't want to know the rules?)

interpersonal attraction
liking or having the desire for a relationship with another person

The Rules of Attraction

WHAT FACTORS GOVERN ATTRACTION AND LOVE, AND WHAT ARE SOME DIFFERENT KINDS OF LOVE?

2   Several factors are involved in the attraction of one person to another, including both superficial physical characteristics, such as physical beauty and proximity, as well as elements of personality.

PHYSICAL ATTRACTIVENESS

3   When people think about what attracts them to other people, one of the topics that usually arises is the physical attractiveness of the other person. Some research suggests that physical beauty is one of the main factors that influence people's choices for selecting people they want to know better, although other factors may become more important in the later stages of relationships.

PROXIMITY—CLOSE TO YOU

proximity
physical or geographical nearness

4   The closer together people are physically, such as working in the same office building or living in the same dorm, the more likely they are to form a relationship. Proximity refers to being physically near someone else. People choose friends and lovers from the pool of people available to them, and availability depends heavily on proximity.

5   One theory about why proximity is so important involves the idea of repeated exposure to new stimuli. The more people experience something, whether it is a song, a picture, or a person, the more they tend to like it. The phrase "it grew on me" refers to this reaction. When people are in physical proximity to each other, repeated exposure may increase their attraction to each other.

BIRDS OF A FEATHER—SIMILARITY

6   Proximity does not guarantee attraction, just as physical attractiveness does not guarantee a long-term relationship. People tend to like being around others who are *similar* to them in some way. The more people find they have in common with others—such as attitudes, beliefs, and interests—the more they tend to be attracted to those others. Similarity as a factor in relationships makes sense when seen in terms of validation of a person's beliefs and attitudes. When other people hold the same attitudes and beliefs and do the same kinds of actions, it makes a person's own concepts seem more correct or valid.

WHEN OPPOSITES ATTRACT

Isn't there a saying that "opposites attract"? Aren't people sometimes attracted to people who are different instead of similar?

7   There is often a grain of truth in many old sayings, and "opposites attract" is no exception. Some people find that forming a relationship with another person who has *complementary* qualities (characteristics in the one person that fill a need in the other) can be very rewarding. Research does not support this view of attraction, however. It is similarity, not complementarity, that draws people together and helps them stay together.

RECIPROCITY OF LIKING

reciprocity of liking
tendency of people to like other people who like them in return

8   Finally, people have a very strong tendency to like people who like them, a simple but powerful concept referred to as reciprocity of liking. In one experiment, researchers paired college students with other students. Neither student in any of the pairs knew the other member. One member of each pair was randomly chosen to receive some information from the experimenters about how the *other* student in the pair felt about the first member. In some cases, target students were led to believe that the other students liked them and, in other cases, that the targets disliked them.

9   When the pairs of students were allowed to meet and talk with each other again, they were friendlier, disclosed more information about themselves, agreed with the other person more, and behaved in a warmer manner *if they had been told* that the other student liked them. The other students came to like these students better as well, so liking produced more liking.

Bettmann/Getty Images

Famed athlete Joe DiMaggio and actress Marilyn Monroe are seen driving away after their 1954 marriage ceremony. While they had in common the fact that they were two of the most famous people in the United States at that time, many people viewed the marriage of the very modest and somewhat shy Joe to the outgoing, vivacious sex symbol that was Marilyn as an example of "opposites attract."

10   The only time that liking someone does not seem to make that person like the other in return is if a person suffers from feelings of low self-worth. In that case, finding out that someone likes you when you don't even like yourself makes you question his or her motives. This mistrust can cause you to act unfriendly to that person, which makes the person more likely to become unfriendly to you in a kind of self-fulfilling prophecy.

Love Is a Triangle—Robert Sternberg's Triangular Theory of Love

11   Dictionary definitions of love refer to a strong affection for another person due to kinship, personal ties, sexual attraction, admiration, or common interests.

But those aren't all the same kind of relationships. I love my family and I love my friends, but in different ways.

12   Psychologists generally agree that there are different kinds of love. One psychologist, Robert Sternberg, outlined a theory of what he determined were the three main components of love and the different types of love that combinations of these three components can produce.

THE THREE COMPONENTS OF LOVE

13   According to Sternberg, love consists of three basic components: intimacy, passion, and commitment.

14   *Intimacy*, in Sternberg's view, refers to the feelings of closeness that one has for another person or the sense of having close emotional ties to another. Intimacy in this sense is not physical but psychological. Friends have an intimate relationship because they disclose things to each other that most people might not know, they feel strong emotional ties to each other, and they enjoy the presence of the other person.

15   *Passion* is the physical aspect of love. Passion refers to the emotional and sexual arousal a person feels toward the other person. Passion is not simply sex; holding hands, loving looks, and hugs can all be forms of passion.

16   *Commitment* involves the decisions one makes about a relationship. A short-term decision might be, "I think I'm in love." An example of a more long-term decision is, "I want to be with this person for the rest of my life."

THE LOVE TRIANGLES

17   A love relationship between two people can involve one, two, or all three of these components in various combinations. The combinations can produce seven different forms of love, as seen in Figure A.

18   Two of the more familiar and more heavily researched forms of love from Sternberg's theory are romantic love and companionate love. When intimacy and passion are combined, the result is the more familiar romantic love, which is sometimes called passionate love by other researchers. Romantic love is often the basis for a more lasting relationship. In many Western cultures, the ideal relationship begins with liking, then becomes romantic love as passion is added to the mix, and finally becomes a more enduring form of love as a commitment is made.

romantic love
type of love consisting of intimacy and passion

FIGURE A   STERNBERG'S TRIANGULAR THEORY OF LOVE

This diagram represents the seven different kinds of love that can result from combining the three components of love: intimacy, passion, and commitment. Notice that some of these types of love sound less desirable or positive than others. What is the one key element missing from the less positive types of love?

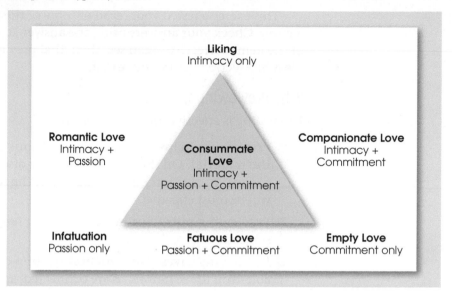

Source: Adapted from Sternberg (1986b).

companionate love
type of love consisting of intimacy and commitment

19   When intimacy and commitment are the main components of a relationship, it is called companionate love. In companionate love, people who like each other, feel emotionally close to each other, and understand one another's motives have made a commitment to live together, usually in a marriage relationship. Companionate love is often the binding tie that holds a marriage together through the years of parenting, paying bills, and lessening physical passion. In many non-Western cultures, companionate love is seen as more sensible. Choices for a mate on the basis of compatibility are often made by parents or matchmakers rather than the couple themselves.

20   Finally, when all three components of love are present, the couple has achieved *consummate love,* the ideal form of love that many people see as the ultimate goal. This is also the kind of love that may evolve into companionate love when the passion lessens during the middle years of a relationship's commitment.

—Ciccarelli and White, *Psychology,* pp. 365–367

EXERCISE 1-3   Evaluating Your Previewing

Directions: Read the following statements and mark each one true (T) or false (F) based on what you learned by previewing the selection above.

_____ 1. *Interpersonal attraction* refers to liking or wanting a relationship with someone else.

_____ 2. Proximity typically guarantees attraction between two people.

_____ 3. People tend to like people who like them.

_____ 4. Intimacy refers to the physical aspect of love.

_____ 5. Consummate love consists of intimacy, passion, and commitment.

This exercise tested your recall of some of the most important ideas in the selection. Check your answers using the answer key below. Did you get most or all of the items correct? You can see, then, that previewing helps you learn the major ideas in a section before you read it.

Why Previewing Is Effective

Previewing is effective for several reasons:

- **Previewing helps you to make decisions about how you will approach the material.** On the basis of what you discover about the assignment's organization and content, you can select the reading and study strategies that will be most effective.

- **Previewing puts your mind in gear.** It helps you start thinking about the subject.

- **Previewing gives you a mental outline of the chapter's content.** It enables you to see how ideas are connected, and since you know where the author is headed, your reading will be easier than if you had not previewed. Previewing, however, is never a substitute for careful, thorough reading.

Make Predictions

We make predictions about many tasks before we undertake them. We predict how long it will take to drive to a shopping mall, how much dinner will cost at a new restaurant, how long a party will last, or how difficult an exam will be. Prediction helps us organize our time and cope with new situations.

Prediction is an important part of active reading as well. It enables you to approach the material systematically. Also, it helps you to read actively because you continually accept or reject your predictions. As you preview, you can predict the development of ideas, the organization of the material, and the author's conclusions. For example, for her philosophy class, a student began to preview an essay titled "Do Computers Have a Right to Life?" From the title, she predicted that the essay would discuss the topic of artificial intelligence: whether computers can "think." Then, as she read the essay, she discovered that this prediction was correct.

In textbook chapters, the boldfaced headings serve as section "titles" and are helpful in predicting content and organization. Considered together, chapter headings often suggest the development of ideas through the chapter. For instance, the following headings appear in "Liking and Loving: Interpersonal Attraction":

The Rules of Attraction

Love Is a Triangle—Robert Sternberg's Triangular Theory of Love

These headings reveal the authors' approach to love and attraction. We can predict that the chapter will discuss the factors that are involved in interpersonal attraction and describe three different kinds of love.

EXERCISE 1-4	## Making Predictions

Directions: Predict the subject and/or point of view of each of the following essays or articles.

1. "The Nuclear Test-Ban Treaty: It's Time to Sign"

   _____

2. "Flunking Lunch: The Search for Nutrition in School Cafeterias"

   _____

3. "Professional Sports: Necessary Violence"

   _____

EXERCISE 1-5	## Making Predictions About "Liking and Loving"

Directions: Based on your previewing of the reading "Liking and Loving" in the Examining Professional Reading section, list at least three topics about which you expect to learn more. Also, predict the authors' purpose for writing.

_____

_____

_____

Form Guide Questions

Did you ever read an entire page or more and not remember anything you read? Have you found yourself going from paragraph to paragraph without really thinking about what the writer is saying? Guide questions can help you overcome these problems. **Guide questions** are questions you expect to be able to answer while or after you read. Most students form them mentally, but you can jot them in the margin of what you are reading if you prefer.

The following tips can help you form questions and use them to guide your reading. It is best to develop guide questions *after* you preview but *before* you read.

How to Form Guide Questions

1. **Turn each major heading into a series of questions.** The questions should ask something that you feel is important to know.

2. **As you read a section, look for the answers to your questions.** Highlight the answers as you find them.

3. **When you finish reading a section, stop and check to see whether you can recall the answers.** Place check marks by those you cannot recall. Then reread.

4. **Avoid asking questions that have one-word answers, like *yes* or *no*.** Questions that begin with *what, why*, or *how* are more useful.

Here are a few textbook headings and some examples of questions you might ask:

HEADING	QUESTIONS
Managing Interpersonal Conflict	What is interpersonal conflict? What are strategies for managing conflict?
Paralegals at Work	What is a paralegal? What do paralegals do?
Kohlberg's Theory of Moral Development	Who was Kohlberg? How did Kohlberg explain moral development?

| EXERCISE 1-6 | Forming Guide Questions |

Directions: Select the guide questions that would be most helpful in improving your understanding of textbook chapter sections that begin with the following headings:

_____ 1. Defining Loneliness
   a. Is loneliness unusual?
   b. What does loneliness mean?
   c. Are adults lonelier than children?
   d. Can loneliness ever be positive?

_____ 2. The Four Basic Functions of Management
   a. How important is management?
   b. Are there other functions of management?
   c. What are management's four basic functions?
   d. Do poor managers cause serious problems?

_____ 3. Surface Versus Depth Listening
   a. Is surface listening difficult?
   b. What is listening?
   c. How do surface and depth listening differ?
   d. Is depth listening important?

_____ 4. The Origins of the Cold War
   a. How did the Cold War start?
   b. Is the Cold War still going on?
   c. How did the United States deal with the Cold War?
   d. Did the Cold War end through compromise?

| EXERCISE 1-7 | Writing Guide Questions for "Liking and Loving" |

Directions: Use the headings in the "Liking and Loving: Interpersonal Attraction" essay in the Examining Professional Writing section of this chapter to write guide questions that would help improve your understanding of the selection.

1. _____
2. _____
3. _____
4. _____
5. _____

Connect the Reading to Your Own Experience

Once you have previewed a reading, try to connect the topic to your own experience. Take a moment to recall what you already know or have read about the topic. This activity will make the reading more interesting and easier to write about. Here are a few suggestions to help you make connections.

How to Make Connections to a Topic

■ **Ask questions and answer them.** Suppose you have just previewed a reading titled "Advertising: Institutionalized Lying." Ask questions such as: *Do ads always lie? If not, why not? What do I already know about deceptive advertising?*

■ **Brainstorm.** Jot down everything that comes to mind about the topic on a sheet of paper or in a computer file. For example, if the topic of a reading is "The Generation Gap," you might list reasons for such a gap, try to define it, or mention names of families in which you have observed it. For more about brainstorming, see the Brainstorming section of Chapter 2.

■ **Think of examples.** Try to think of situations, people, or events that relate to the topic. For instance, suppose you have previewed a reading titled "Fashions, Fads, and Crazes." You might think of recent examples of each: *skinny jeans, hashtags, tongue tattoos.*

Each of these techniques will help you identify ideas or experiences that you may share with the writer and that will help you focus your attention on the reading. In this text, the section titled "Thinking Before Reading," which comes before each selection, lists several questions that will help you make connections between the reading and your own experience.

EXERCISE 1-8	Connecting "Liking and Loving" to Your Own Experience

Directions: Based on your preview of "Liking and Loving: Interpersonal Attraction" in the Examining Professional Writing section of this chapter, use one or more of the above techniques to connect the reading to your own experience. You might consider what factors attract you to other people—in both the early and later stages of a relationship—or think of examples of the different kinds of love in your own life.

During-Reading Strategies

■ **GOAL 3**
Use interactive strategies during reading

You can read textbooks and other college assignments more effectively, remember more of what you read, and review more efficiently if you interact with the text through highlighting and annotating, assess your comprehension, create maps and outlines, analyze visuals, and use the SQ3R reading and study system. Writing *as you read* and writing *in response to reading* increase comprehension and recall as well as aid you in connecting what you are learning to what you already know.

Highlight and Annotate as You Read

Reading is time-consuming. To avoid having to reread an entire essay or chapter in order to review it or locate important ideas, be sure to highlight and annotate as you read.

■ Highlighting is a process of sorting ideas, identifying those that you need to learn, remember, or review.

■ Annotating, or making marginal notes, is a way of recording your thinking as you read.

Highlight to Identify What Is Important

In some cases, the easiest and fastest way to mark important facts and ideas is to **highlight** them. When highlighting, you mark the portions of a reading that you need to study, remember, or locate quickly. Here are a few suggestions for highlighting effectively.

How to Highlight Effectively

- **Read a paragraph or section first,** then go back and highlight what is important.

- **Highlight the topic sentence and any important details you want to remember.**

- **Be accurate.** Make sure your highlighting reflects the content of the reading. Incomplete highlighting may cause you to miss the main point.

- **Use a system for highlighting.** For instance, use two different highlighter colors to distinguish between topic sentences and supporting details.

- **Highlight the right amount.** By highlighting too little, you miss valuable information. By highlighting too much, you are not identifying the most important ideas. As a general rule, the only complete sentences that should be highlighted are topic sentences. In all other sentences, highlight only key phrases or words.

Here is an example of effective highlighting, using paragraphs 4 and 5 from "Liking and Loving: Interpersonal Attraction":

> The closer together people are physically, such as working in the same office building or living in the same dorm, the more likely they are to form a relationship. **Proximity** refers to being physically near someone else. People choose friends and lovers from the pool of people available to them, and availability depends heavily on proximity.
>
> One theory about why proximity is so important involves the idea of repeated exposure to new stimuli. The more people experience something, whether it is a song, a picture, or a person, the more they tend to like it. The phrase "it grew on me" refers to this reaction. When people are in physical proximity to each other, repeated exposure may increase their attraction to each other.

Annotate to Record Your Thinking

Annotation means jotting down your ideas, reactions, and opinions as you read. It is a way to "talk back" to the author—to question, agree, disagree, or comment. Annotations are particularly useful when you are planning to write about what you have read.

Two different types of annotations are useful: *symbols and abbreviations* and *statements and questions*. Depending on your preferences, you may choose to use one or both of these methods.

- **Symbols and abbreviations**. Marking key parts of an essay with symbols or abbreviations can help you clarify meaning and remember key information. Table 1-1 provides a list of useful symbols and abbreviations. You should feel free to add to this list in any way that suits your reading and learning styles.

TABLE 1-1 ANNOTATION SYMBOLS AND ABBREVIATIONS		
Type of Annotation		**Symbol and Example**
Underlining key ideas		The <u>most prominent unions in the United States are among public-sector employees</u> such as teachers and police.
Circling unknown words		One goal of labor unions is to address the apparent (asymmetry) of power in the employer–worker relationship.
Marking definitions	*def.*	To say that the balance of power favors one party over another is to introduce a disequilibrium.
Marking examples	*ex.*	Concessions may include additional benefits, increased vacation time, or higher wages.
Numbering lists of ideas, causes, reasons, or events	④	The components of power include ①self-range, ②population, ③natural resources, and geography.
Placing asterisks (stars) next to important passages	*	Once a dominant force in the United States economy, labor unions have been shrinking over the last few decades.
Putting question marks next to confusing passages	?	Strikes can be averted through the institutionalization of mediated bargaining.
Marking possible test items	T	A *closed shop* is a form of union agreement in which the employer agrees to hire only union workers.
Drawing arrows to show relationships		Standing between managers and employees is the (shop steward) who is both a union employee and a rank-and-file worker within the company that employs union members.
Marking summary statements	*sum.*	The greater the degree of conflict between labor and management, the more sensitive the negotiations need to be.
Marking essential information that you must remember		The largest and most important trade union in the United States, and the one that has had the most influence on labor-union relations, is the AFL-CIO.
Noting author's opinion of or attitude toward the topic	*opinion*	In a world where the gap between rich and poor is increasing, labor unions are essential to ensuring that workers are paid and treated fairly.
Indicating material to reread later	*RR*	At the apex of union density in the 1940s, only about 9.8 percent of public employees were represented by unions, while 33.9 percent of private, nonagricultural workers had such representation. In this decade, those proportions have essentially reversed, with 36 percent of public workers being represented by unions while private sector union density has plummeted to around 7 percent.

Here is an example of annotation using paragraphs 8 and 9 from "Liking and Loving."

Finally, <u>people have a very strong tendency to like people who like them,</u> a *def.* <u>simple but powerful concept referred to as</u> **reciprocity of liking** In one experiment, researchers paired college students with other students. Neither student in any of the pairs knew the other member. One member of each pair was randomly *?* chosen to receive some information from the experimenters about how the *other* student in the pair felt about the first member. In some cases, target students were led to believe that the other students liked them and, in other cases, that the * targets disliked them.

When the pairs of students were allowed to meet and talk with each other again, they <u>were friendlier, disclosed more information about themselves, agreed</u> *sum.* <u>with the other person more, and behaved in a warmer manner</u> *if they had been told* that the other student liked them. The other students came to like these students better as well, so liking produced more liking.

■ **Statements and questions.** In many of your writing assignments, you'll be asked to respond to an author's presentation, opinion, or suggestions. By recording your responses in the margin as you read, you take the first step toward writing about your own ideas.

Table 1-2 lists some types of statements and questions you might write in the margins of a reading. Note that it is perfectly acceptable to use abbreviations in your statements and questions. You should feel free to expand this list in any way that helps you "talk" with the reading.

TABLE 1-2 RESPONDING TO "LIKING AND LOVING" WITH MARGINAL STATEMENTS AND QUESTIONS	
Ways of Responding	Example of Marginal Annotation
Asking questions	What are the factors that become more important later in a relationship?
Challenging the author's ideas	Physical proximity sometimes has the opposite effect—too much closeness can be a bad thing.
Looking for inconsistencies	Authors say complementary qualities can be rewarding so why do they say it is similarity, not complementarity, that draws people together?
Adding examples	In the movie *Titanic*, Rose and Jack are romantic love (intimacy + passion), but Rose and her fiancé are empty love (commitment only).
Noting exceptions	You wouldn't want to limit your relationships only to people with the same attitudes/beliefs—it's more interesting to be around people with different ideas.
Disagreeing with the author	Anyone who bases friendship and attraction on physical beauty is too superficial for me.
Making associations with other sources	What do the authors of my marriage and family textbook say about what makes a relationship last?
Making judgments	This reading has some interesting ideas, but not all of them apply to me.
Making notes to yourself	Try to find that online article from last year with a quiz for rating different types of love relationships.
Asking instructor to clarify	Ask prof: What do the authors mean by the phrase "self-fulfilling prophecy" in paragraph 10?

EXERCISE 1-9   Highlighting and Annotating "Liking and Loving"

Directions: Read, highlight, and annotate "Liking and Loving: Interpersonal Attraction" in the Examining Professional Writing section of this chapter using the techniques described in this section.

Monitor and Strengthen Your Comprehension

For many daily activities, you maintain an awareness of how well you are performing them. In most sports, you know if you are playing a poor game; you actually keep score and deliberately try to correct errors and improve your performance. A similar type of monitoring or checking should occur as you read. You may understand certain ideas you read and be confused by others. At times, comprehension may be incomplete—you may miss certain key ideas and not know you missed them. You need to keep score of how well you understand.

Pay Attention to Comprehension Signals

When you read certain material, does it seem that everything clicks—that is, do ideas seem to fit together and make sense? Is that click noticeably absent at other times? The "Need to Know" box below lists and compares common signals that may help you assess your comprehension. Not all signals appear at the same time, and not all signals work for everyone.

NEED TO KNOW

Comprehension Signals

POSITIVE SIGNALS	NEGATIVE SIGNALS
Everything seems to fit and make sense; ideas flow logically from one to another.	Some pieces do not seem to belong; the material seems disjointed.
You understand what is important.	Nothing or everything seems important.
You are able to see where the author is leading.	You feel as if you are struggling to stay with the author and are unable to predict what will follow.
You are able to make connections among ideas.	You are unable to detect relationships; the organization is not apparent.
You read at a regular, comfortable pace.	You often slow down or reread.
You understand why the material was assigned.	You do not know why the material was assigned and cannot explain why it is important.
You can express the main ideas in your own words.	You must reread often and find it hard to paraphrase the author's ideas.
You recognize most words or can figure them out from the context.	Many words are unfamiliar.
You feel comfortable and have some knowledge about the topic.	The topic is unfamiliar, yet the author assumes you understand it.

EXERCISE 1-10   Assessing Your Comprehension of "Liking and Loving"

Directions: Answer the following questions based on your reading of the selection "Liking and Loving: Interpersonal Attraction" in the Examining Professional Reading section of this chapter.

1. How would you rate your overall comprehension? What positive signals did you sense? Did you feel any negative signals? Did you encounter unfamiliar vocabulary?

2. Did you feel at any time that you had lost, or were about to lose, comprehension? If so, go back to that section now. What made that section difficult to read?

3. Do you think previewing, highlighting, and annotating strengthened your comprehension? If so, how?

Whenever you sense your comprehension is weak or insufficient, take immediate action. Rereading is often *not* the best solution. Instead, try to figure out what is going wrong and change what you are doing. Ask yourself the following questions:

Ways to Strengthen Your Comprehension

- **Could the time, place, or distractions be interfering with my reading?** If so, make changes.

- **Is vocabulary the problem?** If so, slow down, mark words you do not know, and look them up.

- **Is background knowledge the problem?** Often if you lack background information that a writer assumes you have, you will have comprehension difficulties. For example, if you are reading about global climate change, and the author assumes you know what greenhouse gases are but you do not, you would be unable to understand the greenhouse effect. You may have to Google a topic and read a bit about it before returning to the material you are reading.

- **Are you reading too fast?** Difficult, complex, or technical material requires very slow reading; adjust your rate.

- **Will reading aloud help?** Often hearing as well as seeing ideas helps to make them clearer.

- **Will writing help?** Outlining, drawing maps, and highlighting may help you examine each idea separately and then see how they fit together.

EXERCISE 1-11   Strengthening Your Comprehension

WORKING TOGETHER

Directions: Find a difficult section in one of your textbooks; then work with a classmate to read each other's textbook sections and identify which strategies above would be most useful.

Outline and Map to Understand and Organize Information

Organizing information is a useful skill for both readers and writers. As a reader, organizing information will help you understand and learn what you read and see how ideas connect. Numerous studies have shown that information that is connected or grouped together is easier to learn and remember than random, unrelated bits of information. As a writer, organizing information using one or more of the strategies suggested in this chapter will help you see how your ideas fit together and will help you write paragraphs and essays in which the ideas follow logically.

Create Outlines

Outlining is an effective way to organize information and discover relationships between ideas. It forces you to select what is important from each paragraph and determine how it is related to key ideas in other paragraphs. Outlining enables you to learn and remember what you read because the process of selecting what is important and expressing it in your own words requires thought and comprehension and provides for repetition and review. Outlining also prepares you to write. By outlining your ideas before putting them in sentence and paragraph form, you can see how they fit together, rearrange them easily, and see where you need further information.

   Outlining involves listing major and minor ideas and showing how they are related. When you make an outline, follow the writer's organization. An outline usually follows a format like the ones below. On the left, you can see the basic structure of an outline; on the right is the outline of a personal essay about a trip to Texas:

I. First major topic
   A. First major idea
      1. First key supporting detail
      2. Second key supporting detail
   B. Second major idea
      1. First key supporting detail
         a. Minor detail or example
         b. Minor detail or example
      2. Second key supporting detail
II. Second major topic
   A. First major idea

I. Favorite cities
   A. San Antonio—beautiful, interesting history
      1. The Alamo
      2. Riverwalk
   B. Houston—friendly people
      1. Seeing Houston Astros play
         a. Excitement of game
         b. Getting lost after leaving Astrodome

   Notice that the most important ideas are closer to the left margin. The rule of thumb to follow is this: the less important the idea, the more it should be indented.

   Here are a few suggestions for writing outlines:

NEED TO KNOW

How to Outline

■ **Read a section completely before writing.**

■ **Do not worry about following the outline format exactly.** As long as your outline shows an organization of ideas, it will work for you.

■ **Use words and phrases or complete sentences,** whichever is easier for you.

■ **Use your own words, and do not write too much.**

■ **Pay attention to headings.** Be sure that all the information you place underneath a heading explains or supports that heading. In the outline above, for instance, the entries "San Antonio" and "Houston" are correctly placed under the major topic "Favorite Cities." Likewise, "The Alamo" and "Riverwalk" are under the "San Antonio" heading.

EXERCISE 1-12   ## Completing an Outline

Directions: After reading the passage below, fill in the missing information in the outline that follows.

Gossip

There can be no doubt that we spend a great deal of time gossiping. In fact, gossip seems universal among all cultures, and among some groups gossip is a commonly accepted ritual.

Gossip involves making social evaluations about a person who is not present during the conversation; it generally occurs when two people talk about a third party.

In the organization, gossip has particularly important consequences and in many instances has been shown to lead to firings, lawsuits, and damaged careers. And because of the speed and ease with which members of an organization can communicate with each other (instant messaging, e-mail, and blogs, for example) gossip can spread quickly and broadly.

People often gossip in order to get some kind of reward; for example, to hear more gossip, gain social status or control, have fun, cement social bonds, or make social comparisons.

Gossiping, however, often leads others to see you more negatively—regardless of whether your gossip is positive or negative or whether you're sharing this gossip with strangers or with friends.

In addition to its negative impact on the gossiper, gossiping often has ethical implications. In many instances, gossiping would be considered unethical: for example, when you use it to unfairly hurt another person, when you know it's not true, when no one has the right to such personal information, or when you are breaking a promise of secrecy.

—DeVito, *Human Communication*, p. 154

I. Gossip
  A. Popularity of gossip
    1. Occurs in all cultures
    2. _____
  B. _____
    1. Social evaluations about a person not present
    2. Occurs when two people talk about a third
  C. Gossip in organizations
    1. _____
    2. Can spread quickly because of the ease of communication in the organization
  D. Reasons for gossip
    1. _____
      a. Examples: to hear more gossip, to gain social status or control, to have fun, to cement social bonds, to make social comparisons

E. Consequences
  1. _____
  2. _____
    a. Examples: hurting another person, sharing information people have no right to know, breaking promises of secrecy

---

EXERCISE 1-13

Writing an Outline of a Section of "Liking and Loving"

Directions: Write an outline of the section of "Liking and Loving: Interpersonal Attraction" titled "The Rules of Attraction" (pp. 6–8, paragraphs 2–10).

Draw Idea Maps

Mapping is a visual method of organizing information. It involves drawing diagrams to show how ideas in a paragraph or chapter are related. Maps can take many forms. You can hand draw them or use a computer.

 NEED TO KNOW

How to Draw Maps

1. **Identify the overall topic or subject.** Write it in the center or at the top of the page.
2. **Identify major ideas that relate to the topic.** Using a line, connect each piece of information to the central topic.
3. **As you discover supporting details that further explain an idea already mapped, connect those details with new lines.**

Read the following paragraph on fashions, and then study the map that follows it:

> Why do fashions occur in the first place? One reason is that some cultures, like ours, *value change:* what is new is good, even better. Thus, in many modern societies clothing styles change yearly, while people in traditional societies may wear the same style for generations. A second reason is that many industries promote quick changes in fashion to increase sales. A third reason is that fashions usually trickle down from the top. A new style may occasionally originate from lower-status groups, as blue jeans did. But most fashions come from upper-class people who like to adopt some style or artifact as a badge of their status. But they cannot monopolize most status symbols for long. Their style is adopted by the middle class, maybe copied or modified for use by lower-status groups, offering many people the prestige of possessing a high-status symbol.

—Thio, *Sociology*, p. 534

Sample Map

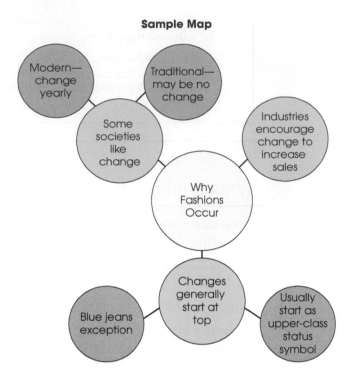

You can use idea maps to help you understand readings by discovering how they are organized and studying how ideas relate to one another. For writing, idea maps can help you organize your own ideas and check to be sure that all the ideas you have included belong in an essay.

Though they take time to draw, idea maps will save you time in the long run. You can avoid rereading, and the content of an essay will stick in your mind, preparing you for class discussions and writing about the reading. Use the model that follows to draw idea maps of articles, essays, or chapters. You may need to add extra boxes or you may not need all the boxes included, depending on the number of ideas and details in the reading selection. The following model shows only the essay's main point (thesis) and the key ideas. You can draw idea maps that include details as well, if it suits your purpose.

Model for Idea Map

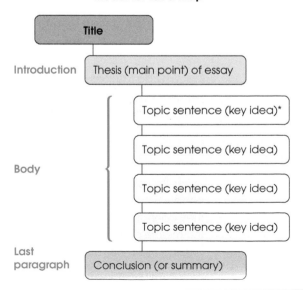

* The number of paragraphs may vary.

Once you are skilled at drawing maps, you can become more creative, drawing different types of maps to fit what you are reading. For example, you can draw a *time line* to show historical events in the order in which they occurred. A time line starts with the earliest event and ends with the most recent.

Sample Time Line

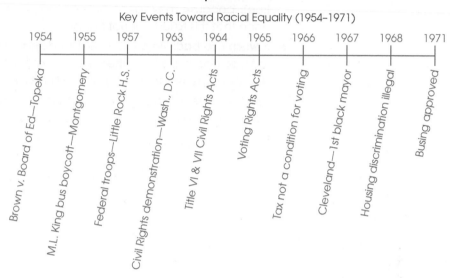

Key Events Toward Racial Equality (1954–1971)

Another type of map is one that shows a process—the steps involved in doing something. This type of map is useful for understanding material written in chronological order or describing a process as well as for writing using these patterns (see Chapter 6).

Sample Process Map

Process: How to Assemble a Birdhouse

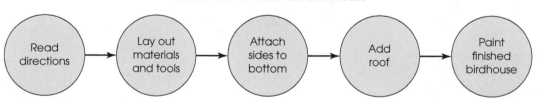

EXERCISE 1-14   Completing a Map

Directions: After reading the following paragraphs, complete each section of the map in which a blank line appears. Fill in the writer's main points as well as some supporting details.

Excuses are explanations designed to reduce the negative effects of your behavior and help to maintain your positive image. Different researchers have classified excuses into varied categories. One of the best typologies classifies excuses into three main types:

- **I didn't do it:** Here you deny that you have done what you're being accused of. You may then bring up an alibi to prove you couldn't have done it or perhaps you may accuse another person of doing what you're being blamed for ("I never said that" or "I wasn't even near the place when it happened"). These "I didn't do it" types are generally the worst excuses (unless they're true), because they fail to acknowledge responsibility and offer no assurance that this failure will not happen again.

- **It wasn't so bad:** Here you admit to doing it but claim the offense was not really so bad or perhaps there was justification for the behavior ("I only padded the expense account by a few bucks").

- **Yes, but:** Here you claim that extenuating circumstances accounted for the behavior; for example, that you weren't in control of yourself at the time or that you didn't intend to do what you did ("I never intended to hurt him; I was actually trying to help").

—DeVito, *The Interpersonal Communication Book*, p. 220

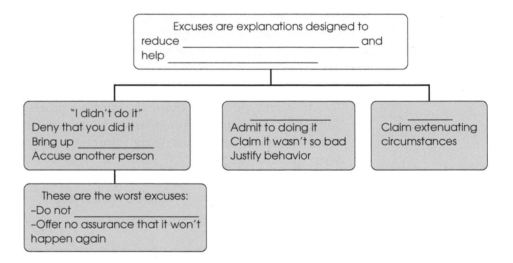

| EXERCISE 1-15 | Drawing an Idea Map of a Section of "Liking and Loving" |

Directions: Draw an idea map of the section titled "Love is a Triangle—Robert Sternberg's Triangular Theory of Love" (paragraphs 11–20) in the professional essay "Liking and Loving: Interpersonal Attraction" using the model shown above as a guide.

Read and Think About Visuals

All **visual aids** share one goal: to illustrate concepts and help you understand them better. Visual aids work best when you read them *in addition to* the text, not *instead of* the text. Keep in mind that the author chose the visual aid, or **graphic**, for a specific purpose. To fully understand the reading, you should be able to explain that purpose.

A General Approach to Reading Graphics

You will encounter many types of graphics in your reading materials. These include photos, graphs, charts, diagrams, and infographics. Here is a step-by-step approach to reading any type of graphic effectively. As you read, apply each step to the figure "Who Ends Up Poor? Poverty by Education and Race-Ethnicity."

1. **Look for the reference in the text**. When you see a reference, finish reading the sentence, and then look at the specific graphic. In some cases, you will need to go back and forth between the text and the graphic, especially if the graphic has multiple parts. Here is a portion of the reference in which the figure "Who Ends Up Poor? Poverty By Education and Race-Ethnicity" originally appeared:

    > You are aware that education is a vital factor in poverty, but you may not know just how powerful it is. Look at Figure 10.10. One of every 4 people who drop out of high school is poor, but only 5 of 100 people who finish college end up in poverty. As you can see, the chances that someone will be poor become less with each higher level of education.

2. **Read the title and caption**. The **title** will identify the subject, and the **caption** will provide important information. In some cases, the caption will specify the graphic's key take-away point. The title of the figure makes the graph's subject clear: *the relationship among education, race-ethnicity, and poverty*.

3. **Examine how the graphic is organized and labeled**. Read all headings and labels. **Labels** tell you what topics or categories are being discussed. Sometimes a label is turned sideways, like the words "Percentage in Poverty."

Who Ends Up Poor? Poverty by Education and Race-Ethnicity

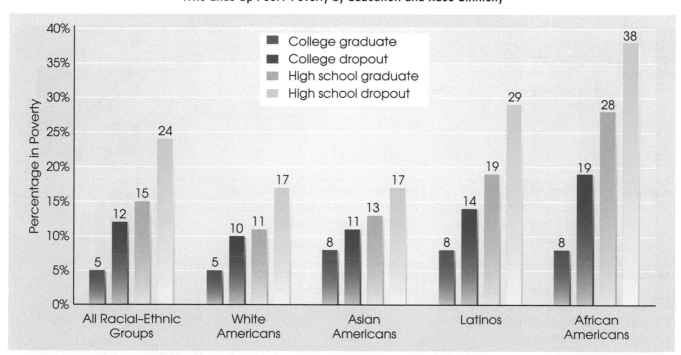

Note that the above graphic has a source note (found at the bottom of the graphic) that provides information on how where the data was obtained.

4. **Look at the legend**. The **legend** is the guide to the graphic's colors, terms, and other important information. In the graphic, the legend appears in the top middle of the graphic and explains the color coding used to designate level of education.

5. **Analyze the graphic**. Based on what you see, determine the graphic's key purpose. For example, is its purpose to show change over time, describe a process, present statistics? The purpose of the figure is clear: it compares the percentage of people of various race-ethncitiy groups in poverty at various educational levels.

6. **Study the data to identify trends or patterns**. If the graphic includes numbers, look for unusual statistics or unexplained variations. What conclusions can you draw from the data?

7. **Make a brief summary note**. In the margin, jot a brief note summarizing the graphic's trend, pattern, or key point. Writing will help cement the idea in your mind. A summary note of the figure might read, "For all race-ethnicity groups, as level of education increases, poverty decreases."

Think Critically About Visuals

Most graphics display information in an abbreviated, more easily accessible form than verbal materials. Because information is condensed and may have little or no interpretation offered by the author of the text in which they are included, it is especially important to analyze and evaluate all visuals. Look at the following chart, which shows how writers and readers use different types of graphics.

TYPE OF GRAPHIC	WRITERS USE THESE TO …	READERS USE THESE TO …	EXAMPLE
Photographs	Spark interest, provide perspective, or offer examples.	Help them visualize the concept and make it easier to remember. Readers can also use photographs as writing prompts.	
Bar graphs	Compare amounts or show changes over time using bars of different lengths. Bars may be horizontal or vertical.	Help them understand the relationship between two ideas. Using bar graphs, readers can make comparisons.	
Line graphs	Show trends or changes over time by connecting points along a line. Line graphs may have a single variable or multiple variables.	Help them understand data about time or events and how it changes.	

TYPE OF GRAPHIC	WRITERS USE THESE TO …	READERS USE THESE TO …	EXAMPLE
Charts	Provide visual method for viewing data quickly. Can be used to show a comparison or relationship or to organize a number of different items of information in an accessible format.	Help them make comparisons and evaluate connections between items of related information.	Regional Corporate Hierarchy & International Support Systems John Takai/Fotolia
Pie charts (Circle graphs)	Show whole/part relationships or how parts of a unit have been divided or classified.	Help them compare the parts with each other or compare each part with the whole.	mhatzapa/Fotolia
Diagrams	Explain an object, idea, or process by showing the appearance, structure, or workings of it.	Help them understand key vocabulary, the parts of a system, relationships between parts, and sequences of a process.	Parietal Lobe Frontal Lobe Occipital Lobe Temporal Lobe Cerebellum Pons Medulla Oblongata Spinal Cord Athanasia Nomikou/Fotolia
Infographics	Combine several types of visual aids into one, often merging photos with text, diagrams, or tables. Infographics are often designed to stand on their own.	Help them gain information about a subject quickly through a combination of text and graphics all in one document.	MEDICAL INFOGRAPHIC incomible/Fotolia

Analyze Photographs

Photographs are particularly powerful because they often have emotional impact and can be used to shape a viewer's impressions or understanding of a situation. Photographs deserve close analysis for the following reasons:

■ **A writer's choice of photo may reveal his or her bias.** For example, in an article about the purpose and function of zoos, a writer who includes a photo of a captive lion unhappily pacing in a tiny yard may reveal that he or she feels zoos mistreat animals.

■ **A photograph may distort a situation, either intentionally or by accident.** A photo of public school teachers participating in a rally opposing school budget reductions may portray them as activists if included with an article that discusses community participation in protests.

- **A photograph may be adjusted, cropped, or otherwise manipulated to control the viewer's perception of the subject or situation.** A photo of a crowd attending a concert may be cropped to show unruly attendees, even if the majority of concert-goers behaved properly.

When analyzing photographs, ask the following questions:

- What is the image intended to show? What is its purpose? Does it reveal bias?
- Is the image representative of the situation it depicts?
- How does the caption direct your attention?
- Examine the foreground and background. What details do they reveal?

EXERCISE 1-16   Analyzing a Photograph

Directions: Study the photograph here and answer the analyzing questions you just learned about.

The bullfight: a cultural experience or animal cruelty?

EXERCISE 1-17   Analyzing the Photograph from "Liking and Loving"

Directions: Answer the questions listed above for the DiMaggio and Monroe photo included in the reading "Liking and Loving" in the Examining Professional Writing section of this chapter. What other photos could have been used to illustrate other concepts discussed in the reading?

Analyze Graphics

Graphics are packed with information, so be sure to take your time when reading and analyzing them. For all graphics, be sure to ask the following questions:

- How does the graphic relate to the text that introduces or discusses it?
- Why was the particular type of graphic chosen? Could others have worked better or provided more complete information?

■ Is the data from a reliable and trustworthy source?

■ Is the data current and accurate?

■ Is the data presented fairly and clearly?

■ Is the title accurately descriptive of its contents?

Now let's apply these questions to the bar graph "Who Ends Up Poor? Poverty by Education and Race-Ethnicity." This bar graph, as the title states, compares the earnings per year of men and women by educational level. The bar graph format was chosen because it dramatically shows two important trends: (1) that men earn more than women at all levels of education and (2) that salaries for both men and women increase as their levels of education increase. The source, the *U.S. Census Bureau*, is a trustworthy and reliable source. The data is dated, having been collected in 2014.

EXERCISE 1-18 Analyzing a Graphic

Directions: For the circle graph below, answer each of the questions listed above and at the bottom of page 28 as well as the following questions:

1. Why is the category "Watching Television and Using Other Technomedia" vague and unclear? Why is the category "Work or School" equally vague?

2. On what group or type of people is the data in the pie chart based? Would you expect the data to be different if the population were only college students?

3. What activities might fall into the "Other Activities" category?

Sample Circle Graph

Average Time Spent at Various Activities

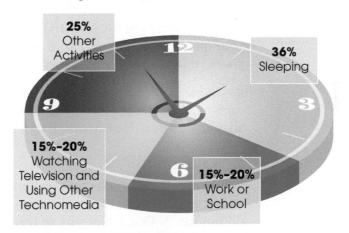

Source: HOMPSON, WILLIAM E.; HICKEY, JOSEPH V., SOCIETY IN FOCUS: AN INTROUDCTION TO SOCIOLOGY, CENSUS UPDATE, 7th Ed., © 2012, p. 10. Reprinted and Electronically reproduced by permission of Pearson Education, Inc., New York, NY.

—Thompson and Hickey, *Society in Focus*, p. 10

Use the SQ3R Reading/Study System

SQ3R is a system that combines reading and study. Instead of reading a chapter one day and studying it later when a test is announced, you can do both at once using SQ3R. The SQ3R system is a model. Once you see how and why SQ3R works, you can adapt it to suit your own academic needs.

Steps in the SQ3R System

The SQ3R system involves five basic steps that integrate reading and study techniques. As you read the following steps, some of them will seem similar to the skills you have already learned.

S—Survey   Try to become familiar with the organization and general content of the material you are to read. This step is the same as previewing (presented earlier in this chapter).

1. **Read the title.**
2. **Read the lead-in or introduction.** (If it is extremely long, read just the first paragraph.)
3. **Read each boldfaced heading and the first sentence that follows it.** If the material lacks headings, read the first sentence of a few paragraphs on each page.
4. **Read the titles of maps, charts, or graphs.**
5. **Read the last paragraph or summary.**
6. **Read the end-of-chapter questions.**

From surveying the material, you should know generally what it is about and how it is organized.

Q—Question   Try to form questions that you can answer as you read. The easiest way to do this is to turn each boldfaced heading into a question. Think of these as similar to the guide questions discussed in the Form Guide Questions section of this chapter.

R—Read   Read the material section by section. As you read each section, look for the answer to the question you formed from the heading of that section.

R—Recite   After you finish each section, stop. Check to see whether you can answer your question for the section. If you cannot, look back to find the answer. Then check your recall again. Be sure to complete this step after you read each section.

R—Review   When you have finished the whole reading assignment, go back to each heading; recall your question and try to answer it. If you cannot recall the answer, be sure to look back and find the answer. Then test yourself again.

Why SQ3R Works

Results of research studies overwhelmingly suggest that students who use the SQ3R system understand and remember what they read much better than students who do not use it. One major way to learn is through repetition, and reading/study systems such as SQ3R provide some of the repetition necessary to ensure learning. SQ3R also has other advantages over ordinary reading:

- Surveying (previewing) gives you a mental organization or structure—you know what to expect.
- You always feel that you are looking for something specific rather than wandering aimlessly through a printed page.
- When you find the information you are looking for, you feel you have accomplished something.
- If you can remember the information in the Recite and Review steps, you know you have learned it.

| EXERCISE 1-19 | Using SQ3R |

Directions: Use the SQ3R method to read and review the professional reading in Chapter 3 titled "Emoji: Trendy Slang or a Whole New Language?" Write the questions you create on a separate sheet of paper, leaving space for the answers. Answer your questions after you have read the section.

Post-Reading Strategies

■ **GOAL 4**
Use post-reading strategies

Your instructors expect you to learn large amounts of textbook material. Rereading to learn is *not* an effective strategy. Writing *is* an effective strategy. In fact, writing is an excellent means of improving both how much you understand and remember. Writing forces you to think about how ideas are related and connected. Writing is a good way of testing your understanding as well. If you can express a writer's ideas in your own words, you probably understand them; if you cannot, this is a warning signal.

Paraphrase to Restate Ideas of Others

A **paraphrase** restates the ideas of a passage in your own words. You retain the author's meaning, but you use your own wording. In speech, we paraphrase frequently. For example, when you relay a message from one person to another, you convey the meaning but do not use the person's exact words. A paraphrase makes a passage's meaning clearer and often more concise.

Paraphrasing is a useful technique for

■ **recording information from reference sources to use in writing a research paper.**

■ **understanding difficult material for which exact, detailed comprehension is required.** For instance, you might paraphrase the steps in solving a math problem or the procedures for a lab setup in chemistry.

■ **reading material that is stylistically complex or with an obvious slant, bias, strong tone, or detailed description.**

Study the following example of a paraphrase of the stylistically difficult preamble to the United States Constitution. Notice that it restates in different words the intent of the preamble.

Preamble

We the People of the United States, in Order to form a more perfect Union, establish Justice, insure domestic Tranquillity, provide for the common defence, promote the general Welfare, and secure the Blessings of Liberty to ourselves and our Posterity, do ordain and establish this Constitution of the United States of America.
Source: U.S. Constitution

Paraphrase

The citizens of the United States established the Constitution to create a better country and to provide rightful treatment, peace, protection, and well-being for themselves and future citizens.

Notice first how synonyms were substituted for words in the original—*citizens* for *people*, *country* for *union*, *protection* for *defense*, and so forth. Next, notice that the order of information was rearranged.

Use the suggestions in the box below to paraphrase effectively.

 NEED TO KNOW

How to Paraphrase

1. **Read the entire material before writing anything.** Read slowly and carefully.

2. **As you read, focus on both exact meanings and relationships between ideas.**

3. **Read each sentence and identify its core meaning.** Use synonyms, replacing the author's words with your words. Look away from the original sentence and write in your own words what it means. Then re-read the original and add any additional or qualifying information.

4. **Do not try to paraphrase word by word.** Instead, work with clauses and phrases (idea groups). If you are unsure of the meaning of a word or phrase, check a dictionary to locate a more familiar meaning.

5. **You may combine several original sentences into a more concise paraphrase.** It is also acceptable to present ideas in a different order from that in the original.

6. **Compare your paraphrase with the original for completeness and accuracy.**

7. **Indicate the source of the material you paraphrase in order to avoid plagiarism** (see Chapter 10 for details on citing sources).

EXERCISE 1-20 Writing a Paraphrase for "Liking and Loving"

Directions: Write a paraphrase of paragraph 19 of "Liking and Loving" in the Examining Professional Writing section of this chapter.

Summarize to Condense Information

A **summary** is a compact restatement of the important points of a passage. Unlike a paraphrase, a summary does not include all the information presented in the original, so you must select what to include. A summary contains only the gist of the text, with limited background, explanation, or detail. Although summaries vary in length, they are often one-quarter or less of the length of the original.

Summaries are useful in a variety of writing situations in which a condensed overview of material is needed. You might summarize information in preparation for an essay exam or key points of news articles required in an economics class. Some class assignments also require summarization. Lab reports for science courses include a summary of results. A literature instructor may ask you to summarize the plot of a short story.

To write a good summary, you need to understand the material and identify the writer's major points. Here are some tips to follow:

NEED TO KNOW

How to Write a Summary

1. **Underline each major idea in the material.**
2. **Write one sentence that states the writer's most important idea.** This sentence will be the topic sentence of your summary.
3. **Be sure to use your own words rather than those of the author.**
4. **Focus on the author's major ideas,** not on supporting details.
5. **Keep the ideas in the summary in the same order as in the original material.**
6. **Indicate the source of the material you summarize to avoid plagiarism** (see Chapter 10 for details on citing sources).

| EXERCISE 1-21 | Practicing Summarizing |

Directions: After reading the following paragraphs, select the choice that best summarizes each one.

_____ 1.   When a group is too large for an effective discussion or when its members are not well informed on the topic, a *panel* of individuals may be selected to discuss the topic for the benefit of others, who then become an audience. Members of a panel may be particularly well informed on the subject or may represent divergent views. For example, your group may be interested in UFOs (unidentified flying objects) and hold a discussion for your classmates. Or your group might tackle the problems of tenants and landlords. Whatever your topic, the audience should learn the basic issues from your discussion.

—Gronbeck et al., *Principles of Speech Communication*, p. 302

a. Panel members are usually well informed on the subject, even though they may express different views. Members of a panel on UFOs, for example, may disagree about whether they exist.

b. Whatever topic a panel discusses, it is important that the audience learns basic information about the topic. For this reason, only well-informed people should participate in panels.

c. If a group is very large, or if its members are not familiar with a particular topic, a panel of people is sometimes chosen to talk about the topic. The rest of the group should get essential information from the panel's discussion.

d. Panels work effectively in large groups, such as in classrooms. Panels also work well when a group's members don't know very much about a topic. For example, a panel might talk about the problems of tenants and landlords to a group that was not familiar with such problems.

_____ 2.   The process of becoming hypnotized begins when the people who will be hypnotized find a comfortable body position and become thoroughly relaxed. Without letting their minds wander to other matters, they focus their attention on a specific object or sound, such as a metronome or the hypnotist's voice. Then, based on both what the hypnotherapist (hypnotist) expects to occur and actually sees occurring, she or he tells the clients how they will feel as the hypnotic process continues. For instance, the hypnotist may say, "You are feeling completely relaxed" or "Your eyelids are becoming heavy." When people being hypnotized recognize that their feelings match the hypnotist's comments, they are likely to believe that some change is taking place. That belief seems to increase their openness to other statements made by the hypnotist.

—Uba and Huang, *Psychology*, p. 148

a. The first step in being hypnotized is for people to feel comfortable and at ease. Then they pay close attention to a particular item or sound while the hypnotist tells them how they will feel. If they believe their feelings are the same as what the hypnotist is saying, they will be more likely to accept other comments the hypnotist makes.

b. If the hypnotist says, "Your eyelids are becoming heavy," then the person being hypnotized would believe such a statement. The person being hypnotized would also continue to believe other statements the hypnotist makes.

c. The most important part of being hypnotized is to feel comfortable and relaxed. If you are uncomfortable at the beginning, you might not be willing to accept what the hypnotist is saying. To feel relaxed, try to focus on changes that are taking place.

d. If the hypnotist says, "You are feeling completely relaxed," people being hypnotized have to believe that this is true. If such belief does not occur, then it is unlikely that hypnosis will happen. Once the subject feels relaxed, his or her eyelids get heavy.

| EXERCISE 1-22 | Writing a Summary of a Section of "Liking and Loving" |

Directions: Write a summary of the material under the heading "Reciprocity of Liking" (paragraphs 8–10) of the reading "Liking and Loving: Interpersonal Attraction" in the Examining Professional Reading section of this chapter using the guidelines in the previous "Need to Know" box.

Review to Strengthen Recall

After finishing reading any essay or chapter once, you probably cannot recall everything you read. After reading, be sure to review and test yourself.

Review Immediately after Reading

Immediate review is done right after you have finished reading an assignment or writing an outline or summary. When you finish any of these, you may feel like breathing a sigh of relief and taking a break. However, it is worth the time and effort to spend another five minutes reviewing what you just read and refreshing your memory. The best way to do this is to go back through the chapter and reread the headings, graphic material, introduction, summary, and any underlining or marginal notes.

Immediate review works because it consolidates, or draws together, the material just read. It also gives a final, lasting impression of the content. Research indicates that review done immediately rather than delayed until a later time makes a large difference in the amount remembered.

Review Periodically

Although immediate review will increase your recall of information, it will not help you retain information for long periods of time. To remember information over time, periodically refresh your memory. This is known as **periodic review**. Go back over the material on a regular basis. Do this by looking again at those sections that carry the basic meaning and reviewing your underlining, outlining, and/or summaries.

Test Yourself

One of the best ways to remember what you read is to test yourself. Self-testing will show you what you do and do not know, thereby making learning more efficient. You will not waste time learning what you already know and can focus on learning what you do not know. Self-testing is good practice for exams too. Use the following steps to test yourself:

1. **Use your guide questions.** Check your ability to answer each.
2. **For textbooks, use all in- and end-of-chapter review materials.** These include self-checks, vocabulary lists, review questions, and discussion questions.
3. **Work with a classmate.** Practice asking and answering questions.

EXERCISE 1-23	Reviewing to Strengthen Your Recall of "Liking and Loving"
WORKING TOGETHER	**Directions:** Working with a classmate, test each other on the selection "Liking and Loving: Interpersonal Attraction." Take turns asking and answering questions about the reading.

Think Critically

■ **GOAL 5**
Think critically

While there will be some overlap between the skills you developed in high school and those you will use in college, the biggest difference between high school and college is the difference in your instructors' expectations of how you *think*.

Much of your elementary and high school education focused on memorization. In college, however, you are expected not only to learn and memorize new information but also to analyze what you are learning, formulate your own opinions, and even conduct your own research. In other words, your college instructors expect you to *think critically*—to interpret and evaluate what you hear and read rather than accept everything you read as "the truth." The term *critical* does not mean "negative." Rather, it means "analytical" and "probing"—that is, thinking more deeply about the subjects you study. And your instructors expect you to demonstrate your critical thinking skills through class participation and in writing essays, research papers, and essay exams.

To succeed in college, then, you will need to combine your basic reading and writing skills with critical thinking skills.

The Value of Critical Thinking

The benefits of developing your critical thinking skills apply to both your college courses and your everyday life. In college, critical thinking skills allow you to

- evaluate whether print and online sources are reliable.
- distinguish good information from bad, incomplete, inaccurate, or misleading information.
- write effective essays and research papers.
- do well on essay exams.

In your everyday life, critical thinking skills will help you

- become a savvy consumer and make good financial choices.
- understand when companies are trying to manipulate you with their advertising or public-relations efforts.
- resolve conflicts or come to acceptable compromises.
- solve problems using a logical, step-by-step process.

College is about opening your mind to new ways of thinking and expressing those thoughts in writing. These new ways of thinking may challenge some of your attitudes, opinions, or beliefs. Be sure to recognize and analyze these different attitudes, opinions, and beliefs. Avoid the temptation to reject them only because they are different from yours.

This text will help you develop your critical thinking skills in several ways. Chapter 9 is devoted to more specific critical reading skills such as distinguishing between fact and opinion, making inferences, and identifying an author's purpose and analyzing his or her intended audience. The questions that follow each end-of-chapter professional reading contain a section titled "Reading and Writing: An Integrated Perspective" that offers you practice in applying critical thinking skills.

| EXERCISE 1-24 | Thinking Critically |

Directions: Answer the following critical thinking questions for the reading "Liking and Loving" presented in the Examining Professional Writing section of this chapter.

1. What is the authors' purpose for writing? How well do they achieve their purpose?

2. Do you think the authors are trying to influence your opinions?

3. Based on the reading, what do you think the authors see as the most important qualities for a lasting relationship?

Liking and Loving: Interpersonal Attraction

Saundra C. Ciccarelli and J. Noland White

In the Examining Professional Writing section of this chapter, you read "Liking and Loving: Interpersonal Attraction" and examined the basic structure of the essay. Now it is time to take a closer look at the reading by responding to the questions that follow.

Writing in Response to Reading

Checking Your Comprehension

Answer each of the following questions using complete sentences.

1. What does *interpersonal attraction* mean?
2. According to the reading, what factors are involved in the attraction of one person to another?
3. Explain the concept of *reciprocity of liking*.
4. What are the three components of Robert Sternberg's theory of love? Define each component.
5. Describe the components of *romantic love, companionate love*, and *consummate love*.

Strengthening Your Vocabulary

Using the word's context, word parts, or a dictionary, write a brief definition of each of the following words as it is used in the reading.

1. interpersonal (paragraph 1) _____
2. superficial (paragraph 2) _____
3. validation (paragraph 6) _____
4. disclosed (paragraph 9) _____
5. prophecy (paragraph 10) _____
6. binding (paragraph 19) _____
7. evolve (paragraph 20) _____

Examining the Reading: Using Idea Maps

Review the reading by completing the missing parts of the following idea map.

VISUALIZE IT!

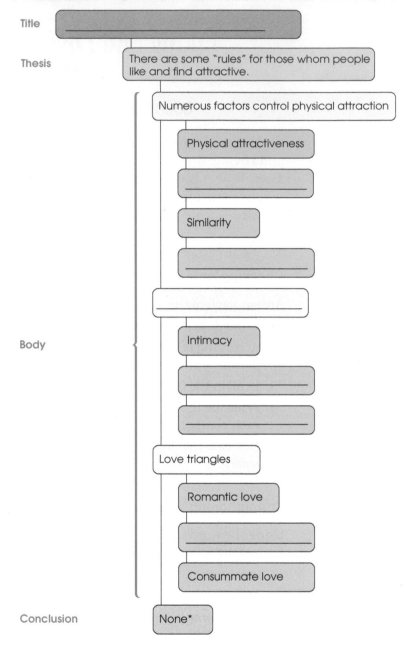

*Although most articles and essays have a conclusion, this reading, because it was excerpted from a college textbook, has no conclusion since it was part of a textbook chapter.

Thinking Critically: An Integrated Perspective

React and respond to the reading by discussing the following:

1. Discuss the idea that opposites attract. Do you find it more rewarding to form a relationship with someone who has similar qualities or complementary qualities?

2. What are the factors that make you want to know someone better? What are the qualities you look for in a friend or romantic interest?

3. Write a journal entry giving examples from your own experience that illustrate the concepts of proximity, similarity, complementarity, and reciprocity of liking.

4. For what audience is this selection written?

5. Why did the authors include the photo of Joe DiMaggio and Marilyn Monroe?

6. Consider the seven different kinds of love shown in Figure A (p. 9). Which types of love sound least desirable or positive? What element is missing from the less positive types of love?

7. What types of evidence do the authors use to support their ideas? How convincing or believable is the evidence?

Paragraph Options

1. Write a paragraph exploring the idea that "liking produces more liking." Have you ever experienced this in your own life?

2. The reading discusses a number of different kinds of love. Write a paragraph identifying the type of love that you consider ideal. Be sure to define it and give reasons for your choice.

3. Write a paragraph giving your own "dictionary definition" of love or different types of love. Include examples of the people you love.

Essay Options

4. Do the "rules of attraction" described in the selection reflect your own experiences? Write an essay exploring the different factors in interpersonal attraction. What qualities make you want to know someone better? How important to you are each of the factors described in the selection?

5. Consider the author's reference to non-Western cultures in which choices for a mate are often made by parents or matchmakers (paragraph 19). How would you respond to someone else's choosing your mate? What advantages and disadvantages can you imagine in this situation? Write an essay exploring the answers.

6. The authors state that one form of love may evolve into another. Do some forms of love remain the same? Have you observed an evolution in any of your relationships or in those of others around you? Consider friendships and family relationships as well as romantic relationships, and write an essay exploring these questions.

Making Connections Between the Readings

This chapter's reading concerns interpersonal relationships, as does Chapter 8. Use the following writing assignments to integrate your ideas about interpersonal relationships. Write a paragraph or an essay in response to one of the following prompts.

1. The authors of "The Woes of Internet Dating" (Chapter 8) and "Finding a Mate: Not the Same as It Used to Be" (Chapter 8) write about technology and dating. How do you think the authors of "Liking and Loving: Interpersonal Attraction" (in this chapter) would respond to the trend of Internet dating? In a paragraph, write a response to the question and explain your response using the Rules of Attraction in this chapter's reading as support.

2. James Henslin writes briefly about arranged marriages in "Finding a Mate: Not the Same as It Used to Be" (Chapter 8). What position do you think Ciccarelli and White (in this chapter) would take on the long-term success of an arranged marriage? In an essay, answer this question and explain why you think the authors would respond as you predict. Be sure to use evidence from "Liking and Loving: Interpersonal Attraction" (in this chapter) as support for your ideas.

3. Which author in Chapter 8, Claire Stroup or James Henslin, would be most likely to agree with Ciccarelli and White, the authors of "Liking and Loving:

Interpersonal Attraction" (in this chapter)? In a paragraph, answer the question and explain your reasoning using support from the readings.

4. If you had to create one title that would be suitable for all three essays, what would it be? Write a paragraph in which you explain why your title is an effective one for the three essays. Be sure to use details from the three essays to support your points.

SELF-TEST SUMMARY

To test yourself, cover the Answer column with a sheet of paper and answer each question in the left column. Evaluate each of your answers as you work by sliding the paper down and comparing your answer with what is printed in the Answer column.

QUESTION	ANSWER
■ **GOAL 1** Use the reading process and read actively What is involved in active reading?	Active reading involves reading each assignment differently, thinking and asking questions as you read, sorting the information as you read, and reviewing after reading.
■ **GOAL 2** Use pre-reading strategies What are some pre-reading strategies?	Pre-reading strategies include previewing, making predictions, forming guide questions, and connecting a reading to your own experience.
What is involved in previewing?	Previewing is a way of quickly familiarizing yourself with the organization and content of written material *before* beginning to read it. See the "Need to Know" box in the Pre-Reading Strategies section of this chapter for specific steps in previewing
■ **GOAL 3** Use interactive strategies during reading What are some strategies to use during reading?	Strategies to use during reading include highlighting, annotating, outlining, mapping, and the SQ3R reading/study system.
How does the SQ3R system help you retain information?	The SQ3R system integrates reading and study techniques through five steps: *survey, question, read, recite,* and *review*.
■ **GOAL 4** Use post-reading strategies What are some post-reading strategies?	Post-reading strategies include paraphrasing, summarizing, and reviewing.
What is a paraphrase?	A paraphrase restates the ideas of a passage in your own words.
What is a summary?	A summary is a compact restatement of the important points of a passage.
■ **GOAL 5** Think critically What is critical thinking?	Critical thinking means interpreting and evaluating what you hear and read rather than accepting everything as "the truth." Critical thinking skills are important in college and in everyday life.

An Overview of the Writing Process (with Reading)

Joerg Steber/Shutterstock

View Apart/Shutterstock

THINK About It!

Suppose you are completing an assignment for your reading–writing class. You are asked to study the photos above, read an essay on cultural differences, and then write an essay in response to that topic. How would you begin? What would you do as you read? How would you find ideas to write about? How would you organize your ideas? How would you be sure that you have written a clear, correct essay? Write a few sentences describing how you would tackle the assignment and what problems or difficulties you anticipate.

This chapter will give you an overview of the writing process and begin to address some of the writing problems you may have identified. In it you will explore the theme of cultural differences by reading a student essay and professional article on the topic.

What Is the Writing Process?

Writing is a skill you can learn with the help of this text, your instructor, and your classmates. Like any other skill, such as basketball, accounting, or cooking, writing requires both instruction and practice. Be sure to focus your attention on new techniques suggested by your instructor as well as the ones given in each chapter of this text. To improve, you often need to be open to doing things differently. Expect success; don't hesitate to experiment.

In this chapter, you will see there is much more to writing than sitting down at your computer and starting to type. It involves reading the ideas of others, generating and organizing your own ideas, and expressing your ideas in sentence, paragraph, and essay form. Writing is a process that involves working through and going back and forth among several steps. Once a draft is written, it also involves reading, rereading, and revising your work. Following the sample student writing in this chapter will give you a good sense of what writing involves.

Practical Advice about Writing

■ GOAL 1
Use strategies to become a successful writer

Use the following suggestions for becoming a successful writer.

Understand What Writing Is and Is Not

The following list explains some correct and incorrect notions about writing:

Writing is ...

- following a step-by-step process of planning, drafting, and revising.
- thinking through and organizing ideas.
- explaining *your* ideas or experiences clearly and correctly.
- using precise, descriptive, and accurate vocabulary.
- constructing clear, understandable sentences.
- a skill that can be learned.

Writing is not ...

- being able to pick up a pen (or sit at a computer) and write something wonderful on your first try.
- developing new, earthshaking ideas no one has ever thought of before.
- being primarily concerned with grammatical correctness.
- showing off a large vocabulary.
- constructing long, complicated sentences.

Get the Most Out of Your Writing Class

Attend all classes. Do not miss any classes, and be sure to come prepared to class with readings and writing assignments complete. Take notes during class, and ask questions about things you do not understand. Be sure to participate in class discussions and attend all writing conferences offered by your instructor.

Take a Positive Approach to Writing

Use the following tips to achieve success:

■ **Think first, then write.** Writing is a thinking process: it is an expression of your thoughts. Don't expect to be able to pick up a pen or sit down at a computer and immediately produce a well-written paragraph or essay. Plan to spend time generating ideas and deciding how to organize them before you write your first draft.

■ **Plan on making changes.** Most writers revise (rethink, rewrite, change, add, and delete) numerous times before they are pleased with their work. For example, I revised this chapter of *In Harmony* five times before I was satisfied with it.

■ **Give yourself enough time to write.** For most of us, writing does not come easily. It takes time to think, select a topic, generate ideas, organize them, draft a piece of writing, revise it, and proofread it. Reserve a block of time each day for writing. Use the time to read this text and to work on its writing exercises and assignments. Begin by reserving an hour per day. Although this may seem like a lot of time, most instructors expect you to spend at least two hours outside of class for every hour you spend in class. If your writing class meets for a total of three hours per week, then you should spend at least six hours per week working on writing.

■ **Develop a routine.** Try to work at the same time each day so you develop a routine that will be easy to follow. Be sure to work at peak periods of concentration. Don't write when you are tired, hungry, or likely to be interrupted.

■ **Take breaks.** If you get stuck and cannot think or write, take a break. Clear your mind by going for a walk, talking to a friend, or having a snack. Set a time limit for your break, though, so you return to work in a reasonable time. When you begin again, start by rereading what you have already written. If you still cannot make progress, use freewriting, brainstorming, and branching techniques (see the Step One: Generate Ideas section of this chapter) to generate more ideas about your topic.

Keep a Journal

A **writing journal** is a collection of your writing and reflections. Keeping a writing journal is an excellent way to improve your writing and keep track of your thoughts and ideas.

How to Keep a Writing Journal

1. Buy an 8.5-by-11-inch spiral-bound notebook. Alternatively, you can use a digital file. Use it exclusively for journal writing.

2. Reserve ten to fifteen minutes a day to write in your journal. Write every day, not just on days when a good idea strikes.

3. Write about whatever comes to mind. You might write about events that happened and your reactions to them or describe feelings, impressions, or worries. If you have trouble getting started, ask yourself some questions:

   ■ What happened at school, work, or home today?

   ■ What world, national, or local events occurred today?

- What am I worried about?
- What is a positive experience I have had lately? Maybe it was eating a good meal, making a new friend, or finding time to wash the car.
- What did I see today? Practice writing descriptions of beautiful, funny, interesting, or disturbing things you've noticed.
- What is the best or worst thing that happened today?
- Who did I talk to? What did I talk about? Record conversations as fully as you can.

Sample Journal Entries

The following student journal entries will give you a better picture of journal writing. They have been edited for easy reading. However, as you write, do not be concerned with neatness or correctness.

Jeffrey The best thing that happened today happened as soon as I got home from work. My cell phone rang. At first, I wasn't going to answer it because I was tired and in one of those moods when I wanted to be by myself. It rang so many times I decided to answer it. Am I glad I did! It was MaryAnn, a long-lost girlfriend whom I'd always regretted losing touch with. She said she had just moved back into the neighborhood, and ... I took it from there.

Acacia This morning while walking across campus to my math class, I stopped for a few minutes under a chestnut tree. Perfect timing! I've always loved collecting chestnuts, and they were just beginning to fall. When I was a kid, I used to pick up lunch bags full of them. I never knew what to do with them once I had them. I just liked picking them up, I guess. I remember liking their cold, sleek, shiny smoothness and how good they felt in my hand. So I picked up a few, rubbed them together in my hand, and went off to class, happy that some things never change.

Benefits of Journal Writing

When you write in your journal, you can practice writing without pressure or fear of criticism. Besides practice, journal writing has other benefits:

- Your journals will become a good source of ideas. When you have a paper assigned and must select your own topic, review your journal for ideas.
- You may find that journal writing becomes a way to think through problems, release pent-up feelings, or keep an enjoyable record of life experiences. Journal writing is writing *for yourself.*

Use Peer Review

Not everything you write in a college writing class needs to be graded by your instructor. Instead, you can get valuable "peer review," or feedback, from other members of your class. Peers (classmates) can tell you what they like and what they think you need to do to improve your writing. You can also learn a lot from reading and commenting on the work of other students. To learn more about peer review, see the Learn from Peer Review section later in this chapter.

Connect the Reading and Writing Processes

■ **GOAL 2**
Compare the reading and writing processes

In college, much of what you write will be in response to what you read. The reading and writing processes complement each other, as shown in Figure 2-1. Active reading, in which you interact with the text, annotate and highlight, take notes, and organize what you learn, is crucial to the writing process, and using the two together is what produces strong, clear, well-organized writing.

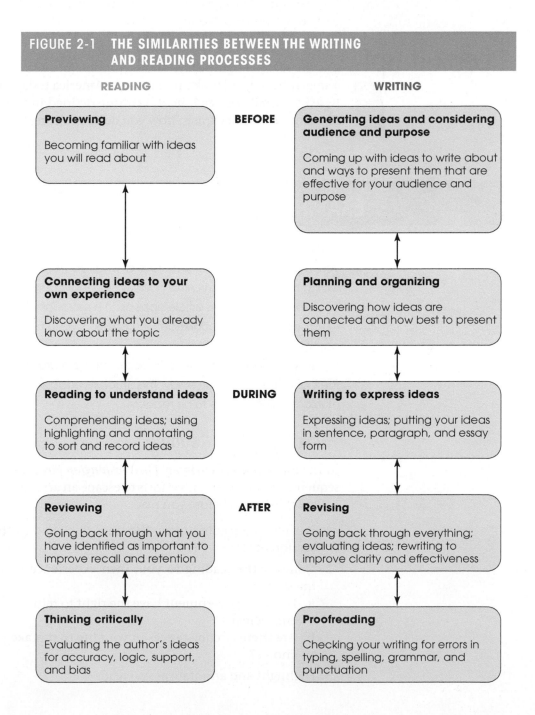

FIGURE 2-1 THE SIMILARITIES BETWEEN THE WRITING AND READING PROCESSES

READING		WRITING
Previewing Becoming familiar with ideas you will read about	**BEFORE**	**Generating ideas and considering audience and purpose** Coming up with ideas to write about and ways to present them that are effective for your audience and purpose
Connecting ideas to your own experience Discovering what you already know about the topic		**Planning and organizing** Discovering how ideas are connected and how best to present them
Reading to understand ideas Comprehending ideas; using highlighting and annotating to sort and record ideas	**DURING**	**Writing to express ideas** Expressing ideas; putting your ideas in sentence, paragraph, and essay form
Reviewing Going back through what you have identified as important to improve recall and retention	**AFTER**	**Revising** Going back through everything; evaluating ideas; rewriting to improve clarity and effectiveness
Thinking critically Evaluating the author's ideas for accuracy, logic, support, and bias		**Proofreading** Checking your writing for errors in typing, spelling, grammar, and punctuation

Chapter Theme: Living Between Two Worlds

In this chapter, you will read a professional and a student essay on the topic of living between two worlds. Each of us navigates the courses between worlds almost daily. Your roles and the expectations that others have of you change as you go from home to school to work and to social activities with friends. At times, the transition from one world to another can be complicated and also very interesting. As you read the two essays in this chapter, consider the worlds that the writers live in and the struggles they encounter as they move between the two worlds. Also, annotate the readings, recording your thoughts on the topic, to be prepared to write about it or a related topic.

Look it up!

Use the search engine on your smartphone (or work with a classmate who has a smartphone) and look up "culture in America today." Review several entries. Based on what you read, how is culture defined in the United States? Write a few sentences that explain how you define culture.

EXAMINING PROFESSIONAL WRITING

Good writing helps readers. By expressing your ideas clearly, logically, and concisely, you are helping readers understand what you are writing about. The professional writing below is an example of good writing that considers its audience and achieves it purpose. Because this article appears in a newspaper, it is written in journalistic style, which appeals to its audience. Journalistic style often includes dialogue and short paragraphs.

As you read the article, look closely at the marginal annotations that highlight the basic structure of an essay. This structure enables the author to effectively communicate his message to his readers.

Thinking Before Reading

In the following article from *The Washington Post*, the author describes the consequences of one woman's efforts to escape an arranged marriage in Afghanistan. Follow these steps before you read:

1. Preview the reading using the steps discussed in the Pre-Reading Strategies section of Chapter 1.
2. Connect the reading to your own experience by answering the following questions:
   a. Does the government have the right to refuse to let a woman cancel her engagement?
   b. Are there circumstances in your life that make you feel as if you have no choice?
3. Highlight and annotate as you read.

The title suggests the thesis

Afghanistan: Where Women Have No Choice

Kevin Sieff

For an Afghan girl dreading marriage to a man she hates, death is often the only escape.

The visual supports the thesis

Westwildwest/Fotolia

The author presents introductory information to capture the reader's attention

1   Just before she leapt from her roof into the streets of Kabul, Farima thought of the wedding that would never happen and the man she would never marry. Her fiancé would be pleased to see her die, she later recalled thinking. It would offer relief to them both.

Introduction: The writer provides important background information

2   Farima, 17, had resisted her engagement to Zabiullah since it was ordained by her grandfather when she was 9. In post-Taliban Kabul, where she walked to school and dreamed of becoming a doctor, she still clawed against a fate dictated by ritual. After 11 years of Western intervention in Afghanistan, a woman's right to study

Thesis statement

and work had long since been codified by the government. Modernity had crept into Afghanistan's capital, Farima thought, but not far enough to save her from a forced marriage to a man she despised.

Body paragraphs support the thesis and explain the key point(s)

Most body paragraphs contain a topic sentence that relates to the thesis; details within each of these paragraphs support the topic sentence

3   Farima's father, Mohammed, was eating breakfast when he heard her body hit the dirt like a tiny explosion. He ran outside. His daughter's torso was contorted. Her back was broken, but she was still alive. In a quick burst of consciousness, Farima recognized that she had survived. It was God's providence, she thought. It was a miracle she hadn't prayed for. But it left her without an escape. Suddenly, she was a mangled version of herself, still desperate to avoid the marriage her family had ordered.

4   She didn't know it yet, but her survival meant that she would become a test case in one of her country's newest and most troubled experiments in modernity: a divorce court guided by Afghanistan's version of Islamic sharia law. Could a disabled teenager navigate a legal system still stacked against women?

sharia

religious law based on the Quran and the example set by the prophet Muhammad

A new paragraph is used for each piece of dialogue; these paragraphs typically do not have topic sentences

5   "We still must get married," Zabiullah told his brother when he heard about Farima's suicide attempt. "The engagement must remain." Her father agreed that Farima's pursuit of a separation was unwise. "We are not a liberal family," Mohammed said. "This is not how we handle our problems."

This sentence serves as a transition; it tells the reader that background information will follow

6   When her marriage was fixed, a 9-year-old Farima crawled into her mother's lap, confused about what it meant to be engaged. Even as Kabul grew more modern, that traditional engagement was unbreakable, her parents told her. The man she was destined to spend her life with was a distant cousin. If the marriage didn't happen, the family could splinter. But when Farima got to know Zabiullah, she couldn't stand him. They talked on the phone, and he chastised her for venturing outside her home. He demanded that she stop speaking even with members of her family. "She was too close with her relatives, getting ice cream and going to the market with her father's cousin," he said.

7   "If he was like that when we were engaged, what would marriage have been like?" Farima said. "I couldn't bear it."

This opening phrase switches readers back to Farima's fall

8   Less than a minute after Farima hit the ground, Mohammed scooped up his daughter. He hailed a taxi, and they sped to Ali Ahmed Hospital, where Taher Jan Khalili performed surgery for three hours. The family was ashamed to tell Khalili the truth. Her father said Farima had fallen by accident.

9   "I wasn't sure if she would survive. Her back was badly broken," Khalili said. In the past year, he has handled nearly a dozen attempted female suicides. Farima spent nine days in the hospital, flickering in and out of consciousness. When she re-entered the world in late September, bandaged and carried on a stretcher, her relatives cried and thanked God that she had survived. "But if not death, then what?" Farima thought.

10   Zabiullah, a plumber, was insistent that the wedding date remain unchanged. He had spent $30,000 on gifts for his fiancée, he said. He had paid for a big engagement party, during which Farima had sat sullen for hours, while relatives sang and danced and ate kebab. "Everyone was having a great night, but she did not," Mohammed said.

11   Dozens of women in Afghanistan kill themselves each year to escape failed, and often violent, marriages. Those tragedies are widely mourned, but they nonetheless offer a resolution recognized by Islamic law: A woman's death, even by her own hand, marks the end of a marriage or engagement. Women who run away face prison sentences of several years.

12   A failed suicide is more complicated to untangle. When Farima awoke in the hospital bruised and broken, her wedding had not yet been canceled. Nearly all of her relatives expected her to follow through with the marriage. She gave up on the prospect of another suicide attempt; she could not walk without assistance and was too weak to inflict much damage on herself. The girl accused of being "too modern" would make another modern decision: She opted to resolve her failing engagement in Kabul's nascent family court. She would have to plead her case in front of a room full of judges and lawyers, who would decide whether she was entitled to a separation. In traditional Afghan culture, men can divorce their wives without the approval of any justice system.

Transitional sentence moves events to two months after the fall

burqa
a loose outer garment covering the entire body and veiling the face, with an opening for the eyes

13   Two months after she left the hospital, her mother and father helped carry her to the third floor of the family court—a faded yellow guesthouse, where a line of burqa-clad women are nearly always waiting outside. Farima wore a black headscarf. Her skin was pallid. She hadn't been outside in weeks, spending most of her time reading novels in her room. The chief judge, Rahima Rasai, looked

across the room at Farima while she adjusted her back brace. "You have ruined your life," Rasai said.

14   The court is a place where a woman is entitled to plead for divorce or custody of her children, but only if she has five male "witnesses," or defenders, and often only if her husband or fiancé condones the separation. The court is funded by Western organizations but adheres strictly to sharia law. Farima sat on the opposite side of the room from her fiancé. She looked at the judge and tried hard not to cry.

15   Every year, Kabul's family court handles about 300 cases, mostly women seeking to divorce their negligent or abusive husbands. Established in 2003, it was seen widely as a leap of progress after the Taliban's stoning of adulterers and dismantling of women's rights. Women whose fiancés emigrated from Afghanistan line up to seek separation from absent partners. Girls whose husbands sold them as prostitutes sink into the court's cushioned chairs, begging for divorce certificates stamped with a government insignia.

16   Last month was a typical one at the court: Some women screamed at their husbands. Some brought their small children to testify. Some beat themselves with their fists to demonstrate the abuse they had endured. Some watched as their husbands were dragged out in handcuffs. Some arrived in burqas, and some in blue jeans. Many were crying as they left the courtroom.

Transitional sentence that announces discussion of the trial

17   On Farima's day in court, her father sat in the corner of the room. For years, he had been trying to avoid this moment. "I told my daughter not to do this. We don't want a bad name. We don't want our family to fall apart," Mohammed said. Farima had told him many times that she was thinking about killing herself, he said. When he looked at her, crumpled and frail, he knew what he could have prevented. "I just never thought she would really do it," he said.

18   "What is wrong with this man?" Rasai asked Farima, pointing to Zabiullah. "He treats me terribly," Farima said. "Our marriage would be hell."

19   Then the judge looked to Zabiullah. He wanted badly not to be there, objecting to the whole idea of a family court. "She is confused," he said. "She has become so liberal," he said.

20   There was a hush in the courtroom. Rasai sipped her tea. She was tired. It was the last case of the morning. Already, the court had heard four women pleading for divorce and protracted arguments over dowry compensation and physical abuse. None of those cases had been resolved. There weren't enough male witnesses, or Rasai wasn't convinced that a separation was warranted; she is reluctant to grant too many. "It haunts me. Even when I'm praying, I think about the sadness of my job," Rasai said later.

21   Although she is one of Afghanistan's few female judges, Rasai is hardly a Western-style advocate of women's rights. She sometimes recommends that men "subdue their wives." Even in seemingly clear-cut cases of domestic abuse, she often resists defendants' initial pleas for separation.

22   When Rasai finally spoke again, she asked Farima what gifts Zabiullah had given her for their engagement. Farima's mother left the courtroom and returned dragging a metal trunk, full of clothes, jewelry and cosmetics. Her mother pulled out one item at a time and held it above her head for the court to see. "Where are the other rings?" Zabiullah burst out. "That's all that you gave me," Farima replied, exasperated.

Karzai
Hamid Karzai, the president of Afghanistan

23   "Even if Karzai demands it, I will not allow my daughter to marry this man!" Farima's mother suddenly exclaimed. It was the kind of support Farima had never received from her parents.

24   Rasai started scribbling. "Your engagement is scrapped," she said. "You no longer have any relation to each other."

25   Farima looked defiant, but she did not smile. She and Zabiullah dipped their thumbs in ink and touched them to certificates pronouncing their separation. "Keep this with you forever," Rasai said, giving each a copy.

26   Farima's parents helped carry her down the stairs. She had lived to get what her family had denied her. Her Afghanistan again showed a flash of modern promise.

27   "I have defended my rights," Farima said in the lobby. Her mother was crying.

28   Two weeks later, Farima was back to spending her days at home. She was reading a book called *The Gift of the Bride*. "It's about relationships between wives and husbands and children," she said. She was no longer attending school. Her father and brothers had asked her to stop during her engagement, and they would not allow her to return.

29   Farima was still basking in the court's judgment, but it left her feeling unmoored. Even in the country's most developed city, opportunities are limited for a single woman unable to walk on her own. "I'm worried that no one will marry my daughter now," her mother said. Zabiullah is sure that he will marry another woman. He has a trunk full of gifts ready for her. Farima has started considering the prospect of a life alone, in her childhood bedroom. "I'm not sure what I will do," she said. "I'm not sure what I can do."

30   In the Afghanistan of her novels, the girls grow up to be happy and marriages are full of love. Husbands are patient and accepting. "For me, it is not always like that," Farima said. "Life is complicated."

The concluding two paragraphs bring the essay to an end, making it clear how complicated the situation is for a young modern woman living in a culture where forced marriages are still the norm

Six Steps in the Writing Process

■ GOAL 3
Use the writing process

Writing, like many other skills, is not a single-step process. Think of the game of football, for instance. Football players spend a great deal of time planning and developing offensive and defensive strategies, trying out new plays, improving existing plays, and practicing. Writing paragraphs and essays involves similar planning and preparation. It also involves testing ideas and working out the best way to express them. Writers often explore how their ideas might "play out" in several ways before settling upon one plan of action. And once they have completed a draft, writers may go back and rework sections or even start over. Writing, then, is not a process that you work through only once from start to finish. Writers go back and forth between and among the steps until they are satisfied with their work.

Writing is often done is response to reading as well. Often college writing assignments ask students to read a chapter, essay, or article and then respond to it. As you learned in Chapter 1, strategies you follow before, during, and after reading will prepare you to write. As part of previewing, you connect the topic of the reading to your own experience, thereby providing ideas and experiences to write about. During reading you highlight and annotate, identifying what is important and recording your initial responses to what you are reading. Both techniques also produce ideas to write about. After reading, paraphrasing, outlining, mapping, and summarizing enable readers to condense ideas and see relationships between and among them.

People have many individual techniques for writing, but all writing involves six basic steps, as shown in the figure "Steps in the Writing Process."

 NEED TO KNOW

The Writing Process

- Writing is a step-by-step process of explaining your ideas and experiences.
- Writing involves six basic steps: generating ideas, considering your audience and your purpose, organizing your ideas, writing a first draft, revising, and proofreading.

FIGURE 2-2   STEPS IN THE WRITING PROCESS

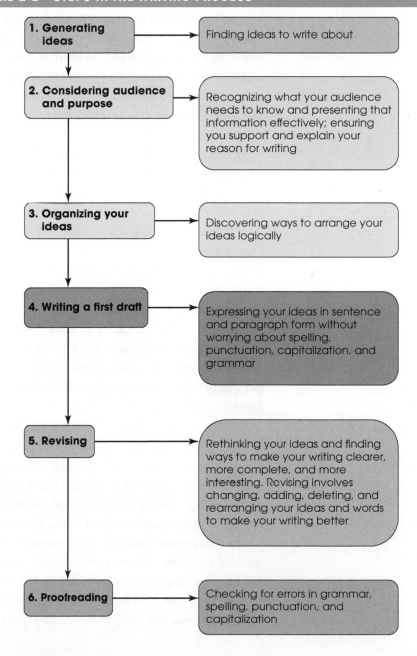

1. Generating ideas → Finding ideas to write about

2. Considering audience and purpose → Recognizing what your audience needs to know and presenting that information effectively; ensuring you support and explain your reason for writing

3. Organizing your ideas → Discovering ways to arrange your ideas logically

4. Writing a first draft → Expressing your ideas in sentence and paragraph form without worrying about spelling, punctuation, capitalization, and grammar

5. Revising → Rethinking your ideas and finding ways to make your writing clearer, more complete, and more interesting. Revising involves changing, adding, deleting, and rearranging your ideas and words to make your writing better

6. Proofreading → Checking for errors in grammar, spelling, punctuation, and capitalization

EXAMINING STUDENT WRITING

Garcia, Santiago Quintana

Below is an essay written by Santiago Garcia. Reading and analyzing other students' writing is one way to develop and improve your writing skills. We will use Santiago's essay throughout the rest of this chapter to illustrate the steps in the writing process.

Santiago Quintana Garcia is a senior at Beloit College in Wisconsin, where he is majoring in literature.

The Space In-Between

Background information on Mexico City and Beloit

1   There are around twenty million people living in Mexico City, and this number is constantly increasing. Mexico is where I was born and grew up, before I moved to Beloit, Wisconsin to attend Beloit College. The town of Beloit has roughly thirty thousand people. This means that about seven hundred towns the size of Beloit would fit inside Mexico City. In Mexico City, I was no more than a speck of dust in a dirty room. In Beloit, if I go have breakfast in one of three downtown cafés, I can be sure that there will be at least one person I know, probably around five or more. Beloit and Mexico City are two completely different worlds that I have come to call home.

Santiago provides information about his physical appearance that makes him an outsider both in Mexico and Beloit

2   I am Mexican. I probably have beautiful cinnamon skin, hair black as night and falling straight like a waterfall to frame two glowing brown eyes. Many people think this is what a "true Mexican" looks like. Drawing a line between what is a true Mexican and what isn't based on looks is not a simple task. I myself think it is impossible. This stereotype has played a role in my life both in Mexico and Beloit. I have white skin, the only blue eyes in my family of brown eyes, and curly light brown hair. When I go to the market to buy vegetables for the week, people don't bother to ask my name. They call me *güerito*, blond. I get asked if I am from the United States or from another country. I was never completely a part of the nation I was born and grew up in. In Beloit though, people are fascinated by my cultural background and ask about my customs and daily life back home. Inevitably, at some point in the conversation they tell me that I don't look Mexican. I live

Thesis statement

between two worlds; being racially "foreign" in Mexico, and being culturally "foreign" in Beloit.

Topic sentence

3   Living a life in-between two worlds, never completely a part of any, is a very complicated and extremely interesting place to be. Living in-between encourages growth and maturity. As a teenager, I struggled with feelings of not belonging and wanting to be a part of a group. I did not play soccer, or the guitar, and suffered from bullying. The impact this had on my life was emotionally wrecking. Often when people find themselves in similar situations, they turn to familiar things for comfort.

Explanation of meaning of "living in-between"

Things like a group they belong to, like a culture, or a race, or a religious group. This was not accessible to me in the same way as it was to others. On the other hand, though, standing on no man's land let me observe the effects of the culture I grew up with on my way of thinking and has greatly influenced my area of focus in my college studies. Standing in this middle ground was a vantage point from which I could analyze the opinions I held and the habits I developed and see my virtues and faults through different eyes. The hardiest weeds live where the pavement meets the prairie. I live where outsider meets insider.

Topic sentence

4   What happens in this middle ground is that concepts such as gender, race, nationality and other identities seem held up by pins. They are extremely volatile and impermanent, constantly changing and molding. This knowledge is present with me every time I say "I am Mexican" or "I am white." I had thought that people who fit snugly into a stereotype would never experience being an outsider. But I soon found out otherwise.

Details of how living "in-between" changes how one views certain concepts

Santiago introduces a friend who lives in a different "in-between" situation

Topic sentence

5   The first time I touched on this subject with a friend of mine, he said that he saw what I meant. I was convinced he didn't. He was the perfect example of the "Mexican" racial stereotype. He explained that he couldn't know about my situation, but that he was having a similar problem with his family. His mom had recently mentioned that he should be going to church more, instead of hanging out with his friends on Sunday mornings. That was his middle place. He identified with these two seemingly separate identities that he had created: his Catholic self and his social self. He was having trouble negotiating between the two. He stood in a place in the middle, where his church community was not understanding about his absences, and his friends made fun of his religious background. At the edges of these groups, he had thought about these two in much greater depth than I ever had, and he shared some incredible insights about the baggage associated with both identities, and how they weren't as solid as he thought; they had blurry edges and a lot of holes subject to interpretation.

Conclusion: Santiago offers a final comment on life "in-between"

6   It is the places in-between where the most potential for growth lives. Everyone has his or her own place where he or she feels like an outsider, or not completely an insider. Realizing that this is where you are standing, and that It Is perfectly fine to have one foot inside and one foot outside, will let the unique reveal itself through you. Being in-between can be difficult, but it is there that the most unexpected and wonderful things happen.

Step One: Generate Ideas

■ GOAL 4
Generate ideas

Before you can write about a topic, you have to collect ideas to write about. Because many students need help with this right away, three helpful techniques are described here: (1) freewriting, (2) brainstorming, and (3) branching. Here is a brief introduction to each.

Freewriting

What is freewriting?   **Freewriting** is writing nonstop about a topic for a specified period of time.

How does freewriting work?   You write whatever comes into your mind, and you do not stop to be concerned about correctness. After you have finished, you go back through your writing and pick out ideas that you might be able to use.

What does it look like?   Here is a sample of freewriting Santiago might have done.

Santiago's Sample Freewriting

Twenty million people live in Mexico City, where I'm from, compared to roughly thirty thousand in Beloit, Wisconsin, where I go to college. That means about seven hundred towns the size of Beloit would fit inside Mexico City! I'm like a speck of dust in Mexico City but if I go out for break- fast in Beloit I always see at least one person I know. Beloit and Mexico City are completely different but both feel like home. And how do I describe myself? White skin, blue eyes, not typical. What do people think a "true Mexican" looks like? I know I don't look like the stereotype. In Mexico, people think I'm American; in Beloit, people want to know what it's like back home. Then they tell me I don't look Mexican. So I'm racially foreign in Mexico and culturally foreign in Beloit. Where do I fit in?

Brainstorming

What is brainstorming?   **Brainstorming** is making a list of everything you can think of that has to do with your topic.

How does brainstorming work?   Try to stretch your imagination and think of everything related to your topic. Include facts, ideas, examples, questions, and feelings. When you have finished, read through what you have written and highlight usable ideas.

What does brainstorming look like?   Here is the brainstorming list that Santiago wrote about his identity.

Identity—Mexican? White? Very arbitrary and flimsy

Easily deconstructed when seen from the edges

Not wrong to subscribe to a certain identity

Everyone has their in-betweens, not all race and nationality

Mexican stereotype: I don't look Mexican. I'm foreign in my own country/race

White: Not quite. I am Mexican after all.

Creates a struggle between the ideal and the reality, from this comes synthesis, movement

Feelings of not belonging as a teenager. No comfort objects. No cushion to fall back to easily,

BUT growth and awareness.

I am Mexican. I still subscribe but with a lot more awareness of how that label is not

representative and exhaustive. It is necessary; practical.

Living in between = energy, movement, growth.

Branching

What is branching?   **Branching** is a way of using diagrams or drawings to generate ideas.

How does branching work?   Begin by drawing a 2-inch oval in the middle of a page. Write your topic in that oval. Think of the oval as a tree trunk. Next, draw lines radiating out from the trunk, as branches would. Write an idea related to your topic at the end of each branch. When you have finished, highlight the ideas you find most useful.

What does branching look like?   Here is a sample of branching Santiago might have created:

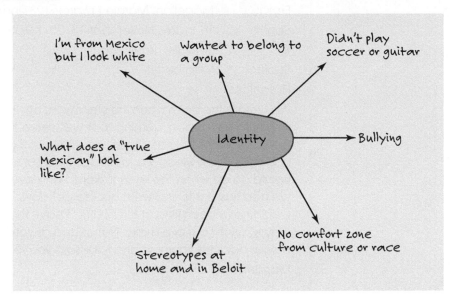

Practicing Generating Ideas

Directions: Choose one of the following topics. Then try out two of the techniques described for generating ideas.

1. Identity theft
2. Paying student athletes
3. Security on college campuses
4. Date rape
5. Mandatory community service in high school or college

6. Role of the Internet in friendships
7. Local food in college cafeterias
8. Cost of a college education
9. Student health concerns
10. Balancing work and college

Step Two: Consider Audience and Purpose

Good writing is directed toward an audience and achieves a purpose.

■ GOAL 5
Consider your audience and purpose

Consider Your Audience

When you write, ask yourself, who will be reading what I write? How should I express myself so that my readers will understand what I write? Considering your audience is essential to good writing.

What is appropriate for one audience may be inappropriate for another. For example, if you were writing about a storm that knocked out the power at your dorm, you would write one way to a close friend and another way to your professor. Because your friend knows you well, she would be interested in all of the details. Conversely, because you and your professor don't know each other well, she would want to know less about your feelings and more about how the storm would affect your course work. Study the following excerpts. What differences do you notice?

E-mail to a Friend

From:	Magellan, Marcie (marcie123@noodle.com)
Sent:	Thursday, November 13, 2017 9:33 AM
To:	Janice@network.com
Subject:	Weather!!!!

Hi Janice,

We were in the dorm when the sirens went off. Pretty scary! We knew there was a thunderstorm warning, but we weren't expecting the hail. There were hailstones the size of golf balls!! The wind was slamming the rain and hail against our window and Megan had just said she thought the power would go off when the lights flickered and everything went dark. Luckily, we had flashlights and were able to get downstairs with everyone else. It would have been kind of fun if I didn't have that Econ paper due and no way to print it out or e-mail it. Not as bad as you, though, because we got power back this morning and Mike says you're still in the dark.

Marcie:)

E-mail to a Professor

From:	Magellan, Marcie (marcie123@noodle.com)
Sent:	Thursday, November 13, 2017 9:45 AM
To:	Luis.T. Fernandez@school.edu
Subject:	Missing Due Date for Second History Paper
Attachment:	Economics of Small Business in Rural United States

Dear Professor Fernandez,

I apologize for submitting my paper late. You may know that the storm caused a power outage last night in the dorms on the west side of campus. The power has just been restored, so I am attaching my paper to this e-mail. I will also bring a printed copy of my paper to your office after my 11:00 class.

Marcie Magellan

While the e-mail to the friend is casual and personal, the note to the professor is businesslike and direct. The writer included details and described her feelings when telling her friend about the storm but focused on missing the deadline in her note to her professor.

Writers make many decisions based on the audience they have in mind. As you write, consider the following:

- How many and what kinds of details are appropriate?
- What format is appropriate (paragraph, essay, letter, e-mail, etc.)?
- What kinds of words should you use (simple, technical, emotional, etc.)?
- What tone should you use (friendly, knowledgeable, formal, etc.)?

Here are four key questions you can ask to assess and write for your audience:

- Who is your audience and what is your relationship with your audience?
- How is your audience likely to respond to your message?
- What does your audience already know about your topic?
- What does your audience need to know to understand your point?

Write for a Purpose

When you call a friend on the phone, you have a reason for calling, even if it is just to stay in touch. When you ask a question in class, you have a purpose for asking. When you describe to a friend an incident you were involved in, you are relating the story to make a point or share an experience. These examples demonstrate that you use spoken communication to achieve specific purposes.

Good writing must also achieve your *intended purpose*. If you write a paragraph on how to change a flat tire, your reader should be able to change a flat tire after reading the paragraph. Likewise, if your purpose is to describe the sun rising over a misty mountaintop, your reader should be able to visualize the scene. If your purpose is to argue that the legal age for drinking alcohol should be 25, your reader should be able to follow your reasoning, even if he or she is not won over to your view. In later chapters, you will learn more about writing to achieve your purpose.

The chapter readings will also show you how other writers accomplish their purposes.

Step Three: Organize Ideas

■ GOAL 6
Organize ideas

Two common methods of organizing ideas are outlining and idea mapping. Understanding each of them will help you decide how to arrange the ideas that you have identified as useful.

Outlining

What is outlining?   **Outlining** is a method of listing the main points you will cover and their subpoints (details) in the order in which you will present them.

How does outlining work?   To make an outline of a paragraph or essay, you list the most important ideas on separate lines at the left margin of a sheet of paper, leaving space underneath each idea. In the space under each main idea, list the details that you will include to explain that main idea. Indent the list of details that fits under each of your most important ideas.

What does outlining look like?   Here is an outline Santiago wrote for paragraph 3 of the first draft of his essay "The Space In-Between" in the Examining Student Writing section of this chapter.

Outline of Paragraph 3 of Santiago's Essay

I. Living in two worlds
   A. Never completely part of either world
      1. Complicated
      2. Interesting

(continued)

B. Living in between encourages growth and maturity

   1. Nothing to hold onto

   2. Effects of culture

C. Living in between offers a vantage point

   1. Analyze opinions and habits

   2. See virtues and faults through different eyes

D. Live where outsider meets insider

Idea Mapping

What is idea mapping?   An **idea map** is a drawing that shows the content and organization of a piece of writing.

How does idea mapping work?   An idea map shows you how ideas are connected and can help you see which ideas are not relevant to the topic of your paragraph or essay.

What does an idea map look like?   Here is a sample idea map drawn for paragraph 5 from **Santiago's** essay:

Idea Map

My friend said he understood what I meant about being an outsider, but I didn't believe him.

His mom wanted him to go to church more often.

He wanted to hang out with his friends instead.

He had difficulty negotiating two separate identities: Catholic and social.

Church community did not understand and friends made fun of his religion.

He shared deep insights with me about identity.

EXERCISE 2-2   ## Using Outlining or Mapping

WRITING IN PROGRESS

Directions: For the topic you chose in Exercise 2-1, use outlining or idea mapping to organize your ideas for a paragraph.

Step Four: Write a First Draft Paragraph or Essay

■ GOAL 7
Write a first draft
paragraph or essay

If you can write a paragraph, you can write an essay, since both have similar parts. A paragraph expresses one main idea and is made up of sentences that explain or support that idea, while an essay consists of multiple paragraphs that all explain one thesis statement. The "Similarities Between Paragraphs and Essays" figure helps you visualize the similarities between the structures of paragraphs and essays.

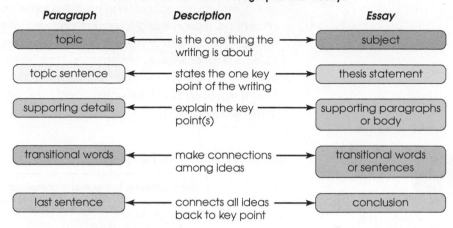

Similarities Between Paragraphs and Essays

Paragraph	Description	Essay
topic	is the one thing the writing is about	subject
topic sentence	states the one key point of the writing	thesis statement
supporting details	explain the key point(s)	supporting paragraphs or body
transitional words	make connections among ideas	transitional words or sentences
last sentence	connects all ideas back to key point	conclusion

Paragraph Structure

A **paragraph** is a group of sentences—usually at least three or four—that expresses one main idea. Paragraphs may stand alone to express one thought, or they may be combined into essays. Paragraphs are one of the basic building blocks of writing, so it is important to learn to write them effectively.

A paragraph's one main idea is expressed in a single sentence called the **topic sentence**. The other sentences in the paragraph, called **supporting details**, explain or support the main idea. You can visualize a paragraph as follows:

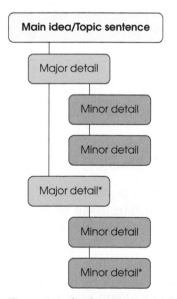

*The number of major and minor details may vary.

Here is a sample paragraph from Santiago's essay, followed by an idea map showing its structure.

> Living a life in-between two worlds, never completely a part of any, is a very complicated and extremely interesting place to be. Living in-between encourages growth and maturity. As a teenager, I struggled with feelings of not belonging and wanting to be a part of a group. I did not play soccer, or the guitar, and suffered from bullying. The impact this had on my life was emotionally wrecking. Often when people find themselves in similar situations, they turn to familiar things for comfort. Things like a group they belong to, like a culture, or a race, or a religious

(continued)

group. This was not accessible to me in the same way as it was to others. On the other hand, though, standing on no man's land let me observe the effects of the culture I grew up with on my way of thinking and has greatly influenced my area of focus in my college studies. Standing in this middle ground was a vantage point from which I could analyze the opinions I held and the habits I developed and see my virtues and faults through different eyes. The hardiest weeds live where the pavement meets the prairie. I live where outsider meets insider.

VISUALIZE IT!

Santiago's Idea Map for Paragraph 3

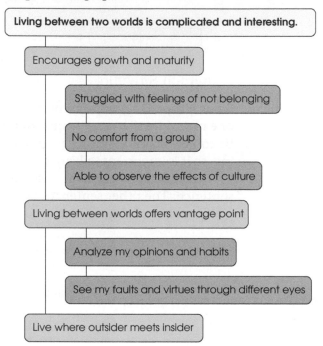

Essay Structure

This text teaches you how to write effective sentences and paragraphs, but you may also be asked to write essays or take essay exams in some of your courses. Some writing instructors prefer that their students write essays right away. Other instructors prefer that their students begin by writing single paragraphs and then progress to essay writing. Regardless of when you begin writing essays, the following introduction to essay techniques will be useful to you. It will show you why good paragraph-writing skills are absolutely necessary for writing good essays.

What Is an Essay?

An **essay** is a group of paragraphs about one subject. It contains one key idea about the subject that is called the **thesis statement**. Each paragraph in the essay supports or explains some aspect of the thesis statement.

How Is an Essay Organized?

An essay follows a logical and direct plan: it introduces an idea (the thesis statement), explains it, and draws a conclusion. Therefore, an essay usually has at least three paragraphs:

■ Introductory paragraph

■ Body (one or more paragraphs)

■ Concluding paragraph

1. Your **introductory paragraph** should accomplish three things:

   ■ It should interest your audience in the topic of your essay.

   ■ It should provide any necessary background information.

   ■ It should present the thesis statement of your essay in an appropriate way for your intended audience.

2. The **body** of your essay should accomplish three things:

   ■ It should provide information that supports and explains your thesis statement.

   ■ It should present each main supporting point in a separate paragraph.

   ■ It should contain enough detailed information to make the main point of each paragraph understandable and believable.

3. Your **concluding paragraph** should accomplish two things:

   ■ It should reemphasize but not restate your thesis statement.

   ■ It should draw your essay to a close.

You can visualize the organization of an essay using the following idea map:

VISUALIZE IT!

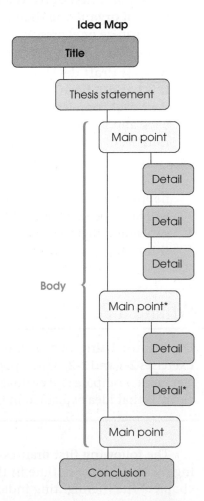

Idea Map

Title

Thesis statement

Main point

Detail

Detail

Detail

Body

Main point*

Detail

Detail*

Main point

Conclusion

*The number of main points and details may vary.

Draft a Paragraph or Essay

Writing a draft of a paragraph or essay is similar to buying a car. When you buy a car, you try out different models, see how different features of the car work together, test drive several, and finally decide what to buy. Similarly, when writing, you have to try out different ideas, see how they work together, try them out, and, after several versions, settle upon what your paper will include. Drafting is a way of trying out ideas to see if and how they work.

A first draft expresses your ideas in sentence form. Work from your list of ideas, and don't be concerned with grammar, spelling, or punctuation at this point. Instead, focus on expressing and developing each idea fully. The following suggestions will help you write effective first drafts:

Guidelines for Effective First Drafts

1. **After you have thought carefully about the ideas on your list, write one sentence that expresses the main point of your paragraph (working topic sentence) or essay (thesis statement).**

2. **Concentrate on explaining your topic sentence or thesis statement, using ideas from your list.** Focus first on those ideas that you think express your main point particularly well. Later in the writing process, you may find you need to add other ideas from your list.

3. **Think of a first draft as a chance to experiment with different ideas and ways of organizing them.** While you are working, if you think of a better way to organize or express your ideas or if you think of new ideas, make changes. Be flexible. Do not worry about getting your wording exact at this point.

4. **As your draft develops, feel free to change your focus or even your topic, if it has not been assigned.** If your draft is not working out, don't hesitate to start over completely. Go back to generating ideas. It is always all right to go back and forth among the steps in the writing process. Most writers make a number of "false starts" before they produce a draft that satisfies them.

5. **Don't expect immediate success.** When you finish your first draft, you should feel that you have the *beginnings* of a paragraph or paper you will be happy with. Now, ask yourself if you have a sense of the direction your paper will take. Do you have a main idea? Do you have supporting details? Is the organization logical? If you can answer "yes" to these questions, you have something on paper to work with and revise.

EXERCISE 2-3	Writing a Paragraph
WRITING IN PROGRESS	

Directions: Using one or more of the ideas you generated and organized in Exercises 2-1 and 2-2, write a paragraph about the topic you chose. Working with a classmate, compare and evaluate each other's paragraphs. Is the opening sentence clear? Is that idea explained in the remainder of the paragraph?

The following first draft essay evolved from Santiago's previous brainstorming list and partial outline in the Brainstorming and Branching sections of this chapter. The highlighting indicates the main points that Santiago developed as he wrote.

First Draft of Santiago's Essay

1   There are around twenty million people living in Mexico City, and this number is constantly increasing. Mexico is where I was born and grew up, before I moved to Beloit, Wisconsin to attend Beloit College. The town of Beloit has roughly thirty thousand people. This means that about seven hundred towns the size of Beloit would fit inside Mexico City. In Mexico City, I was no more than a speck of dust in a dirty room. In Beloit, if I go have breakfast in one of three downtown cafés, I can be sure that there will be at least one person I know, probably around five or more. Beloit and Mexico City are two completely different worlds that I have come to call home.

2   I am Mexican. I probably have beautiful cinnamon skin, hair black as night and falling straight like a waterfall to frame two glowing brown eyes. Many people think this is what a 'true Mexican' looks like. Drawing a line between what is a true Mexican and what isn't based on looks is not a simple task. I myself think it is impossible. This stereotype has played a role in my life both in Mexico and Beloit. I have white skin, the only blue eyes in my family of brown eyes, and curly light brown hair. When I go to the market to buy vegetables for the week, people don't bother to ask my name. They call me *güerito*, blond. I get asked if I am from the United States or from another country. I was never completely a part of the nation I was born and grew up in. In Beloit though, people are fascinated by my cultural background and ask about my customs and daily life back home. Inevitably, at some point in the conversation they tell me that I don't look Mexican. I live between two worlds; being racially 'foreign' in Mexico, and being culturally 'foreign' in Beloit.

3   Living a life in-between two worlds, never completely a part of any, is a very complicated and extremely interesting place to be. Living in-between encourages growth and maturity. On one hand, in my teenage years, when I desperately wanted to feel I was a part of something, there wasn't anything to take refuge in and feel strongly about. On the other, though, this made me see the effects of the culture I grow up in my way of thinking. Standing in this middle grown was a vantage point where I could analyze the opinions I held and the habits I developed and see the virtues and faults through different eyes. The hardiest weeds live where the pavement meets the prairie. I live where outsider meets insider.

4   I became used to being in the middle. I discovered that most questions can have more than one answer, or no answer at all. I realized that people are a lot more complex that I thought, and you really can't stick a label to them that won't become old and fall off. I had thought that people who fit snugly into the stereotype would never experience being an outsider. But I soon found out otherwise. Some had to choose between going to the cinema with their friends and going to church with their family. Some loved playing soccer in the mornings, and then go ballroom dancing in the afternoon. Everyone had their own experience of being in-between two places they sometimes love and sometimes hate.

5   It is the places in-between where the most potential for growth lives. Everyone has their own place where they feel like outsiders, or not completely insiders. Realizing that this is where you are standing, and that it is perfectly fine to have one foot inside and one foot outside, will let the unique reveal itself through you. Being in-between can be difficult, but it is there that the most unexpected and wonderful things happen.

Writing a First Draft of Your Essay

Directions: Using one of the topics you did not use in Exercise 2-1 or the topic you wrote a paragraph about in Exercise 2-3, generate ideas about it using freewriting, brainstorming, or branching. Then create an outline or idea map to organize the ideas that best support your topic, and write a short essay.

Step Five: Revise Drafts

■ **GOAL 8**
Revise a draft

Let's think again about the process of buying a car. At first, you may think you have considered everything you need and are ready to make a decision. Then, a while later, you think of other features that would be good to have in your car; in fact, these features are at least as important as the ones you have already thought of. Now you have to rethink your requirements and perhaps reorganize your thoughts about what features are most important to you. You might eliminate some features, add others, and reconsider the importance of still others.

A similar thing often happens as you revise your first draft. Although when you finish a first draft you may feel more or less satisfied with it, once you reread it later, you will see you have more work to do. When you revise, you have to rethink your entire paragraph or paper, reexamining every part and idea. Revising is more than changing a word or rearranging a few sentences, and it is not concerned with correcting punctuation, spelling errors, or grammar. Make these editing changes later when you are satisfied that you have presented your ideas in the optimal way. Revision is your chance to make significant improvements to your draft. It might mean changing, adding, deleting, or rearranging whole sections.

Here is an excerpt from a later draft of Santiago's essay shown on page 52. In this draft, you will see how he expands his ideas, adding words and details (underlined), and deletes others in paragraphs 3 and 4 of his first draft. After you have read the excerpt once, study the annotations. They will help you see the changes Santiago made.

Santiago's Revision of Paragraphs 3 and 4

3   Living a life in-between two worlds, never completely a part of any, is a very complicated and extremely interesting place to be. Living in-between encourages growth and maturity. As a teenager, I struggled with feelings of belonging and wanting to be a part of a group. I did not play soccer, or the guitar, and suffered from bullying. The impact this had in my life was emotionally wrecking. Often when people find themselves in similar situations, they turn to familiar things for comfort. Things like a group you belong to, like a culture, or a race, or a religious group. This was not accessible to me in the same way as it was to others. ~~On one hand, in my teenage years, when I desperately wanted to feel I was part of something, there wasn't anything to take refuge in and feel strongly about.~~ On the other hand, though, standing on no man's land let ~~this made~~ me observe ~~see~~ the effects of the culture I grew up with on my way of thinking, and has greatly influenced my area of focus in my college studies. Standing in this middle ground was a vantage point from which I could analyze the opinions I held and the habits I developed and see my virtues and faults through different eyes. The hardiest weeds live where the pavement meets the prairie. I live where outsider meets insider.

Santiago adds details to explain living in between

Santiago adds mention of college

Santiago revises to add
specifics about his conflict

4 ~~I became used to being in the middle. I discovered that most questions can have more than one answer, or no answer at all. I realized that people are a lot more complex that I thought, and you really can't stick a label to them that won't become old and fall off.~~ What happens in this middle ground is that concepts such as gender, race, nationality and other identities seem held up by pins. They are extremely volatile and impermanent; constantly changing and molding. This knowledge is present with me every time I say "I am Mexican" or "I am white." I had thought that people who fit snugly into a stereotype would never experience being an outsider. But I soon found out otherwise.

How to Know What to Revise

Peer review means asking one or more of your classmates to read and comment on your writing. It is an excellent way to find out what is good in your draft and what needs to be improved.

Learn from Peer Review

How can you make peer review as valuable as possible? Here are some suggestions:

When You Are the Writer ...

1. Prepare your draft in readable form. Double-space your work and print it on standard 8.5-by-11-inch paper.
2. When you receive your peers' comments, weigh them carefully. Keep an open mind, but do not feel that you must accept every suggestion that is made.
3. If you have questions or are uncertain about your peers' advice, talk with your instructor. *You* are responsible for your writing success.

When You Are the Reviewer ...

1. Read the draft through at least once before making any suggestions.
2. As you read, keep the writer's intended audience in mind. The draft should be appropriate for that audience.
3. Offer positive comments first. Say what the writer did well.
4. Use the Revision Checklists and "Need to Know" boxes in this text to guide your reading and comments. Be specific in your review and offer suggestions for improvement.
5. Be supportive; put yourself in the place of the person whose work you are reviewing. Phrase your feedback in the way you would want to hear it!

EXERCISE 2-5	Revising a Draft

WRITING IN PROGRESS

Directions: Revise the first draft you wrote for Exercise 2-4, following steps 1 through 6 in the "Tips for Revising" box on the next page.

EXERCISE 2-6	Using Peer Review

Directions: Pair with a classmate for this exercise. Read and evaluate each other's drafts written for Exercise 2-4 using peer review guidelines and the "Tips for Revising" box on the next page.

Tips for Revising

Use these suggestions to revise effectively:

1. **Reread the sentence that expresses your main point**. It must be clear, direct, and complete. Experiment with ways to improve it.

2. **Reread each of your other sentences**. Does each relate directly to your main point? If not, cross it out or rewrite it to clarify its connection to the main point. If all your sentences suggest a main point that is different from the one you've written, rewrite the topic sentence or thesis statement.

3. **Make sure your writing has a beginning and an end**. A paragraph should have a clear topic sentence and concluding statement. An essay should have introductory and concluding portions, their length depending on the length of your essay.

4. **Replace words that are vague or unclear with more specific or descriptive words**.

5. **Seek advice**. If you are unsure about how to revise, visit your writing instructor during office hours and ask for advice, or try peer review. Ask a classmate or friend to read your paper and mark ideas that are unclear or need further explanation.

6. **When you have finished revising, you should feel satisfied with what you have said and with the way you have said it**. You will learn additional strategies for revising in Chapter 8.

Step Six: Proofread

■ GOAL 9
Proofread for
correctness

Proofreading is a final reading of your paper to check for errors. In this final polishing of your work, the focus is on correctness, so don't proofread until you have done all your rethinking of ideas and revision. When you are ready to proofread your writing, you should check for errors in:

- sentences (run-ons or fragments).
- grammar.
- spelling.
- punctuation.
- capitalization.

Tips for Proofreading

The following tips will ensure that you don't miss any errors:

1. **Review your paper once for each type of error**. First, read it for run-on sentences and fragments. Take a short break, and then read it four more times, each time paying attention to one of the following: *grammar, spelling, punctuation*, and *capitalization*.

2. **To find spelling errors, read your paper from last sentence to first sentence and from last word to first word**. Reading in this way, you will not get distracted by the flow of ideas, so you can focus on finding errors. Also use the spell-checker on your computer, but be sure to proofread for the kinds of errors it cannot catch: missing words, errors that are themselves words (such as *of* for *or*), and homophones (for example, using *it's* for *its*).

3. **Read each sentence aloud, slowly and deliberately.** This technique will help you catch endings that you have left off verbs or missing plurals.

4. **Check for errors one final time after you submit your paper.** Don't do this when you are tired; you might introduce new mistakes. Ask a classmate or friend to read your paper to catch any mistakes you missed.

Here is a paragraph that shows the errors in grammar, punctuation, and spelling that Santiago corrected during proofreading.

> It is places in-between where the most potential for growth lives. Everyone has his or her own place where he or she feel like an outsiders or not a completely insiders. Realizing that this is where you are standing, and that it is perfectly fine to have one foot inside and one foot outside, will let the unique reveal itself through you. Being in-between can be difficult. But it is there that the most unexpected and wonderful things happen.

The Proofread for Correctness section of Chapter 8 includes a helpful proofreading checklist.

Proofreading

Directions: Revise your essay using suggestions from peer review (Exercise 2-6). Then prepare and proofread the final version of the essay.

READ AND RESPOND: A Student Essay

The Space In-Between

Santiago Quintana Garcia

The questions and activities below refer to Santiago's essay "The Space In-Between" in the Examining Student Writing section of this chapter that we have used as a model throughout the chapter. Now you are ready to think more critically about his writing and write in response to his essay.

Garcia, Santiago Quintana

Examining Writing

1. Compare Santiago's first draft in the Draft a Paragraph or Essay section of this chapter with his final draft. What content did he delete? What did he add? Why do you think he made these decisions?

2. How would you describe Santiago's audience for this essay? What was his purpose in writing it?

3. What does the title refer to in the essay? Evaluate the effectiveness of the title, introduction, and conclusion.

4. What other changes would you recommend to improve this essay?

Writing Assignments

1. The author writes about living between two worlds. Have you ever experienced "living in between"? Do you agree with the author that unexpected and wonderful things can happen in such a place? Write a paragraph describing an experience or aspect of your life in which you felt like an outsider.

2. Brainstorm some ideas about your own identity. How would you describe yourself? How would others describe you? Write a paragraph about who you are.

3. Write a paragraph explaining what the author means by his statement "The hardiest weeds live where the pavement meets the prairie."

READ AND RESPOND: A Professional Essay

Afghanistan: Where Women Have No Choice

Kevin Sieff

In the Examining Professional Writing section of this chapter, you read "Afghanistan: Where Women Have No Choice" and examined the basic structure of the essay. Now it is time to take a closer look at the reading by responding to the questions that follow.

Writing in Response to Reading

Checking Your Comprehension

Answer each of the following questions using complete sentences.

1. Describe Zabiullah through Farima's eyes.

2. Why did Farima's father lie about the cause of her fall?

3. Why did Zabiullah want to keep the wedding date unchanged despite Farima's fall?

4. Describe the court process that an Afghan woman has to follow according to sharia law.

5. What was Farima's life like after she was granted a separation?

Strengthening Your Vocabulary

Using the word's context, word parts, or a dictionary, write a brief definition of each of the following words as it is used in the reading.

1. contorted (paragraph 3) _____

2. chastised (paragraph 6) _____

3. sullen (paragraph 10) _____

4. nascent (paragraph 12) _____

5. pallid (paragraph 13) _____

6. condones (paragraph 14) _____

7. protracted (paragraph 20) _____

8. unmoored (paragraph 29) _____

Examining the Reading: Using Idea Maps

Review the reading by completing the missing parts of the following idea map.

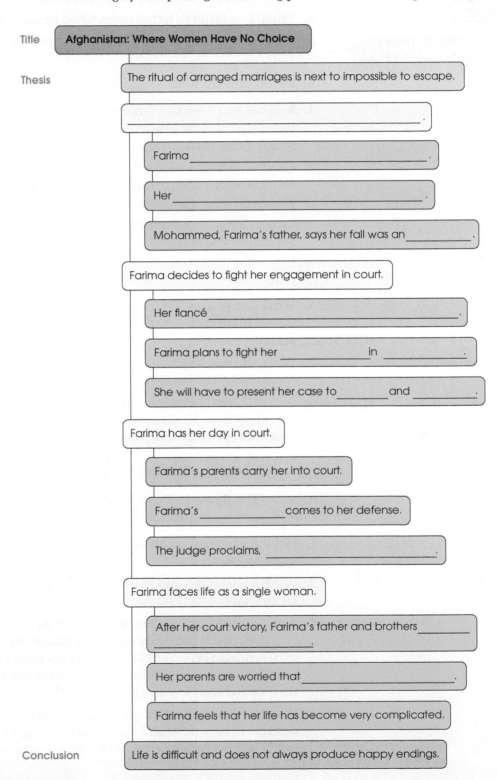

Title   **Afghanistan: Where Women Have No Choice**

Thesis   The ritual of arranged marriages is next to impossible to escape.

_____
_____.

Farima _____.

Her _____.

Mohammed, Farima's father, says her fall was an _____.

Farima decides to fight her engagement in court.

Her fiancé _____.

Farima plans to fight her _____ in _____.

She will have to present her case to _____ and _____.

Farima has her day in court.

Farima's parents carry her into court.

Farima's _____ comes to her defense.

The judge proclaims, _____.

Farima faces life as a single woman.

After her court victory, Farima's father and brothers _____
_____.

Her parents are worried that _____.

Farima feels that her life has become very complicated.

Conclusion   Life is difficult and does not always produce happy endings.

Thinking Critically: An Integrated Perspective

Get ready to write about the reading by discussing the following:

1. What was the author's purpose in writing this article?
2. Write a journal entry explaining what you think of the method of match-making described in this reading.
3. How would you describe Farima's relationship with her father?
4. What does Farima's father mean when he says, "We are not a liberal family?"
5. What details do you notice about the photograph that correspond to the reading?

THINKING VISUALLY

6. ### Paragraph Options

    1. Suppose you lived in a culture in which arranged marriages were the norm. What type of mate would your parents select for you? Write a paragraph describing that mate.
    2. Can you think of a time in your life when you felt so strongly about something that you took a risk and went against the popular opinion? Write a paragraph telling about it.
    3. Choose a friend, a boyfriend/girlfriend, or your mate and write a paragraph about how you met.

Essay Options

4. What can you tell from this reading about the author's attitude toward arranged marriages? Write an essay examining the ways the author reveals his attitude. Include in your essay specific examples from the reading.
5. Write an essay in which you compare and contrast the status of women in Afghanistan and women in the United States.
6. In the novels that Farima reads, "the girls grow up to be happy and marriages are full of love. Husbands are patient and accepting." In an essay, describe your concept of the ideal marriage.

Making Connections Between the Readings

Use both "The Space In-Between" and "Afghanistan: Where Women Have No Choice" to write a paragraph or an essay in response to one of the following prompts.

1. Write a paragraph explaining how both Santiago and Farima lived in "the space inbetween."
2. Write a paragraph summarizing the different identities that Santiago and Farima have.
3. Both Santiago and Farima speak of life as being complicated. Farima says, "For me ... life is complicated," and Santiago states, "Living a life in-between two worlds is a very complicated and extremely interesting place to be." In an essay, discuss the complications that these two people experience. How are they similar and how are they different?
4. What are the worlds that you live in-between? Write an essay in which you describe these worlds and explain how living a life in-between these worlds can be a "very complicated and extremely interesting place to be."

SELF-TEST SUMMARY

To test yourself, cover the Answer column with a sheet of paper and answer each question in the left column. Evaluate each of your answers as you work by sliding the paper down and comparing your answer with what is printed in the Answer column.

QUESTION	ANSWER
■ **GOAL 1** Use strategies to become a successful writer What strategies can you use to become a successful writer?	Strategies for successful writing include understanding what writing is and is not, getting the most out of your writing class, taking a positive approach, keeping a journal, and using peer review.
■ **GOAL 2** Compare the reading and writing processes What are the similarities in the two processes?	Both processes focus on: ■ generating ideas ■ organizing ideas ■ the presentation of key ideas ■ clear communication/understanding of content
■ **GOAL 3** Use the writing process What are the six steps in the writing process?	The writing process has six basic steps: generating ideas, considering audience and purpose, organizing ideas, writing a first draft, revising, and proofreading.
■ **GOAL 4** Generate ideas What are some ways to generate ideas?	Three techniques for generating ideas are freewriting, brainstorming, and branching.
■ **GOAL 5** Consider your audience and purpose How do you consider your audience and purpose?	To consider your audience, ask yourself who will be reading what you write. To consider your purpose, think about what you are trying to achieve through your writing.
■ **GOAL 6** Organize ideas What methods can you use to organize ideas?	Two common methods of organizing ideas are outlining (listing main points and details in the order in which you will present them) and mapping (creating a drawing that shows the content and organization of your writing).

(continued)

QUESTION	ANSWER
■ **GOAL 7** Write a first draft paragraph or essay What is a paragraph?	A paragraph is a group of sentences that expresses one main idea. (See the idea map for a paragraph in the Paragraph Structure section of this chapter.)
What is an essay?	An essay is a group of paragraphs about one subject. (See the idea map for essays in the Essay Structure section of this chapter.)
What is drafting, and how can you write an effective first draft?	Drafting is a way of trying out ideas to see if and how they work. Begin by writing one sentence expressing your main point, and then focus on explaining that sentence. Experiment with different ideas and ways of organizing them.
■ **GOAL 8** Revise a draft Why is revision important?	Revision is your chance to make significant improvements to your draft by changing, adding, deleting, or rearranging parts and ideas. (See the "Tips for Revising" box on p. 66.)
■ **GOAL 9** Proofread for correctness How do you proofread for correctness?	Proofread by checking for errors in sentences, grammar, spelling, punctuation, and capitalization. Read your paper once for each type of error, read your paper from the end to the beginning, read aloud, and check for errors again after you print your paper.

Vocabulary: Working with Words

Antony McAulay/Fotolia

THINK About It!

Study the photograph, showing a slogan that originated in Britain during World War II, was more recently repopularized, and became a meme (a cultural icon that is copied, often altered, and transmitted via various media). This slogan is forceful and engaging; it demonstrates how words can convey attitudes and feelings, in this case providing reassurance and expressing a national sentiment at one time. Can you think of other powerful slogans? Your vocabulary can be equally powerful—it can be lively, interesting, and descriptive, conveying a great deal of information—or it can be dull and uninteresting and convey very little information.

In this chapter, you will learn to express your ideas accurately and in a compelling way. Specifically, you will learn to figure out the meaning of unknown words using context clues and word parts, consult dictionaries and thesauruses effectively, use numerous features of language to express yourself clearly and creatively, and learn strategies for learning vocabulary in college courses. This chapter will also guide you in exploring the theme of digital communication. You will read a professional essay about the use of emojis—a new form of digital communication.

Why Is Vocabulary Important?

In college and in the workplace, as well as in everyday life, you will constantly encounter and be expected to learn new words. Because words are the basic building blocks of language, you need a strong vocabulary to express yourself clearly in both speech and writing. A strong vocabulary identifies you as an effective communicator and an educated person—someone who is able to think, write, and read critically and speak effectively. Vocabulary building is well worth your while and will pay off hundreds of times both in college and on the job.

In college, each course has its own language, and your success in each course depends, in part, on your ability to read, speak, and write in the language of the discipline. In psychology, you are expected to learn and use words such as *conditioned stimulus, endorphins,* and *habituation.* In the workplace, you need to learn and use the terms that refer to products, procedures, policies, and business strategies. As a nurse, you would need to know terms such as *agglutinins, dehiscence,* and *hordeolum.* In everyday life, new words are constantly introduced into the language.

Figure Out Unknown Words: A Strategy

What should you do when you are reading a passage and you come to a word you don't know?

Despite what you might expect, looking up a word in a dictionary is not the first thing to do when you encounter a word you don't know. In fact, a dictionary is your last resort—somewhere to turn when all else fails. Instead, first try to figure out the meaning of the word from the words around it in the sentence, paragraph, or passage that you are reading. The words around an unknown word that contain clues to its meaning are referred to as the context; the clues themselves are called *context clues.* You can use five basic types of context clues in determining word meanings in textbook material: *definition, synonym, example, contrast,* and *inference.*

If a word's context does not provide clues to its meaning, you might try breaking the word into parts. Analyzing a word's parts, which may include its prefix, root, and suffix, also provides clues to its meaning. Finally, if word parts do not help, look up the word in a dictionary. Regardless of the method you use to find a word's meaning, be sure to record its meaning in the margin of the page. Later, transfer its meaning to your vocabulary log (see section titled "Write to Learn: Keeping a Vocabulary Log" later in this chapter). You will learn how to use each of these strategies later in this chapter.

Chapter Theme: Digital Communication

In this chapter, you will read a professional essay on the topic of digital communication. Technology has made communication faster and easier for us and revolutionized the ways we communicate. Texting, in particular, has made it possible for us to get an immediate response to a question or a message, but it also has complicated communication due to its inability to convey tone and voice. But humans are clever, and they quickly created ways to address this problem. As you read the essay in this chapter, consider the evolution of emoji and the dimension that they add to digital communication. Also, annotate the reading, recording your thoughts on the topic, to be prepared to write about it or a related topic.

Look it up!

Use the search engine on your smartphone (or work with a classmate who has a smartphone) and look up "communicating by emoji." Review the first few entries. Based on what you read, how is the use of emoji changing how we communicate? Write a few sentences on how and why you use (or do not use) emojis to communicate.

EXAMINING PROFESSIONAL WRITING

In the following selection from *Wired Magazine,* the author explores the evolution of emoji and their influence on written English. This selection will be used in examples and exercises throughout the chapter to give you practice in reading and learning from professional writing.

Thinking Before Reading

Follow these steps before you read:

1. Preview the reading, using the steps discussed in Chapter 1.
2. Connect the reading to your own experience by answering the following questions:
   a. How do you express emotion when you write a text message or an e-mail?
   b. What is your preferred method of communication, and why do you prefer this method?
3. Highlight and annotate as you read.

Emoji—Trendy Slang or a Whole New Language?

Nick Stockton

Viktoria Kazakova/ Shutterstock

nuance
shades of meaning

1   OH, CRAP. DID you really just send that text? OK, OK, OK… just send a 😘. Oh wait, this is *that* cousin? You're right, 😔 would be bad. How about 🙄? Play it off as an honest mistake. Too candid? OK, why not 😹? After all, you were just joking. Seriously?! The cat thing you told me about last week was this cousin's dad? OK, fine, just use 💩. Your family is so weird.

2   Digital communications have always been a little socially handicapped. Unlike the written and typed communiques that came before, digital mixes immediacy with intimacy in a way that strips nuance and drains context. But emoji are more than emotional punctuation. They add context, enable wordplay, insert **nuance**, and let you speak your mind while taking the edge off your message. They're tone-of-voice for a medium that has no tone and no voice.

3   They might also be changing written English. No, not changing in a way that means the language is abandoning the alphabet and regressing back to ideograms—simple glyphs, symbols, and pictures.

Languages change all the time, and that's OK. It's evolution. The question is whether emoji will ride their cultural appeal long enough to become a discrete, complete means of communication. Or emoji might be a lexical fad, here for now but gone as soon as this wave of digital natives hands control of the global village over to the next generation.

portmanteau
a word that sounds and combines the meaning of two other words (for example, *breakfast + lunch = brunch*)

onomatopoeia
a word that imitates the sound it describes

4   Emoji means picture (e) character (moji). It's a Japanese **portmanteau**, but it sounds like an American **onomatopoeia**. Docomo, a Japanese telecoms giant, invented emoji in the 1990s to sweeten their countrymen to texting. Spoken, written, lived Japanese is rich with context, honorifics, and layers of meaning. Perhaps more than anybody speaking English or a European language could imagine, Japan needed some way to indicate the tone of a text.

5   Of course, emoji weren't the first attempt to add an emotional layer. Before emoji there were kaomoji—those looked kinda like this: (˘~˘), (o__O), and (=`ω'=). And before that there were emoticons :-). Both were created to add emotional context. Cute and creative, but those older forms require a lot of typing, which on phones means tapping, which in the 1990s meant pecking at numeral buttons. By creating a standardized Unicode library of images, emoji took the finger work out of typing context into your texts.

6   But it would be pretty narrow to think of emoji as just emotional punctuation. Emoji are clever, are puns, are art, are jokes about art, are games, are songs, are stories. So when you think about them that way, they start to seem like a language.

analogue
similarity

7   But emoji aren't a language. At least, not yet. They're more like an embryonic language, a cluster of cells that might be a language some day. The closest linguistic **analogue** might be a pidgin. "A pidgin is a new language created when people who have two languages come together," says Susan Herring, a linguist at Indiana University who has been studying the way people talk on the Internet since 1990. Pidgins are typically created out of extreme necessity—they are trade languages, slave languages, refugee languages. Emoji, though, are mostly fun. And the users typically come from the same linguistic background. So not quite a pidgin, but still some of the linguistic structural constraints might still be relevant.

8   "In a pidgin, you have nouns and verbs and not very much grammar," says Herring. Pidgins are article-deficient, conjunction-deprived, and prepositionally challenged. They are used only in the present tense, and rarely accommodate personal pronouns. Pidgins are downright hostile to plurals.

9   Emoji have the same limitations. When was the last time you used emoji to discuss a past or future event when it wasn't in response to a question? Have you ever used emoji to talk about a third party without first teeing up that personal pronoun with boring old letters? And if you're talking about a crowd of people, the only way to pluralize is by tap-tap-tapping a bunch of little faces. Not to mention all the little linking words that we take for granted but give English the power to identify, modify, and look at things far away in space and time. Words like: "the," "in," "around," "into," "apart from," "beside," "by," "as," and "instead."

10   These aspects only come along if a pidgin is passed along to another generation. This is when a pidgin becomes a creole. Creoles have tense, nuance, and grammar. The fact that creoles develop these tells us two things:

emergent
developing

1. Languages are **emergent**.

2. Children evolve languages.

11   But nobody is going to learn emoji as their first language. So even though emoji can answer questions, modify sentences, and give punch lines, they are closer to slang than anything else. And like creoles and slang, the most creative users of emoji are the youth. Emoji may seem like a new language (and an ideographic one at that) to people who don't use them natively. "Adolescents are the real movers and shakers in linguistic change," says Penelope Eckert, a linguist at Stanford University. "They are the ones who lead in the terms of **dialectic** difference and ultimately language difference. You got the romance languages by people speaking language differently. Same goes for regional dialects and ethnic dialects. It's the process of social differentiation. Teenagers are much busier in that process than older people."

dialectic
relating to discussion or debate

12   Adolescent linguistic fads percolate out in a few ways. One, the people who used the lingo grow up. Two, older people catch on. Young people are the disease vectors in linguistic memes.

13   Which is how emoji might die. Think about "groovy." Think about "tubular." Think about "wazzzzzzzuuuuup," or Snoop Dogg's -izzle slang, or people yelling "Yeah Baby!" at each other in fake British accents. Think about when the Oxford English Dictionary added "bling." Think about the first time your mom called something "the bomb." Think about the dork you saw at the mall in a trollface shirt. Think about emoji's long term fate while also thinking about the all-emoji press release Chevrolet proudly shared on Monday.

14   On the other hand, think about cool, whatever, chillin', hanging out. Think about all the ways you use the word 'like' every single day. Think about the fact that hip hop survived some of the worst possible corporate co-opting in the 1990s. Consider emoji in the context of all the other linguistic innovations people owe to digital communication—not just emoticons and kaomoji, but netspeak, lolspeak, dogespeak, 13375p3ak, reaction gifs, memes, lol, brb, jk. "It's possible that emoji, like other Internet languages, will get absorbed into regular online writing," says Herring. Humans love language, and we love playing with language, and any time we find a new method of communicating we are going to play and experiment with it. At least for a while. The fate of emoji is the same as the fate of English: ¯_(ツ)_/¯.

Nick Stockton, "Emoji—Trendy Slang or a Whole New Language?", Wired, June 24, 2015. Nick Stockton/WIRED © Conde Nast.

Reading: Use Context Clues

■ **GOAL 1**
Use context clues

Closely studying the words in a sentence can help you figure out the meaning of a particular word within the sentence. Read the following brief paragraph. Several words are missing. Try to figure out the missing words and write them in the blanks.

> Jayla has never been to Mexico, but she loves _____ food. Her favorite dish is _____, those delicious tortilla chips covered with cheese, beef, and beans. Just thinking about them makes Jayla _____.

Did you insert the word *Mexican* in the first blank, *nachos* in the second blank, and *hungry* in the third blank? You were probably able to correctly identify all three missing words. You could tell from each sentence which word to put in. The words around each word—the sentence **context**—gave you clues as to which word would fit and make sense. Such clues are called **context clues**.

Even though you won't find missing words on a printed page, you will often find words that you do not know. Context clues can help you figure out the meanings of unfamiliar words, as shown in the following examples:

Tony noticed that the **wallabies** at the zoo looked like kangaroos.

From the comparison in this sentence, you can tell that *wallabies* are "animals that look like kangaroos."

Many people have **phobias**, such as a fear of heights, a fear of water, or a fear of confined spaces.

From the examples listed in this sentence, you can figure out that *phobia* means "a fear of specific objects or situations."

When you have trouble with a word, look for five types of context clues: (1) definition, (2) synonym, (3) example, (4) contrast, and (5) inference. Each is described in Table 3-1.

TABLE 3-1 FIVE USEFUL TYPES OF CONTEXT CLUES		
Type of Context Clue	**How It Works**	**Examples**
Definition	Writers often define a word after using it. Words such as *means, refers to*, and *can be defined as* provide an obvious clue that the word's meaning is to follow. Sometimes writers use dashes, parentheses, or commas to separate a definition from the rest of the sentence.	• *Corona* refers to <u>the outermost part of the sun's atmosphere</u>. • <u>Broad flat noodles</u> that are served covered with sauce or butter are called fettuccine. • The judge's candor—<u>his sharp, open frankness</u>—shocked the jury. • Audition, <u>the process of hearing</u>, begins when a sound wave reaches the outer ear.
Synonym	Rather than formally define a word, some writers include a word or brief phrase that is close in meaning to a word you may not know.	The main character in the movie was an amalgam, <u>or combination</u>, of several real people the author met during the war.
Example	Writers often include examples to help explain a word. From the examples, you can often figure out what the unknown word means.	• Toxic materials, <u>such as arsenic, asbestos, pesticides, and lead</u>, can cause bodily damage. (You can figure out that *toxic* means "poisonous.") • Many pharmaceuticals, including <u>morphine and penicillin</u>, are not readily available in some countries. (You can figure out that *pharmaceuticals* are drugs.)
Contrast	Sometimes a writer gives a word that is opposite in meaning to a word you don't know. From the opposite meaning, you can figure out the unknown word's meaning. (Hint: watch for words such as *but, however, though, whereas*.)	• Uncle Sal was quite portly, <u>but his wife was very thin</u>. (The opposite of *thin* is *fat*, so you know that *portly* means "fat.") • The professor advocates the testing of cosmetics on animals, <u>but many of her students oppose it</u>. (The opposite of *oppose* is *favor*, so you know that *advocates* means "favors.")
Inference	Often your own logic or reasoning skills can lead you to the meaning of an unknown word.	Bob is quite versatile: <u>he is a good student, a top athlete, an excellent auto mechanic, and a gourmet cook</u>. (Because Bob excels at many activities, you can reason that *versatile* means "capable of doing many things.") <u>On hot, humid afternoons</u>, I often feel languid. (From your experience you may know that you feel drowsy or sluggish on hot afternoons, so you can figure out that *languid* means "lacking energy.")

EXERCISE 3-1	Reading: Using Definition Clues

Directions: Using the definition clues in each sentence, select the choice that best defines each boldfaced word.

_____ 1. After taking a course in **genealogy**, Xavier was able to create a record of his family's history dating back to the eighteenth century.
    a. the study of ancestry   c. the study of plants
    b. creative writing   d. personal finance

_____ 2. Participants in a **triathlon** compete in long-distance swimming, bicycling, and running.
    a. hiking trail   c. large group
    b. three-part race   d. written test

_____ 3. Louie's **dossier** is a record of his credentials, including college transcripts and letters of recommendation.
    a. briefcase or valise   c. diploma
    b. checking account statement   d. file of documents

_____ 4. **Power**, the ability to control others, is a factor that determines social class.
    a. the ability to disregard others   c. the ability to mislead others
    b. the ability to influence others   d. the ability to defend others

_____ 5. A person who becomes an **entrepreneur** must be willing to take on both the risks and opportunities of his or her new business.
    a. business owner   c. employee
    b. stockbroker   d. designer

EXERCISE 3-2	Reading: Using Synonym Clues

Directions: Using the synonym clues in each sentence, select the choice that best defines each boldfaced word.

_____ 1. The noise in the nursery school was **incessant**; the crying, yelling, and laughing never stopped.
    a. careless   c. bold
    b. harmful   d. continuous

_____ 2. There was a **consensus**—or unified opinion—among the students that the exam was difficult.
    a. requirement   c. disagreement
    b. consequence   d. agreement

_____ 3. The family's decision to donate their land to the park system was **altruistic**; they were unselfish in their desire to do what was best for the community.
    a. shrewd   c. selfless
    b. thoughtless   d. greedy

_____ 4. The mayor worried that the town council was trying to **usurp** her power, but how could she prevent the council members from taking over?
    a. support   c. improve
    b. take away   d. allow

_____ **5.** The old man avoided his family; in fact, he **eschewed** the company of anyone who knew about his past.
a. sought out   c. shunned
b. enjoyed   d. welcomed

EXERCISE 3-3   Reading: Using Example Clues

Directions: Using the example clues in each sentence, select the choice that best defines each boldfaced word.

_____ **1.** Diego's child was **reticent** in every respect; she would not speak, refused to answer questions, and avoided looking at anyone.
a. reserved   c. undisciplined
b. noisy   d. rigorous

_____ **2.** Most **condiments**, such as pepper, mustard, and ketchup, are used to improve the flavor of foods.
a. ingredients   c. sauces
b. seasonings   d. appetizers

_____ **3.** Paul's grandmother is a **sagacious** businesswoman; once she turned a small ice cream shop into a popular restaurant and sold it for a huge profit.
a. old fashioned   c. dishonest
b. shrewd   d. foolish

_____ **4.** Many things about the library make it **conducive** to study, including good lighting and many reference books.
a. unattractive   c. helpful
b. uncomfortable   d. sociable

_____ **5.** Murder, rape, and armed robbery are **reprehensible** crimes.
a. reasonable   c. blameworthy
b. unusual   d. rural

EXERCISE 3-4   Reading: Using Contrast Clues

Directions: Using the contrast clues or antonyms in each sentence, select the choice that best defines each boldfaced word or phrase.

_____ **1.** Little Lola hid shyly behind her mother when she met new people, yet her brother Matthew was very **gregarious**.
a. insulting   c. concerned
b. sociable   d. embarrassed

_____ **2.** The child remained **demure** while the teacher scolded but became violently angry afterward.
a. quiet and reserved c. cowardly
b. boisterous   d. upset and distraught

_____ **3.** I am certain that the hotel will hold our reservation; however, if you are **dubious**, call to make sure.
a. confused   c. sure
b. doubtful   d. energetic

_____ 4. Extroverted people tend to be outgoing and talkative, while introverted people are more **taciturn**.

    a. quiet   c. overbearing
    b. showy   d. helpless

_____ 5. Unlike other male-dominated species, Indian elephants live in a **matriarchal** society.

    a. aggressive   c. led by females
    b. nonthreatening   d. passive

EXERCISE 3-5	Reading: Using Inference Clues

Directions: Using logic and your reasoning skills, select the choice that best defines each boldfaced word.

_____ 1. To **compel** Clare to hand over her wallet, the mugger said he had a gun.

    a. discourage   c. force
    b. entice   d. imagine

_____ 2. Student journalists are taught how to be **concise** when writing in a limited space.

    a. peaceful   c. proper
    b. clear and brief   d. wordy

_____ 3. There should be more **drastic** penalties to stop people from littering.

    a. dirty   c. extreme
    b. suitable   d. dangerous

_____ 4. To **fortify** his diet while weightlifting, Monty took 12 vitamins a day.

    a. suggest   c. avoid
    b. approve of   d. strengthen

_____ 5. On our wedding anniversary, my husband and I **reminisced** about how we first met.

    a. sang   c. argued
    b. remembered   d. forgot

_____ 6. For their own safety, household pets should be **confined** to their own yards.

    a. restricted   c. shown
    b. led   d. used

_____ 7. The quarterback **sustained** numerous injuries: a fractured wrist, two broken ribs, and a hip injury.

    a. caused   c. displayed
    b. noticed   d. experienced

_____ 8. Sam's brother advised him to be **wary** of strangers he meets on the street.

    a. suspicious   c. congenial with
    b. trusting   d. generous toward

_____ 9. The lawyer tried to confuse the jury by bringing in many facts that weren't **pertinent** to the case.

    a. obvious   c. relevant
    b. continuous   d. harmful

_____ **10.** We keep candles in the house to **avert** being left in the dark during power failures.
a. prevent   c. accommodate
b. ensure   d. begin

| EXERCISE 3-6 | Reading: Using Context Clues |

Directions: Using context clues, select the choice that best defines each boldfaced word.

_____ **1.** The cat and her newborn kittens had to be **isolated** from the family dog after he tried to attack them.
a. combined   c. separated
b. heated up   d. rejected

_____ **2.** The protest was held to publicize the **atrocities** that are committed when animals are used for testing the effects of drugs and cosmetics.
a. punishments   c. controls
b. rewards   d. cruelties

_____ **3.** The baby birds needed a place of **refuge** from the summer storm.
a. shelter   c. building
b. rejection   d. separation

_____ **4.** Mike's efforts to buy a car were **futile**, so he continued to ride his bike to work.
a. helpful   c. necessary
b. useless   d. careless

_____ **5.** Janice **persistently** asked her mother to buy a new car, so her mother finally gave in and bought one.
a. constantly   c. briefly
b. lazily   d. unenthusiastically

_____ **6.** The meal was prepared perfectly, but the young woman found it **repugnant**.
a. overpriced   c. distasteful
b. lovely   d. delicious

_____ **7.** Getting our car fixed after the accident was an **ordeal**.
a. good time   c. unexpected event
b. relaxing opportunity   d. painful experience

_____ **8.** Candace wore a red, low-cut dress to the party, but her sister was dressed more **decorously**.
a. fashionably   c. attractively
b. warmly   d. modestly

_____ **9.** Kayla let a few weeks **elapse** before returning her ex-boyfriend's phone call.
a. separate   c. slow down
b. pass   d. speed up

_____ **10.** Gorillas can **convey** messages to humans through gestures and sounds.
a. invent   c. communicate
b. allow   d. approve of

Reading: Using Context Clues

Directions: Write the meaning of the boldfaced word in each of the following sentences.

1. The economy was in a state of continual **flux**; inflation increased one month and decreased the next. _____

2. Ava is always talkative, but Ed is usually **laconic**. _____

3. Many **debilities** of old age, including poor eyesight and loss of hearing, can be treated medically. _____

4. The soap opera contained numerous **morbid** events: the death of a young child, the suicide of her father, and the murder of his older brother. _____

5. Information, as well as gossip and rumors, is quickly spread through the **grapevine**, although is is not recognized as an official channel of communication. _____

6. The newspaper's error was **inadvertent**; the editor did not intend to include the victim's name. _____

7. To save money, we have decided to **curtail** the number of meals we eat out each month. _____

8. Steam from the hot radiator **scalded** the mechanic's hand. _____

9. Sonia's **itinerary** outlined her trip and listed Cleveland as her next stop. _____

10. Chang had very good **rapport** with his father, but he was unable to get along with his mother. _____

Reading: Using Context Clues in "Emoji—Trendy Slang or a Whole New Language?"

Directions: Write the meaning of each boldfaced word from the passage below.

Digital communications have always been a little socially handicapped. Unlike the written and typed communiques that came before, digital mixes immediacy with intimacy in a way that strips nuance and drains context. But emoji are more than emotional punctuation. They add context, enable wordplay, insert nuance, and let you speak your mind while taking the edge off your message. They're tone-of-voice for a **medium** that has no tone and no voice.

They might also be changing written English. No, not changing in a way that means the language is abandoning the alphabet and **regressing** back to ideograms—simple glyphs, symbols, and pictures. Languages change all the time, and that's OK. It's **evolution**. The question is whether emoji will ride their cultural appeal long enough to become a discrete, complete means of communication. Or emoji might be a lexical **fad**, here for now but gone as soon as this wave of digital natives hands control of the global village over to the next generation.

Emoji means picture (e) character (moji). It's a Japanese portmanteau, but it sounds like an American onomatopoeia. Docomo, a Japanese telecoms giant, invented emoji in the 1990s to **sweeten** their countrymen

> to texting. Spoken, written, lived Japanese is rich with context, honorifics, and layers of meaning. Perhaps more than anybody speaking English or a European language could imagine, Japan needed some way to indicate the tone of a text.
>
> When you label something as "good" or "bad," you are using language to create your own vision of how you experience the world. If you tell a friend that the movie you saw last night was vulgar and obscene, you are not only providing your friend with a critique of the movie; you are also communicating your sense of what is appropriate and inappropriate.

1. medium _____

2. regressing _____

3. evolution _____

4. fad _____

5. sweeten _____

Use Word Parts

■ **GOAL 2**
Use word parts

Many students build their vocabulary word by word: if they study ten new words, then they have learned ten new words. However, by learning the meanings of the parts that make up a word, you will be able to figure out the meanings of many more words. For example, if you learn that *pre-* means "before," then you can begin to figure out hundreds of words that begin with *pre-* (*premarital, premix, preemployment*).

Suppose that you came across the following sentence in a human anatomy textbook:

> Trichromatic plates are used frequently in the text to illustrate the position of body organs.

If you did not know the meaning of *trichromatic,* how could you determine it? There are no clues in the sentence context. One solution is to look up the word in a dictionary. An easier and faster way is to break the word into parts and analyze the meaning of each part. Many words in the English language are made up of word parts called *prefixes* (which appear at the beginning of words), *roots* (which carry the core meaning of a word), and *suffixes* (which are word endings that often change the part of speech). These word parts have specific meanings that, when added together, can help you determine the meaning of the word as a whole.

The word *trichromatic* can be divided into three parts: its *prefix, root,* and *suffix.*

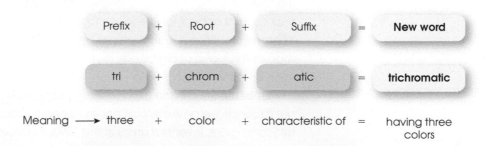

You can see from this analysis that *trichromatic* means "having three colors." Here is another example:

The student was a nonconformist.

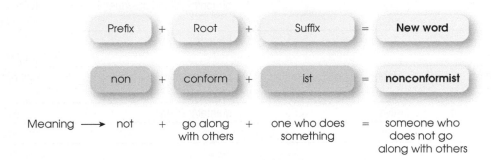

What You Need to Know About Using Word Parts

Before you begin to use word parts to figure out the meaning of new words, there are a few things you need to know:

- **In most cases, a word is built upon at least one root.**
- **Words can have more than one prefix, root, or suffix.**
  - Words can be made up of two or more roots (*geo/logy*).
  - Some words have two prefixes (*in/sub/ordination*).
  - Some words have two suffixes (*beauti/ful/ly*).
- **Words do not always have a prefix and a suffix.**
  - Some words have neither a prefix nor a suffix (*read*).
  - Others have a suffix but no prefix (*read/ing*).
  - Others have a prefix but no suffix (*pre/read*).
- **The spelling of roots may change as they are combined with suffixes.** Some common variations are included in Table 3-2: Common Prefixes.
- **Different prefixes, roots, or suffixes may have the same meaning.** For example, the prefixes *bi-, di-,* and *duo-* all mean "two."
- **Sometimes, you may identify a group of letters as a prefix or root but find that it does not carry the meaning of that prefix or root.** For example, the letters *mis* in the word *missile* are part of the root and are not the prefix *mis-*, which means "wrong, bad."

Prefixes

Prefixes appear at the beginning of many English words and alter the meaning of the root to which they are connected. For example:

re- + read = reread (to read again)
pre- + reading = prereading (before reading)
post- + reading = postreading (after reading)

Table 3-2 includes more than 40 common prefixes grouped according to meaning and shows how they affect the meaning of words they are affixed to.

TABLE 3-2 COMMON PREFIXES

Prefix	Meaning	Sample Words	Definitions
Prefixes referring to amount or number			
mono-/uni-	one	monocle/unicycle	eyeglass for one eye/one-wheel vehicle
bi-/di-/duo-	two	bimonthly/diandrous/duet	twice a month/flower with two stamens/two singers
tri-	three	triangle	a figure with three sides and three angles
quad-	four	quadrant	any of four parts into which something is divided
quint-/pent-	five	quintet/pentagon	a group of five/five-sided figure
deci-	ten	decimal	based on the number ten
centi-	hundred	centigrade	divided into 100 degrees, as a thermometer scale
milli-	thousand	milligram	one thousandth of a gram
micro-	small	microscope	an instrument used to see a magnified image of a small object
multi-/poly-	many	multipurpose/polygon	having several purposes/figure with three or more sides
semi-	half	semicircle	half of a circle
equi-	equal	equidistant	at equal distances
Prefixes meaning "not" (negative)			
a-	not	asymmetrical	not identical on both sides of a central line
anti-	against	antiwar	against war
contra-	against, opposite	contradict	deny by stating the opposite
dis-	apart, away, not	disagree	have a different opinion
in-/il-/ir-/im-	not	incorrect/illogical/irreversible/impossible	wrong/not having sound reasoning/cannot be changed back/not possible
mis-	wrongly	misunderstand	fail to understand correctly
non-	not	nonfiction	writing that is factual, not fiction
pseudo-	false	pseudoscientific	a system of theories or methods mistakenly regarded as scientific
un-	not	unpopular	not popular
Prefixes giving direction, location, or placement			
ab-	away	absent	away or missing from a place
ad-	toward	adhesive	able to stick to a surface
ante-/pre-	before	antecedent/premarital	something that came before/before marriage
circum-/peri-	around	circumference/perimeter	the distance around something/border of an area
com-/col-/con-	with, together	compile/collide/convene	put together/come into violent contact/come together
de-	away, from	depart	leave, go away from
dia-	through	diameter	a straight line passing through the center of a circle
ex-/extra-	from, out of, former	ex-wife/extramarital	former wife/occurring outside marriage

Prefix	Meaning	Sample Words	Definitions
Prefixes giving direction, location, or placement (cont.)			
hyper-	over, excessive	hyperactive	unusually or abnormally active
inter-	between	interpersonal	existing or occurring between people
intro-/intra-	within, into, in	introvert/intramural	turn or direct inward/involving only students within the same school
post-	after	posttest	a test given after completion of a program or course
re-	back, again	review	go over or inspect again
retro-	backward	retrospect	a survey or review of the past
sub-	under, below	submarine	a ship designed to operate under water
super-	above, extra	supercharge	increase or boost the power of something
tele-	far	telescope	an instrument for making distant objects appear nearer
trans-	across, over	transcontinental	extending across a continent

EXERCISE 3-9 — Reading: Using Prefixes to Determine Meaning

Directions: Use the list of common prefixes in Table 3-2 to determine the meaning of each of the following words. Write a brief definition or synonym for each. If you are unfamiliar with the root, you may need to check a dictionary.

1. interoffice: _____
2. supernatural: _____
3. nonsense: _____
4. introspection: _____
5. prearrange: _____
6. reset: _____
7. subtopic: _____
8. transmit: _____
9. multidimensional: _____
10. imperfect: _____

EXERCISE 3-10 — Reading: Identifying Words That Use Prefixes

WORKING TOGETHER

Directions: Working in teams of two, choose two of the following prefixes and list as many words as you can think of that begin with them: *multi-, mis-, trans-, com-, inter-*. Try to work out the meanings of the words based on the prefixes they contain. Check your answers using a dictionary.

EXERCISE 3-11 Using Prefixes to Figure Out Words as You Read

Directions: Read the following paragraphs and use your knowledge of prefixes to identify the meaning of each of the words in boldfaced type. Use a dictionary if necessary.

A. How can we **reconcile** such **contradictory** conclusions about heroin addiction? Certainly William Burroughs' description of his own addiction to heroin (and similar reports by others) is accurate. He did not make it up. At the same time, Johnson and his associates are also accurate. They did not make up their findings either. And other researchers have noted that some people use heroin on an **irregular** basis, such as at weekend parties, without becoming addicted. Where does this leave us? From the mixed reports, it seems reasonable to conclude that heroin is addicting to some people, but not to others. Some people do become addicts and match the **stereotypical** profile. Others use heroin on a recreational basis. Both, then, may be right. With the evidence we have at this point, it would be **inappropriate** to side with either extreme.

—adapted from Henslin, *Social Problems*, p. 118

1. reconcile _____

2. contradictory _____

3. irregular _____

4. stereotypical _____

5. inappropriate _____

B. An especially **unstable** class of molecules are oxygen free radicals, sometimes just called free radicals. Some free radicals are accidentally produced in small amounts during the normal process of energy transfer within living cells. Exposure to chemicals, radiation, **ultraviolet** light, cigarette smoke, and air pollution may also create free radicals. We now know that certain enzymes and nutrients called **antioxidants** are the body's natural defense against oxygen free radicals. Antioxidants may prevent oxidation by **inactivating** them quickly before they can damage other molecules. Many health experts believe that antioxidant vitamins reduce the chance of certain cancers and the risk of **cardiovascular** death.

—adapted from Johnson, *Human Biology*, p. 27

1. unstable _____

2. ultraviolet _____

3. antioxidants _____

4. inactivating _____

5. cardiovascular _____

Roots

Roots carry the basic or core meaning of a word, and knowledge of the meanings of these roots will enable you to unlock the meanings of many words. For example, if you know that the root *dic/dict* means "tell or say," then you would have a clue to the meanings of such words as *dictate* (to speak for someone to write down), *diction* (wording or manner of speaking), or *dictionary* (book that tells what words mean). Table 3-3 lists common roots, their meanings, and definitions of sample words that include them.

TABLE 3-3 COMMON ROOTS			
Common Root	**Meaning**	**Sample Word**	**Definition**
aster/astro	star	astronaut	a person trained to travel in space
aud/audit	hear	audible	able to be heard
bene	good, well	benefit	an advantage gained from something
bio	life	biology	the scientific study of living organisms
cap	take, seize	captive	a person who has been taken prisoner
chron/chrono	time	chronology	the order in which events occur
cog	to learn	cognitive	relating to mental processes
corp	body	corpse	dead body
cred	believe	incredible	difficult/impossible to believe
dict/dic	tell, say	predict	declare something will happen in the future
duc/duct	lead	introduce	bring in or present for the first time
fact/fac	make, do	factory	a building where goods are manufactured
geo	earth	geophysics	the physics of the earth
graph	write	telegraph	a system for sending messages to a distant place
log/logo/logy	study, thought	psychology	the scientific study of the human mind
mit/miss	send	permit/dismiss	allow or make possible
mort/mor	die, death	immortal	everlasting, not subject to death
path	feeling	sympathy	sharing the feelings of another
phon	sound, voice	telephone	a device used to transmit voices
photo	light	photosensitive	responding to light
port	carry	transport	carry from one place to another
scop	seeing	microscope	an instrument that magnifies small objects
scrib/script	write	inscription	a written note
sen/sent	feel	insensitive	lacking concern for others' feelings
spec/spic/spect	look, see	retrospect	a survey or review of the past
tend/tens/tent	stretch or strain	tension	mental or emotional strain
terr/terre	land, earth	territory	a geographic area, a tract of land
theo	god	theology	the study of the nature of God and religious belief
ven/vent	come	convention	a meeting or formal assembly
vert/vers	turn	invert	put upside down or in the opposite position
vis/vid	see	invisible/video	not able to be seen
voc	call	vocation	a person's occupation or calling

EXERCISE 3-12 — Reading: Using Roots to Determine Meaning

Directions: Use the list of common roots in Table 3-3 to determine the meanings of the following words. Write a brief definition or synonym for each, checking a dictionary if necessary.

1. porter: _____
2. credentials: _____
3. speculate: _____
4. terrain: _____
5. audition: _____
6. astrophysics: _____
7. capacity: _____
8. chronicle: _____
9. autograph: _____
10. sociology: _____

EXERCISE 3-13 — Using Roots to Determine Meaning as You Read

Directions: Read each of the following paragraphs and use your knowledge of roots as well as a dictionary to determine the meaning of each of the boldfaced words.

A. Is it possible that humankind is now, at last, at the end of its ability to increase food supplies? The answer to this question is a cautious "probably not." If demographers are correct in their **projections** of Earth's future **population**, the population can be fed. **Humankind** has scarcely begun to maximize **productivity** with the best contemporary technology, and that leading technology has been applied to only a small portion of Earth. Spreading **urbanization** is replacing agriculture in many places, but more lands can still be farmed.

—Bergman and Renwick, *Introduction to Geography*, p. 323

1. projections _____
2. population _____
3. humankind _____
4. productivity _____
5. urbanization _____

B. No country is completely self-sufficient in food. Most countries both import and export food despite the fact that portions of their own populations are **undernourished**. This may be due to **injustice** or civil strife. Political **instability** contributes to hunger. Several African countries, for example, are environmentally richly endowed, yet a great many of their people go hungry. Peter Rosset, director of the Institute for Food and Development Policy, wrote, "There is no relationship between the **prevalence** of hunger in a given country and its population. The world today produces more food per **inhabitant** than ever before."

—Bergman and Renwick, *Introduction to Geography*, p. 329

6. undernourished _____

7. injustice _____

8. instability _____

9. prevalence _____

10. inhabitant _____

Suffixes

Suffixes are word endings that often change the part of speech of a word. For example, adding the suffix -*y* to the noun *cloud* forms the adjective *cloudy*. Accompanying the change in part of speech is a shift in meaning (*cloudy* means "resembling clouds; overcast with clouds; dimmed or dulled as if by clouds"). A list of common suffixes and their meanings appears in Table 3-4.

TABLE 3-4 COMMON SUFFIXES			
Suffix		**Sample Words**	**Meaning**
Suffixes that refer to a state, condition, or quality			
-able	capable of	touchable	capable of being touched
-ance	characterized by	assistance	the action of helping
-ation	action or process	confrontation	an act of confronting or meeting face to face
-ence	state or condition	reference	an act or instance of referring or mentioning
-ible	capable of	tangible	capable of being felt, having substance
-ion	action or process	discussion	
-ity	state or quality	superiority	the quality or condition of being higher in rank or status
-ive	performing action	permissive	characterized by freedom of behavior
-ment	action or process	amazement	a state of overwhelming surprise or astonishment
-ness	state, quality, condition	kindness	the quality of being kind
-ous	possessing, full of	jealous	envious or resentful of another
-ty	characterized by	loyalty	the state of being loyal or faithful
-y	condition, quality	creamy	resembling or containing cream
Suffixes that mean "one who"			
-an		Italian	one who is from Italy
-ant		participant	one who participates
-ee		referee	one who enforces the rules of a game or sport
-eer		engineer	one who is trained in engineering
-ent		resident	one who lives in a place
-er		teacher	one who teaches
-ist		activist	one who takes action to promote or advocate a cause
-or		advisor	one who advises
Suffixes that mean "pertaining to or referring to"			
-al		autumnal	occurring in or pertaining to autumn
-ship		friendship	the state of being friends
-hood		brotherhood	the relationship between brothers
-ward		homeward	leading toward home

Often, several different words can be formed from a single root word by adding different suffixes. The chart below shows how adding a suffix changes the meaning and often the part of speech of a word.

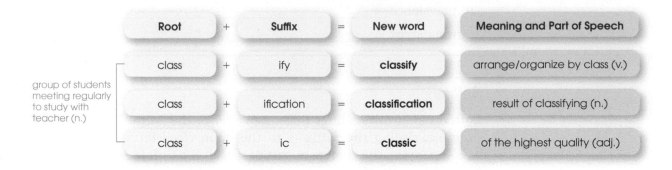

Root		Suffix		New word	Meaning and Part of Speech
class	+	ify	=	**classify**	arrange/organize by class (v.)
class	+	ification	=	**classification**	result of classifying (n.)
class	+	ic	=	**classic**	of the highest quality (adj.)

group of students meeting regularly to study with teacher (n.)

You can expand your vocabulary by learning the variations in meaning that occur when suffixes are added to words you already know. When you find a word that you do not know, look for the root. Then, using the sentence the word is in (its context), figure out what the word means with the suffix added. Occasionally, you may find that the spelling of the root word has been changed. For instance, a final *e* may be dropped, a final consonant may be doubled, or a final *y* may be changed to *i*. Consider the possibility of such changes when trying to identify the root word.

- The article was a **compilation** of facts.
  root + suffix
  compil(e) + -ation = something that has been compiled, or put together into an orderly form
- We were concerned with the **legality** of our decision to change addresses.
  root + suffix
  legal + -ity = lawfulness
- Our college is one of the most **prestigious** in the state.
  root + suffix
  prestig(e) + -ious = having prestige or distinction

EXERCISE 3-14

WORKING TOGETHER

Writing: Adding Suffixes

Directions: Working with a classmate, for each word listed below, write as many new words as you can create by adding suffixes, and note their meanings and parts of speech. Share your findings with the class.

1. compare: _____

2. adapt: _____

3. direct: _____

4. identify: _____

5. will: _____

6. prefer: _____

7. notice: _____

8. like: _____

9. pay: _____

10. promote: _____

| EXERCISE 3-15 | Writing: Using Suffixes to Create New Words |

Directions: For each of the words listed below, add a suffix so that the word will complete the sentence. Write the new word in the space provided. Check a dictionary if you are unsure of the spelling.

> **EXAMPLE**   sex: __Sexist__ language should be avoided in both speech and writing.

1. **eat:** We did not realize that the plant was _____ until we tasted its delicious fruit.

2. **compete:** The gymnastics _____ was our favorite part of the Olympics.

3. **decide:** It was difficult to be _____ in such a stressful situation.

4. **Portugal:** Our favorite restaurant specializes in _____ food.

5. **active:** She gained fame as a civil rights _____ in the 1960s.

6. **parent:** _____ is one of the most rewarding experiences in life.

7. **vaccine:** You must receive several different _____ before your trip to Africa.

8. **member:** We inadvertently allowed our _____ to the botanical garden to lapse.

9. **drive:** The abandoned car did not appear _____ so a tow truck was summoned.

10. **celebrate:** The girls waited at the airport for hours to catch a glimpse of their favorite _____ .

| EXERCISE 3-16 | Reading: Using Prefixes, Roots, and Suffixes to Determine Meaning |

Directions: Read the following paragraphs and use your knowledge of prefixes, roots, and suffixes to determine the meaning of the boldfaced words.

A.   Certain types of crime are easier to get away with than others. Running less risk are **political** criminals who attempt to maintain the status quo and white-collar criminals who commit crimes in the name of a **corporation**, and those who comprise the top levels of organized crime. **Respectability**, wealth, power, and underlings insulate them. Those in the second group are insulated by the corporation's desire to avoid negative **publicity**. Those who run the highest risk of arrest are "soldiers" at the lowest levels of organized crime, who are considered **expendable**.

—adapted from Henslin, *Social Problems*, p. 192

1. political _____

2. corporation _____

3. respectability _____

4. publicity _____

5. expendable _____

B.   The proponents of capital punishment argue that it is an appropriate **retribution** for **heinous** crimes, that it deters, and, of course, that it is an effective **incapacitator**. Its critics argue that killing is never justified. Opponents also argue that the death penalty is **capricious**: Jurors deliberate in secrecy and indulge their prejudices in recommending death, and judges are **irrational**—merciful to some but not to others.

—adapted from Henslin, *Social Problems*, p. 205

6. retribution _____

7. heinous _____

8. incapacitator _____

9. capricious _____

10. irrational _____

EXERCISE 3-17

Reading: Using Prefixes, Roots, and Suffixes in "Emoji—Trendy Slang or a Whole New Language?"

Directions: Use your knowledge of prefixes, roots, and suffixes to determine the meaning of each of the following words that appear in "Emoji—Trendy Slang or a Whole New Language?" in the Examining Professional Writing section of this chapter. Write a synonym or brief meaning for each.

1. regress (paragraph 3) _____

2. emotional (paragraph 6) _____

3. creative (paragraph 11) _____

4. corporate (paragraph 14) _____

How to Use Word Parts

When you come upon a word you do not know, keep the following pointers in mind:

 NEED TO KNOW

How to Use Word Parts

1. **First, look for the root (shown in bold below).** Think of this as looking for a word inside a larger word. Often a letter or two will be missing.

un/**utter**/able	**defens**/ible
inter/**colleg**/iate	re/**popular**/ize
post/**operat**/ive	non/**adapt**/able
im/**measur**/ability	non/**commit**/tal

2. **If you do not recognize the root, then you will probably not be able to figure out the word.** The next step is to check its meaning in a dictionary. For tips on locating words in a dictionary rapidly and easily, see the next section, Use a Dictionary Effectively.

3. **If you did recognize the root word, look for a prefix (shown in bold below).** If there is one, determine how it changes the meaning of the word.

un/utterable	**un** = not
post/operative	**post** = after

4. **Locate the suffix (shown in bold below).** Determine how it further adds to or changes the meaning of the root word.

unutter/**able**	**able** = able to
postoperat/**ive**	**ive** = state or condition

5. **Next, try out the meaning in the sentence in which the word was used.** Substitute your meaning for the word, and see whether the sentence makes sense.

   ■ Some of the victim's thoughts were **unutterable** at the time of the crime.
   unutterable = cannot be spoken

   ■ My sister was worried about the cost of **postoperative** care.
   postoperative = describing state or condition after an operation

Use a Dictionary Effectively

■ GOAL 3
Use a dictionary
effectively

If you cannot determine the meaning of unfamiliar words using context clues and/or word parts, it is time to use a dictionary.

Types of Dictionaries

Every writer needs access to several types of dictionaries:

1. **Print and Online Dictionaries** Desk or collegiate dictionaries are available both in print and online. Widely used dictionaries include the following:
   ■ *The American Heritage Dictionary of the English Language*
   ■ *Merriam-Webster's Collegiate Dictionary*
   ■ *Webster's New World Dictionary of the American Language*

   This type of dictionary typically contains entries for all the commonly used words in the English language and is updated frequently to add words recently entering the language and retire those that have become outdated.

2. **Misspeller's Dictionary** If you have difficulty finding a word because you do not know exactly how it is spelled, consult a misspeller's dictionary. *Webster's New World Misspeller's* Dictionary is available both in print and online.

3. **Unabridged Dictionaries** Typically found in the reference section of the library or available online through subscription, an unabridged dictionary offers the most complete information about each word in the English language, including the word's history.

4. **Bilingual Dictionaries** If you are an ESL student, be sure to purchase a bilingual dictionary. They are available, either in print or online, for most commonly spoken languages. Online versions are easy to use; just type in the English word and the corresponding word in your language appears. Google also offers translations from the main Google search page.

Using a Dictionary

Here is a brief review of the information a dictionary entry contains. Refer to the sections of the sample online dictionary entry below.

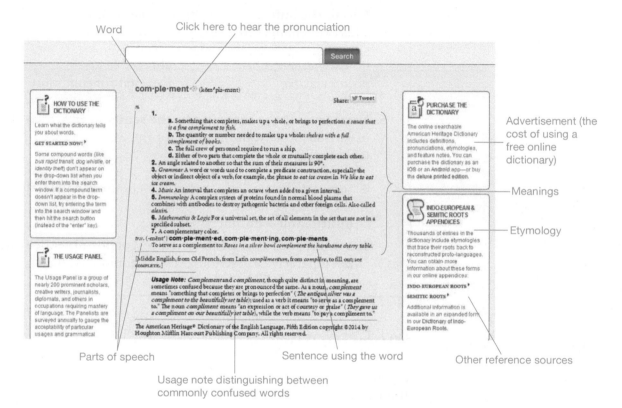

EXERCISE 3-18   Reading: Using a Dictionary

Directions: Use a dictionary to answer the following questions about vocabulary in the professional reading "Emoji—Trendy Slang or a Whole New Language?" in the Examining Professional Writing section of this chapter.

1. How many meanings are listed for the word *mind* (paragraph 2)?

   _____

2. How is the word *portmanteau* (paragraph 4) pronounced? (Record its phonetic spelling.)

   _____

3. Can the word *cluster* (paragraph 7) be used other than as a noun? If so, how?

   _____

4. What is the etymology or origin of the word *language* (paragraph 3)?

   _____

5. The meaning of the word *narrow* as used in paragraph 6 is "limited in scope." What are two other meanings of the word *narrow*?

_____

6. List three synonyms for the word *accommodate* (paragraph 8).

_____

7. List several words that are formed using the word *personal* (paragraph 9).

_____

8. The author uses the word *text* (paragraph 4) to refer to an electronic communication sent and received by mobile phones. What is another meaning of the word?

_____

9. Explain the meaning of the word *nuance* (paragraph 2).

_____

10. Define the word *pecking* (paragraph 5) as it is used in the selection and write a sentence using the word.

_____

_____

Selecting Appropriate Meanings

Because most words have more than one meaning, you must choose the meaning that fits the way the word is used in the context of the sentence. The meanings are often grouped by part of speech and are numbered consecutively in each group. Generally, the most common meanings of the word are listed first, with more specialized, less common meanings appearing toward the end of the entry. Here are a few suggestions for choosing the correct meaning from among those listed in an entry:

1. **If you are familiar with the parts of speech, try to use these to locate the correct meaning.** For instance, if you are looking up the meaning of a word that names a person, place, or thing, you can save time by reading only those entries given after *n.* (noun).

2. **For most types of college reading, you can skip definitions that give slang and colloquial (abbreviated *colloq.*) meanings.** Colloquial meanings refer to informal or spoken language.

3. **If you are not sure of the part of speech, read each meaning until you find a definition that seems correct.** Skip over restrictive meanings that are inappropriate.

4. **Test your choice by substituting the meaning in the sentence with which you are working.** Substitute the definition for the word and see whether it makes sense in context.

For example, suppose you were looking up the word *perceive* from the following sentence:

> "Without emoji, it is difficult to perceive the actual emotion that is supposed to accompany the message."

Perceive is used as a verb. If you look at the definitions listed for *perceive* in a dictionary, definition 1 relates to sight, which is not the meaning here based on context. However, definition 2, "to achieve understanding of," does fit and makes sense: emoji give you a tool for understanding the tone of a text.

EXERCISE 3-19   Reading: Finding the Right Meaning

Directions: Use a dictionary to help you find an appropriate meaning for the boldfaced word in each of the following sentences.

1. The last contestant did not have a **ghost** of a chance.

   _____

2. The visitors were **immersed** in the culture of their host.

   _____

3. The artist was known for having a **fertile** imagination.

   _____

4. The orchestra played the first **movement** of the symphony.

   _____

5. The plane stalled on the **apron**.

   _____

Use a Thesaurus to Find Synonyms and Antonyms

■ GOAL 4
Use a thesaurus to find synonyms and antonyms

Synonyms are words with similar meanings; **antonyms** are words with opposite meanings. Both categories of words are useful to expand and diversify your vocabulary.

When writing or speaking, you may want to find a *synonym*, a word with a more exact, descriptive, or specific meaning than the one that comes to mind. For example, you might want to describe how a person walks. There are many words that mean *walk*, although each may have a different connotation: *strut, meander, stroll, hike, saunter*, and *march*.

Antonyms are useful when making a contrast or explaining differences. You might be describing two different communication styles of friends. One style is *decisive*. Finding antonyms for the word *decisive* may suggest a way to describe the opposite style of the other person such as *faltering, hesitant*, or *wavering*.

Using a Thesaurus

A **thesaurus** is a dictionary of synonyms and antonyms. A thesaurus is particularly useful when you want to

■ locate the precise term to fit a particular situation.

■ find an appropriate descriptive word.

■ replace an overused or unclear word.

■ convey a different or more specific shade of meaning.

■ find a word that means the opposite of another word.

Suppose you are looking for a more precise word for the expression, *look into* in the following sentence:

The marketing manager will **look into** the decline of recent sales in the Midwest.

The thesaurus lists synonyms for "look into." Read the thesaurus entry and underline words or phrases that you think would be more descriptive than *look into*. You might underline words and phrases such as *examine, investigate*, and *scrutinize*.

The most widely used thesaurus is *Roget's Thesaurus*. Inexpensive paperback editions are available in most bookstores. *Merriam-Webster's Collegiate Thesaurus* is available free online (http://www.merriam-webster.com/thesaurus.htm). You can also access a thesaurus at http://www.thesaurus.com.

When you first consult a thesaurus, you will need to familiarize yourself with its format and learn how to use it. The following is a step-by-step approach:

How to Use a Thesaurus

1. **Begin by locating the word you are trying to replace.** Many thesauruses are organized alphabetically, much like a dictionary. Following the word, you will find numerous entries that list the synonyms of that word. Select words that seem like possible substitutes. (The hardback edition of *Roget's* is organized by subject with an index in the back.)

2. **Test each of the words you selected in the sentence in which you will use it.** The word should fit the context of the sentence.

3. **Select the word that best expresses what you are trying to say.**

4. **Choose only words whose shades of meaning you know.** Check unfamiliar words in a dictionary before using them. Remember, misusing a word is often a more serious error than choosing an overused, vague, or general one.

EXERCISE 3-20	Writing: Noting the Differences in Synonyms

Directions: For each of the pairs or sets of synonyms listed, explain the difference in meaning between the words. Use a dictionary if necessary.

EXAMPLE   subject / topic: Both denote the principal idea or point of a speech, a piece of writing, or an artistic work; *subject* is the more general term, whereas *topic* is a subject of discussion, argument, or conversation.

1. form / figure / shape: _____

_____

_____

_____

2. bright / brilliant / radiant: _____

_____

_____

3. offend / insult: _____

_____

_____

4. perform / accomplish / achieve: _____

_____

_____

_____

5. complex / complicated: _____

_____

_____

| EXERCISE 3-21 | Writing: Using Antonyms |

Directions: Find an antonym for each of the following words and then write a sentence using the antonym. Consult a dictionary or thesaurus, if necessary.

1. prohibit _____
2. obtuse _____
3. tedious _____
4. compliant _____
5. rebuke _____

| EXERCISE 3-22 | Writing: Using a Thesaurus |

Directions: Using a thesaurus, replace the boldfaced word or phrase in each sentence with a more precise or descriptive word. Write the word in the space provided. Rephrase the sentence, if necessary.

EXAMPLE   The union appointed Corinne Miller to act as the **go-between** in its negotiations with management. liaison _____

1. The two interviewers **went back and forth** asking questions of the candidate.

   _____

2. On the night of the inauguration, the ballroom looked **very nice.** _____

3. More than anything, he **wanted** a new minivan. _____

4. The town had gone through an economic decline, but now it appeared to be on the verge of an economic **increase.** _____

5. The two brothers were opposites: Chester **liked to talk a lot**, whereas John was content to sit quietly and listen. _____

6. Freshwater lakes that are in the process of accelerated growth of algae are often **cloudy-looking.** _____

7. Daylilies range in color from **dark red** to yellow to almost white. _____

8. Today's trend toward casual clothing in the workplace has made the demand for high-quality custom suits **fall.** _____

9. The children were **so sad** over the loss of their old dog, Chumley. _____

10. The first speaker was interesting, but the second one was so **dull** I almost fell asleep. _____

Understand Denotative and Connotative Language

■ **GOAL 5**
Understand denotative and connotative language

All words have one or more standard meanings; these meanings are called **denotative meanings**. Think of them as those meanings listed in the dictionary. They tell us what the word names. Many words also have connotative meanings. **Connotative meanings** include the feelings and associations that may accompany a word. For example, the denotative meaning of *mother* is female parent. However, the word carries many connotations. For many, *mother* suggests a warm, loving, caring person, but for others it can mean an uncaring, neglectful, or even cruel woman.

Writers and speakers use connotative meanings to stir emotions or to bring to mind positive or negative associations. Suppose a writer is describing how someone walks. The writer could choose words such as *strut, stroll, swagger,* or *amble.* Do you see how each creates a different image of the person? Connotative meanings, then, are powerful tools of language. When you read, be alert for meanings suggested by the author's word choice. When writing or speaking, be sure to choose words with appropriate connotations.

EXERCISE 3-23

WORKING TOGETHER

Writing: Understanding Connotative Meanings

Directions: Working with a classmate, discuss the differences in connotative meaning of each of the following pairs or sets of words. Write the definitions below. Then write a sentence using one word from each of the sets. Consult a dictionary, if necessary.

EXAMPLE   To improve: **mend—reform**
Mend implies repairing something that is broken; reform means changing something, often a document or law, to improve it or eliminate its faults.

1. A competitor: **rival—opponent**

_____

_____

2. Working together: **accomplice—colleague**

_____

_____

3. Old: **antique—old-fashioned—obsolete—dated**

_____

_____

_____

4. Cautious: **wary—vigilant—careful**

_____

_____

5. Trip: **excursion—pilgrimage—vacation—tour**

_____

_____

_____

Reading: Understanding Connotative Meanings in "Emoji—Trendy Slang or a Whole New Language?"

Directions: Working with a classmate, discuss the connotative meaning of each of the following words or phrases from "Emoji—Trendy Slang or a Whole New Language?" and determine whether it is positive or negative. Write the definition of each. Consult a dictionary, if necessary.

1. socially handicapped (paragraph 2) _____

   _____

2. lexical fad (paragraph 3) _____

3. lingo (paragraph 12) _____

4. disease vectors (paragraph 12) _____

5. dork (paragraph 13) _____

Use Creative Language

■ GOAL 6
Use creative language

Figurative language, idioms, and euphemisms are all different ways of using words to convey meaning.

Figurative Language

The purpose of figurative language is to paint a word picture that will help the reader or listener visualize how something looks, feels, or smells. **Figurative language** allows the writer or speaker the opportunity to be creative and to express attitudes and opinions without directly stating them. Figurative language is used widely in literature, as well as many forms of expressive writing.

The two most common types of figurative language are similes and metaphors. A **simile** uses the word *like* or *as* to make a comparison. A **metaphor** states or implies that one thing *is* another thing. If you say, "Mary's dress looks *like* a whirlwind of color," you have created a simile. If you say, "Mary's dress *is* a whirlwind of color," you have created a metaphor. Notice that each compares two unlike things, the dress and the whirlwind. Here are a few examples:

■ I will speak daggers to her, but use none. (metaphor)
—William Shakespeare, Hamlet

■ An aged man is but a paltry thing, / A tattered coat upon a stick . . . (metaphor)
—W. B. Yeats, "Sailing to Byzantium"

■ O my Luve's like the melodie / That's sweetly play'd in tune (simile)
—Robert Burns, "A Red, Red Rose"

■ Announced by all the trumpets of the sky, / Arrives the snow . . . (metaphor)
—Ralph Waldo Emerson, "The Snow-Storm"

EXERCISE 3-25   Reading: Understanding Figurative Expressions

Directions: For the figurative expression indicated in each sentence, select the choice that best explains its meaning.

_____ 1. It was **an uphill battle** to get the insurance claim approved.
   a. dangerous   c. physically tiring
   b. extremely difficult   d. complicated

_____ 2. His face **clouded over** as soon as she said no.
   a. looked unhappy   c. cooled off
   b. cleared up   d. was shaded

_____ 3. At sunset, the surface of the lake was **like a piece of glass**.
   a. sharp   c. wavy
   b. smooth   d. hard

_____ 4. The sound of the chainsaw outside her window was **like a dentist drilling on her nerves.**
   a. a pleasant humming   c. an extremely unpleasant sound
   b. a sound she could ignore   d. an important and necessary sound

_____ 5. His birthday money was **burning a hole in his pocket**!
   a. on fire   c. causing people to look at him
   b. too heavy for his pocket   d. making him anxious to spend it

EXERCISE 3-26   Writing: Using Figurative Language

Directions: Explain the meaning of each of the following figures of speech, and then write a sentence for each, using it figuratively, not literally.

EXAMPLE   a black eye   _A black eye is a mark of shame or dishonor. The flamingo's escape was a black eye for the zoo. [The flamingo's escape caused dishonor to the zoo's reputation.]_

1. piece of cake _____

_____

2. hanging on every word _____

_____

3. dinosaur _____

_____

4. off the wall _____

_____

5. fit to be tied _____

_____

Idioms

Each of the following italicized expressions is an idiom:

■ Does a _flea market_ sell fleas?

■ Does the _graveyard shift_ mean you work in a graveyard?

■ Does _"Close, but no cigar"_ involve tobacco?

Idioms are phrases that have a meaning other than what the common definitions of the words in the phrase indicate. There are thousands of idioms in use in the English language, and they are often particularly puzzling to nonnative speakers. To find the meaning of an idiom, look in a dictionary under one of the key words. For instance, look under *crow* to find the meaning of the idiom *as the crow flies*. In a dictionary, idioms are often labeled "idiom" and followed by the complete phrase and its meaning.

EXERCISE 3-27

Writing: Defining Idioms

Directions: Write a definition of each of the following idioms.

1. to keep tabs on _____
2. to learn the ropes _____
3. like a chicken with its head cut off _____
4. peeping tom _____
5. to steal someone's thunder _____
6. rule of thumb _____
7. straight from the horse's mouth _____
8. in the dark _____
9. under the weather _____
10. let the cat out of the bag _____

Euphemisms

What do each of the following sentences have in common?

- Where is the ladies' room?
- My aunt passed away.
- I work for the sanitation department.

Each uses an expression called a **euphemism**—a word or phrase that is used in place of a word that is unpleasant, embarrassing, or otherwise objectionable. The expression *passed away* replaces the word *died, ladies' room* is a substitute for *toilet*, and *sanitation* is a more pleasing term than *garbage*.

Today, many euphemisms are widely used in both spoken and written language. Here are a few more examples:

- The objective of the air strike was to **neutralize** (kill) the enemy. Some **collateral damage** (death to civilians) occurred as a result of the air strike.
- When it is hot, women **glow** (sweat).

Euphemisms tend to minimize or downplay the importance or seriousness of something. They are often used in politics and advertising. They can be used to camouflage actions or events that may be unacceptable to readers or listeners if bluntly explained. For example, the word *casualties of war* may be used instead of the phrase *dead soldiers* to lessen the impact of troop losses. To say that a politician's statement was *at variance with the truth* is less forceful than to say that the politician *lied*.

When you speak or write, be sure to avoid euphemisms that obscure or interfere with your intended meaning. Euphemisms can lead your listeners or readers to believe that you have something to hide or that you are not being completely truthful with them.

| EXERCISE 3-28 | Writing: Understanding Euphemisms |

Directions: For each of the boldfaced euphemisms, determine the meaning of the term, and then write a new sentence that does not minimize or avoid the term's real meaning.

EXAMPLE   The former mayor was sent to a **correctional facility** after being convicted of accepting bribes.
The former mayor went to prison after being convicted of accepting bribes.

1. The search continued for the **remains** of the victims of the air crash.

2. The advertising campaign was an **incomplete success**.

3. The company announced that it would be **downsizing** several hundred employees over the next few months.

4. The car dealership sold both new and **previously owned** automobiles.

5. The veterinarian recommended that the elderly cat be **put to sleep**.

Learn Vocabulary in College Courses

■ **GOAL 7**
Learn vocabulary in college courses

For each course you take, you encounter an extensive set of words and terms that are used in a particular way in that subject area. One of the most important tasks you face in college is to learn the vocabulary of each course. This task is especially important in introductory courses in which the subject is new and unfamiliar.

Learn Vocabulary in Classes and Lectures

Often, the first few class lectures in a course are devoted to acquainting students with the nature and scope of the field and introducing them to its specialized language. Be sure to record accurately each new term for later review and study. Good lecturers give students clues to what terms and definitions are important to record. They may:

■ write new words on the board, as a means of emphasis.

■ highlight new terms using PowerPoint.

■ slow down, almost dictating, so that students can record definitions.

■ repeat a word and its definition several times or offer several variations of meaning.

As a part of your note-taking system, develop a consistent way of easily identifying new terms and definitions recorded in your notes. Circle, box, or highlight each new term or write "def." in the margin.

Vocabulary in College Textbooks

Because textbooks are written by professors, they know which words you need to learn for a specific discipline.

Textbook Features That Help You Learn Vocabulary

Here are some of the features textbook authors include in their textbooks to help you learn the vocabulary needed to master their courses:

- **Context clues.** Because textbook authors know much of the terminology they use is unfamiliar, they often provide obvious context clues. *Definition, synonym,* and *example clues* are the most common.

> synonyms
>
> (Actus reus) or "guilty deed" occurs when an individual (whether as a principal, accessory, or accomplice) engages in a behavior prohibited by the criminal law. This can involve either doing something wrong (commission) or failing to do something that is legally obligated (omission).

—Fuller, *Criminal Justice*, p. 135

- **Marginal definitions.** Many textbooks include the meaning of unfamiliar terms in the margin next to where the word is first used; words being defined are often set in **bold** or *italic* font. Highlight these definitions as you read. Be sure to check them again as you review and study for exams. If there is a lot of terminology to learn, use the index card system described below.

- **Chapter vocabulary review.** This list identifies key terms introduced during the chapter, often followed by page numbers indicating where the terms were first used. This list may appear either at the beginning or at the end of the chapter. Check this list before you read the chapter so you will know what key words to look for. As you read, highlight each term and its definition. Use the list as a study aid later: test yourself to be sure you can define each term.

- **Glossaries.** Appearing at the end of a text, a glossary is an alphabetical list of new terms introduced in the text. Use it to check the meanings of words not defined in the text or those you may have forgotten. If all the chapters in a text have been assigned, you can use the glossary to review for final exams. Scan the glossary; look for words that are unfamiliar or that you are unable to give a complete definition for and learn their meanings.

EXERCISE 3-29   Reading: Defining Textbook Vocabulary

Directions: Choose a textbook chapter that you have been assigned to read for one of your other courses. Identify ten new words that you are able to determine the meaning of using context clues, marginal definitions, the chapter vocabulary review, or the glossary.

Write to Learn: Keeping a Vocabulary Log

A **vocabulary log** is a list of words you want to learn. You can create a vocabulary log for each of your courses, keep a separate notebook designated as your vocabulary log, or create a digital file. Record the word, its meaning, its pronunciation if unfamiliar, and textbook page reference. An excerpt from one student's vocabulary log for psychology is shown in Figure 3-1 below.

FIGURE 3-1	SAMPLE VOCABULARY LOG FOR A PSYCHOLOGY COURSE	
Word	**Meaning**	**Page**
intraspecific aggression	attack by one animal upon another member of its species	310
orbitofrontal cortex	region of the brain that aids in recognition of situations that produce emotional responses	312
modulation	an attempt to minimize or exaggerate the expression of emotion	317
simulation	an attempt to display an emotion that one does not really feel	319

Use Flashcards

Flashcards are one of the most practical and easy-to-use systems for learning new words. They enable you to record words and learn them through repetition and self-testing. Using index cards, write the word on the front and the meaning on the back. You might also include the word's pronunciation or a diagram or picture if you are a visual learner. Test yourself, and shuffle the pack frequently, sorting the cards into "Know" and "Don't Know" piles. Keep going through the "Don't Know" pile until you have learned all the words. Several Web sites also enable you to create flashcards electronically, including Quizlet.com and Cram.com.

Whatever system you use, you will find that by writing or typing the word and its meaning, you are strengthening your recall, and testing yourself on its meaning prepares you for situations in which you will need to recall or use the word.

Tips for Using the Words You Learn

Here are some suggestions for learning and retaining words. Depending on your learning style, some of the suggestions will work better than others.

- **Write the word immediately.** You will have a better chance of remembering a word if you write it rather than just highlight it. In fact, write it several times, once in the margin of the text and then again on an index card or in your vocabulary log. Write it again as you test yourself.

- **Write a sentence using the word.** Make the sentence personal, about you or your family or friends. The more meaningful the sentence is, the more likely you are to remember the word.

- ■ **Try to visualize a situation involving the word.** For instance, for the word *restore* ("to bring back to its original condition"), visualize an antique car restored to its original condition.
- ■ **Draw a picture or diagram that involves the word.** For example, for the word *squander* ("to waste"), draw a picture of yourself squandering money by setting bills on fire.
- ■ **Try to use the word in your own academic speech or writing as soon as you have learned it.**
- ■ **Give yourself vocabulary tests, or work with a friend to make up tests for each other.**

READ AND RESPOND: A Professional Reading

Emoji—Trendy Slang or a Whole New Language?

Nick Stockton

Earlier in the chapter, you read "Emoji—Trendy Slang or a Whole New Language?" in the Examining Professional Writing section, and you have examined the vocabulary in the essay throughout this chapter. Now it is time to take a closer look at the reading by responding to the questions that follow.

Writing in Response to Reading

Checking Your Comprehension

Answer each of the following questions using complete sentences.

1. What does the word *emoji* mean?
2. What were the two forerunners to emoji?
3. What is the purpose of adding emoji to a text?
4. What is pidgin?
5. Name two ways that adolescent linguistic fads phase out.
6. Name two limitations of emoji.

Strengthening Your Vocabulary

Using the word's context, word parts, or a dictionary, write a brief definition of each of the following words as it is used in the reading.

1. medium (paragraph 2) _____
2. puns (paragraph 6) _____
3. embryonic (paragraph 7) _____
4. linguist (paragraph 7) _____
5. emergent (paragraph 10) _____

Examining the Reading: Using Idea Maps

Review the reading by completing the missing parts of the following idea map.

VISUALIZE IT!

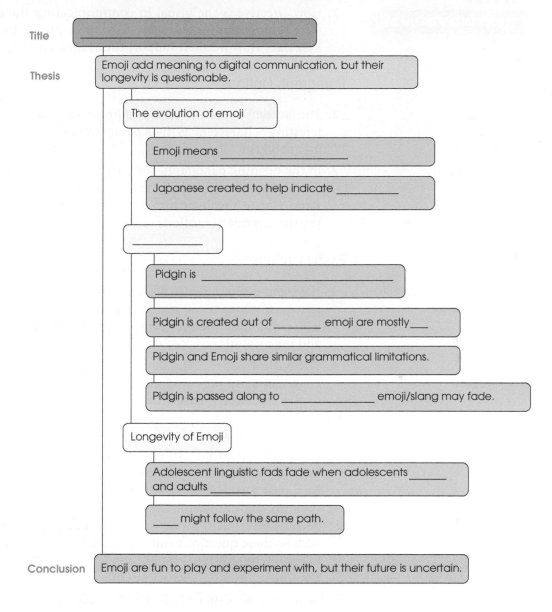

Title _____

Thesis — Emoji add meaning to digital communication, but their longevity is questionable.

The evolution of emoji

Emoji means _____

Japanese created to help indicate _____

_____

Pidgin is _____ _____

Pidgin is created out of _____ emoji are mostly ___

Pidgin and Emoji share similar grammatical limitations.

Pidgin is passed along to _____ emoji/slang may fade.

Longevity of Emoji

Adolescent linguistic fads fade when adolescents _____ and adults _____

____ might follow the same path.

Conclusion — Emoji are fun to play and experiment with, but their future is uncertain.

Thinking Critically: An Integrated Perspective

React and respond to the reading by discussing the following:

1. Why does the author begin the reading with the texting conversation? Discuss why this conversation is relevant to the subject of the reading.

2. What is the thesis (main idea) of the reading?

3. What do the introductory paragraphs (paragraphs 2 and 3) suggest about how the author will approach the subject?

4. Discuss the idea that linguistic fads change when adults catch on. Can you think of an example of this phenomenon?

5. Discuss popular words and expressions that you used five years ago and ones that you and your peers use today. Make a list that you can share with the class. (See paragraphs 13 and 14 for ideas.)

6. Why is it important that there be an emotional layer to communication? Write a journal entry answering this question and discussing the use of emoji to help provide this tone of voice.

7. How effective is the visual in communicating the author's message? If you were responsible for choosing a photograph for the reading, what would it look like? How would it support the author's message?

Paragraph Options

1. The last sentence in the essay addresses the fate of emoji and ends with an interesting "character." Write a paragraph explaining the meaning of the statement and the "character."

2. In the opening paragraph, the author presents a snapshot of a text conversation, complete with emoji, between two people. Your assignment is to do the same. Create a realistic text conversation between you and a friend and convey the intended emotions of the conversation with emoji.

Essay Options

3. Have you ever accidentally sent a text to the wrong person or received a text that wasn't meant for you or heard of someone who did? Write an essay in which you describe the texting incident, the results/fallout of the incident, and the resolution.

4. The author writes, "Humans love language, and we love playing with language, and any time we find a new method of communicating we are going to play and experiment with it. At least for a while." What does this statement mean to you? Write an essay explaining this statement and using examples from your own experience.

5. In paragraph 3, the author addresses the question of the longevity of emoji. What do you think of the questions he posed? Are emoji just a fad? Will they disappear just as soon as something better comes along or when adults use them to communicate? Or will they work their way into our language and become a standard mode of communication? Write an essay in which you address these questions and use examples from your experience and information from the reading as support.

Making Connections Between the Readings

This chapter's reading concerns digital communication and Chapter 5 is about a related topic: life on the grid. Use the following writing assignments to integrate your ideas about digital technology. Using "Emoji—Trendy Slang or a Whole New Language?" (in this chapter), "To Connect or Not to Connect" (Chapter 5), and "Google Is Making You More Forgetful. Here's Why That's a Good Thing" (Chapter 5), write a paragraph or an essay in response to one of the following prompts.

1. The authors of all three of the articles address ways that digital technology has enhanced our daily lives. Using the three articles as support, write a paragraph or an essay about the ways that digital technology has impacted your life as a student.

2. Another theme that runs through the three readings is that of communication. Using the three articles as support, write a paragraph or an essay in which you discuss the three authors' feelings about digital technology and how it has affected communication.

3. How do you think the author of "Google Is Making You More Forgetful. Here's Why That's a Good Thing" (Chapter 5) would respond to the points made by the author of "Emoji—Trendy Slang or a Whole New Language?" (in this chapter)? Write a response to this question, being sure to include support from both readings.

4. Discuss the similarities and differences in the three titles. What do the titles suggest about the authors' attitudes toward the subject?

SELF-TEST SUMMARY

To test yourself, cover the Answer column with a sheet of paper and answer each question in the left column. Evaluate each of your answers as you work by sliding the paper down and comparing your answer with what is printed in the Answer column.

QUESTION	ANSWER
■ **GOAL 1** Use context clues What is context?	Context refers to the words surrounding an unfamiliar word; context often provides clues to a word's meaning.
What are the five types of context clues?	Types of context clues include *definition, synonym, example, contrast,* and *inference*.
■ **GOAL 2** Use word parts What are word parts, and how do they help you learn words?	The beginnings, middles, and endings of words are called *prefixes, roots,* and *suffixes*. By learning the meanings of the parts that make up a word, you can figure out the meaning of the word. (See tips for how to use word parts on p. 94.)
■ **GOAL 3** Use a dictionary effectively What is involved in using a dictionary effectively?	Using a dictionary effectively involves selecting the right type of dictionary for the situation, understanding the kinds of information provided in a dictionary, and choosing the appropriate meaning of a word.
■ **GOAL 4** Use a thesaurus to find synonyms and antonyms What are synonyms and antonyms?	*Synonyms* are words with similar meanings; *antonyms* are words with opposite meanings.
What is a thesaurus?	A *thesaurus* is a dictionary of synonyms and can be used to find a precise term, to replace overused words, and to provide antonyms for words.

(continued)

QUESTION	ANSWER
■ **GOAL 5** Understand denotative and connotative language What are denotative and connotative language?	The *denotative* meaning of a word is its standard, dictionary meaning. The *connotative* meaning of a word includes the feelings and associations that may accompany it.
■ **GOAL 6** Use creative language What is figurative language?	*Figurative language* is a way of describing something that makes sense on an imaginative or creative level but not on a factual or literal level.
What are some types of figurative language?	Two common types of figurative language are *similes* (comparisons using the word *like* or *as*) and *metaphors* (comparisons stating or implying that one thing is another thing).
What is an idiom?	An *idiom* is a phrase that has a meaning other than what the common definitions of the words in the phrase indicate.
■ **GOAL 7** Learn vocabulary in college courses What features are included in college textbooks to help you learn vocabulary?	Textbooks include context clues, marginal definitions, chapter vocabulary reviews, and glossaries.
What are two systems for learning new words?	A vocabulary log and the index card system will help you learn and remember new words.

Main Ideas and Topic Sentences

Khttttithat Weerasirut/Shutterstock

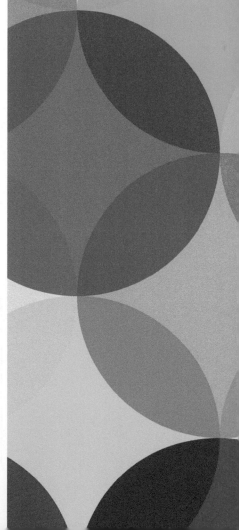

LEARNING GOALS

Learn how to …

■ **GOAL 1**
Understand general versus specific ideas

■ **GOAL 2**
Identify and select topics

■ **GOAL 3**
Read and write topic sentences

THINK About It!

Write a sentence describing the single overall feeling you get from this photograph. Does the food waste shown in this photograph surprise or concern you? Many photographs convey a single impression, as this one does. Details in the photograph support that impression.

In this chapter, you will learn how sentences in a paragraph are organized and how they work together to express a single idea. If you were to write a paragraph describing your response to the photograph, the sentence you wrote could serve as its topic sentence. A topic sentence expresses the main idea or single impression of the paragraph in a single sentence. In this chapter, you will learn how to read and write topic sentences.

This chapter will also guide you in an exploration of food waste. You will read a professional essay on dumpster diving and a student essay on reducing food waste in the United States.

What Are Topics, Main Ideas, and Topic Sentences?

Understanding or writing a paragraph is a step-by-step process. A paragraph focuses on one subject, called the **topic**. The paragraph makes one point about that topic, called the **main idea**. That main idea is often expressed in a single sentence, called the **topic sentence**. The rest of the paragraph, called **details**, explains the main idea.

Here is a sample paragraph from the professional essay you will read next.

> That Reid is able to easily find good food in supermarket dumpsters is evidence of just how widespread the country's food waste problem is. Roughly 40 percent of all food in the U.S. goes uneaten, and yet one in seven American households doesn't have a regular supply of good food. While food is wasted at every step along the supply chain, nearly half of the country's wasted food is lost at supermarkets and restaurants, creating a vast supply of uneaten food sitting in dumpsters and trash cans—ripe for the taking by people who know how to find it.

In this paragraph, the topic is *food waste*. The main idea is that *food waste is widespread in the United States*. The remainder of the paragraph describes the extent of the waste. You can visualize the paragraph as follows:

VISUALIZE IT!

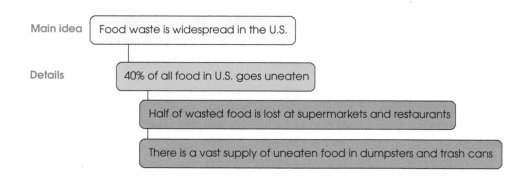

In this chapter, you will learn how to identify topics, main ideas, and topic sentences. You will also learn how to choose effective topics and write topic sentences. In Chapter 5, you will learn to identify and write details that support a topic sentence.

 NEED TO KNOW

Important Terms

Paragraph: a group of sentences that focus on a single idea

Topic: the one subject a paragraph is about

Main idea: the point the paragraph makes about a topic

Topic sentence: the sentence that states the paragraph's main idea

Supporting details: those sentences that explain the topic sentence

Chapter Theme: Food Waste

The chapter theme is food waste, and you will read both a professional essay and a student essay on the topic. The statistics about wasted food in America are startling. Forty percent of the food produced in our country is wasted, while people struggle to put food on the table for their family. Clearly, food waste is a big problem with big consequences, but most people seldom give a thought to the seriousness of the problem. As you read the two essays in this chapter, think about how you can help in the effort to reduce food waste. Also, annotate each reading, recording your thoughts on the topic, to be prepared to write about it or a related topic.

Look it up!

Use the search engine on your smartphone (or work with a classmate who has a smartphone) and look up "dumpster diving." Review several entries. Based on what you read, what are your thoughts about people who retrieve food from dumpsters? If food was scarce, is this something you would do? In a few sentences, describe what you would if you had no money and you needed to get food for you and your family.

EXAMINING PROFESSIONAL WRITING

One of the ways you will learn about topics, main ideas, and topic sentences is by studying a good model. By examining the essay "This Guy Spends $2.75 a Year on Food and Eats Like a King" by Casey Williams, you will learn how to identify topics and topic sentences as you read and how to create clear and concise topic sentences as you write. Throughout this chapter, we will analyze these features in the professional essay and put their use into practice.

Thinking Before Reading

In the following selection, which is an essay that appeared in *The Huffington Post*, the author explains how he spends $2.75 a year for food by eating supermarket food that has been thrown into dumpsters. Follow these steps before you read:

1. Preview the reading, using the steps discussed in the Pre-Reading Strategies section of Chapter 1.

2. Connect the reading to your own experience by answering the following questions:

   a. Have you ever seen someone "dumpster diving" or scrounging through a trash can looking for food? What were your thoughts at the moment you witnessed this behavior?

   b. When was the last time you ate a meal in a restaurant? What did you order, and how much did it cost? Did you eat every bite of the food, or did you leave some on your plate to be thrown away?

This Guy Spends $2.75 a Year on Food and Eats Like a King

Casey Williams

Dumpster diving is legal in the U.S., though it is outlawed in some cities. Here a dumpster diver finds a treasure trove of discarded food.

1   Over the last two years, William Reid has spent just $5.50 on food. Reid is a committed dumpster diver: He dredges unsold grub from supermarket dumpsters and collects food scraps wherever he finds them, and he feasts.

2   A graduate student in film and electronic media at American University in Washington, D.C., Reid forswore store-bought food in August 2014. Since then, he's been munching on found meals of green vegetables, fruits, meat, eggs, milk and candy—really, "anything you can imagine," he said, adding that he's never gotten sick from food he's scavenged, nor has he ever lacked access to healthy meals.

3   "My life isn't tremendously different from other people's," Reid told *The Huffington Post*. "Other people go shopping for their food; I'll go around back and see what's available," he said. "I'm getting to make the same decisions about what I'm eating as another person would."

4   Dumpster diving is legal in the U.S., though some cities have outlawed the practice. In some cases, dumpster diving requires poking around on private property, which can amount to illegal trespassing. Reid said he's never been ticketed or hassled for picking unsold food out of dumpsters. Store employees have even handed him food they were about to toss so he wouldn't have to rummage through trash bins.

5   That Reid is able to easily find good food in supermarket dumpsters is evidence of just how widespread the country's food waste problem is. Roughly 40 percent of all food in the U.S. goes uneaten, and yet one in seven American households doesn't have a regular supply of good food. While food is wasted at every step along the supply chain, nearly half of the country's wasted food is lost at supermarkets and restaurants, creating a vast supply of uneaten food sitting in dumpsters and trash cans—ripe for the taking by people who know how to find it.

6   "I think people would be surprised about the level of quality of food" in dumpsters, Reid said. It's "tremendously disturbing," he added, given how many people don't have enough quality food to eat. "It actually kind of sends me chills," Reid said. "We have tremendous want and need in this country for healthy food, and we have tremendous waste."

7   Reid began casually dumpster diving in early 2014, while volunteering at Food Not Bombs, an organization that collects unsold food from stores and donates it to food pantries. After several months of scrounging for food, he realized that he could eat pretty well without spending any money. "It occurred to me that it might be possible for somebody to survive that way," Reid said.

8   In August of that year, Reid began dining exclusively on discarded and donated food. He has since limited himself to food waste and, earlier this year, decided to eat only vegan food—not because he's vegan, but because finding free food had become "too easy," he said. He needed an added challenge. Going vegan was "difficult," Reid said, noting he's lost weight in recent months. Finding

vegan food requires rummaging through lots of dumpsters. "I don't always have time to cast my net that wide," he told HuffPost.

9   Despite the challenges of finding vegan offerings, Reid said he doesn't actually spend that much time scavenging for food. One of the biggest misconceptions about dumpster diving is that it takes hours to scrape together enough food for a meal, he noted. In reality, it usually doesn't take any longer than it would to shop for groceries at a supermarket. "It's not like I have to go any more often than others," Reid said. "I think people have this idea that there must be a big time commitment, but I go to some dumpsters that are in my neighborhood and, in 15 minutes, get some food and I'm out." Even so, not everyone can do what Reid does. It takes a certain amount of privilege to spend even 15 minutes a day rifling through trash cans for food. If you have a family, inflexible work hours or concerns about how you'll be perceived, dumpster diving might not work for you.

10   Reid recognizes that he's in a relatively unique position. His goal isn't to encourage others to adopt his eating habits, but to shine a light on the absurd amount of food waste in the U.S. He's making a documentary about the issue that he hopes to finish in December and release in early 2017.

11   So, you're probably wondering: If Reid is so good at dumpster diving, what caused him to crack and go on a $5.50 spending spree? A scheduling conflict forced Reid to spend an extra night on Deal Island, in Maryland, where he was shooting a film. He didn't have extra food with him and had to eat what he could find. "I was sort of stranded in a situation, and I needed something to eat and really didn't have any options," Reid said. So he shelled out for a bag of Chex Mix and a protein bar. "I was weak," he added jokingly. "It wasn't even real food."

Reading: Understand General Versus Specific Ideas

Roman Samokhin/Fotolia

■ **GOAL 1**
Understand general versus specific ideas

To successfully identify topics and main ideas in paragraphs, it will help if you understand the difference between general and specific. A **general** idea is a broad idea that applies to a large number of individual items. The term *food* is general because it refers to a large collection of individual items—fruits, vegetables, meats, and so on. A **specific** idea or term is more detailed or particular. It refers to an individual item. The word *bananas,* for example, is a specific term. The phrase *unripe green bananas* is even more specific.

General:	person		**General:**	food
Specific:	dumpster diver		**Specific:**	Chex Mix
	graduate student			protein bar
	vegan			eggs
General:	dumpster finds		**General:**	food outlets
Specific:	green vegetables		**Specific:**	supermarkets
	fruits			food pantries
	milk			restaurants

EXERCISE 4-1   Reading: Identifying General Terms

Directions: Underline the most general term in each group of words.

1. pounds, ounces, kilograms, weights
2. soda, coffee, beverage, wine
3. soap operas, news, TV programs, sports specials
4. home furnishings, carpeting, drapes, wall hangings
5. sociology, social sciences, anthropology, psychology
6. softball, soccer, team sports, basketball
7. dogs, beagles, retrievers, poodles
8. ice cream, brownies, cake, dessert
9. fiction, poetry, literature, drama
10. frown, wink, smile, nonverbal communication

EXERCISE 4-2   Reading: Analyzing General and Specific Ideas

Directions: Read each of the following items and decide what term(s) will complete the group. Write the word(s) in the spaces provided.

1. General: college courses
   Specific: math

   _____

   _____

2. General: _____
   Specific: roses

   tulips

   narcissus

3. General: musical groups
   Specific: _____

   _____

   _____

4. General: art
   Specific: sculpture

   _____

   _____

5. General: types of movies
   Specific: comedies

   _____

   _____

Applying General and Specific to Paragraphs

Now, we will apply the idea of general and specific to paragraph 4 from the professional reading. The main idea is the most general statement the writer makes about the topic. Pick out the most general statement among the following sentences:

1. In some cases, dumpster diving requires poking around on private property, which can amount to illegal trespassing.

2. Store employees have even handed him food they were about to toss so he wouldn't have to rummage through trash bins.

3. Dumpster diving is legal in the U.S., though some cities have outlawed the practice.

4. Reid says he's never been ticketed or hassled for picking unsold food out of dumpsters.

Did you choose sentence 3 as the most general statement? Here is the original paragraph:

> Dumpster diving is legal in the U.S., though some cities have outlawed the practice. In some cases, dumpster diving requires poking around on private property, which can amount to illegal trespassing. Reid says he's never been ticketed or hassled for picking unsold food out of dumpsters. Store employees have even handed him food they were about to toss so he wouldn't have to rummage through trash bins.

In this brief paragraph, the main idea is expressed in the first sentence. This sentence is the most general statement expressed in the paragraph. All the other statements are specific details that explain this main idea.

| EXERCISE 4-3 | Reading: Identifying General Statements |

Directions: For each of the following groups of sentences, select the most general statement the writer makes about the topic.

_____ 1. **a.** Brightly colored annuals, such as pansies and petunias, are often used as seasonal accents in a garden.
   b. Most gardens feature a mix of perennials and annuals.
   c. Some perennials prefer shade, while others thrive in full sun.
   d. Butterfly bushes are a popular perennial.

_____ 2. **a.** Hiring a housepainter is not as simple as it sounds.
   b. You should try to obtain a cost estimate from at least three painters.
   c. Each painter should be able to provide reliable references from past painting jobs.
   d. The painter must be able to work within the time frame you desire.

_____ 3. **a.** Flaxseed is an herbal treatment for constipation.
   b. Some people use kava to treat depression.
   c. Gingko biloba is a popular remedy for memory loss.
   d. A growing number of consumers are turning to herbal remedies to treat certain ailments.

_____ 4. a. Many students choose to live off-campus in apartments or rental houses.

b. Most colleges and universities offer a variety of student housing options.

c. Sororities and fraternities typically allow members to live in their organization's house.

d. On-campus dormitories provide a convenient place for students to live.

_____ 5. a. Try to set exercise goals that are challenging but realistic.

b. Increase the difficulty of your workout gradually.

c. Several techniques contribute to success when beginning an exercise program.

d. Reduce soreness by gently stretching your muscles before you exercise.

Identify and Select Topics

■ GOAL 2
Identify and select topics

Topics are important to both readers and writers. Identifying the topic of a paragraph helps readers to understand what it is about. Choosing focused topics helps writers focus their thoughts and organize their ideas in a paragraph or essay.

Reading: Locate the Topic of a Paragraph

The **topic** is the subject of an entire paragraph. Every sentence in a paragraph in some way discusses or explains this topic. If you had to choose a title for a paragraph, the one or two words you would choose are the topic. To find the topic of a paragraph, ask yourself: What is the one thing the author is discussing throughout the paragraph?

Now read paragraph 9 from the professional reading with that question in mind:

> Despite the challenge of finding vegan offerings, Reid said he doesn't actually spend that much time scavenging for food. One of the biggest misconceptions about dumpster diving is that it takes hours to scrape together enough food for a meal, he noted. In reality, it usually doesn't take any longer than it would to shop for groceries at a supermarket. "It's not like I have to go any more often than others," Reid said. "I think people have this idea that there must be a big time commitment, but I go to some dumpsters that are in my neighborhood and, in 15 minutes, get some food and I'm out." Even so, not everyone can do what Reid does. It takes a certain amount of privilege to spend 15 minutes a day rifling through trash cans for food. If you have a family, inflexible work hours or concerns about how you'll be perceived, dumpster diving might not work for you.

In this example, the author is discussing one topic—the time it takes to scavenge for food—throughout the paragraph. Notice that the word *time* is used several times. Often, the repeated use of a word can serve as a clue to the topic.

EXERCISE 4-4 | Reading: Identifying the Topic

Directions: Read each of the following paragraphs and then select the topic of the paragraph from the choices given.

_____ 1.   People have been making glass in roughly the same way for at least 2,000 years. The process involves melting certain Earth materials and cooling the liquid quickly before the atoms have time to form an orderly crystalline structure. This is the same way that natural glass, called obsidian, is generated from lava. It is possible to produce glass from a variety of materials, but most commercial glass is produced from quartz sand and lesser amounts of carbonate minerals.

—Lutgens et al., *Essentials of Geology*, p. 62

a. Earth
b. atoms
c. glass
d. lava

_____ 2.   The large majority of shoplifting is not done by professional thieves or by people who genuinely need the stolen items. About 2 million Americans are charged with shoplifting each year, but analysts estimate that for every arrest, 18 unreported incidents occur. About three-quarters of those caught are middle- or high-income people who shoplift for the thrill of it or as a substitute for affection. Shoplifting is also common among adolescents. Research evidence indicates that teen shoplifting is influenced by factors such as having friends who also shoplift.

—Solomon, *Consumer Behavior*, p. 35

a. shoplifting
b. shopping
c. professional thieves
d. adolescents

_____ 3. In order to survive, hunting and gathering societies depend on hunting animals and gathering plants. In some groups, the men do the hunting, and the women the gathering. In others, both men and women (and children) gather plants, the men hunt large animals, and both men and women hunt small animals. Hunting and gathering societies are small, usually consisting of only 25 to 40 people. These groups are nomadic. As their food supply dwindles in one area, they move to another location. They place high value on sharing food, which is essential to their survival.

—adapted from Henslin, *Sociology: A Down-to-Earth Approach*, p. 149

a. hunters
b. food supplies
c. hunting and gathering societies
d. survival

EXERCISE 4-5 Writing: Identifying the Topic

Directions: Read each of the following paragraphs and write the topic of the paragraph in the space provided.

1. The word *locavore* has been coined to describe people who eat only food grown or produced locally, usually within close proximity to their homes. Locavores rely on farmers' markets, homegrown foods, or foods grown by independent farmers. Locavores prefer these foods because they are thought to be fresher, are more environmentally friendly, and require far fewer resources to get them to market and keep them fresh for longer periods of time. Locavores believe that locally grown organic food is preferable to large corporation- or supermarket-based organic foods, as local foods have a smaller impact on the environment.

    —adapted from Donatelle, *Health: The Basics*, p. 282

    Topic: _____

2. A monopoly exists when an industry or market has only one producer (or else is so dominated by one producer that other firms cannot compete with it). A sole supplier enjoys nearly complete control over the prices of its products. Its only constraint is a decrease in consumer demand due to increased prices or government regulation. In the United States, laws forbid many monopolies and regulate prices charged by natural monopolies—industries in which one company can most efficiently supply all needed goods or services. Many electric companies are natural monopolies because they can supply all the power needed in a local area.

    —adapted from Ebert and Griffin, *Business Essentials*, p. 12

    Topic: _____

3. Values represent cultural standards by which we determine what is good, bad, right, or wrong. Sometimes these values are expressed as proverbs or sayings that teach us how to live. Do you recognize the phrase, "Life is like a box of chocolates—you never know what you're going to get"? This modern-day saying is popular among those who embrace life's unpredictability. Cultures are capable of growth and change, so it's possible for a culture's values to change over time.

    —Carl, *Think Sociology*, p. 51

    Topic: _____

4. They go by many different names—capsule hotels, modular hotels, and pod hotels—but they all have one thing in common: very efficient use of space in a small footprint. The concept of modular hotels was pioneered by the Japanese, but the idea is sweeping across the world. Priced well below most competitors, these small, 75- to 100-square-foot rooms don't waste any space. Most modular units include the basics: private bathrooms, beds that are designed for two, flat-screen televisions, and a small work space. Weary travelers looking for nothing more than a place to sleep are finding that modular hotels "fit the bill."

    —adapted from Cook et al., *Tourism: The Business of Travel*, p. 347

    Topic: _____

5. Television commercials provide a rich source of material to analyze. Begin by asking, "What reasons am I being given to lead me to want to buy this product?"

Often, commercials do not overtly state the reasons; instead, they use music, staging, gestures, and visual cues to suggest the ideas they want us to have. We probably will not find a commercial that comes right out and says that buying someone a bottle of perfume or piece of jewelry will lead to a fulfilling love life, but several holiday commercials certainly imply as much.

—adapted from Facione, *Think Critically*, p. 90

Topic: _____

Writing: Select a Topic

The first step in writing an effective paragraph is to select a topic that you have some knowledge about and feel comfortable discussing. The Step One: Generate Ideas section of Chapter 2 describes three techniques—freewriting, brainstorming, and branching—that you can use to generate topics to write about.

The student writer we will follow in this chapter, Alex Boyd, was given an assignment to write an essay about a food-related problem facing the United States and possible solutions to it. Once he had determined the main point of his essay, the problem of reducing food waste, he worked on developing topics for each of his supporting paragraphs. Read his essay and then the discussion of how to develop manageable topics and write effective topic sentences.

EXAMINING STUDENT WRITING

Alex Boyd

A good way to learn to read and write essays is to study a model. By examining the student essay below by Alex Boyd, you will learn how to narrow a topic and write clear and effective topic sentence. Throughout the rest of the chapter, we will refer to Alex's essay to illustrate techniques and strategies.

Alex Boyd is a student at Beloit College in Wisconsin. He is double majoring in literary studies and sociology. He wrote the following essay in response to an English class assignment that asked students to write about a food-related problem facing the United States today and possible solutions to the problem.

Title indicates topic of essay

Reducing Food Waste in the United States

Writer begins with a question to capture readers' attention

1   Why is a large portion of the food produced and purchased in the United States thrown away each year? Even as food prices rise and many people struggle to earn enough money to eat well, huge amounts of food are wasted every single day. Food waste in the United States is a problem in various ways at the production level, as in farms and orchards, and at the consumer level, meaning the people who eat the food. Different approaches are required to reduce food waste at the produc-

Thesis statement

tion and consumer levels. While it would be easiest to pin the blame for this issue on just the big food producers or just restaurants or just wasteful individuals, it is necessary to look at how and why food waste occurs at every level of the American food chain, from the farm to the table, in order to truly begin to work on reducing waste.

Topic sentence introduces first reason for food waste

2   Food is often wasted at the production level because of poor practices in harvesting. On large scale farms, fruits and vegetables are often harvested by machinery in order to harvest as much as possible as quickly as possible. For example, on an orange orchard, a large machine drives through the rows of trees and shakes the branches to knock the oranges into a container. This is an efficient method of harvesting, but it leads to a large number of fruits missing the container and being knocked to the ground and not used. While it is necessary for food producers to use this type of harvesting, food waste could be reduced by improving harvesting technologies, or by allowing gleaning, which refers to letting people come in after harvesting and pick up any food missed in the harvest.

Solution #1

Topic sentence is a clear statement of what paragraph is about

3   Even when fruits and vegetables are harvested properly, they may still be thrown away by farmers. Many food producers also choose to simply discard any food that does not look nearly perfect for fear that people will not buy differently shaped fruits and vegetables. Food naturally grows in different shapes and sizes, but many producers only sell food that looks like what consumers have come to expect. People may expect all tomatoes to be perfectly round, or all apples to be one size, so a farmer may not want to waste money transporting fruits or vegetables that look different if they will be rejected. This could be addressed by consumers expressing a willingness to buy food that does not look entirely uniform, as well as restaurants and grocery stores buying and serving these differently shaped and colored foods to change consumers' views on what food should look like.

Writer continues to expand on and support thesis

Solution #2

Topic sentence expresses point of view

4   The role of the consumer in food waste is incredibly important, as they are the end of the food production chain and the driving factor behind what does or does not get thrown away. As discussed before, consumers create demand for different products. If consumers do not want to eat strangely shaped zucchini or carrots in any color besides orange, these foods will go to waste. Consumers can choose to not support businesses that have poor practices with food waste. If it comes out that certain restaurants or grocery stores are throwing away large amounts of food, consumers can choose to not spend their money at these stores until they reduce the amount of food they waste.

Solution #3

Topic sentence

5   While production practices and consumer buying patterns play major roles in how much food is wasted, the largest issue is so simple that it may be overlooked: People throw away too much food. It has become common practice for many people to prepare more food than they will eat, and then instead of packaging what is left over and storing it, they throw away what is left. This is not always drastic; it isn't always people preparing twice as much as they need and eating only half. This can be as small as scraping a few bites off of a dinner plate into the trash, or eating only some of a dish at a restaurant and then deeming what is left to be too little to take home. These actions may seem unimportant at the individual level, but it is crucial to keep in mind that what may seem small and harmless could have huge effects when done by hundreds of millions of people. One spoonful in the trash is small, but a spoonful in the trash for every person in the country adds up to be a massive amount.

Details support topic sentence

Details are easy to relate to

Conclusion: Writer stresses the importance of a collaborative effort in reducing food waste

6   Waste happens in different ways in different situations, production and consumption, but it is all a part of one interconnected food system. Food waste

can only be slowed down or reduced by looking at the system through a wide lens and understanding the way that every link in the chain interacts with every other link, and then devising holistic approaches to the problems. Progress in the reduction of food waste requires responsibility and accountability at all levels of the food system.

Ensure Your Topic Is Not Too Broad or Too Narrow

The topic you choose for a paragraph must not be *too broad* or *too narrow*. It must be the right size to cover in a single paragraph. If you choose a topic that is too broad, you will have too much to say. Your paragraph will wander and seem unfocused. If you choose a topic that is too narrow (too small), you will not have enough to say. Your paragraph will seem skimpy.

Alex wanted to write a paragraph about *food waste during production*. Clearly, this topic is too broad to cover in a single paragraph, as there are many ways food can be wasted at different steps in the production process, so he revised it to address just one stage:

> food waste related to poor harvesting practices

This topic was specific enough that he could discuss it within one paragraph.

Shown below are a few more examples of topics that are too broad. Each one has been revised to be more specific.

TOO BROAD	water conservation
REVISED	lawn-watering restrictions
TOO BROAD	effects of water shortages
REVISED	sinkholes caused by water shortages
TOO BROAD	crop irrigation
REVISED	a system for allocating water for crop irrigation in the San Joaquin Valley

If your topic is too narrow, you will run out of things to say in your paragraph. You also run the risk of straying from your topic as you search for ideas to include. Alex wanted to write a paragraph about the role consumers play in food waste and brainstormed the following topic:

> strangely shaped or colored foods not appealing to consumers

This topic is too specific; there is nothing else to say about it. Alex revised this topic to include a point about the role consumers' preferences play in food waste:

> influence of consumer preferences on food waste

Here are a few other examples of topics that are too narrow. Each one has been revised to be less specific.

TOO NARROW	250 million used tires are discarded each year
REVISED	a solution to the problem of used tires
TOO NARROW	only 4 percent of plastics are recycled
REVISED	how consumers can take plastic recycling seriously
TOO NARROW	consumers receive five cents per can to recycle aluminum cans
REVISED	how money motivates many consumers to recycle

EXERCISE 4-6   Reading: Evaluating Topics

Directions: For each of the following pairs of topics, place a check mark before the one that is more effective (neither too broad nor too narrow).

1. _____ **a.** team sports
   _____ **b.** what a child can learn by participating in team sports

2. _____ **a.** the U.S. Marshal Service
   _____ **b.** the role of U.S. Marshals in witness protection

3. _____ **a.** driving contracts between parents and teenagers
   _____ **b.** driving

4. _____ **a.** birthday traditions in your family
   _____ **b.** holiday celebrations

5. _____ **a.** the percentage of Americans who live on farms
   _____ **b.** a typical visit to your grandparents' farm

EXERCISE 4-7   Writing: Narrowing a Topic

Directions: Choose three of the following topics and narrow each one to a topic manageable in a single paragraph. Use one of the techniques for generating ideas described in the Step One: Generate Ideas section of Chapter 2 to help you.

1. Packaging of products
2. The value of parks and "green spaces"
3. Contact sports
4. Factory farming
5. Building environmental awareness
6. Road trips
7. New electronic devices
8. Superstitions
9. Abuse of prescription medications
10. The importance of pets

Read and Write Topic Sentences

■ GOAL 3
Read and write topic
sentences

You learned earlier that the main idea of a paragraph is the most general state-ment the writer makes about the topic, and it is expressed in a topic sentence.

Reading: Tips for Finding Topic Sentences

Read this paragraph we looked at earlier, and then read the tips for finding topic sentences.

> Despite the challenge of finding vegan offerings, Reid said he doesn't actually spend that much time scavenging for food. One of the biggest misconceptions about dumpster diving is that it takes hours to scrape together enough food for a meal, he noted. In reality, it usually doesn't take any longer than it would to shop for groceries at a supermarket. "It's not like I have to go any more often than others," Reid said. "I think people have this idea that there must be a big time commitment, but I go to some dumpsters that are in my neighborhood and, in 15 minutes, get some food and I'm out." Even so, not everyone can do what Reid does. It takes a certain amount of privilege to spend 15 minutes a day rifling through trash cans for food. If you have a family, inflexible work hours or concerns about how you'll be perceived, dumpster diving might not work for you.

1. **Identify the topic.** As you did earlier, figure out the general subject of the entire paragraph. In this paragraph, the time it takes to scavenge for food is the topic.

2. **Locate the most general sentence, the topic sentence.** This sentence must be broad enough to include all of the other ideas in the paragraph. The first sentence in this paragraph—"Despite the challenge of finding vegan of-ferings, Reid said he doesn't actually spend that much time scavenging for food."—covers all of the other details in that paragraph.

3. **Study the rest of the paragraph.** The main idea expressed in the topic sen-tence must make the rest of the paragraph meaningful. It is the one idea that ties all of the other details together. In this paragraph, sentences 2, 3, 4, 5, 6, and 7 all give specific details about the time it takes to scavenge for food.

Although a topic sentence can be located anywhere in a paragraph, it is usu-ally *first* or *last*.

Topic Sentence First

In many paragraphs, the topic sentence comes first: The author states his or her main point and then explains it as illustrated here:

General   Topic Sentence
                    Detail
Specific   Detail
                    Detail

> You may not worry too much about being able to obtain all your favorite foods tomorrow, next week, and in the years to come, but you should. According to research, America's industrialized agriculture system is using topsoil, fossil fuel, and water—all precious natural resources—at unsustainable rates. We are also degrading the environment, reducing **biodiversity**, and polluting our air and water. Business as usual can't continue as usual if we want the next generation to enjoy the bountiful diet and healthy environment that we have been taking for granted.

In the first sentence, the writer states that we need to worry about being able to obtain all of our favorite foods in the near and distant future. The rest of the paragraph explains why we need to be concerned.

Topic Sentence Last

The second most likely place for a topic sentence to appear is last in a paragraph. When using this arrangement, a writer leads up to the main point and then states it at the end. Here is the preceding paragraph, rewritten so the topic sentence is last:

> According to research, America's industrialized agriculture system is using top-soil, fossil fuel, and water—all precious natural resources—at unsustainable rates. We are also degrading the environment, reducing **biodiversity**, and polluting our air and water. Business as usual can't continue as usual if we want the next generation to enjoy the bountiful diet and healthy environment that we have been taking for granted. <u>You may not worry too much about being able to obtain all your favorite foods tomorrow, next week, and in the years to come, but you should.</u>

This version of the paragraph explains the ways that we are depleting precious natural resources. Then, at the end, the writer states the main idea.

Topic Sentence in the Middle

If a topic sentence is placed neither first nor last, then it may appear somewhere in the middle of a paragraph. In this arrangement, the sentences before the topic sentence lead up to or introduce the main idea. Those that follow the main idea explain or describe it. Here is the original paragraph with the main idea placed in the middle.

> According to research, America's industrialized agriculture system is using topsoil, fossil fuel, and water—all precious natural resources—at unsustainable rates. We are also degrading the environment, reducing **biodiversity**, and polluting our air and water. <u>You may not worry too much about being able to obtain all your favorite foods tomorrow, next week, and in the years to come, but you should.</u> Business as usual can't continue as usual if we want the next generation to enjoy the bountiful diet and healthy environment that we have been taking for granted.

This paragraph begins with two examples of how we are abusing our natural resources and environment. Then the writer states the main idea and continues with one more example.

Topic Sentence First and Last

Occasionally, writers put the main idea at the beginning of a paragraph and again at the end. Writers may do this to emphasize the main point or to clarify it.

> <u>You may not worry too much about being able to obtain all your favorite foods tomorrow, next week, and in the years to come, but you should.</u>
> According to research, America's industrialized agriculture system is using topsoil, fossil fuel, and water—all precious natural resources—at unsustainable rates. We are also degrading the environment, reducing **biodiversity**, and polluting our air and water. Business as usual can't continue as usual if we want the next

(continued)

generation to enjoy the bountiful diet and healthy environment that we have been taking for granted. <u>We must be concerned about the current practices that are harming our resources and our environment if we expect to be able to obtain our favorite foods both now and in the future.</u>

The first and last sentences both state, in slightly different ways, the main idea of the paragraph—that we must be concerned about the future of our resources and environment.

| EXERCISE 4-8 | Reading: Identifying Topic Sentences |

Directions: Underline the topic sentence in each of the following paragraphs. Keep in mind that topic sentences can appear at the beginning, middle, or end of a paragraph.

1.   Fast foods tend to be short on fresh fruits and vegetables, and are low in calcium, although calcium can be obtained in shakes and milk. Pizza is a fast-food exception. It contains grains, meat, vegetables, and cheese, which represent four of the food groups. Pizza is often only about 25 percent fat, most of which comes from the crust. Overall, studies have shown pizza to be highly nutritious.

—Byer and Shainberg, *Living Well*, p. 289

2.   In recent years there have been many cases of college students dying from binge drinking, which involves having at least five drinks in a row for men or four drinks in a row for women. According to Dr. David Anderson, of George Mason University in Fairfax, Virginia, at least 50 college students throughout the United States drink themselves to death every year. While endangering their own lives, binge drinkers also tend to disturb or hurt their fellow students, such as causing them to lose sleep, interrupting their studies, and assaulting them physically or sexually.

—Thio, *Sociology*, p. 141

3.   When consumers are in a store to buy an expensive product, they may feel pressured to purchase immediately. The sales staff may exert pressure, or they may create their own pressure. After all, the trip has cost time and effort, and the buyers don't want to appear indecisive. For important purchases, it is often advisable to invest a bit more time before making a final decision. In fact, consumers should go home and evaluate and weigh the purchase decision. At home consumers are free of external pressures exerted by the sales environment and the sales staff. Consumers can also ask themselves important questions such as "Can I really afford this?" and "Is this the best product I can find for the price?"

4.   Suppose you are preparing to give a speech to a group of people. Assume you are in a position where you can observe the group. What are they wearing? Are they dressed casually, formally, informally, trendily, classily, or wildly? Do they seem well-to-do or frugal? What are their hobbies? What sports are they involved with? To what age range do most of the group members belong? What are their occupations? Are they professional or blue-collar workers? Assessing the characteristics of your audience will allow you to make inferences about its values and interests and enable you to tailor your speech to those interests.

5.   In the United States, Australia, and Western Europe people are encouraged to be independent. Members of these cultures are taught to get ahead, to compete, to win, to achieve their goals, to realize their unique potential, to stand out from the crowd. In many Asian and African countries, people are taught to value an inter-dependent self. Members of these cultures are taught to get along, to help others, and to not disagree or stand out. Thus, there are significant cultural differences in the way people are taught to view themselves.

—adapted from DeVito, *Human Communication*, p. 78

6.   With so many people participating in social networking sites and keeping personal blogs, it's increasingly common for a single disgruntled customer to wage war online against a company for poor service or faulty products. Unhappy customers have taken to the Web to complain about broken computers or poor customer service. Individuals may post negative reviews of products on blogs, upload angry videos outlining complaints on YouTube, or join public discussion forums where they can voice their opinion about the good and the bad. In the same way that companies celebrate the viral spread of good news, they must also be on guard for online backlash that can damage a reputation.

—adapted from Ebert and Griffin, *Business Essentials*, p. 161

7.   Elections serve a critical function in American society. They make it possible for most political participation to be channeled through the electoral process rather than bubbling up through demonstrations, riots, or revolutions. Elections provide regular access to political power, so that leaders can be replaced without being overthrown. This is possible because elections are almost universally accepted as a fair and free method of selecting political leaders. Furthermore, by choosing who is to lead the country, the people—if they make their choices carefully—can also guide the policy direction of the government.

—adapted from Edwards et al., *Government in America*, p. 306

8.   Darwin hypothesized sexual selection as an explanation for differences between males and females within a species. For instance, the enormous tail on a male peacock results from female peahens that choose mates with showier tails. Because large tails require so much energy to display and are more conspicuous to their predators, peacocks with the largest tails must be both physically strong and smart to survive. Peahens can use the size of the tail, therefore, as a measure of the "quality" of the male. When a peahen chooses a male with a large tail, she is making sure that her offspring will receive high-quality genes. Sexual selection explains the differences between males and females in many species.

—adapted from Belk and Maier, *Biology: Science for Life with Physiology*, p. 305

9.   In Japan, it's called kuroi kiri (black mist); in Germany, it's schmiergeld (grease money), whereas Mexicans refer to la mordida (the bite), the French say pot-de-vin (jug of wine), and Italians speak of the bustarella (little envelope). They're all talking about baksheesh, the Middle Eastern term for a "tip" to grease the wheels of a transaction. Giving "gifts" in exchange for getting business is common and acceptable in many countries, even though this may be frowned on elsewhere.

—adapted from Solomon, *Consumer Behavior*, p. 21

10.   The standards of our peer groups tend to dominate our lives. If your peers, for example, listen to rap, rock and roll, country, or gospel, it is almost inevitable that you also prefer that kind of music. In high school, if your friends take math courses, you probably do too. It is the same for clothing styles and dating standards. Peer influences also extend to behaviors that violate social norms. If your peers are college-bound and upwardly striving, that is most likely what you will be; but if they use drugs, cheat, and steal, you are likely to do so too.

—adapted from Henslin, *Sociology: A Down-to-Earth Approach*, p. 85

Writing Effective Topic Sentences

An effective topic sentence must

- identify what the paragraph is about (the topic) and express an attitude or viewpoint about that topic.
- not be too broad.
- not be too narrow.
- not make a direct announcement or statement of intent.
- be a complete thought.

Making a Point About Your Topic

Think of your topic sentence as a headline; it states what your paragraph will contain. It should identify your topic and express an attitude or viewpoint about it. Suppose your topic is *acid rain*. You could make a number of different points about acid rain. Each of the following is a possible topic sentence:

1. Acid rain has caused conflict between the United States and Canada.
2. Acid rain could be reduced by controlling factory emissions.
3. Acid rain has adversely affected the populations of fish in our lakes.

Each of the sentences identifies acid rain as the topic, but each expresses a different point about acid rain. Each would lead to a different paragraph and be supported by different details.

If you write a topic sentence that does not express a viewpoint, you will find you have very little or nothing to write about in the remainder of the paragraph. Look at this topic sentence that Alex wrote for a first draft of a paragraph for his essay:

LACKS POINT OF VIEW	Farmers throw away fruits and vegetables.
EXPRESSES POINT OF VIEW	Even when fruits and vegetables are harvested properly, they may still be thrown away by farmers.

If he used the first topic sentence, what else could he include in his paragraph? When he used the second one, he was able to discuss the reasons why farmers throw away perfectly good fruits and vegetables, even after harvesting them properly.

Notice how the following topic sentences have been revised to express a point of view.

LACKS POINT OF VIEW	Mark wastes food.
REVISED	Mark should be concerned that he throws out half the food in his refrigerator each week. (Details can explain what he discards and its detrimental effects.)
LACKS POINT OF VIEW	My local grocery store refuses to sell imperfect produce.
REVISED	My local grocery store should sell imperfect produce at a lower cost. (Details can describe how the store could select, display, and price imperfect produce.)

Guidelines for Revising Topic Sentences Lacking a Point of View

The following suggestions will help you revise your topic sentence if you discover that it lacks a point of view:

■ **Use brainstorming, freewriting, or branching.** Try to generate more ideas about your topic. Study your results to discover a way to approach your topic.

■ **Ask yourself questions about your topic sentence.** Specifically, ask "Why?" "How?" "So what?" or "Why is this important?" Answering your own questions will give you ideas for revising your topic sentence.

EXERCISE 4-9

WORKING TOGETHER

Writing: Revising Topic Sentences for Point of View

Directions: The following topic sentences lack a point of view. Working with a classmate, revise each one to express an interesting view on the topic.

SENTENCE   I took a biology exam today.

REVISED   _____

1. I am taking a math course this semester.

   REVISED: _____

2. I purchased an iPhone 6 last week.

   REVISED: _____
   _____

3. Soft rock was playing in the dentist's office.

   REVISED: _____
   _____

4. Sam has three televisions and four radios in his household.

   REVISED: _____
   _____

5. There is one tree on the street where I live.

   REVISED: _____

Avoiding Topic Sentences That Are Too Broad

Some topic sentences express a point of view, but they are too broad in scope.

> **TOO BROAD**   The death penalty is a crime against humanity.

This statement cannot be supported in a single paragraph. Lengthy essays, even entire books, have been written to argue this opinion.

A broad topic sentence promises more than you can reasonably deliver in a single paragraph. It leads to writing that is vague and rambling. With a broad topic sentence, you will end up with too many facts and ideas to cover or too many generalities (general statements) that do not sufficiently explain your topic sentence. In the following example, note the broad topic sentence and its effects on paragraph development:

> All kinds of violent crimes in the world today seem to be getting worse. Sometimes I wonder how people could possibly bring themselves to do such horrible things. One problem may be the violent acts shown on television programs. Some people think crime has a lot to do with horror movies and television programs. We have no heroes to identify with other than criminals. News reporting of crimes is too "real"; it shows too much. Kids watch these programs without their parents and don't know what to make of them. Parents should spend time with their children and supervise their play.

The topic sentence above promises more than a good paragraph can reasonably deliver: to discuss all violent crimes in the world today and their worsening nature. In the supporting sentences, the author wanders from topic to topic. She first mentions violence on television and then moves to lack of heroes. Next, she discusses news reporting that is too graphic and then switches to children watching programs alone. Finally, she ends with parental supervision of children. Each point about possible causes of violence or ways to prevent it seems underdeveloped.

Alex wanted to write a paragraph about food waste during production. He wrote the following topic sentence:

> Food is often wasted during production.

Clearly, the topic of food waste during production was too broad to cover in a single paragraph. There are numerous types, causes, effects, and potential solutions. Should he write about causes? If so, could he write about all possible causes in one paragraph? What about effects? Was he concerned with immediate effects? Long-term effects?

Alex decided he could make his topic more manageable by limiting it to a specific type of wastage during production. He considered several factors related to this topic: natural causes like bad weather and insect infestations during the growing period, machine harvesting, agricultural regulations, and consumer buying patterns. He decided to focus on poor practices in harvesting for this paragraph. Here is his revised topic sentence:

> Food is often wasted at the production level because of poor practices in harvesting.

This topic was specific enough that he could discuss it within one paragraph. Shown below are a few more examples of topic sentences that are too broad. Each one has been revised to be more specific.

TOO BROAD   Water conservation is important.

REVISED   Water use restrictions in small towns can be very effective in decreasing water consumption.

TOO BROAD   There are many effects of water shortages.

REVISED   Lack of water has several significant effects on grain crops.

TOO BROAD   Crop irrigation is used throughout the world.

REVISED   A system for allocating water for crop irrigation in the San Joaquin Valley has been very successful in increasing water use efficiency.

Guidelines for Revising Topic Sentences That Are Too Broad

The following suggestions will help you revise your topic sentence if you discover that it is too broad:

- **Narrow your topic.** A topic that is too broad often produces a topic sentence that is too broad. Narrow your topic by subdividing it into smaller topics. Continue subdividing until you produce a topic that is manageable in a single paragraph.

- **Rewrite your topic sentence to focus on one aspect or part of your topic.** Ask yourself, "What is the part of this topic that really interests me or that I care most about? What do I know most about the topic and have the most to say about?" Then focus on *that* aspect of the topic.

- **Apply your topic sentence to a specific time and place.** Ask yourself, "How does this broad topic that I'd like to write about relate to some particular time and place that I know about? How can I make the general topic come alive by using a well-defined example?"

- **Consider using one of your supporting sentences as a topic sentence.** Reread your paragraph; look for a detail that could be developed or expanded.

EXERCISE 4-10   ## Writing: Revising Topic Sentences That Are Too Broad

WORKING
TOGETHER

Directions: Turn each of the following broad topic sentences into a well-focused topic sentence that could lead to an effective paragraph. Remember that your topic sentence must also include a point of view. Then compare your answers with your classmates' answers to see the variety of effective topic sentences that can come from a broad one.

TOO BROAD   Hunting is a worthwhile and beneficial sport.

REVISED: <u>Hunting deer in overpopulated areas is beneficial to the herd.</u>

1. I would like to become more creative.

   REVISED: _____

   _____

2. Brazil is a beautiful country.

   REVISED: _____

3. Pollution is a big problem.

   REVISED: _____

   _____

4. The space program is amazing.

   REVISED: _____

   _____

5. It is very important to learn Japanese.

   REVISED: _____

   ____

Avoiding Topic Sentences That Are Too Narrow

If your topic sentence is too narrow, you will realize it right away because you will not have enough to write about to complete your paragraph. Topic sentences that are too narrow also frequently lack a point of view.

Here are some examples of topic sentences that are too narrow:

TOO NARROW	My birdfeeder attracts yellow songbirds.
REVISED	Watching the different birds at our feeder is a pleasant diversion enjoyed by our entire family, including our cat.
TOO NARROW	My math instructor looks at his watch frequently.
REVISED	My math instructor has a number of nervous habits that detract from his lecture presentations.

Alex wanted to write a paragraph about the role consumers play in food waste. He wrote the following topic sentence:

> If consumers do not want to eat strangely shaped zucchini or carrots in any color besides orange, these foods will go to waste.

This sentence is too specific. It could work as a detail, but it is too narrow to be a topic sentence. Alex revised this sentence to make a larger point about the role consumers play in determining which foods are unnecessarily discarded and made his original topic sentence into a supporting detail. His revised topic sentence is shown on the next page.

> The role of the consumer in food waste is incredibly important, as they are at the end of the food production chain and the driving factor behind what does or does not get thrown away.

He then developed his paragraph as follows:

> The role of the consumer in food waste is incredibly important, as they are the end of the food production chain and the driving factor behind what does or does not get thrown away. As discussed before, consumers create demand for different products. If consumers do not want to eat strangely shaped zucchini or carrots in any color besides orange, these foods will go to waste. Consumers can choose to not support businesses that have poor practices with food waste. If it comes out that certain restaurants or grocery stores are throwing away large amounts of food, consumers can choose to not spend their money at these stores until they reduce the amount of food they waste.

Guidelines for Revising Topic Sentences That Are Too Narrow

The following suggestions will help you revise your topic sentence when it is too narrow:

- **Broaden your topic to include a wider group or range of items or ideas.** For example, do not write about one nervous habit; write about several. Look for patterns and trends that could form the basis of a new, broader topic sentence.

- **Broaden your topic so that it takes in both causes and effects or makes comparisons or contrasts.** For example, do not write only about how fast an instructor lectures. Also write about the effect of his lecture speed on students trying to take notes, or contrast that instructor with others who have different lecture styles.

- **Brainstorm and research; try to develop a more general point from your narrower one.** Ask yourself, "What does this narrow point mean? What are its larger implications?" For example, rather than write about not being able to afford a new pair of jeans this week, expand this idea to discuss the importance or value of making and following a weekly budget.

EXERCISE 4-11

WORKING TOGETHER

Writing: Revising Topic Sentences That Are Too Narrow

Directions: Turn each of the following narrow topic sentences into a broader, well-focused topic sentence that could lead to an effective paragraph. Remember that your topic sentence must also include a point of view. Then compare your answers with your classmates' answers to see the variety of effective topic sentences that can come from a narrow one.

TOO NARROW   Football players wear protective helmets.

REVISED   <u>Football players wear several types of protective equipment to guard. against injuries.</u>

1. I planted a tomato plant in my garden.

   REVISED: _____

   _____

2. The cafeteria served hot dogs and beans for lunch.

   REVISED: _____

3. Orlando sings in a low key.

   REVISED: _____

4. Suzanne bought a stapler for her desk.

   REVISED: _____

5. Koala bears are really marsupials, not bears.

   REVISED: _____

   _____

Avoiding Announcements

Avoid direct announcements or statements of intent such as the following examples:

ANNOUNCEMENT	In this paragraph, I will show that even when harvested properly, fruits and vegetables may still be thrown away by farmers.
REVISED	Even when fruits and vegetables are harvested properly, they may still be thrown away by farmers.

ANNOUNCEMENT	This paragraph will explain why carbon monoxide is a dangerous air pollutant.
REVISED	There are three primary reasons why carbon monoxide is a dangerous air pollutant.

Ensuring Your Topic Sentence Is a Complete Thought

Be sure your topic sentence is a complete thought. If your sentence is a fragment, run-on sentence, or comma splice, your meaning will be unclear or incomplete.

FRAGMENT	While consumers are responsible for throwing away vast quantities of food.
REVISED	While consumers are responsible for throwing away vast quantities of food, they are not the only ones who contribute to the problem of food waste in America.

RUN-ON SENTENCE	Reading and writing are important skills they are essential for college success.
REVISED	Reading and writing are important skills; they are essential for college success.

COMMA SPLICE	Social networks have impacted interpersonal communication, Facebook and Twitter are examples.
REVISED	Social networks, for example Facebook and Twitter, have impacted interpersonal communication.

Chapters 11 and 12 discuss how to spot and correct these errors.

EXERCISE 4-12　Reading: Evaluating Topic Sentences

Directions: Evaluate each of the following topic sentences and mark them as follows:

E = effective	N = not complete thought
G = too general	S = too specific
A = announcement	

_____　1.　I will describe what causes the hiccups and how to cure them.

_____　2.　Summer camps are excellent for children.

_____　3.　Asking a professor for a recommendation is an important part of applying for a summer internship.

_____　4.　Palliative care programs offer many benefits to seriously ill patients and their families.

_____　5.　This paper will explain why the best place to get your next dog or cat is at an animal shelter.

_____　6.　Learning how to drive a manual transmission car.

_____　7.　The number of students who participate in practical work experiences while studying abroad has increased by 35 percent.

_____　8.　African American soldiers played an important role during war time.

_____　9.　There are five factors to consider when choosing a major.

_____　10.　The process of chocolate-making from bean to bar.

EXERCISE 4-13　Writing: Revising Topic Sentences

Directions: Analyze the following topic sentences. If a sentence is too general or too specific, makes a direct announcement, or is not a complete thought, revise it to make it more effective.

1. Short stories are fun to read.

   REVISED: _____

   _____

2. I will explain the steps in teaching a child how to swim.

   REVISED: _____

   _____

3. The Eastern Cougar was declared extinct in 2011.

REVISED: _____

_____

4. Food deserts in urban areas.

REVISED: _____

_____

5. A knowledge of world geography is important for everyone.

REVISED: _____

_____

! NEED TO KNOW

Topic Sentences

Ineffective paragraphs may frustrate, confuse, or bore your reader.

A weak topic sentence may

- lack a point of view or attitude toward the topic.
- be too broad.
- be too narrow.

To revise a topic sentence that lacks a point of view

- use brainstorming, freewriting, or branching.
- ask yourself questions about your topic sentence to focus on a particular viewpoint.

To narrow a topic sentence that is too broad, consider

- narrowing your topic.
- rewriting your topic sentence to focus on one aspect of your topic.
- applying your topic sentence to a specific time and place.
- using one of your supporting sentences as a topic sentence.

To broaden a topic sentence that is too narrow, consider

- broadening your topic to make it more inclusive.
- broadening your topic to consider causes and effects or to make comparisons or contrasts.
- brainstorming and researching to develop a more general point.

READ AND REVISE

The following excerpt is from an essay called "Going to the Movies." This excerpt contains topic sentences that are too broad, are too narrow, or lack a point of view. Underline each topic sentence; then revise the topic sentences to make them more effective.

Going to the Movies

There are many types of movies. People are drawn to action/adventure films for the special effects, nonstop action, big-name stars, and "good guys versus bad guys" plots. Action/adventure films offer the audience pure escapism. Dramas are serious and often realistic, and they attract audiences more interested in character development and storyline than special effects. Comedies are another form of escapism, with plots, dialogue, and action all aimed at getting an audience to laugh. Comedies may also contain romantic elements and even special effects.

Horror movies often feature aliens. Horror movies may overlap with science fiction and other types of movies. Sometimes they even include comic elements. Horror movies may feature elaborate special effects or the most basic and amateurish camerawork. They may have big-name stars or no-name actors, simple or complex plots, high-tech androids or low-tech monsters. Some people enjoy the thrill of a good scare that a horror movie offers, while others would rather see any other type of movie—or just stay home.

READ AND RESPOND: A Student Essay

Reducing Food Waste in the United States

Alex Boyd

The questions below refer to Alex's essay, "Reducing Food Waste in the United States," in the Examining Student Writing section of this chapter. We have used his essay throughout the chapter as an example for how to develop focused topics and write effective topic sentences, and now you are ready to examine his writing more closely.

Examining Writing

1. How did Alex organize the essay?

2. Evaluate Alex's topic sentences. Were any too broad, too narrow, or lacking a viewpoint?

3. What additional information could Alex have provided? Are there places where you felt you needed further explanation or more specific information?

4. Can you think of another reason that food is wasted in the United States? If you were to include another body paragraph about food waste in this essay, what would its topic sentence be?

READ AND RESPOND: A Professional Reading

This Guy Spends $2.75 a Year on Food and Eats Like a King

Casey Williams

The questions and activities below refer to the professional reading, "This Guy Spends $2.75 a Year on Food and Eats Like a King," in the Examining Professional Reading section of this chapter. You have been working with the excerpt throughout the chapter, and now you are ready to examine it, integrate and apply ideas, and write in response to reading it.

Writing in Response to Reading

Checking Your Comprehension

Answer each of the following questions using complete sentences.

1. Where does William Reid find most of the food he eats?

2. Describe the quality of the food that Reid eats.

3. What percentage of wasted food can be attributed to supermarkets and restaurants?

4. What added challenge has Reid imposed upon himself and his hunt for food?

5. What misconception do people have about Reid's hunt for food?

6. How does Reid plan to educate the public about the startling food waste in the United States?

Strengthening Your Vocabulary

Using the word's context, word parts, or a dictionary, write a brief definition of each of the following words as it is used in the reading.

1. dredges (paragraph 1) _____
2. forswore (paragraph 2) _____
3. rummage (paragraph 4) _____
4. vast (paragraph 5) _____
5. scrounging (paragraph 7) _____
6. vegan (paragraph 8) _____

Examining the Reading: Using Idea Maps

Review the reading by completing the missing parts of the following detailed idea map.

VISUALIZE IT!

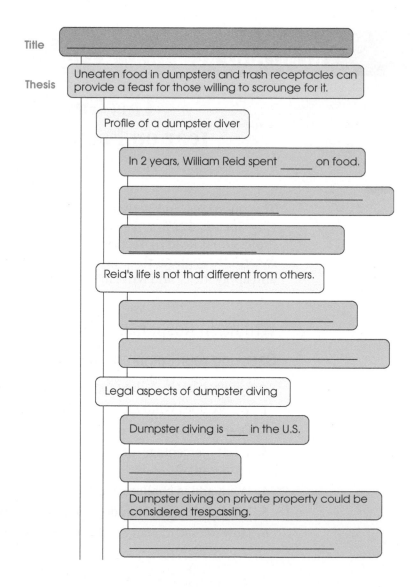

Title _____

Thesis — Uneaten food in dumpsters and trash receptacles can provide a feast for those willing to scrounge for it.

Profile of a dumpster diver

In 2 years, William Reid spent _____ on food.

_____
_____

_____
_____

Reid's life is not that different from others.

_____

_____

Legal aspects of dumpster diving

Dumpster diving is ____ in the U.S.

_____

Dumpster diving on private property could be considered trespassing.

_____

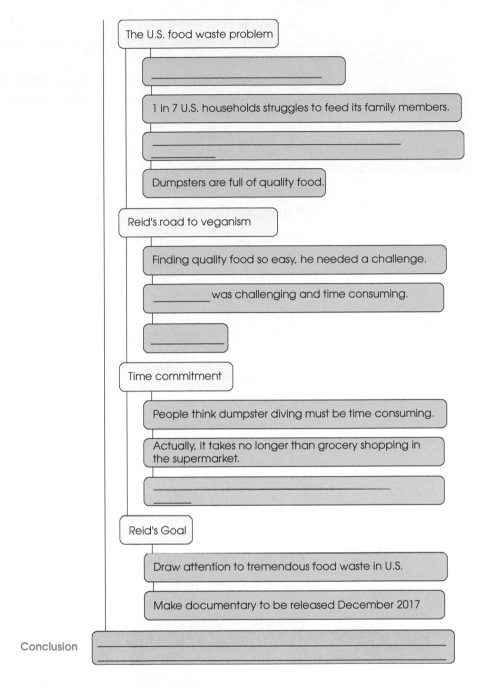

The U.S. food waste problem

_____

1 in 7 U.S. households struggles to feed its family members.

_____

Dumpsters are full of quality food.

Reid's road to veganism

Finding quality food so easy, he needed a challenge.

_____ was challenging and time consuming.

_____

Time commitment

People think dumpster diving must be time consuming.

Actually, it takes no longer than grocery shopping in the supermarket.

_____

Reid's Goal

Draw attention to tremendous food waste in U.S.

Make documentary to be released December 2017

Conclusion _____

Thinking Critically: An Integrated Perspective

Get ready to write about the reading by discussing the following:

1. Discuss the title of this selection. Did it capture your interest and provide a clue to the subject of the selection? Can you think of another title that would be effective?

2. Discuss the types of details the author used in this selection. Which details were most effective? Why?

3. What is the author's purpose in writing this selection?

4. Using your own words, state the conclusion of the reading in one sentence.

5. What does William Reid consider to be _real_ food?

6. The author writes that William Reid "eats like a king" and "feasts." Why do you think the author chose to use these words when talking about food that comes from a dumpster?

7. Are you concerned about the issues raised in this selection? Which issues are most important to you? In a journal entry, discuss your response to these questions.

8. The photograph that originally accompanied the reading shows William Reid sitting atop a dumpster. What other photographs or illustrations would be equally or more effective in drawing attention to the issue of food waste?

Paragraph Options

1. Do you think you could depend solely on dumpster diving for all of your food needs? Why or why not? Write a paragraph that addresses these questions.

2. What steps can you take to reduce food waste on your college campus? Write a paragraph describing the steps and which ones you might try.

3. Write a paragraph describing the statistic or detail in the selection that you found most surprising and why.

Essay Options

1. What do you already do to address the issue of food waste? Write an essay discussing what you do to minimize food waste in your home and what you could do differently to reduce food waste even more.

2. Food waste is a social problem. People are struggling to put food on the table for their families while we are wasting food. What steps could you take in your community to address this problem? Write an essay in which you discuss the proposed steps and explain how you would implement them.

Making Connections between the Readings

Use both "Reducing Food Waste in the United States" and "This Guy Spends $2.75 a Year on Food and Eats Like a King" to write a response to one of the following prompts.

1. In a paragraph, suggest at least three ways supermarkets could have a positive impact on reducing food waste in the United States.

2. Using information from both essays, write an essay suggesting how people in the United States can be more responsible consumers of food.

3. The farm-to-table movement is rapidly gaining support in the United States. Explain what the movement is and how each of the essays relates in some way to this movement.

SELF-TEST SUMMARY

To test yourself, cover the Answer column with a sheet of paper and answer each question in the left column. Evaluate each of your answers as you work by sliding the paper down and comparing your answer with what is printed in the Answer column.

QUESTION	ANSWER
■ **GOAL 1** Understand general versus specific ideas What are general and specific ideas?	A general idea is broad and can apply to many things. A specific idea is detailed and refers to a smaller group or an individual item.
■ **GOAL 2** Identify and select topics How can you identify the topic of a paragraph?	Look for the one idea the author is discussing throughout the entire paragraph.
How does topic breadth affect a paragraph?	In a paragraph with an overly broad topic, the writing will be rambling and unfocused. If the topic is too narrow, you will run out of things to say and have a skimpy paragraph.
■ **GOAL 3** Read and write topic sentences What is a topic sentence?	The topic sentence states the main idea of a paragraph. The topic sentence can be located anywhere in the paragraph. The most common positions are first or last, but the topic sentence can also appear in the middle or first and last.
How do you write an effective topic sentence?	An effective topic sentence must ■ identify what the paragraph is about and express a point about that topic. ■ not be too broad or too narrow. ■ not make a direct announcement. ■ be a complete thought.

5

Details, Transitions, and Implied Main Ideas

LEARNING GOALS

Learn how to …

- **GOAL 1**
  Identify supporting details in a paragraph

- **GOAL 2**
  Select and organize details to support your topic sentence

- **GOAL 3**
  Use transitional words and phrases to read and write paragraphs

- **GOAL 4**
  Identify implied main ideas

Marcio Eugenio/Shutterstock

THINK About It!

Analyze the photograph above to determine what is happening. On the face of it, a woman is heavily involved with electronics, but what is the rest of the story? Why is she so engaged with electronics? Is this a typical or an unusual situation for her? What is the impact of her heavy reliance on electronics on her life, her friends, her family, and her career?

In analyzing the photograph, you went beyond the main point to consider details. A similar process occurs when you read or write a paragraph. First, you discover or express the main point in a topic sentence; then you move on to consider the details that support the topic sentence. You also pay attention to transitions that connect details.

In this chapter, you will learn to read and write details, transitions, and implied main ideas. The theme of this chapter is living on the grid; that is, we will explore our reliance on smartphones, computers, and other technological devices. You will read a professional essay on our overreliance on technology as a memory aid and a student essay on how technology has affected society.

What Are Supporting Details, Transitions, and Implied Main Ideas?

The details of the chapter-opening photograph suggest that this girl is comfortable engaging with digital electronics. Similarly, the details of a paragraph enable a writer to provide more complete information about the paragraph's main idea. **Supporting details** are statements that prove or explain the main idea of a paragraph. Supporting details may be *reasons, examples, statistics, facts, descriptions, steps,* or *procedures*.

In some paragraphs and articles, as in some photographs, the main point is not stated but only suggested or implied. The reader has to figure out the writer's main point (his or her **implied main idea**) by analyzing the details and determining what, when taken together, they all mean.

In photographs, visual clues lead you from one detail to another. Because paragraphs and articles lack the visual clues that photographs offer, writers often use words and phrases, called **transitions**, to lead the reader from one detail to another.

In this chapter, you will learn to recognize supporting details, figure out implied main ideas, and use transitions to guide your reading. You will also learn to use supporting details to support your topic sentence and use transitions to guide your reader. Until you become a very skilled writer, it is usually advisable not to write paragraphs with implied main ideas. Focus instead on writing clear and direct topic sentences.

Chapter Theme: Life "On the Grid"

In this chapter, you will read both a professional and a student essay on the topic of living "on the grid." For many of us, living "on the grid" has become the norm. Smartphones and other technological tools now provide a way for us to communicate, retrieve factual information, get directions, manage our schedule, plug into social media, and perform many other tasks related to daily living. But this reliance, or some say overreliance, on technology is not without drawbacks. As you read the two essays in this chapter, focus on the theme as well as the details, transitions, and implied main ideas. Also, annotate each reading yourself, recording your thoughts on the topic, to be prepared to write about it or a related topic.

Look it up!

Use the search engine on your smartphone (or work with a classmate who has a smartphone) and look up "living off the grid." Review several entries. Based on what you read, what are your thoughts about people who decide to live off the grid? Write a few sentences explaining why this is a lifestyle that would or would not interest you.

EXAMINING PROFESSIONAL WRITING

The following selection originally appeared in *The Washington Post*. In the selection, the author discusses "digital amnesia," a condition that she says results from overreliance on technology as a memory aid. It will be used in this chapter to demonstrate reading techniques.

Thinking Before Reading

Follow these steps before you read:

1. Preview the reading, using the steps discussed in the Pre-Reading Strategies section of Chapter 1.

2. Connect the reading to your own experience by answering the following questions:

   a. Do you memorize phone numbers or rely on your phone to save them for you?

   b. Have you ever used Google Maps or a similar app to help you drive to a place that you once knew from memory how to find?

3. Highlight and annotate as you read.

Google Is Making You More Forgetful. Here's Why That's a Good Thing.

Caitlin Dewey

violetkaipa/Shutterstock.com

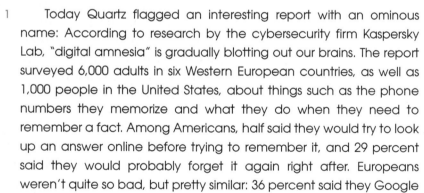

1   Today Quartz flagged an interesting report with an ominous name: According to research by the cybersecurity firm Kaspersky Lab, "digital amnesia" is gradually blotting out our brains. The report surveyed 6,000 adults in six Western European countries, as well as 1,000 people in the United States, about things such as the phone numbers they memorize and what they do when they need to remember a fact. Among Americans, half said they would try to look up an answer online before trying to remember it, and 29 percent said they would probably forget it again right after. Europeans weren't quite so bad, but pretty similar: 36 percent said they Google first and think later; 24 percent admitted they would forget the Googled thing as soon as they closed their browser.

2   Across the board, everybody's obsessed with their smartphones: More than 40 percent say their phone contains "everything they need to know." Granted, you probably don't need a laboratory study or a large-scale survey to confirm a phenomenon you've observed yourself. How many people memorize phone numbers anymore? How many get around without consulting Google Maps?

3   But while it's undeniably true that we rely on technology as a sort of memory aid, the jury is still very much out as to whether that's a positive or negative thing. After all, the issue can be framed in two different ways: Either the Internet is replacing our natural mental capacity, or it's augmenting it. That may seem counterintuitive, but consider

two oft-forgotten (heh) facts about how memory works. First off, memory isn't—and has never been—a solo endeavor, constrained to your head. Research suggests that we've always relied heavily on other people, as well as on tools like diaries and Post-its, to remember all kinds of biographical and general facts. This is called "transactive memory," and it basically means that we store information not just in our brains—but in the objects and people around us. Second, "remembering" isn't an inherently good thing, and forgetting isn't inherently bad. It doubtlessly doesn't seem that way when you're punching in repeated wrong PIN numbers at the ATM. But generally speaking, your brain has only so much space to store memories—rather like your phone. At some point, you have to delete all those old photos and apps to take new ones.

4   This brings us back to the specter of "digital amnesia": the idea that our computers somehow hurt our memory. But when you remember that we've always stored memories in outside people and things, and that we don't have the capacity to remember everything, the phenomenon looks less like amnesia and more like prudent outsourcing. That was, in fact, the conclusion of three psychologists who studied the "Google effect" in 2011: Although their results were widely interpreted as evidence that Google makes us forget, the researchers themselves were far more optimistic. "We are becoming symbiotic with our computer tools," they wrote, "growing into interconnected systems that remember less by knowing information than by knowing where the information can be found."

5   The technologist and Columbia law professor Tim Wu has written what is perhaps the clearest defense of this development: If a time traveler from the early 1900s encountered a modern-day person with a smartphone and spoke to her through a curtain, what would he think? He'd be amazed by her ability to solve complex equations, to answer obscure trivia questions, to quote things in foreign languages. To him, the smartphone user would seem like some kind of genius. (To us, she'd just seem like some chick with a phone.) "With our machines, we are augmented humans and prosthetic gods," Wu writes, "though we're remarkably blasé about that fact, like anything we're used to."

6   Besides, raw human memory isn't all that it's cracked up to be. Take this amnesia report from Kaspersky: It came out four months ago—long enough for us to forget the first round of coverage and start reanalyzing.

Reading: Identify Supporting Details in a Paragraph

■ GOAL 1
Identify supporting
details in a paragraph

Here is paragraph 1 from "Google Is Making You More Forgetful. Here's Why That's a Good Thing." The topic sentence is highlighted in yellow. Notice that all the details in this paragraph concern the results of the survey conducted by Kaspersk Lab, thus supporting the main idea expressed in the topic sentence.

Today Quartz flagged an interesting report with an ominous name: According to research by the cybersecurity firm Kaspersk Lab, "digital amnesia" is gradually blotting out our brains. The report surveyed 6,000 adults in six Western

(continued)

European countries, as well as 1,000 people in the United States, about things such as phone numbers they memorize and what they do when they need to remember a fact. Among Americans, half said they would try to look up an answer online before trying to remember it, and 29 percent said they would probably forget it again right after. Europeans weren't quite as bad, but pretty similar: 36 percent said they Google first and think later: 24 percent admitted they would forget the Googled thing as soon as they closed their browser.

Distinguish Between Major and Minor Details

Some details in a paragraph are more important than others. **Major details** are the most important details in a paragraph; they directly explain or prove the main idea. **Minor details** may provide additional information, offer examples, or further explain one or more of the major details. You can visualize a paragraph as shown here. The less important, minor details appear below the major supporting details that they explain.

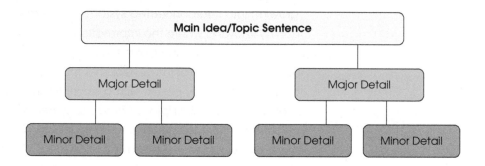

Now study paragraph 3 from "Google Is Making You More Forgetful. Here's Why That's a Good Thing." The major details are highlighted in green, and the topic sentence is underlined.

But while it's undeniably true that we rely on technology as a sort of memory aid, the jury is still very much out as to whether that's a positive or a negative thing. After all, the issue can be framed in two different ways: Either the Internet is replacing our natural mental capacity, or it's augmenting it. <u>That may seem counterintuitive, but consider two oft-forgotten (heh) facts about how memory works.</u> First off, memory isn't—and has never been—a solo endeavor, constrained to your head. Research suggests that we've always relied heavily on other people, as well as on tools like diaries and Post-its, to remember all kinds of biographical and general facts. This is called "transactive memory," and it basically means that we store information not just in our brains—but in objects and people. Second, "remembering" isn't an inherently good thing, and forgetting isn't inherently bad. It doubtlessly doesn't seem that way when you're punching in repeated wrong PIN numbers at the ATM. But generally speaking, your brain has only so much space to store memories—rather like your phone. At some point, you have to delete all those old photos and apps to take new ones.

Each of the major details describes the two facts about how memory works. Now study the details that are not highlighted. What functions do they serve? They elaborate on the major details by providing more description. You can visualize this paragraph as shown here.

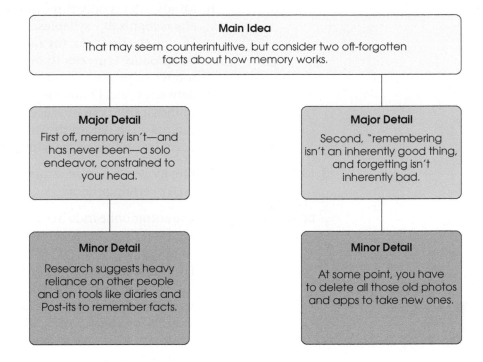

Main Idea

That may seem counterintuitive, but consider two oft-forgotten facts about how memory works.

Major Detail

First off, memory isn't—and has never been—a solo endeavor, constrained to your head.

Major Detail

Second, "remembering isn't an inherently good thing, and forgetting isn't inherently bad.

Minor Detail

Research suggests heavy reliance on other people and on tools like diaries and Post-its to remember facts.

Minor Detail

At some point, you have to delete all those old photos and apps to take new ones.

In this idea map, you can see the major details that explain the two facts about memory. The minor details, such as the information about using diaries and Post-it notes as tools for remembering, provide further information and are less important than the major details.

Look at the paragraph again, and notice how the author has used transitions—words that lead you from one major detail to the next. The phrases "First off" and "Second" are a couple of the transitions that can help you find the major details in this paragraph. Be on the lookout for transitions as you read; they will be discussed more fully later in this chapter.

EXERCISE 5-1

Reading: Identifying Supporting Details

Directions: Each of the following topic sentences states the main idea of a paragraph. After each topic sentence are sentences containing details that may or may not support the topic sentence. Read each sentence and put a check mark beside those that contain major details that support the topic sentence.

1. TOPIC SENTENCE   Many dramatic physical changes occur during adolescence between the ages of 13 and 15.

DETAILS   _____ **a.** Voice changes in boys begin to occur at age 13 or 14.

_____ **b.** Facial proportions may change during adolescence.

_____ **c.** Adolescents, especially boys, gain several inches in height.

_____ **d.** Many teenagers do not know how to react to these changes.

_____ **e.** Primary sex characteristics begin to develop for both boys and girls.

2. TOPIC SENTENCE   The development of speech in infants follows a definite sequence or pattern of development.

DETAILS

_____ **a.** By the time an infant is six months old, he or she can make 12 different speech sounds.

_____ **b.** Mindy, who is only three months old, is unable to produce any recognizable syllables.

_____ **c.** During the first year, the number of vowel sounds a child can produce is greater than the number of consonant sounds he or she can make.

_____ **d.** Between 6 and 12 months, the number of consonant sounds a child can produce continues to increase.

_____ **e.** Parents often reward the first recognizable word a child produces by smiling or speaking to the child.

3. TOPIC SENTENCE   An oligopoly is a market structure in which only a few companies sell a certain product.

DETAILS

_____ **a.** The automobile industry is a good example of an oligopoly, even though it gives the appearance of being highly competitive.

_____ **b.** The breakfast cereal, soap, and cigarette industries, although basic to our economy, operate as oligopolies.

_____ **c.** Monopolies refer to market structures in which only one industry produces a particular product.

_____ **d.** Monopolies are able to exert more control and price fixing than oligopolies.

_____ **e.** In the oil industry there are only a few producers, so each producer has a fairly large share of the sales.

EXERCISE 5-2   Reading: Identifying Details

A. Directions: Read the following paragraph and complete the diagram that follows. Some of the items have been filled in for you.

Communication occurs with words and gestures, but did you know it also occurs through the sense of smell? Odor can communicate at least four types of messages. First, odor can signal attraction. Animals give off scents to attract members of the opposite sex. Humans use fragrances to make themselves more appealing or attractive. Smell also communicates information about tastes. The smell of popcorn popping stimulates the appetite. If you smell a chicken roasting, you can anticipate its taste. A third type of smell communication is through memory. A smell can help you recall an event that occurred months or even years ago, especially if the event was an emotional one. Finally, smell can communicate by creating an identity or image for a person or product. For example, a woman may wear only one brand of perfume. Or a brand of shaving cream may have a distinct fragrance, which allows users to recognize it.

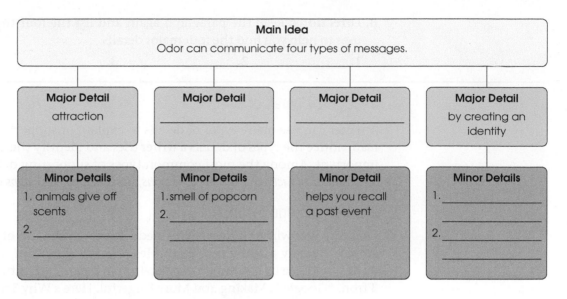

B. Directions: Read the paragraph again and list the four transitions the writer uses to help you find the four major details.

1. _____   2. _____   3. _____   4. _____

The diagram you completed in Exercise 5-2 is a **map**—a visual way of organizing information. By filling in—or drawing—maps, you can "see" how ideas in a paragraph or essay are related. The Draw Idea Maps section of Chapter 1 gives you more information about mapping and about other ways of organizing information.

EXERCISE 5-3

Reading: Understanding Supporting Details

A. Directions: Read the following paragraph and complete the map that follows. Some of the items have been filled in for you.

Small group discussions progress through four phases. The first is orientation, when the members become comfortable with each other. Second is the conflict phase. Disagreements and tensions become evident. The amount of conflict varies with each group. The third phase is known as emergence. The members begin to try to reach a decision. The members who created conflict begin to move toward a middle road. The final phase is the reinforcement phase when the decision is reached. The members of the group offer positive reinforcement toward each other and the decision.

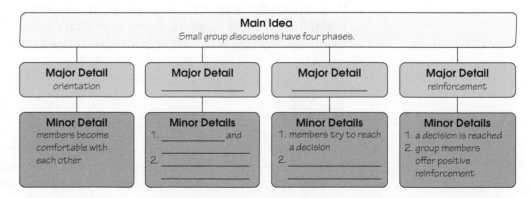

B. Directions: Read the paragraph again and list the four transitions the writer uses to help you find the four major details.

1. _____ 2. _____ 3. _____ 4. _____

Recognize Types of Details

A writer can use many types of details to explain or support a main idea. As you read, notice the types of details a writer uses and identify the details that are most important. Among the most common types of supporting details are *illustrations and examples, facts and statistics, reasons, descriptions,* and *steps* or *procedures*.

Illustrations and Examples

One way you will find ideas explained is through the use of illustrations or examples. Usually a writer uses **examples** to make a concept, problem, or process understandable by showing its application in a particular situation. In paragraph 3 from "Google Is Making You More Forgetful. Here's Why That's a Good Thing," several examples are provided to explain the facts about how memory works. The topic sentence for this paragraph is highlighted in yellow.

> But while it's undeniably true that we rely on technology as a sort of memory aid, the jury is still very much out as to whether that's a positive or a negative thing. After all, the issue can be framed in two different ways: Either the Internet is replacing our natural mental capacity, or it's augmenting it. That may seem counterintuitive, but consider two oft-forgotten (heh) facts about how memory works. First off, memory isn't—and has never been—a solo endeavor, constrained to your head. Research suggests that we've always relied heavily on other people, as well as on tools like diaries and Post-its, to remember all kinds of biographical and general facts. This is called "transactive memory," and it basically means that we store information not just in our brains—but in objects and people. Second, "remembering" isn't an inherently good thing, and forgetting isn't inherently bad. It doubtlessly doesn't seem that way when you're punching in repeated wrong PIN numbers at the ATM. But generally speaking, your brain has only so much space to store memories—rather like your phone. At some point, you have to delete all those old photos and apps to take new ones.

As you read illustrations and examples, be sure to grasp the relationship between the illustration or example and the concept or idea it illustrates.

Facts and Statistics

Another way a writer supports an idea is by including facts or statistics that further explain the main idea. Notice how in the following paragraph from "Google Is Making You More Forgetful. Here's Why That's a Good Thing," (paragraph 1), the main idea (highlighted in yellow below) is explained by the use of facts and statistics.

> Today Quartz flagged an interesting report with an ominous name: According to research by the cybersecurity firm Kaspersk Lab, "digital amnesia" is gradually blotting out our brains. The report surveyed 6,000 adults in six Western European countries, as well as 1,000 people in the United States, about things such as phone numbers they memorize and what they do when they need to remember a fact. Among Americans, half said they would try to look up an answer online before trying to remember it, and 29 percent said they would

(continued)

probably forget it again right after. Europeans weren't quite as bad, but pretty similar: 36 percent said they Google first and think later: 24 percent admitted they would forget the Googled thing as soon as they closed their browser.

When reading paragraphs developed by the use of facts and statistics, you can expect that these details will answer questions such as *what, when, where*, or *how* about the main idea.

Reasons

Certain types of main ideas are most easily explained by giving reasons. Especially in argumentative and persuasive writing, you will find that a writer supports an opinion, belief, or action by discussing *why* the thought or action is appropriate. In paragraph 4 from "Google Is Making You More Forgetful. Here's Why That's a Good Thing," the writer provides reasons to support her argument that computers do not hurt our memory and that the idea of "digital amnesia" may not be an accurate explanation for what is going on with our memory.

This brings us back to the specter of "digital amnesia": the idea that our computers somehow hurt our memory. But when you remember that we've always stored memories in outside people and things, and that we don't have the capacity to remember everything, the phenomenon looks less like amnesia and more like prudent outsourcing. That was, in fact, the conclusion of three psychologists who studied the "Google effect" in 2011: Although their results were widely interpreted as evidence that Google makes us forget, the researchers themselves were far more optimistic. "We are becoming symbiotic with our computer tools," they wrote," growing into interconnected systems that remember less by knowing information than by knowing where the information can be found."

You can see that the writer offers reasons for being skeptical about "digital amnesia": She cites the research by three psychologists who support her belief that what looks like "digital amnesia" might, in fact, be prudent outsourcing.

Descriptions

If the purpose of a paragraph is to help the reader understand or visualize the appearance, structure, organization, or composition of an object, then descriptions are often used as a means of paragraph development. **Descriptive details** help you visualize the person, object, or event being described. The following paragraph describes the 1900s time traveler speaking to a 21st century smartphone user.

The technologist and Columbia law professor Tim Wu has written what is perhaps the clearest defense of this development: If a time traveler from the early 1900s encountered a modern-day person with a smartphone and spoke to her through a curtain, what would he think? He'd be amazed by her ability to solve complex equations, to answer obscure trivia questions, to quote things in foreign languages. To him, the smartphone user would seem like some kind of genius. (To us, she'd just seem like one chick with a phone.) "With our machines, we are augmented humans and prosthetic gods," Wu writes, "though we're remarkably blase about that fact, like anything else we're used to."

Notice how each detail contributes to the impression of the "genius" smartphone user. Details such as the "augmented humans" and the "prosthetic gods" and the use of words such as *amazed* and *blase* help you visually re-create a picture of the "geniuses" we have become thanks to the technologies that enable us to access information on almost any subject. In reading descriptive details, you must pay close attention to each detail as you try to form a visual impression of what is being described.

Steps or Procedures

Paragraphs often explain how to do something or how something works—listing the steps or procedures involved in the process—or discuss events in the order they occurred. If the author were to explain how to use a smartphone for many different tasks, a topic of paragraph 2, she might have written the following paragraph.

Across the board, everybody's obsessed with their smartphones: More than 40% say their phone contains "everything they need to know." Granted, you probably don't need a laboratory study or a large-scale survey to confirm a phenomenon you've observed yourself. Consider what happens when you receive an email that contains an invitation to a birthday party. First, you open the digital invitation to get the details of the party. You then check your digital calendar to make sure you are free on the day of the party. You enter the date on your calendar and reply by email or text to the sender. As the date of the party approaches, you use your phone to order a gift from an online store. Within the next few days, you check the progress of the shipment by entering a tracking number into your phone. Finally, on the day of the party, you Google the address of the party and drive to the location without one wrong turn. Indeed, your phone contained everything you needed to know to navigate this process.

| EXERCISE 5-4 | Reading: Identifying Types of Supporting Details |

WORKING TOGETHER

Directions: Working in pairs, read each of the following topic sentences, and discuss what types of supporting details you would expect to be used to develop a paragraph for each one. Be prepared to justify your answers.

1. On Saturday mornings, the farmers' market is a sea of color, with baskets of yellow, green, red, and purple produce lined up neatly on tables presided over by vendors in straw hats and blue aprons.

   Type of detail: _____

2. The process of becoming a kidney donor begins with a simple blood test.

   Type of detail: _____

3. Laws regulating the sale of certain cold medicines were enacted because chemicals in these medicines were being used to manufacture methamphetamine.

   Type of detail: _____

4. Government documents indicate that the total number of Americans living in poverty has decreased, but the definition of the poverty line has also been changed.

   Type of detail: _____

5. A sudden explosion at 200 decibels can cause massive and permanent hearing loss.

Type of detail: _____

Reading: Identifying Types of Details

Directions: Each topic sentence below is followed by a list of details that could be used to support it. Label each detail as *illustration, example, fact, statistic, reason, description,* or *step/procedure.*

1. Individual behaviors significantly influence your risk for chronic disease.

_____ Physical inactivity and overweight/obesity are each responsible for nearly 1 in 10 deaths in U.S. adults.

_____ Dietary risks such as high salt, low omega-3 fatty acids, and high trans fatty acids have a significant effect on mortality.

_____ Excessive alcohol consumption increases risk through cardiovascular disease, other medical conditions, traffic accidents, and violence.

_____ The first step in changing an unhealthy behavior is to increase your awareness.

—adapted from Donatelle, *My Health: An Outcomes Approach,* pp. 6–8

2. The family, the media, and the schools all serve as important agents of political socialization.

_____ Recent research has demonstrated that one of the reasons for the long-lasting impact of parental influence on political attitudes is simply genetics.

_____ For example, eight years after researchers first interviewed a sample of high school seniors and their parents, they still found far more agreement than disagreement across the generational divide.

_____ Better-educated citizens are more likely to vote in elections, they exhibit more knowledge about politics and public policy, and they are more tolerant of opposing opinions.

_____ The median age of viewers of CBS, ABC, and NBC news programs in 2008 was 61—19 years older than the audience for a typical prime-time program.

—Edwards et al., *Government in America,* pp. 174–175

3. The number of things plants do for human beings is enormous.

_____ In the world today, up to 90 percent of the calories human beings consume come directly from plants.

_____ Then there are the products that human beings have learned to derive from plants, among them lumber, medicines, fabrics, fragrances, and dyes.

_____ Plants are able to provide us with food because they make their own food through photosynthesis.

_____ Plants also produce much of the oxygen that most living things require.

—adapted from Krogh, *Biology: A Guide to the Natural World*, pp. 441–442

EXAMINING STUDENT WRITING

Sarah Frey

A good way to learn to read and write paragraphs is to study the work of other student writers. In this chapter, we will examine the writing of Sarah Frey and see how she creates topic sentences and uses details to support them.

Sarah Frey is a student at the University of North Carolina at Chapel Hill (UNC), where she is pursuing a double major in biology and psychology. She submitted this essay in her sociology class. The assignment she responded to directed her to write an essay on how technology has impacted society.

Title suggests topic

To Connect or Not to Connect
Sarah Frey

Background details

1   According to the *Washington Post*, in 2013 the average American teenager spent about seven and a half hours consuming media, whether it was by watching television or accessing media on a computer or cell phone. Greater than 75% of today's teenagers own a cell phone and most of those seven and a half hours are spent on this one device (Ahuja). The millennial generation is even referred to as the Facebook generation, becoming the first generation to be tied to the technology of their time. Teens are spending increasing amounts of time in front of a screen, taking time away from family and friends, playing outdoors, and even being in touch with reality; however, the Internet and cell phones also beneficially connect users of all ages to news sources, online banking, GPS technology and even emergency alerts from local police.

Thesis statement

2   Where it was the norm for the Baby Boomers to sit down to dinner with their parents every night for dinner, it is now more often than not that families eat only one or two meals together a week, and even then it is not uncommon for cell phones to also be present at the dinner table. Family time now seems to be a foreign concept as parents are competing for attention with the Internet, social media, and their children's friends. Not only is screen time detracting from quality time with parents, it is also taking time away from sleep and school work. In a *Washington Post* article, Zarin Rahman writes about how the more time she spent on social media on her phone and her computer, the worse she felt. Rahman writes that she was "moody and tired, and focusing on classroom lectures and interactions became increasingly difficult, particularly after spending hours online on (her) computer or on (her)

Topic sentence

Writer uses facts to illustrate effect of technology on teenager iPhone." She acknowledges that innovative technology tools can be used to build or destroy aspects of the teenage life, and she urges her peers to take care when using them (Rahman).

Topic sentence 3   The negative effects of screen time are not limited to the social world; there are also a number of health and psychological risks associated with too much screen time. Although more loosely connected, too much screen time can result in cyber bullying and have negative effects on socialization. Furthermore, some children suf-

Examples of other negative effects of technology follow

fer from sleep deprivation because they are online surfing the Web late at night when they should be sleeping. Pediatricians across the country are encouraging parents to limit their children's screen time to less than two hours each day and to keep laptops, TVs, and cell phones out of the bedrooms (CBS). These are all important side effects that have come about since the explosion of technology over the last fifteen years.

Topic sentence 4   Although there are serious risks to the overuse and abuse of being connected, technology is also a major part of today's culture; therefore, it would be a catastrophic change to move away from it completely. For the average college student, being connected is a vital part of his or her life. Aside from the obvious reasons, such as doing research through online databases and submitting homework through online portals, college students use being connected to receive emergency alerts from campus police and information about severe weather in the area. In addition

Writer uses transition to move from one detail to another

to emergency information, college students use their phones and the Internet to break out of the bubble that ties them to their little world on campus.

Topic sentence 5   The benefits of being connected are not limited to college students. GPS is becoming increasingly important in ground and air travel. The ease of knowing where to go and how to get there has made an easy task out of navigating a trip. GPS also makes it possible to locate positions of lost or crashed vehicles or even to find stolen goods. In addition to GPS, online banking has revolutionized the way that

Examples of other benefits of using technology

many people take care of their banking needs. With just the click of a button into a secure server, users can transfer money and pay bills. According to Statistic Brain,

Writer uses statistics to support her point

81% of Americans who managed household finances did so through an online banking system at least once in the past twelve months (Statistic Brain).

Conclusion 6   *Urban Dictionary* defines "going off the grid" as living or being "unrecorded, untraceable through normal means." Living "on the grid" means exactly the opposite—being "plugged in" and traceable at all times. It does not appear that either being totally connected on the grid or going off the grid is better than the other. In reality, there are benefits and drawbacks for both lifestyles. There seems to be no regression of technology now that it has become a way of life for so many. One can only hope that by understanding both the benefits and the drawbacks, users of technology will be able to find a happy medium as they experience life both on and off the grid.

Works Cited

Ahuja, Masuma. "Teens Are Spending More Time Consuming Media, on Mobile Devices." *The Washington Post*, 13 Mar. 2013, www.washingtonpost.com/postlive/teens-are-spending-more-time-consuming-media-on-mobile-devices/2013/03/12/309bb242-8689-11e2-98a3-b3db6b9ac586_story.html.

Kung-fu Jesus. "Off the Grid." *Urban Dictionary*, 26 June 2004, www.urbandiction-ary.com/define.php?term=off+the+grid. Accessed 30 Mar. 2014.

"Online/Mobile Banking Statistics." *Statistic Brain*, 17 Mar. 2015, www.statisticbrain.com/online-mobile-banking-statistics.

"Pediatricians Urge Parents to Limit Kids' 'Screen Time.'" *CBS/The Associated Press*, 28 Oct. 2013, www.cbsnews.com/news/pediatricians-urge-parents-to-limit-kids-screen-time.

Rahman, Zarin. "Fellow Teenagers, Now Is the Time for Us to Limit Our Screen Time." *The Washington Post*, 7 Mar. 2014, www.washingtonpost.com/news/innovations/wp/2014/03/07/fellow-teenagers-now-is-the-time-for-us-to-limit-our-screen-time.

Writing: Select and Organize Details to Support Your Topic Sentence

■ **GOAL 2**
Select and organize details to support your topic sentence

Once you have written a preliminary topic sentence, your next step is to include the details that support it. Using relevant, specific, sufficient, and varied details and arranging them effectively will improve your writing, allowing you to create clear, lively, and interesting paragraphs.

Relevant Details

Relevant details directly relate to or explain a topic sentence. Sarah's early draft of paragraph 3 from "To Connect or Not to Connect" contains two details that do not support the topic sentence, which is shaded. Can you spot them?

> **Tip for Writers**
>
> *Relevant* information is content about the topic being discussed. The opposite is *irrelevant*. If your teacher marks a sentence *irrelevant*, she means it doesn't belong where you have placed it, so it should be deleted or moved to another paragraph.

[1]The negative effects of screen time are not limited to the social world; there are also a number of health and psychological risks associated with too much screen time. [2]Although more loosely connected, too much screen time can result in cyber bullying and have negative effects on socialization. [3]Furthermore, some children suffer from sleep deprivation because they are online surfing the Web late at night when they should be sleeping. [4]Some of the videos and other online content children watch are not even very entertaining. [5]Pediatricians across the country are encouraging parents to limit their children's screen time to less than two hours each day and to keep laptops, TVs, and cell phones out of the bedrooms (CBS). [6]When I was a child, my parents would never have allowed me to have a computer or TV in my room. [7]These are all important side effects that have come about since the explosion of technology over the last fifteen years.

Sentence 4 is not relevant because what the author considers entertaining does not relate to the negative effects of screen time. Sentence 6 is not relevant because it is limited to what the author's parents allowed when she was a child.

EXERCISE 5-6

WORKING TOGETHER

Reading: Selecting Relevant Details

Directions: Each of the topic sentences listed below is followed by a set of details. Working with a classmate, place check marks on the lines before those statements that are relevant supporting details.

1. TOPIC SENTENCE   People should take safety precautions when outside temperatures reach 95 degrees or above.

   DETAILS   _____ **a.** It is important to drink plenty of fluids.

   _____ **b.** If you are exposed to extreme cold or dampness, you should take precautions.

   _____ **c.** To prevent heat exhaustion, reduce physical activity.

   _____ **d.** Infants and elderly people are particularly at risk for heat exhaustion.

2. TOPIC SENTENCE   Freedom of speech, the first amendment to the U.S. Constitution, does not give everyone the right to say anything at any time.

   DETAILS   _____ **a.** The Constitution also protects freedom of religion.

   _____ **b.** Freedom of speech is a right that citizens of most Western countries take for granted.

   _____ **c.** Freedom of speech is restricted by slander and libel laws, which prohibit speaking or publishing harmful, deliberate lies about people.

   _____ **d.** Citizens may sue if they feel their freedom of speech has been unfairly restricted.

3. TOPIC SENTENCE   Family violence against women is a growing problem that is difficult to control or prevent.

   DETAILS   _____ **a.** Abusive partners will often ignore restraining orders.

   _____ **b.** Violence shown on television may encourage violence at home.

   _____ **c.** New laws make it easier for observers of child abuse to report the violence.

   _____ **d.** Battered women frequently do not tell anyone that they have been battered because they are ashamed.

   _____ **e.** Violence against the elderly is increasing at a dramatic rate.

Choose Specific Details

Read the following pairs of statements. For each pair, place a check mark on the line before the statement that is more vivid and that contains more information.

1. _____ **a.** Professor Valquez gives a lot of homework.

   _____ **b.** Professor Valquez assigns 20 problems during each class and requires us to read two chapters per week.

2. _____ **a.** In Korea, people calculate age differently.

   _____ **b.** In Korea, people are considered to be one year old at birth.

3. ____ **a.** It was really hot Tuesday.

   ____ **b.** On Tuesday, the temperature in New Haven reached 97 degrees.

These pairs of sentences illustrate the difference between vague statements and specific statements. Statement a in each pair conveys little information and lacks interest and appeal. Statement b offers specific, detailed information and, as a result, is more interesting. As you generate ideas and draft paragraphs, try to include as many specific details as possible. These details make your writing more interesting and your ideas more convincing.

Sarah's first draft paragraph below lacks detail. Compare it with her revised version. Notice how the revision has produced a much more lively, informative, and convincing paragraph.

Sarah's *First Draft of Paragraph 4*

Although there are risks to being connected, technology is also such a part of today's culture that it would be a big change to move away from it completely. For the average college student, being connected is a big part of his or her life. Aside from obvious reasons, college students use being connected to get information about problems on campus and the weather. In addition, college students use their phones and the internet to find out what's going on off campus.

Sarah's *Revised Paragraph 4*

Although there are serious risks to the overuse and abuse of being connected, technology is also a major part of today's culture; therefore, it would be a catastrophic change to move away from it completely. For the average college student, being connected is a vital part of his or her life. Aside from the obvious reasons, such as doing research through online databases and submitting homework through online portals, college students use being connected to receive emergency alerts from campus police and information about severe weather in the area. In addition to emergency information, college students use their phones and the internet to break out of the bubble that ties them to their little world on campus.

In this revision, Sarah added examples, included more descriptive words, and made all the details more *concrete* and *specific*.

Ways to Include More Specific Details

Here are a few suggestions for how to include more specific details in your writing, using examples from Sarah's essay:

■ Add names, numbers, times, and places.

VAGUE	Many Americans go online to do their banking.
MORE SPECIFIC	According to Statistic Brain, 81% of Americans who managed household finances did so through an online banking system at least once in the past twelve months (Statistic Brain, 2014).

■ Add more facts and explanation.

VAGUE	GPS lets you do a lot.
MORE SPECIFIC	GPS also makes it possible to locate positions of lost or crashed vehicles or even find stolen goods.

■ Use examples.

VAGUE	Overuse of technology causes different problems.
MORE SPECIFIC	Rahman writes that she was "moody and tired, and focusing on classroom lectures and interactions became increasingly difficult, particularly after spending hours online on (her) computer or on (her) iPhone."

■ Draw from your personal experience.

VAGUE	I rely on the internet for school.
MORE SPECIFIC	As a college student, I use the internet to do research through online databases and to submit homework through online portals.

Depending on your topic, you may need to do research to get more specific details. Dictionaries, encyclopedias, and magazine articles are often good sources. Think of research as interesting detective work and a chance to learn. For example, if you are writing a paragraph about the safety of air bags in cars, you may need to locate some current facts and statistics. Your college library and the Internet will be two good sources; a car dealership and a mechanic may be two others.

EXERCISE 5-7	Writing: Revising Sentences to Be More Specific

Directions: Revise each of the following statements to make it more specific.

Example   Biology is a difficult course.

Biology involves memorizing scientific terms and learning some of life's complex processes.

1. I rode the train.

_____

_____

2. Pizza is easy to prepare.

_____

_____

3. The Fourth of July is a holiday.

_____

_____

4. I bought a lawnmower.

_____

_____

5. The van broke down.

_____

_____

| EXERCISE 5-8 | Writing: Developing Relevant and Specific Details |

WRITING IN PROGRESS

Directions: Choose three of the following topics and narrow each of them down to a more manageable one. Develop a topic sentence that expresses one main point about each topic. Then brainstorm three specific details you could use to support each topic sentence.

1. Your favorite book or movie
2. How to end a relationship
3. A sport (or hobby) you would like to take up
4. A childhood memory
5. Your most difficult class
6. How pets help people
7. Your favorite relative or friend
8. A memorable childhood toy
9. Your worst nightmare
10. Your dream vacation

Include Sufficient Details

Including **sufficient details** means including _enough_ details to make your topic sentence believable and convincing. Your details should be as exact and specific as possible. Sarah's first draft of paragraph 2 lacked sufficient detail:

Sarah's _First Draft of Paragraph 2_

> Technology has made the idea of family time into a foreign concept. Everyone is competing for attention. Screen time detracts from quality time with parents and from school. It is too easy to spend hours on social media, whether on your phone or your computer. Obviously, there are many positive aspects of technology, but teenagers have to be careful about how they use technology.

Notice that the paragraph is very general. It does not describe specific negative aspects of technology, nor does it explain how screen time detracts from family time as well as sleep and school work. A revised version is shown below. Notice the addition of numerous details and the more focused topic sentence.

Sarah's *Revised Paragraph 2*

Where it was the norm for the Baby Boomers to sit down to dinner with their parents every night for dinner, it is now more often than not that families only eat one or two meals together a week, and even then it is not uncommon for cell phones to also be present at the dinner table. Family time now seems to be a foreign concept as parents are competing for attention with the internet, social media, and their children's friends. Not only is screen time detracting from quality time with parents, it is also taking time away from sleep and school work. In a *Washington Post* article, Zarin Rahman writes about how the more time she spent on social media on her phone and her computer, the worse she felt. Rahman writes that she was "moody and tired, and focusing on classroom lectures and interactions became increasingly difficult, particularly after spending hours online on (her) computer or on (her) iPhone." She acknowledges that innovative technology tools can be used to build or destroy aspects of the teenage life, and she urges her peers to take care when using them (Rahman).

If you have difficulty thinking of enough details to include in a paragraph, try the following strategies.

Ways to Generate Additional Details

1. **Try brainstorming, freewriting, or branching for more ideas.**
2. **Draft a more focused topic sentence** (as **Sarah** did in the paragraph above). You may then find it easier to develop supporting details.
3. **Review your topic.** If you are still unable to generate additional details, your topic may be too narrow or you may need to do some additional reading or research on your topic. If you use information from another source, be sure to give the author credit by using a citation. Refer to Chapter 10 for more information on documenting sources.

Use a Variety of Types of Supporting Details

As you learned earlier in the chapter, there are many types of details that you can use to explain or support a topic sentence: (1) illustrations or examples, (2) facts or statistics, (3) reasons, (4) descriptions, and (5) steps or procedures.

Using a variety of supporting details to support your topic sentence makes your writing more interesting and engaging for your reader. More important, it also makes your topic sentence more believable, and it is likely that your reader will accept your ideas. For example, if you support a topic sentence asserting that teenage bullying is getting out of control only with examples from your own community, a reader may wonder if your community is the exception rather than the rule. If, however, you offer statistics from a national survey demonstrating that teenage bullying is a common occurrence, then you assure your readers that the problem extends beyond your community.

NEED TO KNOW

Drafting Paragraphs

To draft effective paragraphs, be sure to do the following:

- **Choose a manageable topic.** Your topic should be neither too broad nor too narrow.
- **Write a clear topic sentence.** Your topic sentence should identify the topic and make a point about that topic.
- **Develop your paragraph by providing relevant, specific, sufficient and varied details.** *Relevant details* are those that directly support the topic. *Specific details* are lively, informative, and descriptive. Including *sufficient details* means providing enough details to make your topic sentence believable and convincing. Using a *variety of details* (illustrations or examples, facts or statistics, reasons, descriptions, and steps or procedures) makes your writing more interesting and more believable.

EXERCISE 5-9
WRITING IN PROGRESS

Writing a Paragraph

Directions: Write a paragraph developing one of the topic sentences you wrote in Exercise 5-8. Use the relevant and specific details you listed, adding more if necessary. Be sure you have included sufficient and varied details in your paragraph.

Use Transitional Words and Phrases to Read and Write Paragraphs

■ GOAL 3
Use transitional words and phrases to read and write paragraphs

Transitions are linking words or phrases that lead the reader from one idea to another.

Use Transitions to Read Paragraphs

If you get into the habit of recognizing transitions, you will see that they often help you read a paragraph more easily. In the following paragraph from "Google Is Making You More Forgetful. Here's Why That's a Good Thing" (paragraph 3), notice how the highlighted transitions lead you from one detail to the next.

> But while it's undeniably true that we rely on technology as a sort of memory aid, the jury is still very much out as to whether that's a positive or a negative thing. After all, the issue can be framed in two different ways: Either the Internet is replacing our natural mental capacity, or it's augmenting it. That may seem counterintuitive, but consider two oft-forgotten (heh) facts about how memory works. First off, memory isn't—and has never been—a solo endeavor, constrained to your head. Research suggests that we've always relied heavily on other people, as well as on tools like diaries and Post-its, to remember all kinds of biographical and general facts. This is called "transactive memory,"
>
> *(continued)*

and it basically means that we store information not just in our brains—but in objects and people. Second, "remembering" isn't an inherently good thing, and forgetting isn't inherently bad. It doubtlessly doesn't seem that way when you're punching in repeated wrong PIN numbers at the ATM. But generally speaking, your brain has only so much space to store memories—rather like your phone. At some point, you have to delete all those old photos and apps to take new ones.

Not all paragraphs contain such obvious transitions, and not all transitions serve as such clear markers of details. As you can see, transitions may be used for a variety of reasons. They may alert you to what will come next in the paragraph, they may tell you that an example will follow, or they may predict that a different, opposing idea is coming. Table 5-1 lists some of the most common transitions and indicates what they tell the reader.

TABLE 5-1 COMMON TRANSITIONS		
Type of Transition	**Example**	**What They Tell the Reader**
Time sequence	*first, later, next, finally, after, afterward, at last, at the same time, before, currently, during, eventually, following, in the beginning, meanwhile, now, second, soon, suddenly, then, third, until, when*	The author is arranging ideas in the order in which they happened.
Example	*for example, for instance, to illustrate, such as*	An example will follow.
Enumeration	*first, second, third, last, another, next*	The author is marking or identifying each major point. (Sometimes these may be used to suggest order of importance.)
Continuation	*also, in addition, and, further, another*	The author is continuing with the same idea and is going to provide additional information.
Contrast	*on the other hand, in contrast, however*	The author is switching to a different, opposite, or contrasting idea than previously discussed.
Comparison	*like, likewise, similarly*	The author will show how the previous idea is similar to what follows.
Cause/effect	*because, thus, therefore, since, consequently*	The author will show a connection between two or more things, how one thing caused another, or how something happened as a result of something else.
Spatial	*above, behind, below, beneath, beside, in front of, inside, nearby, next to, on the other side of, outside, to the west (north, etc.) of*	The author will describe a physical location or position in space.
Least/most	*above all, best of all, especially, even more, moreover, most, most important, particularly important, not only, but also*	The author is arranging details from least to most important or from most to least important.

EXERCISE 5-10 | Reading: Understanding Transitions

Directions: Many transitions have similar meanings and can sometimes be used interchangeably. Match each transition in column A with a similar transition in column B. Write your answers in the spaces provided.

	Column A	Column B
_____	1. because	a. therefore
_____	2. in contrast	b. also
_____	3. for instance	c. likewise
_____	4. thus	d. after that
_____	5. first	e. since
_____	6. one way	f. finally
_____	7. similarly	g. on the other hand
_____	8. next	h. one approach
_____	9. in addition	i. in the beginning
_____	10. to sum up	j. for example

EXERCISE 5-11 | Reading: Identifying Transitions

Directions: Read each paragraph below and complete the items that follow.

A.   You can help prevent heat stress by following certain precautions. First, proper acclimatization to hot and/or humid climates is essential. Heat acclimatization increases your body's cooling efficiency; in this process, you increase activity gradually over 10 to 14 days in the hot environment. Second, avoid dehydration by replacing the fluids you lose during and after exercise. Third, wear clothing appropriate for your activity and the environment. And finally, use common sense—for example, on a day when the temperature is 85 degrees and the humidity is 80 percent, postpone your usual lunchtime run until the cool of evening.

—Donatelle, *Health: The Basics*, pp. 290–291

List the transitional words or phrases in this paragraph that suggest enumeration.

1. _____   2. _____   3. _____   4. _____

B.   One indicator of good advertising is, of course, the impression it makes on consumers. But how can this impact be defined and measured? Two basic measures of impact are *recognition* and *recall*. In the typical recognition test, subjects are shown ads one at a time and asked if they have seen them before. In contrast, free recall tests ask consumers to think of what they have seen without being prompted for this information first. Under some conditions, these two memory measures tend to yield the same results; however, recognition scores tend to be more reliable and do not decay over time the way recall scores do. Recall tends to be more important in situations in which consumers do not have product data at their disposal, so they must rely on memory to generate this information. On the other hand, recognition is more likely to be an important factor in a store, where consumers are confronted with thousands of product options and the task may simply be to recognize a familiar package.

—adapted from Solomon, *Consumer Behavior*, pp. 92–93

List the transitional words or phrases in this paragraph that suggest contrast.

1. _____   2. _____   3. _____

C.   Tuition vouchers are a set amount of money given by the government to parents that can only be used to pay for public or private school tuition. Supporters of tuition vouchers argue that by giving parents a choice in where they send their children to school, schools will have to pay more attention to the needs of students and their parents or risk losing students to competitive schools with better services. They also argue that schools that are guaranteed students solely because of their location have no incentive to improve. Further, voucher advocates argue that it is unfair that rich families have the ability to choose which school their children attend, but poor families do not.

—adapted from Edwards et al., *Government in America*, pp. 654–655

List the transitional words or phrases in this paragraph that suggest continuation.

1. _____   2. _____

D.   The process of making an etching begins with the preparation of a metal plate with a *ground*—a protective coating of acid-resistant material that covers the copper or zinc. The printmaker then draws easily through the ground with a pointed tool, exposing the metal. Finally, the plate is immersed in acid. Acid "bites" into the plate where the drawing has exposed the metal, making a groove that varies in depth according to the strength of the acid and the length of time the plate is in the bath.

—Preble and Preble, *Artforms*, p. 144

List the transitional words or phrases in this paragraph that suggest time sequence.

1. _____   2. _____   3. _____

E.   Dangerous and dramatic mass movements, such as rock slides and mudflows, can occur on steep slopes, especially during wet conditions. Steep slopes are prone to rock slides because the force of gravity pushing down on the rocks is likely to exceed the strength of the rocks. Landslides on steep slopes can follow intense rains, because material with a high water content is heavier, weaker, and less able to resist the force of gravity. The sliding material may break down into fluid mud, which flows downhill. Houses built on very steep slopes—along the west coast of North America, for example—risk damage from landslides and mudflows.

—adapted from Bergman and Renwick, *Introduction to Geography*, p. 106

List the transitional words or phrases in this paragraph that suggest the illustration and example pattern.

1. _____   2. _____

Use Transitions When You Organize Paragraphs

Transitional words allow readers to move easily from one detail to another; they show how details relate to one another. You might think of them as words that guide and signal your reader about how your ideas are organized and signal what is to follow.

Here is a first draft of paragraph 3 from Sarah's essay "To Connect or Not to Connect," followed by a later revision. As you read each version, pay particular attention to the order in which she arranged the details in both versions.

Sarah's *First Draft of Paragraph 3*

The negative effects of screen time are not limited to the social world; there are also a number of health and psychological risks associated with too much screen time. Pediatricians across the country are encouraging parents to limit their children's screen time to less than two hours each day and to keep laptops, TVs, and cell phones out of the bedrooms (CBS). Too much screen time can result in cyber bullying and have negative effects on socialization. Children suffer from sleep deprivation because they are online surfing the Web late at night when they should be sleeping. These are all important side effects that have come about since the explosion of technology over the last fifteen years.

Sarah's *Revised Paragraph 3*

The negative effects of screen time are not limited to the social world; there are also a number of health and psychological risks associated with too much screen time. Although more loosely connected, too much screen time can result in cyber bullying and have negative effects on socialization. Furthermore, some children suffer from sleep deprivation because they are online surfing the Web late at night when they should be sleeping. Pediatricians across the country are encouraging parents to limit their children's screen time to less than two hours each day and to keep laptops, TVs, and cell phones out of the bedrooms (CBS). These are all important side effects that have come about since the explosion of technology over the last fifteen years.

Did you find Sarah's revision easier to read? In the first draft, she recorded details as she thought of them. There is no logical arrangement to them. In the second version, she arranged the details from least to most important and used transitions (*although, furthermore*) to indicate the connections between details.

The three common methods for arranging details are as follows:

- time sequence
- spatial arrangement
- least/most arrangement

Time-Sequence Arrangement

When you are describing an event or series of events, it is often easiest to arrange them in the order in which they happened. This arrangement is called **time**

sequence. You can also use time sequence to explain how events happened or to tell a story. For example, you can explain how you ended up living in Cleveland or tell a story about a haunted house. In the following sample paragraph, the student has arranged details in time sequence. Read the paragraph and then fill in the blanks in the time-sequence map that follows it.

Sample Time-Sequence Paragraph

Driving a standard-shift vehicle is easy if you follow these steps. First, push the clutch pedal down. The clutch is the pedal on the left. Then start the car. Next, move the gearshift into first gear. On most cars, this is the straight-up position. Next, give the car some gas, and slowly release the clutch pedal until you start moving. Finally, be ready to shift into higher gears—second, third, and so on. A diagram of where to find each gear usually appears on the gearshift knob. With practice, you will learn to start up smoothly and shift without the car making grinding noises or lurching.

VISUALIZE IT!

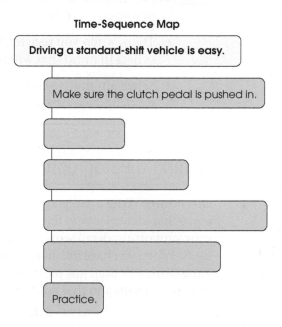

Time-Sequence Map

Driving a standard-shift vehicle is easy.

Make sure the clutch pedal is pushed in.

Practice.

Look again at the sample paragraph. Notice that transitions are used to lead you from one step to another. Try to pick them out; underline those that you find. Did you underline *first, then, next,* and *finally*? Using transitions like those listed below will help you to link details in a time-sequence paragraph.

COMMON TIME-SEQUENCE TRANSITIONS		
first	next	before
second	during	Now
third	at the same time	Later
in the beginning	following	at last
then	after	finally

| EXERCISE 5-12 | Writing: Using Time Sequence |

Directions: Arrange in time sequence the supporting-detail sentences that follow the topic sentence below. Place a "1" on the line before the detail that should appear first in the paragraph, a "2" before the detail that should appear second, and so on.

TOPIC SENTENCE   Registration for college classes requires planning and patience.

SUPPORTING DETAIL SENTENCES

_____ **a.** Find out which of the courses that you need are being offered that particular semester.

_____ **b.** Study your degree requirements and figure out which courses you need to take before you can take others.

_____ **c.** Then start working out a schedule.

_____ **d.** For example, a math course may have to be taken before an accounting or a science course.

_____ **e.** Then, when you register, if one course or section is closed, you will have others in mind that will work with your schedule.

_____ **f.** Select alternative courses that you can take if all sections of one of your first-choice courses are closed.

| EXERCISE 5-13 | Writing a Paragraph Using Time Sequence |

Directions: Write a paragraph on one of the following topics. First, write a topic sentence that identifies your topic and expresses your main point about it. Then arrange your supporting-detail sentences in order. Be sure to use transitions to connect your ideas. When you have finished, draw a time-sequence map of your paragraph (see the Time-Sequence Map just presented). Use your map to check that you have included sufficient details and that you have presented your details in the correct sequence.

1. Going on a disastrous date
2. Closing (or beginning) a chapter of your life
3. Getting more (or less) out of an experience than you expected
4. Having an adventure
5. Having an experience that made you feel like saying, "Look who's talking!"

Spatial Arrangement

Suppose you are asked to describe a car you have just purchased. You want your reader, who has never seen the car, to visualize it. How would you organize your description? You could describe the car from bottom to top or from top to bottom, or from front to back. This method of presentation is called **spatial arrangement**. For other objects, you might arrange your details from inside to outside, from near to far, or from east to west. Notice how, in the following paragraph, the details are arranged from top to bottom.

> My dream house will have a three-level outdoor deck that will be ideal for relaxing on after a hard day's work. The top level of the deck will be connected by sliding glass doors to the family room. On this level there will be a hot tub, a large picnic table with benches, and a comfortable padded chaise. On the middle level there will be a suntanning area, a hammock, and two built-in planters for a mini-herb garden. The lowest level, which will meet the lawn, will have a built-in stone barbeque pit for big cookouts and a gas grill for everyday use.

Can you visualize the deck?

In spatial-arrangement paragraphs, transitions are particularly important since they often reveal placement or position of objects or parts. Using transitions like those listed in the table below will help you to link details in a spatial-arrangement paragraph.

COMMON SPATIAL-ARRANGEMENT TRANSITIONS		
above	next to	nearby
below	inside	on the other side
beside	outside	beneath
in front of	behind	west (or other direction)

EXERCISE 5-14

Writing: Using Spatial Arrangement

Directions: Use spatial arrangement to order the supporting-detail sentences that follow the topic sentence below. Write a "1" on the line before the detail that should appear first in the paragraph, a "2" before the detail that should appear second, and so on.

TOPIC SENTENCE   My beautiful cousin Audry always looks as if she has dressed quickly and given her appearance little thought.

SUPPORTING DETAIL SENTENCES

_____ **a.** She usually wears an oversized, baggy sweater, either black or blue-black, with the sleeves pushed up.

_____ **b.** Black slip-on sandals complete the look; she wears them in every season.

_____ **c.** On her feet, she wears mismatched socks.

_____ **d.** Her short, reddish hair is usually wind-blown, hanging every which way from her face.

_____ **e.** She puts her makeup on unevenly, if at all.

_____ **f.** The sweater covers most of her casual, rumpled skirt.

Writing a Paragraph Using Spatial Arrangement

Directions: Write a paragraph on one of the following topics. First, write a topic sentence that identifies your topic and expresses your main point about it. Then use spatial arrangement to develop your supporting details.

1. A secret hiding place
2. The street that leads to your house
3. A photograph or painting that you like
4. Your dream car
5. The inside of an alien spacecraft

Least/Most Arrangement

Another method of arranging details is to present them in order from least to most or most to least, according to some quality or characteristic. For example, you might choose least to most important, serious, frightening, or humorous. In writing a paragraph explaining your reasons for attending college, you might arrange details from most to least important. In writing about an exciting evening, you might arrange your details from most to least exciting.

As you read the following paragraph, note how the writer has arranged details in a logical way.

> This week has been filled with good news. One night when balancing my checkbook, I discovered a $155 error in my checking account—in my favor, for once! I was even happier when I finally found a buyer for my Chevy Blazer that I had been trying to sell all winter. Then my boss told me he was submitting my name for a $1.50 hourly raise; I certainly didn't expect that. Best of all, I learned that I'd been accepted into the Radiology curriculum for next fall.

In this paragraph, the details are arranged from least to most important.

In least/most paragraphs, transitions help your reader to follow your train of thought. Using transitions like those listed in the table below will help you link details in a least/most paragraph.

COMMON LEAST/MOST TRANSITIONS		
most important	particularly important	moreover
above all	even more	not only … but also
especially	best of all	

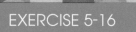

Writing a Paragraph Using Least/Most Arrangement

Directions: Write a paragraph on one of the following topics. First, write a topic sentence that identifies your topic and expresses your main point about it. Then use a least/most arrangement to order your details. When you have finished, draw a map of your paragraph. Use your map to check that you have included sufficient details and that you have arranged your details in least/most order.

1. Your reasons for choosing the dorm or apartment you live in
2. Changes in your life since you began college
3. Why people shop online
4. Why you like a certain book or movie
5. Good (or bad) things that have happened to you recently

EXERCISE 5-17

WORKING TOGETHER

Reading: Identifying Methods of Arrangement

Directions: Find several magazine or newspaper ads. Working in a group, identify the method of arrangement of the advertising copy.

! **NEED TO KNOW**

Developing, Arranging, and Connecting Details

Be sure to use interesting and lively **details** to support your topic sentence.

- Choose details that are specific and concrete.
- Within your paragraphs, arrange details in a **logical order**. Three techniques for arranging details are
  - **time-sequence arrangement**; information is presented in the order in which it happened.
  - **spatial arrangement**; descriptive details are arranged according to their position in space.
  - **least/most arrangement**; ideas are arranged from least to most or most to least according to some quality or characteristic.
- Use transitions to help your reader move easily from one key detail to the next.

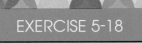

EXERCISE 5-18

WRITING IN PROGRESS

Writing: Revising Your Paragraph

Directions: Reread the paragraph you wrote for Exercise 5-9 and decide on the best way to arrange the details. Then revise your draft using time-sequence, spatial, or least/most arrangement to arrange your details, adding transitions to help your reader move from one key detail to the next.

Reading: Identify Implied Main Ideas

In paragraphs, writers sometimes leave their main idea unstated. The paragraph contains only details. It is up to you, the reader, to infer the writer's main point. You can visualize this type of paragraph as follows:

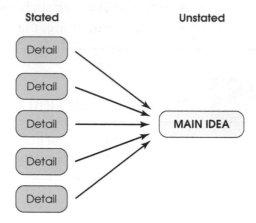

The details, when taken together, all point to a larger, more important idea, an **implied main idea**. Think of the paragraph as a list of facts that you must add up or put together to determine the meaning of the paragraph as a whole. Use the following steps as a guide to find implied main ideas:

1. **Find the topic.** Ask yourself, "What is the one thing the author is discussing throughout the paragraph?"

2. **Decide what the writer wants you to know about that topic.** Look at each detail and decide what larger general idea each explains.

3. **Express this idea in your own words.** Make sure the main idea is a reasonable one. Ask yourself, "Does it apply to all the details in the paragraph?"

Read the following paragraph (paragraph 2) from "Google Is Making You More Forgetful. Here's Why That's a Good Thing"; then follow the three steps listed above to determine the implied main idea.

> Across the board, everybody's obsessed with their smartphones: More than 40% say their phone contains "everything they need to know." Granted, you probably don't need a laboratory study or a large-scale survey to confirm a phenomenon you've observed yourself. How many people memorize phone numbers anymore? How many get around without consulting Google Maps?

The topic of this paragraph is using smartphones to access information. More specifically, it is about the types of information that people access on their smartphones. Two details are given: people use smartphones to access phone numbers and to get directions. Each of these details is a different use that replaces information that people used to know from memory. The main point the writer is trying to make, then, is technology, specifically smartphones, is making people more forgetful. Notice that no single sentence states this idea clearly.

You can visualize this paragraph as follows:

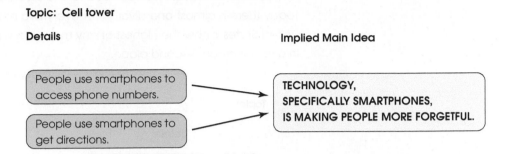

Topic: Cell tower

Details   **Implied Main Idea**

People use smartphones to access phone numbers.

People use smartphones to get directions.

→ TECHNOLOGY, SPECIFICALLY SMARTPHONES, IS MAKING PEOPLE MORE FORGETFUL.

Here is another paragraph. Read it and then fill in the diagram that follows:

> Yellow is a bright, cheery color; it is often associated with spring and hopefulness. Green, since it is a color that appears frequently in nature (trees, grass, plants), has come to suggest growth and rebirth. Blue, the color of the sky, may suggest eternity or endless beauty. Red, the color of both blood and fire, is often connected with strong feelings such as courage, lust, and rage.

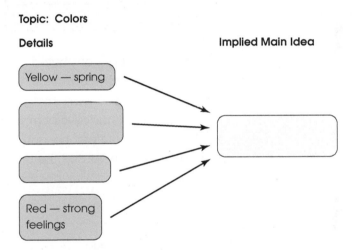

Topic: Colors

Details   **Implied Main Idea**

Yellow — spring

Red — strong feelings

How to Know Whether You Have Made a Reasonable Inference

There is a test you can perform to discover whether you inferred a reasonable main idea. The idea you infer to be the main idea should be broad enough so that every sentence in the paragraph explains the idea you have identified. Work through the paragraph, sentence by sentence. Check to see that each sentence explains or gives more information about the idea you have identified. If some sentences do not explain this idea, your main idea probably is not broad enough. Work on expanding your idea and making it more general.

EXERCISE 5-19

Reading: Analyzing Implied Main Ideas

Directions: After reading each of the following paragraphs, complete the diagram that follows.

1.   In 1920 there was one divorce for every seven marriages in the United States. Fifty years later the rate had climbed to one divorce for every three marriages, and today there is almost one divorce for every two marriages. The divorce rate in the United States is now the highest of any major industrialized nation, while Canada is in a rather distant second place.

—Coleman and Cressey, *Social Problems*, p. 130

Topic: _____

Details	Implied Main Idea

1920 — divorce rate is _____

50 years later — divorce rate is _____

Now the divorce rate is _____ _____ _____

The _____ has _____ dramatically since 1920.

2.   Immigration has contributed to the dramatic population growth of the United States over the past 150 years. It has also contributed to the country's shift from a rural to an urban economy. Immigrants provided inexpensive labor, which allowed industries to flourish. Native-born children of immigrants, benefiting from education, moved into professional and white collar jobs, creating a new middle class. Immigration also increased the U.S. mortality rate. Due to crowded housing and unhealthy living conditions, disease and fatal illness were common.

Topic: _____

Details	Implied Main Idea

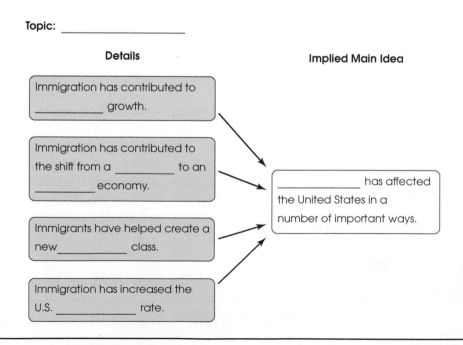

Immigration has contributed to _____ growth.

Immigration has contributed to the shift from a _____ to an _____ economy.

Immigrants have helped create a new _____ class.

Immigration has increased the U.S. _____ rate.

_____ has affected the United States in a number of important ways.

| EXERCISE 5-20 | Reading: Understanding Implied Main Ideas |

Directions: After reading each of the following paragraphs, select the choice that best answers each of the questions below.

Paragraph A

A smooth fabric such as silk is equated with luxury, although denim is considered practical and durable. Fabrics that are composed of scarce materials or that require a high degree of processing to achieve their smoothness or fineness tend to be more expensive and thus are seen as being higher class. Similarly, lighter, more delicate textures are assumed to be feminine. Roughness is often positively valued for men, and smoothness is sought by women.

—Solomon, *Consumer Behavior*, pp. 49–50

_____ 1. What is the topic?
   a. the feel of fabrics
   b. expense in producing fabrics
   c. luxury clothing
   d. roughness in clothing

_____ 2. What is the writer saying about the topic?
   a. Denim is a practical and durable fabric.
   b. Men and women differ in their perception of quality.
   c. Fabrics made of scarce materials are expensive.
   d. The feel of a fabric influences how consumers regard its quality.

Paragraph B

In a classic research study, experimenters told teachers that certain pupils were expected to do exceptionally well—that they were late bloomers. And although the experimenters actually selected the "late bloomers" at random, the students who were labeled "late bloomers" actually did perform at higher levels than their classmates. These students became what their teachers thought they were. The expectations of the teachers may have caused them to pay extra attention to the students and this may have positively affected the students' performance. This same occurrence, called the Pygmalion effect, has been studied in such varied contexts as the courtroom, the clinic, the work cubicle, management and leadership practices, athletic coaching, and stepfamilies.

—adapted from DeVito, *Human Communication*, p. 73

_____ 3. What is the topic?
   a. the struggles of late bloomers
   b. how teachers decide on grades
   c. the impact of research on situations such as courtrooms
   d. how expectations influence results

_____ 4. From the paragraph, it is reasonable to infer that
   a. research studies based on classroom performance cause students to get higher grades.

    b. students for whom teachers have high expectations usually perform better and meet those expectations.

    c. students should be judged based on who they are, not on what teachers think about them.

    d. researchers are expanding their work beyond the classroom into real-life situations.

_____ **5.** Which one of the following details does not directly support the paragraph's implied main idea?

    a. The Pygmalion effect is being studied in the courtroom.

    b. Some students were labeled as late bloomers.

    c. The students labeled as late bloomers performed better than other students.

    d. Teachers' expectations may have resulted in extra attention to the late bloomer students.

READ AND REVISE

The following excerpt is from an essay called "You Have 12 Friend Requests and 15 Messages." As you read, underline the topic sentence and transitions in each paragraph. Then revise the essay by adding or deleting transitions, changing vague words to specific words, and deleting any details that are not relevant.

Facebook gives users a very good way to meet new people and make great new friends. If one doesn't go out much, it's really hard to get to meet new people. Going through Facebook, a user can read about people before taking an interest in them. In addition, if the user is just a shy person and doesn't really like to talk a lot but likes to write, this can be an awesome way to meet new people. Making and meeting new friends through Facebook is the biggest thing right now. Twitter is another way to connect with people. Always remember that the user is the one in control of confirming and ignoring a request to be a friend.

Facebook also has this amazing way of letting the user to create an event so that it can be sent out to all those he or she chooses to invite. A Facebook invite saves money, time, and stamps; stamps are expensive now and so are invitations. t's a quick means to make contact with hundreds of these events. If someone was trying to get a business started they would send out an event invite explaining their new business venture. Free advertisement on Facebook is a money saver for those just getting started. Let's going to be a family reunion; his or her invitation will indicate the date, time, place, and any other special instructions, but the event will only be sent to close family members and be seen by those he or she chooses to invite. Family reunions can be really hard to organize. Another thing that event invites do is raise money for people who are sick and need help paying their medical bills; these kinds of benefits really help the less fortunate. An event can be created in just minutes and the word can be spread rapidly.

READ AND RESPOND: A Student Essay

Sarah Frey

In the Examining Student Writing section of this chapter, you read "To Connect or Not to Connect" and examined various elements of the essay. Now it is time to take a closer look at the reading by responding to the questions that follow.

To Connect or Not to Connect

Sarah Frey

Examining Writing

1. What types of supporting details did Sarah use in this essay?

2. Which details were the most effective?

3. Do the details in each paragraph relate to the topic sentence?

4. Does each paragraph have sufficient details to support the topic sentence?

5. How did Sarah arrange her ideas?

6. Underline transitions throughout the essay. What does each transition indicate? Where might additional transitions be useful in guiding the reader?

7. Evaluate the types of words Sarah used and underline examples of vague and/or specific language in this essay. Choose a couple of sentences and rewrite vague language using specific details (see the Choose Specific Details section of this chapter for suggestions on how to do this).

In the Examining Professional Writing section of this chapter, you read "Google Is Making You More Forgetful. Here's Why That's a Good Thing," which has been used throughout the chapter to illustrate reading techniques. Now it is time to take a closer look at the reading by responding to the questions that follow.

Google Is Making You More Forgetful. Here's Why That's a Good Thing.

Caitlin Dewey

Writing in Response to Reading

Checking Your Comprehension

Answer each of the following questions using complete sentences.

1. How does Tim Wu describe humans with digital machines?
2. What is "digital amnesia"?
3. What is transactive memory?
4. According to the reading, why isn't forgetting necessarily a bad thing?
5. What were the results of the 2011 "Google effect" study?

Strengthening Your Vocabulary

Using the word's context, word parts, or a dictionary, write a brief definition of each of the following words as it is used in the reading.

1. ominous (paragraph 1) _____
2. augmenting (paragraph 3) _____
3. constrained (paragraph 3) _____
4. inherently (paragraph 3) _____
5. prudent (paragraph 4) _____
6. prosthetic (paragraph5) _____

Examining the Reading: Using Idea Maps

Review the reading by completing the missing parts of the following idea map.

VISUALIZE IT!

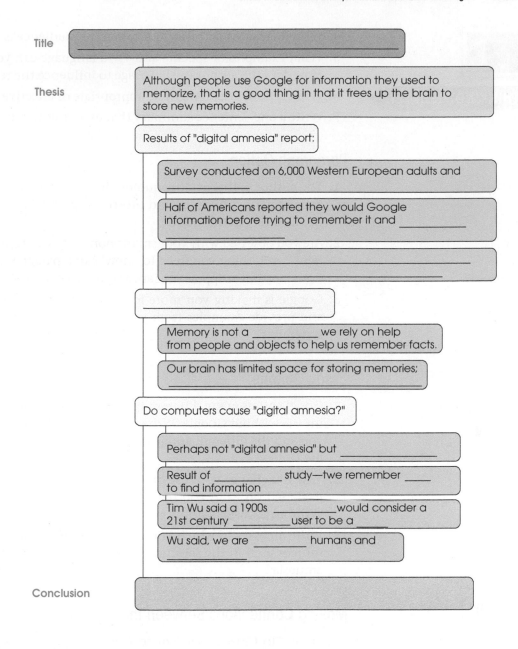

Title _____

Thesis

Although people use Google for information they used to memorize, that is a good thing in that it frees up the brain to store new memories.

Results of "digital amnesia" report:

Survey conducted on 6,000 Western European adults and _____

Half of Americans reported they would Google information before trying to remember it and _____

_____
_____

_____

Memory is not a _____ we rely on help from people and objects to help us remember facts.

Our brain has limited space for storing memories; _____

Do computers cause "digital amnesia?"

Perhaps not "digital amnesia" but _____

Result of _____ study—twe remember _____ to find information

Tim Wu said a 1900s _____ would consider a 21st century _____ user to be a _____

Wu said, we are _____ humans and _____

Conclusion _____

Thinking Critically: An Integrated Perspective

Get ready to write about the reading by discussing the following:

1. Discuss the types of supporting details the author uses to capture your attention and to inform you about the research on memory and Google. Which types of details are most effective and/or convincing?

2. Discuss the effectiveness of the title and the introduction of the reading. Does the title communicate the author's intended message? Can you think of another title for the reading? How does the author capture the attention of the reader in the introduction?

3. How would you describe the author's attitude toward the claim that Google is making people more forgetful? What impression does she leave the reader with at the end of the reading?

THINKING VISUALLY

4. Who do you think the author's intended audience is?

5. What examples of specific and vivid language can you find in the selection? How does the author use language to influence the reader?

6. What type of visual might be appropriate or effective with this subject?

7. Write a one-sentence summary that expresses the main idea of the reading.

Paragraph Options

1. The author of this reading quotes Tim Wu, who says, "With our machines, we are augmented humans and prosthetic gods." Write a paragraph explaining the meaning of this quote.

2. Are you obsessed with your smartphone? Do you believe that your phone contains "everything you need to know"? In a paragraph, answer these two questions. Be sure to support your answers with details from your personal experience.

3. Google is making you more forgetful. In a paragraph, answer this question and provide examples from your own life that either support or refute this statement.

Essay Options

1. Google offers many different types of services, and most people cannot imagine life without Google. Write an essay in which you discuss Google's value to you and the different applications you use in your school, work, and personal life.

2. Will you change your use of technology—or try to limit your dependence on it—based on what you have learned from this selection? Why or why not? Write an essay explaining your answer.

3. Write an essay in which you summarize the findings of each of the different sources used in the selection and draw your own conclusions about "digital amnesia."

Making Connections Between the Readings

Use both "To Connect or Not to Connect" and "Google Is Making You More Forgetful. Here's Why That's a Good Thing" to write a paragraph or an essay in response to one of the following assignments.

1. Although both authors focus on the effects of wireless technology, the types of technology, the examples used, and the tone of the writing are markedly different. In an essay, contrast the two essays on the basis of the three aforementioned points.

2. How do you think the author of the professional essay would respond to the points made by the student author? Write a response to this question, being sure to include support from both of the readings.

3. How are the attitudes of the authors and the conclusions they draw similar or different? Write a response to this question and include details from both writings to support your answer.

SELF-TEST SUMMARY

To test yourself, cover the Answer column with a sheet of paper and answer each question in the left column. Evaluate each of your answers as you work by sliding the paper down and comparing your answer with what is printed in the Answer column.

QUESTION	ANSWER
■ **GOAL 1** Identify supporting details in a paragraph What is the difference between major and minor details?	*Major details* are the most important details in a paragraph; they directly explain or prove the main idea. *Minor details* provide additional information, offer examples, or further explain major details.
What are common types of supporting details?	*Common types of supporting details* include illustrations and examples, facts and statistics, reasons, descriptions, and steps or procedures.
■ **GOAL 2** Select and organize details to support your topic sentence What kinds of details should you use to support your topic sentence?	Details should be ■ relevant (directly support the topic sentence). ■ specific (lively, informative, and descriptive). ■ sufficient (enough to make your topic sentence believable and convincing). ■ varied (containing a variety of types of supporting details).
■ **GOAL 3** Use transitional words and phrases to read and write paragraphs What are transitions?	*Transitions* are linking words or phrases that lead the reader from one idea to another. See Table 5-1: Common Transitions for a list of common transitions.
What are three common methods of arranging details?	Three common methods of arranging details are *time sequence, spatial arrangement,* and *least/most arrangement.*
■ **GOAL 4** Identify implied main ideas How do you find implied main ideas?	Find the topic, decide what the writer wants you to know about that topic based on the details in the paragraph, and express this idea in your own words.

Patterns of Organization: Chronological Order, Process, Narration, and Description

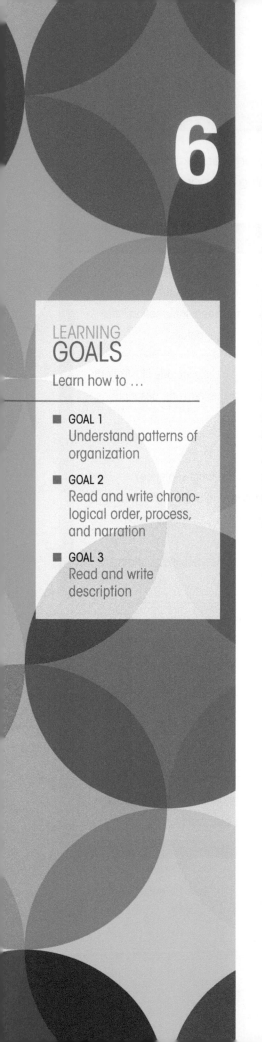

wavebreakmedia/Shutterstock

LEARNING GOALS

Learn how to …

- **GOAL 1**
  Understand patterns of organization

- **GOAL 2**
  Read and write chronological order, process, and narration

- **GOAL 3**
  Read and write description

THINK About It!

The photograph above shows a busy gym. Suppose you had to write a paragraph about the photo. What would you write about? One option would be to describe the physical details of the scene so that someone could visualize what is happening. Or based on your own experience, you could relate the process that the people follow when they arrive at the gym. Or you could tell a story about a person who just joined the gym, explaining the circumstances that brought him or her there.

Each paragraph would be quite different—each would contain different information and be organized differently. This example illustrates that there are a variety of organizational plans, or patterns, that writers use to organize their ideas. In this chapter, you will learn how to recognize specific patterns—*time sequence, chronological order, process, narration*, and *description*—as you read and how to use them to organize your ideas as you write.

In this chapter, you will explore the theme of healthy living. You will read a professional essay on behavioral changes needed for a healthy lifestyle, and a student essay on steps individuals can take toward a healthier lifestyle.

What Are Patterns of Organization?

Organization is important in paragraphs and longer pieces of writing. Good writers follow a clear pattern when they write so that readers can easily find and understand the important points they are making. To learn what patterns of organization are and why they are useful for reading and writing, complete the following activity.

Lists A and B each contain five facts. Which would be easier to learn?

List A

1. Cheeseburgers contain more calories than hamburgers.
2. Christmas cactus plants bloom once a year.
3. Many herbs have medicinal uses.
4. Many ethnic groups live in Toronto.
5. Fiction books are arranged alphabetically by author.

List B

1. Making a lasting change in your behavior requires following certain steps.
2. You must research to get information.
3. You must write up a plan.
4. You must set goals.
5. You must recruit others to help you.

Most likely, you chose list B. There is no connection between the facts in list A; the facts in list B, however, are related. The first sentence makes a general statement, and each remaining sentence gives a particular step for making a lasting change in your behavior. Together, they fit into a pattern.

The details of a paragraph, paragraphs within an essay, events within a short story, or sections within a textbook often fit a pattern. If you can recognize the pattern, you will find it easier to understand and remember the content. You will be able to comprehend the work as a unified whole rather than independent pieces of information.

Patterns are useful when you write as well. They provide a framework within which to organize and develop your ideas and help you present them in a clear, logical manner. This chapter explains how to read and write using each of the patterns of organization shown in the following chart.

PATTERN OF ORGANIZATION	WHAT IT DOES	AN EXAMPLE OF ITS USE
Chronological order	Explains events in the order in which they occurred	Telling how your mother fell and broke her leg, was found hours later, and taken to the emergency room (ER)
Process	Explains how something is done or how something works	Explaining the admission process at the ER
Narration	Tells a story that makes a point	Telling the story of your mother's fall to make the point that frail seniors should have Med Alert services
Description	Uses sensory details to help the reader visualize a topic	Describing the people, activities, sounds, and smells of a busy ER

Additional patterns are covered in Chapter 7.

Chapter Theme: Toward a Healthier Self

In this chapter, you will read both a professional and a student essay on becoming a healthier self. One component of a healthy lifestyle is diet. It has been said that "you are what you eat." If this is so, are you a Snickers bar, a sugary soft drink, or a leafy green vegetable? And do you exercise, get plenty of sleep, and laugh every day? All of these habits help you to have a balanced life and keep your body healthy, and one very important by-product of a balanced lifestyle is your ability to focus in school. So what changes in lifestyle do you need to make that would help you to be a healthier person and a better student? As you read the two essays in this chapter, focus on the authors' suggestions for moving toward a healthier self. Also, annotate each reading, recording your thoughts on the issue, to be prepared to write about it or a related issue.

Look it up!

Use the search engine on your smartphone (or work with a classmate who has a smartphone) and look up "how to live a healthy lifestyle." Review several entries. Based on what you read, which habits contribute to a healthy lifestyle? Which habits do you currently follow? Write a list of those habits you would like to adopt.

EXAMINING PROFESSIONAL WRITING

In the following selection from a health textbook, the authors present seven steps to help you make choices that will benefit your health. As you read, pay special attention to the organizational pattern of the essay.

Thinking Before Reading

Follow these steps before you read:

1. Preview the reading, using the steps discussed in the Pre-Reading Strategies section of Chapter 1.
2. Connect the reading to your own experiences by answering the following questions:
   a. Do you struggle to make the right food choices even when you know what you should be eating? What strategies do you use to help you make wise food choices?
   b. Have you ever created a fitness plan for yourself? If so, what were the components of the plan?
3. Highlight and annotate as you read.

Change Yourself, Change Your World
April Lynch, Barry Elmore, and Jerome Kotecki

1   We can't change our biology or genetics, but we can modify and change individual behaviors. Every day, we encounter opportunities to make choices that will benefit our health. Making the right choices, however, can be a challenge. We often have a good idea of what choices we ought to be making—for instance, eating more fruits and vegetables, setting aside time each day to exercise, or getting more sleep—but actually doing these things and achieving true behavior change is the hard part.

2   Changing your targeted behavior will require more than a quick decision to "just do it." Effective change is a process and starts with information, a SMART goal, and a practical plan. You also need to identify and tackle your barriers, work your environment, promise yourself some rewards—and commit. Let's consider these seven steps one at a time.

Step 1. Get Informed

3   You've identified a goal—"Quit smoking" or "Get fit"—but how much do you really know about the behavior you want to change? For instance, what are the components of fitness, what are the benefits, how is it achieved, and how is it measured? If you're going to set a fitness goal and create a plan for reaching it, you need to be able to answer these questions. So your first step is to do some homework. You can find information at your campus health services center, from your health-care provider, and from reputable professional journals. Jot down the facts that seem most important for changing your targeted behavior. What rate of weight loss is reasonable per week, for instance? Or what's your target heart rate during aerobic exercise? Is it more effective to quit smoking "cold turkey" or gradually? Answering these questions will, among other things, help you identify a more effective behavior-change goal; that is, a SMART goal.

Step 2. Set a SMART Goal

4   If you don't know precisely where you're going, how will you know when you've arrived? Experts in business, education, health care, and personal development agree that goals are more likely to be achieved when they're SMART. The acronym SMART, which was first used in project management in the early 1980s, stands for the five qualities of an effective goal:

- **Specific.** Your goal for change should be well-defined and entirely clear to you. For example, "I'm going to try to lose weight" is not a SMART goal. How much weight do you want to lose? Or if precise numbers don't motivate you, decide specifically how you want to look or feel: "When I'm wearing my new jeans, I want to be able to slide my finger comfortably between me and the waistband."

- **Measurable**. Include in your goal statement objective criteria for evaluating your success. What data would make it clear to anyone that you have succeeded? For instance, "By the end of this semester ... I'll have lost 10 pounds ...

I'll be meditating for at least 20 minutes a day ... I'll have paid off my credit card debt ..."

■ **Attainable.** Does the research you did earlier convince you that you can achieve your goal? If not, you probably won't. So make sure your goal isn't unreasonable. For instance, for most people who are overweight, it's sensible to aim to lose about ½–1 pound of body weight per week; however, 3 pounds a week is not attainable without putting your health at risk.

■ **Relevant.** Don't borrow somebody else's health goal! Make sure that the goal you're working toward feels right for you. For instance, let's say you're overweight, and can't even climb a flight of stairs without feeling winded. You've been looking for some inspiration to get moving when a friend invites you to join him in training for a local marathon. Your friend has been involved in track since middle school. The goal is relevant for him, but it's not SMART for you.

■ **Time based.** A SMART goal has a time frame. For instance: "For the next 6 months, each time I weigh myself—on the 15th and the 30th of each month—I'll have lost at least 1 pound. In 5 months' time, by December 30th, I'll have lost 10 pounds."

5   The National Institutes of Health also advises that your goal be forgiving. That is, it should allow for the occasional intervention of unforeseen events. A goal of walking for 30 minutes a day, 5 days a week, is forgiving. A goal of walking for 30 minutes a day, every day, is not.

Step 3. Make a Plan

6   A SMART goal is like a guiding vision: "In 6 months, I'm going to get on that scale and see that I've lost 20 pounds!" But to make it happen, you need an

Arek malang/Shutterstock

Keep in mind your current situation when setting goals. Set a goal that is **relevant** and **attainable** and you're more likely to reach it.

action plan, and that means you need to break down your goal into specific, achievable, day-to-day actions that will enable you to accomplish it. In doing this, it helps to use a technique called shaping; that is, breaking a big goal into a series of smaller, measurable steps. If you'd like to eventually run a 10K, for instance, set yourself a goal of a shorter distance at first, and then gradually increase your distance a little each week.

Step 4. Identify Barriers and How You'll Overcome Them

7   Barriers are factors that stand in the way of successful change. You can think of them as the "disabling" factors and "negative reinforcers." In an ecological model of behavior change, barriers can emerge from any of the multiple levels of influence on human behavior. For instance, emotional factors like fear and anxiety are common barriers, as is a factor called low self-efficacy. One of the most important psychological factors influencing our ability to change, self-efficacy is both the conviction that you can make successful changes and the ability to take appropriate action to do so. If you believe in your own ability to get in better shape, for example, you'll keep exercising, even if a few workouts leave you tired or frustrated. If you have low self-efficacy, you may give up, or never attempt an exercise program in the first place.

8   Your sense of self-efficacy, and the actions that stem from it, are closely tied to your locus of control. If you have an internal locus of control, you are more likely to believe that you are the master of your own destiny. When a barrier presents itself, you'll look for ways to overcome it. If you have an external locus of control, you are more likely to believe that events are out of your hands—that there's little you can do to overcome barriers.

Jens Briggemann/123RF

Factors in your **environment** can be barriers to behavior change. If you'd like to adopt a more healthy diet, you may want to limit your trips to the bakery!

Step 5. Recruit Some Support

9   Your plan for change will be more likely to succeed if you have different levels of support. Start with your family members and friends. With whom do you feel comfortable sharing your plans for change? Give your support group specific instructions about how they can help; for instance, if you want to lose weight, you might ask your mom to stop sending you care packages loaded with cookies and other sweets. When your motivation wanes, call on your support group to cheer you on. If family members and friends can't provide the consistent support you need, consider joining a campus or community self-help group. Many such programs pair you up with a coach, mentor, or buddy you can call on for advice and caring.

10   Don't ignore campus resources as a source of support for your plan for change. Remember all that campus-services information you got at the start of your freshman year? Take a look back through it, and you may be surprised to find a department or organization ideally suited to support your targeted change.

Step 6. Promise Yourself Rewards

11   Rewards keep you motivated to sustain change. For example, you might promise yourself new clothing after you've reached a target weight goal. However, reinforcement doesn't have to be a material object. For instance, the natural "high" people often feel after physical exercise can be its own positive reinforcement. Many people who are trying to quit smoking set aside the money they would have spent on cigarettes daily, with the promise of travel or another significant reward when they've reached a time goal—say, 6 months or a year—smoke free.

12   End-goal rewards are important, but it's also important to reward yourself for small steps along the way. For instance, if you enroll in an aerobics class held on T/TH throughout the current semester, you might promise yourself that, when you attend both sessions, you'll reward yourself with an act of "self-kindness," such as a long-distance call to a loved one that weekend.

Step 7. Commit in Writing

13   Many people find it helps to write out and sign their name at the bottom of a behavior-change contract—indicating that they've made a pact with themselves that they intend to keep. Make copies of your behavior-change contract, and place them anywhere you want support: on the refrigerator, your full-length mirror … or scan your contract and use it as your screensaver image on your laptop so you see it several times throughout the day!

Believe It!

14   Once you have your contract, it's time to make it happen. When barriers arise—and they will—don't give in to discouragement. Try to fill your mind with positive self-talk—thoughts that affirm your ability to change and acknowledge the help available to you from your environment. At all costs, avoid negative self-talk—the inner chatter that says you can't do this, or you don't have the time or money, or it's not important anyway.

Sleep Deprived

John Dawson/Pearson Education

"Hi, I'm Jasmine. I'm a freshman and I'm a child development major. Each night, I'm very lucky if I get 4 hours of sleep. I'm just a night owl. I like staying up at night. My father's the exact same way. It's like 3 o'clock in the morning and we'll still be up watching the food channel. Around exam time, I find myself awake at 7:30 in the morning, still up—knowing that I have a test at 9:30. Why, I don't know.

I don't think I'm doing my best right now because when I drag myself to class, I'm half asleep. I do need to change and get better rest so that I can do better in school. I don't think I've gotten 8 hours of sleep since I was 13. I'm 19, so that's 6 years of not getting a full night's sleep. That takes a toll on your body and your mind."

1. Write a SMART goal that might help Jasmine address her problem of sleep deprivation.
2. What information should Jasmine obtain to help her achieve this goal?
3. How could Jasmine use shaping to work toward her goal?
4. What barriers might Jasmine expect to encounter?

Reading and Writing Time Sequence: Chronological Order, Process, and Narration

■ **GOAL 2**
Read and write chronological order, process, and narration

Chronological order, process, and narration are all patterns based on time sequence.

What Is Time Sequence?

The terms *chronological order* and *process* both refer to the order in which something occurs or is done. When writers tell a story, they usually present events in **chronological order**. In other words, they start with the first event, continue with the second, and so on. For example, if you were telling a friend about choosing your college, you would probably start by explaining how you identified schools that offered the program you are interested in, continue by describing your visits to each campus, and end with the result—the college you chose was the best fit for you. You would put events in order according to the *time* they occurred, beginning with the first event.

   Process is a pattern used to explain how something is done or how something works. For example, a writer might explain how to apply for a loan or describe how glass is recycled. **Narration** is another pattern that uses time sequence to tell a story. Whether you are reading or writing, time sequence is used whenever ideas are organized according to the order in which they occurred.

VISUALIZE IT!

You can visualize and draw the chronological order and process patterns as follows:

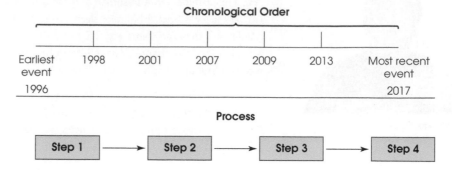

Read Chronological Order and Process

When writers use the chronological order pattern, they often include time transitions (see the box below). They may also use dates to help readers keep track of the sequence of events. In the following passage, time transitions and dates are used to organize details related to the topic of health and hygiene.

> Prior to the 1800s, if you weren't sick, you were not only regarded as lucky, but also healthy. When deadly epidemics such as bubonic plague, influenza, and cholera killed millions of people, survivors were believed to be of hearty stock, and they congratulated themselves on their good fortune. Poor health was often associated with poor hygiene and unsanitary conditions, and a stigma was attached to households that harbored illnesses. Not until the late 1800s did researchers discover that victims of epidemics were not simply dirty or unhealthy. Rather, they were victims of environmental factors (microorganisms found in contaminated water, air, and human waste) over which they had little control. Public health officials moved swiftly to address these problems, and as a result, *health* became synonymous with *good hygiene*.
>
> —Donatelle, *Health: The Basics*, p. 3

COMMON CHRONOLOGICAL ORDER AND PROCESS TRANSITIONS		
first	before	following
second	after	last
later	then	during
next	in addition	when
another	also	until
as soon as	finally	meanwhile

Writers also follow a time sequence when they use the process pattern—when they explain how something is done or made. Transitions are often used to guide you from one step to the next. When writers explain how to put together a bookcase, how to knit a sweater, or how bees make honey, they use steps to show the appropriate order.

The professional reading "Change Yourself, Change the World" is organized using the process pattern; the authors clearly outline the seven steps they believe people should follow in order to change specific behaviors and improve their health. They also use the process pattern within paragraphs. In paragraph 9, for example, the authors describe the process for enlisting support from family and friends in order to achieve one's goals.

Your plan for change will be more likely to succeed if you have different levels of support. Start with your family members and friends. With whom do you feel comfortable sharing your plans for change? Give your support group specific instructions about how they can help; for instance, if you want to lose weight, you might ask your mom to stop sending you care packages loaded with cookies and other sweets. When your motivation wanes, call on your support group to cheer you on. If family members and friends can't provide the consistent support you need, consider joining a campus or community self-help group. Many such programs pair you up with a coach, mentor, or buddy you can call on for advice and caring.

| EXERCISE 6-1 | Reading: Using Chronological Order and Process |

Directions: Using either chronological order or process, put each of the following groups of sentences in the correct order. Write a number from 1 to 4 before each sentence, beginning with the topic sentence.

1. ___ Vassar College opened its doors in 1865, followed by Smith in 1871, Wellesley in 1877, and Bryn Mawr in 1880.

   ___ In spite of varied protests, the 1800s saw the admission of women into higher education.

   ___ Today the great majority of the more than 2,000 institutions of higher learning in the United States are coeducational.

   ___ Meanwhile, the University of Michigan had admitted women in 1870, and by the turn of the century coed colleges and universities were becoming commonplace.

   —adapted from Kephart and Jedlicka, *The Family, Society, and the Individual*, p. 332

2. ___ The blips meant one thing: high levels of radiation.

   ___ The technicians began a frantic search for the problem at their own plant, but they found nothing.

   ___ At 9:00 a.m. on Monday, April 28, 1986, technicians at a nuclear plant sixty miles north of Stockholm began to see alarming blips across their computer screens.

   ___ They concluded that the problem was not with their own facilities but perhaps with the Soviet Union's nuclear plant to the south, at Chernobyl.

   —adapted from Wallace, *Biology*, p. 572

3. ___ He soon had one-third of all Americans over 65 enrolled in his Townsend clubs, demanding that the federal government provide $200 a month for every person over 65—the equivalent of about $2,000 a month today.

   ___ The Great Depression made matters even worse, and in 1930 Francis Townsend, a social reformer, started a movement to rally older citizens.

   ___ Because the Townsend Plan was so expensive, Congress embraced President Franklin Roosevelt's more modest Social Security plan in June 1934.

   ___ In the 1920s, before Social Security provided an income for the aged, two-thirds of all citizens over 65 had no savings and could not support themselves.

   —adapted from Henslin, *Essentials of Sociology*, p. 272

EXERCISE 6-2

Reading: Analyzing Chronological Order/Process Paragraphs

Directions: Read each of the following paragraphs. Identify the topic and write a list of the actions, steps, or events described in each paragraph.

1.   Two important traditions are typically performed when new lodging properties are constructed. First, when the final floor is completed, an evergreen tree is placed on the top of the building. This act signifies that the building will rise no higher. It also symbolically ties the building safely to the ground through the "roots of the tree." The second important tradition is performed when the ceremonial ribbon is cut on opening day. At that time, the key to the front door is symbolically thrown onto the roof because it will never be used again. This is a symbol signifying that the building is more than just a building. It has become a place that will always be open to those who are seeking a home for the night or more appropriately a "home away from home."

—adapted from Cook et al., *Tourism: The Business of Travel*, p. 170

Topic: _____

Steps: _____

2.   In jury selection, the pool of potential jurors usually is selected from voter or automobile registration lists. Potential jurors are asked to fill out a questionnaire. Lawyers for each party and the judge can ask questions of prospective jurors to determine if they would be biased in their decision. Jurors can be "stricken for cause" if the court believes that the potential juror is too biased to render a fair verdict. Lawyers may also exclude a juror from sitting on a particular case without giving any reason for the dismissal. Once the appropriate number of jurors is selected (usually six to twelve jurors), they are impaneled to hear the case and are sworn in. The trial is ready to begin.

—adapted from Goldman and Cheeseman, *The Paralegal Professional*, p. 266

Topic: _____

Steps: _____
_____

3.   At 12:30 on the afternoon of May 1, 1915, the British steamship *Lusitania* set sail from New York to Liverpool. The passenger list of 1,257 was the largest since the outbreak of war in Europe in 1914. Six days later, the *Lusitania* reached the coast of Ireland. The passengers lounged on the deck. As if it were peacetime, the ship sailed straight ahead, with no zigzag maneuvers to throw off pursuit. But the submarine U-20 was there, and its commander, seeing a large ship, fired a single torpedo. Seconds after it hit, a boiler exploded and blew a hole in the *Lusitania's* side. The ship listed immediately, hindering the launching of lifeboats, and in eighteen minutes it sank. Nearly 1,200 people died, including 128 Americans. As the ship's bow lifted and went under, the U-20 commander for the first time read the name: *Lusitania*.

—adapted from Divine et al., *America Past and Present*, p. 596

Topic: _____

Steps: _____
_____

EXAMINING STUDENT WRITING

A good way to learn to read and write essays is to study a model. By examining the student essay below by Kate Atkinson, you will learn how to develop process and narrative paragraphs and write a process essay.

After reading the textbook excerpt in this chapter, Kate did some additional research on health issues and decided to write about the steps low-income people could take to achieve a healthier life.

Once Kate had decided which steps to include in her essay, she created an outline that included her thesis statement and her topic sentences, in the order she planned to use them. After considering her audience—her professor and possibly readers who could benefit from the information she had obtained—and her purpose—explaining the steps a person should follow to become healthier— she began to outline each paragraph, making sure she had plenty of supporting details and noting where she would need to provide additional information or explanation. We will look at the paragraphs she developed in more detail later in the chapter.

Kate Atkinson is a student at Beloit College in Wisconsin, where she is studying sociology and Russian. Kate wrote this essay for a sociology class in response to the article "How Being Poor Makes You Sick." As a sociology major, she has a particular interest in the health of the public and efforts that are being made to improve the overall health of all people, regardless of socioeconomic status.

Kate Atkinson

Title announces subject

How to Pursue a Healthier Lifestyle

Kate Atkinson

1   For many years, doctors' prescriptions have come in the form of pills, syrups, tonics, and topical creams, with occasional suggestions regarding obvious lifestyle changes. For example, it has been easy for doctors to tell patients who are overweight to go on a diet or patients who are chronically short of breath to stop smoking. Now, armed with advances in research and medical science, more doctors are helping patients understand the many factors that influence their health. In fact, some doctors have begun moving beyond a simple "prescription medication" approach toward a holistic type of treatment that looks not only at the patient's body, but also at his or her family, home, and community. In this new approach to leading a healthier life, doctors recommend diet and exercise, help patients manage their stress levels, and refer patients to community-based programs that are intended to raise the well-being of an entire city or neighborhood. For these patients, becoming healthier is not a simple linear process of taking a pill one day and feeling better the next; rather it is an ongoing process of managing their lives to make healthy choices that will benefit them in the short, medium, and long run.

Thesis statement

Topic sentence

Potential problem is identified

2   Many doctors believe that the two keys to health (for people who do not suffer from debilitating diseases or disabilities) are diet and exercise. Yet it is difficult for

Paragraph provides
background information

many people—especially poor people who live in neighborhoods filled with fast-food restaurants—to find healthy food or get the exercise they need. The Centers for Disease Control report that 69 percent of adults over the age of 20 in the United States are considered overweight or obese, thus increasing their likelihood of developing diabetes, heart disease, high cholesterol, and certain cancers. According to a study by Dr. Uri Ladabaum for the Stanford University School of Medicine, Americans have become increasingly sedentary over the past two decades, and their health is suffering as a result (Ladabaum). In the land of desk jobs and pizza parlors, many Americans find it difficult to find time to work exercise and healthy food choices into their daily lives.

Topic sentence presents the
first step

3   The first step that people must take in their quest for better health is to seek help from a medical professional who can help them achieve their goals. More and more doctors are becoming aware of the challenges of treating those individuals who have little money, and they are coming up with creative solutions to help them get the food and exercise they need to lead a healthier life. In her article "How Being Poor Makes You Sick," Olga Khazan highlights a recent experiment in Boston that seems promising. Some doctors have teamed up with Hubway, the city's bike-share program, to help people get more exercise. Doctors can prescribe bike shares at a significant discount to patients who can't afford one or who live in neighborhoods where a bike is likely to be stolen. These bikes have a sturdy design that will accommodate the overweight patients who need exercise the most. For example, the bikes have thicker handlebars than traditional bikes and wider seats for a more comfortable ride. They also have thick, puncture-resistant tires and a light that is powered by the pedals, thus making the bikes safer to ride at night. In terms of helping patients gain access to more nutritious foods, Khazan discusses the work of the Boston Medical Center, which operates a food pantry for families whose access to healthy foods is limited or nonexistent (Khazan).

Descriptive details give more
background

Topic sentence; transition
indicates chronological order

4   After seeking help with food and exercise, low-income individuals must also learn how to better manage the stress in their lives, for leading a healthier life isn't simply a matter of finding the time to ride a bicycle and eating fewer processed foods; it's also about managing stress. Science has shown conclusively that poverty causes illness, and stress underlies many of these illnesses. The anxiety caused by facing scarcity in one's daily life can actually change the way people think and lead to "toxic stress." In fact, one study determined that "the anxiety of living in poverty is a stronger predictor of mental health problems than going to war" (Khazan). Toxic stress makes it difficult to make good decisions and plan for the future. For all these reasons, doctors have begun to teach stress-reduction techniques, such as deep-breathing and relaxation methods. Because money is often a source of stress, doctors recommend free seminars that teach people how to manage and save money—for example, by setting up a budget, conserving on their utility bills, and buying generic medications (acetaminophen costs about $1.99 for 100 caplets, while Tylenol, which is just a brand name for acetaminophen, costs about $9.99 for 100 caplets).

Topic sentence presents
another step of the process

5   Another step that individuals may take in their pursuit of a healthier lifestyle is to seek help from community agencies. Many doctors are partnering with

community agencies to make healthy lifestyles a priority for the entire community, not just for the individuals they treat. When you visit a community-oriented doctor's office, you will often find pamphlets, leaflets, and advertisements for community agencies to which patients can turn for additional support. Many of these community agencies are overseen by doctors whose area of specialization is public health. In New York City, for example, the Department of Health and Mental Hygiene has started a public health poster campaign to get people to take the stairs more. The bright posters, which have been distributed in over 1,000 buildings in the city, tout slogans such as "Burn Calories, Not Electricity. Take the Stairs!" (Lichtman). The campaign acknowledges the fact that technological advancement has resulted in millions of workers sitting at computer screens in high-rise skyscrapers for eight to ten hours a day. As a result, not only have jobs become more sedentary, but also elevators and escalators have created an easier, quicker alternative to stairs. Climbing stairs burns calories and promotes muscle tone; riding an elevator does not. The campaign is part of the "active design" movement, which aims to design buildings that use less energy and promote health at the same time (Lichtman).

Topic sentence

Narrative paragraph

6   My cousin Rosalyn provides a real-world example of the steps a person can take to improve one's health, and her story shows how a patient, a doctor, and a community can all work together to promote a healthier lifestyle. Rosalyn is 32 years old and full of life. She was raised by a single mother who did her best, but they were never healthy eaters. As a result, Rosalyn has been very overweight since she was a little girl. About a year ago, Rosalyn was not feeling well, and although she did not have a lot of money to spend, she finally decided to go to a medical clinic for help. She was diagnosed as being very close to having Type 2 diabetes. Her doctor told her that the best way to prevent herself from becoming diabetic was to lose weight. He then took her down the hallway to meet with a nutrition and diet specialist. The specialist talked to a friend who works at a local health club that offers discounted memberships for people who have to lose weight for medical reasons. Embarking on an exercise regimen was a big step for Rosalyn. Realizing that she couldn't do it alone, she searched the Internet and found a local support group for people who are trying to prevent diabetes, and at the group she made several friends who made a pact to help one another keep exercising and keep losing weight. Rosalyn is now 30 pounds lighter, and her doctor says her blood sugar is under control!

Conclusion

7   Ultimately, Americans today face a number of obstacles in achieving good health, and the poor typically face more challenges than those who are middle-income or wealthy. Not everyone can afford a gym membership and three square meals a day. But as doctors begin to take a more holistic approach to health with all of their patients—the poor and the wealthy—it is likely that the overall health of Americans will improve. By leading patients through a series of steps that teach the importance of diet, exercise, stress management, and community support, doctors are leading the charge in giving patients the control they need to take charge of their health and their lives. Just as life is a journey, not a destination, so is healthy living a process, not simply an outcome.

Works Cited

Khazan, Olga. "How Being Poor Makes You Sick." *The Atlantic*, 21 May 2014, www.theatlantic.com/health/archive/2014/05/poverty-makes-you-sick/371241.

Ladabaum, Uri, et al. "Obesity, Abdominal Obesity, Physical Activity, and Caloric Intake in US Adults: 1988–2010." *The American Journal of Medicine*, vol. 127, no. 8, Aug. 2014, pp. 717-27, doi: 10.1016/j.amjmed.2014.02.026.

Lichtman, Flora. "One Step to Combat Obesity: Make Stairs More Attractive." *National Public Radio*, 4 Aug. 2014, www.npr.org/sections/health-shots/2014/08/04/337126235/one-step-to-combat-obesity-make-stairs-more-attractive.

"Obesity and Overweight." United States, Department of Health and Human Services, Centers for Disease Control and Prevention, www.cdc.gov/nchs/fastats/obesity-overweight.htm. Accessed 17 Apr. 2016.

Kate Atkinson. Reprinted by permission of the author.

Write Process Paragraphs

There are two types of process paragraphs—a "how-to" paragraph and a "how-it-works" paragraph.

- ■ **"How-to" paragraphs explain how something is done.** For example, they may explain how to change a flat tire, aid a choking victim, or locate a reference source in the library.

- ■ **"How-it-works" paragraphs explain how something operates or happens.** For example, they may explain the operation of a pump, how the human body regulates temperature, or how children acquire speech.

Here are examples of both types of paragraphs. The first explains the steps to follow when washing your hands in a medical environment. Read the paragraph, and study the idea map that follows.

"How-to" Paragraph

Washing your hands may seem a simple task, but in a medical environment it is your first defense against the spread of disease and infection, and must be done properly. Begin by removing all jewelry. Turn on the water using a paper towel, thus avoiding contact with contaminated faucets. Next, wet your hands under running water and squirt a dollop of liquid soap in the palm of your hand. Lather the soap, and work it over your hands for two minutes. Use a circular motion, since it creates friction that removes dirt and organisms. Keep your hands pointed downward, so water will not run onto your arms, creating further contamination. Use a brush to clean under your fingernails. Then rinse your hands, reapply soap, scrub for one minute, and rinse again thoroughly. Dry your hands using a paper towel. Finally, use a new dry paper towel to turn off the faucet, protecting your hands from contamination.

VISUALIZE IT!

Idea Map

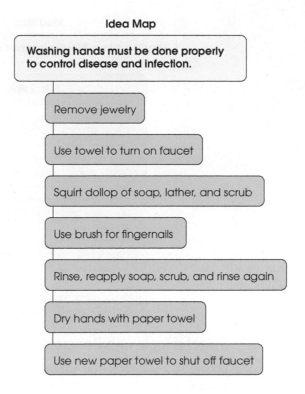

Washing hands must be done properly to control disease and infection.

Remove jewelry

Use towel to turn on faucet

Squirt dollop of soap, lather, and scrub

Use brush for fingernails

Rinse, reapply soap, scrub, and rinse again

Dry hands with paper towel

Use new paper towel to shut off faucet

The second paragraph is taken from Kate's essay, and it explains how doctors are helping low-income people to manage the stress that can underlie many illnesses. Be sure to study the idea map that follows.

"How-It-Works" Paragraph from Kate's Essay

After seeking help with food and exercise, low-income individuals must also learn how to better manage the stress in their lives, for leading a healthier life isn't simply a matter of finding the time to ride a bicycle and eating fewer processed foods; it's also about managing stress. Science has shown conclusively that poverty causes illness, and stress underlies many of these illnesses. The anxiety caused by facing scarcity in one's daily life can actually change the way people think and lead to "toxic stress." In fact, one study determined that "the anxiety of living in poverty is a stronger predictor of mental health problems than going to war" (Khazan). Toxic stress makes it difficult to make good decisions and plan for the future. For all these reasons, doctors have begun to teach stress-reduction techniques, such as deep-breathing and relaxation methods. Because money is often a source of stress, doctors recommend free seminars that teach people how to manage and save money—for example, by setting up a budget, conserving on their utility bills, and buying generic medications (acetaminophen costs about $1.99 for 100 caplets, while Tylenol, which is just a brand name for acetaminophen, costs about $9.99 for 100 caplets).

Idea Map

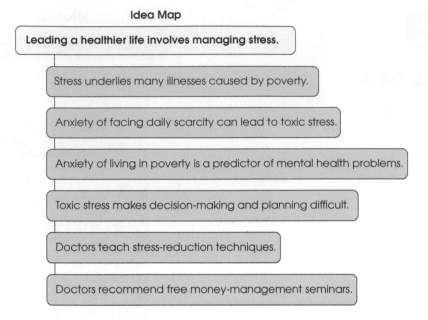

Leading a healthier life involves managing stress.

Stress underlies many illnesses caused by poverty.

Anxiety of facing daily scarcity can lead to toxic stress.

Anxiety of living in poverty is a predictor of mental health problems.

Toxic stress makes decision-making and planning difficult.

Doctors teach stress-reduction techniques.

Doctors recommend free money-management seminars.

Select a Topic and Generate Ideas

Before you can describe a process, you must be very familiar with it. You should have done it often or have a complete understanding of how it works. How-to paragraphs describe steps that occur in a specified order in order to complete a task. Begin developing your paragraph by listing these steps in the order in which they must occur. It is helpful to imagine yourself actually performing the task. For complicated how-it-works descriptions, draw diagrams and use them as guides in identifying the steps and putting them in the proper order.

EXERCISE 6-3

WRITING IN PROGRESS

Writing: Generating Ideas

Directions: Think of a process or procedure you are familiar with, or select one from the following list, and make a list of the steps involved.

1. How to find a good part-time job
2. How to waste time
3. How to learn to like _____
4. How the NFL football draft works
5. How to win at _____
6. How to make a marriage or relationship work
7. How to protect your right to privacy
8. How to improve your skill at _____
9. How to make your boss want to promote you

Write Your Topic Sentence

For a process paragraph, your topic sentence should accomplish two things:

■ **It should identify the process or procedure.**

■ **It should explain to your reader why familiarity with the process is useful or important (*why* he or she should learn about the process).** Your topic sentence should state a goal, offer a reason, or indicate what can be accomplished by using the process.

Here are a few examples of topic sentences that contain both of these important elements.

- Reading maps, a vital skill if you are orienteering, is a simple process, except for the final refolding.
- Because leisure reading encourages a positive attitude toward reading in general, every parent should know how to select worthwhile children's books.

Here are two of the topic sentences Kate wrote, once she had determined which steps for getting healthy she would write about.

- The first step that people must take in their quest for better health is to seek help from a medical professional who can help them achieve their goals.
- Another step that individuals may take in their pursuit of a healthier lifestyle is to seek help from community agencies.

Notice that each sentence includes the overall topic of the essay, becoming healthier, and then a clear point about how to achieve this goal.

EXERCISE 6-4

WORKING TOGETHER

Writing: Revising Topic Sentences

Directions: Working with a classmate, revise these topic sentences to make clear why the reader should learn the process.

1. Making pizza at home involves five steps.
2. Making a sales presentation requires good listening and speaking skills.
3. Bloodhounds that can locate criminals are remarkable creatures.
4. The dental hygienist shows patients how to use dental floss.
5. Here's how to use a search engine.

EXERCISE 6-5

WRITING IN PROGRESS

Writing a Topic Sentence

Directions: Write a topic sentence for the process you selected in Exercise 6-3.

Develop and Sequence Your Ideas: Consider Audience and Purpose

Because your readers may be unfamiliar with your topic, try to include helpful information that will enable them to understand (for how-it-works paragraphs) and follow or complete the process (for how-to paragraphs). Consider including the following:

- **Definitions.** Explain terms that may be unfamiliar. For example, explain the term *debride* when writing about wound care.

- **Needed equipment.** For how-to paragraphs, tell your readers what tools or supplies they will need to complete the process. For a how-to paragraph on caring for minor injuries at home, for example, list the supplies you will need (tweezers, antibacterial cream, and Band-Aids).

- **Pitfalls and problems.** Alert your reader about potential problems and places where confusion or error may occur. For instance, warn your readers that certain types of wounds require professional care and suggest where they should go to obtain it.

Tips for Developing an Effective Process Paragraph

1. **Place your topic sentence first.** This position provides your reader with a purpose for reading.

2. **Present the steps in a process in the order in which they happen.**

3. **Include only essential, necessary steps.** Avoid comments, opinions, or unnecessary information because they may confuse your reader.

4. **Assume that your reader is unfamiliar with your topic** (unless you know otherwise). Be sure to define unfamiliar terms and describe clearly any technical or specialized tools, procedures, or objects.

5. **Use a consistent point of view.** Use either the first person (*I*) or the second person (*you*) throughout. Do not switch between them.

EXERCISE 6-6

WRITING IN PROGRESS

Drafting a Process Paragraph

Directions: Draft a paragraph for the process you chose in Exercise 6-3.

Use Transitions

Transitions are particularly important in process paragraphs because they lead your reader from one step to the next. Specifically, they signal to your reader that the next step is about to begin. Look at paragraphs 3, 4, and 5 in Kate's essay (see the Examining Student Writing section of this chapter), and notice that each paragraph begins with a transition that indicates that a new step is about to follow.

Refer to the box Common Chronological Order and Process Transitions in the Read Chronological Order and Process section of this chapter for a list of commonly used transitional words and phrases that are useful in process paragraphs.

EXERCISE 6-7

WRITING IN PROGRESS

Revising Your Draft

Directions: Revise the draft you wrote for Exercise 6-6. Check transitional words and phrases and add them, as necessary, to make your ideas clearer.

Write Narrative Paragraphs

The technique of making a point by telling a story is called **narration**. Narration is *not* simply listing a series of events—"this happened and then that happened." Narration shapes and interprets events to make a point.

Below is Kate's first draft of paragraph 6 of her essay. Notice that it just lists the events relating to her cousin's story.

Kate's First Draft of Paragraph 6: A Series of Events

> My cousin Rosalyn provides an example of how to improve one's health. Rosalyn is 32 years old and was raised by a single mother. They were never healthy eaters, so Rosalyn has always been overweight. About a year ago, Rosalyn did not feel well and decided to go to a medical clinic for help. She was diagnosed as being very close to having Type II diabetes. Her doctor told her to lose weight and took her to meet with a nutrition and diet specialist. Rosalyn found a local support group for people who are trying to prevent diabetes. She is now 30 pounds lighter and her blood sugar is under control.

In the revised version that follows, she has created a narrative that tells a story and makes a point: working with her doctor and community, Rosalyn was able to significantly improve her health. In this version all the details and events work together to support that point, and Kate has added transitions to connect details and guide her reader.

Kate's Paragraph 6 Revised: A Narrative

> My cousin Rosalyn provides a real-world example of the steps a person can take to improve one's health, and her story shows how a patient, a doctor, and a community can all work together to promote a healthier lifestyle. Rosalyn is 32 years old and full of life. She was raised by a single mother who did her best, but they were never healthy eaters. As a result, Rosalyn has been very overweight since she was a little girl. About a year ago, Rosalyn was not feeling well, and although she did not have a lot of money to spend, she finally decided to go to a medical clinic for help. She was diagnosed as being very close to having Type 2 diabetes. Her doctor told her that the best way to prevent herself from becoming diabetic was to lose weight. He then took her down the hallway to meet with a nutrition and diet specialist. The specialist talked to a friend who works at a local health club that offers discounted memberships for people who have to lose weight for medical reasons. Embarking on an exercise regimen was a big step for Rosalyn. Realizing that she couldn't do it alone, she searched the Internet and found a local support group for people who are trying to prevent diabetes, and at the group she made several friends who made a pact to help one another keep exercising and keep losing weight. Rosalyn is now 30 pounds lighter and her doctor says her blood sugar is under control!

Study the model for a narrative paragraph (left) and then the map for Kate's revised paragraph (right).

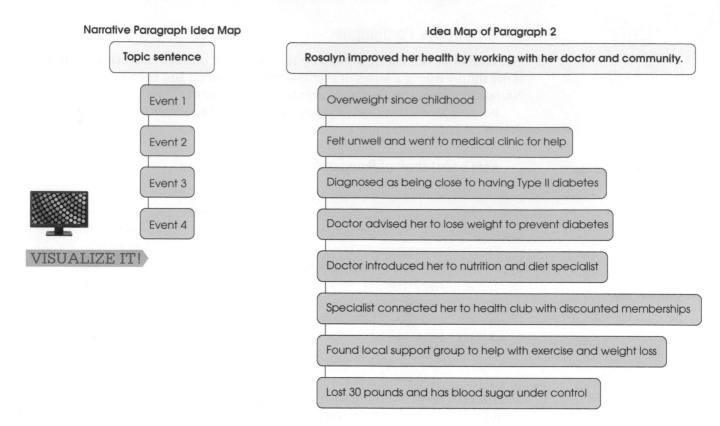

Narrative Paragraph Idea Map

Topic sentence

Event 1

Event 2

Event 3

Event 4

VISUALIZE IT!

Idea Map of Paragraph 2

Rosalyn improved her health by working with her doctor and community.

Overweight since childhood

Felt unwell and went to medical clinic for help

Diagnosed as being close to having Type II diabetes

Doctor advised her to lose weight to prevent diabetes

Doctor introduced her to nutrition and diet specialist

Specialist connected her to health club with discounted memberships

Found local support group to help with exercise and weight loss

Lost 30 pounds and has blood sugar under control

Writing a narrative involves selecting a topic, generating ideas, writing a topic sentence, sequencing and developing your ideas, considering your audience and purpose, and using transitions.

Select a Topic and Generate Ideas

For shorter pieces of writing, such as paragraphs and short essays, it is usually best to concentrate on a single event or experience. Otherwise, you will have too much information to cover, and you will not be able to include sufficient detail. To generate ideas for a narrative, make a list of events. Don't worry, at this point, about expressing each in sentence form or listing them in the order in which they occurred. Record in the margin any feelings you have about the events. Although you may not include them in the paragraph, they will be helpful in writing your topic sentence.

EXERCISE 6-8

WRITING IN PROGRESS

Writing: Generating Ideas

Directions: Assume you are taking an introductory psychology class this semester and your instructor has asked you to describe one of the following scenarios. Begin by making a list of the events that occurred.

1. A situation in which you observed or benefited from altruistic behavior (someone helping another person unselfishly, out of concern and compassion)

2. A vivid childhood memory

3. An experience in which you felt stress

4. A time when you were in danger and how you reacted

5. A situation in which you either rejected or gave in to peer pressure

Write Your Topic Sentence

A **topic sentence** states the main point of your paragraph. Your topic sentence should accomplish two things:

- It should identify your topic—the experience you are writing about.
- It should indicate your view or attitude toward that experience.

For example, suppose you are writing a paragraph about your mother falling and breaking her leg. Your point might be that she should have had a Med Alert system in place or that the medical system did an excellent job once they were involved. Here are a few possible topic sentences that indicate a point of view:

- My mother's recent fall and hours long wait for help convinced me that we needed to arrange for a Med Alert system to be installed.
- Although it was very unfortunate that my mother had to wait so long to get help after her fall, once the ambulance was called she received first class help.

Sometimes you may discover your view toward the experience as you are writing about it. For example, a student drafted the following paragraph about registering for her classes:

> Online registration was supposed to be simple, and it was for my friends. My registration was a nightmare. The computer in my advisor's office went down. When she tried to get back online, she learned the main system in the college had failed. We could not find out what classes were available; we could not check prerequisites; we could not even find the times my courses were being offered. We waited a while, and finally she told me to come back tomorrow. I was afraid that all the classes I wanted would be filled before I had a chance to register.

As she was writing, she realized she wished she had known more about the problems of the online registration process before she began. Then she wrote the following topic sentence:

> My first registration day at college might not have been so frustrating if someone had warned me about the possibility of computer system failures at the college and told me to take a hard copy of class listings with me.

EXERCISE 6-9

WRITING IN PROGRESS

Writing a Topic Sentence

Directions: For the experience or situation you chose in Exercise 6-8, write a topic sentence that expresses your attitude toward the experience.

Consider Your Audience and Purpose

When writing a narrative, your audience and your purpose will help you determine the following:

■ **How much explanation and which definitions to include about each event.** An audience that is unfamiliar with the event may need more detail than readers who are familiar with it. If you are writing about a baseball game and your audience is made up of baseball fans, then you will not need to explain rules, scoring, and so forth. However, if your audience is not made up of baseball enthusiasts, you may need to explain terms such as *batting average, grand slams*, and *errors*.

■ **How much background information to include.** If you are writing about an everyday event, such as a traffic jam, most readers need little explanation about it; however, if you are writing about a holiday such as Cinco de Mayo, you may need to provide your non-Mexican readers with some background about the holiday.

Sequence and Develop Your Ideas

The events in a narrative paragraph are usually arranged in **chronological** order— the order in which they happened. Sometimes, however, you may want to rearrange events to emphasize a point. If you do, make sure the sequence of events is clear enough for the reader to follow. To place the events in the correct sequence, review and number your list of events.

A clear, well-written narrative should provide sufficient detail to allow your readers to understand fully the situation about which you are writing. Try to answer for your readers most of the following questions:

When did it happen?	**What** events occurred?
Where did it happen?	**Why** did they happen?
Who was involved?	**How** did they happen?

Be sure to include only essential and relevant details. Other details will distract readers from the events you are describing.

EXERCISE 6-10

WRITING IN PROGRESS

Drafting a Paragraph

Directions: For the experience or situation you selected for Exercises 6-8 and 6-9, draft a paragraph describing the events in the order in which they occurred.

Use Transitions

As you know from Chapter 5, **transitions** are words that connect ideas to one another. Transitions in narratives lead your readers from one event to another. They make your writing easier to follow and clearly identify important parts of your narrative. Notice in Kate's Paragraph 6 Revised: A Narrative in the Write Narrative Paragraphs section of this chapter how the transitions connect and lead you through the narrative.

Here are some frequently used transitional words and phrases that connect events in a sequence:

COMMON NARRATIVE TRANSITIONS			
after	finally	later	therefore
after that	first	next	third
at last	following	second	while
during	in the beginning	then	

EXERCISE 6-11

WRITING IN PROGRESS

Revising Your Paragraph

Directions: Revise the paragraph you wrote for Exercise 6-10. Check it for transitional words and phrases and add them, as necessary, to make your ideas clearer.

Read and Write Description

■ GOAL 3
Read and write
description

What Is Description?

Descriptive writing creates an impression: it helps the reader visualize the subject. Here is a paragraph from a health textbook that vividly describes the symptoms of a panic attack.

It can happen at any time: while sleeping, while sitting in traffic, just before you deliver your class presentation. Suddenly and unexpectedly your heart starts to race, your face turns red, you can't catch your breath, you feel nauseated, you start to perspire, and you may feel like you are going to pass out. What you are experiencing could be a **panic attack**, a form of acute anxiety reaction that brings on an intense physical reaction. A panic attack typically starts abruptly, peaks within ten minutes, lasts about 30 minutes, and leaves the victim tired and drained. In addition to those described, symptoms can include trembling, dizziness, increased respiration rate, chills, hot flashes, shortness of breath, stomach cramping, chest pain, difficulty swallowing, and a sense of doom or impending death.

—adapted from Donatelle, *Health:
The Basics*, pp. 50–51

The topic of this paragraph is panic attacks, and the topic sentence makes the point that they cause a range of intense physical reactions. This feeling or attitude toward the topic is called the **dominant impression**. The remainder of the paragraph offers details that help the reader visualize the experience of a panic attack and helps explain the dominant impression. Each sentence contains vivid and descriptive words and phrases. These details are called **sensory details** because they appeal to the reader's senses—touch, sight, smell, taste, and hearing. You can visualize a descriptive paragraph as shown below left and the paragraph describing a panic attack as shown below right.

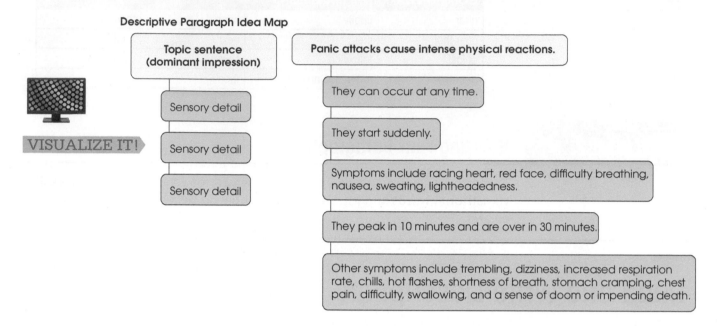

Descriptive Paragraph Idea Map

VISUALIZE IT!

Topic sentence (dominant impression)

Sensory detail

Sensory detail

Sensory detail

Panic attacks cause intense physical reactions.

They can occur at any time.

They start suddenly.

Symptoms include racing heart, red face, difficulty breathing, nausea, sweating, lightheadedness.

They peak in 10 minutes and are over in 30 minutes.

Other symptoms include trembling, dizziness, increased respiration rate, chills, hot flashes, shortness of breath, stomach cramping, chest pain, difficulty, swallowing, and a sense of doom or impending death.

Read Descriptive Paragraphs

A **descriptive paragraph** has three key features—a *dominant impression, sensory details,* and *descriptive language.* As you read descriptive writing, pay attention to each of these features.

- **The dominant impression.** The dominant impression is the one central idea the piece of writing presents. It is the single, main point that all of the details prove or support. To find the dominant impression, ask yourself, "What do all these details and descriptions, taken together, mean or suggest?" Often, this dominant impression is unstated; it is left for you to infer.

- **Sensory details.** Each detail is important, but the details, when added together, create the dominant impression. Be careful not to skip details, and for each, consider what it contributes to the overall meaning. For example, in the description of an accident scene, the detail that a car has a dented fender does not mean much. However, when added together with details of the seventy foot skid marks, shattered shop window, and major injuries to the driver and passenger, it helps create the impression that a serious auto accident has occurred.

- **Descriptive language. Descriptive language** uses words that create a visual or imaginary picture of the topic. As you read, be sure to read slowly enough to allow the language to "sink in." Mark and annotate particularly striking or unusual words and phrases. Stop and reflect, too, about why a particularly descriptive phrase was chosen.

When writing a descriptive paragraph, writers use transitions to orient their readers. Some common transitions are shown on the next page.

COMMON DESCRIPTION TRANSITIONS				
Spatial			**Least/most**	
above	inside	over	first	second
below	outside	beneath	primarily	secondarily
beside	under	on the other side	especially	particularly
across	nearby	to the right	also important	even more
facing	next to	to the west (north, etc.)	most important	of lesser importance
behind	to the left	in front of	above all	of greater importance

EXERCISE 6-12 Reading Descriptive Paragraphs

Directions: Underline the topic sentence in each of the following paragraphs and highlight particularly descriptive details.

1. Earth resembles an egg with a cracked shell. Earth's crust is thin and rigid, averaging 45 kilometers (28 miles) in thickness. Beneath this rigid crust, the rock is like a very thick fluid and is slowly deformed by movements within Earth. While far from the free-flowing substances we know as liquids, the rock just beneath the crust, known as the **mantle**, is fluid enough to move slowly along in convection currents, driven by heat within Earth's core.

    —Dahlman et al., *Introduction to Geography*, p. 90

2. Jackson was one of the most forceful and domineering American presidents. His most striking traits were an indomitable will, an intolerance of opposition, and a prickly pride that would not permit him to forgive or forget an insult or supposed act of betrayal. It is sometimes hard to determine whether principle or personal spite motivated his political actions. As a young man on the frontier, he had learned to fight his own battles. Violent in temper and action, he fought duels and battled the British, Spanish, and Indians with a zeal his critics found excessive. He was tough and resourceful, but he lacked the flexibility successful politicians usually show. Yet he generally got what he wanted.

    —Brands, *American Stories, A History of the United States*, p. 254

3. Sushi preparation is an art that involves careful selection of lovely and delicate ingredients (various seafood or vegetables, or both) to be arranged alongside vinegared rice. Sometimes, sushi is pressed into molds to form long fingers. A familiar style is made by arranging a layer of dried seaweed on a bamboo mat, and then artfully arranging the ingredients on the seaweed before rolling it carefully and tightly to enclose the filling as a long tube. Ultimately, the roll is sliced crosswise for lovely round slices with the seaweed serving as the outer covering.

    —McWilliams, *Food Around the World*, p. 357

Write Descriptive Paragraphs

Writing an effective descriptive paragraph involves considering audience and prupose, creating a dominant impression, using descriptive language, and organizing details and using transitions.

Write a Topic Sentence: Consider Audience and Purpose

The dominant impression of a descriptive paragraph is the overall sense you want to convey about your topic or main idea. It is expressed in your topic sentence, usually at the beginning of the paragraph. Suppose you are the music critic for your college newspaper and you are writing about a recent concert. If you felt the audience was appreciative, you might write the following topic sentence:

> The audience at the recent Rihanna concert appreciated and responded well to both the old and the new songs that Rihanna and her band performed.

Different dominant impressions of the audience are created, however, by the following topic sentences:

- The antics and immature behavior of the audience at the Rihanna concert ruined the event for me.
- Because many in the audience at the recent Rihanna concert were international students, I realized that her music has broad appeal.

If you have difficulty deciding on or thinking of a dominant impression for a topic, brainstorm a list of words to sum up your observations and reactions. For example, for the topic of your college health office, you might write things such as *friendly, helpful, smells like a doctor's office*, or *antiseptic and clean*. This brainstorming eventually could lead you to write about the health office as a place of impersonal, sterile sights and sounds that houses a warm and caring staff.

Descriptive writing is a useful skill. Even when you are not writing a purely descriptive paragraph, you will often need to describe a thing, place, event, experiment, or piece of art in order to make a point in a paragraph or essay. Here is an example from Kate's essay. The paragraph it is from (paragraph 3) is about seeking help from a doctor as a first step toward better health, but she uses description to explain how the bikes in the bike-sharing program are especially deigned to help those who need to use them. Notice the details that provide a vivid image of the specially constructed bikes.

> Some doctors have teamed up with Hubway, the city's bike-share program, to help people get more exercise. Doctors can prescribe bike shares at a significant discount to patients who can't afford one or who live in neighborhoods where a bike is likely to be stolen. These bikes have a sturdy design that will accommodate the overweight patients who need exercise the most. For example, the bikes have thicker handlebars than traditional bikes and wider seats for a more comfortable ride. They also have thick, puncture-resistant tires and a light that is powered by the pedals, thus making the bikes safer to ride at night.

EXERCISE 6-13   Writing Topic Sentences

Directions: For two of the following topics, write three topic sentences that each expresses a different dominant impression.

1. Professional athletes

    a. _____

    b. _____

    _____

    c. _____

    _____

2. A favorite food

    a. _____

    b. _____

    c. _____

3. A film or television show you have seen recently

    a. _____

    b. _____

    c. _____

EXERCISE 6-14   Writing a Topic Sentence That Creates a Dominant Impression

WRITING IN PROGRESS

Directions: Suppose you are taking a business course and are currently studying advertising. Your instructor has asked you to write a paragraph on one of the following topics. For the topic you select, use prewriting techniques to generate ideas and details. Then write a topic sentence that establishes a dominant impression.

1. Find an ad in a newspaper or magazine that contains a detailed scene. Describe the ad and explain whether it is effective. Make note of what props have been placed in the scene, what the models are wearing, and any other details that support your answer.

2. Choose an ad you think is effective. Write a paragraph describing the person you imagine is likely to buy the product. Explain how the ad would appeal to him or her.

3. Suppose you have developed a new product (frozen gourmet pizza or a long-lasting, multicolored highlighter, for example). Write a paragraph describing the product to a company that is interested in distributing it. Be sure to describe your product in a positive, appealing way.

Use Descriptive Language and Consider Audience and Purpose

Descriptive language is exact, colorful, and appealing. It enables the reader to envision what the writer has seen. Here are two sentences about a day in the woods. The first presents lifeless, factual information; the second describes what the writer saw and felt.

■ I walked in the woods.

■ I got up early my first morning camping at Yosemite National Park, and I walked through the aisles of ancient trees that towered two hundred feet above my head, breathing in the cool, clean, piney air.

You might think of descriptive language as the way the reader sees the world through the eyes of the writer.

One of the best ways to help your reader "see" is to use specific words, particularly those that draw on your reader's five senses, to provide sensory details. Use the following questions to help you uncover sensory details about your subject:

- **Touch:** What does it feel like? What is its texture? What is its weight? What is its temperature?

- **Smell:** Is it pleasant or unpleasant? Is it mild or strong? What other smells does it remind you of?

- **Taste:** Is it pleasant or unpleasant? Is it sweet, sour, salty, or bitter? What favorite flavors does it remind you of?

- **Sight:** What is the color? Is there a pattern? What size is it? What shape is it?

- **Sound:** Is it loud or soft? Is it high or low? Is it pleasant or unpleasant? What other sounds does it remind you of?

EXERCISE 6-15   Writing: Using Descriptive Language

Directions: For each of the following items, write a sentence that provides a vivid description and includes sensory details. The first one has been done for you. _____

1. An old coat _____
_____

2. A fast-food meal _____
_____

3. A bride (or groom) _____
_____

4. A sidewalk _____
_____

5. The dog behind a sign that warns "Guard Dog on Premises" _____
_____

All the details in a descriptive paragraph must be relevant to creating your dominant impression. Begin by visualizing the person, place, or experience and brainstorming a list of all the details you can think of that describe your topic. Your details should enable your reader to paint his or her own mental picture of the topic. Here's a list of details a student produced about working at movie theaters:

rude people	crowded concession stands	ticket stubs
fold-up seats	greasy smell of popcorn	lines at the box office
big screen	kids running up the aisle	sticky floors
headaches	squishy seats you sink into	always crowded
people whispering	people annoying others	dim lights
trash on floor	quieting people down	hurrying, pressure

If you have not formed a dominant impression, review your list, looking for a pattern to your details. What feeling or impression do many of them suggest? In the preceding list, many of the details convey the feeling of annoyance or dislike.

After you have decided on an impression, eliminate those details that do not support that impression. For example, the details about the screen, ticket stubs, seats, and lighting in the list above should be eliminated because they do not support the impression of annoyance.

Now read the student's paragraph on the topic of working at movie theaters. Notice how the student developed ideas from the earlier list. The paragraph still contains some details that do not directly support the dominant impression. Watch for them as you read.

Movie theaters are crowded, annoying places to work. I know. I have worked part-time in three different theaters over the past four years. I often leave work with a pounding headache and jangled nerves. There is always time pressure; shows must start on time. Customers are always in a rush. They arrive minutes before a show is about to begin yet demand to be waited on instantly at the concession stand. One regular and particularly annoying guy wearing baggy sweats and a ball cap once shouted: "Hey, over here! Get me a jumbo popcorn and a large Pepsi, and do it fast before I miss my show!" There was no "please," no "thank you," and no consideration of people standing in line ahead of him. This is just the kind of patron who carelessly spreads handfuls of these yellow kernels all over the theater floor and creates a sticky patch of spilled soda that someone has to clean up at the end of the evening. I do not enjoy assisting pushy people who are rude to others, either. Some customers talk loudly, complain about those in front of them, make obscene gestures, and generally make nuisances of themselves during the show. It is my job to quiet them down. I'd rather throw them out. There would be no "ifs," no "ands," and no "buts," just "you're out of here." Although you do get to see some free movies, working at a movie theater is far from the ideal job.

The detail about wanting to throw annoying people out should be deleted because it does not explain why a theater is a difficult place to work.

EXERCISE 6-16   Reading: Identifying Irrelevant Details

Directions: For the following topic sentences, circle the letters of the details that are not relevant to the dominant impression.

1. Gambling is addictive and can lead to financial disaster.

    a. Some people are unable to stop because they want to win just one more time.

    b. Money is exchanged for gambling chips at casinos.

    c. Las Vegas is a place where many people go to gamble.

    d. I know a gambler who often bets his entire paycheck on one horse race.

2. Officials at sporting events must be knowledgeable and skillful and have strong personalities.

    a. Officials must be able to ignore crowd reactions to unpopular calls.

    b. Officials must know the technicalities of the game.

    c. Officials must exert authority and win the respect of the players.

    d. The pay that officials receive is not in proportion to their responsibilities.

3. Starting a travel agency is a high-risk venture.

    a. The manager must have at least two years' experience.

    b. In most areas, there are many competing agencies.

    c. Profit from each individual client is low, so a great many clients are needed.

    d. Total start-up costs are high, ranging up to $150,000.

EXERCISE 6-17

WRITING IN PROGRESS

Writing a Descriptive Paragraph

Directions: Select one of the topic sentences you wrote for Exercise 6-13 or 6-14, determine your audience and purpose, and develop a descriptive paragraph for it.

Organize Details and Use Transitions

The arrangement of details in a description is determined by your topic and by the dominant impression you want to convey. You want to emphasize the most important details, making sure your readers can follow your description.

One of the most common arrangements is spatial organization. If you were describing your college campus, for example, you might start at one end and work toward the other. You might describe a stage set from left to right or a building from bottom to top.

If you were describing a person, you might work from head to toe. But you might prefer to follow another common arrangement: from least to most important. If the dominant impression you want to convey about a person's appearance is messiness, you might start with some characteristics that are only slightly messy (an untied shoe, perhaps) and work toward the most messy (a blue-jean jacket missing one sleeve, stained with paint, and covered with burrs).

Whichever arrangement you choose, transitional words and phrases will help your reader see how details relate to each other and where you are going. For a list of common transitional words and phrases for a spatial arrangement or a least-to-most-important organization, refer to the box on page 211.

EXERCISE 6-18

WRITING IN PROGRESS

Writing: Evaluating and Revising Your Paragraph

Directions: Evaluate the arrangement of details in the paragraph you wrote for Exercise 6-17. Does it support your dominant impression? Revise it and add transitional words and phrases, if needed.

READ AND REVISE

The following excerpt is from an essay called "Salto Waterfall Park." As you read the first two paragraphs, underline sensory details and descriptive language. Then read the last paragraph and revise it by replacing vague words with specific and vivid language and adding more details, based on your own experience of being in a beautiful park.

I was ten years old when my grandparents took me to Salto Waterfall Park in Jalisco, Mexico. It was a warm morning. The sky was endlessly blue, stretching for galaxies through the treetops. There was a great smell of flowers in the park. Roses were all across the bridge. The trees made a beautiful view with the mountains. The only sounds were those from lively mockingbirds, wind passing through the treetops, and the river as it flowed over the rocks.

I remember looking out at the water. It was so crystal clear that I could see exotic and tropical fishes of all different colors swim about with no worries. I strolled along the sidewalk, and every once in a while, I stopped to smell the fragrant white flowers of the coffee trees which were scattered throughout the park. People enjoyed hiking in the mountains while children played in the cascades. Older people watched their grandchildren swim in the water. I sat next to rocks covered with moss and read a book.

Although I am older, I still go to Salto Waterfall Park. It is a special place for me. The park still has a lake, the sound of the birds, and a nice landscape. The smell of flowers is the same. I will never forget my moments at the Salto Waterfall Park.

Read and Respond: A Student Essay

How to Pursue a Healthier Lifestyle

Kate Atkinson

Kate Atkinson

In the Examining Student Writing section of this chapter, you read "How to Pursue a Healthier Lifestyle" and examined various elements of the essay. Now it is time to take a closer look at the reading by responding to the questions that follow.

Examining Writing

1. Does the title of the essay clearly communicate the subject? Can you think of a more effective title?

2. What background information does Kate provide in her introduction? Is it sufficient?

3. Evaluate Kate's explanation of the process of pursuing a healthier lifestyle. Is the process clearly presented? How could she improve her explanation?

4. What other steps might someone take to make his or her lifestyle healthier? Write topic sentences for two additional paragraphs that Kate could have included in her essay.

5. Evaluate the conclusion of Kate's essay. Does she restate her thesis? Does she reemphasize the importance of the process?

Read And Respond: A Textbook Reading

Change Yourself, Change Your World
April Lynch, Barry Elmore, and Jerome Kotecki

In the Examining Professional Writing section of this chapter, you read the textbook excerpt "Change Yourself, Change Your World" and examined various elements of it. Now it is time to take a closer look at the reading by responding to the questions that follow.

Writing in Response to Reading

Checking Your Comprehension

Answer each of the following questions using complete sentences.

1. What is the meaning of the acronym SMART?
2. Why is it important to be informed about the behavior you want to change?
3. Provide an example (not mentioned in the reading) of a measurable goal.
4. Why must a goal be relevant?
5. What is *self-efficacy*?
6. How does *shaping* help you to accomplish your goal?
7. Does an *internal locus of control* or an *external locus of control* help you to overcome barriers? Explain your answer.
8. How do rewards help you achieve your goal?

Strengthening Your Vocabulary

Using the word's context, word parts, or a dictionary, write a brief definition of each of the following words as it is used in the reading.

1. components (paragraph 3) _____
2. reputable (paragraph 3) _____
3. aerobic (paragraph 3) _____
4. acronym (paragraph 4) _____
5. intervention (paragraph 5) _____
6. ecological (paragraph 7) _____
7. wanes (paragraph 9) _____
8. mentor (paragraph 9) _____
9. pact (paragraph 13) _____
10. affirm (paragraph 14) _____

Examining the Readings Using Idea Maps

Review the reading by filling in the missing parts of the following idea map.

VISUALIZE IT!

Title — **Change Yourself, Change Your World**

Thesis — Following a seven-step process can help you change your behavior and become a healthier individual.

Step 1: Get informed

Find facts at _____, _____, and _____

Step 2: _____

Specific: well-defined and clear

Measurable: _____

_____

_____

_____

_____

Use shaping to _____

_____

Sense of _____: the conviction that you can make changes and the ability to take action to do so

_____

Give specific instructions on how to help

_____

End-goal rewards and rewards for small steps

Step 7: Commit in writing

Sign a _____

Conclusion — Following a plan and believing in yourself will help you to make changes in your behavior and become a healthier person.

Thinking Critically: An Integrated Perspective

Get ready to write about the reading by discussing the following:

1. Discuss the title, introduction, and conclusion of the reading. How does the author capture your attention? How effective is the conclusion? What does the title mean?

2. What is the author's purpose in writing this selection? For what audience is this reading intended?

3. How has the author organized the details?

4. Discuss the types of supporting details the author uses to capture your attention and educate you about the steps in becoming a healthier person. What detail in the selection creates the most graphic visual picture in your mind?

5. What is the author's attitude toward the subject of this selection? Support your answer with details from the reading.

6. Discuss with your peers some other steps that you could take to become a healthier person.

7. The author speaks of the importance of "positive self-talk—thoughts that affirm your ability to change and acknowledge the help available to you from your environment." What do you think of this technique for overcoming discouragement? Do you agree that it is helpful? Why or why not? Have you ever used positive self-talk? What were the results? Reflect on this technique by writing a thoughtful entry in your journal.

8. What details do you notice in the two photographs that accompany this essay? What message does each photograph convey? How do the photographs support the author's thesis?

THINKING VISUALLY

Writing About the Reading

Paragraph Options

1. Develop a short-term goal that meets the SMART criteria. In a paragraph, explain how your goal meets each of the five qualities of an effective goal as outlined in Step 2 of "Change Yourself, Change Your World" in the Examining Professional Writing section of this chapter.

2. Using the tips for developing an effective process paragraph/essay as outlined in the Develop and Sequence Your Ideas: Consider Audience and Purpose section of this chapter, evaluate the reading selection. Write a paragraph in which you discuss how each of the five criteria are met or not met in the reading. Cite examples from the reading to support your ideas.

3. The concluding paragraph (paragraph 14 of "Change Yourself, Change Your World" in the Examining Professional Writing section of this chapter) in this selection is not a typical one for an essay. Your job is to improve it. Write a paragraph that effectively concludes this textbook selection.

Essay Options

4. The author writes about barriers that keep you from achieving your goal. What barriers or challenges in your life keep you from becoming a healthier individual? How can you overcome these barriers? Write an essay exploring these questions.

5. This reading focuses on changing behavior in order to become a healthier individual. How about you? What changes do you need to make in your life to improve your overall health and well-being? Do you plan to make these changes? If so, how will you go about it? If not, why not? Write an essay exploring your answers to these questions.

6. The reading mentions having a mentor to support you as you work your plan to become a healthier individual. A mentor is a wise and trusted individual who can provide guidance, advice, and support. Do you have a mentor in your life? If so, who is your mentor and how does he or she provide guidance to you? Write an essay in which you describe this individual and the role he or she plays in your life.

Making Connections between the Readings

Use both "How to Pursue a Healthier Lifestyle" and "Change Yourself, Change Your World" to write in response to one of the following prompts.

1. "Change Yourself, Change Your World" could possibly be the title for *both* of the reading selections. In a paragraph, explain how this title relates to both essays. Be sure to use examples from the readings to support your main points.

2. In an essay, discuss the similarities and differences in the two readings. "How to Pursue a Healthier Lifestyle" focuses on the health needs of low-income people. How do you think the author of this reading selection would respond to the information presented in "Change Yourself, Change Your World"? Be sure to cite examples from each of the readings.

3. In an essay, compare and/or contrast the author's tone, organization, and attitude toward the topic in the two readings.

4. March is National Nutrition Month. In an essay, discuss how you think the two authors would celebrate this month. Be sure to use information from each reading to support your ideas.

SELF-TEST SUMMARY

To test yourself, cover the Answer column with a sheet of paper and answer each question in the left column. Evaluate each of your answers as you work by sliding the paper down and comparing your answer with what is printed in the Answer column.

QUESTION	ANSWER
■ **GOAL 1** Understand patterns of organization What are patterns of organization?	Patterns of organization provide a framework within which to organize and develop your ideas and help you present them in a clear, logical manner.

(continued)

QUESTION	ANSWER
■ **GOAL 2** Read and write chronological order, process, and narration What are time sequence patterns?	Time sequence patterns include chronological order, process, and narration. *Chronological order* is a pattern in which events are presented in order according to when they occurred, beginning with the first event. *Process* is a pattern used to explain how something is done or how something works. *Narration* uses time sequence to tell a story.
How do you recognize that an author is using chronological or process patterns?	Writers often use time transitions when they write using a chronological or process pattern. (See Common Chronological Order and Process Transitions in the Read Chronological Order and Process section of this chapter for a list of time transitions.)
What are two types of process paragraphs?	A "how-to" paragraph explains how something is done, and a "how-it-works" paragraph explains how something operates or happens.
How do you develop effective process paragraphs?	To develop process paragraphs, place your topic sentence first, present the steps in a process in the order in which they happen, include only essential steps, assume that your reader is unfamiliar with your topic, and use a consistent point of view.
What is involved in writing a narrative?	Writing a narrative involves selecting a topic, generating ideas, writing a topic sentence, sequencing and developing your ideas, considering your audience and purpose, and using transitions. Narration shapes and interprets events to make a point.
■ **GOAL 3** Read and write description What is descriptive writing?	Descriptive writing creates an impression by helping the reader visualize the subject.
How do you read descriptive paragraphs?	As you read descriptive paragraphs, pay attention to the dominant impression, sensory details, and descriptive language.
What is involved in writing a descriptive paragraph?	Writing an effective descriptive paragraph involves creating a dominant impression, selecting sensory details, using descriptive language, organizing details, and using transitions.

Patterns of Organization: Example, Cause and Effect, and Comparison and Contrast

LEARNING
GOALS

Learn how to ...

■ GOAL 1
Read and write
example

■ GOAL 2
Read and write cause
and effect

■ GOAL 3
Read and write
comparison and
contrast

Savannah1969/Fotolia

THINK About It!

Suppose you had to research and write a paragraph about playing music. How would you organize your ideas? One option would be to give examples of the type of instruments people enjoy playing. Another would be to explain why people enjoy playing music. A third option would be to compare or contrast the different types of music people play. Regardless of which option you would choose, your paragraph would follow a logical method of organization. In this chapter, you will learn to read and write three methods of organization: *example, cause and effect*, and *comparison and contrast*. You will also explore the theme of creative expression by examining a professional essay on the benefits of listening to music and a student essay on the relationship between poetry and healing.

Why Use Patterns of Organization?

Patterns of organization are useful to both readers and writers. As we discussed in Chapter 6, patterns help readers comprehend and recall what they read, and they help writers organize and present their ideas clearly.

Patterns are useful in a variety of academic situations:

- Professors use patterns to organize their lectures. If you recognize the patterns used to organize a lecture, you will be able to understand and remember it more easily.
- Patterns will help you understand and prepare class assignments, including lab reports, summaries, and case studies.
- Essay exams often contain questions that require you to use one or more patterns. Patterns can also help you present a well-organized, easy-to-read answer.
- Patterns will help you organize your speech, both in formal presentations and in classroom discussions.

Chapter Theme: The Benefits of Creative Expression

In this chapter, you will read both a professional and a student essay on the benefits of creative expression. Do you remember when you used to color, draw, paint, sing, or act when you were a young child? And then as a teenager, perhaps you wrote a song, played an instrument, or joined a band? Unfortunately, many people abandon these expressions of creativity when they get older and become more aware and concerned about being judged by others. In some ways, technology has become a barrier to creativity, but in other ways, it has enhanced it. As you read the essays in this chapter, focus on the benefits of creative expression presented by the authors. Also, annotate each reading, recording your own thoughts on the issue, to be prepared to write about it or a related issue.

Look it up!

Use the search engine on your smartphone (or work with a classmate who has a smartphone) to look up "creativity and the brain." Review a few entries. Based on what you read, how does creativity work within the brain? Write a few sentences about ways that you express yourself (or would like to) creatively.

EXAMINING PROFESSIONAL WRITING

The following selection originally appeared in a music textbook. In the selection, the authors explore the effects of music on the human brain. It will be used in this chapter as an example of good writing and to give you practice with reading patterns.

Thinking Before Reading

Follow these steps before you read:

1. Preview the reading, using the steps discussed in the Pre-Reading Strategies section of Chapter 1.
2. Connect the reading to your own experience by answering the following questions:
   a. How do you feel when you listen to music?
   b. What types of music do you enjoy? Why?
3. Highlight and annotate as you read.

The Benefits of Listening to Music

Steven Cornelius and Mary Natvig

1   Ninety-three-year-old Veva Campbell slumps wordlessly in her wheelchair. A victim of Alzheimer's disease, she has not spoken, walked, fed herself, or recognized friends and family for over two years. This afternoon, her granddaughter, an out-of-town musician, comes to visit. There is nothing to say or do, so she pulls out her violin and begins to play. Miraculously, Mrs. Campbell sits up and begins singing along to the traditional hymns and old-time songs she recognizes from her youth. When the music stops, Mrs. Campbell retreats back into silence.

2   Our story is not apocryphal. Mrs. Campbell was the coauthor's grandmother. And this demonstration of music's power, remarkable as it may be, is not an isolated example. All over the world music unites and heals, transforms and inspires. This appears to have been the case since the beginning of civilization.

Music and the Brain

3   The foundation of musical experience resides deep within the mind. Medical science is just beginning to document these complexities. We know, for example, that severe stutterers, even those unable to get out single spoken words, can sometimes perfectly sing entire sentences. We know that by setting instructions to song, sufferers of autism can learn to execute sequential tasks otherwise far beyond their reach. And we know that when medication fails, those with the neuropsychiatric disorder Tourette syndrome can successfully use drum circles to calm their tics.

4   There is much to learn. Scientists cannot explain the case of Tony Cicoria, a middle-aged physician who, after being struck by lightning, suddenly developed a passion and gift for playing the piano and composing. Nor can they explain the case of Clive Wearing, a British amnesia victim who, despite being able to remember just a few seconds into the past, can still play the piano, read music, and even direct choral rehearsals.

5   The human brain seems to be programmed for song. So fundamental is the human capacity for music that it may have evolved even before speech. Physiologists have shown that a mother's lullaby does double duty by lowering a child's arousal levels while simultaneously increasing the child's ability to focus attention. Music therapists have found that listening to music induces the release

of pleasure-producing endorphins that both lower blood pressure and ease the sensation of physical pain. Social scientists believe that music, by bringing people together to perform and listen, may have provided an early model for social co-operation, cohesion, and even reproductive success. If this is correct, then music would seem to be a fundamental building block in the development of culture.

6   Attentive listening is good for the brain. It helps us organize our thinking, give shape to our consciousness, and focus our ideas. These phenomena seem to happen for a variety of reasons and in a number of ways. Our involuntary nervous system—including heart rate, brain waves, and other basic bodily functions—automatically entrains to the sounds we hear. We also respond to music's emotional qualities. Lovely melodies softly played relax us, whereas beating drums and searing trumpets excite us. A favorite song recalls times gone by, whereas the sounds of a national anthem invite us to reflect upon our identity.

7   Music helps structure the analytical mind. Psychological studies suggest that musical training improves one's organizational skills and can even have a positive effect on IQ. Indeed, scientists hypothesize that while performing, musicians are actually engaged in high-powered brain calisthenics. These skills transfer to other areas of life.

Did You Know?

EARS, BRAIN, AND FINGERS

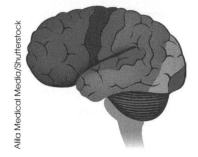

Alila Medical Media/Shutterstock

The human brain, highlighting the auditory cortex.
The auditory cortex (highlighted here in dark blue), which grows with musical training, can be up to 130 percent larger in musicians than in nonmusicians. Brains grow when challenged with physical tasks as well. The part of the brain that governs a violinist's left-hand fingers will be larger than the part that governs the right-hand fingers. Presumably, Jimi Hendrix, who played the guitar "backwards," would have shown more brain growth for the right-hand fingers.

8   Clearly, active musical experience affects consciousness in profound ways. But what does this mean for you? What if you do not play music, sing, or dance? Research shows that one need not perform to reap music's benefits. Simply engaging in *active* listening is enough to set the brain in high gear. And the best part of all this is that the effects of listening skills are cumulative. The better you learn to listen today, the more listening techniques you will have available tomorrow.

—Cornelius and Natvig, *Music: A Social Experience*, pp. 2–3

Reading and Writing Example

■ GOAL 1
Read and write example

Examples help to illustrate and explain what we read and write.

What Is an Example?

Examples are specific instances or situations that explain a general idea or statement. Peaches and plums are examples of fruit. Presidents' Day and Veterans Day are examples of national holidays. Here are a few sample general statements, along with specific examples that illustrate them. In each case, the examples make the general statement clear, understandable, and believable by giving specific illustrations or supporting details.

GENERAL STATEMENT	EXAMPLES
I had an exhausting day.	■ I had two exams.
	■ I worked four hours.
	■ I swam 20 laps in the pool.
	■ I did three loads of laundry.
Research studies demonstrate that reading aloud to children improves their reading skills.	■ Whitehurst (2007) found that reading picture books to children improved their vocabulary.
	■ Crain-Thompson and Dale (2006) reported that reading aloud to language-delayed children improved their reading ability.

Example paragraphs consist of examples that support the topic sentence. You can visualize an example paragraph as shown below:

VISUALIZE IT!

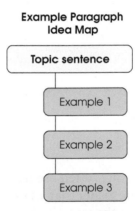

**Example Paragraph
Idea Map**

Topic sentence

Example 1

Example 2

Example 3

Read Examples

The **example** pattern uses specific instances or detailed situations to explain an idea or concept. One of the clearest ways to explain something is to give an example. This is especially true when a subject is unfamiliar. Suppose, for instance, that your younger brother asks you to explain what anthropology is. You might give him examples of the topics you study, such as apes and early humans, and the development of modern humans. Through examples, your brother would get a fairly good idea of what anthropology is all about.

When organizing a paragraph, a writer often states the main idea first and then follows it with one or more examples. In a longer piece of writing, a separate paragraph may be used for each example.

Notice how the example pattern is developed in paragraph 3 from "The Benefits of Listening to Music":

> The foundation of musical experience resides deep within the mind. Medical science is just beginning to document these complexities. We know, for example, that severe stutterers, even those unable to get out single spoken words, can sometimes perfectly sing entire sentences. We know that by setting instructions to song, sufferers of autism can learn to execute sequential tasks otherwise far beyond their reach. And we know that when medication fails, those with the neuropsychiatric disorder Tourette syndrome can successfully use drum circles to calm their tics.

In this paragraph, the writer uses the examples of severe stutterers, sufferers of autism, and people with Tourette syndrome to illustrate that the foundation of musical experience resides in the human mind. You could visualize the paragraph as follows:

VISUALIZE IT!

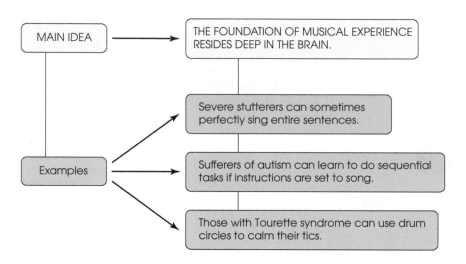

Writers often use transitional words—*for example, for instance*, or *such as*—to signal the reader that an example is to follow. In the paragraph you just read, the writers use the transitional phrase "for example" and repeat the phrase "we know" to indicate that an example is to follow.

EXERCISE 7-1

WORKING
TOGETHER

Writing: Brainstorming Examples

Directions: Working with another student, brainstorm a list of examples to illustrate one of the following statements:

1. Effective teaching involves caring about students.
2. Dogs (or cats) make good companions.
3. Volunteerism has many benefits.

EXERCISE 7-2   Reading: Analyzing the Example Pattern

Directions: The following paragraphs, all of which are about stress, use the example pattern. Read each of them and answer the questions that follow.

A.   Any single event or situation by itself may not cause stress. But, if you experience several mildly disturbing situations at the same time, you may find yourself under stress. For instance, getting a low grade on a biology lab report by itself may not be stressful, but if it occurred the same week during which your car "died," you argued with a close friend, and you discovered your checking account was overdrawn, then it may contribute to stress.

1. What transition does the writer use to introduce the examples?

_____

2. List the four examples the writer provides as possible causes of stress.

a. _____

b. _____

c. _____

d. _____

B.   Every time you make a major change in your life, you are susceptible to stress. Major changes include a new job or career, marriage, divorce, the birth of a child, or the death of someone close. Beginning college is a major life change. Try not to create multiple simultaneous life changes, which multiply the potential for stress.

3. Does the topic sentence occur first, second, or last?

_____

4. The writer gives six examples of major changes. List them briefly.

a. _____   d. _____

b. _____   e. _____

c. _____   f. _____

C.   Because you probably depend on your job to pay part or all of your college expenses, your job is important to you and you feel pressure to perform well in order to keep it. Some jobs are more stressful than others. Those, for example, in which you work under constant time pressure tend to be stressful. Jobs that must be performed in loud, noisy, crowded, or unpleasant conditions—a hot kitchen, a noisy machine shop, with co-workers who don't do their share—can be stressful. Consider changing jobs if you are working in very stressful conditions.

5. Does the topic sentence occur first, second, or last?

_____

6. What transition does the writer use to introduce the first type of job?

_____

7. To help you understand "jobs that must be performed in loud, noisy, crowded, or unpleasant conditions," the writer provides three examples. List these examples in the diagram below.

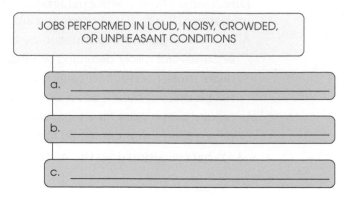

JOBS PERFORMED IN LOUD, NOISY, CROWDED, OR UNPLEASANT CONDITIONS

a. _____

b. _____

c. _____

D.   People who respond well to stress focus on doing the best they can, not on how they might fail. It's not that the potential problems have disappeared—it's that successful people believe in the possibility of success. Once success is seen as possible, you can focus on completing the task to the best of your ability. For example, instead of saying "I cannot do this on time," leave out the word *not*. Ask yourself: "How *can* I finish this task on time?" and "How well *can* I do this?"

8. Does the topic sentence occur first, second, or last?

_____

9. What transition does the author use to introduce the example?

_____

10. What does the example tell you to do?

_____

EXAMINING STUDENT WRITING

Amanda Keithley

A good way to learn to read and write essays is to study a model. By examining the student essay below by Amanda Keithley, you will learn how to develop example and cause and effect paragraphs for use in your writing.

Amanda Keithley is a student at Seattle Pacific University. She is majoring in English literature with a minor in global and urban ministry. After graduation, she plans to walk the Camino de Santiago pilgrimage and travel for a few months in Mediterranean countries before she settles on a career. The English composition assignment she responded to directed her to write an example essay.

Poetry and Healing

Amanda Keithley

Title suggests the subject

1   When asked to write poetry, some people break out in a nervous sweat while others rejoice at the opportunity. Many people think of poetry as an art form reserved for only the most creative writers. Others, frustrated by years of studying it in school and struggling to ever extract an ounce of meaning from abstract words, cannot imagine that there could be any benefit or pleasure derived from writing it. In reality, the hidden meanings that some find frustrating are actually the beauty of the art form. Poetry often expresses a wide range of meanings and can therefore be interpreted in many ways. Poetry allows people to express both their suffering and their joy in a safe space where their voices can be heard. Through poetry, people are able to write about and work through difficult topics such as death, drugs, alcohol, prostitution, injustice, eating disorders, poverty, abuse, and abandonment. The act of writing poetry can be therapeutic, life giving, and ultimately healing.

Thesis statement
Topic sentence makes first point

2   One way poetry can be healing is through writing with other people. As a result of joining with others who share an interest in poetry, writers can find a safe place for their voices to be heard without fear of criticism or shame. Not only can the group experience provide listening ears, but it also can provide inspiration. When a writer gets stuck and the words won't come, the group can ask questions, suggest ideas, encourage, and inspire creativity. Consequently, a group poetry writing session can function similarly to a one-on-one counseling session in which other writers enable a person to think through the issue, put words to feelings, and begin a process that will ultimately lead to healing.

Transitional phrase moves reader from one example to another

Examples of how writing with others is healing

Topic sentence makes second point

3   Reading one's poetry to others can have a healing effect. When a poet shares her poetry aloud with those she trusts, she is able to express emotions, thoughts, and feelings in a safe place that is free from judgment. The act of creating something meaningful out of sorrow, and then sharing this creation with one's peers, is a liberating and healing experience. Emotions that have long been bottled up deep inside are set free when one speaks the words associated with them, and these emotions are no longer silenced. Sharing a difficult story, such as the death of a loved one or a broken relationship, through poetry with one's peers allows one to regain some control over one's life and move forward. As painful as it may be, remembering the death of a parent and putting words to one's sorrow, can bring memories of happy times to the surface and lead to the path of healing. Remembering a failed relationship and being brave enough to write about it and share it can lead to a greater understanding of the problem and move one closer to restoration.

Specific examples of how reading aloud can lead to healing

Transitional phrase guides reader to third point
Topic sentence

4   Although writing and sharing poetry with others is beneficial, a group is not essential to find healing through writing poetry. The functions of poetry are limitless. Poetry is healing, remembering, dancing, chanting, and crying. Poetry can be intensely personal, in fact, too personal to share with others, but the act of writing poetry can do the impossible and reach to the unknowable. Everyday things that might normally seem terrible all of a sudden can sound better when written as poetry. For instance, seeing something positive in a difficult situation can move one past the ugly and onto the path of healing and wholeness. This act of creation

brings healing through making something out of the remembrance of loss and pain. By remembering the suffering, one can find freedom and wholeness. Remembering sorrow, so as not to forget it, is also part of the journey of healing. By reflecting and discovering the sorrow, one is able to take a devastating event and make it better by writing a poem about the experience. For example, writing poetry and emptying oneself of the emotions surrounding an abusive relationship can move one to face fears, admit to insecurities, deal with feelings of rejection and hatred, and gain new insight into the situation as one moves forward with hope and a lighter burden.

Conclusion

5   The act of writing poetry brings hope and healing because even the darkest and deepest suffering can be lightened in a poem. To the poets writing on their own and the ones who participate in writing groups, hope looks like the face of a young girl who is pregnant, homeless, and writes beautiful poems. Hope is in the hand of an Albanian immigrant who writes about injustice and how he wants to change the world so people will not have to endure the hardships he has endured. Hope is the voice of a young man who was abused as a child and now lives on the streets, but who writes poetry and sometimes sings his poems in a tender and gentle voice. Hope is the sound of people clapping after a poem is read or the silence that follows a poem that is too beautiful and moving for words. Hope is the willingness of a man or woman to share his or her story no matter how scary, pain filled, or tragic, it may be. Hope is the healing power of poetry.

Write Examples

Writing paragraphs using examples involves writing a clear topic sentence, selecting appropriate and sufficient examples, arranging your details, and using transitions.

Write Your Topic Sentence

You must create a topic sentence before you can generate examples to support it. Consider what you want to say about your topic and what your main point or fresh insight is. From this main idea, compose a first draft of a topic sentence. Be sure it states your topic and the point you want to make about it. (See Chapter 4, p. 131, if necessary, for a review of developing your point.) You will probably want to revise your topic sentence once you've written the paragraph, but for now, use it as the basis for gathering examples.

EXERCISE 7-3

WRITING IN PROGRESS

Writing a Topic Sentence

Directions: Select one of the topics listed below and write a topic sentence for it.

1. Slang language
2. Daily hassles or aggravations
3. The needs of infants or young children
4. Overcommercialization of holidays
5. Irresponsible behavior of crowds or individuals at public events

Select Appropriate and Sufficient Examples

Use brainstorming to create a list of as many examples as you can think of to support your topic sentence. For paragraph 3, Amanda wanted to provide examples of the different ways she believes poetry can have a healing. effect. Her working topic sentence was "Poetry can have a healing effect," and she brainstormed the following list of examples to support it:

- Sharing poetry with people you trust allows you to express emotions, thoughts, and feelings.
- Sharing the death of a loved one or a broken relationship can help you move forward.
- Sharing poems about the difficult breakup with my partner really helped me deal with the loss.
- Writing about what went wrong in a relationship is very brave and can help you understand what happened and move closer to restoration.

Here is the paragraph she wrote using this list:

Reading one's poetry to others can have a healing effect. When a poet shares her poetry aloud with those she trusts, she is able to express emotions, thoughts, and feelings in a safe place that is free from judgment. The act of creating something meaningful out of sorrow, and then sharing this creation with one's peers, is a liberating and healing experience. Emotions that have long been bottled up deep inside are set free when one speaks the words associated with them, and these emotions are no longer silenced. Sharing a difficult story, such as the death of a loved one or a broken relationship, through poetry with one's peers allows one to regain some control over one's life and move forward. As painful as it may be, remembering the death of a parent and putting words to one's sorrow, can bring memories of happy times to the surface and lead to the path of healing. Remembering a failed relationship and being brave enough to write about it and share it can lead to a greater understanding of the problem and move one closer to restoration.

In Amanda's paragraph, you probably noticed that she used some of her brainstormed examples and not others. She also added new examples. You will probably want to select two to four examples from your list for an average-length paragraph, but the number will vary depending on your purpose for writing. When you revise, you may decide to cut some examples and add ones that better support your point.

Use the following guidelines in selecting details to include.

Guidelines for Selecting Details

- **Each example should illustrate the idea stated in your topic sentence, and you should draw connections between your examples and your main point.** If you find that your examples do not clarify your main point or seem to illustrate something different, your topic is too broad. Narrow your topic, using the suggestions in Chapter 4, page 134. You also want to ensure that you draw connections between your examples and main point so readers understand why you chose them, as Amanda does in paragraph 4 of her essay. Her topic sentence states that there are unlimited functions of poetry, and then she lists several examples and explains how each one supports this point.

> Although writing and sharing poetry with others is beneficial, a group is not essential to find healing through writing poetry. The functions of poetry are limitless. Poetry is healing, remembering, dancing, chanting, and crying. Poetry can be intensely personal, in fact, too personal to share with others, but the act of writing poetry can do the impossible and reach to the unknowable. Everyday things that might normally seem terrible all of a sudden can sound better when written as poetry. For instance, seeing something positive in a difficult situation can move one past the ugly and onto the path of healing and wholeness. This act of creation brings healing through making something out of the remembrance of loss and pain. By remembering the suffering, one can find freedom and wholeness. Remembering sorrow, so as not to forget it, is also part of the journey of healing. By reflecting and discovering the sorrow, one is able to take a devastating event and make it better by writing a poem about the experience. For example, writing poetry and emptying oneself of the emotions surrounding an abusive relationship can move one to face fears, admit to insecurities, deal with feelings of rejection and hatred, and gain new insight into the situation as one moves forward with hope and a lighter burden.

- **Each example should be as specific and vivid as possible, accurately describing an incident or situation.** Suppose your topic sentence is "Celebrities are not reliable sources of information about a product because they are getting paid to praise it." For your first example you write: "Many sports stars are paid to appear in TV commercials." "Many sports stars" is too general. To be convincing, your example has to name specific athletes and products or sponsors: "Tom Brady, star quarterback for the Patriots, endorses UGG Boots and Under Armour; LeBron James, basketball superstar, endorses Nike products."

- **Choose a sufficient number of examples to make your point understandable.** The number you need depends on the complexity of the topic and your reader's familiarity with it. One example is sufficient only if it is well developed. The more difficult and unfamiliar the topic, the more examples you will need. For instance, if you are writing about how poor service at a restaurant can be viewed as an exercise in patience, two examples may be sufficient: your long wait and your rude waiter. However, if you are writing about test anxiety as a symptom of poor study habits, you probably would need several examples: the need to organize one's time, set realistic goals, practice relaxation techniques, and work on self-esteem.

EXERCISE 7-4   Writing: Brainstorm Examples

WRITING IN PROGRESS

Directions: Brainstorm a list of examples that illustrate the topic sentence you wrote in Exercise 7-3.

NEED TO KNOW

Choosing Appropriate Examples

Use the following guidelines in choosing examples:

- **Make sure your example illustrates your topic sentence clearly.** Do not choose an example that is complicated or has too many parts; your readers may not be able to see the connection to your topic sentence clearly.

- **Choose examples that your readers are familiar with and understand.** If you choose an example that is out of the realm of your readers' experience, the example will not help them understand your main point.

- **Choose interesting, original examples.** Your readers are more likely to pay attention to them.

- **Vary your examples.** If you are giving several examples, choose a wide range from different times, places, people, and so on.

- **Choose typical examples.** Avoid outrageous or exaggerated examples that do not accurately represent the situation.

Arrange Your Details

Once you have selected examples to include, arrange your ideas in a logical sequence. Here are a few possibilities:

- **Arrange the examples chronologically.** If some examples are old and others more recent, you might begin with the older examples and then move to the more current ones.

- **Arrange the examples from most to least familiar.** If some examples are more detailed or technical, and therefore likely to be unfamiliar to your reader, place them after more familiar examples.

- **Arrange the examples from least to most important.** You may want to begin with less convincing examples and finish with the strongest, most convincing example, thereby leaving your reader with a strong final impression.

- **Arrange the examples in the order suggested by the topic sentence.**

Use Transitions

Transitional words and phrases are needed in example paragraphs, both to signal to your reader that you are offering an example and to signal that you are moving from one example to another. Notice in the paragraph on page 234 how the transitions connect the examples and make them easy to follow. Also look at how Amanda repeats the word *poetry* at the beginning of two sentences to indicate she is providing an example.

COMMON EXAMPLE TRANSITIONS			
for example	for instance	such as	in particular
to illustrate	an example is	also	when

EXERCISE 7-5

WRITING IN PROGRESS

Writing an Example Paragraph

Directions: Using the list of examples you brainstormed in Exercise 7-4, write a paragraph, arranging your details in a logical sequence and using transitions.

Reading and Writing Cause and Effect

■ **GOAL 2**
Read and write cause and effect

VISUALIZE IT!

What Is Cause and Effect?

Writers use the **cause and effect** pattern to explain why an event or action causes another event or action. For example, if a professor was explaining the therapeutic effects of counseling, she would probably follow a cause and effect pattern. She would tell what caused a person to seek counseling and what happened as a result.

When a single cause has multiple effects, it can be visualized as shown below left. Sometimes, however, multiple causes result in a single effect, as shown below right.

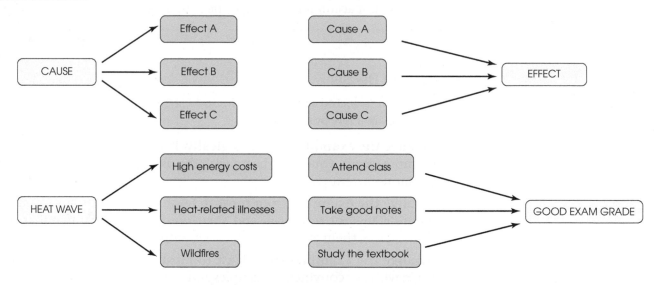

Read Cause and Effect

When you read and study ideas involving cause and effect, focus on the connections between or among the events. Sometimes, a single cause produces a single primary effect. If you get your cell phone wet, it may stop working, for instance. Other times, though, there may be multiple effects.

Read paragraph 6 from "The Benefits of Listening to Music," which discusses the multiple effects of a single cause.

> Attentive listening is good for the brain. It helps us organize our thinking, give shape to our consciousness, and focus our ideas. These phenomena seem to happen for a variety of reasons and in a number of ways. Our involuntary nervous system—including heart rate, brain waves, and other basic bodily functions—automatically entrains to the sounds we hear. We also respond to music's emotional qualities. Lovely melodies softly played relax us, whereas beating drums and searing trumpets excite us. A favorite song recalls times gone by, whereas the sounds of a national anthem invite us to reflect upon our identity.

EXERCISE 7-6   ## Reading: Analyzing Cause and Effect

Directions: After reading the preceding paragraph, answer the following questions.

1. What cause is the writer discussing?

   _____

2. The writer mentions several effects of the cause. List three of them.

   _____

   a. _____

   b. _____

   c. _____

As you worked on Exercise 7-6, did you notice that the topic sentence indicates to the reader that the paragraph will be about the effect of listening on the brain? Topic sentences often provide this important clue in a cause and effect paragraph, so pay close attention to them.

You also may have noticed that in Exercise 7-6, the writers use specific words to show cause and effect: "seem to happen for a variety of reasons," "also respond," "whereas." Writers often use such words to show why one event is caused by another. Look at the following statement:

> Men and women communicate in different ways. *Consequently,* there are many opportunities for miscommunication.

The word *consequently* ties the cause—different communication styles—to the effect—miscommunication. Here is another example:

> The mute Alzheimer's patient began to sing *because* her daughter took out her violin and began to play.

In this sentence, the word *because* ties the effect—the patient singing—to the cause—her daughter playing violin. In both of these examples, the cause and effect words help explain the relationship between two events. As you read, watch for words that show cause and effect; some common ones are listed in the box below.

COMMON CAUSE AND EFFECT TRANSITIONS			
cause	due to	consequently	resulted in
because	reasons	as a result	therefore
because of	effect	one result is	thus
since			

EXERCISE 7-7 | Reading: Analyzing Cause and Effect

A. Directions: After reading the following paragraph, select the cause and effect word or phrase in the box below that best completes each sentence in the paragraph. Write your answer in the space provided. Not all of the words in the box will be used.

consequently	reason	because of
result	effects	causes

The three-car accident on Route 150 had several serious _____. First, and most tragically, two people died when their car overturned. In addition, traffic into the city was delayed for several hours _____ the accident. _____, those who were headed to the fairgrounds for the Fourth of July fireworks never got to see the colorful display. Another _____, which occurred long afterward, was that the state legislature lowered the speed limit in the area where the accident had occurred. After the legislation passed, several legislators stated that the accident was the main _____ for the change.

B. Directions: After reading the preceding paragraph, answer the following questions.

1. What cause is being discussed? _____

2. What four effects does the writer mention?

   a. _____

   b. _____

   c. _____

   d. _____

3. Does the topic sentence tell you that this will be a cause and effect paragraph?

   _____

4. Aside from the cause and effect words, list four transitions that the writer uses to lead the reader through the information.

   a. _____   b. _____   c. _____   d. _____

EXERCISE 7-8 | Reading: Identifying Causes and Effects

Directions: For each of the following paragraphs, list the cause(s) and effect(s) being discussed.

1. Many regions are experiencing high levels of unemployment. Unfortunately, widespread job loss affects more than household income levels. Household tensions and even domestic violence rise. Indeed, some communities see an increase in all crimes. Loss of self-esteem and hope are some of the more personal ways unemployment hurts.

Cause(s): _____

Effect(s): _____

_____

2.   Government leaders need to look harder at the true reasons our violent crime rates have risen. What they will see are people living in poverty, desperately trying to survive. Add to that rampant drug use and you have the perfect conditions for violent gang activity. Furthermore, budget cuts have lessened the police presence and done away with special police programs that were working to keep neighborhoods safe.

Cause(s): _____

_____

Effect(s): _____

3.   The Earth is always moving in one way or another. When there is volcanic activity, an earthquake can occur. Also, shifting plates of the Earth's crust along faults will make the ground shake beneath us. Most earthquakes cannot be felt but are measured by sensitive equipment at seismic centers around the globe.

Cause(s): _____

Effect(s): _____

4.   Low standardized test scores among minorities caused by biased questions lead teachers to "teach to the test." These same students may improve their performance on the next standardized test but do not receive the well-rounded education needed to succeed in school as a whole and ultimately in life.

Cause(s): _____

Effect(s) _____

Write Cause and Effect

Writing a cause and effect paragraph involves writing a clear topic sentence that indicates whether you are talking about causes, effects, or both; providing supporting details; and using transitions.

Write Your Topic Sentence

To write effective topic sentences for cause and effect paragraphs, do the following:

1. **Clarify the cause and effect relationship.** Before you write, carefully identify the causes and the effects. If you are uncertain, divide a sheet of paper into two columns. Label one column "Causes" and the other "Effects." Brainstorm about your topic, placing your ideas in the appropriate column.

2. **Decide whether to emphasize causes or effects.** In a single paragraph, it is best to focus on either causes or effects—not both. For example, suppose you are writing about students who drop out of college. You need to decide whether to discuss why they drop out (causes) or what happens to students who drop out (effects). Your topic sentence should indicate whether you are going to emphasize causes or effects. (In essays, you may consider both causes and effects.)

3. **Determine whether the events are related or independent.** Analyze the causes or effects to discover if they occurred as part of a chain reaction or if they are not related to one another. Your topic sentence should suggest the

type of relationship about which you are writing. If you are writing about a chain of events, your topic sentence should reflect this—for example, "A series of events led up to my sister's decision to drop out of college." If the causes or effects are not related to one another, then your sentence should indicate that—for example, "Students drop out of college for a number of different reasons."

Now read paragraph 2 from "Poetry and Healing." Notice that Amanda's topic sentence makes it clear that she is focusing on the cause (writing poetry in a group setting) that leads to an effect (healing).

> One way poetry can be healing is through writing with other people. As a result of joining with others who share an interest in poetry, writers can find a safe place for their voices to be heard without fear of criticism or shame. Not only can the group experience provide listening ears, but it also can provide inspiration. When a writer gets stuck and the words won't come, the group can ask questions, suggest ideas, encourage, and inspire creativity. Consequently, a group poetry writing session can function similarly to a one-on-one counseling session in which other writers enable a person to think through the issue, put words to feelings, and begin a process that will ultimately lead to healing.

EXERCISE 7-9

WRITING IN PROGRESS

Writing a Topic Sentence

Directions: Select one of the topics below, and write a topic sentence for a paragraph that will explain either its causes *or* effects.

1. Watching too much TV
2. Children who misbehave
3. The popularity of horror films
4. Rising cost of attending college
5. Eating junk food

Provide Supporting Details

Providing supporting details for cause and effect paragraphs requires careful thought and planning. Details must be relevant, sufficient, and effectively organized.

Providing Relevant and Sufficient Details Each cause or effect you describe must be relevant to the situation introduced in your topic sentence. Suppose you are writing a paragraph explaining why you are attending college. Each sentence must explain this topic. You should not include ideas, for example, about how college is different from what you expected.

If, while writing, you discover you have more ideas about how college is different from what you expected than you do about your reasons for attending college, you need to revise your topic sentence in order to refocus your paragraph.

Each cause or reason requires explanation, particularly if it is *not* obvious. For example, it is not sufficient to write, "One reason I decided to attend college was to advance my position in life." This sentence needs further explanation. For example, you could discuss the types of advancement (financial, job security, job satisfaction) you hope to attain.

Jot down a list of the causes or reasons you plan to include. This process may help you think of additional causes and will give you a chance to consider how to explain or support each one. You might decide to eliminate one or to combine several. Here is one student's list of reasons for attending college.

VISUALIZE IT!

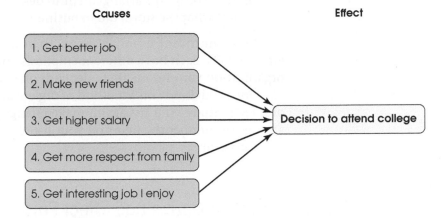

By listing his reasons, this student realized that the first one—to get a better job—was too general and was covered more specifically later in the list, so he eliminated it. He also realized that "get higher salary" and "get interesting job" could be combined. He then wrote the following paragraph:

> There are three main reasons I decided to attend Ambrose Community College. First, and most important to me, I want to get a high-paying, interesting job that I will enjoy. Right now, the only jobs I can get pay minimum wage, and as a result, I'm working in a fast-food restaurant. This kind of job doesn't make me proud of myself, and I get bored with routine tasks. Second, my parents have always wanted me to have a better job than they do, and I know my father will not respect me until I do. A college degree would make them proud of me. A third reason for attending college is to make new friends. It is hard to meet people, and everyone in my neighborhood seems stuck in a rut. I want to meet other people who are interested in improving themselves like I am.

Organizing Your Details There are several ways to arrange the details in a cause and effect paragraph. The method you choose depends on your purpose in writing, as well as your topic. Suppose you are writing a paragraph about the effects of a hurricane on a coastal town. Several different arrangements of details are possible:

■ **Chronological.** A chronological organization arranges your details in the order in which situations or events happened. The order in which the hurricane damage occurred becomes the order for your details. This arrangement is similar to the narration arrangement, which you learned in Chapter 6. A chronological arrangement works for situations and events that occurred in a specific order.

■ **Order of importance.** In an order-of-importance organization, the details are arranged from least to most important or from most to least important. In describing the effects of the hurricane, you could discuss the most severe damage first and then describe lesser damage. Alternatively, you could build up from the least to the most important damage for dramatic effect.

■ **Spatial.** Spatial arrangement of details uses physical or geographical position as a means of organization. In describing the hurricane damage, you could start by describing damage to the beach and work toward the center of town.

■ **Categorical.** This form of arrangement divides the topic into parts or categories. Using this arrangement to describe hurricane damage, you could recount what the storm did to businesses, roads, city services, and homes.

As the hurricane example shows, there are many ways to organize cause and effect details. Each has a different emphasis and achieves a different purpose. The organization you choose, then, depends on the point you want to make.

Once you decide on a method of organization, return to your preliminary list of effects. Study your list again, make changes, eliminate, or combine. Then rearrange or number the items on your list to indicate the order in which you will include them.

EXERCISE 7-10

WRITING IN PROGRESS

Writing a Cause and Effect Paragraph

Directions: Write a paragraph developing the topic sentence you wrote for Exercise 7-9. Be sure to include relevant and sufficient details. Organize your paragraph according to one of the methods described above.

Use Transitions

To blend your details smoothly, use transitional words and phrases. Some common transitions for the cause and effect pattern are listed in the box Common Cause and Effect Transitions in the Read Cause and Effect section of this chapter. The paragraph from Amanda's essay in the Examining Student Writing section of this chapter is a good example of how transitional words and phrases are used. Notice how these transitions function as markers and help you to locate each separate effect.

EXERCISE 7-11

WRITING IN PROGRESS

Writing: Revising a Paragraph

Directions: Reread the paragraph you wrote for Exercise 7-10. Add transitional words and phrases, if needed, to connect your details.

Reading and Writing Comparison and Contrast

■ **GOAL 3**
Read and write
comparison and contrast

What Is Comparison and Contrast?

Often, a writer will explain an object or idea, especially if it is unfamiliar to the reader, by showing how it is similar to or different from a familiar object or idea. At other times, it may be the writer's purpose to show how two ideas, places, objects, or people are similar or different. In each of these situations, a writer commonly uses a pattern called **comparison and contrast**. This pattern emphasizes the similarities or differences between two or more items. There are several variations on this pattern: a paragraph may focus on similarities only, differences only, or both. The comparison pattern can be visualized and mapped as shown below left. For material that focuses on differences, you might use a map like the one below right.

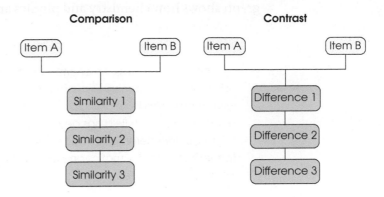

Read Comparison and Contrast

Often, a writer will explain something by using comparison or contrast—that is, by showing how it is similar to or different from a familiar object or idea. Comparison treats similarities, while contrast emphasizes differences. For example, an article comparing two car models might mention these common, overlapping features: hybrid engine, safety features, sunroof, and seating layout. The cars may differ in fuel efficiency, transmission type, navigation system, and entertainment options. When comparing the two models, the writer would focus on shared features. When contrasting the two cars, the writer would focus on individual differences. Such an article might be diagrammed as follows:

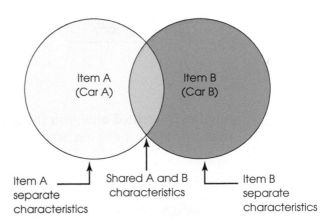

In this diagram, Items A and B are different except where they overlap and share the same characteristics.

In most situations that use the comparison and contrast method, you will find some passages that only compare, some that only contrast, and others that both compare and contrast. To read each type of passage effectively, you must follow the pattern of ideas. Passages that show comparison and/or contrast can be organized in a number of different ways. The organization depends on the author's purpose.

Comparison

If a writer is concerned only with similarities, he or she may identify the items to be compared and then list the ways in which they are alike. The following paragraph shows how chemistry and physics are similar.

> Although physics and chemistry are considered separate fields of study, they have much in common. First, both are physical sciences and are concerned with studying and explaining physical occurrences. To study and record these occurrences, each field has developed a precise set of signs and symbols. These might be considered a specialized language. Finally, both fields are closely tied to the field of mathematics and use mathematics in predicting and explaining physical occurrences.
>
> —Hewitt, *Conceptual Physics*, pp. 82–84

Such a pattern can be diagrammed as follows:

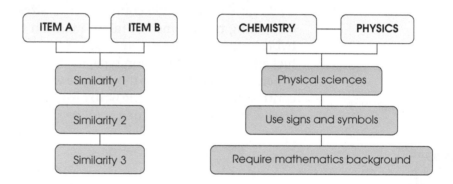

Contrast

A writer concerned only with the differences between sociology and psychology might write the following paragraph:

> Sociology and psychology, although both social sciences, are very different fields of study. Sociology is concerned with the structure, organization, and behavior of groups. Psychology, on the other hand, focuses on individual behavior. While a sociologist would study characteristics of groups of people, a psychologist would study the individual motivation and behavior of each group member. Psychology and sociology also differ in the manner in which research is conducted. Sociologists obtain data and information through observation and survey. Psychologists obtain data through carefully designed experimentation.

Such a pattern can be diagrammed as follows:

Comparison and Contrast

In many passages, a writer will discuss both similarities and differences between subjects. There are two common methods for organizing these types of paragraphs.

■ **Point-by-point.** In this pattern, the writer discusses both of his or her subjects together for each point of comparison or contrast, as in the following paragraph on amphibians and reptiles.

Although reptiles evolved from amphibians, several things distinguish the two kinds of animals. Amphibians (such as frogs, salamanders, and newts) must live where it is moist. In contrast, reptiles (which include turtles, lizards and snakes, and crocodiles and alligators) can live away from the water. Amphibians employ external fertilization, as when the female frog lays her eggs on the water and the male spreads his sperm on top of them. By contrast, all reptiles employ internal fertilization—eggs are fertilized inside the female's body. Another difference between amphibians and reptiles is that reptiles have a tough, scaly skin that conserves water, as opposed to the thin amphibian skin that allows water to escape. Reptiles also have a stronger skeleton than amphibians, more efficient lungs, and a better-developed nervous system.

—adapted from Krogh, *Biology: A Guide to the Natural World*, pp. 466–467, 474

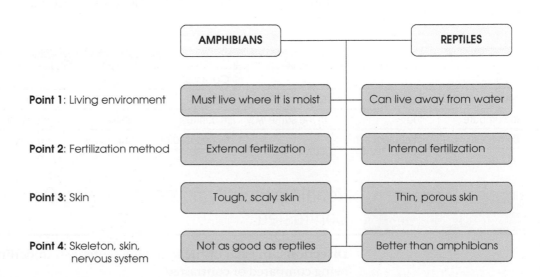

■ **Subject-by-subject.** In this pattern, the writer first discusses all the similarities and differences for one subject and then all the similarities and differences for the second subject. Using this pattern, the paragraph on reptiles and amphibians would look like this:

VISUALIZE IT!

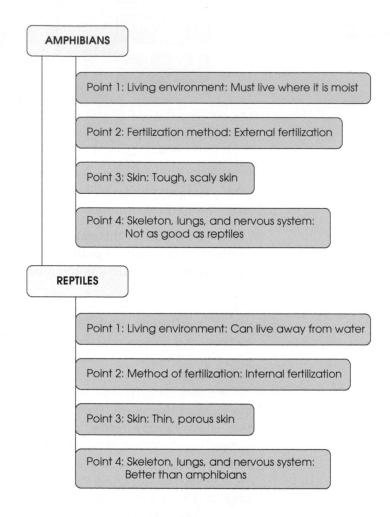

AMPHIBIANS

Point 1: Living environment: Must live where it is moist

Point 2: Fertilization method: External fertilization

Point 3: Skin: Tough, scaly skin

Point 4: Skeleton, lungs, and nervous system: Not as good as reptiles

REPTILES

Point 1: Living environment: Can live away from water

Point 2: Method of fertilization: Internal fertilization

Point 3: Skin: Thin, porous skin

Point 4: Skeleton, lungs, and nervous system: Better than amphibians

Paragraphs and passages that use comparison and contrast often contain transitional words and phrases that guide readers through the material. These include:

COMMON COMPARISON AND CONTRAST TRANSITIONS						
Comparison			**Contrast**			
also	likewise	similarly	although	instead	differs from	on the other hand
to compare	too	in the same way	in contrast	unlike	on the contrary	
both	in comparison		as opposed to	but	however	

EXERCISE 7-12

Reading: Identifying What Is Being Compared and Contrasted

Directions: In each of the following sentences, underline the two items that are being compared or contrasted.

1. Humans are complex organisms made up of many sophisticated systems. Yet humans share several characteristics with primates such as gorillas and New World Monkeys.

2. Educators differ in their approaches to teaching reading. One method, whole language, applies a holistic model to literacy. The other main approach, seen as old-fashioned by some, is phonics, where children learn to read by "sounding out" letters and letter combinations.

3. Face-to-face communication and electronic communication share a common goal—the transmission of information.

4. Many actors believe that stage acting requires more overall skill than movie acting. Unlike filmmaking, where actors can make mistake after mistake, knowing that the scene will just be shot again and again until it is right, live theater demands more concentration and preparation since retakes are not possible.

5. Flame retardant and flame resistant fabrics each provide a degree of protection to the person wearing them.

| EXERCISE 7-13 | Reading: Analyzing Comparison and Contrast |

Directions: Read each of the paragraphs below, and answer the questions that follow.

A.   The term primary group, coined by Charles H. Cooley, refers to small informal groups who interact in a personal, direct, and intimate way. A secondary group, on the other hand, is a group whose members interact in an impersonal manner, have few emotional ties, and come together for a specific purpose. Like primary groups, secondary groups are usually small and involve face-to-face contacts. Although the interactions may be cordial or friendly, they are more formal than primary group interactions. Secondary groups, however, are often just as important as primary groups. Most of our time is spent in secondary groups—committees, professional groups, sales-related groups, classroom groups, or neighborhood groups. The key difference between primary and secondary groups is in the quality of the relationship and the extent of personal intimacy and involvement. Primary groups are person-oriented, whereas secondary groups tend to be goal-oriented.

—Eshleman and Cashion, *Sociology: An Introduction*, p. 88

1. Although the writers are comparing and contrasting primary and secondary groups, what other pattern do they use in the first two sentences?

_____

2. What words do the writers use to indicate similarities and differences?

_____

3. The paragraph includes many similarities and differences between primary and secondary groups. List some of the similarities and differences below.

Primary and Secondary Groups

Similarities

1. _____

   _____

2. _____

   _____

3. _____

   _____

   _____

Differences

1. _____

   _____

2. _____

3. _____

   _____

4. _____

5. _____

   _____

B.   Small businesses are likely to have less formal purchasing processes. A small retail grocer might, for example, purchase a computer system after visiting a few suppliers to compare prices and features, but a large grocery store chain might collect bids from a specified number of vendors and then evaluate those bids according to detailed corporate guidelines. Usually, fewer individuals are involved in the decision-making process for a small business. The owner of the small business, for example, may make all decisions, and a larger business may operate with a buying committee of several people.

—Kinnear, Bernhardt, and Krentler, *Principles of Marketing*, p. 218

1. What are the writers comparing or contrasting in this paragraph?

   _____

2. Why are small retail grocers and grocery store chains mentioned?

   _____

3. What transitional word or phrase suggests the overall pattern of the paragraph?

   _____

4. The paragraph includes two major differences between small and large businesses. Fill in these differences below.

Differences Between Small and Large Businesses

		Small Businesses	*Large Businesses*
1.	Purchasing processes	_____	_____
2.	Decision-making process	_____	_____

Write Comparison and Contrast

Writing a comparison and contrast paragraph involves identifying similarities and differences between two items, writing a topic sentence that indicates the item you will be comparing and contrasting and your point, organizing your paragraph, developing your points, and using transitions.

Identify Similarities and Differences

If you have two items to compare or contrast, the first step is to figure out how they are similar and how they are different. Be sure to select subjects that are neither too similar nor too different. If they are, you will have either too little or too much to say. Follow this effective two-step approach:

1. Brainstorm to produce a two-column list of characteristics.
2. Match up the items and identify points of comparison and contrast.

Brainstorming to Produce a Two-Column List Let's say you want to write about two friends—Rhonda and Maria. Here is how to identify their similarities and differences:

1. Brainstorm and list the characteristics of each person.

RHONDA	MARIA
Reserved, quiet	Age 27
Age 22	Single parent, two children
Private person	Outgoing person
Friends since childhood	Loves to be center of attention
Married, no children	Loves sports and competition
Hates parties	Plays softball and tennis

2. When you finish your list, match up items that share the same point of comparison or contrast—age, personality type, marital status—as shown below.

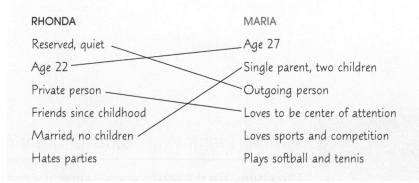

3. **When you have listed an item in a certain category for one person but not for the other, think of a corresponding detail that will balance the lists.** For instance, you listed "friends since childhood" and "hates parties"

for Rhonda, so you could indicate how long you have known Maria and whether she likes parties. This will give you additional points of comparison and contrast.

EXERCISE 7-14

WRITING IN PROGRESS

Listing Similarities and Differences

Directions: Make a two-column list of similarities and differences for two of the following topics:

1. Two professional athletes
2. Two political candidates
3. Two restaurants
4. Two neighborhoods you have lived in
5. Two friends
6. Two vampires

Identifying Points of Comparison and Contrast   The next step is to reorganize the lists so that the items you matched up appear next to each other. Now, in a new column to the left of your lists, write the term that describes or categorizes each set of items in the lists. These are general categories we will call "points of comparison and contrast." **Points of comparison and contrast** are the characteristics you use to examine your two subjects. As you reorganize, you may find it easier to group several items together. For example, you might group some details about Rhonda and Maria together under the category of personality. Study the following list, noticing the points of comparison and contrast in the left-hand column.

POINTS OF COMPARISON AND CONTRAST	RHONDA	MARIA
Personality	Quiet, reserved, private person	Outgoing, loves to be center of attention
Marital status	Married, no children	Single parent, two children
Length of friendship	Friends since childhood	Met at work last year
Shared activities	Go shopping	Play softball together, go to parties

EXERCISE 7-15

WRITING IN PROGRESS

Writing: Identifying Points of Comparison and Contrast

Directions: For the two topics you chose in Exercise 7-14, match up the items and identify points of comparison and contrast.

This two-step process can work in reverse order as well. You can decide points of comparison and contrast first and then fill in characteristics for each point. For example, instead of brainstorming and listing the characteristics of Rhonda and Maria, you could first decide on points to compare them on—such as personality, marital status, length of friendship, and shared activities—and then fill in the details for each of them. You would end up with a three-column chart like the one above.

| EXERCISE 7-16 | Writing: Listing Points of Comparison and Contrast |

Directions: List at least three points of comparison and contrast for each of the following topics. Then choose one topic and make a three-column list on a separate sheet of paper.

1. Two films you have seen recently

   Points of comparison and contrast:

   a. _____

   b. _____

   c. _____

   d. _____

   e. _____

2. Two jobs you have held

   Points of comparison and contrast:

   a. _____

   b. _____

   c. _____

   d. _____

   e. _____

3. Baseball and football players

   Points of comparison and contrast:

   a. _____

   b. _____

   c. _____

   d. _____

   e. _____

Whichever method you choose, once you have completed your three-column list, the next step is to study your list and decide whether to write about similarities, differences, or both. It is usually easier to concentrate on one or the other. If you see similarities as more significant, you might need to omit or de-emphasize differences—and vice versa if you decide to write about differences.

Write Your Topic Sentence

Your topic sentence should do two things:

- ■ It should identify the two subjects that you will compare or contrast.
- ■ It should state whether you will focus on similarities, differences, or both.

It may also indicate what points you will compare or contrast. Suppose you are comparing your two friends: Rhonda and Maria. Obviously, you could not cover every characteristic of these two people in a single paragraph. Instead, you could limit your comparison to their personalities or the activities you share with each friend.

Here are a few sample topic sentences that meet the above requirements:

- ■ Two of my dearest friends, Rhonda and Maria, have completely different personalities.
- ■ The activities I share with my friends Rhonda and Maria are each enjoyable in their own way.

Be sure to avoid topic sentences that announce what you plan to do. Here's an example: "I'll compare my friends Rhonda and Maria and explain how our friendships differ."

EXERCISE 7-17	Writing a Topic Sentence
WRITING IN PROGRESS	

Directions: Write a topic sentence for each of the two topics you worked with in Exercises 7-14 and 7-15.

Organize Your Paragraph

Once you have identified similarities and differences and drafted a topic sentence, you are ready to organize your paragraph, using the subject-by-subject or point-by-point methods.

Subject-by-Subject Organization In the **subject-by-subject method**, you write first about one of your subjects, covering it completely, and then about the other, covering it completely. Ideally, you cover the same points of comparison and contrast for both, and in the same order. (See the idea map showing this method of organization on p. 246.)

To develop each subject, focus on the same kinds of details and discuss the same points of comparison in the same order. If you are discussing only similarities or only differences, organize your points within each topic, using a most-to-least or least-to-most arrangement. If you are discussing both similarities and differences, you might discuss points of similarity first and then points of difference, or vice versa.

Here is a sample paragraph about Rhonda and Maria using the subject-by-subject method and a map showing its organization:

Two of my dearest friends, Rhonda and Maria, present a study in contrasts. The first quality you might notice about Rhonda is that she is very reserved and quiet. Rhonda hates parties but we have a lot of fun when we go shopping together. I have known Rhonda since we were kids and even though she is a private person by nature, she tells me everything about her life. In contrast to Rhonda, Maria is one of the most outgoing people I know. Maria enjoys competition, so we often spend our time together playing softball and tennis. I met Maria last year at work, so we have only known each other a short while, but she is the type of person who has never met a stranger. And unlike my friend Rhonda, Maria loves to be the center of attention.

VISUALIZE IT!

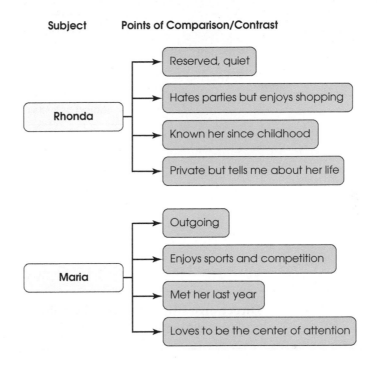

Subject	Points of Comparison/Contrast
Rhonda	Reserved, quiet
	Hates parties but enjoys shopping
	Known her since childhood
	Private but tells me about her life
Maria	Outgoing
	Enjoys sports and competition
	Met her last year
	Loves to be the center of attention

EXERCISE 7-18

WRITING IN PROGRESS

Writing: Using Subject-by-Subject Organization

Directions: Using the subject-by-subject method of organization, write a comparison or contrast paragraph using one of the topic sentences you wrote for Exercise 7-17.

Point-by-Point Organization In the **point-by-point method of organization**, you discuss both of your subjects together for each point of comparison and contrast. When using this organization, maintain consistency by discussing the same subject first for each point. (That is, always discuss Rhonda first and Maria second or vice versa.) If your paragraph focuses only on similarities or only on differences, arrange your points in a least-to-most or most-to-least pattern.

Here is a sample paragraph using the point-by-point method and a map showing its organization:

Two of my dearest friends, Rhonda and Maria, present a study in contrasts. The first quality you might notice about Rhonda is that she is very reserved and quiet, in contrast to Maria, who is one of the most outgoing people I know,

(continued)

Rhonda is a private person by nature, unlike Maria, who loves to be the center of attention. I share different activities with each friend too. Rhonda hates parties but we have a lot of fun shopping together, whereas Maria and I enjoy going to parties and playing competitive sports like softball and tennis. A final difference between the two has to do with the length of our friendships: Rhonda and I have been friends since we were kids, but Maria and I have only known each other since we met last year at work.

VISUALIZE IT!

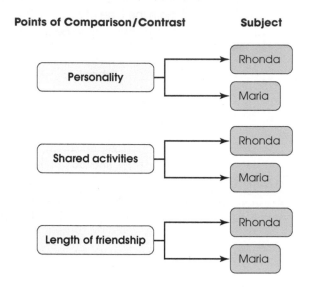

EXERCISE 7-19

WRITING IN PROGRESS

Writing: Using Point-by-Point Organization

Directions: Using the point-by-point method of organization, write a comparison and contrast paragraph using the other topic sentence you wrote for Exercise 7-17.

Develop Your Points of Comparison and Contrast

As you discuss each point, don't feel as if you must compare or contrast in every sentence. Your paragraph should not just list similarities and/or differences. For every point, provide explanation, descriptive details, and examples.

Try to maintain a balance in your treatment of each subject and each point of comparison and contrast. Give equal attention to each point and each subject. If you give an example for one subject, try to do so for the other as well.

Use Transitions

Transitions are particularly important in comparison and contrast writing. Because you are discussing two subjects and covering similar points for each, your readers can easily become confused. Commonly used transitional words and phrases are listed in the box Common Comparison and Contrast Transitions in the section Comparison and Contrast.

Each method of organization uses different transitions in different places. If you choose a subject-by-subject organization, you'll need the strongest transition in the middle of the paragraph, when you switch from one subject to another. You will also need a transition each time you move from one point to another while still on the same subject. Look at the subject-by-subject paragraph in the Organize Your Paragraph section of this chapter, where the transitions are highlighted.

If you choose point-by-point organization, use transitions as you move from one subject to the other. On each point, your reader needs to know quickly whether the two subjects are similar or different. Look at the point-by-point paragraph in the Organize Your Paragraph section of this chapter, where the transitions are highlighted.

EXERCISE 7-20

WRITING IN PROGRESS

Writing: Using Transitions

Directions: Reread the paragraphs you wrote for Exercises 7-18 and 7-19. If necessary, add transitions to make your organization clearer.

 NEED TO KNOW

Organizing Your Details

Regardless of the method of organization you choose, it is important to organize the details in each method so that your paragraph or essay is easy to follow. Use the following suggestions:

For subject-by-subject organization:

- Be sure to cover the same points of comparison for each subject.
- Cover the points of comparison in the same order in each half of your paragraph or essay.
- Make sure you include a strong transition that signals you are moving from one subject to another.

For point-by-point organization:

- As you work back and forth between your subjects, try to mention the subjects in the same order.
- Decide how to organize your points of comparison. You could move from the simplest to the most complex similarity, or from the most obvious to least obvious difference, for example.

READ AND REVISE

The following paragraph was written to compare two colleges its author attended. This first draft is disorganized because the student focused only on getting his ideas down on paper. You can see that he skips around between the two schools and between various points of comparison. Rewrite this paragraph to make it follow a single method of organization. Add transitions as needed. You may delete or add ideas.

> The two colleges I attended are the University of Colorado (UC) in Boulder, Colorado, and Allan Hancock College (AHC) in Santa Maria and both offered me opportunities, but differed greatly in style and focus. AHC offers small classes, and class size is important for getting help when you need it.

(continued)

UC, being a four-year university, offers Bachelor's degrees and preparation for professional schools. AHC is a community college, so most students can affordably live at home. UC offers student clubs that are important in teaching students how to network, communicate, and work together. Classes at UC are taught by a team consisting of a professor, who conducts lectures, a graduate student who conducts recitation classes, and occasionally, a co-seminar class taught by an adjunct professor. At AHC classes are taught by one person, a professor or adjunct. It is nice to be able to feel like your instructor knows you, and that you know him or her. AHC prepares students for careers and transfer to four-year schools. Classes at UC tend to be large. A typical freshman class may have between 150 and 220 students. The environment at UC is competitive; grades are very important. AHC has student clubs, but they don't have the importance that they do at CU. Costs are another factor. Living on campus is expensive at CU.

READ AND RESPOND: A Student Essay

Poetry and Healing

Amanda Keithley

In the Examining Student Writing section of this chapter, you read "Poetry and Healing" and examined various elements of the essay. Now it is time to take a closer look at the reading by responding to the questions that follow.

Examining Writing

1. Evaluate the examples Amanda used to support her thesis statement. Did she provide enough examples? What other kinds of evidence could she have used to support her thesis?
2. How did Amanda organize her essay? Summarize her main points in your own words.
3. Evaluate Amanda's introduction. How does she build interest in her topic?
4. Evaluate the conclusion. How might it be more effective?

In the Examining Professional Writing section of this chapter, you read "The Benefits of Listening to Music." Now it is time to take a closer look at the reading by responding to the questions that follow.

The Benefits of Listening to Music

Steven Cornelius and Mary Natvig

Writing in Response to Reading

Checking Your Comprehension

Answer each of the following questions using complete sentences.

1. What three conditions or disorders do the authors use to illustrate the benefits of listening to music?
2. What are two physiological effects of a mother's lullaby?
3. In what three ways do the authors say attentive listening is good for the brain?
4. What are two psychological effects of musical training?
5. What is the difference between the auditory cortex in musicians and nonmusicians?

Strengthening Your Vocabulary

Using the word's context, word parts, or a dictionary, write a brief definition of each of the following words as it is used in the reading.

1. apocryphal (paragraph 2) _____
2. sequential (paragraph 3) _____
3. induces (paragraph 5) _____
4. cohesion (paragraph 5) _____
5. entrains (paragraph 6) _____
6. profound (paragraph 8) _____

Examining the Reading: Using Idea Maps

Review the reading by completing the missing parts of the following idea map.

VISUALIZE IT!

Title: **The Benefits of Listening to Music**

Thesis: Music has a powerful impact on the human brain.

Medical effects are not understood.

Stuttering, _____

Human brain seems programmed for song

Psychologists showed that mother's lullaby affects child by:

_____

_____

Music therapists found listening to music releases endorphins that:

_____

_____

Social scientists believe music provided early model for _____

Attentive listening helps us to:

_____

_____

_____

Musical training may:

_____

_____

Conclusion: Active musical experience and engaging in active listening both offer health benefits.

Thinking Critically: An Integrated Perspective

React and respond to the reading by discussing the following:

1. What is the purpose of the example of Veva Campbell that is used in the first two paragraphs?

2. What pattern of organization has the author used in this reading? Explain your answer.

3. Why did the author choose to include the information about Tony Cicoria and Clive Wearing in the selection?

4. What type of music do you choose to listen to for different purposes or moods? Write a journal entry describing the types of music you listen to when you are happy, are sad, or need to accomplish a task.

5. Discuss the term "brain calisthenics" (paragraph 7). What other kinds of brain exercises can you think of?

6. Discuss the use of music as a form of therapy. In addition to the examples in the selection, what other applications can you think of for music therapy?

7. What is the purpose of the drawing that accompanies "The Benefits of Listening to Music"?

8. If you were given the responsibility of choosing a photograph to accompany this reading, what would the photograph look like? What message would your photograph convey?

THINKING VISUALLY

Paragraph Options

1. Choose a musical performer or group you enjoy and identify several factors that make the performer or group popular. Give an example illustrating each factor.

2. What makes a song or a particular piece of music appealing to you? Write a paragraph describing three of your favorite songs (or other pieces of music) and explaining why you like them.

3. Write a paragraph comparing listening to recorded music, such as streaming on Spotify to attending a live concert.

Essay Options

4. How do you typically listen to music? What is your favorite music for different activities, such as studying, going out, or relaxing at home? Write an essay answering these questions.

5. What would you say are the three most important reasons you listen to music? Write an essay explaining your answer.

6. Choose two songs that you enjoy or two musical artists that you listen to and write a comparison or contrast essay examining their similarities or differences.

Making Connections between the Readings

Use both "Poetry and Healing" and "The Benefits of Listening to Music" to write a response to one of the following prompts.

1. Both of the essays focus on creative expression. Do you have a talent that you use to express yourself creatively? If not, what form of creative expression do you wish you had a talent for? Write a paragraph response to one or both of the questions.

2. In the two essays, both authors address the healing aspects of creative expression. Write an essay reflecting on a personal experience in which you or someone you know has used music or poetry to promote physical or emotional healing.

3. The two writers also address listening in their essays. In an essay, explain how listening to poetry, music, or even spoken words can bring life, hope, and healing. Use examples from your own life or the lives of your friends and family to support your thesis.

4. In addition to the forms of creative expression and their benefits discussed by the authors, there are many other forms of creative expression and also many more benefits than what the authors have mentioned. Conduct an Internet search and find an article on another form of creative expression and the benefits associated with it. After reading the article, write an essay response to the ideas presented in the reading.

SELF-TEST SUMMARY

To test yourself, cover the Answer column with a sheet of paper and answer each question in the left column. Evaluate each of your answers as you work by sliding the paper down and comparing your answer with what is printed in the Answer column.

QUESTION	ANSWER
■ **GOAL 1** Read and write example What are examples?	*Examples* are specific instances or situations that explain a general idea or statement.
How do writers organize paragraphs when using examples?	Writers often state the main idea first and then follow it with one or more examples.
What is involved in writing paragraphs using examples?	Writing paragraphs using examples involves ■ writing a clear topic sentence. ■ selecting appropriate and sufficient examples. ■ arranging your details. ■ using transitions.
■ **GOAL 2** Read and write cause and effect Why do writers use cause and effect?	Writers use the cause and effect pattern to explain why and/or how an event or action causes another event or action.
How do you read cause and effect?	When you read cause and effect paragraphs, focus on the connections between or among the events being described.
How do you write effective topic sentences for cause and effect paragraphs?	Clarify the cause and effect relationship, decide whether to emphasize causes or effects, and determine whether the events are related or independent.

QUESTION	ANSWER
■ **GOAL 3** Read and write comparison and contrast What does the comparison and contrast pattern do?	The comparison and contrast pattern emphasizes similarities or differences between two or more items.
How do you read comparison and contrast effectively?	To read comparison and contrast effectively, follow the pattern of ideas and look for transitional words and phrases to guide you through the material.
What are two ways of organizing a comparison or contrast paragraph?	In the subject-by-subject method, write first about one of your subjects and then about the other, ideally covering the same points of comparison and contrast for both. In the point-by-point method, discuss both of your subjects together for each point of comparison and contrast.

Revision and Proofreading

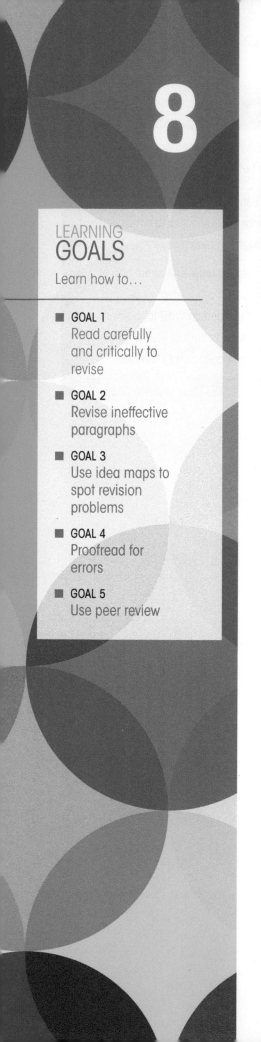

LEARNING GOALS

Learn how to…

- **GOAL 1**
  Read carefully and critically to revise

- **GOAL 2**
  Revise ineffective paragraphs

- **GOAL 3**
  Use idea maps to spot revision problems

- **GOAL 4**
  Proofread for errors

- **GOAL 5**
  Use peer review

Profile

I'm a no-baggage type of guy, and I am not looking for someone with baggage, either.

I love to travel, especially to the Southwest, and to learn about different cultures and see new things.

I just started my own computer repair business, but I have a lot of other good business ideas, too. I intend to be successful by the time I am 30.

Music is a big part of my life. Sports are not a big part of my life.

Some people say I am a hopeless romantic. I agree with them.

My family is important to me, as are my dogs. Kids? Maybe.

If you want to get to know me better, ask me!

THINK About It!

Write a sentence describing the man shown in the photograph above. No doubt, you found there was a limited amount of information in it. You could describe his physical appearance, but not much else. Now write a sentence describing him using both the photograph and the excerpt from his profile on a dating site. How do your descriptions differ?

Many ineffective paragraphs are like the photograph above. They do not provide enough information and leave the reader frustrated and confused. An effective paragraph contains details that explain and illustrate the topic sentence, like the characteristics listed in the profile.

In this chapter, you will learn to read, examine, and analyze your drafts closely to find and revise problems and errors. You will also read both a student essay and a professional article on the theme of dating.

What Are Revision and Proofreading?

Revision is a process of examining and rethinking your ideas as they appear in sentence and paragraph form. It involves finding ways to make your writing clearer, more effective, more complete, and more interesting. When revising you may change, add, delete, or rearrange your ideas and how you have expressed them to improve your writing. Revision also involves careful reading and critical thinking. You have to read closely to determine whether you have said exactly what you meant to say. Then you must be able to step back from what you have written and ask yourself the questions: *Will my readers understand what I have written?* and *Is my message clear?* Using the process of peer review, you may also find suggestions from classmates helpful.

Proofreading focuses on correctness and involves checking for errors in grammar, spelling, punctuation, and capitalization. It also involves formatting your paragraph to make it easy to read. Proofreading requires close and careful reading, working word by word and sentence by sentence, searching for and correcting errors.

Read Carefully and Critically for Revision

■ GOAL 1
Read carefully and
critically to revise

The first step in preparing to revise a draft is to read it critically with the purpose of finding out what works and what does not. Use the following suggestions:

Guidelines for Reading Critically

1. **Create distance.** It is easy to like your own work and see nothing wrong with it. Mentally prepare yourself to look at your writing critically by creating distance between yourself and your work. Try setting it aside for a day or so. Then, when you return, examine it as if someone else wrote it.

2. **Plan on and allow enough time to read your draft several times.** It is difficult to check for all aspects of writing at the same time. Each time, read it for a different purpose, using the following strategy:

   ■ **Step 1: Read the draft once, examining your ideas:** Have you said what you want to say? If not, make the necessary changes.

   ■ **Step 2: Read the draft again, evaluating how effectively you have expressed your ideas, again making changes to improve the draft.** Reread to make sure your changes work.

   ■ **Step 3: Read it a third time, checking for correctness.** You might want to read the draft several times, looking for one common error at a time.

3. **Print a copy of your draft.** It may be easier to see mistakes or problems if you are reading print copy rather than reading from your computer screen.

4. **Read with a pen in hand.** Mark and make notes as you read and reread. If you see something that doesn't sound right or an idea that needs further explanation, mark it so you don't overlook it as you start to rewrite.

5. **Read aloud.** When you hear your ideas, you may realize they sound choppy or that a statement seems to stand alone without adequate explanation or support.

6. **Check with classmates.** After reading the draft several times, if you are still unsure of what to revise, check with a classmate. Ask him or her to read your draft and offer comments and suggestions. For more on this process, called peer review, see the Peer Review section later in this chapter.

Even after giving yourself some distance from your work, it may be difficult to know how to improve your own writing. Simply rereading may not help you discover flaws, weaknesses, or needed changes. This chapter offers guidelines to follow and questions to ask to help you spot problems. It also shows you how to use a revision map, includes a revision checklist to guide your revision, and explains how to use peer review.

Chapter Theme: The World of Dating

In this chapter, you will read both a professional and a student essay on the world of dating. James Henslin summed up the current world of dating when he titled his essay "Finding a Mate: Not the Same as It Used to Be." Truly, the ways that people find a date and actually experience a date have changed drastically. Technology has made it possible for someone to choose a date from a bank of "applicants," exchange messages with a potential dating candidate in order to get to know him or her better, arrange a meeting place, and "drop" a date without ever having to face the person again. Obviously, there are pros and cons to this method. As you read the two essays in this chapter, consider the benefits and drawbacks of the new ways of dating. Also, annotate each reading, recording your own thoughts on the issue, to be prepared to write about it or a related issue.

Look it up!

Use the search engine on your smartphone (or work with a classmate who has a smartphone) to look up "finding love online." Review several entries. Based on what you read, what are the chances of finding love online? Have you (or someone you know) used online dating? If so, what was your experience like? Write a few sentences about your personal experiences with online dating or about the online dating experiences of someone you know.

EXAMINING STUDENT WRITING

Claire Stroup

One of the ways you will learn about revision and proofreading is by studying a model essay. Claire Stroup's essay is used throughout this chapter to illustrate how to identify and revise ineffective paragraphs.

Claire Stroup is a student at North Carolina State University where she is pursuing a degree in history. Upon graduating from college, she plans to teach high school. In her spare time, she enjoys riding and showing horses and working at a horse farm. She submitted this essay for a sociology class assignment that required her to write a response to "Finding a Mate: Not the Same as It Used to Be," the professional essay in the Examining Professional Writing section of this chapter.

The Woes of Internet Dating
Claire Stroup

Title announces subject

1   It is easy to fall in love with an idea. The idea of a six foot tall, dark haired, mysterious, perfectly chiseled man with impeccable manners or a bombshell who can take a truck engine apart and put it back together in under an hour one moment and rock a fussy baby to sleep the next are both highly appealing. On Internet dating sites, people can create an identity completely opposite to that of their true selves. It is easy to lie about appearance, occupation, or income. In an environment where truth often goes untold, Internet dating creates more options for lies, deception, and heartbreak; on a very rare occasion, however, these relationships do work out.

Details provide background leading up to thesis statement

Thesis statement

2   There are obviously some disturbing aspects to online dating. With technology becoming widely available, underage girls and boys have more and more access to the Internet and its terrors (and wonders). Parents probably would love to think that their children are utilizing the Internet for school research purposes, but the appeal of an idea with sweet words can be too great to resist. It is no surprise that a predator can use online dating or other communication to entice victims into his web under the disguise of being a cool teen just like his victims. First dates wind up being late night movie dates, and kids go missing. Abduction, rape, and murder become increasingly simple for creative predators when unsuspecting men, women, and children utilize Internet dating and relationships while throwing caution to the wind in the hopes of finding true love or just friendship.

Topic sentence

Details explain topic sentence

3   While not all those looking for love find themselves on the tail end of a potential romance gone bad, there is a great opportunity for dysfunctional relationships to be founded on little white lies. Even something as trivial as lying about weight because, "I'm going to lose those extra twenty pounds in a month or two anyway," creates an opportunity for a painful relationship. It seems easy to slip into a comfortable relationship behind a screen where people can be slightly tweaked versions of themselves, where they might have a job online when they actually just got laid off, or their profile picture is one from a couple of years back when everything was just a little bit firmer. The fact remains that a relationship, no matter what its roots, must be built on a foundation of truth and honesty. The MTV show *Catfish* illustrates what a large problem deceiving identities have become in online interactions; even if both parties had a real connection, the relationship cannot be based on white lies. These heartbreaking deceptions have become such an issue that MTV created a show about it. Little white lies that seem harmless can be indicators to a partner that his or her lover may have lied about far more than just love handles.

Topic sentence

Details explain and support topic sentence

4   Aside from the basic problems with lying to a lover such as distrust and potential bodily harm, there lies a less tangible effect: heartbreak. Just because a person was not physically injured by another does not make the internal pain less significant. The emotional impact of having taken a risk on a faceless person and failing miserably is without a doubt shattering and life-altering. News media publish plenty of stories about individuals who have lost their lives because of trusting the wrong person online, but they rarely tell the stories of everyone else who got the short end

Topic sentence

Details support topic sentence

of the stick and how that relationship changed their lives. That dishonesty will live with those victims forever, inhibiting their relationships from that point onward.

5   Of course, not all Internet dating relationships are lies, and not all online couples end up hurt and ashamed. Sometimes, a relationship works and is exactly as the two people hoped it would be. These legitimate, truthful relationships usually begin online and turn into face-to-face interactions fairly quickly. Some become long-term relationships, some friendships, some marriages. Then again, some people just hate each other when they actually speak face-to-face because the tone of the person's voice is downright obnoxious. Not all of those looking for love online are creepers, nor are all of them naïve daydreamers. Occasionally, two people looking for the right partner in life find each other online, and all is well.

6   The truth of the matter is that there is no substitute for interpersonal, face-to-face relationships. It is difficult to nourish or sustain a relationship when neither party can see, hear, or touch the other. Although it seems quite simple to slip into easy love with the idea of someone through the keys of a message board, the reality of that person often is shocking and discouraging. Each relationship is unique, so it proves difficult to generalize, but media shares more news about the online relationships that ended badly than those that end in happily ever after. Perhaps online dating is the future, but not as it exists today.

Claire Stroup. Reprinted by permission of the author.

Margin notes:

Topic sentence
Transition moves readers along
Writer includes examples to support the topic sentence

Concluding paragraph
Writer emphasizes the importance of building a relationship on personal, face-to-face contact

Revise Ineffective Paragraphs

■ GOAL 2
Revise ineffective paragraphs

To revise a paragraph, begin by examining your topic sentence and then, once you are satisfied with it, determine whether you have provided adequate details to support it.

Revise Ineffective Topic Sentences

Your topic sentence is the sentence around which your paragraph is built, so be sure it is strong and effective. The most common problems with topic sentences include

- The topic sentence lacks a point of view.
- The topic sentence is too broad.
- The topic sentence is too narrow. Each of these problems is addressed in Chapter 4 (pp. 132–137). Be sure to review this section.

EXERCISE 8-1

WRITING IN PROGRESS

Writing a Paragraph

Directions: Write a paragraph on one of the following topics. Evaluate your topic sentence to determine whether it is too broad, is too narrow, or lacks a point of view.

1. A memorable wedding or funeral
2. Your favorite holiday
3. A favorite character in a book or movie
4. A person who is a hero to you
5. An embarrassing experience

Revise Paragraphs to Add Supporting Details

The details in a paragraph should give your reader sufficient information to make your topic sentence believable. Paragraphs that lack necessary detail are called **underdeveloped paragraphs**. Underdeveloped paragraphs lack supporting sentences to prove or explain the point made in the topic sentence. As you read the following first draft of paragraph 5 from Claire's essay, keep the topic sentence in mind and consider whether the rest of the sentences support it.

Claire's First Draft of Paragraph 5

> Of course, not all Internet dating relationships are lies, and not all online couples end up hurt and ashamed. Sometimes, a relationship works and is exactly as the two people hoped it would be. Then again, some people just hate each other when they actually speak face-to-face. Not all of those looking for love online are creepers. Occasionally, two people find each other, and all is well.

This paragraph begins with a topic sentence that is focused (it is neither too broad nor too narrow) and that includes a point of view. It promises to explain how not all online relationships are dishonest and hurtful. However, the rest of the paragraph does not fulfill this promise. Instead, Claire gives two very general examples of online relationships: (1) sometimes a relationship works as the two people hoped and (2) some people hate each other when they actually speak face-to-face. The third example (not all people looking for love online are creepers) is a little more specific, but it is not developed well. The last sentence suggests, but does not explain, that people can find successful relationships online.

Taking into account the need for more supporting detail, Claire revised her paragraph as follows:

Claire's Revised Paragraph

> Of course, not all Internet dating relationships are lies, and not all online couples end up hurt and ashamed. Sometimes, a relationship works and is exactly as the two people hoped it would be. These legitimate, truthful relationships usually begin online and turn into face-to-face interactions fairly quickly. Some become long-term relationships, some friendships, some marriages. Then again, some people just hate each other when they actually speak face-to-face because the tone of the person's voice is downright obnoxious. Not all of those looking for love online are creepers, nor are all of them naïve daydreamers. Occasionally, two people looking for the right partner in life find each other online, and all is well.

Did you notice that Claire became much more specific in the revised version? She gave an example of relationships that began online and became long-term friendships and marriages. The example of hating someone once they speak face-to-face was explained in more detail: the tone of the person's voice is obnoxious. Finally, Claire provided more detail about the types of people looking for love online and explained how people occasionally can find the right partner online. With the extra details and supporting examples, the paragraph is more interesting and effective.

The following suggestions will help you revise an underdeveloped paragraph:

Tips for Revising Underdeveloped Paragraphs

1. **Analyze your paragraph sentence by sentence.** If a sentence does not add new, specific information to your paragraph, delete it or add to it so that it becomes relevant.

2. **Think of specific situations, facts, or examples that illustrate or support your topic.** Often, you can make a general sentence more specific.

3. **Brainstorm, freewrite, or branch.** To come up with additional details or examples to use in your paragraph, try some prewriting techniques. If necessary, start fresh with a new approach and new set of ideas.

4. **Reexamine your topic sentence.** If you are having trouble generating details, your topic sentence may be the problem. Consider changing the approach.

EXAMPLE	Internet dating is tedious.
REVISED	Internet dating, although tedious, is worth the effort if you take the time to write a good profile, list your criteria for a partner, and invest time in face-to-face meetings with potential partners.

5. **Consider changing your topic.** If a paragraph remains troublesome, look for a new topic and start over.

EXERCISE 8-2

Reading: Evaluating a Paragraph

Directions: The following paragraph is poorly developed. What suggestions would you make to the writer to improve the paragraph? Write them in the space provided. Be specific. Which sentences are weak? How could each be improved?

I am attending college to improve myself. By attending college, I am getting an education to improve the skills that I will need for a good career in broadcasting. Then, after a successful career, I'll be able to get the things that I need to be happy in my life. People will also respect me more.

_____

_____

_____

_____

EXERCISE 8-3 Writing: Revising a Paragraph

Directions: Evaluate the following paragraph by answering the questions that follow it.

> One of the best ways to keep people happy and occupied is to entertain them. Every day people are being entertained, whether it is by a friend for a split second or by a Broadway play for several hours. Entertainment is probably one of the nation's biggest businesses. Entertainment has come a long way from the past; it has gone from plays in the park to films in eight-screen movie theaters.

1. Evaluate the topic sentence. What is wrong with it? How could it be revised?

   _____

   _____

2. Write a more effective topic sentence about entertainment.

   _____

   _____

3. Evaluate the supporting details. What is wrong with them?

   _____

   What should the writer do to develop her paragraph?

   _____

4. Use the topic sentence you wrote in question 2 above to develop a paragraph about entertainment.

 NEED TO KNOW

Adding Supporting Details

To revise an underdeveloped paragraph,

- analyze your paragraph sentence by sentence.
- think of specific situations, facts, or examples that illustrate or support your main point.
- use brainstorming, freewriting, or branching.
- reexamine your topic sentence.
- consider changing your topic.

EXERCISE 8-4 Writing: Revising a Paragraph

WRITING IN PROGRESS

Directions: Revise the paragraph you wrote in Exercise 8-1, ensuring you have an effective topic sentence and sufficient details to support it.

Use Idea Maps to Spot Revision Problems

■ **GOAL 3**
Use idea maps to spot
revision problems

Some students find revision a troublesome step because it is difficult for them to see what is wrong with their own work. After working hard on a first draft, it is tempting to say to yourself that you have done a great job and to think, "This is fine." Other times, you may think you have explained and supported an idea clearly when actually you have not. Almost all writing, however, needs and benefits from revision.

An idea map can help you spot weaknesses and discover what you may not have done as well as you thought. It can also show how each of your ideas fits with and relates to all of the other ideas in a paragraph or essay. In this section, you will learn how to use an idea map to (1) discover problems in a paragraph and (2) guide your revision as you ask and answer the following questions.

■ Does every detail belong? Have I strayed from the topic?

■ Are the details arranged and developed logically?

■ Is the paragraph balanced? Is it repetitious?

Does Every Detail Belong, or Have You Strayed Off Topic?

Every detail in a paragraph must directly support the topic sentence or one of the other details. To spot unrelated details, draw an idea map and ask, "Does this detail directly explain the topic sentence or one of the other details?" If you are not sure, ask, "What happens if I take this out?" If meaning is lost or if confusion occurs, the detail is important. Include it in your map. If you can make your point just as well without the detail, list it under "unrelated details." Unrelated details like these are an indication that you are straying off topic.

Here is Claire's first draft of paragraph 4.

Claire's First Draft of Paragraph 4

Aside from the basic problems with lying to a lover such as distrust and potential bodily harm, there lies a less tangible effect: heartbreak. Just because a person was not physically injured by another does not make the internal pain less significant. And excessive crying from that heartbreak may cause actual physical damage to your eyes, blurring your vision temporarily. Tea bags containing caffeine can help reduce swelling from too much crying and improve your blurred vision. The emotional impact of having taken a risk on a faceless person and failing miserably is without a doubt shattering and life-altering. News media publish plenty of stories about individuals who have lost their lives because of trusting the wrong person online, but they rarely tell the stories of everyone else who got the short end of the stick and how that relationship changed their lives. News media try to gain readers by focusing on sensational stories involving a very small percentage of people. That dishonesty will live with those victims forever, inhibiting their relationships from that point onward.

She was concerned that she had included unrelated details, so she drew the following idea map:

VISUALIZE IT! ▶

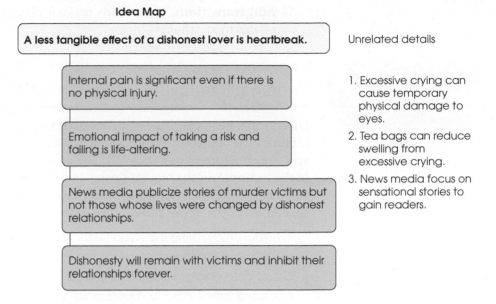

Idea Map

A less tangible effect of a dishonest lover is heartbreak.

Unrelated details

Internal pain is significant even if there is no physical injury.

Emotional impact of taking a risk and failing is life-altering.

News media publicize stories of murder victims but not those whose lives were changed by dishonest relationships.

Dishonesty will remain with victims and inhibit their relationships forever.

1. Excessive crying can cause temporary physical damage to eyes.
2. Tea bags can reduce swelling from excessive crying.
3. News media focus on sensational stories to gain readers.

Once she completed the map, she saw that the details about excessive crying and the use of teabags to reduce swelling do not directly explain the intangible effects of heartbreak. Also, the detail about the news media's focus on sensational stories to gain readers did not explain how people's lives are changed forever by dishonest online relationships. She cut these details in the final version of the paragraph.

What to Do If You Stray Off Topic

Use the following suggestions to revise your paragraph if it strays from your topic:

1. **Locate the last sentence that does relate to your topic, and begin your revision there.** What could you say next that *would* relate to the topic?

2. **Consider expanding your existing ideas.** If, after two or three details, you have strayed from your topic, consider expanding the details you have rather than searching for additional details.

3. **Reread your brainstorming, freewriting, or branching to find more details.** Look for additional ideas that support your topic. Do more brainstorming, if necessary.

4. **Consider changing your topic.** Drifting from your topic is not always a loss. Sometimes by drifting, you discover a more interesting topic than your original one. If you decide to change topics, revise your entire paragraph. Begin by rewriting your topic sentence.

Showing How Details Belong

The following suggestions will help ensure your reader can see the relevance of your details and their connection to your topic sentence:

■ **Add explanations to make the connections between your ideas clearer.** Often, a detail may not seem to relate to the topic because you have not explained *how* it relates. For example, health insurance may seem to have little to do with the prevention of breast cancer deaths until you explain that mammograms, which are paid for by some health care plans, can prevent deaths.

■ **Add transitions.** Transitions make it clearer to your reader how one detail relates to another.

EXERCISE 8-5

Reading: Identifying Unrelated Details

Directions: Read the following first-draft paragraph. Then draw an idea map that includes the topic sentence, only those details that support the topic sentence, and the concluding sentence. List the unrelated details to the side of the map, as in the example on the previous page. Identify where the writer began to stray from the topic, compare your results with those of a classmate, and then decide what specific steps the writer should take to revise this paragraph.

> Your credit rating is a valuable thing that you should protect and watch over. A credit rating is a record of your loans, credit card charges, and repayment history. Credit card charges can really pile up if you only pay the minimum each month, but some credit card companies will waive penalties just one time. You can try to negotiate a lower interest rate too. (No harm in asking!) If you pay a bill late or miss a payment, that information becomes part of your credit rating. It is, therefore, important to pay bills promptly. Some people just don't keep track of dates; some don't even know what date it is today. Errors can occur in your credit rating. Someone else's mistakes can be put on your record, for example. Hackers who break into credit card companies to use clients' accounts should face severe penalties once they are caught. It is a huge hassle to replace your card once your account number has been stolen. Why these credit-rating companies can't take more time and become more accurate is beyond my understanding. It is worthwhile to get a copy of your credit report and check it for errors. Time spent caring for your credit rating will be time well spent.

EXERCISE 8-6

WRITING IN PROGRESS

Writing: Identifying Unrelated Details in Your Paragraph

Directions: Draw an idea map of the paragraph you revised in Exercise 8-4. Check for unrelated details. If you find any, revise your paragraph using the suggestions given above.

Are the Details Arranged and Developed Logically?

Details in a paragraph should follow some logical order. As you write a first draft, you are often more concerned with expressing your ideas than with presenting them in the correct order. As you revise, however, you should make sure you have followed a logical arrangement. Chapter 5 discusses various methods of arranging and developing details. The following "Need to Know" box reviews these arrangements.

! NEED TO KNOW

Methods of Arranging and Developing Details

METHOD	DESCRIPTION
• **Time sequence**	Arranges details in the order in which they happen
• **Spatial**	Arranges details according to their physical location
• **Least/most**	Arranges details from least to most or from most to least, according to some quality or characteristic

Chapters 6 and 7 discuss several methods of organizing and presenting material. The "Need to Know" box below reviews these arrangements.

! NEED TO KNOW

Methods of Organizing and Presenting Material

METHOD	DESCRIPTION
• **Chronological order**	Arranges events in the order in which they occurred
• **Process**	Arranges steps in the order in which they are to be completed
• **Narration**	Makes a point by telling a story
• **Description**	Arranges descriptive details spatially or uses the least/most arrangement
• **Example**	Explains by giving situations that illustrate a general idea or statement
• **Cause and effect**	Explains why something happened or what happened as a result of a particular action
• **Comparison and contrast**	Explains an idea by comparing or contrasting it with another, usually more familiar, idea

Your ideas need a logical arrangement to make them easy to follow. Poor organization creates misunderstanding and confusion. After drafting the following paragraph, Claire drew an idea map of it, shown below.

Claire's First Draft of Paragraph 2

There are obviously some disturbing aspects to online dating. First dates wind up being late night movie dates, and kids go missing. Parents probably would love to think that their children are utilizing the Internet for school research purposes, but the appeal of an idea with sweet words can be too great to resist. With technology becoming widely available, underage girls and boys have more and more access to the Internet and its terrors (and wonders). Abduction, rape, and murder become increasingly simple for creative predators when unsuspecting men, women, and children utilize Internet dating

(continued)

and relationships while throwing caution to the wind in the hopes of finding true love or just friendship. It is no surprise that a predator can use online dating or other communication to entice victims into his web under the disguise of being a cool teen just like his victims.

VISUALIZE IT!

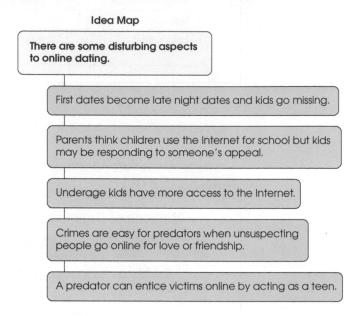

Idea Map

There are some disturbing aspects to online dating.

First dates become late night dates and kids go missing.

Parents think children use the Internet for school but kids may be responding to someone's appeal.

Underage kids have more access to the Internet.

Crimes are easy for predators when unsuspecting people go online for love or friendship.

A predator can entice victims online by acting as a teen.

An idea map lets you see quickly when a paragraph has no organization or when details are out of order. Claire's map showed that her paragraph did not present the potential results of online dating in the most logical arrangement: cause and effect. She therefore reorganized the details and revised her paragraph as follows:

Claire's Revised Paragraph

There are obviously some disturbing aspects to online dating. With technology becoming widely available, underage girls and boys have more and more access to the Internet and its terrors (and wonders). Parents probably would love to think that their children are utilizing the Internet for school research purposes, but the appeal of an idea with sweet words can be too great to resist. It is no surprise that a predator can use online dating or other communication to entice victims into his web under the disguise of being a cool teen just like his victims. First dates wind up being late night movie dates, and kids go missing. Abduction, rape, and murder become increasingly simple for creative predators when unsuspecting men, women, and children utilize Internet dating and relationships while throwing caution to the wind in the hopes of finding true love or just friendship.

Arranging and Developing Details Logically

The following suggestions will help you revise your paragraph if it lacks organization:

1. **Review the methods of arranging and developing details and organizing and presenting material** (see the "Need to Know" boxes on p. 273). Will one of those arrangements work? If so, number the ideas in your idea map

according to the arrangement you choose. Then begin revising your paragraph. If you find one or more details out of logical order in your paragraph, do the following:

- ■ Number the details in your idea map to indicate the correct order, and revise your paragraph accordingly.
- ■ Reread your revised paragraph and draw another idea map.
- ■ Look to see if you've omitted necessary details. After you have placed your details in a logical order, you are more likely to recognize gaps.

2. **Look at your topic sentence again.** If you are working with a revised arrangement of supporting details, you may need to revise your topic sentence to reflect that arrangement.

3. **Check whether additional details are needed.** Suppose, for example, you are writing about an exciting experience, and you decide to use the time-sequence arrangement. Once you make that decision, you may need to add details to enable your reader to understand exactly how the experience happened.

4. **Add transitions.** Transitions help make your organization obvious and easy to follow.

EXERCISE 8-7

Reading: Evaluating Arrangement of Ideas

Directions: Read the following student paragraph, and draw an idea map of it. Evaluate the arrangement of ideas. What revisions would you suggest?

The minimum wage is not an easily resolved problem; it has both advantages and disadvantages. Its primary advantage is that it does guarantee workers a minimum wage. It prevents the economic abuse of workers. Employers cannot take advantage of workers by paying them less than the minimum. Its primary disadvantage is that the minimum wage is not sufficient for older workers with families to support. For younger workers, such as teenagers, however, this minimum is fine. It provides them with spending money and some economic freedom from their parents. Another disadvantage is that as long as people, such as a teenagers, are willing to work for the minimum, employers don't need to pay a higher wage. Thus, the minimum wage prevents experienced workers from getting more money. But the minimum wage does help our economy by requiring a certain level of income per worker.

EXERCISE 8-8

Writing: Evaluating the Arrangement of Ideas in Your Writing

WRITING IN PROGRESS

Directions: Review the paragraph you revised for Exercise 8-6, and use your idea map to evaluate whether your details are logically arranged. Revise if needed.

Is the Paragraph Balanced and Not Repetitious?

In a first draft, you may express the same idea more than once, each time in a slightly different way. Repetitive statements can help you stay on track and keep you writing and generating new ideas. However, it is important to eliminate repetition at the revision stage, as it adds nothing to your paragraph and detracts from its clarity.

An effective paragraph achieves a balance among its points. That is, each idea receives an appropriate amount of supporting detail and emphasis. Here is Claire's first draft of paragraph 3 followed by her idea map of it.

Claire's First Draft of Paragraph 3

While not all those looking for love find themselves on the tail end of a potential romance gone bad, there is a great opportunity for dysfunctional relationships to be founded on little white lies. Even something as trivial as lying about weight because, "I'm going to lose those extra twenty pounds in a month or two anyway," creates an opportunity for a painful relationship. It seems easy to slip into a comfortable relationship behind a screen where people can be slightly tweaked versions of themselves, where they might have a job online when they actually just got laid off, or their profile picture is one from a couple of years back when everything was just a little bit firmer. It is tempting for people to present themselves using a photo from when they were younger or in better shape. It may seem trivial to some but people really should not lie about their weight or age or job status. The fact remains that a relationship, no matter what its roots, must be built on a foundation of truth and honesty. The MTV show *Catfish* illustrates what a large problem deceiving identities have become in online interactions. Little white lies that seem harmless can be indicators to a partner that his or her lover may have lied about far more than just love handles.

VISUALIZE IT!

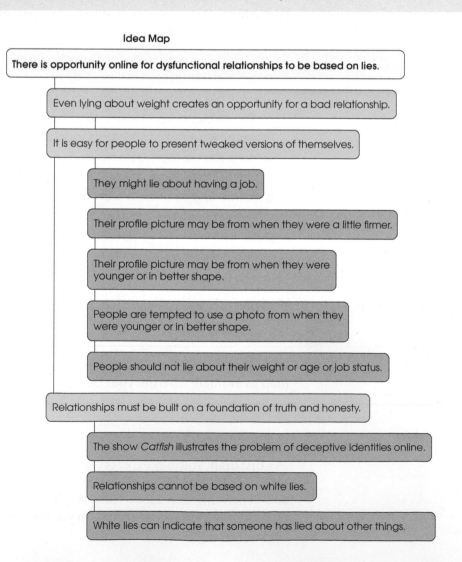

Idea Map

There is opportunity online for dysfunctional relationships to be based on lies.

Even lying about weight creates an opportunity for a bad relationship.

It is easy for people to present tweaked versions of themselves.

They might lie about having a job.

Their profile picture may be from when they were a little firmer.

Their profile picture may be from when they were younger or in better shape.

People are tempted to use a photo from when they were younger or in better shape.

People should not lie about their weight or age or job status.

Relationships must be built on a foundation of truth and honesty.

The show *Catfish* illustrates the problem of deceptive identities online.

Relationships cannot be based on white lies.

White lies can indicate that someone has lied about other things.

As the idea map shows, a major portion of Claire's paragraph is devoted to how people may misrepresent their physical appearance in online descriptions. The example about MTV's show *Catfish* is not as thoroughly explained. To revise for balance, she expanded her treatment of the MTV show and eliminated some of the repetitive details about dishonest profile photos.

Making Sure Your Paragraph Is Balanced

The following suggestions will help you revise your paragraph for balance:

- **Not every point or example must have the *same* amount of explanation.** For example, more complicated ideas require more explanation than simpler, more obvious ones. When you are using a least/most arrangement, the more important details may need more coverage than the less important ones.

- **If two ideas are equally important and equally complicated, they should receive similar treatment.** For instance, if you include an example or statistic in support of one idea, you should do so for the other.

How to Avoid Repetition

The following suggestions will help you revise a paragraph with repetitive ideas:

- **Try to combine ideas.** Select the best elements and wording of each idea and use them to produce a revised sentence. Add more detail if needed.

- **Review places where you make deletions.** When you delete a repetitious statement, check to see whether the sentence before and the sentence after the deletion connect. Often, a transition will be needed to help the paragraph flow easily.

- **Decide whether additional details are needed.** Often, we write repetitious statements when we don't know what else to say. Thus, repetition often signals lack of development. Refer to page 269 for specific suggestions on revising underdeveloped paragraphs.

- **Watch for statements that are only slightly more general or specific than one another.** For example, although the first sentence below is general and the second is more specific, they repeat the same idea.

> Loud noises from other people's apartments can be annoying. The noises coming from my neighbor's apartment last night were very annoying.

To make the second sentence a specific example of the idea in the first sentence, rather than just a repetition of it, the writer would need to add specific details about how the noises throughout the evening were annoying.

> The sounds coming from my neighbor's apartment last night—WXKS-FM played full blast until after 1 A.M., visitors with lead feet, and a screaming match with his girlfriend at 3 A.M.—are all examples of how annoying loud noises can be!

EXERCISE 8-9   Reading: Revising Repetition and Evaluating Balance

Directions: Read the following paragraph and delete all repetitive statements. Draw an idea map, evaluate the balance of details, and indicate where more details are needed.

> Children misbehaving is an annoying problem in our society. I used to work as a waiter at Denny's, and I have seen many incidences in which parents allow their children to misbehave. I have seen many situations that you would just not believe. Once I served a table at which the parents allowed their four-year-old to make his toy spider crawl up and down my pants as I tried to serve the food. The parents just laughed. Children have grown up being rewarded for their actions, regardless of whether they are good or bad. Whether the child does something the parents approve of or whether it is something they disapprove of, they react in similar ways. This is why a lot of toddlers and children continue to misbehave. Being rewarded will cause the child to act in the same way to get the same reward.

EXERCISE 8-10   Writing: Revising Repetition and Evaluating Balance in Your Paragraph

WRITING IN PROGRESS

Directions: Review the paragraph you revised for Exercise 8-8. Use your idea map to identify repetitive statements and evaluate the balance of details. Make any necessary revisions.

 NEED TO KNOW

Using Idea Maps

An idea map is a visual display of the ideas in your paragraph. It allows you to see how ideas relate to one another and to identify weaknesses in your writing. You can use idea maps to answer the following five questions that will help you revise your paragraphs:

- Does the paragraph stray from the topic?
- Does every detail belong?
- Are the details arranged and developed logically?
- Is the paragraph balanced?
- Is the paragraph repetitious?

> ### *Revision Checklist*
>
> #### Paragraph Development
>
> 1. Is the topic manageable (neither too broad nor too narrow)?
> 2. Is the paragraph written with purpose and audience in mind?
> 3. Does the topic sentence identify the topic?
> 4. Does the topic sentence make a point about the topic?
> 5. Does each sentence support the topic sentence?
> 6. Is there sufficient detail?
> 7. Is there a sentence at the end that brings the paragraph to a close?
>
> #### Sentence Development
>
> 8. Are there any sentence fragments, run-on sentences, or comma splices?
> 9. Are ideas combined to produce more effective sentences?
> 10. Are adjectives and adverbs used to make the sentences vivid and interesting?
> 11. Are relative clauses and prepositional phrases like *-ing* phrases used to add detail?
> 12. Are pronouns used correctly and consistently?

Proofread for Correctness

■ GOAL 4
Proofread for errors

Proofreading is a final reading of your paper to check for errors. In this final polishing of your work, the focus is on correctness, so don't proofread until you have done all your rethinking of ideas and revision. When you are ready to proofread your writing, you should check for errors in

- ■ sentences (run-ons or fragments).
- ■ grammar.
- ■ spelling.
- ■ punctuation.
- ■ capitalization.

The "Brief Grammar Handbook" on page 467 gives more detailed information on each topic. The following tips will ensure that you don't miss any errors.

Tips for Proofreading

1. **Review your paper once for each type of error.** First, read it for run-on sentences and fragments. Take a short break, and then read it four more times, each time paying attention to one of the following: *spelling, punctuation, grammar*, and *capitalization*.

2. **To find spelling errors, read your paper from last sentence to first sentence and from last word to first word.** Reading in this way, you will not get distracted by the flow of ideas, so you can focus on finding errors. Also use the spell-checker on your computer, but be sure to proofread for the kinds of errors it cannot catch: missing words, errors that are themselves words (such as *of* for *or*), and homophones (for example, using *it's* for *its*).

3. **Read each sentence aloud, slowly and deliberately.** This technique will help you catch endings that you have left off verbs or missing plurals.

4. **Check for errors one final time after you print your paper.** Don't do this when you are tired; you might introduce new mistakes. Ask a classmate or friend to read your paper to catch any mistakes you missed.

Here is paragraph 2 from Claire's essay, showing a variety of the types of errors that you should look for and correct during proofreading. Notice how the errors in grammar, punctuation, and spelling have been corrected.

There are obviously some disturbing aspects to online dating. With technology becoming widely available, underage girls and boys have more and more ~~axcess~~ *access* to the Internet and ~~it's~~ *its* terrors (and wonders). Parents probably would love to think that ~~there~~ *their* children are utilizing the Internet for school research purposes, but the appeal of *an* idea with sweet words can be too great to resist. It is no ~~suprise~~ *surprise* that a ~~predater~~ *predator* can use online dating or other communication to entice victims into his web under the ~~disgiuse~~ *disguise* of being a cool *teen* just like his victim. First dates wind up being late night movie dates~~. And~~ *, and* kids go missing. Abduction, rape, and murder becomes increasingly simple for creative ~~predaters~~ *predators* when unsuspecting men, ~~woman~~ *women*, and children utilize Internet dating and relationships while ~~thrown~~ *throwing* caution to the wind in the hopes of finding true love or just friendship.

The following checklist will remind you to check for spelling, punctuation, and other mechanical errors.

Proofreading Checklist

1. Does each sentence end with an appropriate punctuation mark (period, question mark, exclamation point, or quotation mark)?
2. Is all punctuation within each sentence correct (commas, colons, semicolons, apostrophes, dashes, and quotation marks)?
3. Is each word spelled correctly?
4. Are capital letters used where needed?
5. Are numbers and abbreviations used correctly?
6. Are any words left out?
7. Are all typographical errors corrected?
8. Are the pages in the correct order and numbered?

EXERCISE 8-11

WRITING IN PROGRESS

Writing: Proofreading Your Paragraph

Directions: Prepare and proofread the final version of the paragraph you revised for Exercise 8-10.

Use Peer Review

■ **GOAL 5**
Use peer review

Classmates can often help you realize what is and what is not effective in a piece of writing. They can provide valuable advice and feedback on what you should revise. And you, in turn, can read the writing of others and offer them helpful ideas. This exchange of ideas is often called **peer review**. Use the following suggestions to make this process work for you.

When You Are the Writer …

1. Prepare your draft in readable form. Double-space your work.

2. When you receive your peers' comments, weigh them carefully. Keep an open mind, but do not feel that you must accept every suggestion that is made.

3. If you have questions or are uncertain about your peers' advice, talk with your instructor.

When You Are the Reader …

1. Read the draft through at least once before making any suggestions.

2. As you read, keep the writer's intended audience in mind (see Chapter 2). The draft should be appropriate for that audience.

3. Offer positive comments first. Say what the writer did well.

4. Use the "Revision Checklist" and "Need to Know" boxes in this text to guide your reading and comments. Be specific in your review and offer suggestions for improvement.

5. Be supportive; put yourself in the place of the person whose work you are reviewing. Phrase your feedback in the way you would want to hear it!

EXERCISE 8-12

WRITING IN PROGRESS

Practicing Peer Review

Directions: Exchange the paragraph you wrote for Exercise 8-1 for the one a classmate wrote for the same exercise. Then the two of you should do the following:

1. List two things the writer did well.

   a. _____

   b. _____

2. List two areas for improvement.

   a. _____

   b. _____

READ AND REVISE

Revise

The paragraph below strays from its topic and includes details that do not belong. Revise the paragraph by deleting repetitive sentences and sentences that do not directly support the thesis. Add transitions as needed.

Do you have trouble getting out of the house on time in the morning? If you are not a naturally well-organized person, you may need to overcompensate by being super organized in the morning. A detailed checklist can help you accomplish the seemingly impossible goal of leaving home exactly when you are supposed to. It is especially difficult to leave on time if you are tired or feeling lazy. When making such a checklist, most people find it helpful to backtrack to the previous evening. Do you have clean clothes for the next day, or do you need to do a load of laundry? Are your materials for school or work neatly assembled, or is there a landslide of papers covering your desk? Do you need to pack a lunch? You get the picture. In your checklist, include tasks to complete the night before as well as a precise sequence of morning tasks with realistic estimates of the time required for each task. If you have children, help them make checklists to keep track of homework assignments. Child development experts stress the importance of predictable structure in children's lives. If you live with a friend or spouse, make sure to divide all chores in an equitable way. Often one person tends to be neater than the other, so you may need to make compromises, but having an explicit agreement about household responsibilities can help prevent resentment and conflict at home.

Proofread

The following excerpt contains run-on sentences and fragments as well as errors in grammar, spelling, punctuation, and capitalization. Proofread the excerpt and correct the errors.

Took me a hole year to get my life back in order from the accedent. Finally, when I did, I started working I even worked on going back to school to get my associate's degree. I wanted to get my degree in Early Childhood Development because, I just love to be around kids. Love how their minds work.

Now that I am working on my dream nothing is going to keep me from it I work my butt off in all my classes, so I can makes somthing of my life. Even though no matter how hard I try to forget everything. I have scars and pictures to remind me not to make the same mistake again. I drive a lot more carefully these days.

READ AND RESPOND: A Student Essay

Earlier in the chapter, you read "The Woes of Internet Dating," and you have examined various elements of the essay throughout the discussion of revision strategies. Now it is time to take a closer look at the reading by responding to the questions that follow.

The Woes of Internet Dating

Claire Stroup

Examining Writing

1. How is this essay organized? Summarize the writer's essay in your own words.
2. Evaluate the details the writer used to support her thesis statement. Are her details relevant and does she provide a sufficient number (see Chapter 5, pp. 160 and 164)?
3. If you were a peer reviewer for this essay, what suggestions for improvement would you make?
4. Evaluate the title, introduction, and conclusion. How might each be more effective?

READ AND RESPOND: A Textbook Reading

The following reading, "Finding a Mate: Not the Same as It Used to Be," is taken from a textbook by James M. Henslin titled *Sociology: A Down-to-Earth Approach, Core Concepts*. As you read this selection, notice how the author uses examples to illustrate his thesis. Follow these steps before you read:

Thinking Before Reading

1. Preview the reading, using the steps discussed in the Pre-Reading Strategies section of Chapter 1.

2. Connect the reading to your own experience by answering the following questions:
   a. How did your parents meet?
   b. What do you think is the best way to find a mate?

3. Highlight and annotate as you read.

Finding a Mate: Not the Same as It Used to Be

James M. Henslin

1   THINGS HAVEN'T CHANGED ENTIRELY. Boys and girls still get interested in each other at their neighborhood schools, and men and women still meet at college. Friends still serve as matchmakers and introduce friends, hoping they might click. People still meet at churches and bars, at the mall and at work. Technology, however, is bringing about some fundamental changes.

2   Among traditional people—Jews, Arabs, and in the villages of China and India—for centuries matchmakers have brought couples together. They carefully match a prospective couple by background—or by the position of the stars, whatever their tradition dictates—arranging marriages to please the families of the bride and groom, and, hopefully, the couple, too.

3   In China, this process is being changed by technology. Matchmakers use computerized records—age, sex, personal interests, and, increasingly significant, education and earnings—to identify compatibility and predict lifelong happiness. But parents aren't leaving the process entirely up to computers. They want their input, too. In one park in Beijing, hundreds of mothers and fathers gather twice a week to try to find spouses for their adult children. They bring photos of their children and share them with one another, talking up their kid's virtues while evaluating the sales pitch they get from the other parents. Some of the parents even sit on the grass, next to handwritten ads they've written about their children.

4   Closer to home, Americans are turning more and more to the Internet with one-third of singles meeting their first dates through the Internet. There are over 1,000 online dating sites. Some are general—they try to appeal to everyone. Others are niche, targeting people by age, race, sexual orientation, or religion. Still others are super-niche. There are sites for Goths, military widows, and pet lovers. One site targets "green singles," people for whom environmental, vegetarian, and animal rights are central. Another targets women who like men with mustaches.

5   The photos on dating sites are fascinating in their variety. Some seem to be lovely people, attractive and vivacious, and one wonders why they are posting their photos and personal information online. Do they have some secret flaw that they need to do this? Others seem okay, although perhaps, a bit needy. Then there are the pitiful, and one wonders if they will ever find a mate, or even a hookup, for that matter. Some are desperate, begging for someone—anyone—to make contact with them: women who try for sexy poses, exposing too much flesh, suggesting the promise of at least a good time; and men who try their best to look like hulks, their muscular presence promising the same.

Snapshots

Tall, Dark, and Handsome chats with Buxom Blonde.

Jason Love/CartoonStock Ltd.

6   Many regular, ordinary people post their profiles. And some do find the person of their dreams—or at least adequate matches. With Internet postings losing their stigma, electronic matchmaking is becoming an acceptable way to find a mate.

7   Matchmaking sites tout "thousands of eligible prospects." Unfortunately, the prospects are spread over the nation, and few people want to invest in a plane ticket only to find that the "prospect" doesn't even resemble the posted photo. You can do a search for your area, but there are likely to be few candidates from it.

8   Do not worry. More technology has come to the rescue. The ease and comfort of "dating on demand" is available. You sit at home, turn on your TV, and use your remote to search for your partner. Your local cable company has done all the hard work— hosting singles events at bars and malls, where they tape singles talking about themselves and what they are looking for in a mate. You can view the videos free. And if you get interested in someone, for just a small fee you can contact the individual.

9   Now all you need to do is to hire a private detective—also available online for another fee—to see if this engaging person is already married, has a dozen kids, has been sued for paternity or child support, or is a child molester or a rapist.

HENSLIN, JAMES M., SOCIOLOGY: A DOWN-TO-EARTH APPROACH, 13th Ed., © 2017. Reprinted and electronically reproduced by permission of Pearson Education, Inc., New York, NY.

Writing in Response to Reading

Checking Your Comprehension

Answer each of the following questions using complete sentences.

1. According to the author, what is the most inconvenient aspect of Internet dating?
2. Explain how "dating on demand" works.
3. How does the author view electronic dating? Is he enthusiastic or skeptical about how technology has changed the process of finding a mate?
4. What is the purpose of the cartoon included with the selection?

Strengthening Your Vocabulary

Using the word's context, word parts, or a dictionary, write a brief definition of each of the following words as it is used in the reading.

1. prospective (paragraph 2) _____
2. compatibility (paragraph 3) _____
3. virtues (paragraph 3) _____
4. vivacious (paragraph 5) _____
5. pitiful (paragraph 5) _____
6. stigma (paragraph 6) _____

Examining the Reading: Using Idea Maps

Review the reading by completing the missing parts of the following idea map.

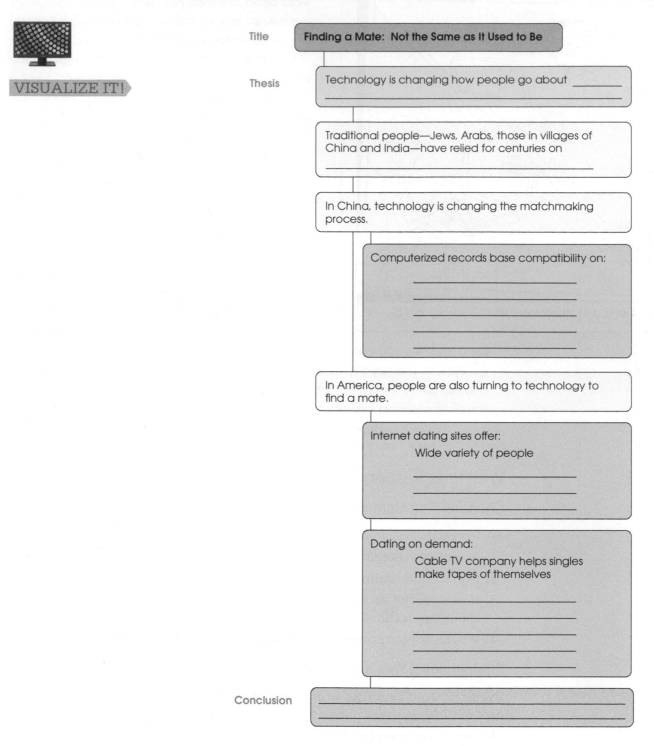

VISUALIZE IT!

Title — **Finding a Mate: Not the Same as It Used to Be**

Thesis — Technology is changing how people go about _____

Traditional people—Jews, Arabs, those in villages of China and India—have relied for centuries on _____

In China, technology is changing the matchmaking process.

Computerized records base compatibility on:

In America, people are also turning to technology to find a mate.

Internet dating sites offer:
 Wide variety of people

Dating on demand:
 Cable TV company helps singles make tapes of themselves

Conclusion

Thinking Critically: An Integrated Perspective

Get ready to write about the reading by discussing the following:

1. What is the author's purpose in writing this essay?

2. How is this essay organized?

3. Discuss the types of supporting details the author uses to capture your attention and to inform you about the various dating practices from around the world. Which types of details are most convincing and/or effective? Can you think of other examples the author might have used to further support his thesis?

4. What do you think of the traditional methods of matchmaking described in this selection? How might technology improve on these methods? Write a journal entry in which you discuss these questions.

5. Evaluate the criteria that matchmakers use in China to identify compatibility and predict happiness. What traits would you add to the list? Which ones would you remove?

6. Would you trust the description of a person you met online? Why or why not? If you became interested in a person you met online, would you use a detective service to look into his or her background?

7. Why was the cartoon included in the reading? What key point does it emphasize?

8. If you were to use a photograph in this reading, what would it look like? Why would you choose that photograph and what message or detail would it support?

THINKING VISUALLY

Paragraph Options

1. Write a paragraph describing how you first met a person who is important in your life.

2. If you are single, have you considered using an electronic dating site? Write a paragraph explaining why or why not.

3. Do you agree that Internet dating sites are losing their stigma? Write a paragraph explaining your answer.

Essay Options

4. Imagine the scene described in paragraph 3, with hundreds of parents trying to make matches for their children in a park in Beijing. If your parents were there, what would they say about you in their "sales pitch" to other parents? Write an essay explaining how you think your parents would describe you. In addition, try writing an ad that your parents might write about you.

5. What can you tell from the reading about the author's attitude toward Internet dating? Write an essay examining the ways the author reveals his feelings toward the subject. Include in your essay specific examples from the selection that show he is sympathetic, suspicious, disapproving, and so on. Also, explain how the selection would be different if it were entirely objective. How does the author's tone add to or detract from the reading?

6. What if you were to make a recording for a "dating on demand" video? Write an essay describing what you would want to include about yourself and the person you are hoping to meet.

Making Connections Between the Readings

Use both "The Woes of Internet Dating" and "Finding a Mate: Not the Same as It Used to Be" to write in response to one of the following prompts.

1. In an essay, compare and/or contrast the author's tone and attitude toward the topic in the two readings.

2. Both of the readings address finding a mate. What do you think are the most important characteristics of a mate? In an essay, discuss your top three most important characteristics of a mate. Be sure to support your three main points with sufficient, relevant, and specific details.

3. The author of "The Woes of Internet Dating" states that "… there is no substitute for interpersonal, face-to-face relationships." Do you think that the author of "Finding a Mate: Not the Same as It Used to Be" would agree with this statement? Use details from his essay to support your opinion.

4. The author of "Finding a Mate: Not the Same as It Used to Be" presents "dating on demand" as a new option for finding a mate. How do you think the author of "The Woes of Internet Dating" would feel about this option? Write an essay supporting your opinion with details from the readings.

SELF-TEST SUMMARY

To test yourself, cover the Answer column with a sheet of paper and answer each question in the left column. Evaluate each of your answers as you work by sliding the paper down and comparing your answer with what is printed in the Answer column.

QUESTION	ANSWER
■ **GOAL 1** Read carefully and critically to revise What strategies can you use when reading a draft for revision?	Create distance, allow enough time to read your draft several times, print a copy of your draft and read it with a pen in hand, read aloud, and ask a classmate for suggestions.
■ **GOAL 2** Revise ineffective paragraphs How do you revise ineffective paragraphs?	Begin revising by examining your topic sentence, and then determine whether you have adequate supporting details.
■ **GOAL 3** Use idea maps to spot revision problems What revision problems do idea maps help you to identify?	Idea maps can identify where the paragraph strays from the topic, whether supporting details are relevant and logically arranged, and whether the paragraph is balanced or repetitious.
■ **GOAL 4** Proofread for errors How do you proofread for correctness?	To proofread for correctness, you should review your paper once for each type of error, find spelling errors by reading your paper in reverse, read each sentence aloud, and check for errors one final time after you print your paper.
■ **GOAL 5** Use peer review What is peer review?	Peer review is an exchange of ideas in which you comment on your classmates' writing and they comment on yours, providing feedback to each other on what to revise.

9

Reading and Thinking Critically About Text

LEARNING GOALS

Learn how to...

- **GOAL 1**
  Read critically

- **GOAL 2**
  Make inferences

- **GOAL 3**
  Identify and focus purpose

- **GOAL 4**
  Analyze and consider audience

- **GOAL 5**
  Distinguish between fact and opinion

- **GOAL 6**
  Recognize bias

Amble Design/Shutterstock

THINK About It!

What is happening in the photograph on this page? Most likely you said that volunteers were helping provide meals to those who are hungry, but how did you know? No doubt, you used clues in the photograph such as the T-shirts worn by the servers, the serving of food, and so forth.

What was the photographer's purpose in taking this photograph? That is, what did he or she want to show or emphasize? Perhaps the photographer wanted to emphasize the importance of volunteerism or charitable acts or the value of community members helping each other. As you read text, you will need to pick up on clues the author provides, especially when ideas are only suggested instead of directly stated. When you write, you want to be sure to give your readers the right clues to make clear your purpose and help them understand your ideas.

In this chapter, you will learn to pick up on clues (called making inferences), evaluate an author's purpose, analyze an author's intended audience, distinguish fact from opinion, and identify bias. In this chapter, you will also read one student essay and one professional essay that explore this chapter's theme—helping others.

What Is Critical Reading?

Critical reading means questioning, reacting to, and evaluating what you read. It is an essential skill because most college instructors expect you to understand what you read *and* respond to it thoughtfully. When using sources to support or explain your ideas in an essay, be sure to read the sources carefully and critically. Critical reading is also important as you read and evaluate your drafts and look for ways to improve them.

Chapter Theme: Paying It Forward

In this chapter, you will read both a professional and a student essay on the topic of paying it forward by helping others. All of us, at some point in our lives, have been the recipient of an act of kindness, often undeserved or unexpected. Our response to that kindness is often to "pay it forward" to someone else who could use a helping hand, a smile, or a kind word. Opportunities to serve others are everywhere, and each of us has the potential to make a difference in the world, one person at a time. As you read the two essays in this chapter, evaluate and analyze the texts and annotate each reading yourself, recording your thoughts on the topic, to be prepared to discuss and write about it or a related topic.

Look it up!

Use the search engine on your smartphone (or work with a classmate who has a smartphone) and look up the phrase "give back by volunteering." Review several entries. Based on what you read, what are some ways that you might volunteer in your community? Write a few sentences about ways that you would like to give back to your community through volunteering.

EXAMINING PROFESSIONAL WRITING

The following selection appeared in *The Huffington Post,* an online site that provides news and analysis on a variety of current issues. In this selection, the author presents a story about nine women who secretly bestowed happiness on others for more than thirty years. It will be used in this chapter to demonstrate how to read and think critically about text.

Thinking Before Reading

Follow these steps before you read:

1. Preview the reading, using the steps discussed in the Pre-Reading Strategies section of Chapter 1.

2. Connect the reading to your own experiences by answering the following questions:
   a. What type of volunteer service have you provided to your community?
   b. If you had a million dollars, how would you spend it?
3. Highlight and annotate as you read.

The Business 9 Women Kept a Secret for Three Decades

Lori Weiss

1   Somewhere in West Tennessee, not far from Graceland, nine women—or "The 9 Nanas," as they prefer to be called—gather in the darkness of night. At 4 a.m., they begin their daily routine—a ritual that no one, not even their husbands, knew about for 30 years. They have one mission and one mission only: to create happiness. And it all begins with baked goods.

2   "One of us starts sifting the flour and another washing the eggs," explained Nana Mary Ellen, the appointed spokesperson for their secret society. "And some-one else makes sure the pans are all ready. We switch off, depending on what we feel like doing that day.

3   "But you make sure to say Nana Pearl is in charge, because she's the oldest!" she added with a wink and a smile.

4   Over the next three hours, the 9 Nanas (who all consider themselves sisters, despite what some of their birth certificates say) will whip up hundreds of pound cakes, as part of a grand scheme to help those in need. And then, before anyone gets as much as a glimpse of them, they'll disappear back into their daily lives. The only hint that may remain is the heavenly scent of vanilla, lemon and lime, lingering in the air.

5   Even the UPS driver, who picks up hundreds of packages at a time, has no clue what these women, who range in age from 54 to 72, are doing. He's just happy to get a hug and a bag filled with special treats. What he doesn't know is that he's part of their master plan. A plan that began 35 years ago—when the "sisters" got together for their weekly card game—something their husbands referred to as "Broads and Bridge."

6   "Pearl says it was all her idea," Mary Ellen teased, "but as I remember it, we were sitting around reminiscing about MaMaw and PaPaw and all the different ways they would lend a hand in the community." MaMaw and PaPaw are the grandpar-ents who raised four of the women, Mary Ellen included, when their mother passed away; and they took in Pearl as their own, when her parents needed some help.

7   "MaMaw Ruth would read in the paper that someone had died," Mary Ellen remembered, "and she'd send off one of her special pound cakes. She didn't have to know the family. She just wanted to put a little smile on their faces. And we started thinking about what we could do to make a difference like that. What if we had a million dollars? How would we spend it?

8   So the ladies began brainstorming.

9 "One of the sisters suggested that we should all start doing our own laundry and put the money we saved to good use. I admit, I protested at first. There's just something about laundering that I don't like. But I was outnumbered! So among the nine of us, we'd put aside about $400 a month and our husbands never noticed a thing. Their shirts looked just fine."

10 And then the women started listening. They'd eavesdrop—all with good intentions, of course—at the local beauty shop or when they were picking up groceries. And when they heard about a widow or a single mom who needed a little help, they'd step in and anonymously pay a utility bill or buy some new clothes for the children.

11 "We wanted to help as much as we could," Mary Ellen said, "without taking away from our own families, so we became coupon clippers. And we'd use green stamps. Remember those? We'd use green stamps and we'd make sure to go to Goldsmith's department store on Wednesdays. Every week they'd have a big sale and you could spend $100 and walk away with $700 worth of merchandise."

12 The Nanas would find out where the person lived and send a package with a note that simply said, "Somebody loves you"—and they'd be sure to include one of MaMaw Ruth's special pound cakes.

13 The more people they helped, the bolder they became.

14 "We gave new meaning to the term drive-by," Mary Ellen said with delight. "We'd drive through low-income neighborhoods and look for homes that had fans in the window. That told us that the people who lived there didn't have air-conditioning. Or we'd see that there were no lights on at night, which meant there was a good chance their utilities had been turned off. Then we'd return before the sun came up, like cat burglars, and drop off a little care package."

15 For three decades, the ladies' good deeds went undetected—that is, until five years ago, when Mary Ellen's husband, whom she lovingly calls "Southern Charmer," started noticing extra mileage on the car and large amounts of cash being withdrawn from their savings account.

16 "He brought out bank statements and they were highlighted!" Mary Ellen said, recalling the horror she felt. "I tried to explain that I had bought some things, but he had this look on his face that I'd never seen before—and I realized what he must have been thinking. I called the sisters and said, 'You all need to get over here right away.'"

17 So 30 years into their secret mission, the 9 Nanas and their husbands gathered in Mary Ellen's living room and the sisters came clean. They told the husbands about the laundry and the eavesdropping—even the drive-bys. And that's where their story gets even better—because the husbands offered to help.

18 "They were amazed that we were doing this and even more amazed that they never knew. We can keep a good secret! All but three of them are retired now, so sometimes they come with us on our drive-bys. In our area, all you need is an address to pay someone's utility bill, so we keep the men busy jotting down numbers."

19 It wasn't long before the couples decided it was also time to tell their grown children. And that's when happiness began to happen in an even bigger way. The children encouraged their mothers to start selling MaMaw Ruth's pound cakes online, so they could raise money to help even more people. And it wasn't long before they were receiving more than 100 orders in a day.

20   "The first time we saw those orders roll in, we were jumping up and down," Mary Ellen said with a laugh. "We were so excited that we did a ring-around-the-rosie! Then we called all the children and said, 'What do we do next?'"

21   That's when the 9 Nanas moved their covert baking operation out of their homes and into the commercial kitchen of a restaurant owned by one of their sons, where they can sneak in before sunrise and sneak out before the staff comes in. They even hired a "happiness coordinator" (whose code name is "Sunny," of course). Her identity needs to be a secret, too, so she can help out with the eavesdropping.

22   "We swore her to secrecy—her parents think she works in marketing. And, really, if you think about it, she is doing public relations and spends a lot of time looking for people to help at the supermarket!"

23   These days, The 9 Nanas are able to take on even bigger projects, given their online success. Recently they donated more than $5,000 of pillows and linens and personal care products to a shelter for survivors of domestic violence. And this August, they'll celebrate their second consecutive "Happiness Happens Month" by sending tokens of their appreciation to one person in every state who has made a difference in their own community.

24   And that million dollars they once wished for? They're almost there. In the last 35 years, the 9 Nanas have contributed nearly $900,000 of happiness to their local community.

25   But that doesn't mean they're too busy to continue doing the little things that make life a bit happier. Sometimes they just pull out the phone book and send off pound cakes to complete strangers. And if the Nanas spot someone at the grocery store who appears to need a little help, it's not unusual for them to start filling a stranger's cart.

26   "Not everyone is as lucky as we were to have MaMaw and PaPaw to take care of them, to fix all those things that are wrong."

27   "So this is our way of giving back," Mary Ellen said. "We want people to know that someone out there cares enough to do something. We want to make sure that happiness happens."

How to Read Critically

■ **GOAL 1**
Read critically

To develop the habit of thinking critically as you read, use the following suggestions each time you work with an assignment:

■ **Read the selection more than once.** Read it several times, if necessary, to understand the author's message; then read it again to analyze and evaluate the author's ideas.

■ **Read with a pen or highlighter in your hand.** Highlight important passages or particularly meaningful or insightful sentences and phrases. Highlighting can be particularly useful for reviewing and summary writing. (For a review of highlighting, see Chapter 1.)

- **Make marginal notes as you read.** Write notes in the margins to record what you are thinking as you read. These notes will be helpful as you write about the reading. (See Chapter 1 for more detailed instructions on annotating.)

- **Ask questions as you read.** Question and challenge the author and the ideas presented. How do the ideas mesh or fit with your own knowledge, experiences, beliefs, and values? If they do not fit, ask why. Do you need to adjust your thinking or do further reading or research on the topic?

Ask Critical Questions

Asking questions is a way of expanding your thinking as well as a way of discovering ideas to write about. Here are a few examples of critical questions you might ask about a particular reading.

- **What do you know about the author?** Many readings provide a brief introduction. This *headnote* often provides information about the writer or the context in which the piece was written. Knowing the author's background can help you better understand or appreciate the reading. (In this text, the headnotes appear just before the "Thinking Before Reading" sections. For an example, see p. 291.)

- **When was the piece written?** Having a sense of the time frame involved can shed light on the issues being discussed. For example, today we take women's rights somewhat for granted. But in the 1800s and early 1900s, women were still struggling for the rights to vote and own property.

- **What emotions does the reading stir in you?** Does it make you thoughtful, cheerful, or angry? Why does the reading have this effect on you?

- **What doesn't sound right or seems impossible or unlikely?** If an idea seems odd or a fact seems not to fit with what you already know, be sure to question it. Check it further through online research or using other sources.

EXERCISE 9-1

Reading Critically: "The Business 9 Women Kept a Secret for Three Decades"

Directions: Read the following paragraphs (paragraphs 1, 4, and 5) from the professional essay, and then think critically and analytically to answer the questions that follow. Write a sentence or two answering each question.

1   Somewhere in West Tennessee, not far from Graceland, nine women—or "The 9 Nanas," as they prefer to be called—gather in the darkness of night. At 4 a.m., they begin their daily routine—a ritual that no one, not even their husbands, knew about for 30 years. They have one mission and one mission only: to create happiness, and it all begins with baked goods.

4   Over the next three hours, the 9 Nanas (who all consider themselves sisters, despite what some of their birth certificates say) will whip up hundreds of pound cakes, as part of a grand scheme to help those in need. And then, before anyone gets as much as a glimpse of them, they'll disappear back into their daily lives. The only hint that may remain is the heavenly scent of vanilla, lemon and lime, lingering in the air.

(continued)

5   Even the UPS driver, who picks up hundreds of packages at a time, has no clue what these women, who range in age from 54 to 72, are doing. He's just happy to get a hug and a bag filled with special treats. What he doesn't know is that he's part of their master plan. A plan that began 35 years ago—when the "sisters" got together for their weekly card game—something their husbands referred to as "Broads and Bridge."

1. Why does the author provide a vague description of the hometown of the 9 Nanas?

   _____

   _____

   _____

   _____

2. Why does the author write that after they bake cakes each morning, "They'll disappear back into their daily lives?"

   _____

3. Why does the author reveal the ages of the 9 Nanas?

   _____

   _____

4. Why does the author include the name, "Broads and Bridge," that the women's husbands used to refer to their weekly card game?

   _____

   _____

   _____

Make Inferences

■ **GOAL 2**
Make inferences

Just as you use inference when you study a photograph, you also use it when you try to figure out why a friend is sad or what an author's message is in a piece of writing. An **inference** is an educated guess about something unknown based on available facts and information. It is the logical connection that you draw between what you observe or know and what you do not know.

Here are two everyday situations. Make an inference for each.

■ You are driving on an expressway and you notice a police car with flashing red lights behind you. You check your speedometer and notice that you are going ten miles per hour over the speed limit.

■ A woman seated alone in a bar nervously glances at everyone who enters. Every few minutes, she checks her watch.

In the first situation, a good inference might be that you are going to be stopped for speeding. However, it is possible that the officer only wants to pass you to get to an accident ahead. In the second situation, one inference is that the woman is waiting to meet someone who is late; another is that she is waiting for someone she has never met, maybe a blind date.

When you make inferences about what you read, you go beyond what a writer says and consider what he or she *means*. You have already done this, to some extent, in Chapters 3 and 5 as you inferred the meanings of words from context and figured out implied main ideas. Thus, you know that writers may directly state some ideas but hint at others. It is left to the reader, then, to pick up the clues or suggestions and to figure out the writer's unstated message.

How to Make Inferences as You Read

Making an inference is a thinking process. As you read, you are following the writer's thoughts. You are also alert for ideas that are suggested but not directly stated. There is no simple, step-by-step procedure to follow. Each inference depends on the situation, the facts provided, and the reader's knowledge and experience. However, here are a few guidelines to keep in mind as you read.

Guidelines for Making Inferences

1. **Be sure you understand the literal meaning.** Before you can make inferences, you need a clear grasp of the facts: the main ideas and supporting details.

2. **Notice details.** Often, a particular detail provides a clue that will help you make an inference. When you spot a striking detail, ask: Why did the writer include this piece of information? Remember that there are many kinds of details, such as descriptions, actions, and conversations.

3. **Add up all the facts.** Ask yourself: What is the writer trying to suggest from this set of facts? What do all these facts and ideas point toward?

4. **Look at the writer's choice of words.** A writer's word choice often suggests his or her attitude toward the subject. Notice, in particular, descriptive words, emotionally charged words, and words that are very positive or negative.

5. **Understand the writer's purpose.** An author's purpose, which is discussed in the next section, affects many aspects of a piece of writing. Ask yourself: Why did the author write this?

6. **Be sure your inference is supportable.** An inference must be based on fact. Make sure there is sufficient evidence to justify any inference you make.

Keep the preceding guidelines in mind as you read the following passage. Try to infer what Charley learns from his experience on the Bay Bridge.

Charley Garfield tells a story about waiting his turn for the toll on the Bay Bridge in Oakland, California. As he's inching his way up to the tollbooth, he hears loud music coming from up ahead. Looking around for the offending car as the music gets louder, Charley gets closer to paying.

Then Charley realizes that the music is coming from his tollbooth and the attendant is smiling right at him. Not only is he smiling, he's dancing in the booth, pausing briefly only to take money from each driver, then resuming his outrageous movements.

(continued)

> When Charley finally hands the smiling attendant his money, he shouts over the thumping music, "Why are you dancing?"
>
> "I'm having a party!" the attendant shouts over the loud music.
>
> "But you're at work."
>
> "I know, but you see the other tollbooths? They're all like coffins," the attendant says to Charley. "Just look at their faces—they're all dead."
>
> "So why are you smiling?"
>
> "Because I've got a great job here. My office has windows on all four walls. And I've got a view of the San Francisco Bay!" The car in back of Charley honked a second time, so he said goodbye to the smiling attendant.
>
> Charley pulls away, also smiling, and with a new appreciation of human nature.
>
> —adapted from Randy Fujishin's *Natural Bridges*, p. 54

By making inferences, you realize that Charley's new appreciation of human nature involves a fresh way of looking at a dull, routine job. He learns that life is what you make of it; how you approach a situation can change it. What clues did the author provide that lead to this inference?

- **Descriptive details.** The writer's descriptions of the thumping music, the smiling attendant, and the tollbooth as having a view of San Francisco Bay all create compelling images.

- **Action details.** The image of the attendant in his booth dancing outrageously while playing loud music creates an impression of a happy, satisfied employee.

- **Conversation details.** The attendant's statement that other tollbooths are "all like coffins" and his instruction to "Just look at their faces—they're all dead" sharply contrast with his description of his tollbooth as an office with "windows on four walls," conveying the idea that one can think of a booth in different ways. The statement "I'm having a party!" effectively summarizes his attitude toward his job.

- **Word choice.** The writer has chosen words to create a vivid image of the attendant in his booth: "smiling," "dancing," "thumping music," and "resuming his outrageous movements."

EXERCISE 9-2　Reading: Analyzing Inferences

Directions: Read each of the following passages. Using inference, determine whether the statements following each passage are true (T) or false (F). Write your answer in the space provided before each statement.

A.　Eye-to-eye contact and response are important in real-life relationships. The nature of a person's eye contact patterns, whether he or she looks another squarely in the eye or looks to the side or shifts his gaze from side to side, tells a lot about the person. These patterns also play a significant role in success or failure in human relationships. Despite its importance, eye contact is not involved in television watching. Yet children spend several hours a day in front of the television set. Certain children's programs pretend to speak directly to each individual child. (Mr. Rogers is an example, telling the child "I like you, you're special," etc.) However, this is still one-way communication and no response is required of the child. How might such a distortion of real-life relationships affect a child's development of trust, of openness, of an ability to relate well to other people?

—Weaver, *Understanding Interpersonal Communication*, p. 291

_____ **1.** To develop a strong relationship with someone, you should look directly at him or her.

_____ **2.** The writer has a positive attitude toward television.

_____ **3.** The writer thinks that television helps children relate well to other people.

_____ **4.** The writer would probably recommend that children spend more time talking to others and playing with other children than watching television.

B. There is little the police or other governmental agencies can't find out about you these days. For starters, the police can hire an airplane and fly over your backyard filming you sunbathing and whatever else is visible from above. A mail cover allows the post office, at the request of another government or police agency, to keep track of people sending you mail and organizations sending you literature through the mail. Police or other governmental agencies may have access to your canceled checks and deposit records to find out who is writing checks to you and to whom you are writing checks. Even the trash you discard may be examined to see what you are throwing away.

No doubt by now you've realized that all of this information provides a fairly complete and accurate picture about a person, including his or her health, friends, lovers, political and religious activities, and even beliefs. Figure that, if the Gillette razor company knows when it's your eighteenth birthday to send you a sample razor, your government, with its super, interconnecting computers, knows much more about you.

—Katz, *Know Your Rights*, p. 54

_____ **5.** The writer seems to trust government agencies.

_____ **6.** The writer would probably oppose forcing libraries to give the police information about the books you read.

_____ **7.** The writer is in favor of strengthening citizens' rights to privacy.

C. George Washington is remembered not for what he was but for what he should have been. It doesn't do any good to point out that he was an "inveterate land-grabber," and that as a young man he illegally had a surveyor stake out some prize territory west of the Alleghenies in an area decreed off limits to settlers. Washington is considered a saint, and nothing one says is likely to make him seem anything less. Though he was a wily businessman and accumulated a fortune speculating in frontier lands, he will always be remembered as a farmer—and a "simple farmer" at that.

Even his personal life is misremembered. While Washington admitted despising his mother and in her dying years saw her infrequently, others maintain that he remembered his mother fondly and considered himself a devoted son. While his own records show he was something of a dandy and paid close attention to the latest clothing designs, ordering "fashionable" hose, the "neatest shoes," and coats with "silver trimmings," practically no one thinks he was vain. Though he loved to drink and dance and encouraged others to join him, the first president is believed to have been something of a prude.

—Shenkman, *Legends, Lies, and Cherished Myths of American History*, pp. 37–38

_____ 8. Washington is usually remembered as saintlike because he was one of the founding fathers and our first president.

_____ 9. The writer considers Washington dishonest and vain.

_____ 10. The writer believes that eventually Americans' attitudes toward Washington will change.

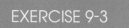
EXERCISE 9-3

Reading: Making Inferences

Directions: After reading the following selection, select the choice that best answers each of the questions that follow.

The Man, the Boy, and the Donkey

A Man and his son were once going with their Donkey to market. As they were walking along by its side a countryman passed them and said: "You fools, what is a Donkey for but to ride upon?" So the Man put the Boy on the Donkey and they went on their way.

But soon they passed a group of men, one of whom said: "See that lazy youngster, he lets his father walk while he rides." So the Man ordered his Boy to get off, and got on himself.

But they hadn't gone far when they passed two women, one of whom said to the other: "Shame on that lazy lout to let his poor little son trudge along." Well, the Man didn't know what to do, but at last he took his Boy up before him on the Donkey.

By this time they had come to the town, and the passers-by began to jeer and point at them. The Man stopped and asked what they were scoffing at. The men said: "Aren't you ashamed of yourself for overloading that poor donkey of yours and your hulking son?" The Man and Boy got off and tried to think what to do. They thought and they thought, till at last they cut down a pole, tied the donkey's feet to it, and raised the pole and the donkey to their shoulders. They went along amid the laughter of all who met them till they came to Market Bridge, when the Donkey, getting one of his feet loose, kicked out and caused the Boy to drop his end of the pole. In the struggle the Donkey fell over the bridge, and his fore-feet being tied together he was drowned.

"That will teach you," said an old man who had followed them: "Please all, and you will please none."

—*Aesop's Fables*

_____ 1. Which of the following words or phrases suggests disapproval?
   a. teach
   b. lout
   c. passers-by
   d. poor little son

_____ 2. Which statement best describes the Man in the fable?
   a. The Man is ignorant and uncaring about animal rights.
   b. The Man is insensitive to the needs of his son.
   c. The Man readily accepts the opinions of others.
   d. The Man does not know how to care for a donkey.

_____ 3. Why did the Man and Boy tie the donkey to the pole?
   a. They attempted to find a solution that met all three criticisms they had received.
   b. They were unable to control the donkey by any other means.
   c. The Man thought he could save the donkey's life.
   d. The son felt threatened by the crowd.

_____ 4. The passersby could best be described as
   a. angry.
   b. well-meaning.
   c. amusing.
   d. thoughtless.

_____ 5. The purpose of the story is to explain that
   a. animals should be treated with respect.
   b. you should ignore the opinions of others.
   c. public opinion is usually untrustworthy.
   d. you cannot make everyone happy.

EXERCISE 9-4

Reading: Making Inferences About "The Business 9 Women Kept a Secret for Three Decades"

Directions: Carefully read the following paragraphs (paragraphs 14, 15, and 16) from the professional essay. Using the guidelines on page 297, determine whether the statements are true (T) or false (F). Write your answer in the space provided before each statement.

"We gave new meaning to the term drive-by," Mary Ellen said with delight. "We'd drive through low-income neighborhoods and look for homes that had fans in the window. That told us that the people who lived there didn't have air-conditioning. Or we'd see that there were no lights on at night, which meant there was a good chance their utilities had been turned off. Then we'd return before the sun came up, like cat burglars, and drop off a little care package."

For three decades, the ladies' good deeds went undetected—that is, until five years ago, when Mary Ellen's husband, whom she lovingly calls "Southern

Charmer," started noticing extra mileage on the car and large amounts of cash being withdrawn from their savings account.

"He brought out bank statements and they were highlighted!" Mary Ellen said, recalling the horror she felt. "I tried to explain that I had bought some things, but he had this look on his face that I'd never seen before—and I realized what he must have been thinking. I called the sisters and said, 'You all need to get over here right away.'"

_____   1. Mary Ellen believes that drive-bys only happen in low-income neighborhoods.

_____   2. Mary Ellen believes that houses that have fans in the windows have no air-conditioning.

_____   3. Mary Ellen believes that houses that are dark at night have no electricity.

_____   4. Mary Ellen believes that the 9 Nanas should deliver pound cakes very early in the morning after the burglars have left the neighborhood.

_____   5. Mary Ellen loves her husband even though he is a southern gentleman who can get his way with most anything.

_____   6. The author believes that Mary Ellen's husband had been withdrawing money secretly from their bank account.

_____   7. The author believes that Mary Ellen's husband kept watch on her wherever she went.

_____   8. Mary Ellen believed that her husband thought she was having an affair.

_____   9. Mary Ellen believes that she needs the help of her sisters to save her marriage.

_____   10. The author believes that the 9 Nanas would be caught sooner or later by their husbands.

Inferences in Your Writing

It is usually better to state your ideas directly and straightforwardly rather than to leave it up to your reader to infer what you mean. Readers can misunderstand or even make incorrect inferences.

Once in a while, when explaining an idea, you may unintentionally omit information or falsely assume your readers have information or background that they do not, forcing them to make inferences. When writing about your career objectives, for example, you may assume that your readers know that nurses must pass state board exams, but in reality, many people not in health fields may not have that information. When reviewing a draft, reread it once to make sure you have provided your readers with full and complete information.

As you read the student essay that follows, you will notice that Juliette writes very straightforwardly, providing plenty of examples to illustrate each topic sentence and not asking the reader to make inferences.

EXAMINING STUDENT WRITING

Rawpixel.com/Fotolia

Although this chapter primarily focuses on reading, Juliette's essay models writing that takes into consideration and applies the same concepts to writing, such as determining audience and purpose, distinguishing between fact and opinion, and evaluating her own possible biases.

Juliette Simmons is a university student pursuing a degree in global studies. She has a passion for serving others and volunteers extensively in her community with the homeless and the aged. In a freshman composition class, she was directed to write an essay about a cause that was important to her and to be prepared to share the essay with classmates. The essay below is her response to the assignment.

"No Man Is an Island": The Importance of Community Service

Juliette Simmons

1   The mainstream American value of individualism is evident in the economics, family life, communication, and social structure of the society. Americans are increasingly communicating through technology rather than face to face interaction, and moving away from a sense of obligation to the community in which they live. So, what is the place for community service in a society that highly values individualism, and why is community service important? There are many different ways to be involved in community service: volunteering at food banks for trash pick-up, in community gardens, and in places such as senior citizen homes, animal shelters, homeless shelters, schools, non-profit organizations, and so on. The experience of participating in community service brings people back to the reality that individuals are not the world, but the world is made up of a community of individuals with different needs, belief systems, and ideas. Through service, people are brought into relationship with each other and into relationship with the earth: therefore, to use language from one of John Donne's poems, "No man is an island."

2   One of the ways in which community service brings people out of a focus on self is by exposing them to situations that cause them to feel sympathy for others. Using the example of doing community service at a homeless shelter, a typical day in this environment would offer the opportunity of communicating with homeless individuals and learning about the ways in which they live their lives. By eating with a homeless man, woman, or child, and having a conversation with him or her, a person is likely to feel a connection with that person on a very basic human level. Through interacting with others and developing relationships through community service, people connect, and, consequently, become more sympathetic towards diverse groups of people.

3   Another aspect of community service that helps to bring people out of themselves is community building. The act of service, whether it be to the environment,

Writer provides background information

Thesis statement includes quote that supports writer's point

Topic sentence supports thesis sentences, as do those that follow. Note use of transition here and in following paragraphs.

Details support topic sentence

Topic sentence

other persons, or animals, is part of the world. Any service project, no matter how small or seemingly insignificant, is a way of helping the community to flourish and grow. When people are exposed to the needs of others and the needs of the earth, they often obtain a broadened perspective that includes the needs of the community and not just their own individual needs. Community building benefits both the individual person and the community at large, and helps remind people that relationships and community are essential to living well.

Topic sentence	4 Community service also promotes the building of bridges and the breaking down of barriers to encourage relationships. An example of bridge building could be volunteering at a retirement or nursing home. As a young person, reaching out to the older generation is an act of bridge building because despite differences in age, and experience, a connection is formed through relationship. By playing cards or sitting down for coffee with an elderly person, space is made in which stories can be told and there can be mutual understanding and companionship. Another example of bridge building and breaking down barriers is doing any kind of community service in which you would have the opportunity to meet people with diverse backgrounds and experiences. Breaking down barriers such as language, religion, and ethnicity cannot be done effectively without building a bridge of connection between the individual self and another.

Examples support topic sentence

Transition moves reader along

Topic sentence	5 An additional reason why participating in community service is important is because the experience helps people to burst the bubble that they are living in and do something for someone else. Every person has his or her own bubble that has been formed over the years that includes people, places, and things that are considered safe and comfortable. It is the purpose of community service to get people to participate in the community, and possibly in part of the community that is unknown to the person. Community service is about being part of something that's bigger than yourself and this, in a sense, goes against the mainstream American values of individualism. Through participation in the life of the community, people are encouraged to move out of their comfort zone and engage with other people and other cultures.

Conclusion repeats thesis and summarizes reasons	6 Through participation in community service, relationships are built and connections made. In today's mainstream culture of individualism, community service works to bring people together through sympathy, community building, building bridges and breaking down barriers, and bursting the bubble of a comfortable individualistic mindset. Community service brings people to a collective "we" perspective rather than the individualistic "I". It is the relational nature of community service that makes it vital to the well-being and healing of human beings and the earth.

Identify and Focus Purpose

■ **GOAL 3**
Identify and focus
purpose

Authors have many different reasons or purposes for writing. Some of the most common purposes are

- **To inform or instruct.** Authors write to present information to their readers.
- **To persuade.** Authors write to convince readers to accept a particular idea or take a particular action.
- **To amuse or entertain.** Authors may write to tell an amusing story, share an entertaining meaningful experience, or make a comment on human behavior.

Identify a Writer's Purpose as You Read

Read the following statements and try to decide why each was written.

1. In 2011, there were nearly 600,000 applications to AmeriCorps—a program with only 80,000 positions, only half of which are full time.

2. Compelling everyone to follow a single path would reduce the value we create as a nation, devalue diversity, and transgress against the right to liberty.

3. I took a job as the beat reporter in Rancho Cucamonga, California. The stories I wrote for a community newspaper were often the only record of important civic happenings in a city of 100,000 people—a huge responsibility, especially for a 22-year-old, and one that caused me to happily work extremely long hours for very modest pay.

The statements above were written (1) to give information, (2) to persuade you to agree with the writer's point of view, and (3) to tell a story to make a point.

In each of the examples, the writer's purpose was fairly clear, as it will be in most textbooks, newspaper articles, and reference books. However, in many other types of writing, authors have less obvious purposes. In these cases, an author's purpose must be inferred. Here's how to discover an author's purpose:

 NEED TO KNOW

Identifying an Author's Purpose

1. **Ask yourself, "What is the writer trying to tell me? What does he or she want me to do or think?"** If you've read carefully and the reading is not too long, you will often be able to answer these questions in one or two sentences.

2. **Pay close attention to the title of the piece and the source of the material because these may offer clues.** Suppose an article is titled "Twenty-Six Reasons to Vote in National Elections." The title suggests that the author's purpose is to urge citizens to vote. If an essay on the lumber industry appears in *Eco-Ideas*, a magazine devoted to environmental preservation, you might predict that the author's purpose is to call for restrictions on the logging industry or for sustainable logging practices.

3. **Look for clues or statements about purpose in the beginning and concluding paragraphs.** Suppose an essay concludes with a statement such as "For all these reasons, it is vitally important to have a job that is rewarding and satisfying." This statement reveals that the author's purpose is to convince readers and win them over to a certain point of view.

| EXERCISE 9-5 | Reading: Identifying the Author's Purpose |

Directions: Based on the title of each of the following articles, predict the author's purpose.

1. Changing Habits: How Online Shopping Can Change Your Life

_____

2. I Got Straight A's, but I Wasn't Happy

_____

3. Animals Can't Speak: We Must Speak for Them

_____

4. Guns Don't Kill People: People Kill People

_____

5. What the Bible Says About the End of the World

_____

6. Sources of Drug Information

_____

7. Holy Week in Spain

_____

8. Two Famous Twentieth-Century Composers

_____

9. Internet Scams: You Could Be Next

_____

10. Biofuels: A Look to the Future

_____

| EXERCISE 9-6 | Reading: Determining the Purpose of Lori Weiss |

WORKING TOGETHER

Directions: Using the guidelines for identifying an author's purpose in the "Need to Know" box on page 305, what do you believe is Lori Weiss' purpose for writing her essay, "The Business 9 Women Kept a Secret for Three Decades"? Discuss your answer and the evidence you used to reach it with a classmate.

Focus Your Purpose When You Write

Identifying your purpose before you begin to write will help you produce a clear and focused draft. Think of purpose as what you hope to accomplish by writing. Once your purpose is clear, you will know the types of information to include, how to organize your ideas, and how to present your ideas clearly. For example, if your purpose is to describe a recent flood in your hometown, you would include descriptive details to help your readers visualize it. Or, if your purpose is to explain the economic impact of the flood on the town's residents, you would include facts and statistics. And, if you were writing to urge rebuilding of your town, you would include reasons and evidence.

Juliette wrote her essay, "'No Man Is an Island': The Importance of Community Service," to explain the benefits of community service. Because she is committed to and involved with volunteering, we may infer that, through this essay, Juliette hopes to encourage her readers to consider becoming involved in community service.

EXERCISE 9-7   Writing with a Purpose

Directions: For each of the following purposes, write a sentence that achieves it.

Example	**Purpose:**	To make a humorous comment about human behavior
	Sentence:	Mark Twain once said, "Never put off until tomorrow what you can do the day after tomorrow."

1. To give advice _____

_____

2. To persuade a friend to eat healthier foods _____

_____

3. To provide information about today's weather _____

_____

4. To give someone directions to your home _____

_____

5. To convey what it feels like to be in love _____

_____

EXERCISE 9-8   Writing: Analyzing Purpose

WORKING TOGETHER

WRITING IN PROGRESS

Directions: For three of the following topics, choose two different purposes and discuss with a classmate how the types of information you would include and the ways you would organize and present your ideas would differ for each. Then choose the topic and purpose you are most interested in and use a prewriting technique to narrow down your topic to be manageable in a paragraph.

1. Organ donation
2. Adoption
3. Performance-enhancing drugs in professional sports
4. Lowering the legal age for drinking
5. Reinstating the draft
6. Furnishing an apartment
7. Universal health care
8. Fertility treatments
9. Free college tuition
10. Assisted suicide

Analyze and Consider Audience

■ **GOAL 4**
Analyze and consider
audience

Writers vary their styles to suit their intended audiences.

Identify a Writer's Audience as You Read

A writer may write for a general-interest audience (anyone who is interested in the subject but is not considered an expert). Most newspapers and periodicals, such as *Time* and *The Washington Post*, appeal to a general-interest audience. On the other hand, a writer may have a particular interest group in mind. A writer may write for medical doctors in the *Journal of American Medicine*, for skiing enthusiasts in *Skiing Today*, or for antique collectors in *The World of Antiques*. A writer may also target his or her writing for an audience with particular political, moral, or religious attitudes. Articles in the *New Republic* often appeal to a particular political viewpoint, whereas the *Catholic Digest* appeals to a specific religious group.

| EXERCISE 9-9 | Reading: Analyzing Intended Audience |

Directions: After reading each of the following statements, select the choice that best describes the audience for whom each was written.

_____ 1. Chances are you're going to be putting money away over the next five years or so. You are hoping for the right things in life. Right now, a smart place to put your money is in mutual funds or bonds.

    a. people who are struggling to pay for basic needs like rent and food
    b. people who are very wealthy and have been investing their money for many years
    c. people with enough income that they can think of investing some for the future
    d. people who are using their extra income to pay off credit-card debt and student loans

_____ 2. Think about all the places your drinking water has been before you drink another drop. Most likely it has been chemically treated to remove bacteria and chemical pollutants. Soon you may begin to feel the side effects of these treatments. Consider switching to filtered, distilled water today.

    a. people who have no interest in environmental issues
    b. chemists
    c. employees of the Environmental Protection Agency
    d. people who are concerned about the environment and their health

_____ 3. Introducing the new, high-powered Supertuner III, a sound system guaranteed to keep your mother out of your car.

    a. drivers who love music
    b. teenagers who own cars
    c. parents of teenage drivers
    d. specialists in stereo equipment

_____ **4.** The life cycle of many species of plants involves an alternation of generations in which individuals of the gametophyte generation produce gametes that fuse and develop into individuals of a sporophyte generation.

—adapted from Wallace, *Biology: The World of Life*, p. 271

a. biology students

b. readers of general-interest magazines

c. gardeners

d. managers of landscaping companies

_____ **5.** As a driver, you're ahead of the repair game if you can learn to spot car trouble before it's too late. If you can learn the difference between the drips and squeaks that occur under normal conditions and those that mean big trouble is just down the road, then you'll be ahead of expensive repair bills and won't find yourself stranded on a lonely road.

a. mechanics

b. managers of auto-parts stores

c. car owners who do the repairs and maintenance on their own cars

d. car owners who are unfamiliar with a car's trouble signs and maintenance

---

EXERCISE 9-10   Reading: Analyzing Intended Audience

Directions: Read each of the following statements, and then write a sentence that describes the intended audience.

1. If you are wondering what you should wear to a job interview, the best advice is to dress as though you already had the job. When in doubt, you will make a better impression by dressing your best rather than wearing casual attire, which might imply that your interest in the job is equally casual.

_____

_____

2. A recent hacking incident revealed that hundreds of computer users have chosen the word "password" as their password and thousands more use sequential numbers such as "123456." To protect yourself from hacking, create a password that includes a mixture of upper- and lowercase letters, numbers, and symbols, and change your password every month.

_____

_____

3. Bright and White laundry detergent removes dirt and stains faster than any other brand.

_____

_____

4. One of the perks of being a college student is that you are eligible for a variety of discounts. By showing your student ID card, you can receive discounts at participating restaurants, theaters, and retail stores, and you can also save money on car insurance, travel, cell phone bills, and tickets for sporting events.

_____

_____

5. Parking around the concert hall is limited, so ticket holders should plan to carpool or take advantage of the free downtown trolley on the night of the concert.

_____

_____

EXERCISE 9-11

WORKING TOGETHER

Reading: Determining the Audience of Lori Weiss

Directions: Review Weiss' essay "The Business 9 Women Kept a Secret for Three Decades," and describe the audience for whom it is intended. Consider both its source, _The Huffington Post_, and the types of evidence she offers to support her ideas. Explain your answer to a classmate.

Consider Your Audience as You Write

What you write and how you say it are, in part, determined by the audience you are writing for. Try this experiment. Suppose the people below made the following comments to you. How would you respond to each person appropriately? Write what you would say to each person.

PERSON	COMMENT	YOUR RESPONSE
Parent or guardian	"Don't you think you should take a course in psychology?"	_____ _____ _____ _____ _____ _____
Employer	"Have you taken a psychology course yet? If not, you should."	_____ _____ _____ _____ _____
College instructor	"I advise you to register for a psychology course."	_____ _____ _____ _____
Close friend	"Why don't you take a psych class?"	_____ _____ _____ _____ _____

Now analyze your responses. Did you choose different words? Did you express and arrange your ideas differently? Did your tone change? Were some responses casual and others more formal?

Your reaction to each person was different because you took into account who the speaker was as well as what each one said. In writing, your readers are your listeners. They are called your **audience**. As you write, keep your audience in mind. What you write about and how you explain your ideas must match the needs of your audience. Through your language and word choice, as well as through the details you include in your paragraphs, you can communicate effectively with your audience.

Remember, your audience cannot see you when you write. Listeners can understand what you say by seeing your gestures, posture, and facial expressions and hearing your tone of voice and emphasis. When you write, all these nonverbal clues are missing, so you must make up for them. You need to be clear, direct, and specific to be sure you communicate your intended meaning.

Juliette's essay, "'No Man Is an Island': The Importance of Community Service," is written for her instructor but also for her classmates. Recognizing that some of her classmates may not have participated in community service, Juliette is careful to include concrete examples to illustrate many of her main points.

| EXERCISE 9-11 | **Writing: Considering Your Audience** |

WORKING TOGETHER

Directions: Select two people from the list below. For each one, write an explanation of why you decided to attend college.

1. Your brother or sister
2. Your favorite teacher
3. Your employer

Do not label which explanation is for which person. In class, exchange papers with a classmate. Ask your classmate to identify the intended audience of each explanation. When you've finished, discuss how the two pieces of writing differ. Then decide whether each piece of writing is appropriate for its intended audience.

| EXERCISE 9-12 | **Writing: Determining Your Audience** |

WRITING IN PROGRESS

Directions: Using the topic you narrowed down in Exercise 9-8, identify three audiences you might write for, choose one, and write a paragraph.

Distinguish Between Fact and Opinion

■ **GOAL 5**
Distinguish between fact and opinion

The ability to distinguish between fact and opinion is an important part of reading critically and writing accurately.

Distinguish Between Facts and Opinions as You Read

You must be able to evaluate ideas you encounter and determine whether they are objective information from a reliable source or whether they are one person's expression of a personal belief or attitude.

Facts

Facts are statements that can be verified. Statements of fact are objective—they contain information but do not tell what the writer thinks or believes about the topic or issue. The statement "My car payments are $250 per month" is a fact. It can be proven by looking at your car loan statement. Here are a few more statements of fact:

Facts

- Entrepreneur Arianna Huffington filed a dispatch yesterday from Aspen, Colorado, where she'll be participating in an effort "to make universal national service a new American rite of passage." (*You can check this by looking at news coverage in* The *Huffington Post.*)
- All over America, there are private schools, religious organizations, civic groups, non-profits, and businesses that either require or enable volunteerism. (*You can check this by looking at various national volunteering sites online, including the U.S. Bureau of Labor Statistics site.*)
- The Peace Corps received 150,000 requests for applications but has funding for only 4,000 new positions each year. (*You can check this by looking at the Peace Corps Web site.*)

Opinions

Opinions are statements that express a writer's feelings, attitudes, or beliefs. They are neither true nor false. They are one person's view about a topic or issue. The statement "My car payments are too expensive" is an opinion. It expresses your feelings about the cost of your auto payments. Others may disagree with you, especially the company that sold you the car or another person paying twice as much as you are paying. As you evaluate what you read, think of opinions as one person's viewpoint that you are free to accept or reject. Here are a few more examples of opinions:

Opinions

- The Washington, D.C., wonks who write the laws won't think of these minorities. (*Policymakers and legislators would disagree.*)
- A great deal of suffering in America today is caused by the evacuation of intermediary structures: the church, the family, voluntary organizations. These intermediary structures are in desperate need of renewal and that can only happen if there is a systematic shift of power, wealth, and influence from state and national governments to local units. (*People who believe power is better held at the state and national government levels rather than at the local level would disagree.*)
- There are some things, like defending the nation and collecting taxes, that government must do. (*Pacifists and people who do not believe in national defense or tax collection would disagree.*)

| EXERCISE 9-13 | Reading: Identifying Fact and Opinion |

Directions: Read the following statements and mark each one as either fact (F) or opinion (O).

_____ 1. After a losing streak that lasted over 100 years, the Chicago Cubs base-ball team won the World Series in 2016.

_____ 2. Alfred Hitchcock was the greatest director in the history of filmmaking.

_____ 3. Organic gardening methods produce the biggest, tastiest vegetables.

_____ 4. Female singers can be classified by pitch as soprano, mezzo-soprano, or contralto.

_____ 5. The Galapagos Islands are located on the equator, 600 miles west of mainland Ecuador.

_____ 6. Cloud storage for digital data is the wave of the future.

_____ 7. A recession is characterized by low prices, high unemployment, and a slowdown in business activity.

_____ 8. Bans on texting while driving should apply to all drivers regardless of age.

_____ 9. The country that became Iran in 1935 had been known for centuries as Persia.

_____ 10. Companies that test their products on animals should be required to disclose their practices to the public.

Informed Opinion

The opinion of experts is known as **informed opinion**. Such opinions are considered more trustworthy and reliable than those of casual observers or nonprofessionals. Here is an example:

> ■ General Stanley McChrystal: "Here is a specific, realistic proposal that would create one million full-time civilian national-service positions for Americans ages 18–28 that would complement the active-duty military—and would change the current cultural expectation that service is only the duty of those in uniform."

Textbook authors, too, often offer informed opinion. As experts in their fields, they may make observations and offer comments that are not strictly factual. Instead, they are based on years of study and research. Here is an example from an American government textbook:

> The United States is a place where the pursuit of private, particular, and narrow interests is honored. In our culture, following the teachings of Adam Smith, the pursuit of self-interest is not only permitted but actually celebrated as the basis of the good and prosperous society.
>
> —Greenberg and Page, *The Struggle for Democracy*, p. 186

The author of this statement has reviewed the available evidence and is providing his expert opinion on what the evidence indicates about American political culture. The reader, then, is free to disagree and offer evidence to support an opposing view.

Some authors are careful to signal the reader when they are presenting an opinion. Watch for words and phrases such as:

apparently	this suggests	in my view	one explanation is
presumably	possibly	it is likely that	according to
in my opinion	it is believed	seemingly	

EXERCISE 9-14

Reading: Identifying Facts and Opinions in the Professional Reading

Directions: Read the following paragraphs (paragraphs 9, 10, and 11) from "The Business 9 Women Kept a Secret for Three Decades," and then list the numbers of the sentences containing facts, opinions, and informed opinions in the spaces below.

[1]"One of the sisters suggested that we should all start doing our own laundry and put the money we saved to good use. [2]I admit, I protested at first. [3] There's just something about laundering that I don't like. [4] But I was outnumbered! [5] So among the nine of us, we'd put aside about $400 a month and our husbands never noticed a thing. [6] Their shirts looked just fine."

[7]Then the women started listening. [8]They'd eavesdrop—all with good intentions, of course—at the local beauty shop or when they were picking up groceries. [9]And when they heard about a widow or a single mom who needed a little help, they'd step in and anonymously pay a utility bill or buy some new clothes for the children.

[10]"We wanted to help as much as we could," Mary Ellen said, "without taking away from our own families, so we became coupon clippers. [11]And we'd use green stamps. [12]Remember those? [13]We'd use green stamps and we'd make sure to go to Goldsmith's department store on Wednesdays. [14]Every week they'd have a big sale and you could spend $100 and walk away with $700 worth of merchandise."

Facts: _____

Opinions: _____

Informed Opinions: _____

Use Facts and Opinions in Your Writing

Facts and opinions both have a place in good writing. Facts are essential in supporting and explaining your ideas, so be sure to provide adequate and sufficient facts in the form of statistics, reasons, quotations, descriptions, observations, and so forth. Opinions may be used to express your own ideas on a subject, but be sure to provide evidence to support them. Unsupported opinions are of little use to your readers and may make them feel as if you "haven't done your homework" in researching and thinking through your topic before writing about it.

Juliette's essay on the importance of volunteering is largely opinion based. Others may disagree with Juliette's position that community service is always enlightening and self-expanding, for example. To improve her essay, Juliette could have researched her topic to find facts that support her ideas or used quotations from experts that support the value of community service.

EXERCISE 9-15	Writing Facts and Opinions

WORKING TOGETHER

Directions: Working with a classmate, write one fact and one opinion for each of the following topics. For each opinion you offer, discuss what types of evidence would be useful in supporting it.

EXAMPLE   Topic: The environment

Fact: Trash, fertilizers, and auto emissions all pollute the environment.

Opinion: Everyone should get involved in efforts to preserve the environment.

1. Eating

Fact: _____

Opinion: _____

2. Cars

Fact: _____

Opinion: _____

3. Dogs

Fact: _____

Opinion: _____

4. The Internet

Fact: _____

Opinion: _____

5. Work

Fact: _____

Opinion: _____

EXERCISE 9-16 | **Writing Facts and Opinions**

WRITING IN PROGRESS

Directions: Reread the paragraph you wrote for Exercise 9-12. Check to see whether you have stated your opinions clearly and whether you need additional facts to bolster your opinions.

Recognize Bias

■ **GOAL 6**
Recognize bias

When a writer or speaker deliberately presents a one-sided picture of a situation, it is known as bias. **Bias** refers to an author's partiality, inclination toward a particular viewpoint, or prejudice. Now, think of a television commercial you have seen recently. Let's say it is for a particular model of car. The ad tells you its advantages—why you want to buy the car—but does it tell you its disadvantages? Does it describe ways in which the model compares unfavorably with competitors? Certainly not. Do you feel the ad writer is being unfair?

Now let's say you know nothing about e-book readers and want to learn about them. You find an article titled "What You Need to Know About E-book Readers." If the author of this article told you all the advantages of e-book readers but none of their disadvantages, would you consider the article unfair? We expect advertisers to present a one-sided view of their products. In most other forms of writing, however, we expect writers to be honest and forthright. If a writer is explaining Instagram, he or she should explain it fully, revealing both strengths and weaknesses. To do otherwise is to present a biased point of view. You can think of bias as a writer's prejudice.

How to Detect Bias as You Read

To detect bias, ask the following questions:

■ Is the author acting as a reporter—presenting facts—or as salesperson—providing only favorable information?

■ Does the author feel strongly about or favor one side of the issue?

■ Does the author seem to be deliberately creating a positive or negative image?

■ Does the author seem emotional about the issue?

■ Are there other views toward the subject that the writer does not recognize or discuss?

The author's language and selection of facts also provide clues about his or her bias. Specifically, words with strong connotative (emotional) meanings or words that elicit an emotional response on the part of the reader suggest bias.

In the following excerpt from the professional reading (paragraphs 24, 25, and 26), the author's choice of words (see highlighting) reveals her attitudes toward the mission of the "9 Nanas".

These days, The 9 Nanas are able to take on even bigger projects, given their online success. Recently they donated more than $5,000 of pillows and linens and personal care products to a shelter for survivors of domestic violence. And this August, they'll celebrate their second consecutive "Happiness Happens

Month" by sending tokens of their appreciation to one person in every state who has made a difference in their own community.

And that million dollars they once wished for? They're almost there. In the last 35 years, the 9 Nanas have contributed nearly $900,000 of happiness to their local community.

But that doesn't mean they're too busy to continue doing the little things that make life a bit happier. Sometimes they just pull out the phone book and send off pound cakes to complete strangers. And if the Nanas spot someone at the grocery store who appears to need a little help, it's not unusual for them to start filling a stranger's cart.

EXERCISE 9-17 | Reading: Recognizing Bias

Directions: Place a check mark in front of each statement that reveals bias.

_____ **1.** Cities should be designed for the pedestrian, not the automobile.

_____ **2.** There are more channels than ever before on cable television.

_____ **3.** The current system of voter registration is a sham.

_____ **4.** Professional sports have become elitist.

_____ **5.** Space exploration costs millions of dollars each year.

EXERCISE 9-18 | Reading: Identifying Bias

Directions: After reading each passage, select the choice that best answers each of the questions that follow.

A.   Summer is often an unpleasant time for Cape Cod residents. By mid-June, the Cape is flooded with tourists who stay until Labor Day. Tourists clog the small village streets with out-of-state cars, minivans, and campers, taking up every available parking spot. Gas prices rocket and local businesses all cash in by raising prices for tourists who are buying food, firewood, ice cream, and souvenirs, but locals are also affected by these price increases. It's best to not even try to eat in a restaurant during the summer if you're a local because the places are packed and the staff overworked. The beaches are filled with families with no room for anyone else to enjoy the natural beauty. Many locals give up and rent out their homes on Airbnb for the summer, collecting high rents while worrying their homes will be trashed by careless tourists. In fact, it is becoming increasingly difficult for everyday working people to afford to keep their homes on the Cape because taxes have been jacked up so high to pay for the amenities and services the tourists require. Tourism is slowly destroying what is so special about Cape Cod.

_____ **1.** The author seems biased against

    a. Cape Cod residents

    b. tourists visiting Cape Cod

    c. restaurant workers

    d. locals who charge high rent

_____ 2. Which of the following phrases best reveals the author's bias?
   a. "services the tourists require"
   b. "tourists who stay until Labor Day"
   c. "trashed by careless tourists"
   d. "pay for the amenities"

B.   Zoos are essential to our understanding of the animal kingdom. For the most part, animals kept in accredited and well-run zoos receive excellent medical care that they would not receive in the wild. They also are assured a stable food supply and won't starve. Zoos allow professionals to protect and conserve endangered species, ensuring they will survive instead of being wiped out in the wild. Many people wrongly complain that zoos constrain animals and reduce their freedom. Most zoos offer large habitats which allows the animals freedom of movement within a reasonable area. Zoos allow scientists to study many species of animals they would not have had access to otherwise and allows them to discover important facts about their behavior, health, and habits. We also absolutely must continue to have zoos so that children have the opportunity to see animals up close and learn to appreciate their beauty and wonder and grow up interested in the conservation of the great diversity of animals on earth.

_____ 3. The author's primary bias concerns the
   a. cruelty to animals.
   b. value of zoos
   c. loss of animal habitats
   d. food supply stability.

_____ 4. Which of the following phrases expresses the author's bias?
   a. "conserve endangered species"
   b. "well-run zoos"
   c. "zoos allow professionals"
   d. "grow up interested"

C.   The lottery might seem like inexpensive fun and a chance to make it rich, but it is in in fact a harmful practice. Americans spend more than $70 billion on lottery tickets every year, more than they spend on all other entertainment and leisure activities. Lotteries are actually a tax because they are used to fund essential state programs, such as education. Because lottery money is available, real taxes are artificially reduced for businesses and wealthier Americans. The people that pay the largest percent of this lottery tax are the poorest citizens who turn to the lottery out of desperation. Lotteries target people who can least afford it. The people who spend the most on lottery tickets do not have college degrees, and live at or below the poverty line. A recent study found that people earning only $13,000 a year spent $645 a year on average on lottery tickets—9% of their income. Lotteries also support and feed addictive behavior, encouraging people to do things against their own self-interest. People who actually win the lottery often lose all of it due to poor money management skills and bad decisions. Lotteries do more harm than good.

_____ 5. The author is biased concerning
   a. unfair lottery taxes.
   b. irresponsible leisure activities.
   c. lottery revenues.
   d. misuses of lotteries exploiting poor people.

_____ **6.** Which phrase best suggests the author's bias?

   a. "feed addictive behavior"
   b. "fund essential state programs"
   c. "lottery money is available"
   d. "people earning only $13,000 a year"

Acknowledging Bias as You Write

Readers appreciate and respect writers who are fair and honest and do not attempt to mislead them. It is acceptable, depending on the assignment and the topic, to express bias, but be sure you acknowledge that you are doing so. You might preface your comments by writing, "In my opinion, ..." or you could say "I agree with people who believe...." Juliette, in her essay on the value of community service, could have made it clearer that she was offering her own opinions by saying "Based on my experience..." or "From working with people from diverse backgrounds, I have observed that..." Adding such phrases would make it clear to her readers that Juliette is offering her own opinions and is aware that she is doing so.

EXERCISE 9-19	Writing: Analyzing Your Paragraph

WRITING IN PROGRESS

Directions: Evaluate the paragraph you wrote during this chapter, using each of the following questions, and make any revisions that are needed.

1. Highlight sentences or sections that require your reader to make inferences. Have you supplied sufficient and detailed information to guide your readers in making any inferences you expect them to make?

2. Is your purpose clear? Does your work accomplish your purpose?

3. Who is your intended audience? How did you adjust your writing to suit them?

4. Underline any statements of opinion. Have you provided reasons, examples, or other evidence for any opinions you offer?

5. Do you express bias? If so, have you done so fairly and openly?

READ AND RESPOND: A Student Essay

Rawpixel.com/Fotolia

"No Man Is an Island": The Importance of Community Service

Juliette Simmons

Earlier in the chapter, you read "No Man Is an Island': The Importance of Community Service" and examined various elements of the essay. Now it is time to take a closer look at the reading by responding to the questions that follow.

Examining Writing

1. Paraphrase Juliette's thesis in your own words.

2. Evaluate the details in this essay. Which reason given by Juliette was the most convincing to you? Why? What other reasons or details can you suggest that would support her thesis?

3. How do the ideas in this essay fit with your own knowledge, experiences, beliefs, and values?

READ AND RESPOND: A Professional Essay

Earlier in the chapter, you read "The Business 9 Women Kept a Secret for Nearly Three Decades" and examined various elements of the essay. Now it is time to take a closer look at the reading by responding to the questions that follow.

Writing in Response to Reading

Checking Your Comprehension

Answer each of the following questions using complete sentences.

1. Where did the 9 Nanas get the idea to make pound cakes for total strangers?

2. How did the 9 Nanas first save money for their happiness project?

3. What were the two places that the 9 Nanas got most of their information about people in need?

4. How did Mary Ellen's husband find out about the 30-year secret mission?

5. According to the 9 Nanas, what is a drive-by?

6. What is "Happiness Happens Month"?

Strengthening Your Vocabulary

Identify at least five words used in the reading that are unfamiliar to you. Using context, word parts, or a dictionary, write a brief definition of each word as it is used in the reading.

Examining the Readings Using Idea Maps

Create an idea map of the reading that starts with the title and thesis and then lists the author's main points. Use the guidelines in Chapter 1.

Thinking Critically: An Integrated Perspective

Get ready to write about the reading by discussing the following:

1. Discuss the title of this selection. Did it capture your interest and provide a clue to the subject of the selection? Can you think of another title that would be effective?

2. Discuss the types of details the author used in this selection. Which details were most effective? Why?

3. Write a journal entry about a time you helped a person in need or participated in a community service project *or* a community service project in which you would like to participate.

4. Mary Ellen says that helping others is her "way of giving back" (paragraph 27). What does she mean by this?

5. Can you detect any bias in this selection? Give examples if you can.

6. Can you find an inference in this selection? Give an example if you can.

7. If you were to include a photograph with this article, what would it look like? Why would you choose that photograph? What part of the author's message would it support?

THINKING VISUALLY

Paragraph Options

1. How do the ideas in this selection reflect your own experiences or beliefs? On what points do you agree or disagree with the author? Write a paragraph giving your answers.

2. Write a paragraph analyzing the author's choice of words and descriptive or emotional language throughout the selection. How would you describe the author's tone?

3. In the essay, Mary Ellen asks the question "What if we had a million dollars? How would we spend it?" Write a paragraph in which you answer those questions for yourself. Be sure to include details to describe how you would spend a million dollars.

Essay Options

4. The 9 Nanas expanded their happiness mission to include every state in the United States. Do you think we should spend our money and time helping those in other states and even other countries rather than helping those who live in our communities? Be sure to provide evidence that will adequately support your opinion.

5. Although many people have not formally volunteered in their community, most have at one point in their life helped someone in need, whether it were a neighbor, family member, or friend. Write an essay about a time that you served someone else. How did you serve? What motivated you to do it? How did you feel after you did it?

6. The 9 Nanas had a dream, and by starting small and persevering, they were able to see that dream come true in an even bigger way than they ever imagined. How about you? What is your dream? Write an essay in which you describe your dream and how you plan to achieve it. Be sure to provide details that will help your reader catch a glimpse of your dream and your passion to pursue it.

Making Connections Between the Readings

Use both "'No Man Is an Island': The Importance of Community Service" and "The Business 9 Women Kept a Secret for Three Decades" to write a response to one of the following prompts.

1. In "'No Man Is an Island,'" the student author poses the question: "What is the place for community service in a society that highly values individualism?" How do you think the author of "The Business 9 Women Kept a Secret for Three Decades" would respond to this question? Write a paragraph in answer to the question and support your thesis with specific details from the professional reading.

2. How do you think the author of "'No Man Is an Island'" would respond to the points made by the professional author? Write an essay to this question, being sure to include support from both of the readings.

3. In "'No Man Is an Island,'" the student author focuses on the building of relationships as the primary benefit of community service. The professional author does not discuss the benefit of building relationships at all; in fact, the "9 Nanas" operated in secret and had no relationship with the recipients of their kindness. Do you think the author agrees that building relationships might be a benefit of community service? Write an essay in response to this question and include details from both writings to support your answer.

SELF-TEST SUMMARY

To test yourself, cover the Answer column with a sheet of paper and answer each question in the left column. Evaluate each of your answers as you work by sliding the paper down and comparing your answer with what is printed in the Answer column.

QUESTION	ANSWER
■ **GOAL 1** Read critically How can you develop the habit of thinking critically when you read? What are four questions that will help you read critically?	Read the selection more than once, read with a pen or highlighter in hand, make marginal notes as you read, and ask questions as you read. Ask yourself: What do you know about the author? When was the piece written? What emotions does the reading stir in you? What doesn't sound right or seems impossible or unlikely?

QUESTION	ANSWER
■ **GOAL 2** Make inferences What is an inference?	An inference is an educated guess or prediction about something unknown based on available facts and information.
How do you make accurate inferences?	Understand the writer's literal meaning first, then notice details, add up the facts, consider the writer's word choices and purpose, and be sure your inference is supportable.
■ **GOAL 3** Identify and focus purpose How do you identify an author's purpose?	Ask yourself what the writer is trying to tell you, pay close attention to the title of the piece and source of the material, and look for clues about purpose in the beginning and concluding paragraphs.
Why is it important to determine your audience before you write?	Identifying your purpose before you begin to write will help you produce a clear and focused draft and help you determine what information to include and how to best organize it.
■ **GOAL 4** Analyze and consider audience How do you determine an author's intended audience?	Examine the site or publication in which the piece of writing appeared, as this can be clue to audience.
How do writers vary their styles to suit their intended audiences?	Writers will change the level of language, choice of words, and method of presentation, depending on the group of people for whom they are writing.
■ **GOAL 5** Distinguish between fact and opinion What is the difference between fact and opinion?	Facts are statements that can be verified; statements of fact are objective. Opinions are statements that express a writer's feelings, attitudes, or beliefs; they are neither true nor false.
What is informed opinion?	The opinion of experts is known as informed opinion.
■ **GOAL 6** Recognize bias What is bias?	Bias refers to an author's partiality, inclination toward a particular viewpoint, or prejudice.
How do you detect bias as you read?	An author's language and selection of facts provide clues about his or her bias. Use of words with strong connotative (emotional) meanings or words that elicit an emotional response on the part of the reader often suggest bias.
Is it acceptable to express bias in your writing?	It is acceptable, depending on the assignment and the topic, to express bias, but be sure you acknowledge that you are doing so by prefacing your comments with phrases like "In my opinion, …" or "I agree with people who believe…"

10

Reading and Writing Essays

kadmy/123RF

THINK About It!

The photograph above shows a security guard observing footage from surveillance cameras. Suppose you were assigned to write an essay either opposing or agreeing with the use of surveillance to monitor the public. How would you begin? What would you do first, how would you decide what to write, where would you find ideas to write about, and how would you be sure you have written a clear and correct essay? This chapter will answer all of these questions and more. You will learn how an essay is structured and how to write an effective thesis statement, support your thesis with evidence, and write effective introductions, conclusions, and titles. You will also learn strategies for reading essays and apply them to a professional essay and a student essay that are tied to the theme of this chapter—the decline of personal privacy. These essays will illustrate the techniques taught in this chapter.

What Is an Essay?

VISUALIZE IT!

If you can read and write a paragraph, you can read and write an essay. The structure is similar, and they have similar parts. A **paragraph** expresses one main idea about a topic in a *topic sentence* and is made up of several additional sentences that support that idea. An **essay** also expresses one key idea called the *thesis*. This is expressed in a sentence called the *thesis statement*. The chart below shows how the parts of the paragraph are very much like the parts of an essay.

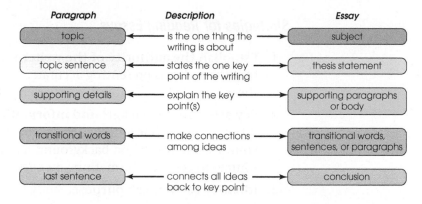

Paragraph	Description	Essay
topic	is the one thing the writing is about	subject
topic sentence	states the one key point of the writing	thesis statement
supporting details	explain the key point(s)	supporting paragraphs or body
transitional words	make connections among ideas	transitional words, sentences, or paragraphs
last sentence	connects all ideas back to key point	conclusion

Think of the organization of an essay as modeling the organization of a paragraph, with one idea explained by supporting details. Because an essay is usually at least three paragraphs long, and often more, it needs an opening paragraph, called the *introduction*, which focuses the reader and provides necessary background information before the thesis is presented. The paragraphs that support the thesis are called the *body* of the essay. Due to length and complexity, an essay also needs a final paragraph, called the *conclusion*, to draw the ideas discussed together and bring it to an end. You can visualize the structure of an essay as shown below.

VISUALIZE IT!

The Structure of an Essay

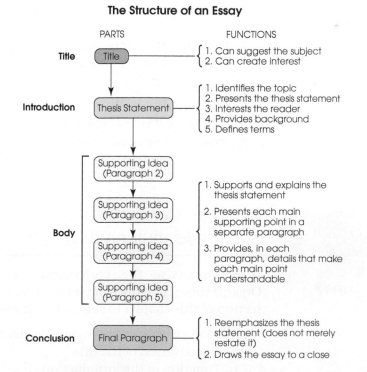

Note: There is no set number of paragraphs that an essay should contain. This model shows six paragraphs, but in actual essays, the number will vary greatly.

Use Strategies for Reading Essays

■ GOAL 1
Use strategies for reading essays

Reading essays provides you with ideas to write about, which can serve as springboards for you to develop your own ideas. By studying the writing of professional writers, you can improve your own writing. You will need to read the essays several times. First, concentrate on understanding them. Then examine the techniques the writers use that you could use in your own writing. Here are a few specific suggestions:

Strategies for Reading Essays

1. **Establish the authority of the writer whenever possible.** In order to trust that the writer is presenting accurate, reliable information, make sure he or she is knowledgeable about or experienced with the subject.

2. **Pay attention to background information the writer provides.** Especially if the subject is one with which you are unfamiliar, you must fill in gaps in your knowledge. If the background supplied is insufficient, consult other sources to get the information you need.

3. **Identify the writer's purpose.** Study how he or she achieves it.

4. **Study the title.** What does it reveal about the essay's content or purpose?

5. **Examine the essay's introduction.** It should do three things: (1) provide needed background information, (2) get you interested in the reading, and (3) state the essay's main point. Observe how the writer accomplishes these things.

6. **Examine the body of the essay.** Study how the writer supports his or her main points.

7. **Examine how paragraphs are organized.** How does the writer state and develop the main point of each paragraph? How are these main points explained or developed?

8. **Examine the sentences the writer creates.** How are the sentences similar to and different from those you write? Are there some sentence patterns you could model?

9. **Examine the writer's use of vocabulary.** What words or phrases seem particularly effective? How could you use them?

10. **Examine the essay's conclusion.** Observe how the writer draws the essay to a close. Could you use this technique?

EXERCISE 10-1

WORKING TOGETHER

Reading "Computer Technology, Large Organizations, and the Assault on Privacy"

Directions: Use the professional reading "Computer Technology, Large Organizations, and the Assault on Privacy" in the Examining Professional Writing section of this chapter to complete this exercise.

1. Working with another student, evaluate the reading in terms of the following:
   a. Effectiveness of the title
   b. Function of the introduction
   c. Effectiveness of the thesis statement

    d. Author's purpose and intended audience

    e. Organization

    f. Adequacy of supporting detail

    g. Function of the conclusion

2. Examine the reading and identify at least two techniques used by the author that you could use to improve your own writing.

Chapter Theme: The Decline of Personal Privacy

In this chapter, you will read both a professional essay and a student essay on the topic of the decline of personal privacy. While technology has simplified life in many ways, it has also brought about the loss of personal privacy. Although many people may not understand how much personal data has been and still is collected on them, it is safe to say that what used to be personal information is now considered public information. Many different organizations want to know even more about you. From law enforcement to financial institutions to the federal government and social media, people's lives have become an open book for those who seek to know more about them and use the data to their advantage. As you read the two essays in this chapter, pay close attention to the many ways in which the public is being watched. Also, annotate each reading yourself, recording your thoughts on the topic, to be prepared to write about it or a related topic.

Look it up!

Use the search engine on your smartphone (or work with a classmate who has a smartphone) to look up the phrase "protecting personal information online." Review some of the material presented. Based on what you read, what are the best ways to protect personal information online? Write a few sentences about your experiences with sharing personal information online and ways you might protect yourself in the future.

EXAMINING PROFESSIONAL WRITING

The following selection is from a sociology textbook. In the selection, the author discusses the decline in personal privacy in today's world. It will be used in this chapter to demonstrate strategies for reading essays.

Thinking Before Reading

Follow these steps before you read:

1. Preview the reading, using the steps discussed in the Pre-Reading Strategies section of Chapter 1.

2. Connect the reading to your own experience by answering the following questions:

    a. Where have you noticed security or surveillance cameras? What is your reaction to seeing them?

    b. Do you think your personal information is secure? How careful are you not to reveal personal information on the Internet?

3. Highlight and annotate as you read.

Computer Technology, Large Organizations, and the Assault on Privacy

John Macionis

1   *Jake completes a page on Facebook, which includes his name and college, e-mail, photo, biography, and current personal interests. It can be accessed by billions of people around the world.*

2   *Late for a meeting with a new client, Sarah drives her car through a yellow light as it turns red at a main intersection. A computer linked to a pair of cameras notes the violation and takes one picture of her license plate and another of her sitting in the driver's seat. Seven days later, she receives a summons to appear in traffic court.*

3   *Julio looks through his mail and finds a letter from a Washington, D.C., data services company telling him that he is one of about 145,000 people whose name, address, Social Security number, and credit file have recently been sold to criminals in California posing as businesspeople. With this information, other people can obtain credit cards or take out loans in his name.*

4   These are all cases showing that today's organizations—which know more about us than ever before and more than most of us realize—pose a growing threat to personal privacy. Large organizations are necessary for today's society to operate. In some cases, organizations using information about us may actually be helpful. But cases of identity theft are on the rise, and personal privacy is on the decline.

5   In the past, small-town life gave people little privacy. But at least if people knew something about you, you were just as likely to know something about them. Today, unknown people "out there" can access information about each of us all the time without our learning about it.

6   In part, the loss of privacy is a result of increasingly complex computer technology. Are you aware that every e-mail you send and every Web site you visit leaves a record in one or more computers? These records can be retrieved by people you don't know as well as by employers and other public officials.

7   Another part of today's loss of privacy reflects the number and size of formal organizations. Large organizations tend to treat people impersonally, and they have a huge appetite for information. Mix large organizations with ever more complex computer technology, and it is no wonder that most people in the United States are concerned about who knows what about them and what people are doing with this information.

8   For decades, the level of personal privacy in the United States has been declining. Early in the twentieth century, when state agencies began issuing driver's licenses, for example, they generated files for every licensed driver. Today, officials can send this information at the touch of a button not only to the police but also to

RayArt Graphics/Alamy stock Photo

all sorts of other organizations. The Internal Revenue Service and the Social Security Administration, as well as government agencies that benefit veterans, students, the unemployed, and the poor, all collect mountains of personal information.

9   Business organizations now do much the same thing, and many of the choices we make end up in a company's database. Most of us use credit—the U.S. population now has more than 1 billion credit cards, an average of five per adult—but the companies that do "credit checks" collect and distribute information about us to almost anyone who asks, including criminals planning to steal our identity.

10   Then there are the small cameras found not only at traffic intersections but also in stores, public buildings, and parking garages and across college campuses. The number of surveillance cameras that monitor our movements is rapidly increasing with each passing year. So-called security cameras may increase public safety in some ways—say, by discouraging a mugger or even a terrorist—at the cost of the little privacy we have left. In the United Kingdom, probably the world leader in the use of security cameras with 4 million of them, the typical resident of London appears on closed-circuit television about 300 times every day, and all this "tracking" is stored in computer files. Here in the United States, New York City already has 4,000 surveillance cameras in the subway system and city officials plan to have cameras installed in 1,500 city buses by 2013.

11   Government monitoring of the population in the United States has been expanding steadily in recent years. After the September 11, 2001, terrorist attacks, the federal government took steps (including the USA PATRIOT Act) to strengthen national security. Today, government officials closely monitor not only people entering the country but also the activities of all of us. These activities may increase national security, but they certainly erode personal privacy.

12   Some legal protections remain. Each of the fifty states has laws that give citizens the right to examine some records about themselves kept by employers, banks, and credit bureaus. The federal Privacy Act of 1974 also limits the exchange of personal information among government agencies and permits citizens to examine and correct most government files. In response to rising levels of identity theft, Congress is likely to pass more laws to regulate the sale of credit information. But so many organizations, private as well as public, now have information about us—experts estimate that 90 percent of U.S. households are profiled in databases somewhere—that current laws simply cannot effectively address the privacy problem.

13   The privacy issues discussed here lead us to consider others, as well. Does the use of surveillance cameras in public places enhance or significantly reduce personal privacy? Is the cost worth the gains in personal security? Does the automatic toll payment on our nation's roads, such as the E-ZPass system, which allows motorists to move quickly through toll gates, but also records information about where you go and when you got there, violate privacy?

—Macionis, *Society*, p. 123

Use the Writing Process to Write Essays

The six steps in the writing process were outlined in Chapter 2, and the basics of writing paragraphs were discussed in Chapters 6 and 7. In this chapter, you will learn how to write essays, using the following essay by Alaina Meyer as a model.

EXAMINING STUDENT WRITING

Nirufft/Fotolia

Alaina Mayer is a community college student who is majoring in nursing. The instructor in her sociology course assigned a short (one- to two-page) essay on a current social issue using MLA style.

Alaina is using MLA style (see p. 352 for details). She gives her name, her professor's name, the course, and date at the top left of the first page of her paper and her last name and the page number top right of every page.

Title: Introduces the topic. Notice you do not bold or underline titles in MLA.

Alaina's paper is double spaced throughout.

Alaina starts her essay by asking questions that get the reader thinking about surveillance.

Thesis statement

Topic sentence

Mayer 1

Alaina Mayer

Professor Thomas

English 101

11 March 2017

Surveillance in America: It's Not Paranoia

If You're Really Being Watched

Have you ever had the feeling that your cell phone is communicating with space? Do you feel like you're constantly being watched? The threat of surveillance today comes not only from shadowy government agencies but more frequently from each other. Well-meaning friends who post blurry video of last Friday night can't be stopped any more than the National Security Agency's (NSA) electronic dragnet. For better or worse, Americans live in a surveillance state. There are many sources and tools for surveillance, and each is a violation of privacy.

One means of surveillance is the monitoring of electronic media by the government. The NSA is a little-known federal agency with a secret budget. It breaks codes and interprets intelligence. The agency is also responsible for "network warfare": hacking. Its goal is the same as that of spies throughout history—to gain an edge by obtaining hard-to-get information and using it

Mayer 2

as they choose. The agency doesn't collect information about Americans, "except pursuant to procedures established by the head of the agency and approved by the Attorney General" ("SIGINT"). In other words, the NSA can only collect information about you if it follows the rules—its rules. Said rules allow an incredible amount of data collection and storage.

According to *Wired* magazine, the NSA collects your Google searches, cell phone calls, emails, and bookstore purchases. It does so partially with the help of 10–20 data centers placed in telecommunications facilities owned by companies such as Verizon. The NSA also eavesdrops on satellites and conducts what's known as "deep packet inspection" (Bamford). In short, it's not just listening to you talk. The agency analyzes everything you do online and sifts it to make sure you're not a danger to the country. Then the information is saved forever to be analyzed by the fastest computers on Earth (Bamford). Electronic surveillance is a powerful intrusion into privacy: your Internet traffic paints an intimate portrait, especially when cross-referenced with Facebook's insight into your social web and cell phone records. The agency can use this combined information to understand you and your relationships in a way that doesn't require questioning or due process. Compiling this data yourself, for your own use, would be almost impossible and a massive intrusion into the privacy of everyone with whom you communicate, yet the federal government is already doing it—to everyone.

The feds are not the only ones keeping an eye on citizens. State governments have taken surveillance a step further, literally watching over their citizens with thousands of surveillance cameras. Nowhere is this more prevalent than in New York City. In Manhattan alone, volunteers counted 4,176 cameras in the 1/6th of the city surveyed (Palmer). Since two horrific murders in 2007, all NYC clubs with a cabaret license are required to have cameras at their entrances and exits (Jones). So you're protected—to the extent that if someone murders you, the police will be able to see grainy footage of the attack if it happened within view of the camera—but you're

Note in-text citation of source (highlighted in purple in this paper). Alaina used all online sources, so no page numbers are included.

Topic sentence

Topic sentence

not free. Whoever's on your shoulder as you stumble will be saved for as long as the camera's owner chooses. You have no way of knowing how long that is or what's going to be done with the footage. It could end up on YouTube or on TV. At least the cameras aren't violating any privacy rights not also held by a random person with a camera—anyone can film you walking out of the bar as long as you remain in public.

Topic sentence

Camera usage isn't limited to major metropolitan areas. A Google search for "cameras installed in the downtown area" came up with reports of cameras currently installed in cities across America: Meriden, CT; Winooski, Brattleboro and Richford, VT; Cohoes, NY; Clemson, SC; Columbia and Maplewood, MO; Houma, LA; Ottumwa, IA; Austin, TX; Colorado Springs, CO; Cheyenne, WY; Klamath Falls, OR; and Los Angeles and the Bay Area of San Francisco, CA, for example. Even small towns have cameras that record you walking into a bank, for instance. Most ATMs have them. International trends show camera surveillance to be on the rise. Great Britain has one camera for every 32 people, according to a recent study (Lewis). Looking at who owns the cameras reveals who's really watching—citizens, not the government!

Topic sentence

Although cameras may violate privacy, a recent study says they are useful tools for fighting crime. After analyzing Baltimore, MD; Washington, DC; and Chicago, IL's police surveillance programs, researchers found that watching gets results. In all three cities the camera systems faced different challenges, but they were shown to be helpful in every step of the criminal justice process, including encouraging witnesses to testify (La Vigne et al.). Slightly more than 95% of the cameras in the study's sample were owned by private entities. Corporations, apartment buildings and restaurants have good reasons to install cameras—loss prevention, protection against liability and overall security concerns make them a reasonable expense for these and many other employers.

Mayer 4

Topic sentence

Companies also use national-security style tactics to profile their customers. The same technologies that predict if you'll make a bomb can tell what coupons you'll like. Store loyalty cards are one of their surveillance tools. In addition to delivering perks and discounts, they track everything you buy. (To avoid this, ask for a store card at the checkout—it usually works for the discounts but not for coupons.) The cards are vital, however, in the case of food recalls. My father recently received a call about some ham salad he'd purchased. It was prepared with Listeria-tainted onions. If he hadn't used the store loyalty card for a discount, the store would have had no way to contact him. Is it worth getting upset about your grocery store knowing you buy only one brand of yogurt if that results in coupons for that brand? However, there are more sophisticated uses for this data. Target's data mining is so precise that a Minneapolis father found out his high-school daughter was pregnant thanks to a targeted mailing she received (Duhigg). The store—rather, the store's marketing algorithms—knew before he did. Predicting due dates is lucrative—if a woman gets hooked into a specific all-purpose store early in her pregnancy, she'll keep shopping there for baby supplies—and keeping a parent informed was just an unexpected bonus.

Topic sentence

Even if you don't see cameras, look around! You might still be trackable via military satellites, for example. That's thanks to E911, the technology introduced in 2002 that required Global Positioning System (GPS) tracking chips in all new cell phones (Koerner). Cell phones aren't just holding the GPS that makes you trackable—the rest of their components make plausible deniability nearly impossible. Cell phones are everywhere and many can take photos, record sound and shoot video. Seconds later, that information can be shared, as fast as the phone and the network can send it.

Conclusion reaffirms the thesis and makes a suggestion.

Big Brother is watching you, and everyone else can be, too. You cannot trust the government, or corporations, banks, stores, or even private individuals to protect your privacy. It is completely up to you. If you want to keep your activities to yourself, conduct them in a windowless room without your cell phone, laptop, or anyone else present.

Mayer 5

Works Cited

Bamford, James. "The NSA Is Building the Country's Biggest Spy Center (Watch What You Say)." *Wired*, 15 Mar. 2012, www.wired.com/2012/03/ ff_nsadatacenter.

Duhigg, Charles M. "How Companies Learn Your Secrets." *The New York Times,* 16 Feb. 2012, www.nytimes.com/2012/02/19/magazine/ shopping-habits.html?_r=0.

Jones, Charisse. "Violence Brings Club Crackdown." *USA Today*, 4 Apr. 2007, usatoday30.usatoday.com/news/nation/2007-04-04-club-violence_N. htm.

Koerner, Brendan I. "Legal Affairs: Your Cellphone Is a Homing Device." *Legal Affairs*, July/Aug. 2003, www.legalaffairs.org/issues/July- August-2003/feature_koerner_julaug03.msp. Accessed 30 July 2012.

La Vigne, Nancy G., et al. "Evaluating the Use of Public Surveillance Cameras for Crime Control and Prevention—A Summary." *Urban Institute*, Sept. 2011, www.urban.org/sites/default/files/alfresco/ publication-pdfs/412401-Evaluating-the-Use-of-Public-Surveillance- Cameras-for-Crime-Control-and-Prevention-A-Summary.PDF.

Lewis, Paul. "You're Being Watched: There's One CCTV Camera for Every 32 People in UK." *The Guardian*, 2 Mar. 2011, www.theguardian.com/ uk/2011/mar/02/cctv-cameras-watching-surveillance.

Palmer, Brian. "Big Apple Is Watching You." *Slate*, 3 May 2010, www.slate. com/articles/news_and_politics/explainer/2010/05/big_apple_is_ watching_you.html.

"SIGINT Frequently Asked Questions." National Security Agency, Central Security Service, 15 Jan. 2009, www.nsa.gov/sigint/faqs.shtml.

Works cited list starts on new page; the title is centered and not in bold or underlined.

Entries are listed alphabetically by authors' last names.

Second and subsequent lines of entries are indented.

If there is no author, entries are listed by title.

Choose a Topic

■ GOAL 2
Choose a topic

You begin the process of writing an essay by selecting a topic, narrowing it to a manageable size, and considering your purpose and audience. Next, you generate ideas and organize them to develop a working thesis statement and plan and outline your essay. Then you research to locate additional information, if needed, and draft your essay using supporting information and transitions to connect your ideas. Finally, you revise and proofread. Although this sounds like a linear process, one step following the next, it is important to remember that as you revise you will revisit all aspects of your essay from the wording of your thesis to the ideas you include and the way you organize and connect them.

The topic for an essay should be broader than for a single paragraph but narrow enough to cover within an essay. Once you have a broad topic in mind, generate ideas about it to help you focus and narrow it to a manageable topic in a similar way that you narrowed down a topic in Chapter 4 (see p. 134).

Ensure Your Topic Is Not Too Broad

One common mistake in writing an essay is choosing a topic that is *too broad*. If your topic is too broad, there will be too much information to include, and you will not be able to cover all the important points with the right amount of detail.

Alaina was asked to write a paper taking a position on a current social issue for her sociology class. If she just wrote down the title "Surveillance" and started writing, she would find that she had too much to say and probably would not know where to start. Should she write about government surveillance programs around the world, privacy concerns on social media and the Internet, or corporate surveillance for marketing and data mining purposes?

Here are a few more examples of topics that are too broad:

- Pollution (Choose one type and focus on causes or effects.)
- Vacations (Choose one trip and focus on one aspect of the trip such as meeting new people.)
- Movies (Choose one movie and concentrate on one feature such as character development, plot, or humor.)

How to Identify Whether a Topic Is Too Broad

Here are the symptoms of a topic that is too broad:

- **You have too much to say.** If it seems as if you could go on and on about the topic, it is probably too broad.
- **You feel overwhelmed.** If you feel the topic is too difficult or the task of writing about it is unmanageable, you may have too much to write about. Another possibility is that you have chosen a topic about which you do not know enough.
- **You are not making progress.** If you feel stuck, your topic may be too broad. It also may be too narrow.
- **You are writing general statements and not explaining them.** Having too much to cover forces you to make broad, sweeping statements that you cannot explain in sufficient depth.

How to Narrow a Broad Topic

One way to narrow a topic that is too broad is to divide it into subtopics. Then choose one subtopic and use it to develop new ideas for your essay.

Another way to limit a broad topic is to answer questions that will limit it. Here are six questions that are useful in limiting your topic to a particular place, time, kind, or type:

Who? What? When? Where? Why? How?

Suppose your topic is surveillance. You realize it is too broad and apply the questions below.

TOPIC: SURVEILLANCE	
Questions	Examples
Who?	Who is conducting surveillance in America? (This question limits the topic to people and agencies that conduct surveillance.)
What?	What types of tools are used for surveillance? (This question limits the topic to specific tools.)
When?	When did NSA surveillance start? (This question limits the topic to a particular time frame.)
Where?	Where are surveillance cameras used? (This question limits the topic to locations such as New York City and other metropolitan areas.)
Why?	Why should surveillance be considered a violation of privacy? (This question limits the topic to the reasons people should object to surveillance.)
How?	How are surveillance programs used to fight crime? (This question limits the topic to one aspect of surveillance.)

EXERCISE 10-2

WORKING TOGETHER

Writing: Narrowing a Broad Topic

Directions: Choose one of the following topics and narrow it down so that it would be suitable for a two-page essay. Exchange your work with a classmate and evaluate each other's work.

1. Organic or health foods
2. Natural disasters
3. Cloning
4. Current fads or fashions
5. Controlling stress
6. Valued possessions
7. An unfortunate accident or circumstance
8. A technological advance
9. Steroid use by athletes
10. Using animals for research

Ensure Your Topic Is Not Too Narrow

Another common mistake is to choose a topic that is *too narrow*. If you decide to write about the effects of the failure of Canada geese to migrate from western New York during the winter, you will probably run out of ideas, unless you are prepared to do extensive library or Internet research. Instead, broaden your topic to the migration patterns of Canada geese. Here are a few more examples of topics that are too narrow:

■ The history of corn mazes in the Ohio River valley
■ Marketing practices for Honda Odyssey minivans
■ Hair color as a determinant of social mobility

How to Identify Whether a Topic Is Too Narrow

Here are examples of a topic that is too narrow:

■ **After a paragraph or two, you have nothing left to say.** If you run out of ideas and keep repeating yourself, your topic is probably too narrow.

■ **Your topic does not seem important.** If your topic seems insignificant, it probably is. One reason it may be insignificant is that it focuses on facts rather than ideas.

■ **You are making little or no progress.** A lack of progress may signal a lack of information.

■ **Your essay is too factual.** If you find you are focusing on small details, your topic may be too narrow.

How to Broaden a Narrow Topic

To broaden a topic that is too narrow, try to extend it to cover more situations or circumstances. If your topic is the price advantage of shopping for your chemistry textbook on the Internet, broaden it to include various other benefits of Internet shopping for textbooks. Discuss price, but also consider convenience and free shipping. Do not limit yourself to one type of textbook. Specifically, to broaden a topic that is too narrow:

■ Think of other situations, events, or circumstances that illustrate the same idea.

■ Think of a larger concept that includes your topic.

EXERCISE 10-3 Writing: Broadening a Narrow Topic

Directions: Broaden three of the following topics to ones that are manageable in a two-page essay.

1. A groom wearing outlandish clothing as a form of social protest
2. Materials needed for a science experiment
3. Evaluating JetBlue's marketing plan
4. Behavior of a celebrity
5. An annoying but effective Internet pop-up
6. McDonald's pricing of hamburgers
7. Speech patterns of a nine-month-old baby
8. Coping with stress caused by a divorce or the end of a long-term relationship

Consider Audience and Purpose

■ GOAL 3
Consider audience and purpose

Once you have chosen a manageable topic, the next step is to consider both your audience and your purpose. Your audience is your intended readers; your purpose is your reason for writing.

Consider Your Audience

You speak differently to different audiences; you would speak differently to your sister than you would to one of your professors, for example. Similarly, you should write differently for different audiences. Before you begin to write, take a few minutes to consider and analyze your audience using the following questions.

- What do my readers know, if anything, about the topic?
- What background, experience, or education do my readers have that will help them understand the topic?
- What attitudes, opinions, or beliefs do my readers hold that may influence how they respond to the topic?
- Do I need to explain any unfamiliar terms, events, parts, or processes?

Once you have answered these questions, keep your answers in mind as you decide what you will say and how you will say it throughout the writing process.

Consider Your Purpose

Every essay should have a clear purpose: it should be written to accomplish a specific goal. Most essays are written to *express ideas*, to *inform*, or to *persuade*. You might write an essay expressing your strong agreement with a new campus regulation. Or you might write an essay informing others about the regulation: why it was instituted, how it will be enforced, and how it will affect students. Or you might write an essay persuading your readers that the regulation is unfair and calling for its repeal.

As you plan, draft, and revise your essay, ask yourself these two questions:

- What do I want to accomplish?
- What do I need to do to meet this goal?

Maintain a focus on these answers as you plan, draft, and revise your essay.

EXERCISE 10-4	Writing: Determining Your Audience and Purpose

WRITING IN PROGRESS

Directions: Based on the topic you chose in Exercise 10-2, determine the audience and purpose of your essay. How will your audience and purpose affect your choice of content, language, and style?

Develop a Thesis Statement

■ GOAL 4
Develop a thesis statement

To develop a sound essay, you must begin with a well-focused thesis statement. A **thesis statement** tells your reader what your essay is about and gives clues to how the essay will unfold. The thesis statement should not only identify your topic but also express the main point about your topic that you will explain or prove in your essay.

A thesis statement rarely springs fully formed into a writer's mind: it evolves and, in fact, may change significantly during the process of prewriting, grouping ideas, drafting, and revising.

The first step in developing a thesis statement is to generate ideas to write about.

Generate and Group Ideas for Your Thesis Statement

Use one of the three prewriting methods you have studied: (1) freewriting, (2) brainstorming, and (3) branching. (Refer to Chapter 2, pp. 53–55, for a review of these strategies.) Once you have ideas to work with, the next step is to group or connect your ideas to form a thesis. Let's see how Alaina produced a thesis following these steps.

After brainstorming a list of various social issues, Alaina decided to write about surveillance in America. She then did a second brainstorming about how and why surveillance is used. She came up with the following list:

federal agencies (NSA)	cameras in NYC and elsewhere
electronic surveillance	state government agencies/police
traffic cameras	hacking
online surveys	privacy concerns (e.g., YouTube footage
customer profiling	that never goes away)
banks and ATMs	international trends
use of cameras to fight crime	private security firms
store loyalty cards	military satellites/GPS

Alaina's next step in writing her essay was to select usable ideas and try to group or organize them logically. In the preceding brainstorming list, she saw three main groups of ideas: *sources of surveillance, types of surveillance tools*, and *violations of privacy*. She sorted her list into categories:

Sources of surveillance: _____

_____

Types of surveillance tools: _____

_____

Violations of privacy: _____

_____

How to Group Ideas

How do you know which ideas to group? Look for connections and relationships among ideas that you generate during prewriting. Here are some suggestions:

- **Look for categories.** Try to discover how you can classify and subdivide your ideas. Think of categories as titles or slots in which you can place ideas. Look for a general term that is broad enough to cover several of your ideas. For example, Alaina broke down surveillance into types of surveillance tools.

Suppose you were writing a paper on favoritism. You could break down the topic by a category, such as place.

> SAMPLE THESIS STATEMENT   Whether it's practiced in the workplace, in a classroom, or on Capitol Hill, favoritism is unfair.

■ **Try organizing your ideas chronologically.** Group your ideas according to the clock or calendar.

> SAMPLE THESIS STATEMENT   From the ancient Mayans to King Henry VIII's court to present-day Congress, personal relationships have always played a role in professional achievement.

■ **Look for similarities and differences.** When working with two or more topics, see if you can approach them by looking at how similar or different they are.

> SAMPLE THESIS STATEMENT   The two great pioneers of psychotherapy, Freud and Jung, agreed on the concept of the libido but completely disagreed on other issues.

■ **Separate your ideas into causes and effects or problems and solutions.** You can often analyze events and issues in this way.

> SAMPLE THESIS STATEMENT   The phrase "it takes a village to raise a child" means that birth parents alone do not determine who an individual will grow up to be.

■ **Divide your ideas into advantages and disadvantages or pros and cons.** When you are evaluating a proposal, product, or service, this approach may work.

> SAMPLE THESIS STATEMENT   Deciding on a major before starting college can either help a student stay focused and on track or keep him or her from discovering new interests.

■ **Consider several different ways to approach your topic or organize and develop your ideas.** As you consider what your thesis statement is going to be, push yourself to see your topic from a number of different angles or from a fresh perspective.

Once Alaina had grouped her ideas into these categories, she could write a thesis statement:

> There are many sources and tools for surveillance, and each is a violation of privacy.

This thesis statement identifies her topic—surveillance—and suggests that the sources and tools for surveillance violate privacy. You can see how this thesis statement grew out of her idea groupings. Furthermore, this thesis statement gives her readers clues as to how she will organize the essay. A reader knows from this preview what aspects of surveillance she will focus on.

Alaina could have examined her brainstorming list and decided to focus only on federal agencies that conduct surveillance, looking more deeply into the NSA and other surveillance programs. In other words, within every topic lie many possible thesis statements.

EXERCISE 10-5

WRITING IN PROGRESS

Writing: Generating and Grouping Ideas

Directions: Generate and group ideas for the topic you narrowed in Exercise 10-2.

A thesis statement should explain what your essay is about, and it should also give your readers clues to its organization. Think of your thesis statement as a promise; it promises your reader what your paper will deliver.

Guidelines for Writing a Strong Thesis Statement

Here are some guidelines to follow for writing an effective thesis statement:

- **It should state the main point of your essay.** It should not focus on details; it should give an overview of your approach to your topic.

TOO DETAILED	Because babies don't know anything about the world around them, parents should allow them to touch toys and other objects.
REVISED	Because babies don't know anything about the world around them when they are born, they need to spend lots of time touching, holding, and exploring the everyday things we take for granted.

- **It should assert an idea about your topic.** Your thesis should express a viewpoint or state an approach to the topic.

LACKS AN ASSERTION	Advertisers promote beer during football games.
REVISED	One of the reasons you see so many beer ads during ball games is that men buy more beer than women.

- **It should be as specific and detailed as possible.** For this reason, it is important to review and rework your thesis *after* you have written and revised drafts.

TOO GENERAL	You need to take a lot of clothes with you when you go camping.
REVISED	Because the weather can change so quickly in the Adirondacks, it is important to pack clothing that will protect you from both sun and rain.

- **It may suggest the organization of your essay.** Mentioning key points that will be discussed in the essay is one way to do this. The order in which you mention them should be the same as the order in which you discuss them in your essay.

DOES NOT SUGGEST ORGANIZATION	Learning to read is important for your whole life.
REVISED	Literacy is a necessary tool for academic, professional, and personal success.

■ **It should not be a direct announcement.** Do not begin with phrases such as "In this paper I will ..." or "My assignment was to discuss ...."

DIRECT ANNOUNCEMENT	What I am going to write about is how working out can make you better at your job.
REVISED	Exercise can dramatically improve the performance of everyone, from front office to assembly-line workers.

■ **It should offer a fresh, interesting, and original perspective on the topic.** A thesis statement can follow the guidelines discussed above, but if it seems dull or predictable, it needs more work.

PREDICTABLE	Complex carbohydrates are good for you.
REVISED	Diets that call for cutting out carbohydrates completely are overlooking the tremendous health benefits of whole grains.

EXERCISE 10-6	Writing a Thesis Statement

WRITING IN PROGRESS

Directions: Using the topic you chose in Exercise 10-2 and the ideas you generated about it in Exercise 10-5, develop a thesis statement.

Plan and Organize Your Essay

■ **GOAL 5**
Plan and organize your essay

Spending time planning and organizing your ideas is well worth the cost. In fact, the more time you spend organizing before and while you write, the less time you will need to spend revising and rewriting later.

Outline and Map

Both outlining and mapping are useful skills to help you fit your ideas together and decide the best way to present them. Outlining and mapping are both covered in detail in Chapter 2.

Outlining is a way of discovering relationships and connections among ideas and will help you discover how to arrange your ideas so they are logically connected and easy to present and understand. Use it when you are considering how to organize your ideas or if you are unsure how to organize them. Experiment with different organizations, moving ideas around to see how they fit together best; this is easy to do if you outline on your computer. As you write an outline, you may discover new ideas or realize where you are missing information as well.

You may also discover that your ideas are imbalanced; it will be easy to see if you have much more information on one topic than another, for example.

Mapping is a method of creating a diagram of how ideas relate. It helps you visualize your ideas. Use mapping if you are a visual learner; you will find it easier to work with than an outline. Also, use mapping when words alone do not seem to tie together easily or when you are having difficulty seeing connections. Mapping makes it easy to identify ideas that are unrelated or not relevant to your topic as well.

Consider Patterns of Development

In Chapters 6 and 7, you learned about several patterns of development: chronological order, process, narration, description, example, cause and effect, and comparison and contrast. These patterns are useful ways to organize your ideas in preparation for drafting your essay. Consider the following questions in selecting a pattern:

- What patterns are appropriate for my topic?
- Which patterns would best suit my audience?
- Which patterns will help me achieve my purpose?

Experiment with various patterns, using either outlining or mapping. Be prepared to discover while drafting that the pattern you chose did not work as well as you thought it would and to select a different pattern.

Locate and Record Sources

- **GOAL 6**
  Locate and record
  appropriate sources

Many assignments in college require you to locate and read several sources of information on a topic and then use them to support and "flesh out" your ideas. At other times, you may be asked to examine certain printed sources and come up with a new idea or thesis about them.

Libraries are filled with sources—print, electronic, and more. They house thousands of books, journals, videos, DVDs, pamphlets, tapes, and newspapers as well as computers that enable you to access the World Wide Web. Yet this very abundance of sources means that one of the hardest parts of doing research is locating the sources that will be the most help to you.

Many books have been written on how to do research and how to use and document print and electronic sources. Therefore, this section gives only a brief overview of the research process and offers advice on how to get started.

Tips for Finding Appropriate Sources

Suppose you are writing an essay about surveillance in America. Although you will find many sources on your topic, not all will be appropriate for your particular assignment. Some sources may be too technical; others may be too sketchy. Some may be outdated, others too opinionated. Your task is to find sources that will give you good, solid, current information or points of view. Use the following tips:

1. **Keep track of all the sources you use.** There are several good reasons for doing this:
   - **When you use sources in a paper, you must acknowledge them** all at the end of your paper in a bibliography or "Works Cited" list. Providing your reader with information on your sources is called **documentation**.

> **Tip for Writers**
>
> A *bibliography* is a list of books and other sources. It may be sources a writer used (the works cited in your research paper), a list of works by a particular author, or a list of sources for information on a particular topic at the end of a textbook chapter.

■ **You may want to refer to the source again.**

■ **You are more likely to avoid plagiarism if you keep accurate records of your sources.** (See p. 345 for a more detailed discussion of plagiarism.)

Record all publication information about each print and electronic source. For print sources, record title, author(s), volume, edition, date of publication, publisher, and page number(s). You may want to use index cards or a small bound notebook to record source information, using a separate card or page for each source. Print the home page of Web site sources and bookmark them in case you need to find them again. You will learn how to document sources you use later in this chapter.

2. **Consult a reference librarian.** If you are unsure of where to begin, ask a reference librarian for advice. It is a reference librarian's job to suggest useful sources. He or she can be very helpful to you.

3. **Use a systematic approach.** Start by using general sources, either print or electronic, such as general reference books and, as needed, move to more specific sources such as periodicals and journals (scholarly magazines written for people focused on a particular area of study).

4. **Use current sources.** For many topics, such as controversial issues or scientific or medical advances, only the most up-to-date sources are useful. For other topics, such as the moral issues involved in abortion or euthanasia, older sources can be used. Before you begin, decide on a cutoff date—a date before which you feel information will be outdated and therefore not useful to you.

5. **Sample a variety of viewpoints.** Try to find sources that present differing viewpoints on the same subject rather than counting on one source to contain everything you need. Various authors take different approaches and have different opinions on the same topic, all of which can increase your understanding of the topic.

6. **Preview articles by reading abstracts or summaries.** Many sources begin with an abstract or end with a summary. Before using the source, check the abstract or summary to determine whether the source is going to be helpful.

7. **Read sources selectively.** Many students spend time needlessly reading entire books and articles thoroughly when they should be reading selectively—skimming to avoid parts that are not on the subject and to locate portions that relate directly to their topic. To read selectively,

■ use indexes and tables of contents to locate the portions of books that are useful and appropriate. In articles, use abstracts or summaries as a guide to the material's organization: the order in which ideas appear in the summary or abstract is the order in which they appear in the source itself.

■ after you have identified useful sections, preview (see p. 4) to get an overview of the material.

■ use headings to select sections to read thoroughly.

8. **Choose reliable, trustworthy sources.** The Internet contains a great deal of valuable information, but it also contains rumor, gossip, hoaxes, and misinformation. Before using a source, evaluate it by checking the author's credentials, considering the sponsor or publisher of the site, checking the date of posting, and verifying links. If you are uncertain about the

---

Tip for Writers

An *abstract* is a short written statement containing the main ideas of a longer work.

information presented on a site, verify the information by cross-checking it with another source.

9. **Look for sources that lead to other sources.** Some sources include a bibliography, which provides leads to other works related to your topic. Follow links included in electronic sources.

Record Information from Sources

As you use sources to research a topic, you will need to record usable information that you find. One option is to photocopy the pages from print sources and download and print information from online sources. This is useful if you plan to directly quote the source. Remember, you will need complete source information so you can cite your sources (see p. 343). However, a good essay does not string together a series of quotations. Instead it uses and combines information to come up with new ideas, perspectives, and responses to what is found in the sources. There are several options for keeping track of information—*annotating, paraphrasing,* and *summarizing* (see Chapter 1 to review annotating, paraphrasing, and summarizing).

What Is Plagiarism?

Plagiarism entails borrowing someone else's ideas or exact words *without giving that person credit.* Plagiarism can be intentional (submitting an essay written by someone else) or unintentional (failing to enclose another writer's words in quotation marks). Either way, it is considered a serious offense. If you plagiarize, you can fail the assignment or even the course.

Cyberplagiarism is a specific type of plagiarism. It takes two forms: (1) using information from the Internet without giving credit to the Web site that posted it or (2) buying prewritten papers from the Internet and submitting them as your own work. For example: If you take information about Frank Lloyd Wright's architecture from a reference source (such as an encyclopedia or Web site) but do not specifically indicate where you found it, you have plagiarized. If you take the six-word phrase "Peterson, the vengeful, despicable drug czar" from a news article on the war on drugs without enclosing it in quotation marks, you have plagiarized.

You can easily avoid plagiarism by building source information into your paper correctly so as to give credit to the authors from whom you borrowed the ideas. You can incorporate researched information into your paper in one of two ways: (1) summarize or paraphrase the information or (2) quote directly from it. In both cases, you must give credit to the authors from whom you borrowed the information by documenting your sources using in-text citations and works cited or references pages so your reader can locate it easily.

Guidelines for Avoiding Plagiarism

Here are some guidelines to help you understand exactly what constitutes plagiarism and how to avoid it:

Plagiarism occurs when you . . .

- use another person's words without crediting that person.
- use another person's theory, opinion, or idea without listing the source of that information.

- do not place another person's exact words in quotation marks.
- do not provide a **citation** (reference) to the original source you are quoting.
- paraphrase (reword) another person's ideas or words without giving him or her credit.
- use facts, data, graphs, and charts without stating their source(s).

*Using commonly known facts or information is **not** plagiarism*, and you need not provide a source for such information. For example, the fact that Neil Armstrong set foot on the moon in 1969 is widely known and does not require documentation.

To avoid plagiarism, do the following:

- When you take notes from any published or Internet source, place anything you copy directly in quotation marks.
- As you read and take notes, separate your ideas from ideas taken from the sources you are consulting. You might use different colors of ink or different sections of a notebook page or Word document for each.
- Keep track of all the sources you use, clearly identifying where each idea comes from.
- When paraphrasing someone else's words, change as many words as possible and try to organize them differently. Credit the original source of the information. (See Chapter 1, p. 31, for more information on paraphrasing.)
- When writing a summary, use your own words to state the author's most important ideas, but keep the ideas in the same order as in the original material. Indicate the source of the material you are summarizing. (For more information on writing a summary, see Chapter 1, p. 32.)
- Use in-text citations to indicate the source of quotations and all information and ideas that are not your own. An **in-text citation** is a notation, set off in parentheses, referring to a complete list of sources provided at the end of the essay. (For more information on citation, see p. 352.)

As you start researching new areas, you may ask yourself, "How can I possibly write a paper without using someone else's ideas? I don't know enough about the subject!" The good news is that it is *perfectly acceptable* to use other people's ideas in your research and writing. The key things to remember are (1) you must credit all information taken from any published or Internet sources, and (2) you must provide specific information regarding the publication from which the information is taken, as described on page 352.

| EXERCISE 10-7 | Identifying Plagiarism |

Directions: Read the following passage. Place a check mark next to each statement in the list that follows that is an example of plagiarism.

Mexican Americans. Currently, Mexican Americans are the second-largest racial or ethnic minority group in the United States, but within two decades they will be the largest group. Their numbers will swell as a result of continual immigration from Mexico and the relatively high Mexican birth rate. Mexican Americans are one of the oldest racial-ethnic groups in the United States. Under the terms of the treaty ending the Mexican-American War in 1848, Mexicans living in territories acquired by the United States could remain there and be treated as American citizens. Those who did stay became known as "Californios," "Tejanos," or "Hispanos."

—Curry, Jiobu, and Schwirian, *Sociology for the Twenty-First Century*, p. 207

_____ 1. Mexican Americans are the second-largest minority in the United States. Their number grows as more people immigrate from Mexico.

_____ 2. After the Mexican-American War, those Mexicans living in territories owned by the United States became American citizens and were known as Californios, Tejanos, or Hispanos (Curry, Jiobu, and Schwirian, 207).

_____ 3. "Mexican Americans are one of the oldest racial-ethnic groups in the United States."

_____ 4. The Mexican-American War ended in 1848.

EXERCISE 10-8

WRITING IN PROGRESS

Writing: Locating and Recording Sources

Directions: Locate at least three reference sources that are useful and appropriate for writing a paper of two to three pages on the topic you have been developing. Make a photocopy of the pages you consulted in each source. Print copies of Web sites used. Be sure to record all the bibliographic information for each source.

Draft Your Essay

■ **GOAL 7**
Draft your essay

Once you have a focused topic, an effective thesis statement, a plan for your essay, and sufficient supporting evidence, you are ready to start your first draft. Once you have drafted your paper, you will be able to see what additional types of supporting information are necessary.

Write Your Introduction

An introductory paragraph has three main purposes.

1. It presents your thesis statement.
2. It interests your reader in your topic.
3. It provides any necessary background information.

Although your introductory paragraph appears first in your essay, it does *not* need to be written first. In fact, it is sometimes best to write it last, after you have drafted your essay.

We have already discussed writing thesis statements earlier in the chapter. Table 10-1 provides some suggestions on how to interest your reader in your topic in your introductory paragraph.

TABLE 10-1	WAYS TO INTEREST YOUR READER IN YOUR TOPIC
Technique	**Example**
Ask a provocative or controversial question	How would you feel if you found out your Facebook account had been under surveillance?
State a startling fact or statistic	Last year, the United States government spent a whopping billion dollars a day on interest on the national debt.
Begin with a story or an anecdote	The day Liam Blake left his parka on the bus was the first day of what would become the worst snowstorm the city had ever seen.
Use a quotation	Robert Frost wrote, "Two roads diverged in a wood, and I — / I took the one less traveled by, /And that has made all the difference."
State a little-known fact, a myth, or a misconception	What was Harry S. Truman's middle name? Stephen? Samuel? Simpson? Actually, it was just plain "S." There was a family dispute over whether to name him for his paternal or maternal grandfather, an argument that was settled by simply using the common initial "S."

A dramatic thesis statement can also capture your reader's interest, as in the following example:

> It is not just the mannequins in Dr. Who that are alive: big name fashion stores are now using bionic mannequins with EyeSee technology to identify criminals and learn about consumer shopping habits.

An introduction should also provide the reader with any necessary background information. Consider what information your reader needs to understand your essay. You may, for example, need to define the term *genetic engineering* for a paper on that topic. At other times, you might need to provide a brief history or give an overview of a controversial issue.

Draft Your Body Paragraphs

Every essay you write should offer substantial evidence in support of your thesis statement. The topic sentence of each paragraph should state an idea that supports or explains your thesis, and each topic sentence should be supported with evidence. **Evidence** can consist of personal experience, anecdotes (stories that illustrate a point), examples, reasons, descriptions, facts, statistics, and quotations (taken from sources).

Many students have trouble locating concrete, specific evidence to support their theses. Though prewriting yields plenty of good ideas and helps you focus your thesis, prewriting ideas may not always provide sufficient evidence. Often you need to brainstorm again for additional ideas. At other times, you may need to consult one or more sources to obtain further information on your topic.

Table 10-2 lists ways to support a thesis statement and gives an example of how Alaina could use each one in her essay on surveillance. Although it offers a

TABLE 10-2   WAYS TO ADD EVIDENCE

Topic: Surveillance	
Support Your Thesis by	**Example**
Telling a story (narration)	Relate a story about a father who found out his daughter was pregnant through Target's customer profiling.
Adding descriptive detail (description)	Give details about crimes recorded on cameras in banks or outside of nightclubs.
Giving an example	Give an example of a benefit of store loyalty cards, such as food recall information.
Giving a definition	Explain the meaning of the term *network warfare*.
Making comparisons	Compare police surveillance programs in three cities.
Making distinctions (contrast)	Compare federal agencies with state agencies.
Explaining how something works (process)	Explain how E911 technology works to track information.
Giving reasons (causes)	Explain why private entities such as corporations and restaurants have good reasons to install cameras.
Analyzing effects	Explain why data collection and storage of personal information are a violation of privacy.

variety of ways Alaina could add evidence to her essay, she would not need to use all of them. Instead, she should choose the ones that are the most appropriate for her audience and purpose. Alaina could also use different types of evidence in combination. For example, she could *describe* a particular city's police camera system and *tell a story* that illustrates its use in the criminal justice system. Use the following guidelines in selecting evidence to support your thesis.

Guidelines for Selecting Evidence

■ **Be sure your evidence is relevant.** That is, it must directly support or explain your thesis.

■ **Make your evidence as specific as possible.** Help your readers see the point you are making by offering detailed, concrete information. For example, if you are explaining the dangers of driving while intoxicated, include details that make that danger seem immediate: victims' names and injuries, types of vehicle damage, statistics on the loss of life, and so on.

■ **Be sure your information is accurate.** It may be necessary to check facts, verify stories you have heard, and ask questions of individuals who may have provided information.

■ **Locate sources that provide evidence.** Because you may not know enough about your topic and lack personal experience, you may be unable to provide strong evidence. When this happens, locate several sources on your topic.

■ **Be sure to document any information that you borrow from other sources.**

Make Connections Among Your Ideas Clear

To produce a well-written essay, be sure to make it clear how your ideas relate to one another. There are several ways to do this:

- **Use transitional words and phrases within paragraphs.** The transitional words and phrases that you learned in Chapters 5, 6, and 7 for connecting ideas help make your essay flow smoothly and communicate clearly. Table 10-3 lists useful transitions for each method of organization.

- **Write a transitional sentence.** This sentence is usually the first sentence in a paragraph. It might come before the topic sentence, or it might *be* the topic sentence. Its purpose is to link the paragraph in which it appears with the paragraph before it. Sometimes it comes at the end of the paragraph and links the paragraph to the following one.

- **Repeat key words.** Repeating key words from either the thesis statement or the preceding paragraph helps your reader see connections among ideas.

TABLE 10-3 USEFUL TRANSITIONAL WORDS AND PHRASES	
Method of Development	**Transitional Words and Phrases**
Least/Most or Most/Least	most important, above all, especially, particularly important, less important
Spatial	above, below, behind, beside, next to, inside, outside, to the west (north, etc.), beneath, near, nearby, next to
Time Sequence	first, next, now, before, during, after, eventually, finally, at last, later, meanwhile, soon, then, suddenly, currently, after, afterward, after a while, as soon as, until
Narration/Process	first, second, then, later, in the beginning, when, after, following, next, during, again, after that, at last, finally
Description	see Least/Most or Most/Least and Spatial above
Example	for example, for instance, to illustrate, in one case
Comparison	likewise, similarly, in the same way, too, also
Contrast	however, on the contrary, unlike, on the other hand, although, even though, but, in contrast, yet
Cause and Effect	because, consequently, since, as a result, for this reason, therefore, thus

Draft Your Conclusion

The final paragraph of your essay has two functions: It should reemphasize your thesis statement and draw the essay to a close. It should not be a direct announcement, such as "This essay has been about ..." or "In this paper I hoped to show that ...."

It's usually best to revise your essay at least once *before* working on the conclusion. During your first or second revision, you often make numerous changes in both content and organization, which may in turn affect your conclusion.

Here are a few effective ways to write a conclusion.

- **Look ahead.** Project into the future and consider outcomes or effects.
- **Return to your thesis.** If your essay is written to prove a point or convince your reader of the need for action, it may be effective to end with a sentence that recalls your main point or calls for action. Do not merely repeat your first paragraph, but reflect on the thoughts you developed in your essay.
- **Summarize key points.** Especially for longer essays, briefly review your key supporting ideas.

If you have trouble writing your conclusion, it's probably a tip-off that you need to work further on your thesis or organization.

Select a Title

Although the title appears first, write it last. It should identify the topic in an interesting way and may also suggest the focus. To select a title, reread your final draft, paying particular attention to your thesis statement and your overall method of development. Here are a few examples of effective titles:

Which Way Is Up? (for an essay on mountain climbing)

A Hare-Raising Tale (for an essay on rabbit farming)

Topping Your Bottom Line (for an essay on how to increase profitability)

To write accurate and interesting titles, try the following tips:

- **Write a question that your essay answers.** For example: "Do You Know Who's Watching You Day and Night?"
- **Use key words that appear in your thesis statement.** If your thesis statement is "Diets rich in lean beef can help teenagers maintain higher levels of usable iron," your title could be "Lean Beef Is Good for Teens."
- **Use brainstorming techniques to generate options.** If in doubt, try out some options on friends to see which is most effective.

Document Your Sources

The Modern Language Association (MLA) uses a system of in-text citation: a brief note in the body of the text that refers to a source that is fully described in the alphabetized "Works Cited" list at the end of the paper. New guidelines now focus on citing sources based on a series of simple principles and elements that can be applied to a wide variety of source types and formats. For a comprehensive review of the new system, consult the *MLA Handbook*, 8th edition, or access the MLA Web site (www.mla.org).

An Overview of MLA Style

When you refer to, summarize, paraphrase, quote, or in any way use an author's words or ideas, you must indicate their original source by inserting an in-text citation that refers your reader to the "Works Cited" list. If you name the author in your sentence, only include the page number in the citation; if you do not name the author, include both the author's name and page number in the citation. When you include a quotation, use an introductory phrase to signal that the quotation is to follow.

> Miller poses the idea that if a good story is supposed to be a condensed version of life, then life should be lived like a good story in the first place (39).
>
> If a good story is supposed to be a condensed version of life, then life should be lived like a good story in the first place (Miller 39).
>
> According to Miller, "[quotation]." As Miller notes, "[quotation]." In the words of Miller, "[quotation]."

When citing a source, use the Elements Diagram below left to select and organize relevant information. MLA uses the term *container* to refer to the larger source (a magazine or journal) in which the specific source (an article) is located. Note that Container 1 provides primary source information for the author and/or title in elements 1 or 2, so include all relevant information for elements 3-9 in the order shown. As the primary source may appear within a second container (e.g., an article may appear in a journal which is then found in a database), you also need to document information relevant to this second container, repeating, as needed, elements 3-9.

ELEMENTS DIAGRAM	CORE ELEMENTS	DESCRIPTION OF ELEMENTS	EXAMPLES
1. Author. 2. Title of source. Container 1 (primary source information)	1. Author.	• Last name, first name • Second author's name written first name, last name • Three or more authors, reverse first name and follow with comma and "et al." • For non-author creators, add labels and spell them out • Treat pseudonyms as author names	• Carr, James I. • Carr, James I., and Martha Hopkins. • Fuentes, José, et al. • García, Emma, editor. • Cook, Douglas, translator. • @Cmdr_Hadfield.
3. Title of container, 4. Other contributors, 5. Version,	2. Title of source.	• Place title in quotation marks if it is part of larger source (e.g., a poem, essay, TV episode, blog post, or tweet), followed by a period. • Place title in italics if it is self-contained (e.g., a book, play, TV series, Web site, or album), followed by a period.	• "The Bee." (poem); "Everybody Dies." (TV episode); "On Noise." (essay); "Inside the Collapse of the New Republic." (blog post) • *Florence Gordon.* (novel); *King Lear.* (play); *House.* (TV series); *The New Yorker.* (Web site); *Cool It.* (album)
6. Number, 7. Publisher,	3. Title of container,	• If the source is part of a larger whole, that whole is considered a container; it is italicized and followed by a comma. • If the title of the source is the whole source, it appears as element 2, and there may be no entry for element 3.	• Ronnie Corbett, performer. "We Love British Comedy." *Facebook,* • Maugham, W. Somerset. *Of Human Bondage.* Viking Penguin, 1963.

ELEMENTS DIAGRAM	CORE ELEMENTS	DESCRIPTION OF ELEMENTS	EXAMPLES
8. Publication date, 9. Location.		• A container can be nested in a second container (see diagram on left).	• Barnard, Neal D., et al. "Vegetarian and Vegan Diets in Type 2 Diabetes Management." *Nutrition Reviews*, vol. 67, no. 5, pp. 255–263. *NCBI*, doi:10.1111/j.1753-4887.2009.00198.x.
Container 2 (where you found the primary source, e.g., database, Web site, online archive)	4. Other contributors,	• Place other important contributors to a work after the title of the container, preceded by a descriptor: *adapted by, performed by, directed by,* or *general editor* or *guest editors,* and followed by a comma.	• Dickinson, Emily. "Griefs." *Emily Dickinson: Selected Poems,* edited by Stanley Applebaum, Dover Thrift Editions, 1990, p. 25.
3. Title of Container,	5. Version,	• Indicate if there is more than one version of the source: *Updated ed., Expanded ed., 13th ed., director's cut,*	• McWhorter, Kathleen. *In Concert: Reading and Writing.* 2nd ed., Pearson, 2016.
4. Other contributors,	6. Number,	• Use abbreviations "vol." and "no." for volume and issue number, separated by a comma.	• Bivins, Corey. "A Soy-free, Nut-free Vegan Meal Plan." *Vegetarian Journal,* vol. 30, no. 1, pp. 14-17.
5. Version, 6. Number,	7. Publisher,	• Name of organization primarily responsible for producing source, followed by a comma. • If two or more organizations are equally responsible, cite both with forward slash between them. • Use "U" for university and "P" for Press.	• Pearson, Penguin, Netflix, Twentieth Century Fox • Lee, Malcolm D., director. *Barbershop: The Next Cut.* Performance by Ice Cube, MGM / New Line Cinema, 2016. • Oxford UP (abbreviation for Oxford University Press)
7. Publisher,	8. Publication date,	• Cite the most relevant date, followed by a comma. If you are citing a print work found online, use the date of the online posting.	• Lilla, Mark. "The President and the Passions." *The New York Times Magazine,* 19 Dec. 2010, p. MM 13.
8. Publication date, 9. Location.	9. Location.	• For print sources, provide page numbers preceded by p. or pp. and followed by a period. • For online sites, MLA recommends providing a URL (check with your professor) or DOI (preferred), followed by a period. Drop "http://" if it appears in URL.	• Maugham, W. Somerset. *Of Human Bondage.* Viking Penguin, 1963, p. 211. • Woolf, Virginia. "A Haunted House." *Monday or Tuesday,* Harcourt Brace, 1921. *Bartleby.com,* www.bartleby.com/85/.

EXERCISE 10-9

WRITING IN PROGRESS

Writing a First Draft of Your Essay

Directions: Draft a first version of your essay. Write an introductory paragraph that will grab your reader's attention, provides background information, if needed, and includes your thesis statement. Write body paragraphs with clear topic sentences that explain and support your thesis and are themselves supported by relevant reasons and evidence. Write a concluding paragraph that looks ahead, returns to your thesis, and/or summarizes your key points. Then brainstorm for a title.

Revise Your Essay

■ GOAL 8
Revise your essay

Revision involves looking both at what you said and how you said it with an eye toward making sure your essay is complete, clear, concise, and well organized. Begin by examining whether you have provided adequate support for your thesis statement and evaluate your organization using a revision map.

Revise Your Thesis Statement

The best time to evaluate and, if necessary, revise your thesis statement is after you have written a first draft. At that time, you can see if your essay delivers what your thesis promises. If it does not, it needs revision, or you need to refocus your essay.

How to Identify a Weak Thesis Statement

Here are the characteristics of a weak thesis statement:

- The essay does not explain and support the thesis.
- The thesis statement does not cover all the topics included in the essay.
- The thesis statement is vague or unclear.
- The thesis statement makes a direct announcement.

How to Revise a Weak Thesis Statement

When evaluating your thesis statement, ask the following questions:

- **Does my essay develop and explain my thesis statement?** As you write an essay, its focus and direction may change. Revise your thesis statement to reflect any changes. If you discover that you drifted away from your original thesis and you want to maintain it, work on revising so that your paper delivers what your thesis statement promises.

- **Is my thesis statement broad enough to cover all the points I made in the essay?** As you develop your first draft, you may find that one idea leads naturally to another. Both must be covered by the thesis statement. For example, suppose your thesis statement is "Because of the number of patients our clinic sees in a day, the need for nurse practitioners has increased dramatically." If, in your essay, you discuss lab technicians and interns as well as nurses, then you need to broaden your thesis statement.

- **Does my thesis statement use vague or unclear words that do not clearly focus the topic?** For example, in the thesis statement "Physical therapy can help bursitis," the word *help* is vague and does not suggest how your essay will approach the topic. Instead, if your paper discusses the effectiveness of physical therapy, this approach should be reflected in your thesis: "When it comes to chronic bursitis, deep tissue massage by a trained physical therapist can be very effective."

- **Does my thesis statement make a direct announcement?** If so, revise to eliminate mention of the essay itself or yourself as the writer. For example, if your thesis statement is "I am going to write about how to reduce cyberbullying," revise it by eliminating mention of yourself and include more about why the issue is important: "Cyberbullying is a growing national problem, and there are obvious steps that can be taken to control it."

EXERCISE 10-10   Evaluating and Revising Thesis Statements

Directions: Identify what is wrong with each of the following thesis statements and revise each one to make it more effective.

1. Most people like to dance.
2. Call the doctor when you're sick.
3. Everyone should read the newspaper.
4. It's important to keep your receipts.
5. Driving in snow is dangerous.
6. This essay is about sexual harassment on the job.

EXERCISE 10-11   Writing: Revising Your Thesis Statement

WRITING IN PROGRESS

Directions: Review the thesis statement you wrote in Exercise 10-6 to see if it is strong. If it has any of the characteristics of a weak thesis, use the list of revision suggestions on page 354 to revise it to be more effective.

Revise an Underdeveloped Essay

An underdeveloped essay is one that lacks sufficient information and evidence to support the thesis.

How to Identify an Underdeveloped Essay

Here are the characteristics of an underdeveloped essay:

- The essay seems to ramble or is unfocused.
- The essay repeats information or says the same thing in slightly different ways.
- The essay makes general statements but does not support them.
- The essay lacks facts, examples, comparisons, or reasons.

How to Revise an Underdeveloped Essay

Use the following suggestions to revise an underdeveloped essay:

1. **Analyze your draft to identify needed information.** Often when writing an essay you will find that you need additional information to support or explain your ideas. Suppose you are writing an essay on one aspect of crime in America. Your thesis states that mandatory minimum sentencing laws for petty crimes should be replaced with sentencing guidelines. In order to present a convincing paper, you need facts, statistics, and evidence to support your opinions. For example, you might need

   - statistics on the numbers of people in prison.
   - statistics on the increase in America's incarceration rate.

- statistics on the amount of money spent on prisoners.
- facts on mandatory minimum sentences.
- facts on countries with successful alternatives to prison for lesser offenses.
- evidence that mandatory minimums are ineffective.

Study your draft and look for statements that require supporting information in order to be believable. For example, suppose you have written the following:

> The prisons in America are bursting with inmates who would be better off in drug treatment programs than locked up with dangerous criminals.

To support this statement, you need statistics on the number of prisoners with drug addictions who have been convicted of minor offenses and incarcerated.

The following types of statements benefit from supporting information:

■ Opinions

EXAMPLE	Judges should be allowed to decide on the appropriate level of punishment.
NEEDED INFORMATION	What evidence supports that opinion?

■ Broad, general ideas

EXAMPLE	Incarcerating people for petty crimes is too harsh a punishment.
NEEDED INFORMATION	What alternatives are available? What constitutes a petty crime?

■ Cause and effect statements

EXAMPLE	Mandatory minimums are the result of politicians wanting to appear tough on crime.
NEEDED INFORMATION	What is the history of mandatory minimum sentencing? Who typically supports or opposes mandatory minimums?

■ Statements that assert what should be done

EXAMPLE	States should work harder to help minor offenders become contributing members of society.
NEEDED INFORMATION	What programs are currently in place? What should states do? How many offenders would be helped?

Make a list of required information, and form questions that need to be answered. Some students find it effective to write each question on a separate index card. As you locate needed information, depending on the source and the requirements of your assignment, you might copy, print and annotate, paraphrase, or summarize it.

As you consult sources, you will probably discover new ideas and perhaps even a new approach to your topic. For example, you may learn that some countries rely on a system of restorative justice, in which the criminal must apologize or provide reparation to the victim instead of going to prison for minor crimes. Record each of these new ideas along with its source.

1. **Revise your paper** by adding or incorporating new supporting information. Then reevaluate your draft, eliminating statements for which you could not locate supporting information, statements that you found to be inaccurate, and statements for which you found contradictory evidence.

2. **Delete sentences that are repetitious and add nothing to the essay.** If you find you have little or nothing left, do additional brainstorming, freewriting, or branching to discover new ideas or consult new sources. If this technique does not work, consider changing your topic to one about which you have more to say.

3. **Go through your essay sentence by sentence and highlight any ideas that you could further develop and explain.** Develop these ideas into separate paragraphs.

4. **Make sure each topic sentence is clear and specific.** Then add details to each paragraph that make it sharp and convincing.

| EXERCISE 10-12 | Writing: Revising to Ensure Adequate Development |

WRITING IN PROGRESS

Directions: Evaluate and revise the essay you wrote in Exercise 10-9, using the suggestions given above.

Revise a Disorganized Essay

A disorganized essay is one that does not follow a logical method of development. A disorganized essay makes it difficult for your readers to follow your train of thought. If readers must struggle to follow your ideas, they may stop reading or lose their concentration. In fact, as they struggle to follow your thinking, they may miss important information or misinterpret what you are saying.

How to Identify a Disorganized Essay

Use the following questions to help you evaluate the organization of your essay:

■ **Does every paragraph in the essay support or explain the thesis statement?**

■ **Do you avoid straying from your topic?**

- Does each detail in each paragraph explain the topic sentence?
- Do you make it clear how one idea relates to another by using transitions?

How to Revise a Disorganized Essay

To improve the organization of your essay, use one of the methods of organization discussed in Chapters 6 and 7. Here is a brief review:

METHOD OF ORGANIZATION	PURPOSE
Process	Describes the order in which things are done
Narration	Presents events in the order in which they happened
Description	Gives descriptive, sensory details
Example	Explains a situation or idea by giving circumstances that illustrate it
Cause and Effect	Explains why things happen or what happens as a result of something else
Comparison and Contrast	Focuses on similarities and differences

Once you have chosen and used a method of development, be sure to use appropriate transitions to connect your ideas.

Another way to spot and correct organizational problems is to draw an idea or revision map, which will help you visualize the progression of your ideas graphically and see which ideas fit and which do not.

EXERCISE 10-13

WRITING IN PROGRESS

Writing: Evaluating Organization

Directions: Evaluate the organization of the essay you worked on in Exercises 10-9 and 10-12. Revise it if needed.

Use a Revision Map

A **revision map** will help you evaluate the overall flow of your ideas as well as the effectiveness of individual paragraphs. To draw an essay revision map, begin by listing your title at the top of the page. Write your thesis statement underneath it, and then list the topic sentence of each paragraph. Next, work through each paragraph, recording your supporting details in abbreviated form. Then write the key words of your conclusion. If you find topic sentences and/or details that do not support the thesis statement, record them to the right of the map.

When you've completed your revision map, conduct the following tests:

1. **Read your thesis statement along with your first topic sentence.** Does the topic sentence clearly support your thesis? If not, revise it to make the relationship clearer. Repeat this step for each topic sentence.

2. **Read your topic sentences, one after the other, without reading the corresponding details.** Is there a logical connection between them? Have you arranged them in the most effective way? If not, revise to make the connection clearer or to improve your organization.

3. **Examine each individual paragraph.** Are there enough relevant, specific details to support the topic sentence?

4. **Read your introduction and then look at your topic sentences.** Does the essay deliver what the introduction promises?

5. **Read your thesis statement and then your conclusion.** Are they compatible and consistent? Does the conclusion agree with and support the thesis statement?

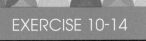

EXERCISE 10-14

WRITING IN PROGRESS

Writing: Using a Revision Map

Directions: Draw a revision map of the essay you wrote and revised throughout this chapter. Make further revisions as needed.

READ AND RESPOND: A Student Essay

Niruft/Fotolia

Surveillance in America: It's Not Paranoia If You're Really Being Watched

Alaina Mayer

Earlier in the chapter, you read "Surveillance in America: It's Not Paranoia If You're Really Being Watched" and examined various elements of the essay. Now it is time to take a closer look at the reading by responding to the questions that follow.

Examining Writing

1. How is the essay organized?

2. Examine Alaina's use of sources. What does each reference used contribute to the essay?

3. Other than sources, what other types of support does Alaina use to explain her thesis?

4. Examine the introduction. Does beginning with questions create an effective opener? If so, what other questions might Alaina have included?

5. For what audience does Alaina seem to be writing?

6. What additional information or additional details could have strengthened Alaina's thesis?

READ AND RESPOND: A Textbook Reading

Computer Technology, Large Organizations, and the Assault on Privacy

John Macionis

Earlier in the chapter, you read "Computer Technology, Large Organizations, and the Assault on Privacy" and examined various elements of the essay. Now it is time to take a closer look at the reading by responding to the questions that follow.

Getting Ready to Write

Checking Your Comprehension

Answer each of the following questions using complete sentences.

1. What three aspects of modern life are used as examples of the decline in privacy?
2. According to the author, what are two reasons for today's loss of privacy?
3. List three examples of government organizations that collect personal information.
4. How many credit cards does the average American adult have?
5. How often does the typical London resident appear on closed-circuit television?
6. What does the federal Privacy Act of 1974 do?

Strengthening Your Vocabulary

Identify at least five words used in the reading that are unfamiliar to you. Using context, word parts, or a dictionary, write a brief definition of each word as it is used in the reading.

Examining the Reading: Creating Idea Maps

Create an idea map of the reading that starts with the title and thesis and then lists the author's main points. Use the guidelines on page 358.

Reading and Writing: An Integrated Perspective

React and respond to the reading by discussing the following:

1. What is the author's purpose in writing this selection? How well does he achieve his purpose?
2. For what audience is this selection written?

3. What types of supporting details does the author use to capture your attention and inform you about the subject of the selection? Which types of details are most effective and/or convincing?

4. What technique does Macionis use in his conclusion? Is it effective? Why or why not?

5. Discuss the title of this selection. Why does the author use the word *assault,* and what does it reveal or imply about his attitude toward the subject? What other word might he have used instead?

6. Do you consider it important to safeguard your personal information on the Internet? Why or why not?

7. Write a journal entry giving your answers to the questions posed in the final paragraph of the essay.

8. What is the purpose of the photo that accompanies the essay? Discuss the types of security or surveillance cameras you have seen in public places. How do these cameras make you feel?

THINKING VISUALLY

Writing About the Reading

Paragraph Options

1. How does the author capture your attention in the first three paragraphs? What do these opening paragraphs tell you about who the author's audience is? Write a paragraph answering these questions and evaluating the introduction.

2. How would you describe the author's attitude toward the subject? Write a paragraph identifying examples of language and details in the selection that reveal the author's attitude.

3. Have you ever received a ticket as the result of a traffic enforcement camera? Have you ever been notified of a breach in the security of your credit or banking information? Write a paragraph describing your experience.

Essay Options

4. Do you think the benefits of security cameras outweigh the costs? Are you willing to make sacrifices in your own privacy in exchange for increased public safety? Why or why not? Write an essay exploring these questions.

5. Are you careful about what personal information you reveal? What steps do you take to protect your personal information? Are you concerned about identity theft? Write an essay explaining how you guard your privacy when you are on the Internet and when you use credit to make purchases. If you do not protect your privacy, explain why.

6. What changes have you noticed in government monitoring of the population in the past decade? How have the federal government's efforts to strengthen national security affected you? If you have traveled by airplane or crossed the border into other countries, what have you noticed about security measures? Write an essay describing your experiences and your reaction to security measures.

Making Connections Between the Readings

Use both "Surveillance in America: It's Not Paranoia If You're Really Being Watched" and "Computer Technology, Large Organizations, and the Assault on Privacy" to write a response to one of the following prompts.

1. In a paragraph, compare and contrast the two reading selections by examining the author's purpose.

2. Write a paragraph discussing the similarities and differences in the two titles. What do the titles suggest about the authors' attitudes toward the subject?

3. Both of the articles mention ways that we unknowingly compromise our personal privacy. Consider your own use of technology. How do you compromise your privacy or the privacy of others when using technology and/or technological applications? Have these articles convinced you that you need to make changes to your practices? If so, what changes do you plan to make? If not, why don't you plan to make any changes? Respond to these questions in an essay.

4. If you had to create a bumper sticker that would serve as a reminder to the public about the necessity of protecting personal information, what would it say? Write an essay in which you describe your bumper sticker and explain why the message is an effective one. Be sure to use details from the two essays to support your point.

SELF-TEST SUMMARY

To test yourself, cover the Answer column with a sheet of paper and answer each question in the left column. Evaluate each of your answers as you work by sliding the paper down and comparing your answer with what is printed in the Answer column.

QUESTION	ANSWER
■ **GOAL 1** Use strategies for reading essays What are some strategies for reading essays?	Establish the writer's authority and pay attention to background information. Identify the writer's purpose. Examine the title, the introduction, the body, and the organization of the essay as well as the writer's use of vocabulary. Finally, examine the essay's conclusion.
■ **GOAL 2** Choose a topic What is involved in choosing a topic?	The topic for an essay should be broader than for a single paragraph but narrow enough to cover within an essay.
How do you narrow a broad topic or broaden a narrow topic?	Narrow a broad topic by asking *who, what, when, where, why,* and *how.* Broaden a narrow topic by thinking of other situations or circumstances that illustrate the same idea or by thinking of a larger concept that includes your topic.

QUESTION	ANSWER
■ **GOAL 3** Consider audience and purpose How do you consider audience and purpose?	Consider your audience by analyzing your readers' knowledge, background, experience, and education. Also consider their attitudes, opinions, and beliefs. Be sure to explain any ideas or concepts that may be unfamiliar to them.
What are three main purposes for writing?	The three main purposes for writing are to express ideas, to inform, and to persuade.
■ **GOAL 4** Develop a thesis statement What does a thesis statement do?	A thesis statement tells your reader what your essay is about and gives clues to how the essay will unfold.
How do you develop a thesis statement?	The first step in developing a thesis statement is to generate ideas by freewriting, brainstorming, or branching. Then group or connect your ideas to form a thesis.
■ **GOAL 5** Plan and organize your essay What strategies are useful in planning and organizing an essay?	Outlining and mapping are useful ways to discover relationships among ideas. Patterns of organization are also helpful. When choosing a pattern, consider which best suits your topic, your audience, and your purpose.
■ **GOAL 6** Locate and record appropriate sources How do you find and record appropriate sources?	Tips for finding appropriate sources include consulting a reference librarian and using a systematic approach to find sources that are current, varied, reliable, and trustworthy. Photocopy pages from print sources and download and print information from online sources. Keep track of information by annotating, paraphrasing, and summarizing.
What is plagiarism?	Plagiarism is using an author's words or ideas without acknowledging that you have done so.
■ **GOAL 7** Draft your essay How do you draft your essay?	Write your introduction; draft your body paragraphs, making connections among your ideas clear; draft your conclusion; select a title; and document your sources (for an overview of MLA style, see p. 352).
■ **GOAL 8** Revise your essay What are common problems in an essay?	Common problems include a weak thesis statement, underdevelopment (a lack of sufficient information and evidence to support the thesis), and disorganization.
What will a revision map do?	A revision map will help you evaluate the overall flow of your ideas as well as the effectiveness of individual paragraphs.

11

Complete Sentences Versus Sentence Fragments

B Christopher /Alamy Stock Photo

THINK About It!

In the photograph above, when you read the banner the activists are carrying, it does not make sense because you do not know who is working for a better planet. You assume it is the activists, but you do not know who they represent. Once you notice the abbreviations that appear on the banner and determine what they mean, then the message on the banner is understandable. SEIU stands for Service Employees International Union, a labor union that represents property service workers including bus drivers, security officers, cleaners, and so forth. 32BJ is a branch of SEIU representing members in northeastern states.

Now, write a sentence that states the message the banner communicates about SEIU workers.

The information about SEIU helped you determine who is "working toward a better planet". The phrase itself is a sentence fragment. A fragment is an incomplete sentence. This fragment lacks a subject.

Fragments are problems for both readers and writers. For readers, the meaning is incomplete, which results in confusion. For writers, fragments are a problem because the intended message is not conveyed clearly and in an understandable way. When meaning is not clear, misunderstandings are possible, leading to a breakdown in communication.

How can the fragment in the photo on the previous page be corrected? It does have a verb—working. To make the caption into a complete sentence, you must add a subject:

	Subject	Verb
COMPLETE SENTENCE	The Service Employees International Union is	working

for a better planet.

The new version now makes sense even without the photograph. This version has a subject and a verb and expresses a complete thought.

In this chapter, you will learn to write effective, complete sentences and to identify and correct fragments. You will also learn how to read sentences effectively by identifying the parts that all complete sentences contain to convey meaning.

What Is a Complete Sentence?

A **complete sentence** is a statement that contains both a subject and a **predicate**—a verb or verbs and the words that govern or modify them—and expresses a complete thought. Being able to identify subjects and predicates will help you avoid errors in writing and will help you read sentences more effectively.

Identify Subjects and Predicates

■ GOAL 1
Identify subjects and predicates

Writing effective sentences involves being able to identify the subject and predicate of a sentence.

Subjects

The **subject** of a sentence is whom or what the sentence is about. It is who or what performs or receives the action expressed in the predicate.

Nouns as Subjects

The **subject** of a sentence is usually a **noun**. (For a review of nouns, see "A Brief Grammar Handbook," p. 469.)

The Babylonians wrote the first advertisements.

The advertisements were inscribed on bricks.

The kings conducted advertising campaigns for themselves.

Pronouns as Subjects

The subject of a sentence can also be a **pronoun**, a word that refers to, or substitutes for, a noun. For example, *I, you, he, she, it, they,* and *we* are all familiar pronouns. (For a review of pronouns, see "A Brief Grammar Handbook," p. 470.)

Early advertisements were straightforward. They carried the names of temples.

The wall was built. It was seen by thousands of people.

Groups of Words as Subjects

The subject of a sentence can also be a group of words:

Inscribing the bricks was a difficult task.

Uncovering the bricks was a surprise.

To build the brick wall was a time-consuming task.

EXERCISE 11-1   Identifying Subjects

Directions: Underline the subject in each of the following sentences.

      EXAMPLE   The Babylonians wrote the first advertisements.

1. The thrush was singing.

2. Digging the hole was a strenuous task.

3. After the lecture, we are going to the movies.

4. Vanessa organized the performance.

5. It was only a raccoon outside.

6. Do you want to eat the last cookie?

7. The weeds spread quickly.

8. To swim the English Channel is my goal.

9. Antoan went running.

10. They circumnavigated the globe.

Compound Subjects

Some sentences contain two or more subjects joined with a coordinating conjunction (*and, but, for, nor, or, so, yet*). Those subjects together form a **compound subject**.

Compound subject

Maria and I completed the marathon.

Compound subject

The computer, the printer, and the DVD player were unusable during the blackout.

Predicates

The **predicate** indicates what the subject does, what happened to the subject, or what is said about the subject. The predicate must include a **verb**, a word or group of words that expresses an action or a state of being (for example, *run, invent, build, know, will decide, become*). The predicate can consist of a single word or several words, including other verbs and words that modify or govern them.

> Joy <u>swam</u> sixty laps.
> The thunderstorm <u>replenished</u> the reservoir.

Sometimes the predicate consists of only one verb, as in the previous examples. Often, however, the main verb is accompanied by a **helping verb**. A helping verb is used with another verb to express time, obligation, possibility, and so forth.

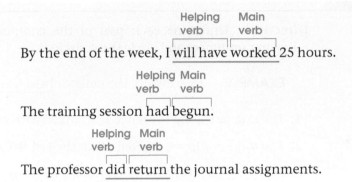

By the end of the week, I <u>will have worked</u> 25 hours.

The training session <u>had begun</u>.

The professor <u>did return</u> the journal assignments.

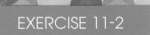

| EXERCISE 11-2 | Identifying Verbs |

Directions: Underline the main verb in each of the following sentences. Circle any helping verbs.

    EXAMPLE   The next blue moon (will) <u>occur</u> in April.

1. May I sit here?

2. Jay practiced the saxophone every day.

3. The divers found the wreckage of an eighteenth-century schooner.

4. Camila had written several articles for the school newspaper.

5. Some whale vocalizations can be heard for many miles.

6. You must wear your seatbelt in my car.

7. She lost her keys down the storm drain.

8. The flood damaged several homes on River Road.

9. A cracking whip does break the sound barrier.

10. Mr. Park hired three new employees.

Compound Predicates

Some sentences have two or more predicates, each of which contains one or more verbs, joined by a coordinating conjunction (*and, but, nor*). These predicates together form a **compound predicate**.

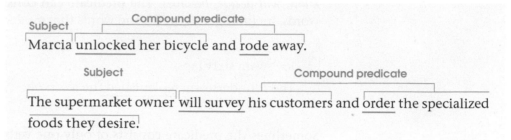

Marcia unlocked her bicycle and rode away.

The supermarket owner will survey his customers and order the specialized foods they desire.

EXERCISE 11-3 | Identifying Compound Predicates

Directions: Underline each part of the compound predicate in each of the following sentences and circle the verbs in it.

EXAMPLE Heating up, the radiator (hissed) and (clanked)

1. The dog ran along the fence and barked with excitement.

2. The toddler slipped and fell down the last few stairs but was unhurt.

3. I can neither snap my fingers nor raise one eyebrow.

4. In the meantime, Diego finished his homework and made himself a snack.

5. The final step is to add the wet ingredients and mix until smooth.

Identify Sentence Fragments

■ GOAL 2
Identify sentence fragments

A **fragment** is a sentence that lacks a subject, a verb, or both or does not express a complete thought. Following are a few more statements taken from magazine ads. Each one is a sentence fragment because each one lacks a subject or a verb or does not express a complete thought. As you read the fragments that follow, they may be difficult to understand. Try to guess what product each sentence fragment describes. Correct answers appear at the bottom of page.

FRAGMENT	PRODUCT
1. At the heart of the image.	1. _____
2. The miracles of science.	2. _____
3. Keeps going and going and going.	3. _____
4. Melts in your mouth, not in your hand.	4. _____

Because advertisers use visuals to complete their messages, they do not have to worry about the confusing nature of sentence fragments. Also, no one requires writers of ads to use complete sentences. Your instructors, however, expect you to write sentences that are complete and correct. You will, therefore, need to know

Answers to sentence fragments 1. Nikon; 2. DuPont; 3. Energizer; 4. M&Ms

how to spot and correct sentence fragments. To do so, you need to understand three sentence elements:

- subjects.
- verbs.
- dependent clauses (also called subordinate clauses).

NEED TO KNOW

Subjects, Verbs, Dependent Clauses, and Sentence Fragments

- The **subject** of a sentence tells you whom or what the sentence is about—who or what does or receives the action of the verb. (Note: The direct object can also receive the action of the verb.)

- A **verb** expresses action or state of being. Sometimes a verb consists of only one word. (The doorbell *rang*.) Often, however, the main verb has a helping verb. (The guest *had arrived*.)

SUBJECT	VERB
Heat	rises.
Joyce	laughed.
Weeds	grow.
Opportunities	exist.

- **Dependent**, or **subordinate**, **clauses** do not express a complete thought.

- A **sentence fragment** is not a complete idea because it lacks a subject and/or a verb or does not express a complete thought. Either it needs to be expanded into a complete sentence through the addition of a subject and/or a verb, or it needs to be connected to a preceding or following sentence to become a complete thought.

Recognize and Correct Fragments Caused by Missing Subjects

- **GOAL 3**
  Recognize and correct fragments caused by missing subjects

A common sentence-writing error is to write a sentence *without a subject*. The result is a sentence fragment. Writers often make this mistake when they think the subject of a previous sentence or a noun in a previous sentence also applies to the next sentence.

Complete sentence | Fragment

Marge lost her keys on Tuesday. And found them on Wednesday.
[The missing subject is *Marge*.]

Complete sentence | Fragment

The instructor canceled class. But did not postpone the quiz.
[The missing subject is *instructor*.]

Complete sentence

Relieved that it had stopped raining, Teresa rushed into the mall.

Fragment

Then remembered her car window was open.
[The missing subject is *Teresa*.]

You can revise a fragment that lacks a subject in two ways:

1. **Add a subject, often a pronoun referring to the subject of the preceding sentence.**

FRAGMENT   And found them on Wednesday.

                        Subject
                           |
REVISED   She found them on Wednesday.

FRAGMENT   Then remembered her car window was open.

                              Subject
                                 |
REVISED   Then she remembered her car window was open.

2. **Connect the fragment to the preceding sentence.**

FRAGMENT   And found them on Wednesday.

                   Subject   Verb   Connecting word   Verb
                      | | | |
REVISED   Marge lost her keys on Tuesday and found them on
                Wednesday.

FRAGMENT   But did not postpone the quiz.

                         Subject   Verb   Connecting word   Verb
                            | | | |
REVISED   The instructor canceled class but did not postpone
                the quiz.

Each of these sentences now has a subject and a compound verb.

EXERCISE 11-4   Revising Fragments by Adding Subjects

Directions: Each of the following items consists of a complete sentence followed by a sentence fragment that lacks a subject. Make each fragment into a complete sentence by adding a subject. You may need to take out words, add new ones, capitalize words, or make them lowercase as you revise.

                                                            He

EXAMPLE   Bert threw the basketball. ~~And~~ cheered when it went in the
                          hoop.

1. The president waved as he left the building. Then got in the car and drove away.

2. The novel was complex. Was also long and poorly written.

3. The scissors were not very sharp. Were old and rusty.

4. Hundreds of students waited to get into the bookstore. Milled around until the manager unlocked the door.

5. My roommate, whose name is Speed, is an excellent skater. Gets teased sometimes about her name.

6. The computer printed out the list of names. Then beeped loudly.

7. Fans crowded the stadium. And cheered after each touchdown.

8. Many guests arrived early for the wedding. But were not seated until ten o'clock.

9. The delivery person dropped the large package. Then split open and spilled on the sidewalk.

10. The big black dog sat obediently. But growled nonetheless.

EXERCISE 11-5

WRITING IN PROGRESS

Writing About an Advertisement

Directions: Write a paragraph describing an advertisement you have seen or heard recently. Explain to whom the advertisement appeals and why. After you have finished revising and proofreading your paragraph, underline the subject of each sentence. Exchange papers with a peer reviewer and see if you agree on the identification of subjects. Discuss any differences of opinion with another peer reviewer or with your instructor. Save your paper. You will need it for another exercise in this chapter.

Recognize and Correct Fragments Caused by Missing Verbs

■ GOAL 4
Recognize and correct fragments caused by missing verbs

A **verb** is a word or word group that indicates what the subject does or what happens to the subject. Most verbs express action or a state of being, for example, *run, invent, build, know, be.* (For a review of verbs, see "A Brief Grammar Handbook," p. 474).

Sometimes a verb consists of only one word.

Advertising is bland without a slogan.

Slogans promote a specific product.

The announcer speaks.

Often, however, the main verb is accompanied by one or more helping (auxiliary) verbs such as *will, can,* and forms of *be, have,* or *do.* (For a review of helping verbs, see "A Brief Grammar Handbook," p. 474).

          Helping verb   Main verb

The announcer will speak.

          Helping verb   Main verb

The announcer will be speaking.

           Helping verb   Main verb

The first trademark was registered in 1870.

Helping verb   Main verb

Do any companies use animals as trademarks?

Helping verb   Main verb

The lion has been MGM's trademark for a long time.

EXERCISE 11-6 — Identifying Verbs

Directions: Underline the verb(s), including any helping verb(s), in each of the following sentences.

> **EXAMPLE** The lectures in psychology <u>have been focusing</u> on instinctive behavior lately.

1. Preschools teach children social and academic skills.

2. Exercise clubs offer instruction and provide companionship.

3. Millions of people have watched soap operas.

4. Essay exams are given in many college classes.

5. The audience will be surprised by the play's ending.

> **Tip for Writers**
>
> The simple present tense is used for repeated action. "Allison *walks* across campus after lunch" means she does this regularly. On the other hand, "Allison is walking" (present continuous tense) means right now or at some stated future time (perhaps to-morrow) she is or will be walking.

How to Revise Fragments Without Complete Verbs

Fragments often occur when word groups begin with words ending in *-ing* or with phrases beginning with the word *to*. These words and phrases are verb forms and may look like verbs, but they cannot function as verbs in sentences.

How to Revise Fragments with *-ing* Verbs

Note the *-ing* word in the fragment below:

> **FRAGMENT** <u>Walking</u> across campus after lunch.

In this word group, *walking* has no subject. Who is walking? Now let's add a subject and see what happens:

> *Allison* <u>walking</u> across campus after lunch.

The word group still is not a complete sentence; the verb form *walking* cannot be used alone as a sentence verb. You can make the word group a complete sentence by adding a helping verb (for example, *is, was, has been*) or by using a different verb form (*walked* or *walks*).

> Helping verb added
> **REVISED** Allison <u>was walking</u> across campus after lunch.

> Verb form changed to present tense
> **REVISED** Allison <u>walks</u> across campus after lunch.

Now the word group is a complete sentence.

You can correct fragments beginning with *-ing* words in four ways:

1. **Add a subject and change the *-ing* verb form to a verb that completes the sentence.**

	Fragment
FRAGMENT	Morris was patient. Waiting in line at the bank.

	Subject Verb changed to past tense
REVISED	Morris was patient. He waited in line at the bank.

2. **Add a subject and a form of *be* (such as *am, are, will be, has been, is, was, were*) as a helping verb.**

	Fragment
FRAGMENT	Juan was bored. Listening to his sister complain about her boyfriend.

	Subject Form of *be* Main verb
REVISED	Juan was bored. He was listening to his sister complain about her boyfriend.

3. **Connect the fragment to the sentence that comes before or after it.**

	Fragment
FRAGMENT	Mark finished lunch. Picking up his tray. Then he left the cafeteria.

	Modifies *he*
REVISED	Mark finished lunch. Picking up his tray, he left the cafeteria.

4. **If the *-ing* word is *being*, change its form to another form of *be* (*am, are, is, was, were*).**

	Fragment
FRAGMENT	Jayla failed the math quiz. Her mistakes being careless errors.

	Verb form changed
REVISED	Jayla failed the math quiz. Her mistakes were careless errors.

How to Revise Fragments with *To* Phrases

A phrase beginning with *to* cannot be the verb of the sentence. When it stands alone, it is a sentence fragment.

FRAGMENT	To review for the psychology test.

This word group lacks a subject and a verb that completes the sentence. To make a complete sentence, you need to add a subject and a verb.

	Subject Verb
REVISED	Deon plans to review for the psychology test.

You can revise fragments that begin with *to* in two ways:

1. **Add a subject and a verb that complete the sentence.**

FRAGMENT   To reach my goal.

                          Subject Verb

REVISED   I hope to reach my goal.

2. **Connect the *to* phrase to a nearby sentence.**

FRAGMENT   To earn the highest grade. Antonio studied for eight hours.

REVISED   To earn the highest grade, Antonio studied for eight hours.

EXERCISE 11-7

WORKING TOGETHER

Correcting Fragments by Adding Verbs

Directions: Each of the following word groups is a fragment. Revise each one to form a complete sentence, and then compare your revisions with those of a classmate.

EXAMPLE

FRAGMENT   Walking along the waterfront.

COMPLETE SENTENCE   Andrea was walking along the waterfront.

1. Photographing the wedding.

_____

2. To have a family.

_____

3. Hanging up the suit in the closet.

_____

4. Deciding what to have for dinner.

_____

5. To attend the awards ceremony.

_____

6. Writing the speech.

_____

7. To sketch a diagram.

_____

8. To quit her job.

_____

9. Making the paper less repetitious.

_____

10. Being old and in disrepair.

Revising Your Paragraph

Directions: Go back to the paragraph you wrote in Exercise 11-5 and circle the verb(s) in each sentence. Exchange papers with a peer reviewer and check each other's work.

Recognize and Correct Fragments Caused by Dependent Clauses

■ **GOAL 5**
Recognize and correct fragments caused by dependent clauses

A sentence not only must contain a subject and a verb but also *must express a complete thought*. That is, a sentence should not leave a question in your mind as to its meaning or leave an idea unfinished. To spot and avoid sentence fragments in your writing, you must be able to recognize the difference between independent and dependent (or subordinate) clauses.

A **clause** is a group of related words that contains a subject and its verb. There are two types of clauses: independent and dependent. An **independent clause** expresses a complete thought and can stand alone as a complete sentence. A **dependent** (or **subordinate**) **clause** does not express a complete thought. When a dependent clause stands alone, it is a fragment.

Recognize Independent Clauses

An **independent clause** has a subject and a verb and can stand alone as a complete and correct sentence. It expresses a complete thought.

COMPLETE THOUGHT

Independent clause

Subject   Verb

Advertising was not halted during World War II.

COMPLETE THOUGHT

Independent clause

Subject   Verb

Advertisers prominently displayed brand names.

COMPLETE THOUGHT

Independent clause

Subject   Verb

Produce will be in short supply this year.

Recognize Dependent (or Subordinate) Clauses

A **dependent clause** has a subject and a verb but cannot stand alone as a complete and correct sentence. It does not express a complete thought. A dependent clause makes sense only when it is joined to an independent clause. When a dependent clause stands alone, it is a **dependent clause fragment**. A dependent clause fragment leaves an unanswered question in your mind.

INCOMPLETE THOUGHT

Dependent clause fragment

Subject   Verb

After World War II ended. [What happened after World War II ended?]

INCOMPLETE THOUGHT

Dependent clause fragment

Subject   Verb

If new products are developed. [What happens if new products are developed?]

INCOMPLETE THOUGHT

Dependent clause fragment

Subject   Verb

When magazine circulation increased. [What happened when circulation increased?]

How can you spot dependent clauses? A dependent clause often begins with a word or group of words called a subordinating conjunction.

A **subordinating conjunction** explains the relationship between the dependent clause and the independent clause to which it is joined. Subordinating conjunctions signal dependent clauses. When you see a clause beginning with one of these words (shown in the "Need to Know" box on p. 377), make sure the clause is attached to an independent clause.

Dependent clause   Independent clause

After World War II ended, advertising became more glamorous.

Subordinating conjunction

Independent clause   Dependent clause

There will be new advertising campaigns if new products are developed.

Subordinating conjunction

Dependent clause   Independent clause

When magazine circulation increased, magazines became a popular new

Subordinating conjunction

advertising medium.

NEED TO KNOW

Subordinating Conjunctions

A clause beginning with a subordinate conjunction is a **dependent clause**. It cannot stand alone. It must be connected to an independent clause. Here is a list of common subordinating conjunctions:

after	even though	than
although	if	that
as	inasmuch as	though
as far as	in case	unless
as if	in order that	until
as long as	in order to	when
as soon as	now that	whenever
as though	once	where
because	provided that	whereas
before	rather than	wherever
during	since	whether
even if	so that	while

EXERCISE 11-9   Identifying Clauses

Directions: Decide whether the following clauses are independent or dependent. Write *I* for independent or *D* for dependent before each clause.

_____   **1.** While Arturo was driving to school.

_____   **2.** *Sesame Street* is a children's educational television program.

_____   **3.** Samantha keeps a diary of her family's holiday celebrations.

_____   **4.** Because Aretha had a craving for chocolate.

_____   **5.** Exercise can help to relieve stress.

_____   **6.** When Peter realized he would be able to meet the deadline.

_____   **7.** A snowstorm crippled the Eastern Seaboard states on New Year's Eve.

_____   **8.** Unless my uncle decides to visit us during spring break.

_____   **9.** Long-distance telephone rates are less expensive during the evening than during the day.

_____   **10.** As long as Jacqueline is living at home.

Correct Dependent Clause Fragments

You can correct a dependent clause fragment in two ways:

1. **Join the dependent clause to an independent clause to make the dependent clause fragment part of a complete sentence.**

FRAGMENT	Although competition increased.
COMPLETE SENTENCE	Although competition increased, the sales staff was still getting new customers.
FRAGMENT	Because market research expanded.
COMPLETE SENTENCE	The company added new accounts because market research expanded.
FRAGMENT	Although statistics and market research have become part of advertising.
COMPLETE SENTENCE	Although statistics and market research have become part of advertising, consumers' tastes remain somewhat unpredictable.

2. **Take away the subordinating conjunction, and the dependent clause fragment becomes an independent clause that can stand alone as a complete sentence.**

FRAGMENT	Although competition increased.
COMPLETE SENTENCE	Competition increased.
FRAGMENT	Because market research expanded.
COMPLETE SENTENCE	Market research expanded.
FRAGMENT	Although statistics and market research have become part of advertising.
COMPLETE SENTENCE	Statistics and market research have become part of advertising.

Keep in mind that, when you join a dependent clause to an independent clause, you need to think about punctuation:

■ **If the *dependent* clause comes first, follow it with a comma.** The comma separates the dependent clause from the independent clause and helps you know where the independent clause begins.

	Dependent clause	Independent clause
COMMA NEEDED	After World War II ended,	humor and sex were used in commercials.

■ If the *independent* clause comes first, do *not* use a comma between the two clauses.

	Independent clause
NO COMMA NEEDED	Humor and sex were used in commercials

Dependent clause

after World War II ended.

EXERCISE 11-10   Revising Fragments by Adding Independent Clauses

Directions: Make each of these dependent clause fragments into a sentence by adding an independent clause before or after the fragment. Add or remove punctuation if necessary.

> EXAMPLE   After we got to the beach,*/* we put on sunscreen.

1. Since the surgery was expensive.

   _____

2. As long as my boss allows me.

   _____

3. Because I want to be a journalist.,

   _____

4. Until the roof is repaired.

   _____

5. Once I returned the library books.

   _____

6. So that I do not miss class.

   _____

7. Provided that Marietta gets the loan.

   _____

8. Unless you would rather go to the movies.

   _____

9. If the thunderstorm comes during the barbecue.

   _____

10. Although we visited Disney last summer.

   _____

Recognize Dependent Clauses Beginning with Relative Pronouns

Dependent clauses also may begin with relative pronouns. A **relative pronoun** relates groups of words to nouns or other pronouns and often introduces other clauses. (For more information on relative pronouns, see "A Brief Grammar Handbook," p. 470.)

> ### ❗ NEED TO KNOW
>
> **Relative Pronouns**
>
> | RELATIVE PRONOUNS THAT REFER TO PEOPLE | | RELATIVE PRONOUNS THAT REFER TO THINGS | |
> | --- | --- | --- | --- |
> | who | whom | that | whichever |
> | whoever | whomever | which | whatever |
> | whose | | | |

The relative pronoun that begins a dependent clause connects the dependent clause to a noun or pronoun in the independent clause. However, the verb in the dependent clause is *never* the main verb of the sentence. The independent clause has its own verb, which is the main verb of the sentence and expresses a complete thought.

The following sentence fragments each consist of a noun followed by a dependent clause beginning with a relative pronoun. They are not complete sentences because the noun does not have a verb and the fragment does not express a complete thought.

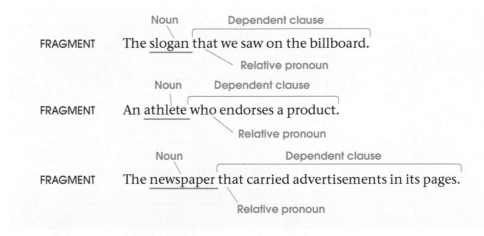

You can correct this type of fragment by adding a verb to make the noun the subject of an independent clause. Often the independent clause will be split, and the dependent clause will appear between its parts.

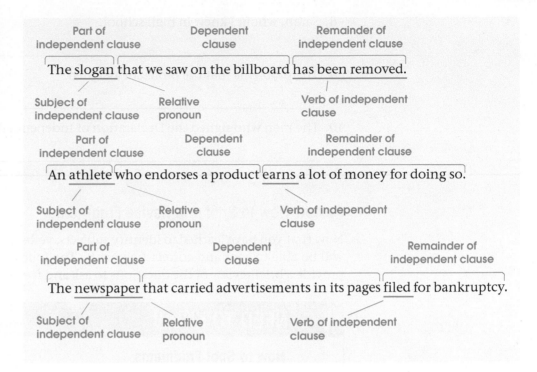

EXERCISE 11-11   Revising Fragments

Directions: Make each of these fragments into a complete sentence. Add words, phrases, or clauses, and punctuation as needed.

EXAMPLE   The usher who was available.  led us to our seats.

1. The radio that Trevor had purchased last night.

   _____

2. The official who had signed the peace treaty.

   _____

3. The athlete who won the tennis tournament.

   _____

4. Mark, whose nose had been broken in a fight.

   _____

5. The advice that his lawyer gave him.

   _____

6. The student who needed the scholarship the most.

   _____

7. The refrigerator that is in the kitchen.

   _____

8. Sarah, whom I knew in high school.

_____

9. The problems that the professor assigned.

_____

10. The men who signed the Declaration of Independence.

_____

Review How to Spot and Revise Fragments

Now that you have learned to identify subjects, verbs, and dependent clauses, you will be able to spot and correct fragments. The following "Need to Know" boxes provide a brief review of the questions to ask and the actions to take to do so.

 NEED TO KNOW

How to Spot Fragments

Use the following questions to check for fragments:

- **Does the word group have a subject?** The subject is a noun or pronoun that performs or receives the action of the sentence. To find the subject, ask _who_ or _what_ performs or receives the action of the verb.
- **Does the word group have a verb?** Be sure that the verb is complete and correct. Watch out for sentences that begin with an _-ing_ word or a _to_ phrase.
- **Does the word group begin with a subordinating conjunction (_since, after, because, as, while, although,_ and so forth), introducing a dependent clause?** Unless the dependent clause is attached to an independent clause, it is a fragment.
- **Does the word group begin with a relative pronoun (_who, whom, whose, whoever, whomever, that, which, whatever_), introducing a dependent clause?** Unless the dependent clause forms a question, is part of an independent clause, or is attached to an independent clause, it is a fragment.

 NEED TO KNOW

How to Revise Fragments

Once you spot a fragment in your writing, correct it in one of the following ways:

- **Add a subject if one is missing.**

FRAGMENT	Appeared on television ten times during the game.
REVISED	The advertisement for Pepsi appeared on television ten times during the game.

- **Add a verb if one is missing.** Add a helping verb if one is needed, or change the verb form.

FRAGMENT	An action-packed commercial with rap music.
REVISED	An action-packed commercial with rap music advertised a new soft drink.

- **Combine the** dependent-**clause fragment with an independent clause to make a complete sentence.**

FRAGMENT	Because advertising is expensive.
REVISED	Because advertising is expensive, companies are making shorter commercials.

- **Remove the subordinating conjunction or relative pronoun so the group of words can stand alone as a sentence.**

FRAGMENT	Since viewers can fast forward through commercials on DVRs.
REVISED	Viewers can fast forward though commercials on DVRs.

EXERCISE 11-12   Revising Fragments

Directions: Make each of the following sentence fragments a complete sentence by adding the missing subject or verb, combining it with an independent clause, or removing the subordinating conjunction or relative pronoun.

EXAMPLE

FRAGMENT	Many environmentalists are concerned about the spotted owl. Which is almost extinct.
COMPLETE SENTENCE	_Many environmentalists are concerned about the spotted owl, which is almost extinct._

1. Renting a DVD of the movie *Casablanca*.

   _____

   _____

2. Spices that have been imported from India.

   _____

   _____

3. The police officer walked to Jerome's van. To give him a ticket.

   _____

   _____

4. My English professor, with the cup of tea he brought to each class.

_____

_____

5. After the table is refinished.

_____

_____

6. Roberto memorized his lines. For the performance tomorrow night.

_____

_____

7. A tricycle with big wheels. painted red.

_____

_____

8. On the shelf, an antique crock used for storing lard.

_____

_____

9. Because I always wanted to learn to speak Spanish.

_____

_____

10. Looking for the lost keys. I was late for class.

_____

_____

EXERCISE 11-13 Revising a Paragraph

Directions: The following paragraph is correct except that it contains sentence fragments. Underline each fragment. Then revise the paragraph by rewriting or combining sentences to eliminate fragments.

Social networks such as Instagram, Snapchat, and Twitter appeal to college students for a variety of reasons. Social networks are a way of having conversations. Staying in touch with friends without the inconvenience of getting dressed and meeting them somewhere. Friends can join or drop out of a conversation whenever they want. Social networks also allow college students to meet new people and make new friends. Members can track who is friends with whom. Students may choose to share only portions of their profiles. To protect their privacy. Some students use social networks to form groups. Such as clubs, study groups, or special interest groups. Other students use networks to screen dates. And discover who is interested in dating or who is already taken.

EXERCISE 11-14 — Revising Sentence Fragments

WRITING IN PROGRESS

Directions: Review the paragraph you wrote for Exercise 11-5, checking for sentence fragments. If you find a fragment, revise it.

EXERCISE 11-15 — Revising Sentence Fragments

Directions: The following paragraph contains numerous fragments. Underline each fragment and then revise each to eliminate the fragment.

> More than 300 million cubic miles. That's how much water covers our planet. However, 97 percent being salty. Which leaves 3 percent fresh water. Three-quarters of that fresh water is in icecaps. And in glaciers. Sixteen thousand gallons. That's how much water the average person drinks in a lifetime. Each family of four, using more than 300 gallons per day. Although the world's demand for water has more than doubled since 1960. There is still a sufficient supply to take care of humanity's needs. However, regular water shortages in certain parts of the world. Because the pattern of rainfall throughout the world is uneven. For instance, 400 inches of rain per year in some parts of India, but no rain for several years in other parts of the world.

READ AND REVISE

The following excerpt is from a student essay called "Coming to America." This excerpt contains sentence fragments that were subsequently corrected in a later draft. Read the excerpt, and underline the sentence fragments caused by missing subjects, verbs, or dependent clauses. Then write out a revised version of the paragraph, correcting the errors using the techniques discussed in this chapter.

> There are many events that happened during my lifetime, but the main one that echoes in my mind. Coming to America. I'm originally from Port-au-Prince, Haiti. I moved to the United States at the age of 10. Which changed my life in many ways. Coming to America took away all the pain and suffering I went through growing up as a child. I didn't have an education, and now it's possible. The hardest thing to learn a new language.
>
> Imagine living in a place where there is severe violence, hunger, and poverty. Where there are no jobs. Kids and adults crying from hunger, waiting for a miracle. Most of the time they have to steal or make a kill to have

something on their plate. Losing friends and family members day by day from sickness or disease. Because there was no hospital to go to. People were killing themselves because they're suffering too much and can't take the pain anymore. That's something I had to see every day. For the 10 years that I lived in Haiti. My father was in America, and I prayed every day that he would come and get me and my brother. Until one day my prayers were answered. We were coming to a better place. Haiti is not the best place to live, but I respect and cherish where I am from for who I am today.

SELF-TEST SUMMARY

To test yourself, cover the Answer column with a sheet of paper and answer each question in the left column. Evaluate each of your answers as you work by sliding the paper down and comparing your answer with what is printed in the Answer column.

QUESTION	ANSWER
■ **GOAL 1** Identify subjects and predicates What are subjects and predicates?	The **subject** of a sentence is whom or what the sentence is about. The subject is often a noun or a pronoun. The **predicate** indicates what the subject does, what happened to the subject, or what is being said about the subject. The predicate must include a **verb**, a word or group of words that expresses an action or a state of being.
■ **GOAL 2** Identify sentence fragments What is a fragment?	A fragment is an incomplete sentence that lacks a subject, a verb, or both or does not express a complete thought.
■ **GOAL 3** Recognize and correct fragments caused by missing subjects What are two ways to revise a fragment that lacks a subject?	1. Add a subject, often a pronoun referring to the subject of the preceding sentence. 2. Connect the fragment to the preceding sentence.

QUESTION	ANSWER
■ **GOAL 4** Recognize and correct fragments caused by missing verbs What are two common ways that fragments without complete verbs occur, and how can you correct them?	Fragments without complete verbs often occur when word groups begin with -*ing* words or with *to* phrases. Correct -*ing* fragments by (1) adding a subject and changing the -*ing* verb to one that will complete the sentence; (2) adding a subject and a form of *be* as a helping verb; (3) connecting the fragment to a sentence that comes before or after it; and (4) if the -*ing* word is *being*, changing it to another form of *be*. Correct fragments caused by *to* phrases by adding a subject and verb that complete the sentence or connecting the fragment to a nearby sentence.
■ **GOAL 5** Recognize and correct fragments caused by dependent clauses What are two ways to correct dependent clause fragments?	A dependent clause does not express a complete thought and often begins with a subordinating conjunction. It can be corrected in two ways: 1. Join the dependent clause to an independent clause. 2. Take away the subordinating conjunction.

Run-On Sentences and Comma Splices

Ian G Dagnall / Alamy Stock Photo

THINK About It!

Read the passage below.

> Food trucks mobile kitchens that sell food are popular in many cities some trucks have fixed locations others move about daily customers can track a truck's location and menu changes on Facebook often operated by laid off chefs from expensive restaurants some trucks offer gourmet food choices long lines of hungry customers eager to buy tacos lobster rolls or specialty burgers for example can be seen at lunch and dinner hours food trucks are successful because they are convenient accessible and inexpensive some traditional restaurant owners feel they are losing business to food trucks and some cities have passed laws prohibiting food trucks from parking within a specified distance of restaurants

Did you have trouble reading this paragraph? Why? Write a sentence explaining your difficulty. Most likely you said that the paragraph lacked punctuation. You could not see where one idea ended and another began. It is important to pay attention to punctuation to avoid confusion when you are writing. When reading, it is important to pay attention to punctuation because it provides helpful clues about the relationships among and relative importance of ideas.

What Is Punctuation, and Why Is It Important to Use It Correctly?

■ **GOAL 1**
Use punctuation correctly within and between sentences

Punctuation is a useful tool as it helps writers communicate their thoughts clearly and helps readers follow and understand those thoughts. **Punctuation** serves one primary purpose: to separate. Periods, question marks, and exclamation points separate complete sentences from one another. Think of these punctuation marks as *between*-sentence separators. All other punctuation marks—*commas, colons, semicolons, hyphens, dashes, quotation marks,* and *parentheses*—separate parts *within* a sentence. To avoid or correct run-on sentences and comma splices that can cause a reader confusion, you need a good grasp of both between-sentence and within-sentence punctuation.

Between-Sentence Punctuation

The period, question mark, and exclamation point all mark the end of a sentence. Each has a different function.

! NEED TO KNOW

Between-Sentence Punctuation

PUNCTUATION	FUNCTION	EXAMPLE
Period (.)	Marks the end of a complete statement or command	*The lecture is about to begin. Please be seated.*
Question mark (?)	Marks the end of a direct question	*Are you ready?*
Exclamation point (!)	Marks the end of statements of excitement or strong emotion	*We are late! I won an award!*

Within-Sentence Punctuation

Commas, colons, semicolons, hyphens, dashes, quotation marks, and parentheses all separate parts of a sentence from one another. For a complete review of how and when to use each, refer to "A Brief Grammar Handbook," pages 522–532.

The comma is the most commonly used within-sentence punctuation mark and is the most commonly misused. The **comma** separates parts of a sentence from one another. In this chapter, we will be concerned with just one type of separation: the separation of two complete thoughts, or independent clauses. An **independent clause** has a subject and a verb and can stand alone as a sentence.

A comma can be used to separate two complete thoughts within a sentence *if and only if* it is used along with one of the coordinating conjunctions (*for, and, nor, but, or, yet, so*). **Coordinating conjunctions** are words that link and relate equally important parts of a sentence. The comma is not a strong enough separator to be used between complete thoughts without one of the coordinating conjunctions.

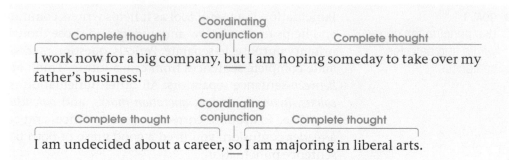

I work now for a big company, but I am hoping someday to take over my father's business.

I am undecided about a career, so I am majoring in liberal arts.

Recognize and Correct Run-On Sentences

■ **GOAL 2**
Recognize and correct run-on sentences

When you do not separate two complete thoughts (two independent clauses) with the necessary punctuation, the two clauses run together and form a **run-on sentence.**

How to Recognize Run-On Sentences

■ **Read each sentence aloud.** Listen for a break or change in your voice midway through the sentence. Your voice automatically pauses or slows down at the end of a complete thought. If you hear a break but have no punctuation at that break, you may have a run-on sentence. Try reading the following run-on sentences aloud. Place a slash mark (/) where you hear a pause.

RUN-ON   The library has a copy machine it is very conveniently located.

RUN-ON   The Career Planning Center on campus is helpful one of the counselors suggested I take a career-planning course.

RUN-ON   My major is nursing I do enjoy working with people.

Did you mark the sentences as follows?

The library has a copy machine / it is very conveniently located.

The Career Planning Center on campus is helpful / one of the counselors suggested I take a career-planning course.

My major is nursing / I do enjoy working with people.

The pause in each indicates the need for punctuation.

■ Look for sentences that contain two complete thoughts (independent clauses) without punctuation to separate them.

Complete thought (independent clause)

RUN-ON   Houseplants are pleasant additions to a home or office

Complete thought
(independent clause)

they add color and variety.

| Complete thought (independent clause) | Complete thought (independent clause) |

RUN-ON   My sister decided to wear black I chose red.

| Complete thought (independent clause) | Complete thought (independent clause) |

RUN-ON   Having a garage sale is a good way to make money it unclutters the house, too.

| Complete thought (independent clause) | Complete thought (independent clause) |

RUN-ON   We bought a portable air conditioner then we had to add brackets to support the weight of the unit.

■ Look for long sentences. Not every long sentence is a run-on, but run-ons do tend to occur more frequently in longer sentences than in shorter ones.

RUN-ON   Choosing a mate is one of the most important decisions you will ever make unless you make the right choice, you may be unhappy.

RUN-ON   I plan to work in a day-care center some days taking care of my own kids is enough to make me question my career choice.

Tip for Writers

Then cannot be used to connect two independent clauses even if it is preceded by a comma. When using *then* as a connector, write the sentence one of these ways:

■ We adopted a dog, **and then** we adopted four cats.

■ We adopted a dog; **then** we adopted four cats.

■ We adopted a dog **and then** four cats.

| EXERCISE 12-1 | Identifying Run-On Sentences |

Directions: Read each sentence aloud. Place a check mark before each sentence that is a run-on. Use a slash mark to show where punctuation is needed. Not all of these sentences are run-ons.

_____ 1. Parking spaces on campus are limited often I must park far away and walk.

_____ 2. Before exercising, you should always stretch and warm up to prevent injury.

_____ 3. Theodore's car wouldn't start fortunately Phil was able to use jumper cables to help him get it started.

_____ 4. The skydiver jumped from the plane when she had fallen far enough she released her parachute.

_____ 5. Radio stations usually have a morning disc jockey whose job is to wake people and cheer them up on their way to work.

_____ 6. It continued to rain until the river overflowed many people had to be evacuated from their homes.

_____ 7. Calla bought a bathrobe for her brother as a birthday gift it was gray with burgundy stripes.

_____ 8. The rooms in the maternity section of the hospital have colorful flowered wallpaper they are cheerful and pleasant.

_____ 9. Because my cousin went to nursing school and then to law school, she is going to practice medical malpractice law.

_____ 10. We watched *The Fighter* on Netflix later we practiced boxing moves.

How to Correct Run-On Sentences

There are four possible ways to correct run-on sentences:

1. Create two separate sentences.
2. Use a semicolon.
3. Use a comma and a coordinating conjunction.
4. Make one thought dependent.

Create Two Separate Sentences

Below, each of the run-on sentences has been corrected so they are two complete sentences. The first corrected sentence ends with a *period, question mark* or an *exclamation mark* if one is needed. The second corrected sentence begins with a capital letter.

	Complete thought.	Complete thought.
RUN-ON	Many students do not have a specific career goal they do have some general career directions in mind.	
CORRECT	Many students do not have a specific career goal. They do have some general career directions in mind.	
RUN-ON	Are there really students who choose courses without studying degree requirements these students may make unwise choices.	
CORRECT	Are there really students who choose courses without studying degree requirements? These students may make unwise choices.	
RUN-ON	Some people love their jobs they are delighted that someone is willing to pay them to do what they enjoy.	
CORRECT	Some people love their jobs. They are delighted that someone is willing to pay them to do what they enjoy.	
RUN-ON	Some people hate their jobs going back to school may be a good idea in these cases.	
CORRECT	Some people hate their jobs! Going back to school may be a good idea in these cases.	

The separation method is a good choice if the two thoughts are not closely related or if joining the two thoughts correctly (by one of the methods described in the next sections) creates an extremely long sentence.

EXERCISE 12-2

WRITING IN PROGRESS

Correcting Run-On Sentences by Making Separate Sentences

Directions: Revise the run-on sentences you identified in Exercise 12-1 by creating two separate sentences in each case.

Use a Semicolon

Use a **semicolon** (;) to connect two complete thoughts that will remain parts of the same sentence.

<u>Complete thought</u>   ;   <u>complete thought.</u>

RUN-ON	Our psychology instructor is demanding he expects the best from all his students.
CORRECT	Our psychology instructor is demanding; he expects the best from all his students.
RUN-ON	Sunshine is enjoyable it puts people in a good mood.
CORRECT	Sunshine is enjoyable; it puts people in a good mood.
RUN-ON	A course in nutrition may be useful it may help you make wise food choices.
CORRECT	A course in nutrition may be useful; it may help you make wise food choices.

Use this method when your two complete thoughts are closely related and the relationship between them is clear and obvious.

EXERCISE 12-3

Correcting Run-On Sentences Using Semicolons

Directions: Place a check mark before each sentence that is a run-on. Correct each run-on by using a semicolon. Not all of these sentences are run-ons.

_____ 1. The economic summit meeting was held in Britain many diplomats attended.

_____ 2. I especially enjoy poetry by Emily Dickinson her poems are intense, concise, and revealing.

_____ 3. The Use and Abuse of Drugs is a popular course because the material is geared for non-science majors.

_____ 4. The food festival offered a wide selection of food everything from hot dogs to elegant desserts was available.

_____ 5. Since the flight was turbulent, the flight attendant suggested that we remain in our seats.

_____ **6.** The bowling alley was not crowded most of the lanes were open.

_____ **7.** Swimming is an excellent form of exercise it gives you a good aerobic workout.

_____ **8.** When the disabled aircraft landed safely, the onlookers cheered.

_____ **9.** The two-lane highway is being expanded to four lanes even that improvement is not expected to solve the traffic congestion problems.

_____ **10.** Before visiting Israel, Carolyn read several guidebooks they helped her plan her trip.

Use a Comma and a Coordinating Conjunction

Use a **comma** _and_ a **coordinating conjunction** to separate two complete thoughts placed within one sentence. The "Need to Know" box below lists the seven coordinating conjunctions, along with a handy trick to help you remember them. Note that whenever you separate two complete thoughts by using a coordinating conjunction, you must also use a comma.

Complete thought, **coordinating conjunction** complete thought.

When you use a coordinating conjunction to separate two complete thoughts, be sure to use the right one. Since each coordinating conjunction has a particular meaning, you should choose the one that shows the right relationship between the two thoughts. For example, the conjunction _and_ indicates that the ideas are equally important and similar. The words _but_ and _yet_ indicate that one idea is contrary to or in opposition to the other. _For_ and _so_ emphasize cause and effect connections. _Or_ and _nor_ indicate choice.

NEED TO KNOW

How to Use Coordinating Conjunctions

There are seven coordinating conjunctions. An easy way to remember them is the acronym FANBOYS (_for, and, nor, but, or, yet,_ and _so_). Choose the one that shows the right relationship between the two complete thoughts in a sentence.

COORDINATING CONJUNCTION	MEANING	EXAMPLE
for	since, because	Sarah is taking math, _for_ she is a chemistry major.
and	added to, in addition, along with	Budgeting is important, _and_ it is time well spent.
nor	and not, or not, not either	Sam cannot choose a career, _nor_ can he decide on a major.
but	just the opposite, on the other hand, however	I had planned to visit Chicago, _but_ I changed my mind.
or	either	I will major in liberal arts, _or_ I will declare myself "undecided."
yet	but, despite, nevertheless	I plan to become a computer programmer, _yet_ a change is still possible.
so	as a result, consequently	Yolanda enjoys mathematics, _so_ she is considering it as a career.

The following examples show how to use a comma and an appropriate coordinating conjunction to correct a run-on sentence:

RUN-ON	Interests change and develop throughout life you may have a different set of interests 20 years from now.
	Comma and conjunction so used to show cause and effect relationship
CORRECT	Interests change and develop throughout life, so you may have a different set of interests 20 years from now.
RUN-ON	Take courses in a variety of disciplines you may discover new interests.
	Comma and conjunction for used to show cause and effect relationship
CORRECT	Take courses in a variety of disciplines, for you may discover new interests.
RUN-ON	Alexis thought she was not interested in biology by taking a biology course, she discovered it was her favorite subject.
	Comma and conjunction but used to show contrast
CORRECT	Alexis thought she was not interested in biology, but, by taking a biology course, she discovered it was her favorite subject.
RUN-ON	The weather forecast threatened severe thunderstorms just as the day ended, the sky began to cloud over.
	Comma and conjunction and used to show addition
CORRECT	The weather forecast threatened severe thunderstorms, and just as the day ended, the sky began to cloud over.

This method of correcting run-ons allows you to indicate to your reader how your two ideas are connected. Use this method for correcting run-on sentences when you want to explain the relationship between the two thoughts.

Correcting Run-On Sentences Using Commas and Conjunctions

EXERCISE 12-4

WORKING TOGETHER

Directions: Working with a classmate, correct each of the following run-on sentences by using a comma and a coordinating conjunction. Think about the relationship between the two thoughts, and then choose the best coordinating conjunction. (These are the coordinating conjunctions you should use: *for, and, nor, but, or, yet, so.*)

EXAMPLE   I thought I had left for class in plenty of time ‸, but I was two minutes late.

1. Jameel got up half an hour late he missed the bus.

2. My creative-writing teacher wrote a book our library did not have a copy.

3. Ford is an interesting first name we did not choose it for our son.

4. Smoking cigarettes is not healthy it can cause lung cancer.

5. My paycheck was ready to be picked up I forgot to get it.

6. The window faces north the room gets little sun.

7. I may order Chinese food for dinner I may bake a chicken.

8. Miranda had planned to write her term paper about World War I she switched her topic to the Roaring Twenties.

9. The journalist arrived at the fire she began to take notes.

10. The table is wobbly we keep a matchbook under one leg to stabilize it.

Make One Thought Dependent

Make one thought dependent by making it a dependent clause. A **dependent clause** depends on an independent clause for its meaning. It cannot stand alone because it does not express a complete thought. In a sentence, a dependent clause must always be linked to an independent clause, which expresses a complete thought. By itself, a dependent clause always leaves a question in your mind; the question is answered by the independent clause to which it is joined.

Dependent clause raises a question

Because I missed the bus   [What happened?]

Independent clause answers the question

Because I missed the bus, I was late for class.

Dependent clause raises a question

When I got my exam back   [What did you do?]

Independent clause answers the question

When I got my exam back, I celebrated.

Did you notice that each dependent clause began with a word that made it dependent? In the above sentences, the words that make the clauses dependent are *because* and *when*. These words are called subordinating conjunctions. **Subordinating conjunctions** let you know that the sense of the clause that follows them depends on another idea, an idea you will find in the independent clause of the sentence. Some common subordinating conjunctions are *after, although, before, if, since,* and *unless.* (For a more complete list of subordinating conjunctions, see Chapter 11, p. 377.)

You can correct a run-on sentence by changing one of the complete thoughts into a dependent clause and joining the ideas in the two clauses with a subordinating conjunction. This method places more emphasis on the idea expressed in the complete thought (independent clause) and less emphasis on the idea in the dependent clause.

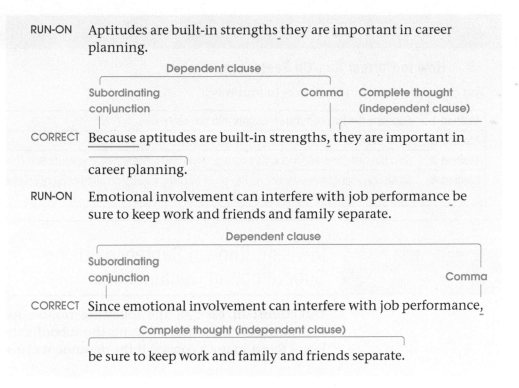

RUN-ON   Aptitudes are built-in strengths they are important in career planning.

CORRECT   Because aptitudes are built-in strengths, they are important in career planning.

RUN-ON   Emotional involvement can interfere with job performance be sure to keep work and friends and family separate.

CORRECT   Since emotional involvement can interfere with job performance, be sure to keep work and family and friends separate.

Note: A dependent clause can appear before or after an independent clause. If the dependent clause appears first, it must be followed by a comma, as in the examples above. If the complete thought comes first, then no comma is needed.

dependent clause comma **complete thought**
independent clause no comma **dependent clause**

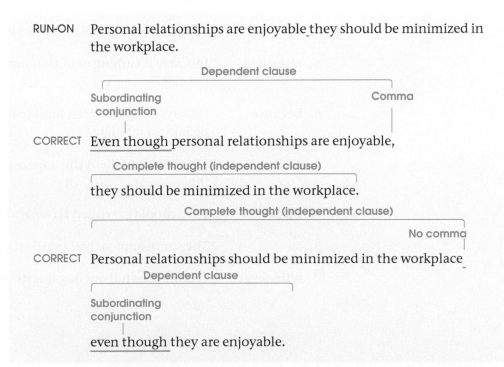

RUN-ON   Personal relationships are enjoyable they should be minimized in the workplace.

CORRECT   Even though personal relationships are enjoyable, they should be minimized in the workplace.

CORRECT   Personal relationships should be minimized in the workplace even though they are enjoyable.

> ## ! NEED TO KNOW
>
> ### How to Correct Run-On Sentences
>
> You can correct run-on sentences in four ways:
>
> | Method 1 | Separate the two complete thoughts into two sentences. |
> |---|---|
> | Method 2 | Separate the two complete thoughts with a semicolon. |
> | Method 3 | Join the two complete thoughts with a comma and a coordinating conjunction (*and, but, for, nor, or, so, yet*). |
> | Method 4 | Make one thought dependent on the other by using a subordinating conjunction (see the list of subordinating conjunctions on p. 377). |

EXERCISE 12-5

Revising Run-On Sentences Using Subordinating Conjunctions

Directions: In each of the following run-on sentences, make one thought dependent on the other by using the subordinating conjunction in boldface. Don't forget to use a comma if the dependent clause comes first.

EXAMPLE

until   Until w
~~We~~ called the plumber ‸ we were without water.

1. **even though**   David wants a leather jacket it is very expensive.

2. **so that**   Margery runs ten miles every day she can try out for the cross-country squad in the spring.

3. **when**   The television program ended Gail read a book to her son.

4. **because**   The pool was crowded it was 95 degrees that day.

5. **although**   Industry is curbing pollution our water supply still is not safe.

6. **because**   I always obey the speed limit speeding carries a severe penalty in my state.

7. **while**   The crowd fell silent the trapeze artist attempted a quadruple flip.

8. **since**   The school year ended I have had more time for my hobbies.

9. **as**   The storm approached I stocked up on batteries.

10. **whenever**   The moon is full our dog is restless.

Revising Sentences

Directions: Write five sentences, each of which has two complete thoughts. Then revise each sentence so that it has one dependent clause and one complete thought (independent clause). Use a comma, if needed, to separate the two clauses. You may want to refer to the list of subordinating conjunctions on page 377.

Recognize and Correct Comma Splices

■ GOAL 3
Recognize and correct
comma splices

A **comma splice** occurs when you use *only* a comma to separate two complete thoughts. A comma alone is not sufficient to divide the two thoughts. A stronger, clearer separation is necessary. You can visualize a comma splice this way:

<u>Complete thought</u> , <u>complete thought.</u>

COMMA SPLICE	Spatial aptitude is the ability to understand and visualize objects in physical space, it is an important skill for engineers and designers.
COMMA SPLICE	Some people have strong mechanical ability, they often prefer hands-on tasks.
COMMA SPLICE	Verbal reasoning is important to many careers, it is the ability to think through problems.

How to Recognize Comma Splices

To avoid comma splices, you have to make sure that you do not place *only a comma* between two complete thoughts. To test a sentence to see if you have written a comma splice, take the sentence apart at the comma. If the part before the comma is a complete thought and the part after the comma is a complete thought, then you need to check whether the second clause starts with a coordinating conjunction (*for, and, nor, but, or, yet, so*). If you do not have a coordinating conjunction to separate the two complete thoughts, then you have a comma splice.

How to Correct Comma Splices

To correct comma splices, use any one of the four methods you used to correct run-ons:

1. **Separate the thoughts into two complete sentences, deleting the comma.**

<u>Complete thought. Complete thought.</u>

2. **Separate the two thoughts with a semicolon, deleting the comma.**

Complete thought; complete thought.

3. **Separate the two thoughts by adding a coordinating conjunction after the comma.**

Complete thought, **coordinating conjunction** complete thought.

4. **Make one thought dependent on the other by using a subordinating conjunction to separate the two thoughts.** (For a complete list of subordinating conjunctions, see p. 377.)

Subordinating conjunction dependent clause, independent clause.

Independent clause **subordinating conjunction** dependent clause.

! NEED TO KNOW

How to Correct Comma Splices

Correct comma splices the same way you correct run-on sentences:

Method 1	Separate the two complete thoughts into two sentences.
Method 2	Separate the two complete thoughts with a semicolon.
Method 3	Join the two complete thoughts with a comma and a coordinating conjunction (*for, and, nor, but, or, yet, so*).
Method 4	Make one thought dependent on the other by using a subordinating conjunction. (See the list on p. 377.)

EXERCISE 12-7   Correcting Comma Splices

Directions: Some of the following sentences have comma splices. Correct each comma splice by using one of the four methods described in this chapter. Write *OK* before each sentence that is correct.

_____ 1. The stained glass window is beautiful, it has been in the church since 1880.

_____ 2. Replacing the spark plugs was simple, replacing the radiator was not.

_____ 3. School buses lined up in front of the school, three o'clock was dismissal time.

_____ 4. The gymnast practiced her balance-beam routine, she did not make a single mistake.

_____ **5.** A huge branch fell on the driveway, it just missed my car.

_____ **6.** The receptionist answered the phone, she put the caller on hold.

_____ **7.** The couple dressed up as zombies for Halloween, but their bandages kept falling off.

_____ **8.** Bill left his notebook in the cafeteria, he was confused later when he was unable to find it.

_____ **9.** The strawberries are red and sweet, the blueberries are not ripe yet.

_____ **10.** There had been a severe drought, so the waterfall dried up.

EXERCISE 12-8

Identifying and Correcting Run-On Sentences and Comma Splices

Directions: Identify each sentence as a run-on sentence (*RO*), a comma splice (*CS*), or a correct sentence (*C*). Then correct the faulty sentences using one of the four methods discussed.

EXAMPLE ___CS___ ~~The~~ When t The children chased the ball into the street, cars screeched to a halt.

_____ **1.** Inez packed for the camping trip she remembered everything except insect repellant.

_____ **2.** A limousine drove through our neighborhood, everybody wondered who was in it.

_____ **3.** The defendant pleaded not guilty the judge ordered him to pay the parking fine.

_____ **4.** Before a big game, Louis, who is a quarterback, eats a lot of pasta and bread he says it gives him energy.

_____ **5.** Four of my best friends from high school have decided to go to law-school, I have decided to become a legal secretary.

_____ **6.** Felicia did not know what to buy her parents for their anniversary, so she went to a lot of stores she finally decided to buy them a camera.

_____ **7.** After living in a dorm room for three years, Jason found an apartment the rent was very high, so he had to get a job to pay for it.

_____ **8.** The cherry tree had to be cut down, it stood right where the new addition was going to be built.

_____ **9.** Amanda worked every night for a month on the needlepoint pillow that she was making for her grandmother.

_____ **10.** Driving around in the dark, we finally realized we were lost, Dwight went into a convenience store to ask for directions.

EXERCISE 12-9

Identifying and Correcting Run-On Sentences and Comma Splices

Directions: Find and correct the run-on sentence and three comma splices in the following paragraph.

If you work in an office with cubicles—small partitioned workspaces—make sure to observe cubicle etiquette. Most cubicles are composed of three chest-high partitions, the fourth side is an open entryway. Cubicle etiquette is designed to minimize invasions of personal space for example as you walk past a cubicle, resist the temptation to peer down at the person. If you need to talk to a cubicle occupant, do not startle the person by entering abruptly or speaking loudly. Similarly, do not silently lurk in the entryway if the person's back is turned, speak quietly to announce your presence. Try to keep cubicle conversations or phone calls brief, in deference to your co-workers in adjacent cubicles. Finally, remember that odors as well as noise can "pollute" the cubicle environment, don't even think about eating leftover garlic pasta at your desk!

EXERCISE 12-10

Revising a Paragraph

Directions: Revise the following paragraphs, correcting the run-on sentences and comma splices.

1. The oldest map we have dates back to ancient Babylonia, it shows an estate surrounded by mountains. As in so many other undertakings, the Greeks were ahead of their time in mapmaking their maps showed the world as round rather than flat, the Greeks also developed a system of longitude and latitude for identifying locations. The Romans were excellent administrators and military strategists therefore, it was no surprise that they made reliable road maps and military maps. The most famous mapmaker of ancient times was Claudius Ptolemy of Alexandria, Egypt, he created a comprehensive map of the world.

_____

_____

_____

_____

_____

_____

_____

2. It seems there is a problem on the Internet with certain types of messages that people post. There are people who argue that anyone has the right to say anything on the Internet people do have the right of free speech, but the line should be drawn when it comes to hate messages. It is immoral—and should be illegal—to make remarks that are racist, sexist, and anti-Semitic. After all, these verbal attacks are no longer tolerated in the classroom or in the workplace, why should the Internet be different? The problem with the Internet is that there seem to be no established rules of etiquette among users, maybe there should be some guidelines about what

people should and should not say on the Internet. Why should people be subjected to hate-filled speech in order to preserve the right of free speech?

_____

_____

_____

_____

_____

_____

_____

_____

_____

_____

READ AND REVISE

The following excerpt is from a student essay called "Little Miracles." Read the excerpt, and underline the run-on sentences and comma splices. Then write out a revised version of the paragraph, correcting the errors using the techniques discussed in this chapter.

Everyone in their lives faces a life changing experience. February 9, 2015 was the day I became a mother on this very day my daughter Kamber was born, and my life from that point on has been different in every aspect. The responsibilities and obstacles I face, who I am, and the joy that comes along with being a mother are just a few things that have changed. There are no words that sum up the feeling I had when she was placed in my arms on that day, all that mattered was that she was the greatest gift I have ever been blessed with. The impact that a child has on a parent is tremendous, it molds you into a whole new human being.

Life is a revolving cycle. We grow into adults, have children, and raise them then they follow our steps and have a family of their own, and it just repeats itself. Maybe I wasn't ready financially for having a child, but I believe things happen for a reason. I use a lot of the same techniques my mother did with me, I also develop my own. There are sad times as a mother such as when your child is sick or gets hurt. The feeling of your child only wanting her mommy at those times is overwhelming. We all fall in love in our lives the love of a child is such a different but amazing emotion.

SELF-TEST SUMMARY

To test yourself, cover the Answer column with a sheet of paper and answer each question in the left column. Evaluate each of your answers as you work by sliding the paper down and comparing your answer with what is printed in the Answer column.

QUESTION	ANSWER
■ **GOAL 1** Use punctuation correctly within and between sentences Can a comma be used to separate two complete thoughts?	A comma can be used to separate two complete thoughts within a sentence *only* if it is accompanied by a coordinating conjunction.
■ **GOAL 2** Recognize and correct run-on sentences What is a run-on sentence?	A run-on sentence occurs when two complete thoughts are joined without punctuation or a connecting word.
What are four ways to correct run-on sentences?	1. Create two separate sentences. 2. Use a semicolon. 3. Use a comma and a coordinating conjunction. 4. Make one thought dependent on the other by using a subordinating conjunction.
■ **GOAL 3** Recognize and correct comma splices What is a comma splice?	A comma splice is a sentence error that occurs when only a comma separates two complete thoughts.
How can a comma splice be corrected?	It can be corrected using one of the four techniques listed above for correcting run-on sentences.

Using Verbs Correctly

Celeste Cota /123RF

"Then she was like, 'I gotta go,' and I was like, 'Okay,' and she was like, 'Later,' and I was like, 'Go already!'"

THINK About It!

Have you ever stopped to listen to the way people misuse or overuse verbs? Write a sentence evaluating this teenager's use of language.

Did you notice that in this teenager's sentence, she used *was like* instead of more interesting and descriptive verbs such as *yell/yelled, retort/retorted, say/said, reply/replied, snort/snorted,* or *exclaim/exclaimed*? Verbs are words that express action. Using them correctly is essential to good writing and can make the difference between something that is dull or difficult to read and something that is interesting or fun to read. In this chapter, you will focus on using verb tenses correctly as you write and learn how to avoid some common verb errors.

What Is a Verb?

A **verb** is a part of speech that expresses action or a state of being. Verbs are important to writers because they allow them to explain what action occurred or is occurring or in what state of being something is.

ACTION	The dog <u>leaped</u> over the fence.
STATE OF BEING	Instagram <u>is</u> popular among college students.

Verbs are important to readers because they carry a great deal of information. They give a sense of·time, telling when something *is* happening, *has* happened, or *will* happen. They also can be very descriptive, allowing you to create a mental picture of an action. A grammatically correct sentence has at least one verb in it.

Recognize Forms of the Verb

■ GOAL 1
Identify verb forms

The primary function of **verbs** is to express action or a condition. However, verbs also indicate time. **Verb tenses** tell us whether an action takes place in the present, past, or future. The three basic verb tenses are the *simple present, simple past*, and *simple future*. There are also nine other verb tenses in English.

There are two types of verbs: *regular* and *irregular*. The forms of **regular verbs** follow a standard pattern of endings; the forms of **irregular verbs** do not. The English language contains many more regular verbs than irregular verbs.

All verbs except *be* have five forms: the **base form** (or dictionary form), the *past tense*, the *past participle*, the *present participle*, and the *-s form* (see Table 13-1). The first three forms are called the verb's **principal parts**. For regular verbs, the past tense and past participle are formed by adding *-d* or *-ed* to the base form. Irregular verbs follow no set pattern to form their past tense and past participle.

Verbs change form to agree with their subjects in person and number (see p. 417 in the section titled "Avoid Errors in Subject–Verb Agreement"); to express the time of their action (**tense**); to express whether the action is a fact, command, or wish (**mood**); and to indicate whether the subject is the doer or the receiver of the action (**voice**).

TABLE 13-1	THE FIVE VERB FORMS	
Tense	**Regular**	**Irregular**
Base form	work	eat
Past tense	worked	ate
Past participle	worked	eaten
Present participle	working	eating
-s form	works	eats

Understand Verb Tense: An Overview

■ **GOAL 2**
Identify verb tenses

The tenses of a verb express time. They convey whether an action, process, or event takes place in the present, past, or future.

The three simple tenses are *present, past*, and *future*. The **simple present tense** is the base form of the verb (and the *-s* form of third-person singular subjects); the **simple past tense** is the past-tense form; and the **simple future tense** consists of the helping verb *will* plus the base form.

The **perfect tenses**, which indicate completed action, are *present perfect, past perfect*, and *future perfect*. They are formed by adding the helping verbs *have* (or *has*), *had*, or *will have* to the past participle. These are discussed in "A Brief Grammar Handbook," page 477.

Use the Simple Tenses

■ **GOAL 3**
Use simple verb tenses correctly

The simple present, simple past, and simple future are the most basic of the verb tenses. You will need to make frequent use of them in your writing, so it is important to become adept in these tenses.

The Simple Present Tense

The **present tense** indicates action that is occurring at the time of speaking or describes regular, habitual action.

HABITUAL ACTION	Maria works hard.
ACTION AT TIME OF SPEAKING	I see a rabbit on the lawn.

In the simple present tense, the verb for first person (*I* or *we*), second person (*you*), or third-person plural (*they*) is the same as the base form; no ending is added. The verb for third-person singular subjects (noun or pronoun) must end in *-s*. (See Table 13-2.)

TABLE 13-2	SIMPLE PRESENT TENSE FORMS OF *LIKE*		
Singular		**Plural**	
Subject	*Verb*	*Subject*	*Verb*
I	like	we	like
you	like	you	like
he, she, it	likes	they	like
Sam	likes	Sara and Marisa	like

To most third-person singular base verbs, just add *-s (I run, she runs)*. If the verb ends in *s, sh, ch, x*, or *z*, add *-es* to make the third-person singular form (*I crunch, she crunches*). If the verb ends in a consonant plus *y*, change the *y* to *i*, and then add *-es (I hurry, he hurries)*. If the verb ends in a vowel plus *y*, just add *-s. (I stay, he stays)*.

Third-person singular subjects include the pronouns *he, she*, and *it* and all singular nouns (*a desk, the tall man*). In addition, uncountable nouns (*money, music, homework*, abstractions such as *beauty* and *happiness*, liquids, and so on) are followed by third-person singular verbs. (*Water is essential for life.*) Singular collective nouns, such as *family, orchestra, team,* and *class,* also usually take a third-person singular verb since they refer to one group.

In speech, we often use nonstandard verb forms, and these forms are perfectly acceptable in informal conversation. However, these nonstandard forms are *not* used in college writing or in career writing. In the examples in Table 13-3, note the nonstandard forms of the verb *lift* and the way these forms differ from the correct, standard forms that you should use in your writing.

TABLE 13-3 NONSTANDARD AND STANDARD FORMS OF *LIFT*			
Nonstandard Present	Standard Present	Nonstandard Present	Standard Present
Singular	*Singular*	*Plural*	*Plural*
I lifts	I lift	we lifts	we lift
you lifts	you lift	you lifts	you lift
she (he) lift	she (he) lifts	they lifts	they lift

EXERCISE 13-1 Identifying Verb Forms

Directions: The sentences below are in the simple present tense. First, underline the subject or subjects in each sentence. Then circle the correct verb form.

> **EXAMPLE**   Sal (pick, picks) apples.

1. Planes (take, takes) off from the runway every five minutes.
2. I (enjoy, enjoys) sailing.
3. She (own, owns) a pet bird.
4. We (climb, climbs) the ladder to paint the house.
5. Engines (roar, roars) as the race begins.
6. They always (answer, answers) the phone on the first ring.
7. That elephant (walk, walks) very slowly.
8. You (speak, speaks) Spanish fluently.
9. He (say, says) his name is Luis.
10. Dinosaur movies (scare, scares) me.

EXERCISE 13-2 Using the Present Tense

Directions: For each of the following verbs, write a sentence using the simple present tense. Use a noun or *he, she, it,* or *they* as the subject of the sentence.

> **EXAMPLE**   prefer   *Priya prefers to sit in the front of the bus.*

1. call   _____
2. request   _____

3. laugh _____

4. grow _____

5. hide _____

Tip for Writers

Subject Pronouns

Remember, in English you must include the subject pronoun with the verb. In some languages, you do not need to do this because the verb ending indicates the person (first, second, or third) and number (singular or plural) of the sentence's subject.

EXAMPLE

He goes to the store.

Tip for Writers

Occasionally, *shall* (rather than *will*) is used as the first-person helping verb in the *simple future* and *future continuous* tenses. It may be used in these situations:

TALKING ABOUT A SERIOUS MATTER

Our country shall win this war no matter how long it takes!

MAKING A SUGGESTION OR AN OFFER

Shall we go now? Shall I get you some tea?

The Simple Past Tense

The **past tense** refers to action that was completed in the past. To form the simple past tense of regular verbs, add *-d* or *-ed* to the verb (see Table 13-4). Note that with the simple past tense, the verb form does not change with person or number.

In nonstandard English, the *-d* or *-ed* is often dropped. You may hear "Last night I work all night" instead of "Last night I work*ed* all night." In written English, be sure to include the *-d* or *-ed* ending.

TABLE 13-4   SIMPLE PAST TENSE FORMS OF *WORK*

Singular		Plural	
Subject	*Verb*	*Subject*	*Verb*
I	worked	we	worked
you	worked	you	worked
he, she, it	worked	they	worked
Sam	worked	Sara and Marisa	worked

The Simple Future Tense

The **future tense** refers to action that *will* happen in the future. Form the simple future tense by adding the helping verb *will* before the verb (see Table 13-5). Note that the verb form does not change with person or number.

TABLE 13-5   SIMPLE FUTURE TENSE FORMS OF *WORK*

Singular		Plural	
Subject	*Verb*	*Subject*	*Verb*
I	will work	we	will work
you	will work	you	will work
he, she, it	will work	they	will work
Sam	will work	Sara and Marisa	will work

NEED TO KNOW

Verb Tense

- **Verb tense** indicates whether an action takes place in the present, past, or future.
- There are three basic verb tenses: *simple present*, *simple past*, and *simple future*.

- The **simple present tense** is used to describe regular, habitual action or can be used for nonaction verbs. It can also indicate action that is occurring at the time of speaking. The ending of a simple present tense verb must agree with the subject of the verb.
- The **simple past tense** refers to action that was completed in the past. For regular verbs, the simple past tense is formed by adding *-d* or *-ed*.
- The **simple future tense** refers to action that will happen in the future. The simple future tense is formed by adding the helping verb *will* before the verb.

EXERCISE 13-3 Using the Simple Past and Simple Future Tenses

Directions: For each of the following verbs, write a sentence using the simple past tense and one using the simple future tense.

EXAMPLE   overcook   <u>The chef overcooked my steak.</u>
<u>I know he will overcook my steak.</u>

1. dance   _____

_____

2. hunt   _____

_____

3. joke   _____

_____

4. watch   _____

_____

5. photograph   _____

_____

EXERCISE 13-4 Writing a Paragraph

WRITING IN PROGRESS

Directions: Write a paragraph on one of the following topics, using either the simple past tense or the simple future tense.

1. Selecting a movie to download

2. Cleaning your apartment after a party

3. Selecting an internship program

4. Buying clothes for a special event

5. Caring for a three-year-old child

Use Irregular Verbs Correctly

■ **GOAL 4**
Use irregular verbs
correctly

Errors in verb tense can occur easily with irregular verbs. Irregular verbs do not form the simple past tense according to the pattern we have studied. A regular verb forms the simple past tense by adding *-d* or *-ed.* An **irregular verb** forms the simple past tense by changing its spelling internally (for example, *I feed* becomes *I fed*) or by not changing at all (for example, *I cut* in present form remains *I cut* in past form).

<table>
<tr><td colspan="2">

Tip for Writers

Helping Verbs
A helping verb is used before the main verb to form certain tenses.

helping verb   main verb

Ericka will sit in front of the television for hours.

Common helping verbs include:

have	has	had
be	am	is
do	does	did
are	was	were
being	been	

The following verbs can be used only as helping verbs:

can	could
will	would
shall	should
may	might
must	ought to

</td></tr>
</table>

Three Troublesome Irregular Verbs

The verbs *be, do,* and *have* can be especially troublesome. You should master the correct forms of these verbs in both the present tenses and the past tenses since they are used so often.

1. **Irregular Verb:** *Be*

TABLE 13-6	FORMS OF THE IRREGULAR VERB *BE*		
Present		**Past**	
Singular	*Plural*	*Singular*	*Plural*
I am	we are	I was	we were
you are	you are	you were	you were
he, she, it is	they are	he, she, it was	they were

■ It is nonstandard to use *be* for all present tense forms.

INCORRECT	I be finished.
CORRECT	I am finished.

INCORRECT	They be surprised.
CORRECT	They are surprised.

■ Another error is to use *was* instead of *were* for plural past tenses or with *you.*

INCORRECT	We was late.
CORRECT	We were late.

INCORRECT	You was wrong.
CORRECT	You were wrong.

■ Note that the verb *to be* never takes an object.

2. **Irregular Verb:** *Do*

TABLE 13-7	FORMS OF THE IRREGULAR VERB *DO*		
Present		**Past**	
Singular	*Plural*	*Singular*	*Plural*
I do	we do	I did	we did
you do	you do	you did	you did
he, she, it does	they do	he, she, it did	they did

Tip for Writers

The pronoun *you* is always grammatically plural in English. Use plural verbs (*are, have,* or *were*) with *you,* not singular forms such as *is, has,* or *was.* Use a plural verb with *you* even when you are speaking or writing to one person.

Tip for Writers

Does, as a main verb or a helping verb, is used only with third-person singular such as *he, Maria, the book* or with uncountable subjects such as *homework, music,* or *an idea*. Use *do,* not *does,* after *I, you,* or *they.*

A common error is to use *does* instead of *do* for present plural forms.

| INCORRECT | We does our best. |
| CORRECT | We do our best. |

| INCORRECT | They doesn't know the answer. |
| CORRECT | They don't know the answer. |

■ Another error is to use *done* instead of *did* for past plural forms.

| INCORRECT | We done everything. You done finish. |
| CORRECT | We did everything. You did finish. |

6. Irregular Verb: *Have*

TABLE 13-8   FORMS OF THE IRREGULAR VERB *HAVE*

Present		Past	
Singular	*Plural*	*Singular*	*Plural*
I have	we have	I had	we had
you have	you have	you had	you had
he, she, it has	they have	he, she, it had	they had

■ A common nonstandard form uses *has* instead of *have* for the present plural.

| INCORRECT | We has enough. They has a good reason. |
| CORRECT | We have enough. They have a good reason. |

■ Another error occurs in the past singular.

| INCORRECT | I has nothing to give you. You has a bad day. |
| CORRECT | I had nothing to give you. You had a bad day. |

EXERCISE 13-5   Using Standard Verb Forms

Directions: Circle the correct, standard form of the verb in each of the following sentences.

EXAMPLE   Last April, Anne (was, were) in Nevada.

1. After I watched the news, I (does, did) my homework.

2. You (be, were) lucky to win the raffle.

3. The electrician (have, has) enough time to complete the job.

4. When I am reading about the Civil War, I (am, be) captivated.

5. All the waitresses I know (have, has) sore feet.

6. We (was, were) at the grocery store yesterday.

7. He (do, does) his studying at the library.

8. We (did, done) the jigsaw puzzle while it rained.

9. Alice Walker (be, is) a favorite author of mine.

10. You (was, were) in the audience when the trophy was awarded.

EXERCISE 13-6   ## Using Irregular Verbs

Directions: Write sentences for each pair of irregular verbs shown below. Try to write several sentences that ask questions.

EXAMPLE   am   _I am going to the Bulls game tonight._

be   _Will you be at home tonight?_

1. do   _____

does   _____

2. was   _____

were   _____

3. is   _____

be   _____

4. do   _____

did   _____

5. am   _____

was   _____

EXERCISE 13-7   ## Using Irregular Verbs

Directions: Write sentences for each pair of irregular verbs shown below. Use a plural pronoun (*we, you, they*) or a plural noun.

EXAMPLE   be   _We will be at my dad's house._

were   _The horses were happy to see us._

1. do   _____

did   _____

2. are   _____

be   _____

3. have
    had
 _____

4. are
    were
 _____

5. be
    were
 _____

EXERCISE 13-8

WORKING TOGETHER

Correcting Verb Errors

Directions: Working with a classmate, read the following student paragraph and correct all verb errors.

> Sometimes first impressions of people is very inaccurate and can lead to problems. My brother, Larry, learn this the hard way. When he was 17, Larry and I was driving to the mall. Larry decided to pick up a hitchhiker because he looks safe and trustworthy. After the man got in the car, we notice that he was wearing a knife. A few miles later, the man suddenly tell us to take him to Canada. So my brother said we'd have to stop for gas and explained that he did not have any money. The man get out of the car to pump the gas. When he goes up to the attendant to pay for the gas, we took off. We do not stop until we reach the police station, where we tell the officer in charge what happens. The police caught the man several miles from the gas station. He be serving time in prison for burglary and had escaped over the weekend. Later, Larry said, "I was lucky that my first impression were not my last!"

Other Irregular Verbs

Among the other verbs that form the past tense in irregular ways are *become* (*became*), *drive* (*drove*), *hide* (*hid*), *stand* (*stood*), and *wear* (*wore*). For a list of the past-tense forms of other common irregular verbs, see "A Brief Grammar Handbook," page 475. If you have a question about the form of a see verb, consult this list or your dictionary.

Confusing Pairs of Irregular Verbs

Two particularly confusing pairs of irregular verbs are *lie/lay* and *sit/set*.

Lie/Lay

Lie means to recline. *Lay* means to put something down. The past tense of *lie* is *lay*. The past tense of *lay* is *laid*.

TABLE 13-9 VERB FORMS OF *LIE* AND *LAY*	
Simple Present	**Simple Past**
Command the dog to <u>lie</u> down.	The dog <u>lay</u> down.
<u>Lay</u> the boards over here.	The carpenter <u>laid</u> the boards over there.

Sit/Set

Sit means to be seated. *Set* means to put something down. The past tense of *sit* is *sat*. The past tense of *set* is *set*.

TABLE 13-10 VERB FORMS OF *SIT* AND *SET*	
Simple Present	**Simple Past**
Please <u>sit</u> over here.	We <u>sat</u> over here.
<u>Set</u> the books on the table.	He <u>set</u> the books on the table.

NEED TO KNOW

Irregular Verbs

■ An irregular verb does not form the simple past tense with *-d* or *-ed*.

■ Three particularly troublesome irregular verbs are *be, do*, and *have*.

■ Two confusing pairs of verbs are *lie/lay* and *sit/set*. Each has a distinct meaning.

EXERCISE 13-9   Using Correct Verbs

Directions: Circle the correct verb in each of the following sentences.

   EXAMPLE   Eric plans to (lay, lie) in bed all day.

1. The chef (sat, set) the mixer on "high" to beat the eggs.

2. I prefer to (lie, lay) in the hammock rather than on the hard futon.

3. The students (sit, set) in rows to take the exam.

4. After putting up the wallboard, Santiago (lay, laid) the hammer on the floor.

5. Bags of grain (set, sat) on the truck.

6. I'm going to (lie, lay) down and take a short nap.

7. Because we came late, we (sat, set) in the last row.

8. The kitten (lay, laid) asleep in the laundry basket.

9. Bob (sat, set) the groceries on the counter.

10. Completely exhausted, Shawna (lay, laid) on the sofa.

Understanding Voice: Using Active Instead of Passive Voice

■ **GOAL 5**
Use active instead of passive voice in most situations

Transitive verbs (those that take objects) may be in either the active voice or the passive voice. In an **active-voice** sentence, the subject performs the action described by the verb; that is, the subject is the actor. In a **passive-voice** sentence, the subject is the receiver of the action. The passive voice of a verb is formed by using an appropriate form of the helping verb *be* and the past participle of the main verb.

	Subject	Active
	is actor	voice
ACTIVE VOICE	Dr. Hillel <u>delivered</u> the report on global warming.	

	Subject is receiver	Passive voice
PASSIVE VOICE	The report on global warming <u>was delivered</u> by Dr. Hillel.	

The following passive-voice sentences do not name the person who wiped away the fingerprints or broke the vase. Passive-voice sentences seem indirect, as if the writer were purposefully avoiding giving information the reader might need or want.

PASSIVE VOICE   The fingerprints <u>had been</u> carefully <u>wiped</u> away.

PASSIVE VOICE   The vase <u>had been broken</u>.

Both active and passive voices are grammatically correct. However, the active voice is usually more effective because it is simpler, more informative, and more direct. Use the active rather than the passive voice unless

■ **you do not know who or what performs the action of the verb.**

PASSIVE   The broken window <u>had been wiped</u> clean of fingerprints.

■ **you want to emphasize the object of the action rather than who or what performs the action.**

PASSIVE   The poem "The Chicago Defender Sends a Man to Little Rock" by Gwendolyn Brooks <u>was discussed</u> in class. (Here, exactly who discussed the poem is less important than what poem was discussed.)

As a general rule, try to avoid writing passive-voice sentences. Get in the habit of putting the subject—the person or thing performing the action—at the beginning of each sentence. If you do this, you will usually avoid the passive voice.

NEED TO KNOW

Active and Passive Voices

■ When a verb is in the **active voice**, the *subject performs* the action.

■ When a verb is in the **passive voice**, the *subject receives* the action.

■ Because the active voice is straightforward and direct, use it unless you do not know who or what performed the action or unless you want to emphasize the object of the action rather than who or what performed it.

EXERCISE 13-10   Using Active Voice

Directions: Revise each of the following sentences by changing the verb from passive to active voice.

EXAMPLE   The china cups and saucers were painted carefully by Lois and her friends.

REVISED   *Lois and her friends carefully painted the china cups and saucers.*

1. *Goodnight Moon* was read by the mother to her daughter.

   _____

2. The maple tree was trimmed by the telephone company.

   _____

3. The vacuum cleaner was repaired by Mr. Fernandez.

   _____

4. Many bags of groceries were donated by the corporation.

   _____

5. Six quarts of strawberries were made into jam by Alice.

   _____

Avoid Errors in Subject–Verb Agreement

■ GOAL 6
Avoid errors in subject–verb agreement

A subject and its verb must agree (be consistent) in person (first, second, third) and in number (singular, plural). (For more on pronoun forms, see "The Brief Grammar Handbook," p. 470.)

The most common problems with subject–verb agreement occur with third-person present-tense verbs, which are formed for most verbs by adding *-s* or *-es*. (For the present-tense and past-tense forms of certain irregular verbs, see p. 411.)

Agreement Rules

■ **If a verb's subject is third-person singular, use the present tense ending -s or -es.** For first and second person, no ending is added. (See Table 13-11.)

TABLE 13-11	THIRD-PERSON SINGULAR PRESENT TENSE ENDINGS		
Singular Subject	Verb	Singular Subject	Verb
I	talk	it	talks
you	talk	Santiago	talks
he	talks	a boy	talks
she	talks		

- For a plural subject (more than one person, place, thing, or idea), use a plural form of the verb. (See Table 13-12.)

TABLE 13-12	VERB FORMS FOR PLURAL SUBJECTS		
Plural Subject	**Verb**	**Plural Subject**	**Verb**
we	talk	Santiago and Nina	talk
you	talk	boys	talk
they	talk		

Common Errors

The following circumstances often lead to errors in subject–verb agreement:

- **Third-person singular** A common error is to omit the *-s* or *-es* in a third-person singular verb in the present tense. The subjects *he, she,* and *it* or a noun that could be replaced with *he, she,* or *it* all take a third-person singular verb.

INCORRECT	She act like a professional.
CORRECT	She acts like a professional.

INCORRECT	Professor Simmons pace while he lectures.
CORRECT	Professor Simmons paces while he lectures.

- **Verbs before their subjects** When a verb comes before its subject, as in sentences beginning with *Here* or *There*, it is easy to make an agreement error. Because *here* and *there* are adverbs, they are never subjects of a sentence and do not determine the correct form of the verb. Look for the subject *after* the verb and, depending on its number, choose a singular or plural verb.

  Singular verb   Singular subject

  There is a pebble in my shoe.

  Plural verb   Plural subject

  There are two pebbles in my shoe.

  Note: Using contractions such as *here's* and *there's* leads to mistakes because you cannot "hear" the mistake. "Here's two pens" may not sound incorrect, but "Here is two pens" does.

- **Words between the subject and its verb** Words, phrases, and clauses coming between the subject and its verb do not change the fact that the verb must agree with the subject. To check that the verb is correct, mentally remove everything between the subject and its verb and make sure that the verb agrees in number with its subject.

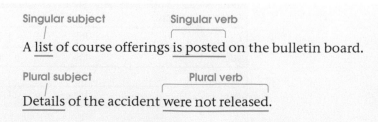

Singular subject   Singular verb

A list of course offerings is posted on the bulletin board.

Plural subject   Plural verb

Details of the accident were not released.

Note: Phrases beginning with prepositions such as *along with, together with, as well as,* and *in addition to* are not part of the subject and should not be considered in determining the number of the verb.

Singular subject   Singular verb

The stereo, together with the radios, televisions, and lights, goes dead during electrical storms.

- **Compound subjects** Two or more subjects joined by the coordinating conjunction *and* require a plural verb, even if one or both of the subjects are singular.

INCORRECT	Anita and Mark plays cards.
CORRECT	Anita and Mark play cards.

When both of the subjects refer to the same person or thing, however, use a singular verb.

The president and chairman of the board is in favor of more aggressive marketing.

When a compound subject is joined by the conjunction *or* or *nor* or the correlative conjunction *either/or, neither/nor, both/and, not/but,* or *not only/but also,* the verb should agree in number with the subject nearer to it.

Neither the books nor the article was helpful to my research.

Yesenia or the boys are coming tomorrow.

- **Indefinite pronouns as subjects** Some indefinite pronouns (such as *everyone, neither, anybody, nobody, one, something,* and *each*) take a singular verb.

Everyone appreciates the hospital's volunteers.

Of the two applicants, neither seems well qualified.

- The indefinite pronouns *both, many, several,* and *few* always take a plural verb. Some indefinite pronouns, such as *all, any, most, none,* and *some,* may take either a singular or plural verb. Treat the indefinite pronoun as singular if it refers to something that cannot be counted and as plural if it refers to more than one of something that can be counted.

Some of the ice is still on the road.

Some of the ice cubes are still in the tray.

All of the spaghetti tastes overcooked.

All of the spaghetti dishes taste too spicy.

- **Collective nouns** A collective noun refers to a group of people or things (*audience, class, flock, jury, team, family*). When the noun refers to the group as one unit, use a singular verb.

The herd stampedes toward us.

When the noun refers to the group members as separate individuals, use a plural verb.

> The <u>herd</u> <u>scatter</u> in all directions.

- **Nouns with plural forms but singular meaning** Some words appear plural (that is, they end in -s or -es) but have a singular meaning. *Measles, hysterics, news,* and *mathematics* are examples. Use a singular verb with them.

> <u>Mathematics</u> <u>is</u> a required course.

Note: Other nouns look plural and have singular meanings but take a plural verb: *braces, glasses, trousers, slacks, jeans, jodhpurs,* and *pajamas.* Even though they refer to a single thing (to one pair of jeans, for example), these words take a plural verb.

> His <u>pajamas</u> <u>were</u> <u>covered</u> with pictures of tumbling dice.

- **Relative pronouns in adjective clauses** The relative pronouns *who, which,* and *that* sometimes function as the subject of an adjective clause. When the relative pronoun refers to a singular noun, use a singular verb. When the pronoun refers to a plural noun, use a plural verb.

> Anita is a person <u>who</u> never <u>forgets</u> faces. [*Who* refers to *person,* which is singular.]
>
> The students <u>who</u> lost their keys <u>are</u> here. [*Who* refers to *students,* which is plural.]

 NEED TO KNOW

Subject–Verb Agreement

- A **subject** of a sentence must agree (be consistent) with the **verb** in person (first, second, or third) and in number (singular or plural).
- Watch for errors when using the third-person singular, placing verbs before their subjects, using compound subjects, and adding words, phrases, or clauses between the subject and the verb.

EXERCISE 13-11   Choosing Correct Verbs

Directions: Circle the verb that correctly completes each sentence.

   EXAMPLE   The newspapers (is, ⟨are⟩) on the desk.

1. The hubcaps that fell off the car (was, were) expensive to replace.

2. The conductor and orchestra members (ride, rides) a bus to their concerts.

3. A Little League team (practice, practices) across the street each Tuesday.

4. Here (is, are) the flash drive I borrowed.

5. Not only the news reporters but also the weather forecaster (are broadcasting, is broadcasting) live from the circus tonight.

6. Nobody older than 12 (ride, rides) the merry-go-round.

7. The discussion panel (offer, offers) its separate opinions after the debate.

8. Terry's green shorts (hang, hangs) in his gym locker.

9. Several of the cookies (taste, tastes) stale.

10. A mime usually (wear, wears) all-black or all-white clothing.

 **EXERCISE 13-12**   Choosing Correct Verbs

Directions: Circle the verb that correctly completes each sentence.

> **EXAMPLE**   Everybody (like, likes) doughnuts for breakfast.

1. Physics (is, are) a required course for an engineering degree.

2. Most of my courses last semester (was, were) in the morning.

3. The orchestra members who (is, are) carrying their instruments will be able to board the plane first.

4. Suzanne (sing, sings) a touching version of "America the Beautiful."

5. Here (is, are) the performers who juggle plates.

6. Kin Lee and his parents (travel, travels) to Ohio tomorrow.

7. A box of old and valuable stamps (is, are) in the safe-deposit box at the bank.

8. The family (sit, sits) together in church each week.

9. Judith and Erin (arrive, arrives) at the train station at eleven o'clock.

10. Directions for the recipe (is, are) on the box.

 **EXERCISE 13-13**   Correcting Subject–Verb Agreement Errors

Directions: Revise any sentences that contain errors in subject–verb agreement.

Los Angeles have some very interesting and unusual buildings. There is the Victorian houses on Carroll Avenue, for example. The gingerbread-style trim and other ornate architectural features makes those houses attractive to tourists and photographers. The Bradbury Building and the Oviatt Building was both part of the nineteenth-century skyline. They was restored as office buildings that now houses twentieth-century businesses. Some of the architecture in Los Angeles seem to disguise a building's function. One of the most startling sights are a building that look like a huge ship.

EXERCISE 13-14   Revising a Paragraph

Directions: The following student paragraph has been revised to correct all errors except for those in subject–verb agreement and shifts in person and number. Complete the revision by correcting all such problems.

Now that the fascination with exercise has been in full swing for a decade, the public are starting to get tired of our nation's overemphasis on fitness. It seems as though every time you turn on the TV or pick up a newspaper or talk with a friend, all we hear about is how we do not exercise enough. The benefits of exercise is clear, but do we really need to have them repeated to us in sermonlike fashion every time we turn around? Each of us are at a point now where we are made to feel almost guilty if we have not joined a health club or, at the very least, participated in some heavy-duty exercise every day. It may be time you realized that there's better ways to get exercise than these. Americans might be better off just exercising in a more natural way. Taking a walk or playing a sport usually fit in better with our daily routines and isn't so strenuous. It could even be that our obsession with extreme forms of exercise may be less healthy than not exercising at all.

EXERCISE 13-15   Revising a Paragraph

WRITING IN PROGRESS

Directions: Reread the paragraph you wrote in Exercise 13-4. Check for subject–verb agreement errors and for sentences you wrote in the passive voice. Revise as necessary.

READ AND REVISE

The following excerpt is from a student essay titled "Alone but Not Lonely." This excerpt contains verb usage errors that were subsequently corrected in another draft. Read the excerpt, and then revise it to correct verb usage errors.

The summer I turned ten, I learned the difference between being alone and being lonely. Growing up in a large family, I never had much time to myself, but that summer I visit my aunt for three weeks. She lived in the country, and I was the only kid for miles around. At first, I had felt lonely without my brothers and sisters, but then I discover the boulders in the woods. The jumble of huge rocks were endlessly fascinating. Some days I was an explorer, moving from one rock to another, surveying the countryside from the tallest boulder. Some days, I retired to my secret fort, tucked in a shadowy crevice. I furnished my rocky fort with an old cushion to set on and a cigar box for collecting treasures. On sunny mornings, before the air has lost its early chill, I laid on the flattest boulder, its smooth surface warming my skinny arms and legs. The boulders were my audience when I read aloud the stories I had wrote. I remember many things about my time alone in the woods that summer, but I don't recall ever feeling lonely.

SELF-TEST SUMMARY

To test yourself, cover the Answer column with a sheet of paper and answer each question in the left column. Evaluate each of your answers as you work by sliding the paper down and comparing your answer with what is printed in the answer column.

QUESTION	ANSWER
■ **GOAL 1** Identify verb forms What are the five forms of a verb?	The five verb forms are the *base form*, the *past tense*, the *past participle*, the *present participle*, and the *-s form*.
■ **GOAL 2** Identify verb tenses What is the function of verb tenses?	Verb tenses express time. They indicate whether an action, process, or event takes place in the present, past, or future.

(continued)

QUESTION	ANSWER
■ **GOAL 3** Use simple verb tenses correctly In the simple present tense, the verb form for which person ends in *-s*?	In the simple present tense, the verb for third-person singular subjects ends in *-s*. (For first-person, second-person, or third-person plural, the base form of the verb is used.)
■ **GOAL 4** Use irregular verbs correctly How does an irregular verb form the simple past tense?	An irregular verb forms the simple past tense, not by adding *-d* or *-ed* but either by changing its spelling internally or by not changing it at all.
■ **GOAL 5** Use active instead of passive voice in most situations What is the difference between the active and passive voices, and why is active voice usually preferred?	In an active-voice sentence, the subject performs the action. In a passive-voice sentence, the subject receives the action. Active voice is usually more effective than passive voice because it is simpler and more direct.
■ **GOAL 6** Avoid errors in subject–verb agreement How must a subject and its verb agree?	A subject of a sentence must agree with its verb in person and in number.

Combining and Expanding Your Ideas

LEARNING GOALS

Learn how to …

- **GOAL 1**
  Recognize independent and dependent clauses

- **GOAL 2**
  Combine ideas of equal importance

- **GOAL 3**
  Combine ideas of unequal importance

- **GOAL 4**
  Write compound–complex sentences

THINK About It!

Study the six photographs shown above one at a time (cover the others with your hands as you look at them). What is happening in each one? It is probably difficult to tell because there is not enough information in each one to convey what is happening in the complete picture, which tells the whole story. Now look at the six photographs all together. When you do this, it is clear what is happening. Write a sentence that states the main point of the combined photographs.

The six photographs seen separately are difficult to understand because each one contains limited information, and it is unclear if and how each is related to the others. A similar uncertainty can occur in writing when a writer uses too many very short sentences in a paragraph and the relationship between them is unclear: The reader has difficulty piecing together the meaning and grasping the larger, more important ideas.

In this chapter, you will learn to combine your ideas to make your sentences more effective and more interesting. You will also learn how to use sentence arrangement to show the relationships and the logical connections between and among your ideas.

What Are Independent and Dependent Clauses?

■ GOAL 1
Recognize independent and dependent clauses

A **clause** is a group of words that contains a subject and a verb. There are two types of clauses—independent and dependent. An **independent clause** can stand by itself and express a complete thought. A **dependent clause** hinges on another clause to complete its meaning. You can think of these two types of clauses in the following way. If you are financially independent, you alone accept full responsibility for your finances. If you are financially dependent, you depend on someone else to pay your living expenses. Similarly, clauses either stand alone and accept responsibility for their own meaning, or they depend on another clause to complete their meaning. Independent clauses can stand alone as sentences. Dependent clauses can never stand alone because they are not complete sentences.

When writing, the key to combining and expanding your ideas is to recognize this difference between independent and dependent clauses. The various combinations of independent and dependent clauses shown in the "Need to Know" box below allow you to link your ideas to one another, to expand and explain ideas, and to show relationships.

When reading, it is useful to pay attention to how a writer combines clauses because relationships and connections are often suggested by how independent and dependent clauses are combined into sentences. The relative importance of ideas is also suggested.

NEED TO KNOW

Independent and Dependent Clauses

Sentences are made up of various combinations of independent and dependent clauses. Here are the possible combinations:

■ **Simple sentence** A simple sentence has one independent clause and no dependent clauses.

> Independent clause
> Richard hurried to his car.

■ **Compound sentence** A compound sentence has two or more independent clauses and no dependent clauses.

> Independent clause   Independent clause
> Richard hurried to his car, but he was already late for work.

- **Complex sentence** A complex sentence has one independent clause and one or more dependent clauses.

  Independent clause | Dependent clause

  Richard hurried to his car because he was late for work.

- **Compound–complex sentence** A compound–complex sentence has two or more independent clauses and one or more dependent clauses.

  Dependent clause | Independent clause | Independent clause | Dependent clause

  As Richard hurried to his car, he knew he would be late for work, so he texted his boss that he had been delayed.

Combine Ideas of Equal Importance

- GOAL 2
  Combine ideas of equal importance

Many times, ideas are of equal importance. For example, in the following sentence, it is just as important to know that the writer never has enough time as it is to know that she always rushes.

I never have enough time, so I always rush from task to task.

Complete thoughts (independent clauses) of equal importance are combined by using a technique called **coordination**. *Co-* means "together." *Coordinate* means "to work together." When you want two complete thoughts to work together equally, you can combine them into a single sentence by using coordination.

There are two basic ways to join two ideas that are equally important:

METHOD 1   Join them by using a *comma* and a *coordinating conjunction (for, and, nor, but, or, yet, so).*

Complete thought , coordinating conjunction   complete thought.

METHOD 2   Join them by using a *semicolon.*

Complete thought ; complete thought.

Method 1: Use a Comma and a Coordinating Conjunction

The most common way to join ideas is by using a *comma and a coordinating conjunction.* (Use a semicolon only when the two ideas are *very* closely related and the connection between the ideas is clear and obvious.)

The following two sentences contain equally important ideas:

Samantha works 20 hours per week.

Samantha manages to find time to study.

You can combine these ideas into one sentence by using a comma and a coordinating conjunction.

Idea 1	Idea 2
Comma	Conjunction

Samantha works 20 hours per week, but she manages to find time to study.

A **coordinating conjunction** joins clauses and adds meaning to a sentence. A coordinating conjunction indicates how the ideas are related. Table 14-1 provides a brief review of the meaning of each coordinating conjunction and the relationship it expresses.

TABLE 14-1	COORDINATING CONJUNCTIONS AND THE RELATIONSHIPS THEY EXPRESS	
Coordinating Conjunction	**Meaning**	**Relationship**
and	in addition	The two ideas are added together.
but	in contrast	The two ideas are opposite.
for	because	The idea that follows *for* is the cause of the idea in the other clause.
nor, or	not either, either	The ideas are choices or alternatives.
so	as a result	The second idea is the result of the first.
yet	in contrast	The two ideas are opposite.

Note: Do *not* use the words *also, plus,* and *then* to join complete thoughts. They are *not* coordinating conjunctions.

Here are a few examples of Method 1:

SIMPLE SENTENCES	Time is valuable. I try to use it wisely.
COMBINED SENTENCE	Time is valuable, so I try to use it wisely.

SIMPLE SENTENCES	Many students try to set priorities for work and study. Many students see immediate results.
COMBINED SENTENCE	Many students try to set priorities for work and study, and they see immediate results.

SIMPLE SENTENCES	I tried keeping lists of things to do. My friend showed me a better system.
COMBINED SENTENCE	I tried keeping lists of things to do, but my friend showed me a better system.

EXERCISE 14-1   Using Coordinating Conjunctions

Directions: For each of the following sentences, add the coordinating conjunction that best expresses the relationship between the two complete thoughts.

EXAMPLE   I never learned to manage my time, _____so_____ I am planning to attend a time-management workshop.

1. I might study math, _____ I might review for my history exam.

2. The average person spends 56 hours a week sleeping, _____ the average person spends seven hours a week eating dinner.

3. Checking Instagram is tempting, _____ I usually log out before I start studying.

4. I do not feel like starting my research paper, _____ do I feel like reviewing math.

5. I am never sure of what to work on first, _____ I waste a lot of time deciding.

6. A schedule for studying is easy to follow, _____ it eliminates the need to decide what to study.

7. My cousin has a study routine, _____ she never breaks it.

8. Ernesto studies his hardest subject first, _____ then he takes a break.

9. I know I should not procrastinate, _____ I sometimes postpone an unpleasant task until the next day.

10. I had planned to study after work, _____ my exam was postponed.

EXERCISE 14-2   ## Completing Sentences

Directions: Complete each of the following sentences by adding a second complete thought. Use the coordinating conjunction shown in bold.

> **EXAMPLE**   I feel torn between studying and spending time with friends, **but** I usually choose to study.

1. My psychology class was canceled, **so** _____

2. I waste time doing unimportant tasks, **and** _____

3. The cell phone used to be a constant source of interruption, **but** _____ _____

4. I had extra time to study this weekend, **for** _____ _____

5. I had hoped to finish reading my biology chapter, **but** _____ _____

6. Every Saturday I study psychology, **or** _____

7. I had planned to finish work early, **yet** _____ _____

8. I can choose a topic to write about, **or** _____

9. I had hoped to do many errands this weekend, **but** _____ _____

10. I tried to study and watch television at the same time, **but** _____ _____

EXERCISE 14-3 ## Combining Sentences Using Coordinating Conjunctions

Directions: Combine each of the following pairs of sentences by using a comma and a coordinating conjunction (*for, and, nor, but, or, yet, so*). Change punctuation, capitalization, and words as necessary. Be sure to insert a comma before the coordinating conjunction.

EXAMPLE
  a. I have a free hour between my first and second classes.
  b. I use that free hour to review my biology notes.

I have a free hour between my first and second class, so I use that hour
to review my biology notes.

1. **a.** Some tasks are more enjoyable than others.
   b. We tend to put off unpleasant tasks.

_____

_____

2. **a.** Many people think it is impossible to do two things at once.
   b. Busy students soon learn to combine routine activities.

_____

_____

3. **a.** Marita prioritizes her courses.
   b. Marita allots specific blocks of study time for each.

_____

_____

4. **a.** Marcus may try to schedule his study sessions so they are several hours apart.
   b. Marcus may adjust the length of his study sessions.

_____

_____

5. **a.** Emily studies late at night.
   b. Emily does not accomplish as much as she expects to.

_____

_____

6. **a.** Marguerite studies without breaks.
   b. Marguerite admits she frequently loses her concentration.

_____

_____

7. **a.** Mateo studies two hours for every hour he spends in class.
   b. Mateo earns high grades.

_____

_____

8. **a.** Deadlines are frustrating.
   b. Deadlines force you to make hasty decisions.

_____

_____

9. a. Juan thought he was organized.
   b. Juan discovered he was not.

   _____

   _____

10. a. Hannah sets goals for each course.
   b. Hannah usually attains her goals.

   _____

   _____

   _____

Method 2: Use a Semicolon

A semicolon can be used alone or with a transitional word or phrase to join independent clauses. These transitional words and phrases are called conjunctive adverbs. **Conjunctive adverbs** are adverbs that *join*. As you can see in these examples, a semicolon comes before the conjunctive adverb, and a comma follows it.

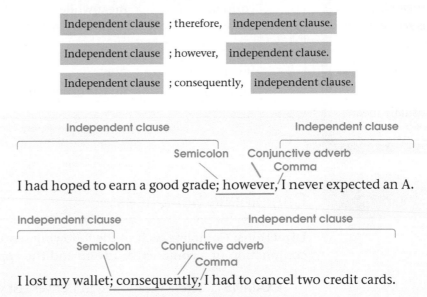

| Independent clause | ; therefore, | independent clause. |

| Independent clause | ; however, | independent clause. |

| Independent clause | ; consequently, | independent clause. |

Independent clause   Independent clause

Semicolon   Conjunctive adverb
                        Comma

I had hoped to earn a good grade; however, I never expected an A.

Independent clause   Independent clause

Semicolon   Conjunctive adverb
                        Comma

I lost my wallet; consequently, I had to cancel two credit cards.

Use this method when the relationship between the two ideas is clear and requires no explanation. Be careful to choose the correct conjunctive adverb. Table 14-2 shows a list of conjunctive adverbs and their meanings.

TABLE 14-2	CONJUNCTIVE ADVERBS AND THEIR MEANINGS	
Common Conjunctive Adverbs	**Meaning**	**Example**
as a result, therefore, consequently, thus, hence	cause and effect	I am planning to become a nurse; *consequently,* I'm taking a lot of science courses.
however, instead, nevertheless, nonetheless, otherwise, conversely	differences or contrast	We had planned to go bowling; *however,* we went to hear music instead.
further, furthermore, in addition, moreover, also	addition; a continuation of the same idea	To save money, I am packing my lunch; *also,* I am walking to school instead of taking the bus.
similarly, likewise	similarity	I left class as soon as I finished the exam; *likewise,* other students left.
then, subsequently, next, finally, now, meanwhile	sequence in time	I walked home; *then* I massaged my aching feet.

Note: If you join two independent clauses with only a comma and fail to use a co-ordinating conjunction or semicolon, you will produce a comma splice. If you join two independent clauses without using a punctuation mark and a coordinating conjunction, you will produce a run-on sentence. (See Chapter 12 for a review.)

Tip for Writers

These words mean the same as **and:** *also, besides, further-more,* and *in addition.* These mean the same as **but:** *however, nevertheless, on the other hand,* and *still.* These mean the same as **so** when it is used to introduce a result: *therefore, con-sequently,* and *as a result. Otherwise* and *unless* usually mean "if not."

 NEED TO KNOW

How to Use Conjunctive Adverbs

Use a conjunctive adverb to join two equal ideas. Remember to put a semicolon before the conjunctive adverb and a comma after it. Here is a list of common conjunctive adverbs:

also	in addition	otherwise
as a result	instead	similarly
besides	likewise	still
consequently	meanwhile	then
finally	nevertheless	therefore
further	next	thus
furthermore	now	undoubtedly
however	on the other hand	

EXERCISE 14-4   ## Completing Sentences

Directions: Complete each of the following sentences by adding a coordinating conjunction or a conjunctive adverb and the appropriate punctuation.

> **EXAMPLE**   Teresa vacationed in Denver last year_____ ; similarly, _____ Jan will go to Denver this year.

1. Our professor did not complete the lecture_____ did he give an assign-ment for the next class.

2. A first-aid kit was in her backpack_____ the hiker was able to treat her cut knee.

3. The opening act performed at the concert_____ the headline band took the stage.

4. I always put a light on when I leave the house_____ I often turn on a radio to deter burglars.

5. Shania politely asked to borrow my car_____ she thanked me when she returned it.

6. My roommate went to the library_____ I had the apartment to myself.

7. Steve and Tomás will go to a baseball game_____ they will go to a movie.

8. Mia looks like her father_____ her hair is darker and curlier than his.

9. Mi-Cha took a job at a bookstore_____ she was offered a job at a museum.

10. Our neighbors bought a barbecue grill_____ we decided to buy one.

EXERCISE 14-5 · Writing Compound Sentences

Directions: Write five compound sentences about how you study for tests or how you spend your weekends. Each sentence should contain two complete thoughts. Join the thoughts by using a comma and a coordinating conjunction. Use a different coordinating conjunction in each sentence.

EXERCISE 14-6 · Writing Using Compound Sentences

Directions: Write a paragraph evaluating how well you manage your time. Use at least two compound sentences.

Combine Ideas of Unequal Importance

■ **GOAL 3**
Combine ideas of
unequal importance

Consider the following two simple sentences:

> Pete studies during his peak periods of attention.
>
> Pete accomplishes a great deal.

Reading these sentences, you may suspect that Pete accomplishes a great deal *because* he studies during peak periods of attention. With the sentences separated, however, that cause and effect relationship is only a guess. Combining the two sentences makes the relationship between the ideas clear.

> Because Pete studies during his peak periods of attention, he accomplishes a great deal.

Let's look at another pair of sentences:

> TaShayla analyzed her time commitments for the week.
>
> TaShayla developed a study plan for the week.

You may suspect that TaShayla developed the study plan *after* analyzing her time commitments. Combining the sentences makes the connection in time clear.

> After TaShayla analyzed her time commitments for the week, she developed a study plan.

In each of these examples, the two complete thoughts were combined so that one idea depended on the other. This process of combining ideas so that one idea is dependent on another is called **subordination**. *Sub-* means "below." Think of subordination as a way of combining an idea of lesser or lower importance with an idea of greater importance.

Make Less Important Ideas Dependent on More Important Ones

Ideas of unequal importance can be combined by making the less important idea depend on the more important one. Notice how, in the following sentence, the part before the comma doesn't make sense without the part after the comma.

> While Malcolm was waiting for the bus, he studied psychology.

If you read only the first half of the sentence, you will find yourself waiting for the idea to be completed, wondering what happened while Malcolm was waiting. The word *while* (a subordinating conjunction) makes the meaning of the first half of the sentence incomplete by itself. Thus, the first half of the sentence is a *dependent clause*. It depends on the rest of the sentence to complete its thought. A dependent clause can never be a complete sentence. It must always be joined to an *independent clause* to make a complete thought. The dependent clause can go at the beginning, in the middle, or at the end of a sentence.

Use **subordinating conjunctions** to indicate how a less important idea—a dependent clause—relates to another, more important idea—an independent clause. (You can also use subordinating conjunctions to correct fragments.) Table 14-3 lists subordinating conjunctions that are commonly used to begin dependent clauses.

TABLE 14-3 SUBORDINATING CONJUNCTIONS AND THEIR MEANINGS		
Subordinating Conjunction	**Meaning**	**Example**
before, after, while, during, until, when, once	time	*When* you set time limits, you are working toward a goal.
because, since, so that	cause or effect	*Because* I felt rushed, I made careless errors.
whether, if, unless, even if	condition	*If* I finish studying before nine o'clock, I will read more of my mystery novel.
as, as far as, as soon as, as long as, as if, as though, although, even though, even if, in order to	circumstance	*Even if* I try to concentrate, I still am easily distracted.

Note: Relative pronouns (*who, whom, whose, that, which, whoever, whomever, whichever*) can also be used to show relationships and to join a dependent clause with an independent clause.

Use Punctuation to Combine Dependent and Independent Clauses

When you combine a dependent clause with an independent clause and the dependent clause comes *first* in the sentence, use a comma to separate the clauses.

> Dependent clause   ,   Independent clause.

> Dependent clause   Comma Independent clause
> When I follow a study schedule, I accomplish more.

When the dependent clause comes in the *middle* of the sentence, set it off with a *pair* of commas if the information is **not** essential to the meaning of the sentence. You can distinguish essential and nonessential clauses by using the following test. Remove the clause. If the meaning is not changed after removing it, it is not essential.

First part of independent clause , Dependent clause , Remainder of independent clause.

Subject of independent clause | Dependent clause | Remainder of independent clause

Comma   Comma

Malcolm, while he was waiting for a ride, studied psychology.

If the dependent clause is essential to the meaning of the sentence, do not use commas to set it apart.

First part of independent clause Dependent clause Remainder of independent clause

Subject of the independent clause | Dependent clause | Remainder of the independent clause

Those of us who did not attend the lecture on Tuesday were unprepared for the pop quiz on Thursday.

If the dependent clause comes at the *end* of the sentence, do not use a comma to separate it from the rest of the sentence.

Independent clause   Dependent clause.

Independent clause   No comma   Dependent clause

I accomplish more when I follow a study schedule.

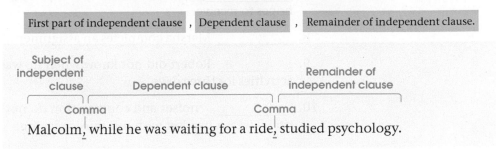

EXERCISE 14-7   Adding Subordinating Conjunctions

Directions: For each of the following sentences, add a subordinating conjunction that makes the relationship between the two ideas clear. Try to use as many different subordinating conjunctions as possible.

EXAMPLE ____When____ I finish studying, I am mentally exhausted.

1. _____ math requires peak concentration, I always study it first.

2. _____ Andres starts to lose concentration, he takes a short break.

3. Julia never stops in the middle of an assignment _____ she is too tired to finish.

4. _____ she likes to wake up slowly, Shannon sets her alarm for ten minutes before she needs to get up.

5. _____ Sofia took a five-minute study break, she felt more energetic.

6. Alan worked on his math homework _____ he did the laundry.

7. _____ Jamille increases his study time, he may not earn the grades he hopes to receive.

8. _____ Marsha completes an assignment, she crosses it off her to-do list.

9. _____ Robert did not know when he wasted time, he kept a log of his activities for three days.

10. _____ noises and conversation do not interfere with my concentration, I wear a headset with soft music playing.

Completing Sentences

Directions: Make each of the following sentences complete by adding a complete thought. Be sure the meaning fits the subordinating conjunction used in the sentence.

EXAMPLE   <u>I edited my essay</u>   while the ideas were fresh in my mind.

1. _____
   after I finished studying.

2. Because my job is part-time, _____
   _____

3. Once I finish college, _____
   _____

4. _____
   when I was not concentrating.

5. If you schedule blocks of study time, _____
   _____

6. _____
   unless I carry a pocket planner.

7. Although English is my favorite subject, _____
   _____

8. _____
   as far as I can tell.

9. Even if I finish by eight o'clock, _____
   _____

10. As soon as I decide what to do, _____
    _____

EXERCISE 14-9   ## Combining Sentences

Directions: Combine each of the following pairs of sentences by using a subordinating conjunction and a comma. Try to vary the position of the dependent clause (first or last). Change punctuation, capitalization, and words as necessary. You may wish to refer to the list of subordinating conjunctions on page 434.

 EXAMPLE   **a.** Yi-Min is taking voice lessons.

 b. Yi-Min always sings scales in the shower.

 Because Yi-Min is taking voice lessons, she always sings scales in the shower.

1. a. Christine has a six-month-old child.
 b. She must study while the baby sleeps.

_____

_____

2. a. Taj is often distracted by stray thoughts.
 b. Taj jots stray thoughts on a notepad to clear them from his mind.

_____

_____

3. a. Gary finished a difficult biology assignment.
 b. He rewarded himself by ordering a pizza.

_____

_____

4. a. It takes Anthony 45 minutes to drive to school.
 b. Anthony records lectures and listens while he drives.

_____

_____

5. a. Ada felt disorganized.
 b. Ada made a priority list of assignments and due dates.

_____

_____

6. a. Juanita walked from her history class to her math class.
 b. She observed the brilliant fall foliage.

_____

_____

7. a. Kevin skipped meals and ate junk food.
 b. Kevin signed up for a cooking class.

_____

_____

8. **a.** Lian joined the soccer team.
   b. Lian became the first woman to do so.

   _____

   _____

9. **a.** John ate dinner on Saturday night.
   b. John reviewed his plans for the week with his less-than-fascinated date.

   _____

   _____

10. **a.** Frank waited for his history class to begin.
    b. He wondered if he was in the right room.

    _____

    _____

EXERCISE 14-10   Writing Complex Sentences

Directions: Working with a classmate, write ten complex sentences on a subject that interests both of you. Each must contain one dependent clause and one independent clause. Use a comma to separate the clauses when the dependent clause comes first. Use two commas to set off a dependent clause in the middle of the sentence. You do not need a comma when the dependent clause comes last.

EXERCISE 14-11   Writing Complex Sentences

Directions: Write a paragraph on one of the following topics. Include at least two complex sentences.

1. Planning a vacation
2. Shopping online
3. Visiting a theme park
4. Advantages of credit cards
5. A favorite possession

Write Compound–Complex Sentences

■ **GOAL 4**
Write compound–complex sentences

A **compound–complex sentence** is made up of two or more independent clauses and one or more dependent clauses. This type of sentence is often used to express complicated relationships. Look at the following examples of compound–complex sentences.

■ Here, a dependent clause is followed by two independent clauses:

Dependent clause	Independent clause

Even though Marsha needed to be better organized, she avoided weekly

Independent clause

study plans, and she ended up wasting valuable time.

■ Here, an independent clause containing a dependent clause is followed by a second independent clause with a dependent clause:

First part of independent clause	Dependent clause	Remainder of independent clause

The new students, who had just arrived, wanted a tour of the town;

Independent clause	Dependent clause

Lamar told them that he had no time because of his new work schedule.

■ Here, the sentence is made up of a dependent clause, an independent clause containing a dependent clause, and another independent clause:

	Independent clause
Dependent clause	Dependent clause

Although Amanda changed her work schedule, she found that she

	Independent clause

still needed more time to study, and she ended up quitting her job.

Refer to page 434 to determine when and when not to use commas to set apart a dependent clause that falls within an independent clause.

The key to writing effective and correct compound–complex sentences is to link each clause in the correct way to the one that follows it. The rules you have already learned in this chapter apply. For example, if you have two independent clauses followed by a dependent clause, link the two independent clauses as you would in a compound sentence by using a comma and a coordinating conjunction. Then link the second independent clause to the dependent clause by using a subordinating conjunction.

Independent clause	Independent clause	Dependent clause

I got up early, and I left the house before rush hour because I wanted to be

on time for my interview.

EXERCISE 14-12   Adding Conjunctions

Directions: Each of the following sentences is made up of at least three clauses. Read each sentence, and then make it correct by adding the necessary subordinating and/or coordinating conjunctions in the blanks.

EXAMPLE   ____Because____ they both got home from work late, Ted grilled hamburgers ____while____ Alexa made a salad.

1. _____ Sarah's sociology class required class discussion of the readings, she scheduled time to review sociology before each class meeting _____ she would have the material fresh in her mind.

2. _____ making a to-do list takes time, Deka found that the list actually saved her time, _____ she accomplished more when she sat down to study.

3. _____ Terry's history lecture was over, he reviewed his notes, _____ when he discovered any gaps, he was usually able to recall the information.

4. Many students have discovered that distributing their studying over several evenings is more effective than studying in one large block of time _____ it gives them several exposures to the material, _____ they feel less pressured.

5. We have tickets for the concert, _____ we may not go _____ Jeff has a bad cold.

EXERCISE 14-13   Writing a Compound–Complex Sentence

Directions: Write a compound–complex sentence, and then label its dependent and independent clauses.

READ AND REVISE

The following excerpt is from a student essay called "A Victim of Circumstance." This excerpt contains errors that were subsequently corrected in another draft. Revise the excerpt by adding coordinating conjunctions, conjunctive adverbs, or subordinating conjunctions where appropriate. Change punctuation as necessary.

I was a victim, a victim of circumstance. I was introduced to this life as a small child. I was the baby out of ten children, five boys and five girls. I watched my parents work for little or nothing. My mom worked odd jobs as a CNA, a waitress, and a short order cook. My dad worked in a restaurant for as little as two dollars and fifty cents per hour. He did earn small tips that helped a little. There were many hardships. He never complained. My mom and dad would come home, their feet would be swollen. They would have burns on their arms. They still did not have enough money to feed the family. Often I would think, "It's going to be another long night of hunger. Or maybe just peanut butter on a spoon."

I watched this same scene repeat itself over and over again until I was about thirteen years old. That's when my life became almost the same as theirs. I was speaking with one of my closest friends, I trusted her deeply. I described to her my life and the situations I faced. I told her I faced them every day. It was at that moment she told me that her mother owned a farm. People under the age of sixteen were allowed to work there. They were paid minimum wage. They were allowed to take home second-day old produce. They could also take produce that was spotted or not top quality. I thought to myself, "Yes! I can help my parents feed my brothers and sisters now."

SELF-TEST SUMMARY

To test yourself, cover the Answer column with a sheet of paper and answer each question in the left column. Evaluate each of your answers as you work by sliding the paper down and comparing your answer with what is printed in the answer column.

QUESTION	ANSWER
■ **GOAL 1** Recognize independent and dependent clauses What is the difference between independent and dependent clauses?	An *independent clause* can stand alone as a sentence. A *dependent clause* does not express a complete thought. It must be joined to an independent clause to make a complete sentence.

(continued)

QUESTION	ANSWER
■ **GOAL 2** Combine ideas of equal importance What are two ways to combine independent clauses?	1. Join two independent clauses by using a comma and a coordinating conjunction. 2. Join two independent clauses by using a semicolon with or without a conjunctive adverb.
■ **GOAL 3** Combine ideas of unequal importance What is subordination?	Subordination is the process of using a subordinating conjunction to combine ideas so that an idea of lesser importance is dependent on an idea of greater importance.
■ **GOAL 4** Write compound–complex sentences What is a compound–complex sentence?	A compound–complex sentence has two or more independent clauses combined with one or more dependent clauses.

Revising Confusing and Inconsistent Sentences

Tony Lilley/Alamy Stock Photo

LEARNING
GOALS

Learn how to …

■ **GOAL 1**
Use pronouns clearly
and correctly

■ **GOAL 2**
Avoid shifts in person,
number, and verb
tense

■ **GOAL 3**
Avoid misplaced and
dangling modifiers

■ **GOAL 4**
Use parallelism

THINK About It!

The situation shown in the photo seems "not right." Inconsistencies in your writing can also make it seem "not right" or confusing. Here are a few examples from a book titled *Anguished English* by Richard Lederer that show how errors create confusion and sometimes unintentional humor.

■ We do not tear your clothing with machinery. We do it carefully by hand.

■ Have several very old dresses from grandmother in beautiful condition.

■ Tired of cleaning yourself? Let me do it.

Sometimes sentence errors create unintentional humor, as in Lederer's examples. Most often, though, they distract or confuse your reader. They may also convey the impression that you have not taken time to check and polish your work. In this chapter, you will learn to avoid several common types of sentence errors.

What Is a Confusing or Inconsistent Sentence?

A **confusing** or **inconsistent sentence** is one in which the meaning is unclear. Usually, the confusion is unintentional. That is, the writer did not realize that information is missing or that several possible interpretations are possible.

Use Pronouns Clearly and Correctly

■ **GOAL 1**
Use pronouns clearly and correctly

A **pronoun** is a word that substitutes for, or refers to, a noun or another pronoun. *I, you, he, she, it, we, they, his, mine, yours, who,* and *whom* are all examples of pronouns. The noun or pronoun to which a pronoun refers is called the pronoun's **antecedent**. To use pronouns correctly, you need to make sure that the antecedent of the pronoun—the word to which the pronoun refers—is clear to your reader and that the pronoun and antecedent agree in number (singular or plural) and in gender.

Pronoun Reference

If your pronoun reference is unclear, your sentence may be confusing and difficult to follow. Note the confusing nature of the following sentences:

The aerobics instructor told the student that *she* made a mistake.

(Who made the mistake?)

They told Kevin that he was eligible for a Visa card. (Who told Kevin?)

Aaron bought a bowling ball at the garage sale *that* he enjoyed. (Did Aaron enjoy the garage sale or the bowling ball?)

The following suggestions will help you make sure that all your pronoun references are clear:

■ **Make sure there is only one possible antecedent for each pronoun.** The antecedent (the word to which the pronoun refers) should come before the pronoun (*ante-* means "before") in the sentence. The reader should not be left wondering what the antecedent of any given pronoun is.

UNCLEAR	The father told the child that *he* was sunburned.
REVISED	The father told the child, "I am sunburned."

■ **Avoid using vague pronouns that lack an antecedent.** *They* and *it* are often mistakenly used this way.

| UNCLEAR | *They* told me my loan application needs a cosigner. |
| REVISED | The loan officer told me my loan application needs a cosigner. |

■ **Eliminate unnecessary pronouns.** If a sentence is clear without a pronoun, delete the pronoun.

| UNCLEAR | The manager, *he* says that the store will close at midnight. |
| REVISED | The manager says that the store will close at midnight. |

■ **Always place the pronoun as close as possible to its antecedent.**

| UNCLEAR | Lucia saw a dress at the mall *that* she wanted. |
| REVISED | At the mall, Lucia saw a dress that she wanted. |

■ **Use the pronoun *you* only if you are directly addressing the reader.**

| UNCLEAR | *You* need daily exercise to keep physically fit. |
| REVISED | Everyone needs daily exercise to keep physically fit. |

Tip for Writers

Don't write both a noun and a pronoun for the same subject.

INCORRECT
My teacher she is very tall.
CORRECT
My teacher is very tall.
(or) She is very tall.

EXERCISE 15-1 | Correcting Pronoun Reference Errors

Directions: Revise each of the following sentences to correct problems in pronoun reference.

                   was
EXAMPLE   The glass, ~~it~~ filled to the rim.

1. One should try to be honest, so you do not get caught telling lies.

2. When I bought the shirt, I told him that I would pay with my credit card.

3. Jamal told Rob, he had received an A in the course.

4. James talked with Bill because he did not know anyone else at the party.

5. The teachers told the school board members that they needed more preparation time.

6. The board of directors, they decided that the company would have to declare bankruptcy.

7. The gallery owner hung a painting on the wall that was blue.

8. They sent our grades at the end of the semester.

9. The Constitution says you have the right to bear arms.

10. They filled the parking lot on Sunday.

EXERCISE 15-2 — Revising Sentences

Directions: Revise each of the following sentences to correct problems in pronoun reference. If a sentence contains no errors, write *Correct* beside it.

         The professor's note
EXAMPLE ~~It~~ said that the grades would be posted on Tuesday.

_____ 1. On the company home page it says there will be a flash sale today.

_____ 2. Laverne and Louise they pooled their money to buy a new virtual reality headset.

_____ 3. They said on the news that the naval base will be shut down.

_____ 4. The street that was recently widened is where I used to live.

_____ 5. Ivan sat on the couch in the living room that he bought yesterday.

_____ 6. "Sarah," the tutor advised, "you should underline in your textbooks for better comprehension."

_____ 7. Christina handed Maggie the plate she had bought at the flea market.

_____ 8. Bridget found the cake mix in the aisle with the baking supplies that she needed for tonight's dessert.

_____ 9. Rick told Larry, he was right.

_____ 10. It said in the letter that my payment was late.

EXERCISE 15-3 — Writing a Paragraph

WRITING IN PROGRESS

Directions: Write a paragraph on one of the following topics. After you have written your first draft, reread it to be certain your pronoun references are clear. Make corrections if needed.

1. A recent clothing fad
2. Advice columns
3. Horoscopes
4. Remembering names
5. An extreme weather condition (heat wave, storm, blizzard, flood) that you lived through

Pronoun–Antecedent Agreement

A pronoun must "agree" with its antecedent—that is, a pronoun must have the same number (singular or plural) as the noun or pronoun it refers to or replaces. Singular nouns and pronouns refer to one person, place, or thing; plural nouns and pronouns refer to more than one.

Always check your sentences for pronoun–antecedent agreement.

	Plural Singular
INCORRECT	The dogs are in its kennels.
CORRECT	The dogs are in their kennels.

	Plural Singular
INCORRECT	Marcia and Megan called all her friends about the party.
CORRECT	Marcia and Megan called all their friends about the party.

Use the following guidelines to make sure the pronouns you use agree with their antecedents:

■ **Use singular pronouns with singular nouns.**

> Singular noun Singular pronoun
>
> Teresa sold her bicycle.

■ **Use plural pronouns with plural nouns.**

> Plural noun   Plural pronoun
>
> The neighbors always shovel their walks when it snows.

■ **Use a plural pronoun to refer to a compound antecedent joined by *and* unless both parts of the compound refer to the same person, place, or thing.**

> Plural antecedent   Plural pronoun
>
> Demond and Keith bought their concert tickets.

> Singular antecedent   Singular pronoun
>
> The pitcher and team captain broke her ankle.

■ **When antecedents are joined by *or, nor, either … or, neither … nor, not … but,* or *not only … but also,* the pronoun agrees in number with the nearer antecedent.**

> Plural noun   Plural pronoun
>
> Either the professor or the students will present their views.

Note: When one antecedent is singular and the other is plural, avoid awkwardness by placing the plural antecedent second in the sentence.

AWKWARD	Neither the salespersons nor the manager has received his check.
REVISED	Neither the manager nor the salespersons have received their checks.

- **Avoid using *he*, *him*, or *his* to refer to general, singular words such as *child, person, everyone*.** These words exclude females. Use *he or she, him or her*, or *his or hers*, or rewrite your sentence to use a plural antecedent and a plural pronoun that do not indicate gender.

INCORRECT	A <u>person</u> should not deceive <u>his</u> friends.
REVISED	A <u>person</u> should not deceive <u>his or her</u> friends.
BETTER	<u>People</u> should not deceive <u>their</u> friends.

- **With collective nouns (words that refer to a group of people such as *army, class, congregation, audience*), use a singular pronoun to refer to the noun when the group acts as a unit.**

   The <u>audience</u> showed <u>its</u> approval by applauding.

   The <u>team</u> chose <u>its</u> captain.

   Use a plural pronoun to refer to the noun when each member of the group acts individually.

   The <u>family</u> exchanged <u>their</u> gifts.

   The <u>team</u> changed <u>their</u> uniforms.

   To avoid using a plural verb or pronoun after a collective noun, write "the members of the family" or "the members of the team," which gives you a plural subject (members).

EXERCISE 15-4	Correcting Agreement Errors

Directions: Revise each of the following sentences to correct errors in pronoun–antecedent agreement.

> **EXAMPLE**   Usually when a driver has been caught speeding, ~~they~~ ^{he or she} readily admit_s the mistake.

1. Each gas station in town raised their prices in the past week.

2. Neither the waitress nor the hostess received their paycheck from the restaurant.

3. The committee put his or her signatures on the document.

4. An infant recognizes their parents within the first few weeks of life.

5. The Harris family lives by his or her own rules.

6. Lonnie and Jack should put his ideas together and come up with a plan of action.

7. An employee taking an unpaid leave of absence may choose to make their own health-insurance payments.

8. The amount of time a student spends researching a topic depends, in part, on their familiarity with the topic.

9. Alex and Susana lost her way while driving through the suburbs of Philadelphia.

10. Neither the attorney nor the protesters were willing to expose himself to public criticism.

Agreement with Indefinite Pronouns

Indefinite pronouns (such as *some, everyone, any, each*) are pronouns without specific antecedents. They refer to people, places, or things in general. When an indefinite pronoun is an antecedent for another pronoun, mistakes in pronoun agreement often result. Use the following guidelines to make your pronouns agree with indefinite pronoun antecedents:

■ **Use singular pronouns to refer to indefinite pronouns that are singular in meaning.**

> ### Tip for Writers
>
> *Everybody, everyone,* and *everything* refer to a group of people or things, but these words are grammatically singular, so use a singular verb with them:
>
> When there's a snowstorm, <u>everyone gets</u> to class late.

another	either	nobody	other
anybody	everybody	no one	somebody
anyone	everyone	nothing	someone
anything	everything	one	something
each	neither		

Singular antecedent   Singular pronoun

Some<u>one</u> left <u>his</u> dress shirt in the locker room.

Singular antecedent   Singular compound pronoun

Every<u>one</u> in the office must pick up <u>his or her</u> paycheck.

Note: To avoid the awkwardness of *his or her*, use plural antecedents and pronouns.

Plural antecedent   Plural pronoun

Office <u>workers</u> must pick up <u>their</u> paychecks.

■ **Use a plural pronoun to refer to indefinite pronouns that are plural in meaning.**

both	few	many	more	several

Plural antecedent   Plural pronoun

<u>Both</u> of the police officers said that as far as <u>they</u> could tell, no traffic violations had occurred.

■ **The indefinite pronouns** *all, any, more, most,* **and** *some* **can be singular or plural, depending on how they are used.** If the indefinite pronoun refers to something that cannot be counted, use a singular pronoun to refer to it. If the indefinite pronoun refers to two or more of something that can be counted, use a plural pronoun to refer to it.

Most of the students feel they can succeed.

Most of the air on airplanes is recycled repeatedly, so it becomes stale.

! NEED TO KNOW

Pronouns

■ **Pronouns** substitute for or refer to nouns or other pronouns.

■ The noun or pronoun to which a pronoun refers is called its **antecedent**.

■ Make sure that it is always clear to which noun or pronoun a pronoun refers.

■ A pronoun must agree with its antecedent in number (singular or plural) and gender. Singular nouns and pronouns refer to one thing; plural nouns and pronouns refer to more than one thing.

■ **Indefinite pronouns** are pronouns without specific antecedents. Follow the rules given in this chapter to make indefinite pronouns agree with their antecedents.

EXERCISE 15-5 | Correcting Pronoun–Antecedent Errors

Directions: Revise each of the following sentences to correct errors in pronoun–antecedent agreement.

EXAMPLE	No one could remember their student number.
REVISED	No one could remember his or her student number.
BETTER	The students could not remember their student numbers.

1. Someone left their jacket in the car.

2. Everything Todd said was true, but I did not like the way he said them.

3. In my math class, everyone works at their own pace.

4. When someone exercises, they should drink plenty of liquids.

5. No one should be forced into a curriculum that they do not want.

6. No one will receive their exam grades before Friday.

7. Many of the club members do not pay his or her dues on time.

8. Both of the cooks used her own secret recipes.

9. No one was successful on their first attempt to run the race in less than two hours.

10. Each of the workers brought their own tools.

EXERCISE 15-6 — Correcting Agreement Errors

Directions: Revise the sentences below that contain agreement errors. If a sentence contains no errors, write *Correct* beside it.

> his or her
> **EXAMPLE**   Somebody dropped ~~their~~ ring down the drain.

_____ 1. Many of the residents of the neighborhood have had their homes tested for radon.

_____ 2. Each college instructor established their own grading policies.

_____ 3. The apples fell from its tree.

_____ 4. Anyone may enter their painting in the contest.

_____ 5. All the engines manufactured at the plant have their vehicle identification numbers stamped on them.

_____ 6. No one requested that the clerk gift wrap their package.

_____ 7. Either Professor Judith Marcos or her assistant, Maria, graded the exams, writing their comments in the margins.

_____ 8. James or his parents sails the boat every weekend.

_____ 9. Most classes were not canceled because of the snowstorm; it met as regularly scheduled.

_____ 10. Not only Ricky but also the Carters will take his children to Disneyland this summer.

EXERCISE 15-7 — Revising a Paragraph

WRITING IN PROGRESS

Directions: Reread the paragraph you wrote for Exercise 15-3 to be certain that there are no errors in pronoun–antecedent agreement. Revise as needed.

Avoid Shifts in Person, Number, and Verb Tense

■ **GOAL 2**
Avoid shifts in person, number, and verb tense

The parts of a sentence should be consistent. Shifts in person, number, or verb tense within a sentence make it confusing and difficult to read.

Shifts in Person

Person is the grammatical term used to identify the speaker or writer (**first person:** *I, we*), the person spoken to (**second person:** *you*), and the person or thing spoken about (**third person:** *he, she, it, they*, or any noun, such as *Joan* or *children*). Be sure to refer to yourself, your audience (or readers), and people and things you are writing about in a consistent way throughout your sentence or paragraph.

In the following paragraph, note how the writer shifts back and forth when addressing her audience:

> A person should know how to cook. You can save a lot of money if you make your own meals instead of eating out. One can also eat more healthily at home if one cooks according to principles of good nutrition.

Here the writer shifts from sentence to sentence, first using the indefinite phrase *a person*, then the more personal *you*, and then the more formal *one*.

In the next paragraph, the writer shifts when referring to himself.

> Arizona has many advantages for year-round living, so I am hoping to move there when I graduate. One reason I want to live in Arizona is that you never need to shovel snow.

In this paragraph, the writer shifts from the direct and personal *I* to the indirect and more general *you*.

To avoid making shifts in references to yourself and others, decide before you begin to write how you will refer to yourself, to your audience, and to those about whom you are writing. Base your decision on whether you want your paragraph to be direct and personal or more formal. In academic writing, most instructors prefer that you avoid using the personal pronoun *I* and try to write in a more formal style.

PERSONAL	I want to live in Florida for a number of reasons.
MORE FORMAL	Living in Florida is attractive for a number of reasons.
PERSONAL	I have difficulty balancing school and a part-time job.
MORE FORMAL	Balancing school and a part-time job is difficult.

Shifts in Number

Number distinguishes between singular and plural. A pronoun must agree in number with its antecedent. Related nouns within a sentence must also agree in number.

SHIFT	All the women wore a dress.
CONSISTENT	All the women wore dresses.

EXERCISE 15-8 — Correcting Shifts in Person and Number

Directions: Revise each of the following sentences to correct shifts in person or number.

EXAMPLE   I perform better on exams if the professor doesn't hover over ~~you~~. *me*

1. Each student has to plan their schedules for the semester.

2. Eva said she doesn't want to go to the wedding because you would have to bring a gift.

3. In some states, continuing education is required for doctors or lawyers; after you pass the board or bar exam, you are required to take a specified number of credits per year in brush-up courses.

4. Construction workers must wear a hard hats.

5. I swim with a life vest on because you could drown without it.

6. A good friend is always there when you need them most.

7. The first and second relay racers discussed his strategies.

8. I always tell yourself to think before acting.

9. Patients often expect their doctors to have all the answers, but you should realize doctors are not miracle workers.

10. Each giraffe stretched their neck to reach the leaves in the trees.

Shifts in Verb Tense

Use the same verb tense (past, present, future, etc.) throughout a sentence and paragraph unless meaning requires you to make a shift.

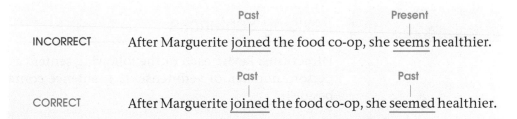

REQUIRED SHIFT   After the moon rises, we will go for a moonlight swim.

Incorrect shifts in verb tense can make a sentence confusing. One of the most common incorrect shifts is between present and past tenses.

INCORRECT   After Marguerite joined the food co-op, she seems healthier.

CORRECT   After Marguerite joined the food co-op, she seemed healthier.

NEED TO KNOW

Shifts in Person, Number, and Verb Tense

■ *Person* is a term used to identify the speaker or writer (**first person:** *I, we*), the person spoken to (**second person:** *you*), and the person or thing spoken about (**third person:** *he, she, it, they*, or any noun, such as *desk* or *Robert*). Be sure to use first, second, and third person consistently throughout a piece of writing.

■ **Number** distinguishes between singular and plural. A pronoun must agree in number with its antecedent.

■ **Verb tense** is the form of a verb that indicates whether the action or state of being that the verb tells about occurs in the past, present, or future. Unless there is a specific reason to switch tenses, be sure to use a consistent tense throughout a piece of writing.

EXERCISE 15-9 — Correcting Shifts in Verb Tense

Directions: Revise each of the following sentences to correct shifts in verb tense.

                                                  waited

EXAMPLE   I ~~was waiting~~ for the hailstorm to end, and then I dashed into the restaurant.

1. In the morning, the factory workers punch in, but have not punched out at night.

2. José looked muscular; then he joined a gym and looks even more so.

3. I run two miles, and then I rested.

4. Quinne called me but hangs up on my voicemail.

5. Until I took physics, I will not understand the laws of aerodynamics.

6. While the rain fell, the campers take shelter in their tent.

7. Because the moon will be full, the tide was high.

8. Katie drives me to work, and I worked until 9:30 p.m.

9. Richard went to the mall because he need to buy a suit for his job interview.

10. The speaker stands at the podium and cleared his throat.

EXERCISE 15-10 — Revising Sentences

Directions: Revise each of the following sentences to correct errors in shift of person, number, or verb tense. If a sentence contains no errors, write *Correct* beside it.

                                                docks

EXAMPLE   Boats along the river were tied to their ~~dock~~.

_____ 1. When people receive a gift, you should be gracious and polite.

_____ 2. When we arrived at the inn, the lights are on and a fire is burning in the fireplace.

_____ 3. Before Trey drove to the cabin, he packs a picnic lunch.

_____ 4. The artist paints portraits and weaves baskets.

_____ 5. The lobsterman goes out on his boat each day and will check his lobster traps.

_____ 6. All the cars Honest Bob sells have a new transmission.

_____ 7. Rosa ran the 100-meter race and throws the discus at the track meet.

_____ 8. Public schools in Florida have an air-conditioning system.

_____ 9. Office workers sat on the benches downtown and are eating their lunches outside.

_____ 10. Before a scuba diver goes underwater, you must check and recheck your breathing equipment.

EXERCISE 15-11

WRITING IN PROGRESS

Writing and Revising a Paragraph

Directions: Write a paragraph on one of the following topics. After you have written your first draft, reread it, checking for shifts in person, number, and verb tense. Revise as needed.

1. Registering to vote

2. The most beautiful place you have visited

3. A current food trend

4. The message of your favorite childhood book

5. Making polite conversation with relatives you see infrequently

Avoid Misplaced and Dangling Modifiers

■ **GOAL 3**
Avoid misplaced and dangling modifiers

A **modifier** is a word, phrase, or clause that describes, qualifies, or limits the meaning of another word. Modifiers that are not correctly placed can confuse your reader.

Types of Modifiers

The following list will help you review the main types of modifiers:

■ **Adjectives modify nouns and pronouns**

It is an interesting photograph.

She is very kind.

■ **Adverbs modify verbs, adjectives, or other adverbs.**

I walked quickly.

The cake tasted extremely good.

The flowers are very beautifully arranged.

■ **Prepositional phrases modify nouns, adjectives, verbs, or adverbs.**

The woman in the green dress is stunning.

They walked into the store to buy milk.

■ ***-ing* phrases modify nouns or pronouns.**

Waiting for the bus, Joe studied his history notes.

■ **Dependent clauses modify nouns, adjectives, verbs, or adverbs.** (A dependent clause has a subject and verb but is incomplete in meaning.)

After I left campus, I went shopping.

I left because classes were canceled.

The kitten that I found in the bushes was frightened.

Misplaced Modifiers

Placement of a modifier in a sentence affects meaning:

I need only to buy Marcos a gift. (Buying the gift is the only thing I need to do.)

Only I need to buy Marcos a gift. (I'm the only one who needs to buy Marcos a gift.)

I need to buy only Marcos a gift. (Marcos is the only person for whom I need to buy a gift.)

If a modifier is placed so that it does not convey the meaning you intend, it is called a **misplaced modifier.** Misplaced modifiers can make a sentence confusing.

MISPLACED	Anthony found a necklace at the mall that sparkled and glittered. (Which sparkled and glittered—the mall or the necklace?)
MISPLACED	The president announced that the club picnic would be held on August 2 at the beginning of the meeting. (Is the picnic being held at the beginning of the meeting on August 2, or did the president make the announcement at the beginning of the meeting?)

You can avoid a misplaced modifier if you make sure that the modifier immediately precedes or follows the word it modifies.

CORRECT	Anthony found a necklace that sparkled and glittered at the mall.
CORRECT	The club president announced at the beginning of the meeting that the picnic would be held on August 2.

Dangling Modifiers

Dangling modifiers are words or phrases that do not clearly describe or explain any part of the sentence. Dangling modifiers create confusion and sometimes unintentional humor. To avoid dangling modifiers, make sure that each modifying phrase or clause has a clear antecedent.

DANGLING	Uncertain of which street to follow, the map indicated we should turn left. (The opening modifier suggests that the map was uncertain of which street to follow.)
CORRECT	Uncertain of which street to follow, we checked a map, which indicated we should turn left.
DANGLING	My shoes got wet walking across the street. (The modifier suggests that the shoes were walking across the street by themselves.)
CORRECT	My shoes got wet as I crossed the street.
DANGLING	To pass the test, careful review is essential. (Who will pass the test?)
CORRECT	To pass the test, I must review carefully.

There are two common ways to revise dangling modifiers.

1. **Add a word or words that the modifier clearly describes.** Place the new material immediately after the modifier, and rearrange other parts of the sentence as necessary.

DANGLING	While walking in the garden, gunfire sounded. (The opening modifier implies that the gunfire was walking in the garden.)
CORRECT	While walking in the garden, Carol heard gunfire.

2. **Change the dangling modifier to a dependent clause.** You may need to change the verb form in the modifier.

DANGLING	While watching television, the cake burned.
CORRECT	While Pat was watching television, the cake burned.

 NEED TO KNOW

Misplaced and Dangling Modifiers

- A **modifier** is a word, phrase, or clause that describes, qualifies, or limits the meaning of another word.
- A **misplaced modifier** is placed in a way that does not convey the sentence's intended meaning. To avoid misplaced modifiers, be sure that you place the modifier immediately before or after the word it modifies.
- A **dangling modifier** is a word or phrase that does not clearly describe or explain any part of the sentence. To revise a dangling modifier, you can add a word or words that the modifier clearly describes, or you can change the dangling modifier to a dependent clause.

EXERCISE 15-12 | Correcting Misplaced or Dangling Modifiers

Directions: Revise each of the following sentences to correct misplaced or dangling modifiers.

> **EXAMPLE**   Jerome mailed a bill at the post office that was long overdue.
>
> **REVISED**   At the post office, Jerome mailed a bill that was long overdue.

1. Running at top speed, dirt was kicked up by the horse.

   _____

   _____

2. Swimming to shore, my arms got tired.

   _____

   _____

3. The helmet on the soldier's head with a red circle represented his nationality.

   _____

   _____

4. To answer your phone, the receiver must be lifted.

   _____

   _____

5. Walking up the stairs, the book dropped and tumbled down.

   _____

   _____

6. Twenty-five band members picked their instruments up from chairs that were gleaming and began to play.

   _____

   _____

7. Laughing, the cat chased the girl.

   _____

   _____

8. When skating, skate blades must be kept sharp.

   _____

   _____

9. The ball bounced off the roof that was round and red.

_____

_____

10. Ducking, the snowball hit Andy on the head.

_____

_____

| EXERCISE 15-13 | Correcting Misplaced or Dangling Modifiers |

Directions: Revise each of the following sentences to correct misplaced or dangling modifiers.

EXAMPLE   Deciding which flavor of ice cream to order, another customer cut in front of Roger.

REVISED   While Roger was deciding which flavor of ice cream to order, another customer cut in front of him.

1. Tricia saw an animal at the zoo that had black fur and long claws.

_____

_____

2. Before answering the door, the phone rang.

_____

_____

3. I could see large snowflakes falling from the bedroom window.

_____

_____

4. Honking, Felicia walked in front of the car.

_____

_____

5. After leaving the classroom, the door automatically locked.

_____

_____

6. Applauding and cheering, the band returned for an encore.

_____

_____

7. The waiter brought a birthday cake to our table that had 24 candles.

_____

_____

8. Books lined the library shelves about every imaginable subject.

_____

_____

9. While sobbing, the sad movie ended and the lights came on.

_____

_____

10. Turning the page, the book's binding cracked.

_____

_____

EXERCISE 15-14

WRITING IN PROGRESS

Revising a Paragraph

Directions: Reread the paragraph you wrote for Exercise 15-11. Check for dangling or misplaced modifiers. Revise as needed.

Use Parallelism

■ **GOAL 4**
Use parallelism

Study the following pairs of sentences. Which sentence in each pair reads more smoothly?

PAIR 1
1. Seth, a long-distance biker, enjoys swimming and drag races cars.
2. Seth enjoys long-distance biking, swimming, and drag racing.

PAIR 2
3. The dog was large, had a beautiful coat, and was friendly.
4. The dog was large, beautiful, and friendly.

Do sentences 2 and 4 sound better than 1 and 3? Sentences 2 and 4 have balance. Similar words have similar grammatical form. In sentence 2, _biking, swimming,_ and _drag racing_ are all nouns ending in _-ing._ In sentence 4, _large, beautiful,_ and _friendly_ are all adjectives. The method of balancing similar elements within a sentence is called **parallelism**. Parallelism makes your writing smooth and makes your ideas easier to follow.

EXERCISE 15-15

Examining Parallelism

Directions: In each group of words, circle the element that is not parallel.

EXAMPLE   walking, running, (to jog,) dancing

1. intelligent, successful, responsibly, mature

2. happily, quickly, hurriedly, hungry

3. wrote, answering, worked, typed

4. to fly, parachutes, to skydive, to drive

5. were painting, drew, were carving, were coloring

6. sat in the sun, played cards, scuba diving, ate lobster

7. thoughtful, honestly, humorous, quick-tempered

8. rewrote my résumé, arranging interviews, buying a new suit, getting a haircut

9. buy stamps, cash check, dry cleaning, return library books

10. eating sensibly, eight hours of sleep, exercising, drinking a lot of water

What Should Be Parallel?

When you write, be sure to keep each of the following elements parallel:

- **Nouns in a series**

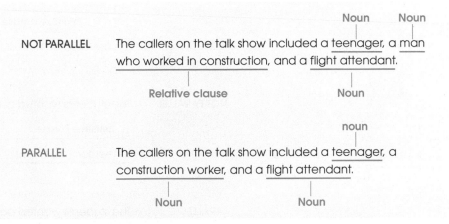

- **Adjectives in a series**

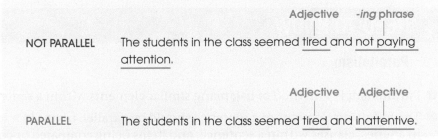

■ **Verbs in a series** (They should have the same tense.)

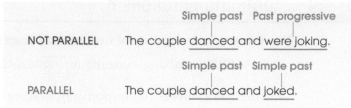

	Simple past	Past progressive
NOT PARALLEL	The couple <u>danced</u> and <u>were joking</u>.	

	Simple past	Simple past
PARALLEL	The couple <u>danced</u> and <u>joked</u>.	

■ **Clauses within sentences**

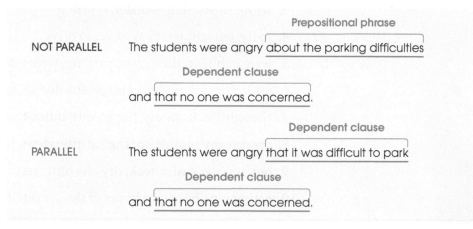

		Prepositional phrase
NOT PARALLEL	The students were angry	about the parking difficulties

Dependent clause
and that no one was concerned.

		Dependent clause
PARALLEL	The students were angry	that it was difficult to park

Dependent clause
and that no one was concerned.

■ **Items being compared or contrasted**

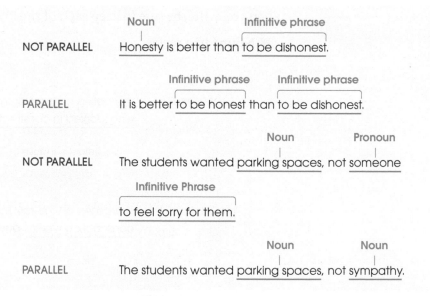

	Noun		Infinitive phrase
NOT PARALLEL	Honesty is better than	to be dishonest.	

	Infinitive phrase	Infinitive phrase
PARALLEL	It is better to be honest than to be dishonest.	

	Noun	Pronoun
NOT PARALLEL	The students wanted parking spaces, not someone	

Infinitive Phrase
to feel sorry for them.

	Noun	Noun
PARALLEL	The students wanted parking spaces, not sympathy.	

! NEED TO KNOW

Parallelism

■ **Parallelism** is a method of balancing similar elements within a sentence.

■ The following elements of a sentence should be parallel: nouns in a series, adjectives in a series, verbs in a series, clauses within a sentence, and items being compared or contrasted.

EXERCISE 15-16   Correcting Parallelism Errors

Directions: Revise each of the following sentences to correct errors in parallel structure.

demanded hard work
EXAMPLE   The instructor ~~was demanding~~ and insisted on high standards.

1. Accuracy is more important than being speedy.

2. The teller counted and recounts the money.

3. Newspapers are blowing away and scattered on the sidewalk.

4. Judith was pleased when she graduated and that she received an honors diploma.

5. Thrilled and exhausting, the runners crossed the finish line.

6. Our guest speakers for the semester are a radiologist, a student of medicine, and a hospital administrator.

7. Students shouted and were hollering at the basketball game.

8. We enjoyed seeing the Grand Canyon, riding a mule, and photography.

9. Laughing and relaxed, the co-workers enjoyed lunch at the Mexican restaurant.

10. Professor Higuera is well known for his humor, clear lecturing, and scholarship.

EXERCISE 15-17   Correcting Parallelism Errors

Directions: Revise each of the following sentences to achieve parallelism.

EXAMPLE   Rosa has decided to study nursing instead of ~~going into~~ accounting.

1. The priest baptized the baby and congratulates the new parents.

2. We ordered a platter of fried clams, a platter of corn on the cob, and fried shrimp.

3. Lucy entered the dance contest, but the dance was watched by June from the side.

4. Léon purchased the ratchet set at the garage sale and buying the drill bits there, too.

5. The exterminator told Brandon the house needed to be fumigated and spraying to eliminate the termites.

6. The bus swerved and hit the dump truck, which swerves and hit the station wagon, which swerved and hit the bicycle.

7. Channel 2 covered the bank robbery, but a python that had escaped from the zoo was reported by Channel 7.

8. Sal was born when Reagan was president, and Clinton was president when Rob was born.

9. The pediatrician spent the morning with sore throats, answering questions about immunizations, and treating bumps and bruises.

10. Belinda prefers to study in the library, but her brother Marcus studies at home.

EXERCISE 15-18　Revising a Paragraph

WRITING IN PROGRESS

Directions: Reread the paragraph you wrote for Exercise 15-11. Correct any sentences that lack parallelism.

EXERCISE 15-19　Revising Sentences

Directions: Now that you have learned about common errors that produce confusing or inconsistent sentences, turn back to the confusing sentences used to introduce the chapter on page 443. Identify each error, and revise the sentences so they convey the intended meaning.

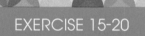

EXERCISE 15-20　Revising a Paragraph

WORKING TOGETHER

Directions: Working with a classmate, revise this student paragraph by correcting all instances of misplaced or dangling modifiers, shifts in verb tense, and faulty parallelism.

> Robert Burns said that the dog is "man's best friend." To a large extent, this statement may be truer than you think. What makes dogs so special to humans is their unending loyalty and that they love unconditionally. Dogs have been known to cross the entire United States to return home. Unlike people, dogs never made fun of you or criticize you. They never throw fits, and they seem happy always to see you. This may not necessarily be true of your family, friends, and those who live near you. A dog never lies to you, never betrays your confidences, and never stayed angry with you for more than five minutes. Best of all, he never expects more than the basics from you of food and shelter and a simple pat on the head in return for his devotion. The world would be a better place if everyone could only be more like their dogs.

EXERCISE 15-21　Revising a Paragraph

Directions: Revise the following paragraph so that all words or phrases in a series, independent clauses joined by a coordinating conjunction, and items being compared are parallel. Write your corrections above the lines.

The first practical pair of roller skates was made in Belgium in 1759 and is designed like ice skates. The skates had two wheels instead of being made with four wheels as they are today. The wheels were aligned down the center of the skate, but were containing no ball bearings. The skates had a life of their own. Without ball bearings, they resisted turning, then were turning abruptly, and then refuse to stop. Finally, they jammed to a halt on their own. Until 1884, when ball bearings were introduced, roller-skating was unpopular, difficult, and it was dangerous for people to do. However, when skating technology improved, roller-skates began to compete with ice-skating. Later, an American made roller skates with sets of wheels placed side-by-side rather than by placing them behind one another, and that design lasted until recently. Since 1980, however, many companies have been manufacturing skates based on the older design. In other words, in-line skates are back, and more and more people are discovering Rollerblading joys and that it benefits their health.

READ AND REVISE

The following excerpt is from a student essay called "High Tide." This excerpt contains confusing and inconsistent sentences that were corrected in a later draft. Read the excerpt and underline pronoun reference errors, shifts in person, misplaced or dangling modifiers, and parallelism errors.

High Tide

The tide rolls in. Two girls, sisters, are stuck in the water, not realizing that the water is rising all around them. The ocean not only is a picture of beauty but a picture of danger and destruction. The girls have two choices of fate: either you will see the ocean's beauty again, or it will be their deathbed.

Visiting their grandparents in Massachusetts, the trip is very exciting and fun for them. The grandparents have a lot planned to stay busy while they are there. The one event that does not have to be scheduled is going out on your grandfather's boat. In fact, it is their favorite part of the entire visit. They feel peaceful on the boat with the wind blowing one's hair, seagulls crying above them, and the sun beams down on the waves. The ocean feels free and inviting.

One sunny day, the ocean beckons the sisters. The day will start out as usual. Their grandma is in the kitchen making sandwiches, their father and grandfather are in the living room talking, and everyone else put on their bathing suits. The girls told her parents they were too excited to wait another minute to rush into the ocean. Little did they know that fate would provide a test of their courage and strength.

SELF-TEST SUMMARY

To test yourself, cover the Answer column with a sheet of paper and answer each question in the left column. Evaluate each of your answers as you work by sliding the paper down and comparing your answer with what is printed in the Answer column.

QUESTION	ANSWER
■ **GOAL 1** Use pronouns clearly and correctly What is a pronoun? How do you use pronouns correctly?	A *pronoun* is a word that substitutes for, or refers to, a noun or another pronoun. To use pronouns correctly, make sure that your pronoun reference is clear to your reader and that the pronoun and antecedent agree in number and in gender.
■ **GOAL 2** Avoid shifts in person, number, and verb tense . What do first, second, and third person refer to?	*First person* refers to the speaker, *second person* to the person spoken to, and *third person* to the person or thing spoken about.
What should you consider when choosing a person for your writing?	When choosing the person, consider whether you desire a personal or formal tone in your writing.
■ **GOAL 3** Avoid misplaced and dangling modifiers What are misplaced and dangling modifiers?	A *misplaced modifier* is placed in such a way that it does not convey the writer's intended meaning. A *dangling modifier* does not clearly describe or explain any part of the sentence it appears in.
What are two ways to revise dangling modifiers?	1. Add a word or words that the modifier clearly describes. 2. Change the dangling modifier to a dependent clause.
■ **GOAL 4** Use parallelism What is parallelism?	Parallelism involves using a similar grammatical form for each element of equal importance in a sentence.
Which elements of a sentence should be parallel?	The following elements of a sentence should be parallel: nouns in a series, adjectives in a series, verbs in a series, clauses within sentences, and items being compared or contrasted.

PART FIVE A Brief Grammar Handbook

Overview

Most of us know how to communicate in our language. When we talk or write, we put our thoughts into words and, by and large, we make ourselves understood. But many of us do not know the specific terms and rules of grammar. Grammar is a system that describes how language is put together. Grammar must be learned, almost as if it is a foreign language.

Why is it important to study grammar, to understand grammatical terms like *verb, participle*, and *gerund* and concepts like *agreement* and *subordination*? There are several good reasons. Knowing grammar will allow you to

- **recognize an error in your writing and correct it.** Your papers will read more smoothly and communicate more effectively when they are error free.

- **understand the comments of your teachers and peers.** People who read and critique your writing may point out a "fragment" or a "dangling modifier." You will be able to revise and correct the problems.

- **write with more impact.** Grammatically correct sentences are signs of clear thinking. Your readers will get your message without distraction or confusion.

As you will see in this part of the text, the different areas of grammatical study are highly interconnected. The sections on parts of speech, sentences, punctuation, mechanics, and spelling fit together into a logical whole. To recognize and correct a run-on sentence, for example, you need to know both sentence structure *and* punctuation. To avoid errors in capitalization, you need to know parts of speech *and* mechanics. If grammar is to do you any good, your knowledge of it must be thorough. As you review the following "basics," be alert to the interconnections that make language study so interesting.

Grammatical terms and rules demand your serious attention. Mastering them will pay handsome dividends: error-free papers, clear thinking, and effective writing.

Understanding the Parts of Speech

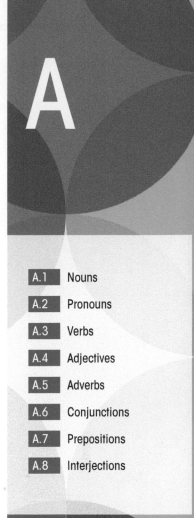

A

The eight parts of speech are **nouns**, **pronouns**, **verbs**, **adjectives**, **adverbs**, **conjunctions**, **prepositions**, and **interjections**. Each word in a sentence functions as one of these parts of speech. Being able to identify the parts of speech in sentences allows you to analyze and improve your writing and to understand grammatical principles discussed later in this section.

It is important to keep in mind that *how* a word functions in a sentence determines *what* part of speech it is. Thus, the same word can be a noun, a verb, or an adjective, depending on how it is used.

> Noun
> He needed some blue <u>wallpaper</u>.

> Verb
> He will <u>wallpaper</u> the hall.

> Adjective
> He went to a <u>wallpaper</u> store.

A.1 Nouns

A **noun** names a person, place, thing, or idea.

People	*woman, winner, Maria Alvarez*
Places	*mall, hill, Indiana*
Things	*lamp, ship, air*
Ideas	*goodness, perfection, harmony*

The form of many nouns changes to express **number** (**singular** for one, **plural** for more than one): *one bird, two birds; one child, five children.* Most nouns can also be made **possessive** to show ownership by the addition of -'s: *city's, Allison's.*

Sometimes a noun is used to modify another noun:

> Noun modifying diploma
> Her goal had always been to earn a <u>college</u> diploma.

Nouns are classified as proper, common, collective, concrete, abstract, count, and noncount.

1. **Proper nouns** name specific people, places, or things and are always capitalized: *Martin Luther King, Jr.; East Lansing; Ford Taurus.* Days of the week and months are considered proper nouns and are capitalized.

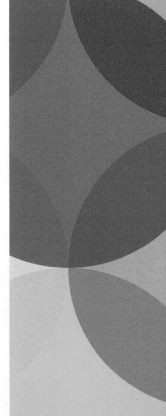

Proper noun   Proper noun   Proper noun

In September, Allen will attend Loyola University.

2. **Common nouns** name one or more of a general class or type of person, place, thing, or idea and are not capitalized: *president, city, car, wisdom*.

Common noun   Common noun   Common noun   Common noun

Next fall, the students will enter college to receive an education.

3. **Collective nouns** name a whole group or collection of people, places, or things: *committee, team, jury*. They are usually singular in form.

Collective noun   Collective noun

The flock of mallards flew over the herd of bison.

4. **Concrete nouns** name tangible things that can be tasted, seen, touched, smelled, or heard: *sandwich, radio, pen*.

Concrete noun   Concrete noun

The frozen pizza was stuck in the freezer.

5. **Abstract nouns** name ideas, qualities, beliefs, and conditions: *honesty, goodness, poverty*.

Abstract nouns   Abstract noun

Their marriage was based on love, honor, and trust.

6. **Count nouns** name items that can be counted. Count nouns can be made plural, usually by adding *-s* or *-es: one river, three rivers; one box, ten boxes*. Some count nouns form their plural in an irregular way: *man, men; goose, geese*.

Count noun   Count noun   Count noun

The salespeople put the invoices in their files.

7. **Noncount nouns** name ideas or qualities that cannot be counted. Noncount nouns almost always have no plural form: *air, knowledge, unhappiness*.

Noncount noun   Noncount noun

As the rain pounded on the windows, she tried to find the courage to walk home from work.

A.2 Pronouns

A **pronoun** is a word that substitutes for or refers to a noun or another pronoun. The noun or pronoun to which a pronoun refers is called the pronoun's **antecedent**. A pronoun must agree with its antecedent in person, number, and gender (these terms are discussed later in this section).

After the campers discovered the cave, they mapped it for the next group, which was arriving next week. [The pronoun *they* refers to its antecedent, *campers*; the pronoun *it* refers to its antecedent, *cave*; the pronoun *which* refers to its antecedent, *group*.]

The eight kinds of pronouns are **personal**, **demonstrative**, **reflexive**, **intensive**, **interrogative**, **relative**, **indefinite**, and **reciprocal**.

1. **Personal pronouns** take the place of nouns or pronouns that name people or things. A personal pronoun changes form to indicate **person, gender, number**, and **case.**

   Person is the grammatical term used to distinguish the speaker (**first person**: *I, we*); the person spoken to (**second person**: *you*); and the person or thing spoken about (**third person**: *he, she, it, they*). **Gender** is the term used to classify pronouns as **masculine** (*he, him*); **feminine** (*she, her*); or **neuter** (*it*). **Number** classifies pronouns as **singular** (one) or **plural** (more than one). Some personal pronouns also function as adjectives modifying nouns (*our house*).

	Singular	*Plural*
First person	I, me, my, mine	we, us, our, ours
Second person	you, your, yours	you, your, yours
Third person		
Masculine	he, him, his	}
Feminine	she, her, hers	they, them, their, theirs
Neuter	it, its	

First-person singular

First-person singular (pronoun/adjective)

Third-person singular

I called my manager about my new clients. She wanted to know as soon as they placed their first orders. "Your new clients are important to us," she said.

Third-person plural

Third-person plural (pronoun/adjective)

Second-person singular (pronoun/adjective)

First-person plural

Third-person singular

A pronoun's **case** is determined by its function as a subject (**subjective** or **nominative case**) or an object (**objective case**) in a sentence. A pronoun that shows ownership is in the **possessive case**. (See p. 509 for a discussion of pronoun case.)

2. **Demonstrative pronouns** refer to particular people or things. The demonstrative pronouns are *this* and *that* (singular) and *these* and *those* (plural). (*This, that, these,* and *those* can also be demonstrative adjectives when they modify a noun.)

   This is more thorough than that.

   The red shuttle buses stop here. These go to the airport every hour.

Tip for Writers

This, that, these, and *those* all refer to a thing, a person things, or people within the speaker's sight, but *that* and *those* refer to things farther away. *This* and *these* refer to what is close to the speaker or writer.

Distance	Singular	Plural
near	this	these
far	that	those

3. **Reflexive pronouns** indicate that the subject performs actions to, for, or upon itself. Reflexive pronouns end in *-self* or *-selves*.

	Singular	*Plural*
First person	myself	ourselves
Second person	yourself	yourselves
Third person	himself herself itself	themselves

We excused <u>ourselves</u> from the table and left.

4. An **intensive pronoun** emphasizes the word that comes before it in a sentence. Like reflexive pronouns, intensive pronouns end in *-self* or *-selves*.

The filmmaker <u>herself</u> could not explain the ending.

They <u>themselves</u> repaired the copy machine.

Note: A reflexive or intensive pronoun should not be used as a subject of a sentence. An antecedent for the reflexive pronoun must appear in the same sentence.

INCORRECT	<u>Myself</u> create colorful sculpture.
CORRECT	I <u>myself</u> create colorful sculpture.

5. **Interrogative pronouns** are used to introduce questions: *who, whom, whoever, whomever, what, which, whose.* The correct use of *who* and *whom* depends on the role the interrogative pronoun plays in a sentence or clause. When the pronoun functions as the subject of the sentence or clause, use *who.* When the pronoun functions as an object in the sentence or clause, use *whom* (see p. 493).

<u>What</u> happened?

<u>Which</u> is your street?

<u>Who</u> wrote *Ragtime*? [*Who* is the subject of the sentence.]

<u>Whom</u> should I notify? [*Whom* is the object of the verb *notify: I should notify whom?*]

6. **Relative pronouns** relate groups of words to nouns or other pronouns and often introduce adjective clauses or noun clauses (see p. 502). The relative pronouns are *who, whom, whoever, whomever,* and *whose* (referring to people) and *that, what, whatever,* and *which* (referring to things).

In 1836, Charles Dickens met John Forster, <u>who</u> became his friend and biographer.

Jason did not understand <u>what</u> the consultant recommended.

We read some articles <u>that</u> were written by former astronauts.

7. **Indefinite pronouns** are pronouns without specific antecedents. They refer to people, places, or things in general.

<u>Someone</u> has been rearranging my papers.

<u>Many</u> knew the woman, but <u>few</u> could say they knew her well.

Here are some frequently used <u>indefinite pronouns:</u>

SINGULAR		PLURAL
another	nobody	all
anybody	none	both
anyone	no one	few
anything	nothing	many
each	one	more
either	other	most
everybody	somebody	others
everyone	someone	several
everything	something	some
neither		

Tip for Writers

Be sure to use a *singular verb* after the *indefinite pronouns* that are grammatically singular: <u>Everybody</u> <u>is</u> here now. Let's eat! (Even though *everybody* means at least three people, it's grammatically singular.)

8. The **reciprocal pronouns** *each other* and *one another* indicate a mutual relationship between two or more parts of a plural antecedent.

> Armando and Sharon congratulated <u>each other</u> on their high grades.

EXERCISE 1

Identifying Nouns and Pronouns

Directions: In each of the following sentences, (a) circle each noun and (b) underline each pronoun.

> **EXAMPLE** (Jamila) parked <u>her</u> (car) in the (lot) that is reserved for (commuters) like her.

1. Shakespeare wrote many plays that have become famous and important.

2. Everyone who has visited Disneyland wishes to return.

3. Jonathan himself wrote the report that the president of the company presented to the press.

4. That desk used to belong to my boss.

5. My integrity was never questioned by my co-workers.

6. The class always laughed at jokes told by the professor, even though they were usually corny.

7. When will humankind be able to travel to Mars?

8. Whoever wins the lottery this week will become quite wealthy.

9. As the plane landed at the airport, many of the passengers began to gather their carry-on luggage.

10. This week we are studying gravity; next week we will study heat.

A.3 Verbs

Verbs express action or state of being. A grammatically complete sentence has at least one verb in it.

There are three kinds of verbs: **action verbs**, **linking verbs**, and **helping verbs** (also known as **auxiliary verbs**).

1. **Action verbs** express physical and mental activities.

> Mr. Royce <u>dashed</u> for the bus.
>
> The incinerator <u>burns</u> garbage at high temperatures.
>
> I <u>think</u> that seat is taken.
>
> The Web designer <u>worked</u> until 3:00 A.M.

Action verbs are either **transitive** or **intransitive**. The action of a **transitive verb** is directed toward someone or something, called the <u>**direct object**</u> of the verb. Direct objects receive the action of the verb. Transitive verbs require direct objects to complete the meaning of the sentence.

> Transitive Direct
> Subject verb   object
>
> Amalia <u>made</u> clocks.

Tip for Writers

A *direct object* answers the question *Who?* or *What?* about the verb.

An **intransitive verb** does not need a direct object to complete the meaning of the sentence.

> Intransitive
> Subject   verb
>
> The traffic <u>stopped</u>.

Some verbs can be both transitive and intransitive, depending on their meaning and use in a sentence.

> INTRANSITIVE   The traffic <u>stopped</u>. [No direct object.]
>
>   Direct object
>
> TRANSITIVE   The driver <u>stopped</u> the <u>bus</u> at the corner.

2. A <u>**linking verb**</u> expresses a state of being or a condition. A linking verb connects a noun or pronoun to words that describe the noun or pronoun. Common linking verbs are forms of the verb *be* (*is, are, was, were, being, been*), *become, feel, grow, look, remain, seem, smell, sound, stay,* and *taste.*

> Their child <u>grew</u> tall.
>
> The office <u>looks</u> messy.
>
> Mr. Davenport <u>is</u> our accountant.

Tip for Writers

Be sure to use an adjective, not an adverb, after a *linking verb*. Use adverbs to describe other verbs: He <u>seems nice</u>. (but) He <u>paints nicely</u>.

3. A **helping (auxiliary) verb** helps another verb, called the **main verb**, to convey when the action occurred (through verb tense) and to form questions. One or more helping verbs and the main verb together form a **verb phrase**. Some helping verbs, called **modals**, are always helping verbs:

can, could	shall, should
may, might	will, would
must, ought to	

The other helping verbs can sometimes function as main verbs as well:

am, are, be, been, being, did, do, does

had, has, have

is, was, were

The verb *be* is a very irregular verb, with eight forms instead of the usual five: *am, are, be, being, been, is, was, were.*

Helping Main
verb verb

The store will close early on holidays.

Helping   Main
verb   verb

Will the store close early on New Year's Eve?

Forms of the Verb

All verbs except *be* have five forms: the **base form** (or dictionary form), the **past tense**, the **past participle**, the **present participle**, and the **-s form**. The first three forms are called the verb's **principal parts**. The infinitive consists of "to" plus a base form: *to go, to study, to talk*. For **regular verbs**, the past tense and past participle are formed by adding *-d* or *-ed* to the base form. **Irregular verbs** follow no set pattern to form their past tense and past participle.

	Regular	*Irregular*
Infinitive	work	eat
Past tense	worked	ate
Past participle	worked	eaten
Present participle	working	eating
-s form	works	eats

Verbs change form to agree with their subjects in person and number (see p. 406); to express the time of their action (**tense**); to express whether the action is a fact, command, or wish (**mood**); and to indicate whether the subject is the doer or the receiver of the action (**voice**).

Principal Parts of Irregular Verbs

Consult the following list and your dictionary for the principal parts of irregular verbs.

BASE FORM	PAST TENSE	PAST PARTICIPLE
be	was	been
become	became	become
begin	began	begun

(continued)

A. Parts of Speech

BASE FORM	PAST TENSE	PAST PARTICIPLE
bite	bit	bitten
blow	blew	blown
burst	burst	burst
catch	caught	caught
choose	chose	chosen
come	came	come
dive	dived, dove	dived
do	did	done
draw	drew	drawn
drive	drove	driven
eat	ate	eaten
fall	fell	fallen
find	found	found
fling	flung	flung
fly	flew	flown
get	got	gotten
give	gave	given
go	went	gone
grow	grew	grown
have	had	had
know	knew	known
lay	laid	laid
lead	led	led
leave	left	left
lie	lay	lain
lose	lost	lost
ride	rode	ridden
ring	rang	rung
rise	rose	risen
say	said	said
set	set	set
sit	sat	sat
speak	spoke	spoken
swear	swore	sworn
swim	swam	swum
tear	tore	torn
tell	told	told
throw	threw	thrown
wear	wore	worn
write	wrote	written

Tense

The **tenses** of a verb express time. They convey whether an action, process, or event takes place in the present, past, or future.

The three **simple tenses** are **present**, **past**, and **future**. The **simple present** tense is the base form of the verb (and the *-s* form of third-person singular subjects; see p. 507); the **simple past** tense is the past-tense form; and the **simple future** tense consists of the helping verb *will* plus the base form.

The **perfect tenses**, which indicate completed action, are **present perfect**, **past perfect**, and **future perfect**. They are formed by adding the helping verbs *have* (or *has*), *had*, and *will have* to the past participle.

In addition to the simple and perfect tenses, there are six progressive tenses. The **simple progressive tenses** are the **present progressive**, the **past progressive**, and the **future progressive**. The progressive tenses are used for continuing actions or actions in progress. These progressive tenses are formed by adding the present, past, and future forms of the verb *be* to the present participle. The **perfect progressive tenses** are the **present perfect progressive**, the **past perfect progressive**, and the **future perfect progressive**. They are formed by adding the present perfect, past perfect, and future perfect forms of the verb *be* to the present participle.

The following chart shows all the tenses for a regular verb and an irregular verb in the first person. (For more on tenses, see p. 504.)

TENSE	REGULAR	IRREGULAR
Simple present	I talk	I go
Simple past	I talked	I went
Simple future	I will talk	I will go
Present perfect	I have talked	I have gone
Past perfect	I had talked	I had gone
Future perfect	I will have talked	I will have gone
Present progressive	I am talking	I am going
Past progressive	I was talking	I was going
Future progressive	I will be talking	I will be going
Present perfect progressive	I have been talking	I have been going
Past perfect progressive	I had been talking	I had been going
Future perfect progressive	I will have been talking	I will have been going

Mood

The **mood** of a verb indicates the writer's attitude toward the action. There are three moods in English: **indicative**, **imperative**, and **subjunctive**.

1. The **indicative mood** is used for ordinary statements of fact or questions.

> The light <u>flashed</u> on and off all night.
>
> <u>Did</u> you <u>check</u> the batteries?

2. The **imperative mood** is used for commands, suggestions, or directions. The subject of a verb in the imperative mood is *you*, though it is not always included.

> <u>Stop</u> shouting!
>
> <u>Come</u> to New York for a visit.
>
> <u>Turn</u> right at the next corner.

3. The **subjunctive mood** is used for wishes, requirements, recommendations, and statements contrary to fact. For statements contrary to fact or for wishes, the past tense of the verb is used. For the verb *be*, only the past-tense form *were* is used.

> If I <u>had</u> a million dollars, I'd take a trip around the world.
>
> If my supervisor <u>were</u> promoted, I would be eligible for her job.

To express suggestions, recommendations, or requirements, the infinitive form is used for all verbs.

> I recommend that the houses <u>be</u> sold after the landscaping is done.
>
> The registrar required that Maureen <u>pay</u> her bill before attending class.

Voice

Transitive verbs (those that take objects) may be in either the active voice or the passive voice (see p. 415). In an **active-voice** sentence, the subject performs the action described by the verb; that is, the subject is the actor. In a **passive-voice** sentence, the subject is the receiver of the action. The passive voice of a verb is formed by using an appropriate form of the helping verb *be* and the past participle of the main verb.

> Subject   Active
> is actor   voice
>
> Dr. Hillel <u>delivered</u> the report on global warming.
>
> Subject is receiver   Passive voice
>
> The report on global warming <u>was delivered</u> by Dr. Hillel.

EXERCISE 2   Changing Tenses

Directions: Revise the following sentences, changing each verb from the present tense to the tense indicated.

EXAMPLE	I <u>know</u> the right answer.
PAST TENSE	I knew the right answer.

1. Allison <u>loses</u> the sales to competitors.

SIMPLE PAST _____

2. Malcolm <u>begins</u> classes at the community college.

PAST PERFECT _____

3. The microscope <u>enlarges</u> the cell.

PRESENT PERFECT _____

4. Reports <u>follow</u> a standard format.

SIMPLE FUTURE _____

5. Meg Ryan <u>receives</u> excellent evaluations.

FUTURE PERFECT _____

6. Juanita <u>writes</u> a computer program.

PRESENT PERFECT _____

7. The movie <u>stars</u> Brad Pitt.

SIMPLE FUTURE _____

8. Dave <u>wins</u> medals at the Special Olympics.

SIMPLE PAST _____

9. Many celebrities <u>donate</u> money to AIDS research.

PRESENT PERFECT _____

10. My nephew <u>travels</u> to Michigan's Upper Peninsula on business.

PAST PERFECT _____

A.4 Adjectives

Adjectives modify nouns and pronouns. That is, they describe, identify, qualify, or limit the meaning of nouns and pronouns. An adjective answers the question *Which one? What kind?* or *How many?* about the word it modifies.

WHICH ONE?	The <u>twisted</u>, <u>torn</u> umbrella was of no use to its owner.
WHAT KIND?	The <u>spotted</u> owl has caused heated arguments in the Northwest.
HOW MANY?	<u>Many</u> customers waited for <u>four</u> days for cable service to be restored.

In form, adjectives can be **positive** (implying no comparison), **comparative** (comparing two items), or **superlative** (comparing three or more items). (See p. 511 for more on the forms of adjectives.)

Positive

The computer is <u>fast</u>.

Comparative

Your computer is <u>faster</u> than mine.

Superlative

This is the <u>fastest</u> computer I have ever used.

A. Parts of Speech

There are two general categories of adjectives. **Descriptive adjectives** name a quality of the person, place, thing, or idea they describe: *mysterious man, green pond, healthy complexion*. **Limiting adjectives** narrow the scope of the person, place, or thing they describe: *my computer, this tool, second try*.

Descriptive Adjectives

A **regular** (or **attributive**) adjective appears next to (usually before) the word it modifies. Several adjectives can modify the same word.

> The enthusiastic new hair stylist gave short, lopsided haircuts.
>
> The wealthy dealer bought an immense blue vase.

Sometimes nouns function as adjectives modifying other nouns:

> *tree house, hamburger bun*

A **predicate adjective** follows a linking verb and modifies or describes the subject of the sentence or clause (see p. 501 on clauses).

> Predicate adjective
>
> The meeting was long. [Modifies the subject, *meeting*]

Limiting Adjectives

1. The **definite article**, *the*, and the **indefinite articles**, *a* and *an*, are classified as adjectives. *A* and *an* are used when it is not important to specify a particular noun or when the object named is not known to the reader (*A radish adds color to a salad*). *The* is used when it is important to specify one or more of a particular noun or when the object named is known to the reader or has already been mentioned (*The radishes from the garden are on the table*).

   > A squirrel visited the feeder that I just built. The squirrel tried to eat some bird food.

2. When the possessive pronouns *my, your, his, her, its, our*, and *their* are used as modifiers before nouns, they are considered **possessive adjectives** (see p. 510).

   > Your friend borrowed my laptop for his trip.

3. When the demonstrative pronouns *this, that, these*, and *those* are used as modifiers before nouns, they are called **demonstrative adjectives** (see p. 471). *This* and *these* modify nouns close to the writer; *that* and *those* modify nouns more distant from the writer.

   > Buy these hot pink shoes, not those ugly black ones.
   >
   > This freshman course is a prerequisite for those advanced courses.

4. **Cardinal adjectives** are words used in counting: *one, two, twenty*, and so on.

   > I read four biographies of Jack Kerouac and seven articles about his work.

5. **Ordinal adjectives** note position in a series.

> The <u>first</u> biography was too sketchy, whereas the <u>second</u> one was too detailed.

6. **Indefinite adjectives** provide nonspecific, general information about the quantities and amounts of the nouns they modify. Some common indefinite adjectives are *another, any, enough, few, less, little, many, more, much, several,* and *some.*

> <u>Several</u> people asked me if I had <u>enough</u> blankets or if I wanted the thermostat turned up a <u>few</u> degrees.

7. The **interrogative adjectives** *what, which,* and *whose* modify nouns and pronouns used in questions.

> <u>Which</u> television station do you like? <u>Whose</u> local news do you prefer?

8. The words *which* and *what,* along with *whichever* and *whatever,* are **relative adjectives** when they modify nouns and introduce subordinate clauses.

> She couldn't decide <u>which</u> job she wanted to take.

9. **Proper adjectives** are adjectives derived from proper nouns: *Spain* (noun), *Spanish* (adjective); *Freud* (noun), *Freudian* (adjective); see page 469. Most proper adjectives are capitalized.

> Shakespeare lived in <u>Elizabethan</u> England.
> The speaker used many <u>French</u> expressions.

EXERCISE 3   Adding Adjectives

Directions: Revise each of the following sentences by adding at least three adjectives.

| **EXAMPLE** | The cat slept on the pillow. |
| **REVISED** | The old yellow cat slept on the expensive pillow. |

1. Before leaving on a trip, the couple packed their suitcases.

_____

_____

2. The tree dropped leaves all over the lawn.

_____

_____

3. While riding the train, the passengers read newspapers.

_____

_____

4. The antiques dealer said that the desk was more valuable than the chair.

_____

_____

5. As the play was ending, the audience clapped their hands and tossed roses onstage.

_____

_____

6. Stew is served nightly at the shelter.

_____

_____

7. The engine roared as the car stubbornly jerked into gear.

_____

_____

8. The tourists tossed pennies into the fountain.

_____

_____

9. Folders were stacked on the desk next to the monitor.

_____

_____

10. Marina's belt and shoes were made of the same material and complemented her dress.

_____

_____

A.5 Adverbs

Adverbs modify verbs, adjectives, other adverbs, or entire sentences or clauses (see p. 501 on clauses). Like adjectives, adverbs describe, qualify, or limit the meaning of the words they modify.

An adverb answers the question *How? When? Where? How often?* or *To what extent?* about the word it modifies.

HOW?	Lian moved <u>awkwardly</u> because of her stiff neck.
WHEN?	I arrived <u>yesterday</u>.
WHERE?	They searched <u>everywhere</u>.
HOW OFTEN?	He telephoned <u>repeatedly</u>.
TO WHAT EXTENT?	Simon was <u>rather</u> slow to answer his e-mail.

Many adverbs end in *-ly* (*lazily, happily*), but some adverbs do not (*fast, here, much, well, rather, everywhere, never, so*), and some words that end in *-ly* are not adverbs (*lively, friendly, lonely*). Like all other parts of speech, an adverb may be best identified by examining its function within a sentence.

> I quickly skimmed the book. [Modifies the verb *skimmed*]
>
> Very angry customers crowded the service desk. [Modifies the adjective *angry*]
>
> He was injured quite seriously. [Modifies the adverb *seriously*]
>
> Apparently, the job was bungled. [Modifies the whole sentence]

Like adjectives, adverbs have three forms: **positive** (does not suggest any comparison), **comparative** (compares two actions or conditions), and **superlative** (compares three or more actions or conditions; see also p. 512).

> Positive   Positive
> Julian rose early and crept downstairs quietly.
>
> Comparative   Comparative
> Isaiah rose earlier than Julian and crept downstairs more quietly.
>
> Superlative   Superlative
> Cody rose earliest of anyone in the house and crept downstairs most quietly.

Some adverbs, called **conjunctive adverbs** (or **adverbial conjunctions**)—such as *however, therefore*, and *besides*—connect the ideas of one sentence or clause to those of a previous sentence or clause. They can appear anywhere in a sentence. (See p. 527 for how to punctuate sentences containing conjunctive adverbs.)

> Conjunctive adverb
> James did not want to go to the library on Saturday; however, he knew the books were overdue.
>
> Conjunctive adverb
> The sporting goods store was crowded because of the sale. Leila, therefore, was asked to work extra hours.

Some common conjunctive adverbs are listed below, including several phrases that function as conjunctive adverbs.

COMMON CONJUNCTIVE ADVERBS			
accordingly	for example	meanwhile	otherwise
also	further	moreover	similarly
anyway	furthermore	namely	still
as a result	hence	nevertheless	then
at the same time	however	next	thereafter
besides	incidentally	nonetheless	therefore
certainly	indeed	now	thus
consequently	instead	on the contrary	undoubtedly
finally	likewise	on the other hand	

EXERCISE 4 | Using Adverbs

Directions: Write a sentence using each of the following comparative or superlative adverbs.

EXAMPLE better: My car runs better now than even before.

1. farther: _____

_____

2. most: _____

_____

3. more: _____

_____

4. best: _____

_____

5. least neatly: _____

_____

6. louder: _____

_____

7. worse: _____

_____

8. less angrily: _____

_____

9. later: _____

_____

10. earliest: _____

_____

A.6 Conjunctions

Conjunctions connect words, phrases, and clauses. There are three kinds of conjunctions: **coordinating**, **correlative**, and **subordinating**. **Coordinating** and **correlative conjunctions** connect words, phrases, or clauses of equal grammatical rank. (A **phrase** is a group of related words lacking a subject, a predicate, or both. A **clause** is a group of words containing a subject and a predicate; see p. 490 and 491.)

1. The **coordinating conjunctions** are *and, but, nor, or, for, so,* and *yet.* These words must connect words or word groups of the same kind. Therefore, two

nouns may be connected by *and*, but a noun and a clause cannot be. *For* and *so* can connect only independent clauses.

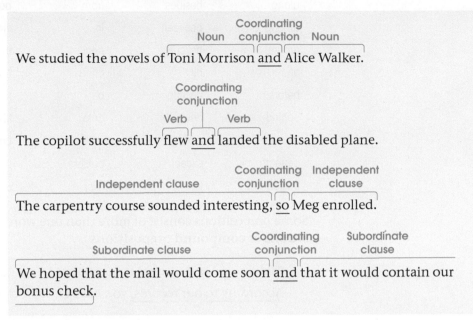

Coordinating
Noun   conjunction   Noun

We studied the novels of Toni Morrison and Alice Walker.

Coordinating
conjunction
Verb   Verb

The copilot successfully flew and landed the disabled plane.

Coordinating   Independent
Independent clause   conjunction   clause

The carpentry course sounded interesting, so Meg enrolled.

Coordinating   Subordinate
Subordinate clause   conjunction   clause

We hoped that the mail would come soon and that it would contain our bonus check.

2. **Correlative conjunctions** are pairs of words that link and relate grammatically equivalent parts of a sentence. Some common correlative conjunctions are *either/or, neither/nor, both/and, not/but, not only/but also*, and *whether/or*. Correlative conjunctions are always used in pairs.

Correlative conjunctions
Either the electricity was off, or the bulb had burned out.

3. **Subordinating conjunctions** connect dependent, or subordinate, clauses to independent clauses (see p. 501). Some common subordinating conjunctions are *although, because, if, since, until, when, where*, and *while*.

Subordinating conjunction
Although the movie got bad reviews, it drew big crowds.

Subordinating conjunction
She received a lot of mail because she was a reliable correspondent.

A.7 Prepositions

A **preposition** links and relates its **object** (a noun or a pronoun) to the rest of the sentence. Prepositions often show relationships of time, place, direction, and manner.

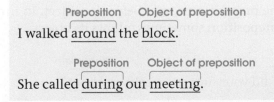

Preposition   Object of preposition
I walked around the block.

Preposition   Object of preposition
She called during our meeting.

COMMON PREPOSITIONS

along	besides	from	past	up
among	between	in	since	upon
around	beyond	near	through	with
at	by	off	till	within
before	despite	on	to	without
behind	down	onto	toward	
below	during	out	under	
beneath	except	outside	underneath	
beside	for	over	until	

Some prepositions consist of more than one word; they are called **phrasal prepositions** or **compound prepositions**.

> Phrasal preposition   Object of preposition
> <u>According to</u> our <u>records</u>, you have enough credits to graduate.

> Phrasal preposition   Object of preposition
> We decided to make the trip <u>in spite of</u> the <u>snowstorm</u>.

COMMON COMPOUND PREPOSITIONS

according to	in addition to	on account of
aside from	in front of	out of
as of	in place of	prior to
as well as	in regard to	with regard to
because of	in spite of	with respect to
by means of	instead of	

The object of the preposition often has modifiers.

> Prep.   Modifier   Obj. of prep.   Prep.   Modifier   Obj. of prep
> Not a sound came <u>from</u> the <u>child's room</u> <u>except</u> a <u>gentle snoring</u>.

Sometimes a preposition has more than one object (a **compound object**).

> Preposition   Compound object of preposition
> The laundromat was <u>between</u> <u>campus</u> and <u>home</u>.

Usually the preposition comes before its object. In interrogative sentences, however, the preposition sometimes follows its object.

> Object of preposition   Preposition
> <u>What</u> did your supervisor ask you <u>about</u>?

The preposition, the object or objects of the preposition, and the object's modifiers all form a **prepositional phrase**.

Tip for Writers

Throughout means "all through." *Alongside* means "next to."

Prepositional phrase

The scientist conducted her experiment throughout the afternoon and early evening.

There may be many prepositional phrases in a sentence.

Prepositional phrase   Prepositional phrase

The water from the open hydrant flowed into the street.

The noisy kennel was underneath the beauty salon, despite the complaints of customers.

Alongside the weedy railroad tracks, an old hotel with faded grandeur stood near the abandoned brick station on the edge of town.

Prepositional phrases frequently function as adjectives or adverbs. If a prepositional phrase modifies a noun or pronoun, it functions as an adjective. If it modifies a verb, adjective, or adverb, it functions as an adverb.

The auditorium inside the conference center has a special sound system. [Adjective modifying the noun *auditorium*]

The doctor looked cheerfully at the patient and handed the lab results across the desk. [Adverbs modifying the verbs *looked* and *handed*]

EXERCISE 5   Expanding Sentences Using Prepositional Phrases

Directions: Expand each of the following sentences by adding a prepositional phrase in the blank.

    EXAMPLE   A cat hid under the car when the garage door opened.

1. Fish nibbled _____ as the fisherman waited.

2. The librarian explained that the books about Africa are located _____.

3. When the bullet hit the window, shards flew _____.

4. _____, there is a restaurant that serves alligator meat.

5. Polar bears are able to swim _____.

6. Heavy winds blowing _____ caused the waves to hit the house.

7. One student completed her exam _____.

8. A frog jumped _____.

9. The bus was parked _____.

10. Stacks of books were piled _____.

A.8 Interjections

Interjections are words that express emotion or surprise. They are followed by an exclamation point, comma, or period, depending on whether they stand alone or serve as part or all of a sentence. Interjections are used in speech more than in writing.

<u>Wow</u>! What an announcement!

<u>So</u>, was that lost letter ever found?

<u>Well</u>, I'd better be going.

Understanding the Parts of Sentences

A **sentence** is a group of words that must expresses a complete thought about something or someone. A sentence contain a **subject** and a **predicate**.

Subject	*Predicate*
Telephones	ring.
Cecilia	laughed.
Time	will tell.

Depending on their purpose and punctuation, sentences are **declarative**, **interrogative**, **exclamatory**, or **imperative**.

1. A **declarative sentence** makes a statement. It ends with a period.

   Subject Predicate
   The snow fell steadily.

2. An **interrogative sentence** asks a question. It ends with a question mark (?).

   Subject Predicate
   Who called?

3. An **exclamatory sentence** conveys strong emotion. It ends with an exclamation point (!).

   Subject Predicate
   Your photograph is in the company newsletter!

4. An **imperative sentence** gives an order or makes a request. It ends with either a period or an exclamation point, depending on how mild or strong the command or request is. In an imperative sentence, the subject is *you*, but this often is not included.

   Predicate
   Get me a fire extinguisher now! [The subject *you* is understood: (*You*) get me a fire extinguisher now!]

B.1 Subjects

The **subject** of a sentence is whom or what the sentence is about. It is who or what performs or receives the action expressed in the predicate.

1. The subject is often a **noun**, a word that names a person, place, thing, or idea.

   <u>Adriana</u> worked on her math homework.

   The rose <u>bushes</u> must be watered.

   <u>Honesty</u> is the best policy.

2. The subject of a sentence can also be a **pronoun**, a word that refers to or substitutes for a noun.

   <u>She</u> revised the memo three times.

   <u>I</u> will attend the sales meeting.

   Although the ketchup spilled, <u>it</u> did not go on my shirt.

3. The subject of a sentence can also be a group of words used as a noun.

   <u>Reading e-mail from friends</u> is my idea of a good time.

Simple Versus Complete Subjects

1. The <u>simple subject</u> is the noun or pronoun that names what the sentence is about. It does not include any **modifiers**—that is, words that describe, identify, qualify, or limit the meaning of the noun or pronoun.

   Simple subject

   The bright red concert <u>poster</u> caught everyone's eye.

   Simple subject

   High-speed <u>computers</u> have revolutionized the banking industry.

   When the subject of a sentence is a proper noun (the name of a particular person, place, or thing), the entire name is considered the simple subject.

   Simple subject

   <u>Martin Luther King, Jr.,</u> was a famous leader.

   The simple subject of an imperative sentence is *you*.

   Simple subject

   [You] Remember to bring the sales brochures.

2. The **complete subject** is the simple subject plus its modifiers.

   Complete subject

   Simple subject

   <u>The sleek, black limousine</u> waited outside the church.

   Complete subject

   <u>Fondly remembered as a gifted songwriter, fiddle player, and storyteller, Quintin Lotus Dickey</u> lived in a cabin in Paoli, Indiana.

   Simple subject

Tip for Writers

The simple subject is *reading*, a gerund, a noun made from a verb. It takes a singular verb, in this case, *is*.

Compound Subjects

Some sentences contain two or more subjects joined with a coordinating conjunction (*and, but, nor, or, for, so, yet*). Those subjects together form a **compound subject**.

> Compound subject
>
> Maria and I completed the marathon.

> Compound subject
>
> The computer, the printer, and the cable box were not usable during the blackout.

B.2 Predicates

The **predicate** indicates what the subject does, what happened to the subject, or what is being said about the subject. The predicate must include a **verb**, a word or group of words that expresses an action or a state of being (for example, *run, invent, build, know, will decide, become*).

> Joy swam 60 laps.
>
> The thunderstorm replenished the reservoir.

Sometimes the verb consists of only one word, as in the previous examples. Often, however, the main verb is accompanied by a **helping verb** (see p. 474).

> Helping   Main
> verb   verb
>
> By the end of the week, I will have worked twenty-five hours.

> Helping Main
> verb   verb
>
> The training session had begun.

> Helping Main
> verb   verb
>
> The professor did return the journal assignments.

Tip for Writers

Did return is an emphatic past form. This form is often used (instead of the usual past, *returned*) when someone has made a mistake:

Alex said, "The professor didn't return our last essays."

Vera replied, "He did return them. He handed them back the day you were absent."

Simple Versus Complete Predicates

The **simple predicate** is the main verb plus its helping verbs (together known as the **verb phrase**). The simple predicate does not include any modifiers.

> Simple predicate
>
> The proctor hastily collected the blue books.

> Simple predicate
>
> The moderator had introduced the next speaker.

The **complete predicate** consists of the simple predicate, its modifiers, and any complements (words that complete the meaning of the verb; see p. 493). In general, the complete predicate includes everything in the sentence except the complete subject.

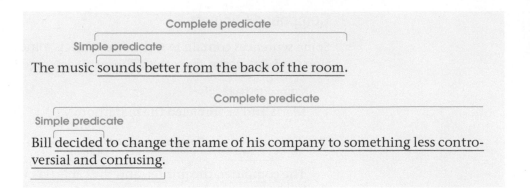

Compound Predicates

Some sentences have two or more predicates joined by a coordinating conjunction (*and, but, or,* or *nor*). These predicates together form a **compound predicate**.

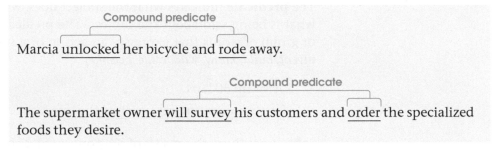

EXERCISE 6

Identifying Single Subjects and Simple and Compound Predicates

Directions: Underline the simple subject(s) and circle the simple or compound predicate(s) in each of the following sentences.

> **EXAMPLE** Pamela Wong ⟨photographed⟩ a hummingbird.

1. A group of nurses walked across the lobby on their way to a staff meeting.

2. The campground for physically challenged children is funded and supported by the Rotary Club.

3. Forty doctors and lawyers had attended the seminar on malpractice insurance.

4. Sullivan Beach will not reopen because of pollution.

5. The police cadets attended classes all day and studied late into each evening.

6. Greenpeace is an environmental organization.

7. Talented dancers and experienced musicians performed and received much applause at the open-air show.

8. Some undergraduate students have been using empty classrooms for group study.

9. A police officer, with the shoplifter in handcuffs, entered the police station.

10. The newly elected senator walked up to the podium and began her first speech to her constituents.

B.3 Complements

A **complement** is a word or group of words used to complete the meaning of a subject or object. There are four kinds of complements: **subject complements**, which follow linking verbs; **direct objects** and **indirect objects**, which follow transitive verbs (verbs that take an object); and **object complements**, which follow direct objects.

Linking Verbs and Subject Complements

A linking verb (such as *be, become, seem, feel, taste*) links the subject to a **subject complement**, a noun or adjective that renames or describes the subject. (See p. 474 for more about linking verbs.) Nouns that function as complements are called **predicate nominatives** or **predicate nouns**. Adjectives that function as complements are called **predicate adjectives**.

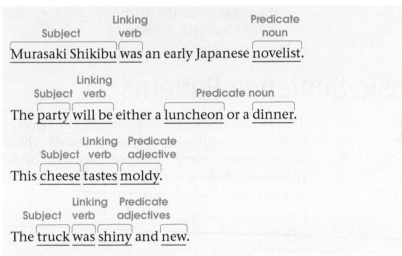

Murasaki Shikibu [Subject] was [Linking verb] an early Japanese novelist [Predicate noun].

The party [Subject] will be [Linking verb] either a luncheon [Predicate noun] or a dinner [Predicate noun].

This cheese [Subject] tastes [Linking verb] moldy [Predicate adjective].

The truck [Subject] was [Linking verb] shiny [Predicate adjectives] and new.

Direct Objects

A **direct object** is a noun or pronoun that receives the action of a transitive verb (see p. 474). A direct object answers the question *What?* or *Whom?*

The pharmacist helped [Transitive verb] us [Direct object]. [The pharmacist helped *whom?*]

Jillian borrowed [Transitive verb] a bicycle and a visor [Direct objects]. [Jillian borrowed *what?*]

Indirect Objects

An **indirect object** is a noun or pronoun that receives the action of the verb indirectly. Indirect objects name the person or thing *to whom* or *for whom* something is done.

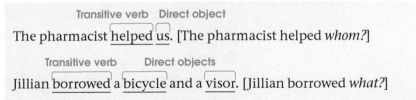

The computer technician gave [Transitive verb] me [Indirect object] the bill [Direct object]. [He gave the bill *to whom?*]

Tip for Writers

In sentences that tell both *whom* and *what* after the verb, follow the word order shown here:

Amir gave his sister a gift. (Do not use *to*.)

Amir gave a gift to his sister. (Use *to*.)

If you mention the person before the thing, don't use *to*.

Transitive verb	Indirect objects		Direct objects	

Eric bought his wife and son some sandwiches and milk. [He bought food *for whom?*]

Object Complements

An **object complement** is a noun or adjective that modifies (describes) or renames the direct object. Object complements appear with verbs like *name, find, think, elect, appoint, choose,* and *consider.*

	Direct object		Noun as object complement

We appointed Dean our representative. [*Representative* renames the direct object, *Dean.*]

		Direct object	Adjective as object complement

The judge found the defendant innocent of the charges. [*Innocent* modifies the direct object, *defendant.*]

B.4 Basic Sentence Patterns

There are five basic sentence patterns in English. They are built with combinations of subjects, predicates, and complements. The order of these elements within a sentence may change, or a sentence may become long and complicated when modifiers, phrases, or clauses are added. Nonetheless, one of five basic patterns stands at the heart of every sentence.

PATTERN 1

Subject	+	*Predicate*
I		shivered.
Cynthia		swam.

PATTERN 2

Subject	+	*Predicate*	+	*Direct Object*
Anthony		ordered		a new desk.
We		wanted		freedom.

PATTERN 3

Subject	+	*Predicate*	+	*Subject Complement*
The woman		was		a welder.
Our course		is		interesting.

PATTERN 4

Subject	+	*Predicate*	+	*Indirect Object*	+	*Direct Object*
My friend		loaned		me		a laptop.
The company		sent		employees		a questionnaire.

PATTERN 5

Subject	+	*Predicate*	+	*Direct Object*	+	*Object Complement*
I		consider		her singing		exceptional.
Lampwick		called		Jiminy Cricket		a beetle.

EXERCISE 7   Adding Complements

Directions: Complete each sentence with a word or words that will function as the type of complement indicated.

> **EXAMPLE**   The scientist acted _____proud_____ as he announced his
> latest invention.   predicate adjective

1. The delivery person handed _____ the large brown package.
   indirect object

2. Ronald Reagan was an American _____.
   predicate noun

3. The chairperson appointed Yesenia our _____.
   object complement

4. Protesters stood on the corner and handed out _____.
   direct object

5. The receptionist gave _____ the messages.
   indirect object

6. Before the storm, many clouds were _____.
   predicate adjective

7. The beer advertisement targeted _____.
   direct object

8. The Super Bowl players were _____.
   predicate noun

9. The diplomat declared the Olympics _____.
   object complement

10. Shopping malls are _____ before Christmas.
    predicate adjective

B.5 Expanding the Sentence with Adjectives and Adverbs

A sentence may consist of just a subject and a verb.

> Linda studied.
>
> Rumors circulated.

Most sentences, however, contain additional information about the subject and the verb. Information is commonly added in three ways:

- by using adjectives and adverbs.
- by using phrases (groups of words that lack either a subject or a predicate or both).
- by using clauses (groups of words that contain both a subject and a predicate).

Using Adjectives and Adverbs to Expand Your Sentences

Adjectives are words used to modify or describe nouns and pronouns (see p. 511). Adjectives answer questions about nouns and pronouns such as *Which one? What kind? How many?* Using adjectives is one way to add detail and information to sentences.

WITHOUT ADJECTIVES	Dogs barked at cats.
WITH ADJECTIVES	Our <u>three</u> <u>large</u>, <u>brown</u> dogs barked at the <u>two</u> <u>terrified</u>, <u>spotted</u> cats.

Note: Sometimes nouns and participles are used as adjectives (see p. 498 on participles).

Noun used as adjective

People are rediscovering the <u>milk</u> bottle.

Present participle used as adjective   Past participle used as adjective

Mrs. Simon had a <u>swimming</u> pool with a <u>broken</u> drain.

Adverbs add information to sentences by modifying or describing verbs, adjectives, or other adverbs (see p. 482). An adverb usually answers the question *How? When? Where? How often?* or *To what extent?*

WITHOUT ADVERBS	I will clean.
	The audience applauded.
WITH ADVERBS	I will clean <u>very</u> <u>thoroughly</u> <u>tomorrow</u>.
	The audience applauded <u>loudly</u> and <u>enthusiastically</u>.

B.6 Expanding the Sentence with Phrases

A **phrase** is a group of related words that lacks a subject, a predicate, or both. A phrase cannot stand alone as a sentence. Phrases can appear at the beginning, middle, or end of a sentence.

WITHOUT PHRASES	I noticed the stain.
	Sal researched the topic.
	Manuela arose.
WITH PHRASES	<u>Upon entering the room</u>, I noticed the stain <u>on the expensive carpet</u>.
	<u>At the local aquarium</u>, Sal researched the topic <u>of shark attacks</u>.
	<u>An amateur astronomer</u>, Manuela arose <u>in the middle of the night</u> to observe the lunar eclipse but, <u>after waiting ten minutes in the cold</u>, gave up.

There are eight kinds of phrases: **noun; verb; prepositional; verbal (participial, gerund,** and **infinitive); appositive;** and **absolute.**

Noun and Verb Phrases

A noun plus its modifiers is a **noun phrase** (*red shoes, the quiet house*). A main verb plus its helping verb is a **verb phrase** (*had been exploring, is sleeping* see p. 474 on helping verbs).

Prepositional Phrases

A **prepositional phrase** consists of a preposition (for example, *in, above, with, at, behind*), an object of the preposition (a noun or pronoun), and any modifiers of the object. (See p. 486 for a list of common prepositions.) A prepositional phrase functions like an adjective (modifying a noun or pronoun) or an adverb (modifying a verb, adjective, or adverb). You can use prepositional phrases to tell more about people, places, objects, or actions. A prepositional phrase usually adds information about time, place, direction, manner, or degree.

As Adjectives

The woman with the briefcase is giving a presentation on meditation techniques.

Both of the telephones behind the partition were ringing.

As Adverbs

The fire drill occurred in the morning.

I was curious about the new human resources director.

The conference speaker came from Australia.

With horror, the crowd watched the rhinoceros's tether stretch to the breaking point.

A prepositional phrase can function as part of the complete subject or as part of the complete predicate, but should not be confused with the simple subject or simple predicate.

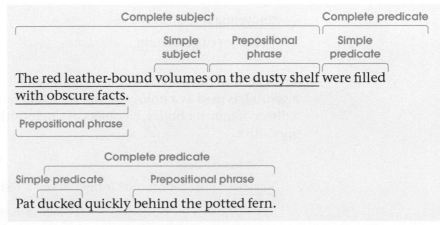

B. Parts of Sentences

Verbal Phrases

A **verbal** is a verb form that cannot function as the main verb of a sentence. The three kinds of verbals are **participles**, **gerunds**, and **infinitives**. A **verbal phrase** consists of a verbal and its modifiers.

Participles and Participial Phrases

All verbs have two participles: present and past. The **present participle** is formed by adding *-ing* to the infinitive form (*walking, riding, being*). The **past participle** of regular verbs is formed by adding *-d* or *-ed* to the infinitive form (*walked, baked*). The past participle of irregular verbs has no set pattern (*ridden, been*). (See p. 475 for a list of common irregular verbs and their past participles.) Both the present participle and the past participle can function as adjectives modifying nouns and pronouns.

> Past participle   Present participle
> as adjective   as adjective
>
> Irritated, Martha circled the confusing traffic rotary once again.

A **participial phrase** consists of a participle and any of its modifiers.

> Participial phrase
>
> Participle
>
> We listened for Isabella climbing the rickety stairs.
>
> Participial phrase
>
> Participle
>
> Disillusioned with the whole system, Kay sat down to think.
>
> Participial phrase
>
> Participle
>
> The singer, having caught a bad cold, canceled his performance.

Gerunds and Gerund Phrases

A **gerund** is the present participle (the *-ing* form) of the verb used as a noun.

> Shoveling is good exercise.
>
> Rex enjoyed gardening.

A **gerund phrase** consists of a gerund and its modifiers. A gerund phrase, like a gerund, is used as a noun and can therefore function in a sentence as a subject, a direct or indirect object, an object of a preposition, a subject complement, or an appositive.

> Gerund phrase
>
> Reviewing the report took longer than La Tisha anticipated. [Subject]
>
> Gerund phrase
>
> The director considered making another monster movie. [Direct object]

Gerund phrase

She gave <u>running</u> three miles daily credit for her health. [Indirect object]

Gerund phrase

Before <u>learning</u> Greek, Omar spoke only English. [Object of the preposition]

Gerund phrase

Her business is <u>designing</u> collapsible furniture. [Subject complement]

Gerund phrase

Hana's trick, <u>memorizing</u> license plates, has come in handy. [Appositive]

Infinitives and Infinitive Phrases

The **infinitive** is the base form of the verb as it appears in the dictionary preceded by the word *to*. An **infinitive phrase** consists of the word *to* plus the infinitive and any modifiers. An infinitive phrase can function as a noun, an adjective, or an adverb. When it is used as a noun, an infinitive phrase can be a subject, object, complement, or appositive.

Infinitive phrase

<u>To love</u> one's enemies is a noble goal. [Noun used as subject]

Infinitive phrase

The season <u>to sell</u> bulbs is the fall. [Adjective modifying *season*]

Infinitive phrase

The chess club met <u>to practice</u> for the state championship. [Adverb modifying *met*]

Sometimes the *to* in an infinitive phrase is not written.

Jacob helped us <u>learn</u> the new accounting procedure. [The *to* before *learn* is understood.]

Note: Do not confuse infinitive phrases with prepositional phrases beginning with the preposition *to*. In an infinitive phrase, *to* is followed by a verb; in a prepositional phrase, *to* is followed by a noun or pronoun.

Appositive Phrases

An **appositive** is a noun that explains, restates, or adds new information about another noun. An **appositive phrase** consists of an appositive and its modifiers. (See p. 526 for punctuation of appositive phrases.)

Appositive

Claude Monet completed the painting *Water Lilies* around 1903. [Adds information about the noun *painting*]

Appositive phrase

Appositive

Francis, <u>my neighbor</u> with a large workshop, lent me a wrench. [Adds information about the noun *Francis*]

Absolute Phrases

An **absolute phrase** consists of a noun or pronoun and any modifiers followed by a participle or a participial phrase (see p. 500). An absolute phrase modifies an entire sentence, not any particular word within the sentence. It can appear anywhere in a sentence and is set off from the rest of the sentence with a comma or commas. There may be more than one absolute phrase in a sentence.

Absolute phrase

The winter being over, the geese returned.

Absolute phrase

Senator Arden began his speech, his voice rising to be heard over the loud applause.

Absolute phrase

A vacancy having occurred, the hotel manager called the first name on the reservations waiting list.

EXERCISE 8

Expanding Sentences with Adjectives, Adverbs, and Phrases

Directions: Expand each of the following sentences by adding adjectives, adverbs, and/or phrases (prepositional, verbal, appositive, or absolute).

EXAMPLE   The professor lectured.

EXPANDED   Being an expert on animal behavior, the professor lectured about animal-intelligence studies.

1. Randall will graduate. _____

_____

2. The race began. _____

_____

3. Walmart is remodeling. _____

_____

4. Hillary walked alone. _____

_____

5. Manuel repairs appliances. _____

_____

6. The motorcycle was loud. _____

_____

7. My term paper is due Tuesday. _____

_____

8. I opened my umbrella. _____

_____

9. Austin built a garage. _____

_____

10. Lucas climbs mountains. _____

_____

B.7 Expanding the Sentence with Clauses

A **clause** is a group of words that contains a subject and a predicate. A clause is either **independent** (also called **main**) or **dependent** (also called **subordinate**).

Independent Clauses

An **independent clause** can stand alone as a grammatically complete sentence.

Independent clause   Independent clause
Subject Predicate   Subject Predicate
The alarm sounded, and I awoke.

Independent clause   Independent clause
Subject   Predicate   Subject   Predicate
The scientist worried. The experiment might fail.

Independent clause   Independent clause
Subject   Predicate   Subject   Predicate
He bandaged his ankle. It had been sprained.

Dependent Clauses

A **dependent clause** has a subject and a predicate, but it cannot stand alone as a grammatically complete sentence because it does not express a complete thought. Most dependent clauses begin with either a **subordinating conjunction** or a **relative pronoun**. These words connect the dependent clause to an independent clause.

Tip for Writers

Remember that some of these words have two meanings. For example, *once* can mean "one time" or "after." *While* can mean "at the same time" or "but."

COMMON SUBORDINATING CONJUNCTIONS		
after	in as much as	that
although	in case	though
as	in order that	unless
as far as	in so far as	until
as if	in that	when
as soon as	now that	whenever
as though	once	where

(continued)

COMMON SUBORDINATING CONJUNCTIONS		
because	provided that	wherever
before	rather than	whether
even if	since	while
even though	so that	why
how	supposing that	
if	than	

RELATIVE PRONOUNS	
that	which
	who (whose, whom)
whatever	whoever (whomever)

These clauses do not express complete thoughts and therefore cannot stand alone as sentences. When joined to independent clauses, however, dependent clauses function as adjectives, adverbs, and nouns and are known as **adjective** (or **relative**) **clauses**, **adverb clauses**, and **noun clauses**. Noun clauses can function as subjects, objects, or complements.

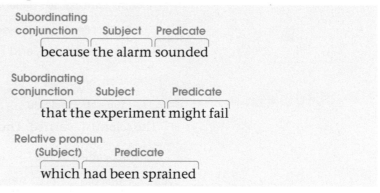

Adjective Clause

Dependent clause

He bandaged his ankle, <u>which had been sprained</u>. [Modifies *ankle*]

Adverb Clause

Dependent clause

<u>Because the alarm sounded</u>, I awoke. [Modifies *awoke*]

Noun Clause

Dependent clause

The scientist worried <u>that the experiment might fail</u>. [Direct object of *worried*]

Elliptical Clause

Sometimes the relative pronoun or subordinating conjunction is implied or understood rather than stated. Also, a dependent clause may contain an implied predicate. When a dependent clause is missing an element that can clearly be supplied from the context of the sentence, it is called an **elliptical clause**.

Elliptical clause

The circus is more entertaining than television [is]. [*Is* is the understood predicate in the elliptical dependent clause.]

Elliptical clause

Canadian history is among the subjects [that] the book discusses. [*That* is the understood relative pronoun in the elliptical dependent clause.]

Relative pronouns are generally the subject or object in their clauses. *Who* and *whoever* change to *whom* and *whomever* when they function as objects (see p. 511).

C Writing Correct Sentences

C.1 Uses of Verb Tenses

The **tense** of a verb expresses time. It conveys whether an action, process, or occurrence takes place in the present, past, or future. There are 12 tenses in English, and each is used to express a particular time. (See p. 505 for information about how to form each tense.)

The **simple present tense** expresses actions that are occurring at the time of the writing or that occur regularly. The **simple past tense** is used for actions that have already occurred. The **simple future tense** is used for actions that will occur in the future.

SIMPLE PRESENT	The chef cooks a huge meal.
SIMPLE PAST	The chef <u>cooked</u> a huge meal.
SIMPLE FUTURE	The chef <u>will cook</u> a huge meal.

The **present perfect tense** is used for actions that began in the past and are still occurring in the present or are finished by the time of the writing. The **past perfect tense** expresses actions that were completed before other past actions. The **future perfect tense** is used for actions that will be completed in the future.

PRESENT PERFECT	The chef <u>has cooked</u> a huge meal every night this week.
PAST PERFECT	The chef <u>had cooked</u> a huge meal before the guests canceled their reservation.
FUTURE PERFECT	The chef <u>will have cooked</u> a huge meal by the time we arrive.

The six progressive tenses are used for continuing actions or actions in progress. The **present progressive tense** is used for actions that are in progress in the present. The **past progressive tense** expresses past continuing actions. The **future progressive tense** is used for continuing actions that will occur in the future. The **present perfect progressive**, **past perfect progressive**, and **future perfect progressive tenses** are used for continuing actions that are, were, or will be completed by a certain time.

PRESENT PROGRESSIVE	The chef <u>is cooking</u> a huge meal this evening.
PAST PROGRESSIVE	The chef <u>was cooking</u> a huge meal when she ran out of butter.
FUTURE PROGRESSIVE	The chef <u>will be cooking</u> a huge meal all day tomorrow.
PRESENT PERFECT PROGRESSIVE	The chef <u>has been cooking</u> a huge meal since this morning.

| PAST PERFECT PROGRESSIVE | The chef <u>had been cooking</u> a huge meal before the electricity went out. |
| FUTURE PERFECT PROGRESSIVE | The chef <u>will have been cooking</u> a huge meal for eight hours when the guests arrive. |

Writing all forms of a verb for all tenses and all persons (first, second, and third, singular and plural) is called **conjugating** the verb. Irregular verbs have an irregularly formed past tense and past participle (used in the past tense and the perfect tenses). (See p. 475 for a list of the forms of common irregular verbs.) Here is the complete conjugation for the regular verb *walk*.

CONJUGATION OF THE REGULAR VERB *WALK*

	Singular	Plural
Simple present tense	I walk you walk he/she/it walks	we walk you walk they walk
Simple past tense	I walked you walked he/she/it walked	we walked you walked they walked
Simple future tense	I will (shall) walk you will walk he/she/it will walk	we will (shall) walk you will walk they will walk
Present perfect tense	I have walked you have walked he/she/it has walked	we have walked you have walked they have walked
Past perfect tense	I had walked you had walked he/she/it had walked	we had walked you had walked they had walked
Future perfect tense	I will (shall) have walked you will have walked he/she/it will have walked	we will (shall) have walked you will have walked they will have walked
Present progressive tense	I am walking you are walking he/she/it is walking	we are walking you are walking they are walking
Past progressive tense	I was walking you were walking he/she/it was walking	we were walking you were walking they were walking
Future progressive tense	I will be walking you will be walking he/she/it will be walking	we will be walking you will be walking they will be walking
Present perfect progressive tense	I have been walking you have been walking he/she/it has been walking	we have been walking you have been walking they have been walking
Past perfect progressive tense	I had been walking you had been walking he/she/it had been walking	we had been walking you had been walking they had been walking
Future perfect progressive tense	I will have been walking you will have been walking he/she/it will have been walking	we will have been walking you will have been walking they will have been walking

Following are the simple present and simple past tenses for the irregular verbs *have*, *be*, and *do*, which are commonly used as helping verbs (see p. 474).

IRREGULAR VERBS *HAVE, BE,* AND *DO*

	Have	Be	Do
Simple present tense	I have you have he/she/it has we/you/they have	I am you are he/she/it is we/you/they are	I do you do he/she/it does we/you/they do
Simple past tense	I had you had he/she/it had we/you/they had	I was you were he/she/it was we/you/they were	I did you did he/she/it did we/you/they did

Special Uses of the Simple Present Tense

Besides expressing actions that are occurring at the time of the writing, the simple present tense has several special uses.

HABITUAL OR RECURRING ACTION	She works at the store every day.
GENERAL TRUTH	The sun rises in the east.
DISCUSSION OF LITERATURE	Gatsby stands on the dock and gazes in Daisy's direction.
THE FUTURE	He leaves for Rome on the 7:30 flight.

Emphasis, Negatives, and Questions

The simple present and the simple past tenses of the verb *do* are used with main verbs to provide emphasis, to form negative constructions with the adverb *not*, and to ask questions.

SIMPLE PRESENT	Malcolm does want to work on Saturday.
SIMPLE PRESENT	He does not want to stay home alone.
SIMPLE PRESENT	Do you want to go with him?
SIMPLE PAST	Judy did write the proposal herself.
SIMPLE PAST	She did not have the money to pay professionals.
SIMPLE PAST	Did she do a good job?

The modal verbs *can, could, may, might, must, shall, should, will*, and *would* are also used to add emphasis and shades of meaning to verbs. Modals are used only as helping verbs, never alone, and do not change form to indicate tense. Added to a main verb, they are used in the following situations, among others:

CONDITION	We can play tennis if she gets here on time.
PERMISSION	You may have only one e-mail address.
POSSIBILITY	They might call us from the airport.
OBLIGATION	I must visit my mother tomorrow.

Tips for Writers

The usual simple present tense form is this: Malcolm wants to work on Saturday. The *emphatic form* is sometimes used to correct a mistake:

Ivan says, "Malcolm does not want to work on Saturday."

Maria replies, "He does want to work on Saturday." (or) "Yes, he does."

Common Mistakes to Avoid with Verb Tense

Check your writing carefully to make sure you have avoided these common mistakes with verb tenses.

1. **Make sure the endings *-d* and *-ed* (for past tenses) and *-s* and *-es* (for third-person singular, simple present tense) are on all verbs that require them.**

INCORRECT	I <u>have walk</u> three miles since I left home.
CORRECT	I <u>have walked</u> three miles since I left home.

2. **Use irregular verbs correctly** (see p. 475).

INCORRECT	I will <u>lay</u> down for a nap.
CORRECT	I will <u>lie</u> down for a nap.

3. **Use helping verbs where they are necessary to express the correct time.**

INCORRECT	I <u>go</u> to class tomorrow.
CORRECT	I <u>will go</u> to class tomorrow.

4. **Avoid colloquial language or dialect in writing.** Colloquial language is casual, everyday language often used in conversation. Dialect is the language pattern of a region or an ethnic group.

INCORRECT	I didn't <u>get</u> the point of that poem.
CORRECT	I didn't <u>understand</u> the point of that poem.
INCORRECT	The train <u>be</u> gone.
CORRECT	The train <u>has</u> gone.

Other common mistakes with verbs are failing to make the verb agree with the subject (see p. 417) and using inconsistent or shifting tenses.

EXERCISE 9

Correcting Verb Form and Tense Errors

Directions: Correct any of the following sentences with an error in verb form or verb tense. If a sentence contains no errors, write "C" for correct beside it.

EXAMPLE   You ~~is~~ _are_ next in line.

_____ 1. Mercedes called and ask Jen if she wanted a ride to the basketball game.

_____ 2. Eric went to a party last week and meets a girl he knew in high school.

_____ 3. I cook spaghetti every Wednesday, and my family always enjoys it.

_____ 4. A package come in yesterday's mail for my office mate.

_____ 5. Louisa wears a beautiful red dress to her sister's wedding last week.

_____ 6. Marni answered a letter she receive from her former employer.

_____ 7. Rob waited until he was introduced, and then he run on stage.

_____ 8. The audience laughed loudly at the comedian's jokes and applauds spontaneously at the funniest ones.

_____ 9. The group had ordered buffalo-style chicken wings, and it was not disappointed when the meal arrived.

_____ 10. Julie spends the afternoon answering correspondence when sales were slow.

C.2 Subjunctive Mood

Tip for Writers

In *subjunctive* (contrary-to-fact) present-tense statements, use a past tense verb in the *if* clause and a modal auxiliary plus an infinitive verb in the main clause:

<u>If I lived</u> in Minnesota, <u>I would need</u> a good pair of winter boots.

The **mood** of a verb conveys the writer's attitude toward the expressed thought. There are three moods in English. The **indicative mood** is used to make ordinary statements of fact and to ask questions. The **imperative mood** is used to give commands or make suggestions. The **subjunctive mood** is used to express wishes, requirements, recommendations, and statements contrary to fact (see p. 478).

INDICATIVE	Laurel <u>lies</u> in the sun every afternoon.
IMPERATIVE	<u>Lie</u> down and rest!
SUBJUNCTIVE	It is urgent that she <u>lie</u> down and rest.

The subjunctive mood requires some special attention because it uses verb tenses in unusual ways. Verbs in the subjunctive mood can be in the present, past, or perfect tense.

PRESENT	His mother recommended that he <u>apply</u> for the job. If truth <u>be</u> told, Jacob is luckier than he knows.
PAST	If she <u>walked</u> faster, she could get there on time. She ran as if she <u>were</u> five years old again.
PERFECT	If I <u>had known</u> his name, I would have said hello.

Tip for Writers

Note that in *contrary-to-fact statements*, the verb in the main clause usually begins with a modal auxiliary or *wish*.

Here are several rules for using the subjunctive correctly:

1. **For requirements and recommendations, use the present subjunctive (the infinitive) for all verbs, including *be*.**

   Mr. Kenefick requires that his students <u>be</u> drilled in safety procedures.

   The dentist recommended that she <u>brush</u> her teeth three times a day.

2. For present <u>conditions contrary to fact</u> and for present wishes, use the past subjunctive (the simple past tense) for all verbs; use *were* for the verb *be* for all subjects.

> I wish that the workday <u>began</u> later.
>
> If Andrew <u>were</u> not so stubborn, he would admit that Adele is right.

3. For past <u>conditions contrary to fact</u> and for past wishes, use the perfect subjunctive (*had* plus the past participle) for all verbs, including *be*.

> If Roman <u>had been</u> at home, he would have answered the phone when you called.
>
> When Peter told me what an exciting internship he had abroad last summer, I wished I <u>had gone</u> with him.

C.3 Pronoun Case

A pronoun changes **case** depending on its grammatical function in a sentence. Pronouns may be in the **subjective case**, the **objective case**, or the **possessive case**.

PERSONAL PRONOUNS			
SINGULAR	**SUBJECTIVE**	**OBJECTIVE**	**POSSESSIVE**
First person	I	me	my, mine
Second person	you	you	your, yours
Third person	he, she, it	him, her, it	his, her, hers, its
PLURAL	**SUBJECTIVE**	**OBJECTIVE**	**POSSESSIVE**
First person	we	us	our, ours
Second person	you	you	your, yours
Third person	they	them	their, theirs
RELATIVE OR INTERROGATIVE PRONOUNS			
	SUBJECTIVE	**OBJECTIVE**	**POSSESSIVE**
Singular and plural	who	whom	whose
	whoever	whomever	

Pronouns in the Subjective Case

Use the **subjective case** (also known as the **nominative case**) when the pronoun functions as the subject of a sentence or clause (see p. 471) or as a subject complement (also known as a predicate nominative; see p. 493). A predicate nominative is a noun or pronoun that follows a linking verb and identifies or renames the subject of the sentence.

Subject

She has won recognition as a landscape architect.

Subject complement

Cathie volunteers at the local hospital. The most faithful volunteer is she.

The subjective case is also used when a pronoun functions as an appositive to a subject or subject complement.

The only two seniors, she and her best friend, won the top awards.

Pronouns in the Objective Case

Use the objective case when a pronoun functions as a direct object, indirect object, or object of a preposition (see pp. 493 and 494).

Direct object

Gabriel helped her with the assignment.

Indirect object

Gabriel gave her a book.

Objects of the preposition

Gabriel gave the book to him and her.

The objective case is also used when the pronoun functions as the subject of an infinitive phrase or an appositive to an object.

Subject of infinitive   Infinitive phrase

I wanted him to go straight home.

Direct object   Appositive to object

The district manager chose two representatives, Lauren and me.

Note: When a sentence has a compound subject or compound objects, you may have trouble determining the correct pronoun case. To determine how the pronoun functions, mentally recast the sentence without the other noun or other pronoun in the compound construction. Determine how the pronoun functions by itself and then decide which case is correct.

Subjective case

They and Teresa brought the beverages. [Think: "*They* brought the beverages." *They* is the subject of the sentence, so the subjective case is correct.]

Objective case

Behind you and me, the curtains rustled. [Think: "Behind *me.*" *Me* is the object of the preposition *behind,* so the objective case is correct.]

Pronouns in the Possessive Case

Possessive pronouns indicate to whom or to what something belongs. The possessive pronouns *mine, yours, his, hers, its, ours,* and *theirs* function just as nouns do.

Subject

Hers is the letterhead with the bright blue lettering.

Direct object

I liked hers the best.

The possessive pronouns *my, your, his, her, its, our*, and *their* are used as adjectives to modify nouns and gerunds (see p. 498).

Our high-school reunion surprised everyone by its size.

Your attending that reunion will depend on your travel schedule.

Who and *Whom* as Interrogative Pronouns

When *who, whoever, whom*, and *whomever* introduce questions, they are interrogative pronouns. How an interrogative pronoun functions in a clause determines its case. Use *who* or *whoever* (the subjective case) when the interrogative pronoun functions as a subject or subject complement (see p. 493). Use *whom* or *whomever* (the objective case) when the interrogative pronoun functions as a direct object or an object of a preposition.

	Subject
SUBJECTIVE CASE	Who is there?

	Object of preposition
OBJECTIVE CASE	To whom did you give the letter?

Who and *Whom* as Relative Pronouns

When *who, whoever, whom*, and *whomever* introduce subordinate clauses, they are relative pronouns. How a relative pronoun functions in a clause determines its case. Use *who* or *whoever* (subjective case) when a relative pronoun functions as the subject of the subordinate clause. Use *whom* or *whomever* (objective case) when a relative pronoun functions as an object in the subordinate clause.

SUBJECTIVE CASE	The lecturer, who is a journalist from New York, speaks with great insight and wit. [*Who* is the subject of the subordinate clause.]
OBJECTIVE CASE	The journalist, whom I know from college days, came to give a lecture. [*Whom* is the direct object of the verb *know* in the subordinate clause.]

C.4 Correct Adjective and Adverb Use

Adjectives and adverbs modify, describe, explain, qualify, or restrict the words they modify (see pp. 479 and 482). **Adjectives** modify nouns and pronouns. **Adverbs** modify verbs, adjectives, and other adverbs; adverbs can also modify phrases, clauses, or whole sentences.

ADJECTIVES	<u>red</u> car; the <u>quiet</u> one
ADVERBS	<u>quickly</u> finish; <u>only</u> four reasons; <u>very</u> angrily

Comparison of Adjectives and Adverbs

Positive adjectives and adverbs modify but do not involve any comparison: *green, bright, lively*.

 Comparative adjectives and adverbs compare two persons, things, actions, or ideas.

COMPARATIVE ADJECTIVE	Michel is <u>taller</u> than Latoya.
COMPARATIVE ADVERB	Antonio reacted <u>more calmly</u> than Robert.

Here is how to form comparative adjectives and adverbs. (Consult your dictionary if you are unsure of the form of a particular word.)

1. **If the adjective or adverb has one syllable, add *-er*. For certain two-syllable words, also add *-er*.**

   cold → colder   slow → slower   narrow → narrower

2. **For most words of two or more syllables, place the word *more* in front of the word.**

   reasonable → more reasonable   interestingly → more interestingly

3. **For two-syllable adjectives ending in *y*, change the *y* to *i* and add *-er*.**

   drowsy → drowsier   lazy → lazier

 Superlative adjectives and adverbs compare more than two persons, things, actions, or ideas.

SUPERLATIVE ADJECTIVE	Michael is the <u>tallest</u> member of the team.
SUPERLATIVE ADVERB	She studied <u>most diligently</u> for the test.

Here is how to form superlative adjectives and adverbs:

1. **Add *-est* to one-syllable adjectives and adverbs and to certain two- syllable words.**

   cold → coldest   fast → fastest   narrow → narrowest

2. **For most words of two or more syllables, place the word *most* in front of the word.**

   reasonable → most reasonable   interestingly → most interestingly

3. **For two-syllable adjectives ending in *y*, change the *y* to *i* and add *-est*.**

   drowsy → drowsiest   lazy → laziest

Tip for Writers

When writing *superlative statements*, always use *the*. Use *much* only in questions and negatives. In affirmative statements, use *a lot of* or *some*.

Do you have <u>much</u> time for painting now that you're going to school?

Yes, I still have <u>a lot of</u> time for painting. (or) No, I <u>don't have much time.</u>

Irregular Adjectives and Adverbs

Some adjectives and adverbs form their comparative and superlative forms in irregular ways.

<table>
<tr><td>

Tip for Writers

Use *littler* and *littlest* for size; use *less* and *least* for amount (quantity). Use *little/less/least* before noncount nouns; use *few/fewer/fewest* before plural nouns:

The littlest of Lana's eight children is only two years old; Lana has less time to spend with her friends now that she has a big family. She has *fewer* friends now.

</td></tr>
</table>

POSITIVE	COMPARATIVE	SUPERLATIVE
Adjectives		
good	better	best
bad	worse	worst
little	littler, less	littlest, least
Adverbs		
well	better	best
badly	worse	worst
Adjectives and Adverbs		
many	more	most
some	more	most
much	more	most

Common Mistakes to Avoid

1. **Do not use adjectives to modify verbs, other adjectives, or adverbs.**

INCORRECT	Peter and Mary take each other serious.
CORRECT	Peter and Mary take each other seriously. [Modifies the verb *take*]

2. **Do not use the adjectives *good* and *bad* when you should use the adverbs *well* and *badly*.**

INCORRECT	Juan did good on the exam.
CORRECT	Juan did well on the exam. [Modifies the verb *did*]

3. **Do not use the adjectives *real* and *sure* when you should use the adverbs *really* and *surely*.**

INCORRECT	Jan scored real well on the exam.
CORRECT	Jan scored really well on the exam. [Modifies the adverb *well*]
INCORRECT	I sure was surprised to win the lottery.
CORRECT	I surely was surprised to win the lottery. [Modifies the verb *was surprised*]

4. **Do not use *more* or *most* with the -er or -est form of an adjective or adverb. Use one form or the other, according to the rules above.**

INCORRECT	That was the most tastiest dinner I've ever eaten.
CORRECT	That was the tastiest dinner I've ever eaten.

5. **Avoid double negatives—that is, two negatives in the same clause.**

| INCORRECT | He did <u>not</u> want <u>nothing</u> in the refrigerator. |
| CORRECT | He did <u>not</u> want <u>anything</u> in the refrigerator. |

6. **When using the comparative and superlative forms of adverbs, do not create an incomplete comparison.**

| INCORRECT | The heater works <u>more efficiently</u>. [More efficiently than what?] |
| CORRECT | The heater works <u>more efficiently than it did before we had it repaired.</u> |

7. **Do not use the comparative form for adjectives and adverbs that have no degree.** It is incorrect to write, for example, *more square, most perfect, more equally,* or *most straight.* Do not use a comparative or superlative form for any of the following adjectives and adverbs:

ADJECTIVES				
complete	equal	infinite	pregnant	unique
dead	eternal	invisible	square	universal
empty	favorite	matchless	supreme	vertical
endless	impossible	parallel	unanimous	whole
ADVERBS				
endlessly	infinitely	uniquely		
equally	Invisibly	universally		
eternally	perpendicularly			
impossibly	straight			

EXERCISE 10   Using Adjectives and Adverbs Correctly

Directions: Revise each of the following sentences so that all adjectives and adverbs are used correctly. If the sentence is correct, write "C" for correct beside it.

       EXAMPLE   I answered the question polite_^.   *ly*

_____ 1. Michael's apartment was more expensive.

_____ 2. When I heard the man and woman sing the duet, I decided that the woman sang best.

_____ 3. Our local movie reviewer said that the film's theme song sounded badly.

_____ **4.** The roller coaster was excitinger than the merry-go-round.

_____ **5.** *The Casual Vacancy* is more good than *The Hive*.

_____ **6.** Susan sure gave a rousing speech.

_____ **7.** Last week's storm seemed worst than a tornado.

_____ **8.** Some women thought that the Equal Rights Amendment would guarantee that women are treated more equally.

_____ **9.** Taking the interstate is the most fast route to the outlet mall.

_____ **10.** Professor Reed had the better lecture style of all my instructors.

C.5 Sentence Variety

Good writers use a variety of sentence structures to avoid wordiness and monotony and to show relationships among thoughts. To achieve **sentence variety**, do not use all simple sentences or all complex or compound sentences, and do not begin or end all sentences in the same way. Instead, vary the length, the amount of detail, and the structure of your sentences.

1. **Use sentences of varying lengths.**

2. **Avoid stringing simple sentences together with coordinating conjunctions (and, but, or, and so on).** Instead, use some introductory participial phrases (see p. 498).

SIMPLE	There was a long line at the deli, <u>so</u> Chris decided to leave.
VARIED	<u>Seeing the long line at the deli</u>, Chris decided to leave.

3. **Begin some sentences with a prepositional phrase.** A preposition shows relationships between things (*during, over, toward, before, across, within, inside, over, above*). Many prepositions suggest chronology, direction, or location (see p. 485).

<u>During the concert</u> the fire alarm rang.

<u>Inside the theater</u> the crowd waited expectantly.

4. **Begin some sentences with a present or past participle** (*cooking, broken*; see p. 475).

<u>Barking</u> and <u>jumping</u>, the dogs greeted their master.

<u>Still laughing</u>, two girls left the movie.

<u>Tired</u> and <u>exhausted</u>, the mountain climbers fell asleep quickly.

5. **Begin some sentences with adverbs** (see p. 482).

<u>Angrily</u>, the student left the room.

<u>Patiently</u>, the math instructor explained the assignment again.

6. **Begin some sentences with infinitive phrases** (*to* plus the infinitive form: *to make, to go*; see p. 499).

> <u>To get breakfast ready on time</u>, I set my alarm for 7 A.M.

7. **Begin some sentences with a dependent clause introduced by a subordinating conjunction** (see p. 501).

> <u>Because</u> I ate shellfish, I developed hives.

8. **Begin some sentences with a conjunctive adverb.**

> <u>Consequently</u>, we decided to have steak for dinner.

EXERCISE 11   Practicing Sentence Construction Techniques

Directions: Combine each of the following pairs of simple sentences into one sentence, using the technique suggested in brackets.

EXAMPLE	**a.** The dog barked and howled.
	b. The dog warned a stranger away. [Use present participle (-*ing* form).]
COMBINED	*Barking and howling, the dog warned a stranger away.*

1. **a.** Professor Clark has a Civil War battlefield model.

   b. He has it in his office.
   [Use prepositional phrase.]

   _____

   _____

2. **a.** Toby went to Disneyland for the first time.

   b. He was very excited.
   [Use past participle (-*ed* form).]

   _____

   _____

3. **a.** Teresa received a full scholarship.

   b. She does not need to worry about paying her tuition.
   [Use subordinating conjunction.]

   _____

   _____

4. **a.** Lance answered the phone.

   b. He spoke with a gruff voice.
   [Use adverb.]

   _____

   _____

5. **a.** The truck choked and sputtered.

   b. The truck pulled into the garage.
   [Use present participle (-*ing* form).]

   _____

   _____

6. **a.** Rich programmed his DVR.

   b. He recorded his favorite sitcom.
   [Use infinitive (*to*) phrase.]

   _____

   _____

7. **a.** The postal carrier placed a package outside my door.

   b. The package had a foreign stamp on it.
   [Use prepositional phrase.]

   _____

   _____

8. **a.** The instructor asked the students to take their seats.

   b. She was annoyed.
   [Use past participle (-*ed* form).]

   _____

   _____

9. **a.** Shyla stood outside the student union.

   b. She waited for her boyfriend.
   [Use present participle (-*ing* form).]

   _____

   _____

10. **a.** Bo walked to the bookstore.

    b. He was going to buy some new highlighters.
    [Use infinitive (*to*) phrase.]

    _____

    _____

C.6 Redundancy and Wordiness

Redundancy results when a writer says the same thing twice. **Wordiness** results when a writer uses more words than necessary to convey a meaning. Both redundancy and wordiness detract from clear, effective sentences by distracting and confusing the reader.

Eliminating Redundancy

A common mistake is to repeat the same idea in slightly different words.

> The <u>remaining</u> chocolate-chip cookie is the <u>only one left</u>, so I saved it for you. [*Remaining* and *only one left* mean the same thing.]
>
> The vase was <u>oval in shape</u>. [Oval is a shape, so *in shape* is redundant.]

To revise a redundant sentence, eliminate one of the redundant elements.

Eliminating Wordiness

1. **Eliminate wordiness by cutting out words that do not add to the meaning of your sentence.**

WORDY	In the final analysis, choosing the field of biology as my major resulted in my realizing that college is hard work.
REVISED	Choosing biology as my major made me realize that college is hard work.
WORDY	The type of imitative behavior that I notice among teenagers is a very important, helpful aspect of their learning to function in groups.
REVISED	The imitative behavior of teenagers helps them learn to function in groups.

   Watch out in particular for empty words and phrases.

Phrase	*Substitute*
until such time as	until
due to the fact that	because
at this point in time	now
in order to	to

2. **Express your ideas simply and directly, using as few words as possible.**
   Often by rearranging your wording, you can eliminate two or three words.

   > the fleas that my dog has → my dog's fleas
   >
   > workers with jobs that are low in pay → workers with low-paying jobs

3. Use strong, active verbs that convey movement and give additional information.

WORDY	I was in charge of two other employees and needed to watch over their work and performance.
REVISED	I supervised two employees, monitored their performance, and checked their work.

4. **Avoid sentences that begin with *"There is"* and *"There are."*** These empty phrases add no meaning, energy, or life to sentences.

WORDY	There are many children who suffer from malnutrition.
REVISED	Many children suffer from malnutrition.

EXERCISE 12   Eliminating Redundancy and Wordiness

Directions: Revise each of the following sentences to eliminate redundancy and wordiness.

EXAMPLE	Janice, who is impatient, usually cannot wait for class to end and packs up all of her books and notebooks in her backpack before the class is over.
REVISED	Janice is impatient and usually packs everything in her backpack before class ends.

1. My co-workers are friendly, nice, and cooperative and always willing to help me.

2. Eva and Joe are returning again to the branch office where they met.

3. Lynn changed from her regular clothes into her shorts and T-shirt in order that she could play basketball.

4. Due to the fact that Professor Reis assigned 100 pages of reading for tomorrow, I will be unable to join the group of my friends at the restaurant tonight.

5. In my mythology class, we discussed and talked about the presence of a Noah's ark–type story in most cultures.

6. Darryl offered many ideas and theories as to the reason why humans exist.

7. There are many children who have not been immunized against dangerous childhood diseases.

8. Scientists have been studying the disease cancer for many years, but they have been unable to find a cure for the disease.

9. The brown-colored chair was my father's favorite chair.

10. The briefcase that Julio has carried belonged to his brother.

C.7 Diction

Diction is the use and choice of words. Words that you choose should be appropriate for your audience and express your meaning clearly. The following suggestions will help you improve your diction:

1. **Avoid slang expressions.** Slang refers to the informal, special expressions created and used by groups of people who want to give themselves a unique identity. Slang is an appropriate and useful way to communicate in some social situations and in some forms of creative writing. However, it is not appropriate for academic or career writing.

SLANG	My sister seems permanently out to lunch.
REVISED	My sister seems out of touch with the world.
SLANG	We pigged out at the ice cream shop.
REVISED	We consumed enormous quantities of ice cream at the ice cream shop.
SLANG	My friend's new haircut is sick!
REVISED	My friend's new haircut is stylish and flattering
SLANG	That guy keeps staring at me, and I'm totally skeeved out.
REVISED	That guy keeps staring at me, and it is making me uncomfortable.

2. **Avoid colloquial language.** Colloquial language refers to casual, everyday spoken language. It should be avoided in formal situations. Words that fall into this category are labeled *informal* or *colloquial* in your dictionary.

COLLOQUIAL	I almost flunked bio last sem.
REVISED	I almost failed biology last semester.
COLLOQUIAL	What are you all doing later?
REVISED	What are you doing later?

3. **Avoid nonstandard language.** Nonstandard language consists of words and grammatical forms that are used in conversation but are neither correct nor acceptable standard written English.

Nonstandard	*Standard*
hisself	himself
knowed	known, knew
hadn't ought to	should not
she want	she wants
he go	he goes

4. **Avoid trite expressions.** Trite expressions are old, worn-out words and phrases that have become stale and do not convey meaning as effectively as possible. These expressions are also called *clichés*.

Trite Expressions		
needle in a haystack	sadder but wiser	as old as the hills
hard as a rock	white as snow	pretty as a picture
face the music	gentle as a lamb	

EXERCISE 13   Practicing Correct Diction

Directions: Revise each of the following sentences by using correct diction.

> **EXAMPLE**   This here building is Clemens Hall.
>
> **REVISED**   This building is Clemens Hall.

1. Jean freaked out when I told her she won the $500 gift card.

2. He go to the library.

3. The campus is wider than an occan.

4. Marty sits next to me in chem.

5. Sandy's new car audio system is totally cool and has an awesome sound.

6. We went nuts when our team won the game.

7. Them home theater systems sure are expensive.

8. I think Nathan is as sharp as a tack because he got every question on the exam right.

9. Nino blew class off today to go rock climbing with his pals.

10. Dr. Maring's cell phone rang in the middle of the meeting, and she had to hightail home.

D Using Punctuation Correctly

D.1 End Punctuation

When to Use Periods

Use a period in the following situations:

1. **To end a sentence unless it is a question or an exclamation.**

   > We washed the car even though we knew a thunderstorm was imminent.

   Note: Use a period to end a sentence that states an indirect question or indirectly quotes someone's words or thoughts.

INCORRECT	Samantha wondered if she would be on time?
CORRECT	Samantha wondered if she would be on time.

2. **To punctuate many abbreviations.**

   > M.D.   B.A.   P.M.   B.C.   Mr.   Ms.

   Do not use periods in acronyms, such as *NATO* and *AIDS*, or in abbreviations for most organizations, such as *NBC* and *NAACP*.

   Note: If a sentence ends with an abbreviation, the sentence has only one period, not two.

   > The train was due to arrive at 7:00 P.M.

When to Use Question Marks

Use question marks after direct questions. Place the question mark within the closing quotation marks.

> She asked the grocer, "How old is this cheese?"

Note: Use a period, not a question mark, after an indirect question.

> She asked the grocer how old the cheese was.

Tip for Writers

Punctuation

Using punctuation incorrectly can sometimes change the meaning of your sentences. Here are two examples:

1. The children who stayed outside got wet. (Only some of the children got wet.) The children, who stayed outside, got wet. (All of the children got wet.)

2. Did she finally marry Roger? Did she finally marry, Roger?

When to Use Exclamation Points

Use an exclamation point at the end of a sentence that expresses particular emphasis, excitement, or urgency. Use exclamation points sparingly, however, especially in academic writing.

> What a beautiful day it is!   Dial 911 right now!

D.2 Commas

The **comma** is used to separate parts of a sentence from one another. If you omit a comma when it is needed, you risk making a clear and direct sentence confusing.

When to Use Commas

Use a comma in the following situations:

1. **Before a coordinating conjunction that joins two independent clauses** (see p. 394).

   > Terry had planned to leave work early, but he was delayed.

2. **To separate a dependent (subordinate) clause from an independent clause when the dependent clause comes first in the sentence** (see p. 394).

   > After I left the library, I went to the computer lab.

3. **To separate introductory words and phrases from the rest of the sentence.**

   > Unfortunately, I forgot my umbrella.
   >
   > To pass the baton, I will need to locate my teammate.
   >
   > Exuberant over their victory, the football team members carried the quarterback on their shoulders.

4. **To separate a nonrestrictive phrase or clause from the rest of a sentence.** A **nonrestrictive** phrase or clause is added to a sentence but does not change the sentence's basic meaning.

   To determine whether an element is nonrestrictive, read the sentence without the element. If the meaning of the sentence does not essentially change, then the commas are *necessary*.

   > My sister, who is a mail carrier, is afraid of dogs. [The essential meaning of this sentence does not change if we read the sentence without the subordinate clause: *My sister is afraid of dogs*. Therefore, commas are needed.]
   >
   > Mail carriers who have been bitten by dogs are afraid of them. [If we read this sentence without the subordinate clause, its meaning changes considerably: *Mail carriers are afraid of (dogs)*. It seems to say that *all* mail carriers are afraid of dogs. In this case, adding commas is not correct.]

5. **To separate three or more items in a series.**

   Note: A comma is *not* used *after* the last item in the series.

   > I plan to take math, psychology, and writing next semester.

6. **To separate coordinate adjectives: two or more adjectives that are not joined by a coordinating conjunction and that equally modify the same noun or pronoun.**

   > The <u>thirsty</u>, <u>hungry</u> children returned from a day at the beach.

   To determine if a comma is needed between two adjectives, use the following test. Insert the word *and* between the two adjectives. Also try reversing the order of the two adjectives. If the phrase makes sense in either case, a comma is needed. If the phrase does not make sense, do not use a comma.

   > The <u>tired</u>, <u>angry</u> child fell asleep. [*The tired and angry child* makes sense; so does *The angry, tired child.* Consequently, the comma is needed.]

   > Sarah is an <u>excellent psychology</u> student. [*Sarah is an excellent and psychology student* does not make sense, nor does *Sarah is a psychology, excellent student.* A comma is therefore not needed.]

7. **To separate parenthetical expressions from the clauses they modify.** Parenthetical expressions are added pieces of information that are not essential to the meaning of the sentence.

   > Most students, <u>I imagine</u>, can get jobs on campus.

8. **To separate a transition from the clause it modifies.**

   > <u>In addition</u>, I will revise the bylaws.

9. **To separate a quotation from the words that introduce or explain it.**

   Note: The comma goes *inside* the closed quotation marks.

   > "Shopping," Julia explained, "is a form of relaxation for me."

   > Julia explained, "Shopping is a form of relaxation for me."

10. **To separate dates, place names, and long numbers.**

    > October 10, 2001, is my birthday.

    > Dayton, Ohio, was the first stop on the tour.

    > Participants numbered 1,777,716.

11. **To separate phrases expressing contrast.**

    > Jorge's good nature, <u>not his wealth</u>, explains his popularity.

EXERCISE 14	Adding Commas

Directions: Revise each of the following sentences by adding commas where needed.

> **EXAMPLE**   Until the judge entered, the courtroom was noisy.

1. "Hello " said the group of friends when Joan entered the room.

2. Robert De Niro the actor in the film was very handsome.

3. My parents frequently vacation in Miami Florida.

4. Drunk drivers I suppose may not realize they are not competent to drive.

5. Jeff purchased a television couch and dresser for his new apartment.

6. Luckily the windstorm did not do any damage to our town.

7. Frieda has an early class and she has to go to work afterward.

8. After taking a trip to the Galápagos Islands Mark Twain wrote about them.

9. The old dilapidated stadium was opened to the public on September 15 1931.

10. Afterward we will go out for ice cream.

D.3 Unnecessary Commas

It is as important to know where *not* to place commas as it is to know where to place them. The following rules explain where it is incorrect to place them:

1. **Do not place a comma between a subject and its verb, between a verb and its complement, or between an adjective and the word it modifies.**

	Adjective Subject
INCORRECT	The stunning, imaginative, and intriguing, painting, became the hit of the show. Verb
CORRECT	The stunning, imaginative, and intriguing painting became the hit of the show.

2. **Do not place a comma between two verbs, subjects, or complements used as compounds.**

	Compound verb
INCORRECT	Marisol called, and asked me to come by her office.
CORRECT	Marisol called and asked me to come by her office.

3. **Do not place a comma before a coordinating conjunction joining two dependent clauses** (see p. 394).

	Dependent clause
INCORRECT	The city planner examined blueprints that the park designer had submitted, and that the budget officer had approved.
	Dependent clause
CORRECT	The city planner examined blueprints that the park designer had submitted and that the budget officer had approved.

4. **Do not place commas around restrictive clauses, phrases, or appositives.** Restrictive clauses, phrases, and appositives are modifiers that are essential to the meaning of the sentence.

INCORRECT	The girl, who grew up down the block, became my lifelong friend.
CORRECT	The girl who grew up down the block became my lifelong friend.

5. **Do not place a comma before the word *than* in a comparison or after the words *like* and *such* as in an introduction to a list.**

INCORRECT	Some snails, such as, the Oahu tree snail, have more colorful shells, than other snails.
CORRECT	Some snails, such as the Oahu tree snail, have more colorful shells than other snails.

6. **Do not place a comma next to a period, a question mark, an exclamation point, a dash, or an opening parenthesis.**

INCORRECT	"When will you come back?," Dillon's son asked him.
CORRECT	"When will you come back?" Dillon's son asked him.
INCORRECT	The bachelor button, (also known as the cornflower) grows well in ordinary garden soil.
CORRECT	The bachelor button (also known as the cornflower) grows well in ordinary garden soil.

7. **Do not place a comma between cumulative adjectives.** Cumulative adjectives, unlike coordinate adjectives (see p. 524), cannot be joined by *and* or rearranged.

INCORRECT	The light, yellow, roses blossom was a pleasant birthday surprise. [*The light and yellow and rose blossom* does not make sense, so the commas are incorrect.]
CORRECT	The light yellow roses blossom was a pleasant birthday surprise.

D.4 Colons and Semicolons

When to Use a Colon

A **colon** follows an independent clause and usually signals that the clause is to be explained or elaborated on. Use a colon in the following situations:

1. **To introduce items in a series after an independent clause.** The series can consist of words, phrases, or clauses.

   > I am wearing three popular colors: magenta, black, and white.

2. **To signal a list or a statement introduced by an independent clause ending with the *following* or *as follows*.**

   > The directions are as follows: take Main Street to Oak Avenue and then turn left.

3. **To introduce a quotation that follows an introductory independent clause.**

   > My brother made his point quite clear: "Never borrow my car without asking me first!"

4. **To introduce an explanation.**

   > Mathematics is enjoyable: it requires a high degree of accuracy and peak concentration.

5. **To separate titles and subtitles of books.**

   > *Biology: A Study of Life*

Note: A colon must always follow an independent clause. It should not be used in the middle of a clause.

INCORRECT	My favorite colors are: red, pink, and green.
CORRECT	My favorite colors are red, pink, and green.

When to Use a Semicolon

A **semicolon** separates equal and balanced sentence parts. Use a semicolon in the following situations:

1. **To separate two closely related independent clauses not connected by a coordinating conjunction** (see p. 484).

   > Sam had a 99 average in math; he earned an A in the course.

2. **To separate two independent clauses joined by a conjunctive adverb** (see p. 483).

   > Margaret earned an A on her term paper; consequently, she was exempt from the final exam.

3. **To separate independent clauses joined with a coordinating conjunction if the clauses are very long or if they contain numerous commas.**

> By late afternoon, having tried on every pair of black jeans in the mall, Marsha was tired and cranky; but she still had not found what she needed to complete her outfit for the play.

4. **To separate items in a series if the items are lengthy or contain commas.**

> The soap opera characters include Marianne Loundsberry, the heroine; Ellen and Sarah, her children; Barry, her ex-husband; and Louise, her best friend.

5. **To correct a comma splice or run-on sentence** (see p. 390).

EXERCISE 15	Correcting Sentences Using Colons and Semicolons

Directions: Correct each of the following sentences by placing colons and semicolons where necessary. Delete any incorrect punctuation.

EXAMPLE   Samuel Clemens disliked his name; therefore, he used Mark
Twain as his pen name.

1. The large, modern, and airy, gallery houses works of art by important artists, however, it has not yet earned national recognition as an important gallery.

_____

_____

2. Rita suggested several herbs to add to my spaghetti sauce, oregano, basil, and thyme.

_____

_____

3. Vic carefully proofread the paper, it was due the next day.

_____

_____

4. Furniture refinishing is a great hobby, it is satisfying to be able to make a piece of furniture look new again.

_____

_____

5. The bridesmaids in my sister's wedding are as follows, Judy, her best friend Kim, our sister, Franny, our cousin, and Sue, a family friend.

_____

_____

6. Mac got a speeding ticket, he has to go to court next Tuesday.

_____

_____

7. I will go for a swim when the sun comes out, it will not be so chilly then.

_____

_____

8. Carlos was hungry after his hockey game, consequently, he ordered four hamburgers.

_____

_____

9. Sid went to the bookstore to purchase _Physical Anthropology Man and His Makings_, it is required for one of his courses.

_____

_____

10. Here is an old expression, "The way to a man's heart is through his stomach."

_____

_____

D.5 Dashes, Parentheses, Hyphens, Apostrophes, Quotation Marks

Dashes (—)

The **dash** is used to (1) separate nonessential elements from the main part of the sentence, (2) create a stronger separation, or interruption, than commas or parentheses, and (3) emphasize an idea, create a dramatic effect, or indicate a sudden change in thought.

> My sister—the friendliest person I know—will visit me this weekend.
>
> My brother's most striking quality is his ability to make money—or so I thought until I heard of his bankruptcy.

Do not leave spaces between the dash and the words it separates.

Parentheses ()

Parentheses are used in pairs to separate extra or nonessential information that often amplifies, clarifies, or acts as an aside to the main point. Unlike dashes, parentheses de-emphasize information.

> Some large breeds of dogs (golden retrievers and Newfoundlands) are susceptible to hip deformities.
>
> The prize was dinner for two (maximum value, $50) at a restaurant of one's choice.

Tip for Writers

Its, your, his, and *their* are *possessive* forms that go before nouns. Their meanings are possessive, so don't use an apostrophe in these words. On the other hand, *it's, you're, he's,* and *they're* are all contractions of pronouns with *is* or *are,* so an apostrophe is needed in each of these words.

Hyphens (-)

Hyphens have the following primary uses:

1. **To split a word when dividing it between two lines of writing or typing** (see p. 536).

2. **To join two or more words that function as a unit, either as a noun or as a noun modifier.**

mother-in-law	single-parent families
20-year-old	school-age children
state-of-the-art sound system	

Apostrophes (')

Use **apostrophes** in the following situations:

1. **To show ownership or possession.** When the person, place, or thing doing the possessing is a singular noun, add -'s to the end of it, regardless of what its final letter is.

The man's football tickets	John Keats's poetry
Aretha's best friend	

With plural nouns that end in -s, add only an apostrophe to the end of the word.

the twins' bedroom	postal workers' hours
teachers' salaries	

With plural nouns that do not end in -s, add -'s.

children's books	men's slacks

Do not use an apostrophe with the possessive adjective *its.*

INCORRECT	It's frame is damaged.
CORRECT	Its frame is damaged.

2. **To indicate omission of one or more letters in a word or number.** Contractions are used in informal writing, but usually not in formal academic writing.

it's [it is]	hasn't [has not]
doesn't [does not]	'57 Ford [1957 Ford]
you're [you are]	class of '99 [class of 1999]

Quotation Marks (" ")

Quotation marks separate a direct quotation from the sentence that contains it. Here are some rules to follow in using quotation marks.

1. **Quotation marks are always used in pairs.**

   Note: A comma or period goes at the end of the quotation, inside the quotation marks.

   > Marge declared, "I never expected Peter to give me a gift for Christmas."
   >
   > "I never expected Peter to give me a watch for Christmas," Marge declared.

2. **Use single quotation marks for a quotation within a quotation.**

   > My literature professor said, "Byron's line 'She walks in beauty like the night' is one of his most sensual."

   Note: When quoting long prose passages of more than four typed lines, do not use quotation marks. Instead, set off the quotation from the rest of the text by indenting each line one-half inch from the left margin. This format is called a **block quotation.**

   > The opening lines of the Declaration of Independence establish the purpose of the document:
   >
   > > When in the Course of human events it becomes necessary for one people to dissolve the political bonds which have connected them with another, and to assume among the powers of the earth, the separate and equal station to which the Laws of Nature and of Nature's God entitle them, a decent respect to the opinions of mankind requires that they should declare the causes which impel them to the separation.

3. **Use quotation marks to indicate titles of songs, short stories, poems, reports, articles, and essays.** Books, movies, plays, operas, paintings, statues, and the names of television series are italicized (or underlined to indicate italics).

   > "Rappaccini's Daughter" (short story)
   >
   > *60 Minutes* [or 60 Minutes] (television series)
   >
   > "The Road Not Taken" (poem)

4. **Colons, semicolons, exclamation points, and question marks, when not part of the quoted material, go outside of the quotation marks.**

   > What did George mean when he said, "People in glass houses shouldn't throw stones"?

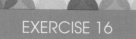

EXERCISE 16   Adding Appropriate Punctuation Marks

Directions: To the following sentences, add dashes, apostrophes, parentheses, hyphens, and quotation marks where necessary.

    EXAMPLE   "You are not going out dressed that way!" said Frank's roommate.

1. My daughter in law recently entered medical school.

   _____

   _____

2. At the bar I worked at last summer, the waitresses tips were always pooled and equally divided.

   _____

   _____

3. Youre going to Paris next summer, aren't you?

   _____

   _____

4. The career counselor said, The computer field is not as open as it used to be.

   _____

   _____

5. My English professor read aloud Frost's poem Two Look at Two.

   _____

   _____

6. Frank asked me if I planned to buy a big screen television for our Super Bowl party.

   _____

   _____

7. Rachel the teaching assistant for my linguistics class spent last year in China.

   _____

   _____

8. Macy's is having a sale on womens boots next week.

   _____

   _____

9. Trina said, My one year old's newest word is bzz, which she says whenever she sees a fly.

   _____

   _____

10. Some animals horses and donkeys can interbreed, but they produce infertile offspring.

    _____

    _____

Managing Mechanics and Spelling

E.1 Capitalization

In general, **capital letters** are used to mark the beginning of a sentence, to mark the beginning of a quotation, and to identify proper nouns. Here are some guidelines on capitalization:

What to Capitalize	*Example*
1. First word in every sentence	Prewriting is useful.
2. First word in a direct quotation	Sarah commented, "That exam was difficult!"
3. Names of people and animals, including the pronoun *I*	Aladdin Maya Angelou Spot
4. Names of specific places, cities, states, nations, geographic areas or regions	New Orleans the Southwest Lake Erie
5. Government and public offices, departments, buildings	Williamsville Library House of Representatives
6. Names of social, political, business, sporting, cultural organizations	Boy Scouts Buffalo Bills
7. Names of months, days of the week, holidays	August Tuesday Halloween
8. In titles of works: the first word following a colon, the first and last words, and all other words except articles, prepositions, and conjunctions	*Biology: A Study of Life* "Once More to the Lake"
9. Races, nationalities, languages	African American, Italian, English
10. Religions, religious figures, sacred books	Hindu, Hinduism, God, Allah, the Bible
11. Names of products	Tide, Buick
12. Personal titles when they come right before a name	Professor Rodriguez Senator Hatch
13. Major historic events	World War I
14. Specific course titles	History 201, Introduction to Psychology

EXERCISE 17   Practicing Capitalization

Directions: Capitalize words as necessary in the following sentences.

M
EXAMPLE   Farmers in the ~~m~~idwest were devastated by floods last summer.

1. My mother is preparing some special foods for our hanukkah meal; rabbi epstein will join us.

2. My american politics professor used to be a judge in the town of evans.

3. A restaurant in the galleria mall serves korean food.

4. A graduate student I know is writing a book about buddha titled *the great one: ways to enlightenment.*

5. at the concert last night, cher changed into many different outfits.

6. An employee announced over the public address system, "attention, customers! we have pepsi on sale in aisle ten for a very low price!"

7. Karen's father was stationed at fort bradley during the vietnam war.

8. Last tuesday the state assembly passed governor allen's budget.

9. Boston is an exciting city; be sure to visit the museum of fine arts.

10. Marcos asked if i wanted to go see the bolshoi ballet at shea's theatre in november.

E.2 Abbreviations

An **abbreviation** is a shortened form of a word or phrase that is used to represent the whole word or phrase. The following is a list of common acceptable abbreviations:

What to Abbreviate	*Example*
1. Some titles before or after people's names	Mr. Ling Samuel Rosen, M.D. *but* Professor Ashe
2. Names of familiar organizations, corporations, countries	CIA, IBM, VISTA, USA
3. Time references preceded or followed by a number	7:00 A.M. 3:00 P.M. A.D. 1973
4. Latin terms when used in footnotes, references, or parentheses	i.e. [*id est*, "that is"] et al. [*et alii*, "and others"]

Here is a list of things that are usually *not* abbreviated:

	Example	
What Not to Abbreviate	***Incorrect***	***Correct***
1. Units of measurement	thirty in.	thirty inches
2. Geographic or other place names when used in sentences	N.Y. Elm St.	New York Elm Street
3. Parts of written works when used in sentences	Ch. 3	Chapter 3
4. Names of days, months, holidays	Tues.	Tuesday
5. Names of subject areas	psych.	psychology

EXERCISE 18	Correcting Inappropriate Use of Abbreviations

Directions: Correct the inappropriate use of abbreviations in the following sentences. If a sentence contains no errors, write "C" for correct beside it.

EXAMPLE   We live 30 ~~mi.~~ outside ~~NYC.~~

<u>We live 30 miles outside New York City.</u>

_____ **1.** Frank enjoys going to swim at the YMCA on Oak St.

_____

_____ **2.** Prof. Jorge asked the class to turn to pg. 8.

_____

_____ **3.** Because he is seven ft. tall, my brother was recruited for the high school b-ball team.

_____

_____ **4.** When I asked Ron why he hadn't called me, he said it was Northeast Bell's fault (i.e., his phone hadn't been working).

_____

_____ **5.** Tara is flying Southwest to KC to visit her parents next Wed.

_____

_____ **6.** At 8:30 P.M., we turned on NBC to watch *Dancing with the Stars*.

_____

_____ **7.** Last wk. I missed my chem. lab.

_____

_____ **8.** The exam wasn't too difficult; only ques. number 15 and ques. no. 31 were extremely difficult.

_____

_____ **9.** Dr. Luc removed the mole from my rt. hand using a laser.

_____

_____ **10.** Mark drove out to L.A. to audition for a role in MGM's new movie.

_____

E.3 Hyphenation and Word Division

Tip for Writers

A *syllable* is a group of letters with one vowel sound, such as *tall* or *straight*. In a dictionary, the first, bold-faced listing of a world has dots to show where the word can be divided with a hyphen and continued on the next line:

trans•por•ta•tion

On occasion you must divide and hyphenate a word on one line and continue it on the next. Here are some guidelines for dividing words.

1. **Divide words only when necessary.** Frequent word divisions make a paper difficult to read.

2. **Divide words between syllables.** Consult a dictionary if you are unsure how to break a word into syllables.

di-vi-sion	pro-tect

3. **Do not divide one-syllable words.**

4. **Do not divide a word so that a single letter is left at the end of a line.**

INCORRECT	a-typical
CORRECT	atyp-ical

5. **Do not divide a word so that fewer than three letters begin the new line.**

INCORRECT	**visu-al**
CORRECT	**vi-sual**
INCORRECT	**caus-al [This word cannot be divided at all.]**

6. **Divide compound words only between the words.**

some-thing	any-one

7. **Divide words that are already hyphenated only at the hyphen.**

ex-policeman

EXERCISE 19   Practicing Division

Directions: Insert a diagonal (/) mark where each word should be divided. Mark "N" beside it if the word should not be divided.

   EXAMPLE   every/where

_____ **1.** enclose   _____ **6.** disgusted

_____ **2.** house   _____ **7.** chandelier

_____ **3.** saxophone   _____ **8.** headphones

_____ **4.** hardly   _____ **9.** swings

_____ **5.** well-known   _____ **10.** abyss

E.4 Numbers

Numbers can be written as numerals (600) or words (six hundred). Here are some guidelines for when to use numerals and when to use words:

When to Use Numerals	*Example*
1. Numbers that are spelled with more than two words	375 students
2. Days and years	August 10, 2016
3. Decimals, percentages, fractions	56.7 59 percent 1¾ cups
4. Exact times	9:27 A.M.
5. Pages, chapters, volumes; acts and lines from plays	Chapter 12 volume 4
6. Addresses	122 Peach Street
7. Exact amounts of money	$5.60
8. Scores and statistics	23–6 5 of every 12

When to Use Words	*Example*
1. Numbers that begin sentences	Two hundred ten students attended the lecture.
2. Numbers of one or two words	sixty students, two hundred women

EXERCISE 20   Practicing Correct Number Usage

Directions: Correct the misuse of numbers in the following sentences. If a sentence contains no errors, write "C" for correct beside it.

EXAMPLE   The reception hall was filled with 500 guests.
            The reception hall was filled with five hundred guests.

_____ **1.** At 6:52 A.M. my roommate's alarm clock went off.

_____ **2.** I purchased 9 turtlenecks for five dollars and fifty-five cents each.

_____ **3.** 35 floats were entered in the parade, but only 4 received prizes.

_____   **4.** Act three of *Othello* is very exciting.

_____

_____   **5.** Almost fifty percent of all marriages end in divorce.

_____

_____   **6.** The Broncos won the game 21–7.

_____

_____   **7.** We were assigned volume two of *Don Quixote*, beginning on page 351.

_____

_____   **8.** The hardware store is located at three forty-four Elm Street, 2 doors down from my grandmother's house.

_____

_____   **9.** Maryanne's new car is a 2-door V-8.

_____

_____   **10.** Our anniversary is June ninth, two thousand ten.

_____

E.5   Suggestions for Improving Spelling

Correct spelling is important to a well-written paragraph or essay. The following suggestions will help you submit papers without misspellings:

1. **Do not worry about spelling as you write your first draft.** Checking a word in a dictionary at this point will interrupt your flow of ideas. If you do not know how a word is spelled, spell it the way it sounds. Circle or underline the word so you remember to check it later.

2. **Keep a list of words you commonly misspell.** This list can be part of your error log.

3. **Every time you catch an error or find a misspelled word on a paper returned by your instructor, add it to your list.**

4. **Study your list.** Ask a friend to quiz you on the words. Eliminate words from the list after you have passed several quizzes on them.

5. **Develop a spelling awareness.** You'll find that your spelling will improve just by your being aware that spelling is important. When you encounter a new word, notice how it is spelled and practice writing it.

6. **Pronounce words you are having difficulty spelling.** Pronounce each syllable distinctly.

7. **Review basic spelling rules.** Your college library or learning lab may have manuals, workbooks, or computer programs that cover basic rules and provide guided practice.

8. **Be sure to have a dictionary readily available when you write.**

9. **Read your final draft through once, checking only for spelling errors.** Look at each word carefully, and check the spelling of those words of which you are uncertain.

E.6 Six Useful Spelling Rules

The following six rules focus on common spelling trouble spots:

1. **Is it *ei* or *ie*?**

   Rule: Use *i* before *e*, except after *c* or when the syllable is pronounced *ay* as in the word *weigh.*

   > *i* before *e:* bel<u>ie</u>ve, n<u>ie</u>ce
   >
   > except after *c:* rec<u>ei</u>ve, conc<u>ei</u>ve
   >
   > or when pronounced *ay:* n<u>ei</u>ghbor, sleigh

Exceptions:	either	neither	foreign	forfeit
	height	leisure	weird	seize

2. **When adding an ending, do you keep or drop the final *e*?**

   Rules: a. Keep the final *e* when adding an ending that begins with a consonant. (Vowels are *a, e, i, o, u,* and sometimes *y;* all other letters are consonants.)

   > hope → hopeful   aware → awareness
   >
   > live → lively   force → forceful

   b. Drop the final *e* when adding an ending that begins with a vowel.

   > hope → hoping   file → filing
   >
   > note → notable   write → writing

Exceptions:	argument	truly	changeable
	awful	<u>manageable</u>	courageous
	judgment	<u>noticeable</u>	outrageous
	acknowledgment		

   ## Tip for Writers

   The final *e* must remain on a word (before adding an ending) if the *e* is needed to keep a "soft" *c* sound (like *s*) or a "soft" *g* sound (like *j*) on the preceding letter. Two examples are *noticeable* and *manageable.*

3. **When adding an ending, do you keep the final *y*, change it to *i*, or drop it?**

   Rules: a. Keep the *y* if the letter before the *y* is a vowel.

   > delay → delaying   buy → buying   prey → preyed

    b. Change the *y* to *i* if the letter before the *y* is a consonant, but keep the *y* for the *-ing* ending.

> defy → defiance   marry → married
>
>   → defying   → marrying

4. When adding an ending to a one-syllable word, when do you double the final letter if it is a consonant?

    Rules: **a.** In one-syllable words, double the final consonant when a single vowel comes before it.

> drop → dropped   shop → shopped   pit → pitted

           b. In one-syllable words, *don't* double the final consonant when two vowels or a consonant comes before it.

> repair → repairable   sound → sounded
>
> real → realize

5. When adding an ending to a word with more than one syllable, when do you double the final letter if it is a consonant?

    Rules: **a.** In multisyllable words, double the final consonant when a single vowel comes before it *and* the stress falls on the last syllable. (Vowels are *a, e, i, o, u,* and sometimes *y.* All other letters are consonants.)

> begin' → beginning   transmit' → transmitted
>
> repel' → repelling

           b. In multisyllable words, do *not* double the final consonant (a) when two vowels or a vowel and another consonant come before it *or* (b) when the stress is not on the last syllable.

> despair → despairing   ben'efit → benefited
>
> conceal → concealing

6. To form a plural, do you add *-s* or *-es*?

    Rules: **a.** For most nouns, add *-s.*

> cat → cats   house → houses

           b. Add *-es* to words that end in *-o* if the *-o* is preceded by a consonant.

> hero → heroes   potato → potatoes

               Note: *Zoos, radios, ratios,* and other words ending with two vowels are made plural by adding *-s.*

           c. Add *-es* to words ending in *-ch, -sh, -ss, -x,* or *-z.*

> church → churches   fox → foxes   dish → dishes

Error Correction Exercises

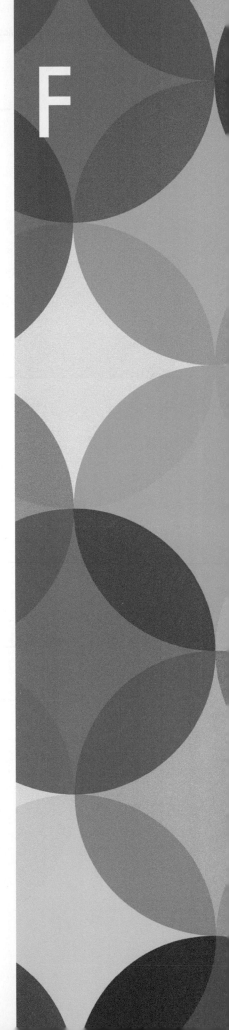

Revise each of the following paragraphs. Look for errors in sentence structure, grammar, punctuation, mechanics, and spelling. Rewrite these paragraphs with corrections.

EXERCISE 21

Jazz is a type of music, originating in new orleans in the early Twenties, and contained a mixture of African and European musical elements. There are a wide variety of types of jazz including: the blues, swing, bop and modern. Jazz includes both hard and soft music. Unlike rock music, jazz does not goes to extremes. Rock bands play so loud you can't understand half of the words. As a result, jazz is more relacking and enjoyable.

_____

_____

_____

_____

_____

EXERCISE 22

every one thinks vacations are great fun but that isnt allways so. Some people are to hyper to relax when their on vaccation. My sister Sally is like that. She has to be on the move at alltimes. She can never slow down and take it easy. She goes from activity to activity at a wild pace. When Sally does have a spare moment between activities, she spends her freetime thinking about work problems and her family and their problems and what she should do about them when she gets back. Consequently, when Sally gets back from a vacation she is exhausted and more tense and upset then when she left home.

_____

_____

_____

_____

_____

_____

_____

EXERCISE 23

Soap operas are usually serious eposodes of different people in the world of today. There about fictuous people whom are supposed to look real. But each character has their unique prblems, crazzy relationships and nonrealistical quirks and habits. In real live, it would never happen. The actors are always getting themself into wiered and unusall situation that are so of the wall that they could never be real. Its just to unreal to have 20 looney people all good frinds.

_____

_____

_____

_____

EXERCISE 24

Here are two forms of music, we have rock music and we have country music. First, these two sound differen. Rock music is very loud and with a high base sound, sometimes you can't even understand the words that the singer is singing. On the other hand, country music is a bit softer with a mellow but up beat sound. Although country music sometimes sounds boring, at least you can understand the lyrics when listening to it. Country singers usually have a country western accent also unlike rock singers.

_____

_____

_____

_____

EXERCISE 25

What a Good Friend Is

I have this friend Margaret who is really not too intelligent. It took awhile before I could accept her limitations. But, I had to get to know Margaret and her feelings. We are like two hands that wash each other. I help her, she helps me. when I need her to babysit for me while I'm at work it's done. If she needs a ride to the dentist she's got it. All I need is to be given time to do them. We help each other and that is why we are friends.

Good friends; Friends that do for one another. To tell the friend the truth about something that is asked of them. And for the other to respect your views as you would theirs. A friend is there to listen if you have a problem and to suggest something to help solve the problem but, yet not telling you just what to do. Or just to be the shoulder to cry on. Good friends go places and do things together. Good Friends are always there when you need them.

_____

_____

_____

_____

_____

_____

_____

_____

_____

_____

Putting Labels on People

People tend to label someone as stupid if they are slower and takes more time in figuring out an assignment or just trying to understand directions. My friend Georgette is a good example. People make fun of her. When a person has to deal with this type of ridicule by her fellow students or friend she start to feel insecure in speaking up. She start to think she is slower mentally, she gets extremely paranoid when asked to give answer in class. She feels any answer out of her mouth will be wrong. Her self-image shoots down drastically, like a bottom less pit. that She will avoyd in answering all answers even when she's almost positive she's right. It's the possibility of being wrong that will keep her from speaking. Then when some one else gives the answer she seess she was right, she would become extremely anoid at herself for not answering the question. As a result, she start to run away from all challenges, even the slightest challenge will frighten her away. Do from the teasing of her friends, Georgette will lock herself away from trying to understand and her famous words when facing to a challenge will be I can't do it!

Therefore, when a person makes a mistake, you should think of what you say before you say it and be sure it's not going to hurt the person. You comments may help destroy that person self confidence.

_____

_____

_____

_____

_____

_____

_____

_____

_____

_____

_____

_____

_____

PART SIX THEMATIC READER

Writing in Response to Reading

Kzenon/Shutterstock

Robert Hainer/Fotolia

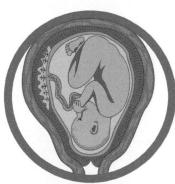

Ianamaster/Fotolia

Theme 1
Poverty in America

Poverty is a global issue affecting millions of people and crossing lines of age, race, and gender. Although the World Bank defines poverty as living on less than $2 a day, poverty thresholds vary from country to country. In the United States, for example, the Census Bureau determines a family's poverty status by assigning it one of 48 possible poverty thresholds, depending on the family's size and the age of its members. The different criteria established for poverty levels do not change the meaning of poverty—a condition where basic needs for food, clothing, and shelter are not being met—or address the significant and often dire effects of poverty. In the United States alone, the U.S. Census Bureau reported that more than 43 million Americans lived in poverty in 2015.

The readings in this theme look at various aspects of poverty in America, examining how children are affected by poverty, how certain events or situations can lead to poverty, and the impact of food and housing insecurity on college students.

> Reading 1: **"A Doctor's Call for Action on Childhood Poverty" by Daniel R. Taylor**
>
> Reading 2: **"Event Poverty" by William Kornblum and Joseph Julian**
>
> Reading 3: **"Hungry, Homeless, and in College" by Sara Goldrick-Rab and Katharine M. Broton**

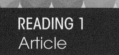

READING 1
Article

A Doctor's Call for Action on Childhood Poverty

Thinking Before Reading

The following article, "A Doctor's Call for Action on Childhood Poverty," was originally published in *The Philadelphia Inquirer* in 2016. The author, Daniel R. Taylor, D.O., is an associate professor at the Drexel University College of Medicine and director of community pediatrics and child advocacy at St. Christopher's Hospital for Children.

As you read, note how the author uses a variety of evidence to support his thesis.

1. Preview the reading, using the steps discussed in Chapter 1, page 4.

2. Connect the reading to your own experience by answering the following questions:

   a. When and where have you encountered poverty? What has been your response?

   b. In your experience, what does the typical "face" of poverty look like?

3. Mark and annotate as you read.

A Doctor's Call for Action on Childhood Poverty

Daniel R. Taylor

"Many things we need can wait. The child cannot. Now is the time his bones are being formed, his blood is being made, his mind is being developed. To him we cannot say tomorrow, his name is today."

—Gabriela Mistral, Chilean Poet, Nobel Laureate

1   The main aim of pediatrics is prevention. Prevention of diseases, of injury, of emotional problems, of developmental and intellectual delays. Our armamentarium includes vaccines; screening instruments; and guidance on development, safety, and nutrition. It's time to add one more item to our tool kit: screening our young patients for health and emotional problems related to poverty.

2   At St. Christopher's Hospital for Children in the heart of North Philadelphia, we see 15 to 20 newborns a day, brought in for their checkups. Many are at high risk of developmental delays, school failure, ADHD, heart disease and even premature death—all because they were born into the most concentrated poverty in Pennsylvania. This is the lottery of birth for millions of similar children across the United States.

3   The most common—and serious—disease in American children is poverty. The daily grind of living without knowing whether there will be enough to eat, whether the lights will come on, whether the landlord will fix the roof or seek to evict for not paying the rent has direct, dire health consequences.

4   Areas of deep poverty, where more than 40 percent of the population lives on less than $24,000 a year for a family of four, have doubled to include 13.8 million people since 2000. That's the highest level ever recorded. More than 135,000 Philadelphia children—16 million children nationwide—live in such circumstances, and it literally is killing them. A child from the most violent part of the city, North Strawberry Mansion/Swampoodle, has an average life expectancy of 68, which is about two decades less than a child from Old City/Society Hill, according to a recent study from the Robert Wood Johnson Foundation.

5   In an unprecedented move, the American Academy of Pediatrics (AAP) and the Academic Pediatric Association (APA) simultaneously released policy statements this month describing the epidemic of childhood poverty, the deleterious effects of poverty on the developing child, and what should be done about it. The reports help bring this issue to the forefront.

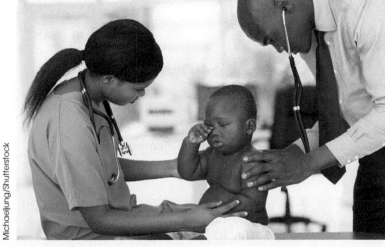

Michaeljung/Shutterstock

6   So does the science. Evolution has gifted us with the ability to become stronger, to think faster, to jump higher when faced with a stressful situation. The brain senses danger and the adrenal glands secrete cortisol that bathes our bloodstream and attaches itself to muscle cells, our heart, our brain. All that helps us react in a productive or even lifesaving way.

7   But what happens when that stress is prolonged, chronic, and toxic, exacerbated by poverty? A study in JAMA Pediatrics showed that poverty was associated with smaller brain volumes in areas of the brain that are responsible for memory, for language, for self control, for executive functioning. Another 2015 study of more than 1,000 children and young adults revealed that in poor children, small differences in income were associated with relatively larger differences in brain surface area. Is it then a surprise that only 14 percent of fourth graders in Philadelphia's public schools are reading at grade level? That there are epidemics of sexually transmitted diseases and violence, both of which require self-control and executive functioning to prevent?

8   Cardiovascular disease continues to be the leading killer of adults in the United States, and recent evidence shows heart damage starts early for children raised in poverty. Teenagers facing adversity such as poverty have more circulating Endothelin-1, which causes blood vessels to constrict, raising blood pressure and damaging the delicate vessels around the heart, the brain, the kidneys, a recent study in the journal Hypertension found. Another study in JAMA Pediatrics in March, "Childhood Psychosocial Factors and Coronary Artery Calcification in Adulthood," demonstrated that the more adversity a child had, the more likely that child was to have coronary artery disease 28 years later, even adjusted for traditional CVD risk factors such as smoking, obesity, depression, and lack of social support. Childhood poverty and stress even creep into our DNA, creating changes that get passed on to the next generation, affecting how babies respond to stress.

9   So what works to ameliorate the effects of child poverty? The Earned Income Tax Credit and Temporary Assistance for Needed Families can help lift children out of poverty. CHIP and the Affordable Care Act have decreased uninsurance rates among children to an all-time low of 6 percent. Investments in early childhood education like Pre-K for Pa. have been shown to have long-lasting health benefits, as do nutrition programs such as WIC, SNAP, and school meals. Home visiting and parenting programs help children bond with the most important buffer against poverty, a stable, supportive adult in their lives. Increasing the minimum wage is also of vital importance.

10   Social Security and Medicare have cut poverty among seniors. We cannot wait to do the same for our children. We need to act today.

Getting Ready to Write

Checking Your Comprehension

Answer each of the following questions using complete sentences.

1. What does the author say is the main goal of pediatrics?

2. According to the author, what items are already in a pediatrician's "tool kit"? What item does the author want to add?

3. What "unprecedented move" did the American Academy of Pediatrics (AAP) and the Academic Pediatric Association (APA) make? Why was this move important?

4. What does the author say is the most common and serious disease in American children?

5. According to the author, what works to ameliorate the effects of child poverty?

Strengthening Your Vocabulary

Identify at least five words from the reading that are unfamiliar to you. Using context clues, word parts, or a dictionary, if necessary, write a brief definition of each word as it is used in the reading.

Examining the Reading: Using Idea Maps

Create an idea map of "A Doctor's Call for Action on Childhood Poverty." Start with the title and thesis and include the main points of the selection.

Thinking Critically: An Integrated Perspective

1. The author writes about the physical and emotional effects of poverty on children. Write a journal entry summarizing the effects described in the article.

2. The author begins the article with a quote from Chilean poet Gabriela Mistral. How does this quote relate to the content of the article? Is the quote effective in capturing your attention and motivating you to read the article? How does the author return to the quote at the end of the selection?

3. Do you agree with the author that the most important buffer against poverty is a stable, supportive adult in children's lives? Write a journal entry explaining why or why not.

4. How does the author's background make him uniquely qualified to write about this topic? Do you think this article would have been less effective if a news reporter had written it instead of a physician? Why or why not?

5. Evaluate the conclusion of the article, which constitutes a "call for action." Do you think the author is optimistic about promoting change with respect to childhood poverty? Why or why not?

Thinking Critically

For a review of critical-thinking skills, see Chapter 9.

1. As a pediatrician and child advocate, the author of this article, Daniel Taylor, is personally and professionally invested in the care of patients affected by poverty. Would you therefore say that this article is biased? Why or why not?

2. How would you describe the intended audience for this article? To answer this question, consider its original source as well as its content.

3. Why did the author include a comparison of life expectancies for children born in two different parts of the city? What inference can you make about the Old City/Society Hill neighborhood?

4. What types of evidence did the author use to support his thesis? How effective was it? What other types of evidence might have been convincing?

5. What was the author's purpose in writing this article?

Writing About the Reading

1. What does poverty look like in your town or neighborhood? How do you respond to poverty when you see it? How should society respond? Write an essay in which you explore your answers.

2. The author refers to "the lottery of birth" in the United States. What does he mean by this phrase? How would you describe the "lottery" of your own birth? What factors do you think are most important or have the most potential to improve one's chances at overcoming a poor beginning? Write an essay in which you explore some of the author's suggestions as well as your own ideas about addressing childhood poverty.

3. The author describes how our bodies have evolved to respond productively when faced with a stressful situation. Think about a stressful situation in your own life. What was your physical reaction? Did you have an emotional reaction as well? Consider how those effects might become damaging to your health if they were prolonged, chronic, and exacerbated by other factors (such as poverty) and write an essay in which you describe the stressful situation and your responses and explore the potential long-term effects.

READING 2
Textbook

Event Poverty

The following excerpt, "Event Poverty," was originally published in the sociology textbook *Social Problems*. As you read, note how the authors organize their discussion of the events and situations that can lead to poverty.

1. Preview the reading, using the steps discussed in Chapter 1, page 4.

2. Connect the reading to your own experience by answering the following questions:

   a. What do you think is the most likely cause of poverty? Have you seen or can you predict situations or events that might push a person or family below the poverty level?

   b. How would you define the phrase "working poor"?

3. Mark and annotate as you read.

Event Poverty

William Kornblum and Joseph Julian

1   Some families are prone to what is known as *event poverty*. In the event of illness, loss of one of the jobs, marital discord, or pregnancy, for example, the family could easily lose half its income and then plunge well below the official poverty level. When a manufacturing plant or other place of employment closes abruptly, hundreds of workers may be thrown out of work. Or a family may become impoverished because of high medical bills or, as Americans have seen so dramatically in the last decade, because they have lost everything in a storm or other natural disaster. The following sections discuss some of the events and situations that can lead to poverty.

2   **A SEVERE RECESSION** The recession that began in 2008 has largely abated at this writing in late 2015. Today, unemployment rates hover around 5 percent for all U.S. residents and around 10 percent for blacks, but in 2010, unemployment rates were twice as high (Bureau of Labor Statistics, 2015b). Many breadwinners lost their jobs (or worried that they would) or had their income reduced. They lost their homes to foreclosure, used their retirement savings to live on, and racked up tremendous credit card debt, often filing for personal bankruptcy.

3   Take a moment to consider some of these financial problems and related issues in more depth. What does it feel like to look for work week after week, and find no job offers? When even the lowest-tier jobs in our economy have stiff competition, many people who would like to work feel psychologically wounded by the lack of employment opportunities. A Gallup Poll based on a nationally representative sample found that people who have been unemployed more than six months are far more likely than those who are employed to feel stress, sadness, and worry (Marlar, 2010).

4   "Rhonda" is one of many people who are looking for a good job with good pay (Seccombe, 2015). She has a high school diploma, but does not have a college degree. She is a single mother, and would like to raise her young son Bobby without relying on government assistance. Rhonda, who wants a permanent full-time job but has been stymied by the tremendous growth in part-time, temporary positions, explains (Seccombe, 2015, p. 177):

> Hopefully I can get me a job. A permanent job. My sister's trying to get me a job where she works. I put my application in last week. And it would be a permanent job. When you go through those agencies, it's just temporary work. It's just whenever they need you, and it's unfair too. Every job I've found is through this temporary agency, like Manpower, but it's only temporary. And they cut my check and my food stamps, and when my job ends, it's like you're stuck again. So I'm trying to find a permanent steady job. But it's hard around here. I've been out looking for work, and hoping that something comes through.

5   Rhonda may be surprised to learn that temporary agencies are doing very well in this recessionary economy. Manpower is one of the largest private employers in the United States, ranked 129 in the Fortune 500 list of large companies, and has revenues of about $21 billion worldwide. It serves over 400,000 employer clients and has placed 12 million workers in more than 80 countries and territories (ManpowerGroup, 2015). Rhonda's experience with temporary agencies is not unique, however, and the success of these agencies reflects the growing divide between the haves and the have-nots.

6   As the recession begins to improve, it is also apparent that immigration and the fate of the nation's immigrants also hinge to a large degree on the changing feelings of economically pinched Americans and their elected officials.

7   **IMMIGRATION** Immigration is a different kind of life event that may be associated with poverty or with efforts to escape from it. In many of the world's

wealthier nations, particularly in the United States, an increasing proportion of poor people are immigrants. Almost 25 percent of the increase in poverty since the early 1970s has occurred among recent immigrants and their children. Although it is important to remember that the majority of Hispanics and Asians are neither impoverished nor immigrants, poor people from Mexico, Central America, the Caribbean, and Southeast Asia are among the largest immigrant groups today (Motel and Patten, 2013; Pew Research Center, April 4, 2013). Many live in the poorest city neighborhoods and rural counties. Most of the adults work full-time, often in the lowest-paying and most undesirable jobs. Most lack health insurance, and many fear that changes in welfare laws will make it impossible for them to send their children to school or to receive the same benefits as others who pay taxes.

8   The issue of whether poor and unskilled immigrants drive down the wages of those who are working and poor and represent a burden to taxpayers generates a great deal of controversy. Politicians who wish to capitalize on the resentment some Americans already feel toward immigrants often use this argument. For example, Arizona passed a law giving police authorization to check on the immigration status of anyone they reasonably suspect of being in the United States illegally. The failure to carry identification of one's legal status would be a crime. Opponents argue that such a law violates civil liberties and encourages racial profiling.

working poor

Individuals who, within a year, spent at least 27 weeks in the labor force (working or looking for work), but whose incomes fell below the official poverty level.

9   **LOW WAGES**   We see poor people working all around us, in restaurant kitchens, on landscaping crews, installing roofs in the hot sun, and taking care of our loved ones. According to the U.S. Department of Labor, the "working poor" are individuals who spent at least 27 weeks in the labor force (working or looking for work), but whose incomes fell below the official poverty level. Of all the people in the labor force for at least 27 weeks, about 10 million people, or about 7 percent of the nation's labor force, are working at wages so low that they remain below the official poverty threshold (Bureau of Labor Statistics, 2014). The majority of the working poor are women.

10   The situation of those who are working and poor has deteriorated over the past few decades. There are several reasons for this downhill slide, including technological changes that eliminate certain kinds of jobs, globalization (which exports jobs to lower-wage regions of the world), the reluctance of the middle and upper classes to share their wealth with less fortunate members of society, and the general attitude of Americans toward poverty.

11   **UNEMPLOYMENT OR LIMITED PART-TIME WORK**   In addition to those who are working but cannot escape from poverty because of low wages, an increasing proportion of people in the United States either are working part-time or are out of the labor force and receiving minimal benefits. These people live on a bare- bones budget and have difficulty providing for the basics in life. Their numbers are growing at a rapid rate. Sociologists often consider "extremely" poor people or households to be those living at 50 percent of the poverty threshold, which would amount to roughly $13,000 a year for a family of four or about $6,000 for one person. Using this definition, over 20 million Americans, 7 million of whom are children, live in extreme poverty.

12   Others apply the criterion used by the World Bank in international work: A person is described as living in extreme poverty if he or she lives on less than $2 a day (Shaefer and Edin, 2012). In recent years, the percentage of the population

considered extremely poor has reached the highest point in four decades. A University of Michigan study notes that 1.5 million U.S. households, comprising about 2.8 million children, were living on $2 or less in income per person per day in a given month. This figure represents almost 20 percent of all poor non-elderly households with children. About 866,000 households appear to live in extreme poverty across a full calendar quarter.

Getting Ready to Write

Checking Your Comprehension

Answer each of the following questions using complete sentences.

1. What is event poverty? What is an example of an event that may trigger event poverty?
2. How do unemployment rates today compare to those in 2010?
3. What did the law passed in Arizona authorize police to do with regard to immigrants?
4. How does the U.S. Department of Labor define the "working poor"?
5. What four reasons do the authors give for why the situation of the working poor has deteriorated over the past few decades?

Strengthening Your Vocabulary

Identify at least five words from the reading that are unfamiliar to you. Using context clues, word parts, or a dictionary, if necessary, write a brief definition of each word as it is used in the reading.

Examining the Reading: Using an Idea Map

Create an idea map of "Event Poverty." Start with the title and thesis and include the main points of the selection.

Thinking Critically: An Integrated Perspective

1. Which fact or statistic in this selection did you find most shocking? Why? Write a journal entry explaining your answer.
2. Suppose that you were faced with one of the life events that the authors describe. How would you respond? Write a journal entry about how you would cope and whether you have a "safety net" that would help you avoid difficulties or even poverty.
3. What types of evidence do the authors use to support their key points? What other types of evidence would be effective?
4. Why do the authors include the description of Rhonda's situation and her statement in paragraph 4?
5. In paragraph 8, the authors mention the controversy generated by the issue of immigrants in the work force. Do you think immigrants drive down wages and represent a burden to taxpayers? Why or why not?

Thinking Critically

For a review of critical-thinking skills, see Chapter 9.

1. What is the authors' primary purpose for writing this selection?

2. Who is the authors' intended audience? Would you say that this selection is written for a specific or a general audience? How can you tell?

3. Are the authors of this article biased in any way? If so, how?

4. Consider the following statement from paragraph 6. Is it a fact or an opinion? "As the recession begins to improve, it is also apparent that immigration and the fate of the nation's immigrants also hinge to a large degree on the changing feelings of economically pinched Americans and their elected officials."

Writing About the Reading

1. In paragraph 3, the authors write, "Take a moment to consider some of these financial problems and related issues in more depth. What does it feel like to look for work week after week, and find no job offers?" Write an essay exploring your response.

2. In their discussion of the working poor, the authors point to a reluctance of some to share wealth with less fortunate members of society as well as the general attitude of Americans toward poverty. What do you think explains this reluctance? How would you describe your attitude toward poverty? Your community's attitude? Write an essay in which you explore ways to address this reluctance and perhaps alter attitudes toward the working poor.

3. According to a Gallup poll, people who have been unemployed more than six months are more likely than those who are employed to feel stress, sadness, and worry. What would you say to someone in this situation? What information from the selection might you use to offer encouragement? Write an essay in the form of a letter to a friend, family member, or stranger who is facing long-term unemployment.

READING 3
Article

Hungry, Homeless and in College

Thinking Before Reading

The following article, "Hungry, Homeless and in College," was originally published in *The New York Times* in December 2015. As you read, note how the authors carry a particular example throughout the article while arguing their case with other evidence as well. How does this example illustrate the problem and make it more real to readers?

1. Preview the reading, using the steps discussed in Chapter 1, page 4.

2. Connect the reading to your own experience by answering the following questions:

   a. Have you ever had to go without food or shelter? How common do you think this experience is among your fellow students?

   b. What college costs do you find most challenging?

3. Mark and annotate as you read.

Hungry, Homeless and in College

Sara Goldrick-Rab and Katharine M. Broton

1   Three months after starting college, Brooke Evans found herself without a place to live. She was 19. She slept in libraries, bathrooms and her car. She sold plasma and skipped meals. It was hard to focus or participate in class, and when her grades fell, her financial aid did, too. Eventually, she left college and began sleeping on the street, in debt, without a degree.

2   As researchers who study why students don't finish college, we happen to have first met people like Ms. Evans in universities and community colleges in Wisconsin. But just how common was it across the country for college students to struggle to come up with enough money for food or shelter?

3   We asked the Association of Community College Trustees and the national nonprofit Single Stop to help us find out. Our organization, the Wisconsin HOPE Lab, along with the Healthy Minds Study, fielded a survey at 10 community colleges in New York, New Jersey, California, Pennsylvania, Louisiana, Wisconsin and Wyoming. Participants included more than 4,300 students who look broadly similar to the national community college population.

4   One in five of those students said that, in the last 30 days, she had gone hungry because of a lack of money. Thirteen percent had experienced a form of homelessness in the last year, having been thrown out or evicted, lived in shelters or abandoned buildings, or gone without a place to sleep at all. Far more—just over half—were at risk of each of those conditions. A majority had financial aid and jobs, but it wasn't enough.

5   Such high rates of food and housing insecurity among hard-working college students indicate that the nation faces a serious crisis. Much of the conversation in Washington concerning college costs—whether it's about simplifying the financial aid application or refinancing student loans—seems almost trivial in comparison with the problems these students face.

6   "Without a home and without meals, I felt like an impostor," Ms. Evans told us. "I was shamefully worrying about food, and shamefully staring at the clock to make it out of class in time to get in line for the local shelter when I should have been giving my undivided attention to the lecturer." When this is what college is like, is it any wonder that students drop out?

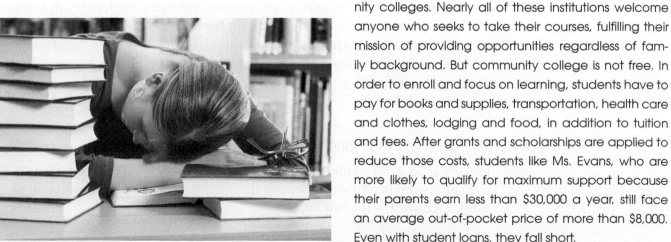

Kzenon/Shutterstock

7   More than 10.5 million students attend community colleges. Nearly all of these institutions welcome anyone who seeks to take their courses, fulfilling their mission of providing opportunities regardless of family background. But community college is not free. In order to enroll and focus on learning, students have to pay for books and supplies, transportation, health care and clothes, lodging and food, in addition to tuition and fees. After grants and scholarships are applied to reduce those costs, students like Ms. Evans, who are more likely to qualify for maximum support because their parents earn less than $30,000 a year, still face an average out-of-pocket price of more than $8,000. Even with student loans, they fall short.

8   By 2020, about two-thirds of all jobs will require education and training beyond high school. If current trends hold, the United States will face a shortfall of five million college-educated workers that year. This problem won't be solved if we don't ensure that students have their basic needs met so that they can manage their schoolwork and finish their degrees.

9   The College and University Food Bank Alliance helps institutions set up and maintain food pantries, and Scholarship America's Dreamkeepers program, along with some college foundations, supports efforts to provide emergency financial aid and counseling. Ms. Evans is back in college now, benefiting from these types of assistance. Single Stop helps community college students use all of the possible social benefits programs to which they are entitled. It also counsels them on how to manage their finances. Programs like these need to be quickly scaled up to alleviate the crisis.

10   But we will have to do much more to ensure that this problem doesn't get worse. This will require changing both our social and educational policies, while also reducing college costs. To give one example, the National School Lunch Program supports schoolchildren but not college students. Subsidized housing and transportation are often available when a student is in high school but not once he enters college. Even if the students are technically adults, this is shortsighted thinking.

11   From President Obama on down, our political leaders are urging people to do the right thing and stay in college. Students are trying—so hard that they sometimes go hungry to learn. When will we match their level of determination? A college education is a great tool for overcoming poverty, but students have to be able to escape the conditions of poverty long enough to finish their degrees or we're wasting their time.

Getting Ready to Write

Checking Your Comprehension

Answer each of the following questions using complete sentences.

1. Who is Brooke Evans?

2. For the authors' survey of community college students, what states were included?

3. Of the students in the survey, what percentage had gone hungry in the past 30 days or experienced homelessness in the past year?

4. According to the authors, what is the average out-of-pocket price of community college for students who qualify for maximum financial support?

5. What are two ways the national nonprofit Single Stop helps community college students?

Strengthening Your Vocabulary

Identify at least five words from the reading that are unfamiliar to you. Using context clues, word parts, or a dictionary, if necessary, write a brief definition of each word as it is used in the reading.

Examining the Reading: Using an Idea Map

Create an idea map of "Hungry, Homeless and in College." Start with the title and thesis and include the main points of the selection.

Thinking Critically: An Integrated Perspective

1. Why do the authors begin with the description of Brooke Evans? Does this introduction capture your attention and motivate you to continue reading? In what ways does the introduction make the issues of hunger and homelessness more relevant to you?

2. What prediction do the authors make about how current trends will affect the job market in 2020? How does this prediction support their argument? Can you think of other aspects of the issue that would support the authors' argument? Write a journal entry exploring these questions.

3. The authors make several calls for action in this selection. Write a journal entry summarizing at least three things the authors say need to happen.

4. Why do the authors mention former President Obama and other political leaders in the last paragraph? Do you agree with the authors' assertions in the last line of the selection? Why or why not?

5. Evaluate the types of details the authors use to support their thesis. Which details are most effective or persuasive? Why?

Thinking Critically

For a review of critical-thinking skills, see Chapter 9.

1. What inferences can you make about Brooke Evans? Consider what the authors tell you about her as well as what she says in paragraph 6.

2. What is the authors' primary purpose for writing this selection? Who is the intended audience?

3. Identify at least two opinions in the article. Would you classify these opinions as informed or uninformed, biased, or unbiased?

4. In paragraph 2, the authors state that they are researchers who study why students don't finish college. Does their research make them biased? Why or why not? Evaluate the authors' bias (or lack of bias) in this article.

Writing About the Reading

1. The authors offer several suggestions for assisting students in the selection, such as offering school lunch programs and subsidized housing and transportation for college students. Choose the suggestion you think has the most merit (or one of your own) and write an essay explaining why you think it would be effective and how it would work.

2. The authors mention programs that offer financial counseling to students. How do you manage your finances? Who taught you? What do you consider the most important aspect(s) of managing the costs of college? Imagine that you have been asked to advise or counsel a younger person on managing his or her finances and write an essay exploring the answers to these questions.

3. Do you agree with the authors' claim that the nation faces a serious crisis regarding food and housing insecurity among college students? Why or why not? What other crises do you think college students face? How would you go about changing the conversation in Washington to address either the authors' view or your own observation? Write an essay exploring your ideas.

Read and Respond to the Theme

Making Connections

1. All of the readings in this section talk about the effects of poverty. What other elements do the readings have in common?

2. How would you describe the scope of each of these readings? Which of the readings focuses on a problem at a local or regional level? Which reading(s) are concerned with problems that are broader in scope?

3. Now that you have read three articles on the topic of poverty, make a list of at least ten facts about poverty that you did not know before reading these articles.

Writing About the Readings

1. How would you describe the writing style in each of the readings? What one word would you use to describe the tone of each reading? In an essay, evaluate how the authors approached the subject of poverty in each of the readings, explaining which approach or style you found most effective and why.

2. Based on what you've read in this theme, how has your attitude toward poverty changed? Write an essay exploring your ideas, keeping in mind that the authors of these readings may have very different opinions on this topic.

3. All of the readings in this section talk about poverty, but each has a different focus: childhood poverty, event poverty, and poverty among college students. Which of these topics did you find most relevant or compelling? Which seemed least important? Explain your answer in an essay.

Theme 2
Relationships: The Expected and Unexpected

When they hear the word *relationship,* many people think primarily of romantic relationships. At a more general level, the word refers to the way in which two or more people, concepts, or objects are connected. For example, as a student you have a relationship not only with your romantic partner but also with your parents, your school, your community, your instructors, your boss and co-workers, and even your country.

The readings in this theme explore aspects of a variety of relationships, including cultural differences regarding romantic love and marriage, the profound bond between humans and their pets (particularly dogs), and the difficulties and joys inherent in parenthood.

> Reading 1: **"Love Across Cultures" by Nijole V. Benokraitis**
>
> Reading 2: **"Your Dog Can Make You Feel Better, and Here's Why" By Marlene Cimons**
>
> Reading 3: **"How to Enjoy the Often Exhausting, Depressing Role of Parenthood" by Alice G. Walton**

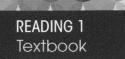

READING 1
Textbook

Love Across Cultures

Thinking Before Reading

The following excerpt, "Love Across Cultures," was originally published in the sociology textbook *Marriages and Families*. In this excerpt, the author explores how and why love varies across cultures. As you read, notice the details the author uses to illustrate cultural differences with regard to love and marriage.

1. Preview the reading, using the steps discussed in Chapter 1, page 4.

2. Connect the reading to your own experience by answering the following questions:

   a. Do you know anyone who has had an arranged marriage? How does this marriage compare to marriages you know of that were based on love?

   b. What factor(s) do you consider key to a successful relationship?

3. Mark and annotate as you read.

Love Across Cultures

Nijole V. Benokraitis

1   The meaning and expression of love vary from one culture to another. In Western societies that emphasize individualism and free choice, love is a legitimate reason for dating, living together, getting married, or getting a divorce ("the spark is gone"). In cultures that stress the group and the community, arrangements between families are more important than romantic love.

Romantic Love

2   The early colonists believed that marriage was far too important to be based on love; politics and economics, not romance, were the key factors in selecting a partner. It was only in the early twentieth century that people came to expect marriage to be based on love, sexual attraction, and personal fulfillment.

Monkey Business/Fotolia

3   Because romantic love exists in at least 89 percent of societies, it's a nearly universal phenomenon. A number of studies in China, Hong Kong, Taiwan, and Hawaii have found that many people, especially the young, believe in passionate love.

4   Romance is least important in societies where kin ties take precedence over individual relationships. In Burma, India, and Mexico, college students said that storgic, agapic, and pragmatic love are more desirable than manic, erotic, and ludic love styles. In much of China, similarly, love is tempered by recognition that a match needs parental approval. In Saudi Arabia and some other Middle Eastern countries, public embracing between men and women is taboo, the sexes can't mix in public, and a woman who is caught with an unrelated man can be flogged, arrested, or killed.

5   The Indian government endorses marriage across castes, but not everyone supports such policies. Also, some radical groups have denounced celebrating Valentine's Day—especially popular among young, middle-class urbanites—as offensive to Indian culture and have tried to disrupt businesses that sell Valentine's Day gifts and cards.

6   In Japan, which has one of the highest divorce rates in the world, expressing love and affection is uncommon, especially among men, who rarely see their wives and children; many companies pressure men to put their job first and to demonstrate their loyalty by working long hours. To increase husbands' appreciation of their wives, a man founded a Devoted Husband Organization and declared January 31 as "Beloved Wives Day," during which a husband is supposed to tell his wife that he loves her for all that she does every day for him and their family. Beloved Wives Day hasn't become a national holiday, but more men are joining the organization to show respect and affection for their wives and to avoid divorce.

Arranged Love

7   In the United States and other Western countries, people often become engaged and then inform family and friends. Worldwide, a more typical pattern is **arranged marriage**, in which parents or relatives choose the children's partners. It's expected that the partners' love for each other will grow over time.

arranged marriage
Parents or relatives choose the children's partners.

8   In many countries, arranged marriages are the norm because respect for parents' wishes, family traditions, the kin group, and the well-being of the community are more important than the individual's feelings. In fact, people in many societies find American beliefs about dating and romance at least as strange as some Americans find the concept of arranged marriages.

9   In India, the majority of marriages are arranged by parents or elders: "There has never been any room for romantic marriage in Indian society on the line of Western societies". Arranged marriages help maintain social and religious traditions, preserve group solidarity, and can augment a family's reputation and financial assets.

10   There are variations in different regions and social classes, however. Educated, upper-middle-class women are allowed to marry whomever they want, but many opt for arranged marriages. One young woman explained: "Love is important, but it's not sufficient." She's reportedly happily married to a man whom she had met just three times before their engagement. In most cases, children can reject undesirable candidates.

11   A young Indian American has convinced her parents to let her date instead of having an arranged marriage. She says, however, "In college, I just could not understand why anyone would marry someone without falling in love first. But as I've seen (my parents') love grow over the years, I have had a deeper appreciation for their arranged marriage".

12   Why do arranged marriages persist in much of India? Shy people can end up with a good partner because parents and relatives seem to do a good job in choosing mates. Also, arranged marriages offer stability because the couple's families stand behind them: "If the relationship between the couples is about to go haywire ... parents of both spouses make concerted efforts to resolve the crisis".

13   Arranged marriages also persist because of family ties. Even financially independent couples usually live with the husband's parents. As a result, similar backgrounds and compatibility with in-laws are more important in India than in the West. The advantage is considerable family support if a marriage runs into trouble. These may be some of the reasons why India has one of the lowest divorce rates in the world.

14   In arranged marriages in Sri Lanka, men and women who fall in love usually tell their parents about their choices. In Turkey, about 52 percent of women live in arranged marriages, but there is a trend toward love marriages among younger, better-educated, and urban women. In Canada, some second-generation Muslim Pakistani women are rebelling against arranged marriages. Others participate willingly because they can't find a suitable partner on their own or believe that their parents know best.

15   Studies of arranged marriages in India and Bangladesh show that, in most cases, love gradually increases and becomes stronger (Epstein, 2010) but that's not always the case. If the husband is abusive in an arranged marriage, women can't escape. In some countries such as Afghanistan, Iran, and Iraq, women who defy arranged marriages are stoned, burned to death, hanged, or shot, often by male family members or men in the community.

Getting Ready to Write

Checking Your Comprehension

Answer each of the following questions using complete sentences.

1. What two factors were key in selecting a partner among the early colonists?

2. What is an arranged marriage?

3. What is the purpose of "Beloved Wives Day" in Japan?

4. What explanation does the author give for why arranged marriages are the norm in many countries?

5. What percentage of women in Turkey live in arranged marriages?

6. What happens to women who defy arranged marriages in countries such as Afghanistan, Iran, and Iraq?

Strengthening Your Vocabulary

Identify at least five words from the reading that are unfamiliar to you. Using context clues, word parts, or a dictionary, if necessary, write a brief definition of each word as it is used in the reading.

Examining the Reading: Using Idea Maps

Create an idea map of "Love Across Cultures." Start with the title and thesis and include the main points of the selection.

Thinking Critically: An Integrated Perspective

1. Although people in Western countries often inform their families after becoming engaged, the author states that arranged marriage is a more typical pattern worldwide. What reasons does the author give for this difference? What other explanations can you think of?

2. The author includes several examples illustrating behaviors and beliefs about love in different cultures. Write a journal entry exploring your reaction to the cultural belief or behavior that you found most interesting or surprising.

3. In paragraph 12, the author discusses the persistence of arranged marriages in India. Write a journal entry summarizing the reasons why India has one of the lowest divorce rates in the world.

4. Evaluate the introduction. What important aspect(s) of "Love Across Cultures" does the author introduce in her opening paragraph?

5. What main points does the author make about romantic love?

6. The author supports her thesis using a variety of details, including statistics, facts, and examples. Which details are most effective? What other types of details might she have included in this selection?

7. Why does the author include negative aspects of relationships and marriage in other countries (paragraphs 4, 6, and 15)?

8. Evaluate the last paragraph of the selection. Does the selection end on an optimistic note or a pessimistic note? Explain.

9. Describe the photo that accompanies the reading on page 560. What aspect(s) of the reading does this photo illustrate? What other types of photos might the author have used to help support her key ideas?

10. This selection is an excerpt from a chapter titled "Love and Loving Relationships." What other topics do you predict are discussed in this chapter?

THINKING VISUALLY

Thinking Critically

For a review of critical-thinking skills, see Chapter 9.

1. Consider how the author addresses the topics of romantic love and arranged love. Is the author biased in any way? If so, how?

2. Why does the author quote the young Indian American woman in paragraph 10?

3. Who is the intended audience for this selection?

4. What is the author's purpose for writing "Love Across Cultures"? How would you describe her approach to the topic?

5. What inference can you make from this statement in paragraph 10? "Love is important, but it's not sufficient."

6. What inference can you make from this statement in paragraph 12? "If the relationship between the couples is about to go haywire...parents of both spouses make concerted efforts to resolve the crisis."

Writing About the Reading

1. Consider the various factors for selecting a partner discussed in this selection, from politics and economics to love and sexual attraction to traditions and family ties. Which of the factors in this selection do you consider most important? Least important? What other factors do you consider in choosing a partner? Write an essay addressing this issue.

2. Do you think marriages should always be based on love, or do you think an arranged marriage has the best chance for success? Imagine that you are trying to convince a friend from another country or culture that either romantic love or arranged love is the best way, and write an essay giving persuasive reasons in support of your argument.

3. Paragraph 6 describes the Devoted Husband Organization, a Japanese man's effort to increase husbands' appreciation of their wives. Do you think this was a good idea? Why or why not? Write an essay on the topic of showing appreciation for loved ones. Consider how you would want the people you care about to show their appreciation for you.

4. How does popular culture promote the idea of romantic love? How realistic is the depiction of love and marriage in music, movies, art, and literature? Choose an aspect of popular culture that interests you and write an essay about the ways in which love, romance, and marriage are portrayed.

READING 2
Article

Your Dog Can Make You Feel Better, and Here's Why

Thinking Before Reading

The following article, "Your Dog Can Make You Feel Better, and Here's Why," by Marlene Cimons was originally published in *The Washington Post* in 2016. The article looks at the close bond between humans and dogs (and other pets) and the many benefits of that bond. As you read, underline any information you find particularly insightful or interesting.

1. Preview the reading, using the steps discussed in Chapter 1, page 4.

2. Connect the reading to your own experience by answering the following questions:

   a. Do you have a pet or animal companion? If so, does he or she feel like a member of the family?

   b. Would you rush into a burning building to save your pet?

3. Mark and annotate as you read.

Your Dog Can Make You Feel Better, and Here's Why

Marlene Cimons

1   Wayne Pacelle has a demanding job as president and chief executive of the Humane Society of the United States. This is one of the reasons he brings Lily, his beagle mix, to work with him. He is convinced that animals "are a necessary ingredient in our emotional well-being," he says. "I deal with many stressful issues, and I see terrible cruelty," he adds. "But when Lily puts her head on my lap, it calms me." Pacelle can't scientifically document the positive effects he gains from his connection with Lily (and Zoe, his cat.) But his experience supports what researchers who study human/animal interaction have concluded: Pets, especially dogs, seem to be good for our health.

2   "Dogs make people feel good," says Brian Hare, an associate professor of cognitive neuroscience at Duke University, who points out that dogs are found now in some courtrooms, exam study halls, hospitals, nursing homes, hospice-care settings, classrooms, airports and elsewhere, "and their only job is to help people in stressful situations feel better. Many people seem to respond to dogs in a positive way". Scientists believe that the major source of people's positive reactions to pets come from oxytocin, a hormone whose many functions include stimulating social bonding, relaxation and trust, and easing stress.

3   Research has shown that when humans interact with dogs, oxytocin levels increase in both species. "When parents look at their baby and their baby stares into their eyes, even though the baby can't talk, parents get an oxytocin boost just by eye contact," Hare says. "Dogs have somehow hijacked this oxytocin bonding pathway, so that just by making contact, or (by) playing and hugging our dog, the oxytocin in both us and our dog goes up. This is why dogs are wonderful in any kind of stressful situation." Miho Nagasawa, a postdoctoral fellow at Jichi Medical University in Shimotsuke, Japan, has found that mutual gazing between humans and their dogs increases the owners' oxytocin levels. This helps decrease anxiety and arousal levels, and slow the heart rate. "The positive interaction between humans and dogs via mutual gazing may reduce stress activity for each other," she says.

4   Both the Centers for Disease Control and Prevention and the National Institutes of Health are interested in the potential health value of having pets: NIH first raised the human/pet connection nearly 30 years ago, recommending that scientists take pets into account when conducting health research, and the agency has funded a number of studies into the impact of pet ownership.

5   Lori Kogan, an associate professor of clinical sciences at the Colorado State University College of Veterinary Medicine and the editor of the Human-Animal

Dogs may not be people, but there's a reason we think of them as members of our families.

Interaction Bulletin, says that pets can be especially helpful for people facing emotional difficulties. "Dogs have a positive impact on depression and anxiety," Kogan says. "When someone loses a spouse or partner, for example, having a dog provides a reason to get up and be social," she says. For many older people, "it's the only relationship they have." In one study, researchers concluded that women living alone were "significantly more lonely" than those who were living with pets, and noted that having a pet might "compensate for the absence of human companionship." This may explain the value many people find in therapy dogs, which are trained to help people deal with worry, unhappiness, and anxiety, and have been found to even reduce the perception of pain.

6   While dogs are most frequently used for therapy purposes, says Mary Margaret Callahan of Pet Partners, the group's registry of available therapy animals also includes cats, horses, rabbits, guinea pigs, llamas, potbellied pigs, birds and domesticated rats.

7   Therapy dogs are widely used to help veterans cope with post-traumatic stress disorder and have been used to help calm autistic children. In June, therapy dogs were brought in to relax swimmers competing in the U.S. Olympic trials in Omaha suffering from pre-race jitters. Therapy golden retrievers from Lutheran Church Charities were sent to Orlando in June to comfort survivors as well as those who lost loved ones in the Pulse nightclub shooting that left dozens dead. A New York funeral home provides mourners with a dog that even "prays" with them. A recently released study found that therapy pets can help first-year university students suffering from homesickness and possibly help in lowering college dropout rates.

8   Of course, there are times when the emotional interaction with pets can be difficult. When they misbehave or are sick (or worse) we feel it. "Dogs are just like kids: They can be the sources of enormous joy and enormous worry," says Hare, who has two children and two dogs. "But overall, despite the worry and pain, most dog owners I know, including me, would say that there is overwhelming benefit."

Getting Ready to Write

Checking Your Comprehension

Answer each of the following questions using complete sentences.

1. In what settings are dogs commonly found, and what is their primary purpose in these settings?
2. What role does the hormone oxytocin play in the relationship between humans and dogs?
3. In addition to dogs, what other pets also serve in therapeutic situations?
4. Why might dogs be so well suited to people who have lost a spouse or partner?
5. In what ways can therapy pets help first-year college students?

Strengthening Your Vocabulary

Identify at least five words from the reading that are unfamiliar to you. Using context clues, word parts, or a dictionary, if necessary, write a brief definition of each word as it is used in the reading.

Examining the Reading: Using Idea Maps

Create an idea map of "Your Dog Can Make You Feel Better, and Here's Why." Start with the title and thesis and include the main points of the selection.

Thinking Critically: An Integrated Perspective

1. What is the meaning of the quote "dogs are just like kids" (last paragraph)?

2. Would the author agree or disagree with the following statement? "The human bond with dogs is primarily chemical." Write a journal entry explaining your answer.

3. In paragraph 5, the author reports on a study showing that women living alone were significantly more lonely than women living with pets. Why do you think this is the case?

4. Evaluate the title of this article. Does it stimulate your interest? Does it motivate you to read the article? What can you predict about the content of the article based on the title?

5. Why does the author begin the article by talking about Wayne Pacelle and his dog Lily?

6. Throughout the article, the author presents evidence in support of dogs and other pets as stress reducers. What argument could be made for dogs and pets *not* having a positive affect on humans?

7. Write a caption to accompany the photo that appears on page 564. What other types of photos might the author have used to help support her key ideas?

THINKING VISUALLY

Thinking Critically

For a review of critical-thinking skills, see Chapter 9.

1. Is the author's opinion on the topic of this reading selection ever in doubt? Explain how the author's opinion is evident throughout the article and in the last paragraph.

2. What is the author's purpose for writing "Your Dog Can Make You Feel Better, and Here's Why"?

3. Who is the intended audience for this selection? Would you say the intended audience is composed solely of dog lovers?

4. What inference can you make from this statement in the last paragraph 8? "Of course, there are times when the emotional interaction with pets can be difficult. When they misbehave or are sick (or worse) we feel it."

5. What inference can you make from this statement in paragraph 3? "Dogs have somehow hijacked this oxytocin bonding pathway..."

6. Do you think the author's opinion on the role of dogs in human life affects her presentation of the facts? In other words, do you perceive the reading as biased? Why or why not?

Writing About the Reading

1. The idea that animals have rights is alluded to in this reading. Write an essay in which you answer the question "Is it ethical for scientists to experiment on animals?"

2. Write an essay about a pet you have owned. What was its personality like? Did it have likes and dislikes? What effect did it have on you, your friends, and/or your family? How did it communicate its needs to you?

3. It's often said that there are "cat people" and "dog people." Write an essay exploring the differences between these two types of pets and the people who own them.

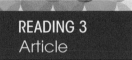

READING 3
Article

How to Enjoy the Often Exhausting, Depressing Role of Parenthood

Thinking Before Reading

The following article from *The Atlantic* magazine, "How to Enjoy the Often Exhausting, Depressing Role of Parenthood," looks at a side of parenthood that is not often discussed: the difficulties of being a parent. As you read, consider how the information provided in the article may challenge the more idealistic views of parenthood you may see on television or in advertisements.

1. Preview the reading, using the steps discussed in Chapter 1, page 4.

2. Connect the reading to your own experience by answering the following questions:

   a. Do you have a child or children? Have you found raising children to be easy, difficult, or somewhere in between?

   b. Think about parents who have young children. What sorts of stresses do you see them dealing with?

3. Mark and annotate as you read.

How to Enjoy the Often Exhausting, Depressing Role of Parenthood

Alice G. Walton

1   Judging from Huggies commercials, Gerber ads, and perhaps a select number of oddly giddy parents on the playground, there's no more blissful experience than becoming a parent. One's days are filled with the laughter of little children; the pride of school recitals; and the rapture of bake sales, soccer game victories, and family vacations. However, many research studies—and an awful lot of parents if you ask them to be candid—paint another picture. While there's certainly a lot of joy involved in parenthood, it is not unusual to also feel overwhelmed with negative feelings: anxiety, confusion, frustration,

depression. Parenthood also puts a lot of pressure on a parent's relationships, which can lead to more stress.

2 Take heart. If you're feeling the downside of being a parent lately, know that you're not alone. Parents all feel the weight of parenthood at some time or another—some more than others. Here we'll go over what scientists have to say about the demands of parenthood and offer some advice based on research to make the less-than-camera-ready moments a little easier.

Parenthood Is Exhausting

3 More and more mothers have been speaking up about postpartum depression, and today most people see it as a normal physiological response experienced by some new mothers. What's less talked about is that negative feelings can extend much beyond the first few months of a baby's life: they can be felt throughout much of your child's grade school and teenage years.

4 As most parents know, taking care of a child and his or her many, many needs can be physically exhausting. Young babies need almost-constant care: they need to be fed every couple of hours; they wake up multiple times per night (making a good night's sleep a thing of the past for you); and they may require specific (and bizarre) rituals to get them to eat, stop crying, or fall asleep. And then there is the never-ending supply of dirty diapers, soiled clothes, and the array of bodily fluids they bestow upon their parents with uncanny regularity.

5 The constant attendance to another person and lack of sleep can leave parents feeling physically run down and haggard. Studies have shown that when parents are fatigued, this can affect their overall well-being, as well as their ability to respond to their children with sensitivity and confidence. Fatigued parents also show more frustration and irritability toward their kids, which means that it's all the more important to learn how to cope with it.

6 The physical exhaustion of parenthood is, of course, tightly coupled to mental exhaustion: in fact, it's difficult to separate the two. The very act of taking care of a baby or child can be draining on many levels—emotionally, cognitively, and psychologically. Let's be honest, playing with teddy bears or transformers for hours on end is not the most stimulating activity for an adult. Focusing one's attention on child games and kid-oriented activities can be wearying, so often parents just zone out. It's easy to beat oneself up for not feeling mentally present 100 percent of the time, but these are feelings that most parents grapple with at some time or another.

Parents Are at Risk for Depression

7 Because of all the work and exhaustion that accompany parenthood, it can bring a rise in depression as much as a boost in happiness. A number of studies have found that people are not only less

Scientists have studied the demands of parenthood and offered advice to make the process a little easier to get through.

happy after having children, compared to their pre-child levels, they are less happy than their childless counterparts.

8   Significantly, once kids leave home, things seem to improve. The same study suggested that the happiness level of empty-nesters was comparable to people who never had children. The authors suggest that while kids are still living at home, "the emotional demands of parenthood may simply outweigh the emotional rewards of having children."

9   While postpartum depression usually dissipates within a few months or a year after the birth of a child, regular old parental blues can wax and wane over the entire period during which your child is living at home. There are additional factors, beyond the fatigue associated with caring for a child, that contribute to it. Luckily, there are ways to combat it.

How Your (Parental) Relationship Affects Parenthood

10   Another important reason that parenthood can be so difficult is that it puts an enormous strain on the central relationship in the family: the relationship of the parents. Couples can often experience a drop in marital happiness that affects their overall well-being. After having a child, people often notice that they are not communicating as well with their partners as they did in their pre-child relationship; they may not handle conflicts as well, and may report an overall loss of confidence in the relationship. In fact, the negative changes can seem to outweigh the positive. Though people who don't have kids also experience a decline in happiness throughout their marriage, it is gradual, without the sudden drop associated with having kids.

11   Other factors, like age and how settled you are in life may also influence how parenthood affects you. Older parents are generally less at risk for depression than younger ones. Parents still in their early 20s appear to have the hardest time because they are struggling with their own move from adolescence to adulthood while at the same time learning to be parents. This may be because younger first-time parents aren't totally grown up themselves, and there is more risk for a "disordered transition from adolescence to adulthood."

12   Other factors that can affect both your relationship with your significant other and your feelings about parenthood include whether the pregnancy was planned or not, one's mood before the birth of a child, and the degree of sleep disruption you experience as a new parent.

13   Though not all of the variables that affect our relationship to parenthood are within our control (age, our partner's behaviors, our children's specific needs), there is a lot that *is* within our power. Changing our attitudes toward parenthood can make a big difference in our perception of it. Below are some things one can do to derive more joy from the experience and minimize the melancholy.

Learning to Enjoy the Ride

14   Despite all of the evidence that parenthood can be hard on the psyche, parents also experience times of fulfillment that are hard to beat. Sometimes it's the little moments of parenting—like the way your toddler says "bsghetti" or how she hums when she is coloring—that make the difference, and paying attention to these can have a big impact. Some studies have found that when people are

actively parenting, it's these specific moments in time that are linked to the highest levels of happiness.

Remember the Cost, Idealize the Benefit

15   Having kids generally entails some level of sacrifice, as some parents are eager to remind their kids. "What I did for you!" can be a common refrain in some households, which is probably not the healthiest sentiment to impart on one's children. But reminding yourself of the cost (and the benefits) can actually help your attitude toward parenting. It may sound a little dire, but recalling how much you have sacrificed to have your own kids can actually help you appreciate the endeavor more. When people were asked to recall the financial sacrifices they'd made for their kids, they also reported being much happier as parents than those who were not asked to recall the financial pain of parenthood.

16   This could be viewed as simply a rationalization, but the same study found that parents who were first encouraged to idealize parenthood and visualize all the pleasant things involved reported many fewer feelings of negativity about being a parent. Focusing on the positive also minimized the negative.

17   Rather than lamenting the costs associated with your child's education, try to focus on the many ways in which it will benefit him or her. Say to yourself, "Yes, it costs a lot, but my child is getting a good education, learning to think critically, making friends, and learning to play violin and basketball." Shifting attention from the cons to the pros is, as in any aspect of life, the most productive approach.

Take Time for Yourself, and Your Spouse

18   As most parents will tell you, leisure time—doing fun activities by yourself or with your spouse—is a key to parental happiness. In fact, studies have found that after women became mothers, they enjoyed their leisure time more than before (which is not surprising, since there is much less of it after the baby comes along).

19   Personal time, either by yourself or with your partner, is an important part of maintaining your sense of self—and your sanity. Pursue a project you want to do; take a walk, visit a museum, listen to a CD you love. (In the same study, women also rated their moods as less negative toward their relatives after the birth of the child, which could suggest that having a baby makes one a little less hard on family members.)

20   Spending time with your spouse is also an important tool for getting through parenthood. Though couples' alone time drops off sharply after a baby is born, it tends to climb in the months after—maybe not to pre-baby levels, but still. And the kind of leisure time couples spent *before* the baby is born has a lot to do with how well the relationship works after the baby is born. For example, women who spend more time enjoying leisure activities with their husbands before having a child are generally happier in the first year of their child's life. For men, the situation is similar: the fewer leisure activities men do by themselves, the less conflict they experience after the baby is born.

21 So make sure that you have a night out with your significant other, whether or not you're a parent. If you haven't yet had a child, make the most of your time together, because it will translate to the strength of your relationship postnatally. And if you already have kids, make sure to give yourselves a night off once in a while, since doing so can increase your bond with each other, which will be a benefit to your child as well.

Take Yourself (and Your Child) a Little Less Seriously

22 Parents are a self-conscious, self-serious group these days. The "helicopter" phenomenon—parents who monitor their kids' every move and pack their kids' schedules full of extracurricular or educational activities—is becoming more widespread. But as helpful as we try to be, sometimes we do too much. And doing less can also make parenting more pleasurable.

23 At the playground, stand back and be slower to step in. Kids need play—as much as parents—to help them learn their way in the world. Studies have found a decline in free play in the last few decades that is not only linked to, but may actually cause, the increased levels of depression, anxiety, feelings of helplessness and loss of control, and other negative effects that we seeing increasing in kids these days.

24 Free play, the kind kids do totally on their own (as opposed to structured or supervised activity) is critically important in how kids develop basic cognitive abilities, like decision-making, problem-solving, and self-control. The trial-and-error nature of unstructured play is an essential practice for the trial-and-error nature of life—and taking it away from kids can actually be a great disservice to their overall mental well-being.

25 Our tendency to strive for parental perfection is understandable given the amount of information to which we have access nowadays. But over-parenting can lead to more anxiety than there needs to be. Learning to have fun with your child—and let him have fun, too—will not only make the experience more pleasant, it will be a big help to your child's development.

We're in It Together

26 Parenthood is a big change—bigger than many anticipate. This aspect, in and of itself, can lead to negative feelings, since it is so easy to feel lost and ineffectual. Any change is hard for people to cope with—but especially difficult is one that involves responsibility for another life (particularly a screaming, crying, bodily-fluid-producing one). Even beyond the baby days, a school-aged child can present a whole new set of challenges, like scheduling activities, restricting screen-time, discipline, and homework management.

27 But childhood goes by fast. The early days of colic and diapers give way to action figures and tea parties, to college applications, to proms, and, finally, to empty-nesting. Approaching parenthood as a process can help keep you sane through it all. Take it seriously but not too seriously. As harrowing as the bad times are, keep in mind that they too shall pass—and the good times go by just as quickly.

Getting Ready to Write

Checking Your Comprehension

Answer each of the following questions using complete sentences.

1. What effects does physical exhaustion have on parents?

2. Rank the following groups of people according to their happiness level, from lowest to highest: parents of infants, couples before they have children, couples who are childless.

3. What are some of the possible negative effects experienced by couples who have recently had a child?

4. Which age group of parents appears to struggle the most with parenting: parents in their 20s, 30s, or 40s? Explain.

5. What is the "helicopter phenomenon"?

Strengthening Your Vocabulary

Identify at least five words from the reading that are unfamiliar to you. Using context clues, word parts, or a dictionary, if necessary, write a brief definition of each word as it is used in the reading.

Examining the Reading: Using Idea Maps

Create an idea map of "How to Enjoy the Often Exhausting, Depressing Role of Parenthood." Start with the title and thesis and include the main points of the selection.

Thinking Critically: An Integrated Perspective

1. What does the author mean by the phrase "less-than-camera-ready moments" in paragraph 2?

2. Write a journal entry summarizing the things that parents can do to maximize their own relationship while making the most of parenthood.

3. Do you or did you have "helicopter parents"? What are the pros and cons of having such involved parents?

4. Evaluate the title of this article. Does it appear to challenge the conventional wisdom about parenting? Does it motivate you to read the article? Why or why not?

5. The author summarizes many research studies to help support her key points. Does she provide specific information about the sources she used? How might providing more specific research citations help readers?

6. Write a caption to replace the caption that appears on page 568. What other types of photos might the author have used to help support her key ideas?

THINKING VISUALLY

Thinking Critically

For a review of critical-thinking skills, see Chapter 9.

1. What is the author's purpose for writing "How to Enjoy the Often Exhausting, Depressing Role of Parenthood"?

2. Who is the intended audience for this selection? Would you say that the selection provides good advice for its intended audience?

3. What inference can you make from this statement in paragraph 4? "They may require specific (and bizarre) rituals to get them to eat, stop crying, or fall asleep."

4. Consider the following statement from paragraph 15. Is it a fact or an opinion? "'What I did for you!' can be a common refrain in some households, which is probably not the healthiest sentiment to impart on one's children."

5. How would you describe the author's approach to the topic? Does she appear to be sympathetic to parents, or is she impatient with them?

6. Consider the author's presentation of two topics: the helicopter phenomenon and free play (paragraphs 22–25). Would you consider her presentation of these topics to be biased or balanced? Explain.

Writing About the Reading

1. Consider this situation: You are in the fortunate position of being able to stay at home to take care of your children full-time. Would this be something you would be interested in doing? Why or why not? Write an essay discussing your feelings; alternatively, write an essay in which you explore the pros and cons of working while raising a child or children.

2. Some people have more than one child because they do not want their first child to be lonely. What is your opinion of the idea of having no more than one child? Write an essay examining this question. (If you are an only child, you might choose to write an essay about your experience of growing up as an only child.)

3. Given the content of this article, it may not be surprising that more and more people have decided not to have children. Write an essay in which you explore the idea of childlessness. What are its pros and cons, both for individuals and for society?

Read and Respond to the Theme
Making Connections

1. Of the readings in this theme, which did you find most relevant to your life? Which were less relevant? Which did you enjoy the most and why?

2. Compare the writing style among the three readings. Which did you find the most engaging and well written? What techniques did the writer use to engage your interest?

3. What role does oxytocin play in romantic relationships and families? What are the pros and cons of oxytocin in terms of society?

4. List at least three types of human relationships other than those discussed in this theme. How is each of these relationships relevant to your life?

Writing About the Readings

1. Choose a type of relationship in which you are interested. Write an essay about it. (For example, you might write about the relationships between brothers and sisters, between two friends, or between a person and his or her community.)

2. Based on this set of readings, do you think it is a good idea for a couple who has recently had a child to also adopt a pet? Why or why not? Write an essay exploring your answer.

3. What different challenges do you think people in arranged marriages face compared with those in marriages based on love? How might the divorce rate change in Western countries if more people embraced the idea of arranged marriage? Write a paragraph or essay in which you explore your answers to these questions.

4. In what ways do all of the readings in this theme relate in some way to romantic relationships? What other elements do the readings have in common? Write an essay that answers one of these questions.

Theme 3

Medical Ethics: Issues in Health Care and Human Well-Being

Ethics is the study of a society's moral principles—what is right, what is wrong, and what lies in between. A specific branch of ethics called *medical ethics* looks deeply at the moral implications of health care and the difficult decisions that must sometimes be made. For example, is euthanasia (mercy killing) ever acceptable? How much money should be spent trying to cure one particular person? Should cloning be permitted?

Most of the academic disciplines touch on questions of medical ethics. Within the sciences, questions range from the morality of experimenting on animals to the ethics of developing chemicals that can be used for destructive purposes (such as warfare). Within the business disciplines, debates rage over the huge profits made by pharmaceutical companies as well as the high costs of medical care. In the social sciences, psychologists study the effects of health on human well-being, while sociologists often compare the medical systems of different countries. The readings in this theme examine contemporary issues in medical ethics: the idea of selecting the sex of your unborn child, using executed prisoners as a source of human organ donations, and how honest doctors are when communicating with their patients.

Reading 1: "Would You Like a Boy or a Girl?" by Michael D. Johnson

Reading 2: "Kidneys from Felons? Prisoner Organ Donation Spurs Debate" by Kate Bennion

Reading 3: "Dishonest Doctors: Why Physicians Lie" by Otis Brawley

Would You Like a Boy or a Girl?

Thinking Before Reading

The following excerpt, "Would You Like a Boy or a Girl?," was originally published in a human biology textbook. It begins the chapter titled "Reproductive Systems." As you read, note how the author uses evidence to support both sides of the controversy.

1. Preview the reading, using the steps discussed in Chapter 1, page 4.

2. Connect the reading to your own experience by answering the following questions:

   a. If you were to have a child, would you want a boy or a girl? If you already have children, did you have a preference for boys or girls?

   b. Do you think it is ethical for parents to use artificial means to increase their chances of having a boy or a girl? Why or why not?

3. Mark and annotate as you read.

Would You Like a Boy or a Girl?

Michael D. Johnson

1   Your parents probably did not know whether you were a boy or a girl until the very moment you were born, unless ultrasound was performed sometime around 18–26 weeks of pregnancy. They certainly had no way of selecting a child for its gender. But with the advent of DNA technology and advanced fertility methods, all that is changing.

Early Gender Detection—Good Idea or Not?

2   Back in 2005 a biotech company called Acu-Gen Biolab, Inc., started offering a gender testing service and kit called Baby Gender Mentor™. According to the company, Baby Gender Mentor could determine the gender of an unborn child with 99.9% accuracy as early as five weeks after fertilization. For $275, the company would analyze a small blood sample from the mother and provide confidential results via e-mail, generally within 48 hours. Baby Gender Mentor was based on the principle that a small amount of fetal DNA is generally present in the mother's blood plasma. The presence of Y-chromosomal material in the mother's blood plasma indicates the presence of a boy fetus; the presence of only X-chromosomal material indicates a girl.

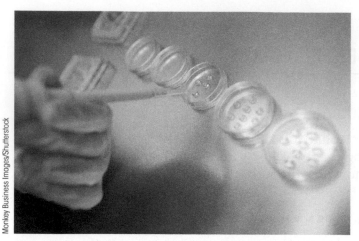

DNA technology and advanced fertility methods are shaping gender selection.

3   Baby Gender Mentor was a big news story when it first came out. But within a year parents who had used the service were suing the company, claiming that it was not nearly as accurate as claimed. The company filed for Chapter 11 bankruptcy in 2009 and the product was taken off the market.

4   Then and even now, some ethicists question whether knowing a fetus's gender as early as five weeks serves any useful purpose. The one obvious purpose is that it would provide couples with an opportunity to have an elective abortion if the fetus is not of the desired gender. In India, where there is a strong preference for male children, prenatal testing and selective abortions are thought to be responsible for a deficit of girls every year. There is no evidence of a similar gender imbalance in the United States, however.

Gender Selection Is Now Possible

5   If you would prefer to have a child of a specific gender without resorting to an elective abortion, there's a relatively easy way to at least increase the odds. A procedure called *sperm sorting* is based on the fact that the X (female) chromosome is larger and carries more DNA than the Y (male) chromosome. First, the sperm in a semen sample from the would-be father are labeled with a fluorescent dye that attaches to DNA. Because sperm with the female (X) chromosome have more DNA, they fluoresce more brightly than sperm with the male (Y) chromosome. The sperm are then sorted on the basis of light intensity by a machine called a *flow cytometer*. After sorting, either the "female-enriched" or the "male-enriched" sperm sample is used to artificially inseminate the mother. For couples who want a girl, sperm sorting produces girls 91% of the time; for boys the odds are a bit lower (only 76%), but that's still a lot better than random chance.

6   Could a couple choose their next child's gender with absolute 100% certainty? Yes, they could, but the techniques involved are expensive. According to the standard procedure at most fertility clinics, eggs and sperm would be collected from the prospective couple and mixed together. Once the early-stage embryos had begun to develop, each one would be tested for the presence or absence of the Y-chromosome by a technique called *preimplantation genetic diagnosis (PGD)*. The presence of a Y-chromosome would indicate a male embryo, whereas the absence of a Y-chromosome would indicate a female embryo. A couple wanting only a boy, then, could choose to have only a boy-embryo implanted into the prospective mother.

7   The American Society of Reproductive Medicine does not endorse PGD for gender selection. Nevertheless, a number of fertility clinics will perform PGD for this purpose. To avoid controversy over the ethics of gender selection, the clinics may describe gender selection as a way to select against certain diseases (females don't get prostate cancer for example, and males are at very low risk for breast cancer).

Beyond Gender Selection

8   In addition to gender selection, PDG can be used to test for genetic disorders. It can also be used to select embryos for certain specific genotypes, including being a compatible tissue match for a sibling.

9   Molly Nash was born with Fanconi's anemia, a rare, incurable disease in which the bone marrow does not produce blood cells normally. Typically people with this condition die in their early 20s. Fanconi's anemia is a genetic disorder. Although neither of Molly's parents have the disease, they both carry the gene that causes it. In a desperate attempt to save their daughter, Molly's parents turned to a fertility clinic that performed PGD. Eggs were harvested from the mother's ovaries, fertilized, and then tested for the abnormal Fanconi gene, among other genetic disorders. Embryos that lacked the fatal gene were screened further to determine whether they would be a safe tissue donor match for Molly. Only embryos that lacked the fatal gene and that were a good tissue donor match for Molly were implanted into the mother's uterus. After four attempts Molly's mother gave birth to a healthy boy, whom the couple named Adam. Shortly after Adam's birth, blood-forming stem cells harvested from Adam's umbilical cord blood were infused into Molly. Apparently, enough of these cells became blood-forming stem cells in Molly that she was cured. Today both children are healthy, and Molly has started school.

10   When the Nash story first hit the press it caused a firestorm of controversy. The media labeled Adam the "savior sibling" and predicted dire effects on his future mental health from knowing that he had been brought into being to save his sister. Molly's parents insisted that they wanted more children anyway, so this procedure enabled them to have a healthy child and also save their daughter's life. However, many people questioned whether it is ethical to have a child for the purpose of being a tissue donor. And of course when multiple eggs are fertilized *in vitro* but only one or two are implanted, there is always the issue of what happens to the embryos not selected for implantation.

11   There's no doubt that as reproductive technologies improve, our ability to screen for genetic abnormalities will also improve. But beyond just avoiding genetic diseases, what about using PGD to influence physical characteristics such as hair, skin, and eye color, intelligence, even musical ability? If we could pick and choose from a menu of specific traits for our offspring, would we want to?

Getting Ready to Write

Checking Your Comprehension

Answer each of the following questions using complete sentences.

1. What did Baby Gender Mentor claim that it could do? Was the company successful?

2. If a developing fetus has a Y chromosome, which sex will the baby be?

3. In which countries is a strong preference for male children found?

4. Which technique could prospective parents use to ensure that they have a male or female child? How does this technique work?

5. How did Molly Nash's parents save her life?

Strengthening Your Vocabulary

Identify at least five words from the reading that are unfamiliar to you. Using context clues, word parts, or a dictionary, if necessary, write a brief definition of each word as it is used in the reading.

Examining the Reading: Using Idea Maps

Create an idea map of "Would You Like a Boy or a Girl?" Start with the title and thesis and include the main points of the selection.

Thinking Critically: An Integrated Perspective

1. Write a journal entry discussing some reasons why parents may have a strong preference for either male or female children.
2. Do you think the decision Jack and Linda Nash made was ethical? Why or why not?
3. The author includes three subheadings in this selection. Which one of the three subheadings does *not* accurately summarize the contents of the section?
4. Identify two paragraphs that identify a key term and provide a detailed description of a process.
5. The author closes the selection with rhetorical questions, which are questions designed to ask a reader to consider a particular issue or viewpoint. Why do you think the author closes this selection with rhetorical questions?

Thinking Critically

For a review of critical-thinking skills, see Chapter 9.

1. Does the author show any bias in this selection? If so, point to specific examples where the author's bias is evident.
2. Would you describe this selection as predominantly factual or predominantly opinion-based?
3. Who is the intended audience for this selection?
4. List at least two valid inferences that you might make after reading paragraph 11.
5. Why might ethicists argue that knowing a fetus's gender serves no useful purpose (paragraph 4)?
6. What is the author implying in the last sentence of paragraph 10?

Writing About the Reading

1. Modern technologies, including the ultrasound discussed in paragraph 1, help parents learn the sex of their unborn child. If you were expecting a child, would you want to know the baby's sex? Write an essay in which you explore the pros and cons of knowing a baby's sex before it is born.
2. Paragraph 4 refers to a "gender imbalance," which exists when there are more people of one gender than of the other. What types of problems might occur in a society that has too many females? A society that has too many males? Write an essay in which you discuss some possible answers to these questions.
3. Would you be willing to have another child in order to help a very sick child, as Linda and Jack Nash did? Why or why not? Write an essay in which you express your feelings about the matter.

Kidneys from Felons? Prisoner Organ Donation Spurs Debate

Thinking Before Reading

The following article, "Kidneys from Felons? Prison Organ Donation Spurs Debate," was originally published in the *Deseret News*. As you read, note how the author uses headings to break the article into smaller chunks. Also evaluate whether the author makes her opinions known within the article.

1. Preview the reading, using the steps discussed in Chapter 1, page 4.

2. Connect the reading to your own experience by answering the following questions:

   a. Have you ever known a person who received an organ transplant or a person who is on a waiting list for an organ?

   b. Do you think prisoners should have the same rights as citizens who are not in jail? Why or why not?

3. Mark and annotate as you read.

Kidneys from Felons? Prisoner Organ Donation Spurs Debate

Kate Bennion

1   After reading the story of a 10-year-old boy with a fatal muscle-wasting disease in the *Deseret News* on February 20, Marco Guizar sent the newspaper a letter. "I am a healthy 37-year-old male and am currently in the Davis County Correctional Facility," said the letter. "If this little boy can be saved by a heart donation, I would like to offer my heart to him."

2   Guizar is being held without bail for allegedly shooting at a truck on Legacy Highway and exchanging fire with police officers. Charged with aggravated attempted murder and assault, he faces 15–20 years in prison. "I am a registered donor and believe I have every right to donate my organs to whomever I choose, and I can't think of any worthier cause or individual," wrote Guizar. "I have made a mess of my life ... but what I can do is offer to make someone's life better and make someone's family happy."

3   Such a donation is illegal, and Guizar is unlikely to be a match for a 10-year-old. But according to the National Organ Donor Registry, 117,784 people are waiting for an organ in the United States. Eighteen die each day while waiting. Almost 2 million people are incarcerated in prisons across the nation, and dozens are executed each year—a largely untapped population, some say, of potential donors. There are significant legal and ethical hurdles, but inmates, states, and families are still asking: why not let prisoners donate organs?

Signing Up in the Southwest

4   The Maricopa County, Arizona, Sheriff's Office complex is one of the largest jail systems in the country. With an average daily inmate population of 7,700 and constant turnover, arrests and subsequent bookings are frequent. The county has an unusual addition to the booking process, however—one that's been in place since 2007. "Whenever an inmate is booked into jail, they're given an opportunity to register as an organ donor," said Lt. Chris Luginbuhl. Somewhere between frisking and fingerprinting, those who opt in are given access to the state donor registry site, and then the criminal justice system process continues as usual.

5   As of January 28 of this year, the office has registered 14,124 inmates for the state organ donor program. Those booked into the county jail are pre-sentence and pre-trial detainees or sentenced to a year or less. If they're released, they are no longer considered by the organ registry to be at high risk for health complications— and remain on the state organ donor registry. Similar measures are taking off elsewhere. Texas and California allow for deceased donation from their inmates, and in January, state legislation passed unanimously in Utah that allows prisoners to voluntarily sign up for the donor registry, a move that was applauded by organ donation advocacy groups.

6   There are more than 100 million registered organ donors in the United States, and the incarcerated population of 2 million may add only a drop to the bucket. However, for those in need of an organ, all it takes is one. "Any way we can possibly expand the donor pool, we're in favor of," says Alex McDonald, director of public education for Intermountain Donor Services, which serves Utah, southeastern Idaho, and western Wyoming. McDonald said that in a period of six weeks, 237 inmates have already registered to be organ donors in the state of Utah. If an inmate dies and his or her organs are transferrable, those on the waiting list are informed of the incarceration status of the donor and asked if they want to accept an organ. "If they have a patient that's not terribly ill, they might say, 'Well, we're going to hold off until a non-prisoner organ comes along,'" says McDonald. "Whereas, a (more ill) patient might be willing to take that chance."

7   Not everyone is enthusiastic about prisoners becoming donors. Inmates have a higher rate of diseases and infections that could make transplantation dangerous or impossible, such as HIV and hepatitis. Organs and tissues are tested before transplantation, but bacterial infections and unknown disease are still a risk. Considered a "high-risk" population, the incarcerated can donate living tissue or organs (such as kidneys or bone marrow) to immediate family members only. Most states do not allow deceased donation for inmates.

8   Greater still are ethical concerns. The United Network for Organ Sharing views policies that reduce sentences or give parole in exchange for donation as "valuable compensation," rendering them unethical. And while prisoners can receive organs and are placed on the national waiting list, donation is different. "Many maintain that prisoners cannot consent freely,

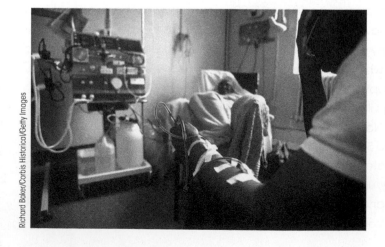

Richard Baker/Corbis Historical/Getty Images

given the nature of the environment in which they live," wrote Arthur Caplan of the University of Pennsylvania for the *American Journal of Bioethics* in 2011. He argues that prisoners aren't allowed to participate in medical research for the same reason. "The ability to comprehend the facts about donation and to make a voluntary choice must be carefully weighed," wrote Caplan. It's too difficult to ensure the decision isn't a compromised one—for prisoners, true informed consent isn't possible. Some recipients are also reluctant to accept life from those that once took it.

9   Wesley Hill, a Salt Lake City resident who received a heart transplant with only days to spare, said as long as the organs and tissues are healthy, he doesn't see why inmates shouldn't be able to donate. But his concern grows with the length of the rap sheet—could he accept a heart from a murderer? Hill says he'd be opposed to receiving an organ from someone on death row, but the decision is tough. "It's just so hard. You're on your deathbed. How desperate are you?" Hill says. "If they had nothing else, I'd think twice about it."

More Need, More Executions?

10   After nine months of living with a painful cracked cornea in his right eye, Kay Wells was delighted when his doctor informed him he had a donor. Kay received his first cornea transplant the morning of January 17, 1977—two hours after convicted murderer Gary Gilmore was executed by firing squad. After surgery, he scarcely batted an eye when the *National Inquirer* tracked him down and told him it was Gilmore's. "(The reporter) asked me if my attitude toward life had changed with a killer's eye," recalls Wells, now 63. "I said, 'Yeah, I really hate reporters now.'"

11   Jokes aside, after the paper confronted him, Wells confirmed with his eye doctor, ophthalmologist Oliver Richards Jr., that he did indeed have Gilmore's cornea. With several patients in need of cornea transplants, Richards told Wells he had visited the Utah State Prison and asked Gilmore to consider donation. The prisoner, who had pleaded for the death penalty, agreed.

12   Richards has since died, so there's no way to confirm the story. But true or not, years later, Wells has no qualms about having possibly received a "killer's eye" and remains firmly pro-donation. "I was just grateful I was able to get the cornea," Wells said. "I think we need as many organs as we can get…. I'll give 'em anything they want, and I'll support anyone that does, whether they're a man on the side of the street or a man in prison."

13   While only 1 to 2 percent of deaths allow for organ donation, state executions, which occur under highly controlled circumstances, could provide a unique opportunity for transplantation. Execution practices in the United States today preclude organ or tissue donation, but death row inmate Christian Longo made a stir in 2011 with a letter to the *New York Times* requesting to donate his organs after execution. "If I donated all of my organs today, I could clear nearly one percent of my state's organ waiting list," wrote Longo. "I am 37 years old and healthy; throwing my organs away after I am executed is nothing but a waste." Longo also founded the organization Gifts of Anatomical Value From Everyone to encourage tissue, organ and blood donation from populations not currently accepted, such as prisoners and gay men.

14   However, in a nation that remains on the fence about the death penalty, it's a fine line between "wasteful" and "cruel and unusual." The few methods of execution deemed to be constitutional don't lend themselves to donation. "It's a very narrow set of circumstances where someone has the potential to be an organ donor," says McDonald. "Something like a lethal injection or firing squad would preclude that."

15   Death row donorship also compounds the ethical questions of prison organ donation. China, with the highest capital punishment rate in the world (around 5,000 are executed each year), currently has no national organ donor registry because all needed organs and tissues are supplied by executed prisoners. The controversial system is due to be phased out this year. While the United States has far fewer executions than China (there were 43 in the United States in 2012), death row donations raise concerns that the justice system could be compromised or the need for organs could influence verdicts. "Any legitimization of the use of executed prisoners in the U.S. may make it more difficult to protest cruel and unjust execution practices in other nations," argued Caplan. He said ethicists object to a practice that makes the death penalty more palatable and acceptable. "Prosecutors, judges or juries may be more likely to insist on the death penalty, knowing that lives might be saved."

16   Mitchell Jones, the 10-year-old boy in Utah, has since quietly passed away. And Guizar still thinks allowing prisoners to donate, especially to children, is "something that should be looked into. I've got kids myself, grandkids," Guizar told the *Deseret News* in an interview. "I'm almost 40. I should be able to decide if I live or die, if I can help someone." A registered organ donor before his arrest, he said many of his fellow prisoners feel similarly. Organ donation could mean redemption, he said. "There are bad people in prison, but there are good people too, especially when it comes to helping kids," Guizar said. "We're just sitting here in a warehouse wasting our lives."

Getting Ready to Write

Checking Your Comprehension

Answer each of the following questions using complete sentences.

1. Which country has the world's highest rate of prison executions?

2. Which facet of the criminal booking system in Maricopa County, Arizona, is unique?

3. What are three key reasons that some people are opposed to prisoners becoming organ donors?

4. Why are prisoners not permitted to take part in medical research?

Strengthening Your Vocabulary

Identify at least five words from the reading that are unfamiliar to you. Using context clues, word parts, or a dictionary, if necessary, write a brief definition of each word as it is used in the reading.

Examining the Reading: Using Idea Maps

Create an idea map of "Kidneys from Felons? Prisoner Organ Donation Spurs Debate." Start with the title and thesis and include the main points of the selection.

Thinking Critically: An Integrated Perspective

1. Suppose you are awaiting an organ transplant and you are offered an organ from a convicted murderer. Would you accept the organ? Why or why not? Write a journal entry exploring these questions.
2. Provide at least two additional reasons (not discussed in the article) why organ donation from prisoners should (or should not) be permitted.
3. Did the *National Inquirer* have the right (or the responsibility) to inform Kay Wells of the source of his donated cornea? Why or why not?
4. Why does the author include the story of Kay Wells's cornea transplant?
5. Does the photo that accompanies this reading show support for or opposition to the idea of prisoner organ donation? Or would you consider the photo "neutral"? Explain.

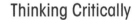

THINKING VISUALLY

Thinking Critically

For a review of critical-thinking skills, see Chapter 9.

1. What is the author's purpose for writing this article? Is she trying to inform/instruct, or is she trying to persuade?
2. Paragraph 13 provides an opinion provided by Christian Longo. Identify at least two other opinions in the article. Also identify at least two facts.
3. Does the article show any signs of bias? If so, point to specific examples where the author's bias is evident.
4. How would you describe the intended audience for this article? To answer this question, consider its original source as well as its content.
5. In paragraph 10, Kay Wells is quoted as saying, "Yeah, I really hate reporters now." From this statement, what can you infer about Mr. Wells's interest in knowing about the source of his cornea donation?
6. Why would Marco Guizar's heart not be a good match for the person he was trying to help? Why would this type of donation be illegal in the United States?
7. What does Alex McDonald mean when he says (paragraph 6), "Any way we can possibly expand the donor pool, we're in favor of"? Do you see any ethical limits to McDonald's statement?
8. Why might the United Network for Organ Sharing consider "policies that reduce sentence or give parole in exchange for donation" unethical (paragraph 8)?

Writing About the Reading

1. Write an essay in which you summarize the arguments in favor of and in opposition to organ donation by prisoners.
2. Until recently, China required organ donation by executed prisoners and for that reason (combined with China's high rate of capital punishment) the

country did not need a national organ donor registry. Write an essay in which you argue in favor of or against this system.

3. Many people in the United States are waiting for organ donations. Write an essay in which you suggest some ways to increase voluntary organ donations. (For example, might the families of donors be paid for these donations?)

4. What criteria should be used in deciding who receives a donated organ? For example, should younger people be given preference over elderly people? Write an essay in which you state and support your opinion.

READING 3
Article

Dishonest Doctors: Why Physicians Lie

Thinking Before Reading

The following article, "Dishonest Doctors: Why Physicians Lie," originally appeared in 2012 on CNN.com, the online version of the CNN news channel. The author, Otis Brawley, is a medical doctor.

1. Preview the reading, using the steps discussed in Chapter 1, page 4.

2. Connect the reading to your own experience by answering the following questions:

   a. If you have a regular physician, how would you describe your doctor–patient relationship?

   b. Do you want your doctor to tell you the truth about your health, no matter how difficult it may be to hear?

3. Mark and annotate as you read.

Dishonest Doctors: Why Physicians Lie

Otis Brawley

1   The doctor-patient relationship is a complex one. It occurs at a stressful and busy time for both the patient and the doctor. Because it involves at least two humans, there are usually at least three versions of the conversation: the doctor's, the patient's and the true version.

2   A survey published this week in the journal *Health Affairs* reflects this complex relationship. Lisa Iezzoni and her colleagues surveyed 1,891 physicians nationwide about how honest they are with their patients regarding medical mistakes and a patient's prognosis. The survey found that although two-thirds of doctors agree they should share serious medical errors with their patients, one-third did not completely agree. Nearly two-fifths of the respondents said they did not disclose their

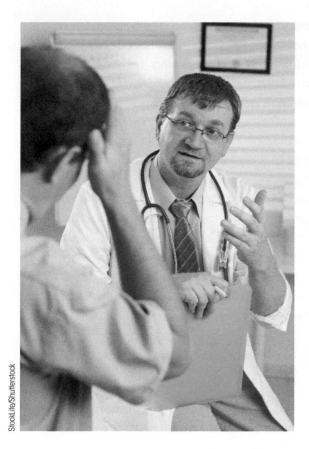

financial relationships with drug and device companies. And more than 55% of physicians said they often or sometimes described a patient's prognosis in a more positive manner than the facts might support.

3   These survey results are unsettling. We all want to think of medicine as an honorable profession and that the people in it work with integrity. While we should all be appalled that a doctor would deceive or lie to a patient, we should also look beyond the white coat for an explanation. While it is not a vindication, the fact is physicians are human. They have all the feelings and failings of humans. Please keep in mind, medical errors can be due to negligence, but they are more often a failure to analyze data appropriately.

4   Many doctor errors are simply a matter of bad luck: The doctor was not good enough that day and would have done better the day before or the day after. Some bad outcomes are not really the physician's fault. Some doctors do not admit error out of fear of litigation. But my experience is that the discomfort of addressing one's own failings or weakness is more commonly the reason for not coming forward.

5   It is a normal human tendency to not want to admit an error. Confession is difficult, especially when you have to admit responsibility to the person you have hurt. In the case of a "bad luck" outcome, the physician may be unwilling to admit their lack of control. This is often due to a lack of communication during the consenting process – when doctors explain the possible outcomes or side effects – and can lead to patient anger when things go badly. Ironically, when I have seen a doctor admit an error, the patient or patient's family is usually forgiving and rarely sues.

6   So why would a doctor not be honest about a patient's disease or prognosis? This is likely because doctors are not always the best communicators. Medical explanations involve defining some complicated things. This is difficult and it is often easier to just not do it. Sometimes there is a tendency to simplify to the point of not telling the truth.

7   It is unfortunate that our medical system pays doctors handsomely to do medical procedures, but does not reimburse well for talking to, counseling and spending time with patients. In a normal office environment, a physician is often forced to see four or more patients per hour. Questions go unanswered or half answered as the physician moves from room to room assessing the patient, reading a patient's history and lab research, documenting and looking things up. It's a rare private practice physician who can block extra time for a patient with special needs. This can be costly.

8   Telling a patient bad news is horribly difficult. It is always an emotional struggle for any caring human being. The emotional incentive is to hold back information or be less than honest. It is harder for me to tell a patient that they are dying – and that all we can reasonably do is try to keep them comfortable – than it is to tell a family member that a patient has died.

9   As someone who studies how health care is provided and how health care is consumed, this survey's findings do not surprise me and the solutions are not simple. We need to transform health care. This involves empowering the patient. Patients need to take an interest in their own health. Ask good questions and expect if not demand answers. Some patients will need advocates or navigators to help them. The transformation also involves more members of the medical profession coming to realize the meaning of the term "profession." A "profession" is a group of people who put their own interests secondary to the interests of the people they serve. A profession is also a group that educates and polices itself.

10   My greatest concern is many doctors and patients fail to comprehend just how complicated medicine can be. Even doctors fail to remember that medicine is a science and an art, often with unclear answers. There are things in medicine that are scientifically known, and things that are unknown. There are also things that are believed. The wise physician draws a distinction between the three. The unwise doctor often confuses what he believes with what he knows. These unwise doctors may not know they are not telling their patients the truth.

Getting Ready to Write

Checking Your Comprehension

Answer each of the following questions using complete sentences.

1. What does the author say are the three versions of the conversation in a doctor–patient relationship?

2. According to the survey in *Health Affairs*, what percentage of physicians said they described a patient's prognosis in a more positive manner than the facts might support?

3. What does the author say is the most likely reason a doctor would not be honest about a patient's disease or prognosis?

4. According to the author, in what two ways does health care need to be transformed?

5. The author says a wise physician is able to draw a distinction between three aspects of medicine. What are these three aspects?

Strengthening Your Vocabulary

Identify at least five words from the reading that are unfamiliar to you. Using context clues, word parts, or a dictionary, if necessary, write a brief definition of each word as it is used in the reading.

Examining the Reading: Using Idea Maps

Create an idea map of "Dishonest Doctors: Why Physicians Lie." Start with the title and thesis and include the main points of the selection.

Thinking Critically: An Integrated Perspective

1. Do you believe it is ethical to lie in order to spare someone from a painful truth? Write a journal entry explaining your answer.

2. Suppose you have to convey a piece of bad news to a friend or loved one. How do you typically go about this? Do you try to soften the facts, or is it more important to you to be completely honest? How does your friend or loved one's personality affect the way you convey information?

3. Why does the author think it is important to remind readers that physicians are human? What other reasons does the author offer to explain the results of the *Health Affairs* survey? Which explanation did you find most convincing or reasonable? Which one did you find least convincing? Write a journal entry exploring your answers.

4. What comparison does the author make in his conclusion? Explain the difference between these two types of doctors.

5. How does the author, who is a doctor, incorporate his own experience as support for his main points? Would specific examples have been more effective?

6. Summarize the author's calls for action in this selection. What does he think doctors and patients can do to improve the doctor–patient relationship?

Thinking Critically

For a review of critical-thinking skills, see Chapter 9.

1. What does the author mean by the "true version" of the conversation (paragraph 1)?

2. Explain what the author means when he refers to "a bad luck outcome" (paragraphs 4–5).

3. Would you describe this selection as predominantly factual or predominantly opinion-based? Find at least two examples of opinions and identify the phrases that signal the author is presenting an opinion.

4. Does the article show any signs of bias? If so, point to specific examples where the author's bias is evident.

5. What is the author's purpose for writing? Who is the intended audience?

6. List at least two valid inferences that you might make after reading paragraph 9.

Writing About the Reading

1. Write an essay in which you explore the following questions: In which circumstances is lying acceptable? In which circumstances is lying not acceptable?

2. Write an essay about a lie you told, either recently or in the past. What was your motivation for doing so? Looking back, do you think telling the lie was justified? Why or why not?

3. Suppose you want to audition for a talent competition, such as *America's Got Talent* or *The Voice*. The problem is this: You really cannot sing, but you think you can. Would you want your friends and family to encourage you to audition, or would you prefer that they tell you the truth? Write an essay exploring this question.

Read and Respond to the Theme

Making Connections

1. Summarize the opposing sides of the argument for all three of the readings included in this theme.

2. How is the controversial nature of these readings evident in the titles of all three of them? In other words, what one element do the titles of all these readings have in common?

3. Do you think the government should be involved in making decisions regarding the issues discussed in this set of readings? If so, to what extent should the government be involved? Or is it up to medical professionals to make ethical decisions in all of these matters?

4. Compile a list of at least ten facts that you did not know before reading these selections.

Writing About the Readings

1. "Dishonest Doctors: Why Physicians Lie" asks serious questions about the doctor–patient relationship. Given what you read in "Kidneys from Felons?" do you think doctors should encourage their patients to donate their organs? Why or why not? Explain your answer in a paragraph.

2. Consider the three topics discussed in these readings: the right to choose the sex of your child, the right to donate your organs, and the right to have your doctor be honest with you. Which of these rights is most important to you? Which is the least important? Write an essay exploring your answer.

3. Select another topic related to medical ethics and write an essay about an aspect of that topic. For example, you might write about the idea of health care rationing (for example, younger people may receive better care than older people who are near the end of their lives) or confidentiality in medical testing.

Credits

Chapter 1

p. 6: CICCARELLI, SAUNDRA K.; WHITE, J. NOLAND, *PSYCHOLOGY,* 5th Ed., ©2017. Reprinted and electronically reproduced by permission of Pearson Education, Inc., New York, NY.; **p. 9**: Sternberg, Robert. "A Triangular Theory of Love," *Psychological Review,* vol. 93, no. 2 (1986), pp. 119-135. Published by the American Psychological Association.; **p. 20**: DeVito, Joseph. *Human Communication,* p. 154, Pearson Education, 2009.; **p. 21**: Thio, Alex. *Sociology,* Thio, Sociology, p. 534, Pearson Education, 1998.; **p. 23**: DeVito, Joseph. *The Interpersonal Communication Book,* p. 220, *The Interpersonal Communication Book,* Pearson Education, 2013.; **p. 33**: Gronbeck, Bruce E et al. *Principles of Speech Communication,* HarperCollins, 1995.; **p. 34**: Uba, Laura and Huang, Karen. *Psychology,* Pearson Education, 1999.

Chapter 2

p. 52: Reprinted by permission of the author.

Chapter 3

p. 88: Henslin, James M. *Social Problems,* Pearson Education. 2003.; **p. 90**: Bergman, Edward F. and Renwick, William H. *Introduction to Geography: People, Places, and Environment,* Pearson Education, 2002.; **p. 90**: Bergman, Edward F. and Renwick, William H. *Introduction to Geography: People, Places, and Environment,* Pearson Education, 2002.; **p. 93**: Henslin, James M. *Social Problems,* Pearson Education, 2003.; **p. 94**: Henslin, James M. *Social Problems,* Pearson Education, 2003.; **p. 102**: Sailing to Byzantium (1 line) W.B. Yeats, "Sailing to Byzantium," The Tower 1928. https://www.poets.org/poetsorg/poem/sailing-byzantium; **p. 102**: Waldo Emerson, Ralph. "The Snow-Storm," *Dial,* 1841.; **p. 102**: Burns, Robert. "A Red, Red Rose," 1794.; **p. 102**: Shakespeare, William. *Hamlet,* 1603.

Chapter 4

p. 123: Reprinted by permission of the author.; **p. 121**: Frederick K. et al. *Essentials of Geology,* Pearson Education, 2009.; **p. 121**: Henslin, James M. *Sociology: A Down-to-Earth Approach,* Pearson Education, 2010.; **p. 121**: Solomon, Michael R. *Consumer Behavior: Buying, Having and Being,* Pearson Education, 2009.; **p. 122**: Donatelle, Rebecca J. *Health: The Basics, Green Edition,* Pearson Education, 2011.; **p. 122**: Ebert, Ronald and Griffin, Ricky. *Business Essentials,* Pearson Education, 2009.; **p. 122**: Carl, John D. *Think Sociology,* Pearson Education, 2010.; **p. 122**: Cook, Roy; Yale, Laura; Marqua, Joseph. *Tourism: The Business of Travel,* Pearson Education, 2010.; **p. 122**: Facione, Peter A. *Think Critically,* Pearson Education, 2011.; **p. 129**: Shainberg, Louis and Byer, Curtis. *Living Well: Health in Your Hands,* HarperCollins Publishers, 1995.; **p. 129**: Thio, Alex. *Sociology: A Brief Introduction,* Pearson Education, 2008.; **p. 130**: Belk, Colleen and Maier, Borden. *Biology: Science for Life with Physiology,* Pearson Education, 2010.; **p. 130**: DeVito, Joseph A. *Human Communication: The Basic Course,* Pearson Education, 1997.; **p. 130**: Griffin, Ricky and Ebert, Ron. *Business Essentials,* Pearson Education, 2009.; **p. 130**: Edwards, III, George C. et al. *Government in America: People, Politics, and Policy,* Pearson Education, 2009.; **p. 130**: Solomon, Michael. *Consumer Behavior: Buying, Having and Being,* Pearson Education, 2009.; **p. 131**: Henslin, James M. *Sociology: A Down-to-Earth Approach,* Pearson Education, 2010.

Chapter 5

p. 158: Sarah Frey. Reprinted by permission of the author.; **p. 157**: Donatelle, Rebecca. *My Health: An Outcomes Approach,* Pearson Education, 2013.; **p. 157**: Edwards III, George C. et al. *Government in America: People, Politics and Policy, Pearson Education,* 2011.; **p. 158**: Krogh, David. *Biology: A Guide to the Natural World,* Pearson Education, 2011.; **p. 168**: Donatelle, Rebecca J. *Health: The Basics,* Pearson Education, 2003.; **p. 169**: Edwards III, George C. et al, *Government in America: People, Politics and Policy,* Pearson Education, 2002.; **p. 169**: Preble, Duane and Preble, Sarah. *Artforms: An Introduction to the Visual Arts,* Pearson Education, 2002.; **p. 169**: Solomon, Michael R. *Consumer Behavior: Buying, Having and Being,* Pearson Education, 2002.; **p. 169**: Bergman, Edward F. and Renwick, William H. *Geography: People, Places, and Environment,* Pearson Education, 2003.; **p. 178**: Coleman, James. *Social Problems,* HarperCollins Publishers, 1996.; **p. 179**: DeVito, Joseph. *Human Communication: The Basic Course,* Pearson Education, 2009.; **p. 179**: Solomon, Michael R. *Consumer Behavior: Buying, Having and Being,* Pearson Education, 1999.

Chapter 6

p. 194: Donatelle, Rebecca J. *Health: The Basics,* Pearson Education, 2007.; **p. 195**: Kephart, William M., and Jedlicka, Davor. *The Family, Society, and the Individual,* Pearson Education, 1991.; **p. 195**: Wallace, Robert A. *Biology: The World of Life,* Pearson Education, 1997.; **p. 195**: Henslin, James M. *Essentials of Sociology,* Pearson Education, 1998.; **p. 196**: Cook, Roy A., et al., *Tourism: The Business of Travel,* Pearson Education,

2010.; **p. 196**: Goldman, Thomas F. and Cheeseman, Henry R. *The Paralegal Professional,* Pearson Education, 2011.; **p. 196**: Divine, Robert A. et al. *America: Past and Present, Combined Volume,* Pearson Education, 2011.; **p. 209**: Donatelle, Rebecca J. *Health: The Basics,* Pearson Education, 2007.; **p. 211**: Dahlman, Carl H. and Renwick, William H. *Introduction to Geography: People, Places, and Environment,* Pearson Education, 2011.; **p. 211**: Brands, H. W. *American Stories: A History of the United States,* Pearson Education, 2012.; **p. 211**: McWilliams, Margaret. Food Around the World: A Cultural Perspective, Pearson Education, 2011.

Chapter 7

p. 225: Republished with permission of Taylor & Francis, Steven Cornelius and Mary Natvig, *Music: A Social Experience,* Taylor & Francis, 2012; permission conveyed through Copyright Clearance Center, Inc.; **p. 231**: Amanda Keithley. Reprinted by permission of the author.; **p. 244**: Hewitt, Paul G. *Conceptual Physics,* Hachette Books, 1958.; **p. 245**: Krogh, David. *Biology: A Guide to the Natural World,* Pearson Education, 2009.; **p. 247**: Eshleman, Ross and Cashion, Barbara. *Sociology: An Introduction,* Pearson Education, 1985.; **p. 248**: Kinnear, Thomas C. et al. *Principles of Marketing,* HarperCollins, 1995.

Chapter 9

p. 297: Fujishin, Randy. *Natural Bridges,* Routledge, 2016; **p. 298**: Weaver, Richard L. *Understanding Interpersonal Communication,* Pearson Education, 1987.; **p. 299**: Katz, Lewis. *Know Your Rights,* Banks-Baldwin Law Publishing Co., 1993.; **p. 299**: Shenkman, Richard. *Legends, Lies, and Cherished Myths of American History,* Random House, 1988.; **p. 300**: Aesop, *Aesop's Fables.*; **p. 303**: Reprinted by permission of the author.

Chapter 10

p. 328: MACIONIS, JOHN J., *SOCIETY: THE BASICS,* 14th Ed., ©2017. Reprinted and Electronically reproduced by permission of Pearson Education, Inc., New York, NY.; **p. 346**: Curry, Tim; Jiobu, Robert; Schwirian, Kent. *Sociology for the Twenty-First Century,* Pearson Education 2002.

Index

Pearson

www.pearson.com

ISBN-13: 978-0-13-474667-8
ISBN-10: 0-13-474667-8